Visit us at

www.syngress.com

T0227085

Syngress is committed to publishing high-quality books for IT Professionals and delivering those books in media and formats that fit the demands of our customers. We are also committed to extending the utility of the book you purchase via additional materials available from our Web site.

SOLUTIONS WEB SITE

To register your book, visit www.syngress.com/solutions. Once registered, you can access our solutions@syngress.com Web pages. There you may find an assortment of valueadded features such as free e-books related to the topic of this book, URLs of related Web sites, FAQs from the book, corrections, and any updates from the author(s).

ULTIMATE CDs

Our Ultimate CD product line offers our readers budget-conscious compilations of some of our best-selling backlist titles in Adobe PDF form. These CDs are the perfect way to extend your reference library on key topics pertaining to your area of expertise, including Cisco Engineering, Microsoft Windows System Administration, CyberCrime Investigation, Open Source Security, and Firewall Configuration, to name a few.

DOWNLOADABLE E-BOOKS

For readers who can't wait for hard copy, we offer most of our titles in downloadable Adobe PDF form. These e-books are often available weeks before hard copies, and are priced affordably.

SYNGRESS OUTLET

Our outlet store at syngress.com features overstocked, out-of-print, or slightly hurt books at significant savings.

SITE LICENSING

Syngress has a well-established program for site licensing our e-books onto servers in corporations, educational institutions, and large organizations. Contact us at sales@syngress.com for more information.

CUSTOM PUBLISHING

Many organizations welcome the ability to combine parts of multiple Syngress books, as well as their own content, into a single volume for their own internal use. Contact us at sales@syngress.com for more information.

SYNGRESS®

Securing Citrix XenApp Server in the Enterprise

Tariq Bin Azad Technical Editor

Connie Wilson
Michael Wright

KEY	SERIAL NUMBER
001	HJIRTCV764
002	PO9873D5FG
003	829KM8NJH2
004	BAL923457U
005	CVPLQ6WQ23
006	VBP965T5T5
007	HJJJ863WD3E
008	2987GVTWMK
009	629MP5SDJT
010	IMWQ295T6T

PUBLISHED BY
Syngress Publishing, Inc.
Elsevier, Inc.
30 Corporate Drive
Burlington, MA 01803

Securing Citrix XenApp Server in the Enterprise

Printed and bound by CPI Group (UK) Ltd, Croydon, CR0 4YY

Transferred to Digital Print 2011

ISBN 13: 978-1-59749-281-2

Publisher: Andrew Williams   Page Layout and Art: SPI
Copy Editor: Mike McGee   Indexer: SPI
Project Manager: Gary Byrne   Cover Designer: Michael Kavish

For information on rights, translations, and bulk sales, contact Matt Pedersen, Commercial Sales Director and Rights, at Syngress Publishing; email m.pedersen@elsevier.com.

Technical Editor

Tariq Bin Azad is the Principal Consultant and founder of NetSoft Communications Inc., a consulting company located in Toronto, Canada. He is considered one of the best IT professionals by his peers, coworkers, colleagues, and customers. He obtained this status by continuously learning and improving his knowledge in the field of information technology. Currently, he holds more than 100 certifications, including MCSA, MCSE, MCTS, and MCITP (Vista, Mobile 5.0, Microsoft Communication Server 2007, Windows 2008 and Microsoft Exchange Server 2007), MCT, CIW-CI, CCA, CCSP, CCEA, CCI, VCP, CCNA, CCDA, CCNP, CCDP, CSE, and many more.

He brings over 15 years of management, technology, infrastructure designing, and assessment experience to NetSoft's team of experts and specialists. He has been working in the information technology industry for the past 15 years, eight of which have been as a System Analyst/Consultant specializing in thin client, Active Directory, and messaging solutions in various industries, including government, defense, telecom, manufacturing, pharmaceutical, retail, health care, technology, and financial fields. He is a well-known subject matter expert in the areas of IT infrastructure, terminal services, AD, Citrix, Exchange, and Windows Server 2008. Throughout his career, Tariq has had the opportunity to work on a diverse set of technical projects and to participate in the development of several business solutions. Some projects involved in-depth technical knowledge, while other projects took advantage of his soft skills where he was involved in defining and executing a product vision and strategy, driving the product road map, conducting research, as well as assisting key customers with implementation. He provides comprehensive solutions focused on Citrix and Microsoft technologies for clients ranging from 50 to 100,000 users, focusing mainly on architecting and deploying access infrastructure solutions for enterprise customers. He serves the company as a strategic business unit leader with both technical and managerial responsibilities. He is responsible for providing high-assurance thin client solutions to a worldwide enterprise. He provides day-to-day technical leadership and guidance as he and his staff develop enterprisewide solutions, processes, and methodologies focused on client organizations. He was recently hand-selected to lead enterprise-changing projects by senior executives of the clients he serves.

His work touches every part of a system's life cycle—from research and engineering to operational management and strategic planning. One of Tariq's primary focuses is developing best practices, processes, and methodologies surrounding access infrastructure that integrate with virtually every part of a customer's infrastructure.

Tariq enjoys working with customers and accomplishing different challenges and business goals on daily basis. During the latter portion of his career, Tariq has been concentrating mostly on Microsoft Windows 2000/2003/2008, Exchange 2000/2003/2007, Active Directory, and Citrix implementations. He is a professional speaker and has trained architects, consultants, and engineers on topics such as Windows 2008 Active Directory, Citrix Presentation Server, and Microsoft Exchange 2007. In addition to owning and operating an independent consulting company, Tariq not only has worked in a capacity of senior consultant but has utilized his training skills in numerous workshops, corporate training, and presentations. Tariq holds both a Bachelor of Science in Information Technology from Capella University, USA, and a Bachelor's degree in Commerce from University of Karachi, Pakistan. He is also exploring options to achieve his ALMIT (Masters of Liberal Arts in Information Technology) from Harvard University, in Cambridge, MA.

Tariq has coauthored multiple books, including the best-selling *MCITP: Microsoft Exchange Server 2007 Messaging Design and Deployment Study Guide: Exams 70-237* and *70-238* (ISBN: 047018146X), *The Real MCTS/MCITP Exam 640 Preparation Kit* (ISBN: 978-1597492355), *The Real MCTS/MCITP Exam 646 Preparation Kit* (ISBN: 978-1597492485), and *The Real MCTS/MCITP Exam 647 Preparation Kit* (ISBN: 978-1597492492). Tariq has worked on projects or provided training for major companies and organizations, including Rogers Communications Inc. Flynn Canada, HP, Citrix Systems Inc., Unicom Technologies, Gibraltar Solutions, and many others. He is a globally renowned Citrix, Active Directory, and Microsoft Exchange expert, speaker, and author who has presented at trainings and presentations around the world. He lives in Toronto, Canada, and would like to thank his father, Azad Bin Haider, and his mother, Sitara Begum, for his lifetime of guidance for their understanding and support to give him the skills that have allowed him to excel in work and life.

Contributors

Connie Wilson (CAN, MSCE, CCA) is a Senior Network Engineer with GE Capital in a designated "Center of Excellence" technology site. Currently, she has ultimate responsibility for design, implementation, and ongoing oversight of multiple Microsoft and MetaFrame servers supporting national and international GE divisions. Her specialties are troubleshooting, new product testing, thin client intercompany consulting, and systems optimization. Connie has a broad technology background with 15 years in progressively challenging IT work and a B.S. in Telecommunications. Before joining GE as an employee, Connie was an IT Consultant for GE, contracted primarily to bring a chronically problematic MetaFrame server farm to a high level of reliability.

Michael Wright (MCSE, CCEA, CISSP) is a Senior Security Engineer with Professional Resource Group, Inc., a Pennsylvania-based consulting firm providing resources to the Department of Defense in the areas of information security and information assurance. With more than 20 years of professional experience in the information technology fields, Michael has spent the last seven years working as both an IT and INFOSEC consultant working on projects for a variety of organizations, including the Pennsylvania Turnpike Commission, Computer Sciences Corporation, and the Defense Information Systems Agency (DISA).

Michael has submitted Citrix Security configuration documents to the Department of Defense and produced a white paper on FIPS-140 Compliancy and Smart Card Authentication for Citrix Presentation Sever 4.0. His professional affiliations include the Information Systems Security Association (ISSA) and the Institute of Electrical and Electronics Engineers (IEEE). Michael guest lectures on topics of information security and information assurance and serves as a volunteer for the Boy Scouts of America. A U.S. Marines veteran and a *magna cum laude* graduate from Harrisburg University of Science and Technology, Michael currently resides in Central Pennsylvania with his wife, Linda, and two children.

Contents

Chapter 1

Introduction to Security

Solutions in this chapter:

- Defining Security

- Understanding the Security Design Process

- Designing a Framework for Implementing Security

- Reviewing Compliancy

- Explaining Security Technologies

- Defining Authentication Models

☑ Summary

☑ Solutions Fast Track

☑ Frequently Asked Questions

Introduction

What is *security*? The answer we provide you may be surprising. Frankly, most of security is mental. How do you perceive what you are securing? How do you perceive threats to your environment? Do you believe the situation is manageable, or do you believe the situation is overwhelming? Are you willing to implement security into your daily operations? Do you consider security a ubiquitous part of overall operations? The list can go on. How you answer these questions will determine the level of security you will achieve.

Likewise, if you want to believe that computer hackers are invincible, you will do nothing to protect yourself. After all, why waste your money trying to stop someone you can't stop? If you approach information and computer security like they are manageable, then they are. If you throw up your hands in defeat, you will be defeated. The way you think affects the way that you perceive and approach the problem. If you believe security is manageable, you will perform basic research, determine reasonable security measures, and implement those measures. It is only then that you can say that you are taking personal responsibility for your security.

Consider the exploits of such infamous hackers as Kevin Mitnick, Adrian Lamo and Kevin Poulsen. Mitnick is best known for his social engineering feats which allowed him to hack the networks of Motorola, NEC, Nokia, Sun Microsystems and Fujitsu Siemens. Mitnick was eventually caught, prosecuted and served time in prison for his illegal activities. His activities did raise public awareness of security issues involving computer networks and their security.

Defining Security

There are lots of books about security, but the fact of the matter is that security is unattainable. You can never be completely secure. According to the *American Heritage Dictionary* and the *Random House Unabridged Dictionary*, the primary definition of security is essentially:

Freedom from risk or danger.

Your information will never be free of risk or danger. Anyone who tells you that they can provide you with perfect security is either a fool or a liar. Likewise corporate security programs are bound to fail, unless they really define their mission to their organization. Security is not about achieving freedom from risk. It is about the *management of risk*. Anyone who expects to achieve a perfect security solution will drive themselves crazy.

So fundamentally, security is about the management of loss or risk. Information security is about the management of loss of information and the resulting cost of that loss, or risk. It is therefore important to define risk.

Defining Risk

There are many different definitions of what is considered *risk*. It is useful at this point to provide a practical definition of risk. You can use the formula in Figure 1.1 to express risk.

Figure 1.1 Defining Risk

$$Risk = \left(\frac{Threat \times Vulnerability}{Countermeasures}\right) \times Value$$

Risk itself is basically the potential loss resulting from the balance of *threats*, *vulnerabilities*, *countermeasures*, and *value*. Usually it is a monetary loss; however, sometimes risk can even be measured in lives. To quickly break down the components of risk:

- **Threats** are the people or entities that can do you harm.

- **Vulnerabilities** are the weaknesses that allow the threat to exploit you.

- **Countermeasures** are the precautions you take.

- **Value** is the potential loss you can experience.

Defining Value

Value is the most important component of risk. Without value, there is no risk. You technically have nothing to lose. Usually though, you have some value embedded in most things that you own or do.

Let's look at an example of value in something that might seem inconsequential. If you have a piece of paper containing the location where you ate lunch yesterday, that would appear to be generally worthless. However, let's say that you left your wallet at the restaurant. That piece of paper could then be worth a very large amount of money to you.

Instead of leaving your wallet at the restaurant, let's assume that you are an executive for a large company, and you were meeting with people from another company that you were thinking of acquiring, or potentially were going to do business with. In this case, the information about the restaurant and meeting could help divulge the attendees and their potential business relationship. If a competitor or even a person who buys and sells stock learned of a meeting, they could profit from the information.

On the other hand, nobody may care. As you see though, Value is a relative and fluid issue. There are three different types of value: *monetary*, *nuisance*, and *competitor*.

- **Monetary Value** is the actual financial worth of information or other assets. If you lose the asset, you lose money. This is a hard value. Sometimes it is difficult to put a hard value on something, but you can find a way to estimate it. If you don't, your insurance people will.

- **Nuisance Value** is the potential cost of dealing with a loss. For example, while you may not have a financial loss related to an identity theft, the aggravation is costly. For example, there is the time lost in dealing with cleaning up a credit report. While you might not be found liable for someone running up bills in your name, you have to take the time to prove that the bills are not yours. This process can take months of your time. Nuisance value must be considered in any calculation of risk.

- **Competitor Value** is the value of an asset in the eyes of an adversary. For example, credit card receipts are generally worthless to an individual after a transaction is completed. People usually take the receipt home and throw it out. However, if the credit card receipt contains the full credit card number, it can be very valuable to a criminal. In the business world, a draft business proposal, for example, can be modified and the draft is then worthless to the business itself. However, if a competitor gets their hands on the draft, they can know exactly what they are competing against. So while something might not have an immediate value to you, its competitor value means that it might cost you value in the future.

When assessing risk, you first have to start with how much you have to lose. If you have nothing to lose, you don't have to worry about anything else. The reality though is that there is always something to lose, so you can't live in a dream world. However, it is critical to know how much you have to lose to temper how much you spend on your security program.

Defining Threat

The *threat* is essentially the *who* or *what* that can do you harm if given the opportunity. They cannot do you harm on their own. They require that you leave yourself vulnerable. Also, while people generally assume that Threats are malicious in nature, most threats that you face do not intend to cause you any harm.

First, you should consider that threats can be either malicious or malignant (we will break this down even further, later in this chapter). Malicious threats intend to do you harm. They include terrorist actions, malicious insiders, hackers, competitors, generic criminals, spies, and foreign countries. The type of harm they can cause you can vary by the type of intent they have. Again though, they have intent.

Malignant threats are threats which are always present. They do not have intent; however, they have the possibility to cause you harm. Malignant threats are present in everyday life. Unfortunately, the more you combat malicious threats, the more you enable malignant threats. For example, the Department of Homeland Security wants to remove markings on train cars that indicate the type of poisonous materials inside the car. They believe that terrorists might specifically target rail cars with poisonous materials, like chlorine, as they enter large cities. However, local fire departments need to know what is inside a rail car to know the potential dangers they face if a train catches fire, derails, and so on. Clearly, terrorists are a malicious threat, while fires and derailments are malignant threats that actually happen quite frequently.

A *who threat* is a person or group of people. These are entities that can do you harm. They can be insiders with malicious intentions, or they just might be uneducated employees. Threats can be competitors, foreign intelligence agencies, or hackers. There are also many nonmalicious people and groups that don't intend to cause you harm, but do. These are malignancies. There are millions of people on the Internet who leave their computers vulnerable. Their vulnerable computers can be taken over by a third party, who uses the computers to attack you. There are a seemingly infinite number of entities that may do you harm.

A *what threat* is an occurrence such as a hurricane, earthquake, flood, or snowstorm. These threats are completely uncontrollable and agnostic in their intent. They do however cause more damage than any malignant threat could ever hope to. For example, Hurricane Katrina caused tens of billions of dollars in damage and the loss of thousands of lives. Power outages have a cumulative cost of billions of dollars as well, and are caused by a wide variety of natural disasters, or even something as simple as a tree limb falling down. Tornados may seem like movie occurrences to many, but likewise cause the loss of billions of dollars and hundreds of lives each year.

When determining your risk, you have to evaluate which threats are relevant to your circumstances. Even though you might believe that you potentially face every threat in the world, the reality is that some threats are much more likely than others. As we will discuss in the next section on vulnerabilities, the threats are actually less of a factor than the vulnerabilities that they compromise.

Defining Vulnerability

Vulnerabilities are basically the weaknesses that allow the threat to exploit you. Threats are entities. By themselves, they cause you no harm. When there is vulnerability to exploit, you have risk. For example, let's say there is a hacker on the Internet. If you don't have a computer, there is no way for the hacker to exploit you. Having a computer does present a low-level vulnerability in and of itself. However, it doesn't have to be a major vulnerability. There can be many vulnerabilities in various software packages. The software itself, assuming it is not updated, is a vulnerability that can lead to a computer being compromised simply by being connected to the Internet. Some sources believe that the Microsoft Windows Meta File vulnerability that led to at least 57 malware entities cost the industry $3.75 billion. There are four categories of vulnerabilities: *technical*, *physical*, *operational*, and *personnel*.

- **Technical vulnerabilities** are problems specifically built into technology. All software has bugs of one form or another. A bug that creates information leakage or elevated privileges is a security vulnerability. Any technology implemented improperly can create a vulnerability that can be exploited.

- **Physical vulnerabilities** are infamous. They range from unlocked doors to apathetic guards to computer passwords taped to monitors. These are vulnerabilities that provide for physical access to an asset of value.

- **Operational vulnerabilities** are vulnerabilities that result from how an organization or person does business or otherwise fails to protect their assets. For example, Web sites can give away too much information. Stories about teenagers providing too much information on MySpace.com, which led to sexual assaults, are commonplace. While people are quick to condemn teenagers, the U.S. military currently finds that military personnel are putting sensitive information in their personal blogs. Corporate public relations departments have released corporate secrets in their marketing efforts.

- **Personnel vulnerabilities** involve how an organization hires and fires people within organizations. It can also involve the contractors involved in the organization. For example, if a company does not check references, it is opening itself up to fraud. Likewise, if there are problem employees, a company needs to make sure that they identify the problems and treat them appropriately. For example, in an organization that does not remove access for people who have left the company, those people can create future damage. While that might sound silly, there have been countless cases where a fired employee was able to access company computers and steal information or sabotage their former employer.

Defining Countermeasures

Countermeasures are the precautions that an organization takes to reduce risk. Theoretically, when you look at the risk formula, the assumption is that a countermeasure addresses a threat or vulnerability.

You can decrease your risk by decreasing value, but that is foolish. Decreasing value is a good way to get yourself fired. Ideally, you want to keep increasing your risk as the value of your organization grows. Likewise, it is probably better to have $1,000,000 dollars in a bank account that could be lost, instead of giving away all of the money so that you don't have anything to lose if someone hacks your bank. Just like vulnerability, there are four categories of countermeasures: *technical*, *physical*, *operational*, and *personnel*.

- **Technical countermeasures** are generally synonymous with computer and network security controls. They include utilities like antivirus software and hardware tokens that basically provide one-time passwords. These days there are thousands of software and hardware tools available as technical countermeasures.

- **Physical countermeasures** provide physical security. These countermeasures include locks, fences, security guards, and access badges. Anything that stops a physical theft, or physically limits access to something of value, is a physical countermeasure.

- **Operational countermeasures** are policies, procedures, and policies that are intended to mitigate the loss of value. This could include reviews of Web site content, policies as to what not to talk about outside of work spaces, and data classification. Any practice that intends to limit loss is an operational countermeasure.

- **Personnel countermeasures** specifically mitigate the handling of how people are hired and fired. They include background checks, policies for removing computer access upon an employee resigning, and policies to limit user access.

It is important to state that technical countermeasures do not necessarily intend to mitigate technical vulnerabilities. The same is true for physical countermeasures and physical vulnerabilities. For example, if you are concerned about passwords being taped to computer monitors, which is a physical vulnerability, a great countermeasure is a one-time password token, which is a technical countermeasure.

You Really Can't Counter Threat

When you look at the risk formula, it would appear that countermeasures can address both threats and vulnerabilities. In theory, that is correct. In the real world, it is really difficult to counter threat. The good news is that it doesn't really matter.

Let's examine why you cannot counter threat. Fundamentally, you cannot stop a hurricane, earthquake, flood, or other *what* threats. They will occur no matter what you do. At the same time, you cannot really counter a *who* threat. Maybe a background check can weed out known criminals; however this doesn't stop unknown criminals. While there is a war on terror, there are still more than enough terrorists to create a terror threat.

Again though, the good news is that you don't have to address the threat. If you counter vulnerability, you are essentially countering any threat that may exploit it. With regard to a natural disaster, like a hurricane, while you cannot stop a hurricane, you can eliminate the vulnerabilities that lead to loss. For example, you can locate facilities outside of areas vulnerable to a hurricane. You can create backup facilities outside of hurricane vulnerable areas. Although you cannot stop a script kiddie from existing, you can counter the underlying computer vulnerabilities that allow the hacker to exploit you. When you take this action, you stop the script kiddie from exploiting you, but you also stop competitors, cybercriminals, malicious employees, and all other threats from exploiting known computer vulnerabilities.

NOTE

A *script kiddie* (sometimes spelled kiddy) is a term typically given to an often immature, but nonetheless, dangerous exploiter of system security vulnerabilities found on the Internet. Script kiddies are different from typical hackers in that script kiddies use well-known and existing programs, techniques, and scripts to exploit weaknesses for their own pleasure. Hackers typically view script kiddies with contempt because the script kiddie does nothing to support the "art" of hacking. Hackers take pride in their work and go to great lengths to cover their tracks, whereas script kiddies seek out the attention for the results of their mischief.

What Is a Security Program?

Now that risk is fundamentally defined, we can address what security programs are supposed to do in theory. First, it is important to remember that you cannot stop all loss if you function in the real world. No matter what you do, you must acknowledge that you will experience some type of loss. Actually, you will experience many types of loss.

In business terms, you may contend that the goal of a security program is to identify the vulnerabilities that can be exploited by any of the threats that you face. Once you identify those vulnerabilities, you then associate the value of the loss that is likely to result from the given vulnerabilities.

The goal of a security program is then to choose and implement cost-effective countermeasures that mitigate the vulnerabilities that will potentially lead to loss.

The previous paragraph is possibly the most important paragraph in the book for people involved in the security profession. In truth, many professionals cannot succinctly and adequately state what their job functions are in business terms. How many times have you met a *book engineer* (someone who has simply studied and passed a certification examination with little or no practical experience) that has ended up doing more harm than good? Just because a person has the educational credentials to meet the expectations of a job, does not necessarily prepare that person for the position. In many cases, organizations do not adequately state the full description of job functions to be performed, especially as they relate to IT security. Consequently, improperly qualified personnel can be placed in jobs, thereby creating a security vulnerability.

Optimizing Risk

It is extremely important to point out that you are not trying to remove all risk. Again you can never be completely secure, and it is foolish to try. This is why your goal is to *optimize*, not minimize, risk.

Let's first discuss the concept of optimization versus minimization of risk. Minimization of risk implies that you want to remove as much risk, or loss, as possible. Using a typical home as an example, first examine what there is to lose. Assuming you have the typical household goods, various insurance companies might say that a house contains $20,000 to $50,000 of value, and the house itself has a value of $200,000. There is also the intangible value of the safety and wellbeing of your family.

Then consider the potential things that could happen to compromise the home. Obviously, you have physical thefts. There is also the potential for a fire. There have actually been cases of a car crashing into a home. You can also not ignore that objects, including airplanes, have fallen onto homes, destroying them and all of their occupants. You have tornados, earthquakes, floods, and other natural disasters. If you want to minimize risk, you must account for all possible losses, including some of the most bizarre ones.

If you are not in an earthquake prone area, you might think about ignoring this risk. However, even if you want to just limit your countermeasures to account for theft, you may consider improving locks on all the doors. What about the windows? Are you going to make all glass shatterproof? Then consider that most homes are made of wood. There is technically nothing to stop a motivated thief from taking a chainsaw to the side of your house. Do you then armor plate the entire house?

So you can see that minimizing your risk can lead to spending money on a lot of countermeasures that are not reasonable. The typical homeowner is not likely to do that. You cannot, however, just broadly discount a great deal of risk. *Optimization* implies that there is some thought to the process. You don't completely ignore any threat or vulnerability, but make a conscious decision that the likelihood of a loss combined with the value of the loss cannot be cost-effectively mitigated. So while it would generally be feasible to install a home alarm system for $300, and pay $25 per month for monitoring as a security countermeasure to protect $50,000 from theft, and to provide personal wellbeing, it would generally not be cost effective to install armor around the home to protect against the extremely unlikely case of a criminal using a chainsaw to get in your house.

You can use the chart in Figure 1.2 to represent risk and also to demonstrate clearly why you cannot completely minimize risk. The curve that begins in the upper left corner represents vulnerabilities and the cost associated with them. The line that begins on the bottom left represents the cost of countermeasures.

Figure 1.2 Cost of Minimizing Risk

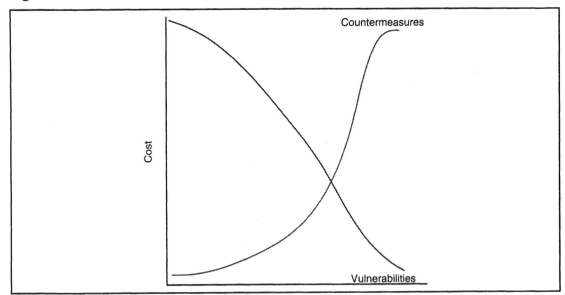

As you begin to implement countermeasures, their cost goes up; however, vulnerabilities and potential losses decrease. Assuming you implement countermeasures that actually address vulnerabilities, there can actually be a drastic decrease in potential loss. It is similar to the 80/20 rule, where you solve 80 pecent of the problems with 20 percent of the effort. You can contend that in the security field, you can solve 95 percent of the problems with 5 percent of the effort.

Since you will never have a situation of *no* potential loss, the vulnerability line never reaches 0 and is asymptotic. The potential cost of countermeasures, however, can keep increasing forever. So at some point, the cost of countermeasures is more than the potential loss of the vulnerabilities. It is illogical to ever spend more to prevent loss than the actual loss itself, so you never want to reach that point.

You also don't want to come close to that point either. The reason is that the potential loss is only *potential* loss. While it is theoretically possible to experience a complete loss, it is extremely unlikely. You need to base the cost of countermeasures on the likelihood of the loss combined with the cost of the loss. This is the concept of *risk optimization*. Figure 1.3 overlays a sample risk optimization line on the initial graph. This is the point that you have determined is the amount of loss you are willing to accept and the cost of the countermeasures that will get you to that point.

Figure 1.3 Understanding Risk Optimization

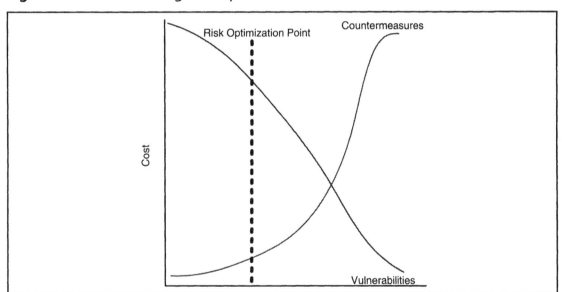

While we wish it was feasible to say that an entire security program should be based on this methodology, the reality is that most organizations are far from implementing this on a macro level. Instead, we recommend that people approach risk optimization on a micro level.

For example, if you were to take a specific vulnerability, such as bad passwords, and determine the potential loss, statistics show that it costs $40 per password reset. A large organization might average one password reset per employee per year. For an organization with 10,000 people, that is a cost of $400,000 per year just in resetting forgotten passwords. This does not even address the loss resulting from the compromise of passwords which could be tens of millions of dollars a year in a large corporation.

If the cost of a single sign-on tool, such as Citrix Password Manager, or one-time password token system costs approximately $1 million, and is good for four years, the average cost is $250,000 per year. The countermeasure is mitigating a hard cost of at least $400,000 per year as well as the loss of intellectual property totaling millions of dollars a year, so the $250,000 is clearly cost effective.

A thorough vulnerability assessment can go through this process for all likely vulnerabilities and countermeasures.

Consciously Accept Risk

The big issue to consider is that risk should be a result of careful deliberation. Whether you are deciding risk for yourself or your organization, you need to realize that you risk should be a consciously accepted fact. It is not a random result of a security program, but the basis for that security program.

If you were asked, "how much risk do you face?" would you have been able to answer accurately before reading this chapter? Do you know that answer now that you have read it? If you don't, you need to figure it out now.

Understanding the Security Design Process

Securing a Citrix XenApp enterprise network is hardly a small undertaking, but it becomes quite manageable if you approach it in an organized and systematic way. Before we can get into the specifics of configuring software, services, and protocols to meet your organization's security needs, we first need to determine what those needs are. The importance of understanding the *why?* will assist you with the *what?* and *how?* of your security design process.

In attempting to answer that all-important *why?*, we open this section with a look at analyzing a company's business requirements for securing its network and data. This includes examining any existing security policies and procedures with an eye toward how they might be incorporated into the new design, or how they might need to change to accommodate a new security framework. This step includes technical elements such as analyzing security requirements for different kinds of data—for example, some financial or medical data might be subject to specific security or financial policies like Sarbanes-Oxley and medical regulations such as HIPAA (Health Insurance Portability and Accountability Act of 1996)— and more human elements such as managing user expectations of security versus usability, and designing security awareness training to transform a user base from obstacle to ally.

Once you've determined your organization's security needs, your next questions is, "Whom are we securing our data against?" ("Know your enemy" is a mantra to live by, whether you're Sun Tzu or a network security administrator.) This section delves into the kinds of common attacks that an enterprise network might face, and what motivates both internal and external attackers. Later in this book, we also look at the steps needed to create a workable *Incident Response Plan*. After all, no matter how well you design your security system, you will almost certainly find yourself the victim of some type of security incident; it's how you respond to such an incident that can make or break a company's network.

The CIA Triad

No matter what kind of data you are dealing with, your task as a security professional is to ensure that it remains accessible, intact, and private. When securing data, a common phrase that you should be familiar with is *CIA Triad*, which stands for *confidentiality*, *integrity*, and *availability*. Taken as a whole, these are the three most important areas to consider when attempting to secure your network's assets and resources. The CIA triad (shown in Figure 1.4) makes up all of the principles of network security design. Depending on the nature of the information you're securing, some of the principles might have varying degrees of importance to you. However, all three will come into play at some point during the design process.

> **TIP**
>
> You've probably heard the information about the CIA triad regarding Confidentiality, Integrity, and Availability before. We re-enforce it (and it will come up again throughout this book) because it is important to truly understand how the three areas interact and will help you in making your network more secure.

Figure 1.4 Defining the CIA Triad

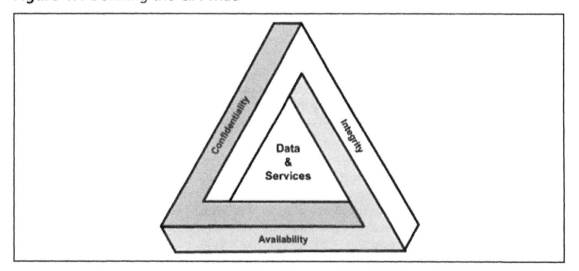

Confidentiality prevents any unauthorized disclosure of your data, and ensures that information will only be available to those people authorized to access it. Confidentiality is crucial when dealing with matters of privacy and protecting personal data such as credit card information, Social Security numbers, or other unique identifiers. It's also a critical matter when attempting to secure the kinds of intellectual property that we've already discusse; once a piece of "secret" information has been disclosed, there is no real way to *un*disclose it. However, determining the confidentiality of data is not only a matter of determining whether a piece of information is secret. When considering confidentiality, you also need to control *how* data can be accessed. For example, a sales representative using a database query to generate a list of follow-up customer service calls would not be a breach of your data's confidentiality. However, that same sales representative querying the same database for a list of e-mail addresses to use in her own personal mass e-mailing would be another matter entirely. Therefore, the confidentiality of data depends not only on *who* can access it, but *how* they are doing so.

To prevent attackers from gaining access to your network's confidential data, you can use any number of technical, administrative, and physical countermeasures. Physical controls can include a secure safe-deposit box to house items like birth certificates or medical records. From a technical standpoint, users might be allowed to access confidential data only from a specific location or by using a specific application. The use of cryptography and file encryption can ensure that only the owner of a file can access it, even if it is somehow transferred to a different location. In addition, end-user and administrative training can guard against an attacker using a so-called social engineering attack to obtain access to an employee's username and password. Whole texts have been dedicated to social engineering. In his 2002 book, *The Art of Deception*, Kevin Mitnick states that he compromised computers solely by using passwords and codes that he gained by social engineering.

The next item in the CIA triad, *integrity*, refers to measures that preserve the accuracy and consistency of data against fraudulent or unauthorized alteration. Data integrity safeguards should ensure that only authorized persons are allowed to make *changes* to network data. Protecting data integrity also means making sure that authorized users cannot make unauthorized changes to corporate data. While a bank teller should be authorized to view your checking account information, he certainly shouldn't be able to transfer monies from your account into someone else's without your approval.

TIP

Confidentiality of data is concerned with who can see a piece of data. Integrity moves into the question of who can modify that data.

Mechanisms that are designed to ensure data integrity need to address attacks on both data storage and data transmission across the network. If an attacker intercepts and changes data traveling from a server to a user's workstation, it is just as detrimental as if the attacker had altered the data on the server hard drive itself. It's important to note that not all attacks against data integrity are necessarily malicious; users can enter invalid data into an application, or an application error can cause an error in processing. (If anyone remembers the Monopoly game card that read "Bank Error in Your Favor, Collect $100," you have a good idea of this type of integrity failure.) Data integrity safeguards should protect against any type of integrity attack, whether intentional or innocuous. This can include administrative safeguards such as user training about the importance of accurate data entry, or technical controls in applications to ensure that 2 + 2 always equals 4, or to flag any unusual transactions for manual approval in case they were the result of an error. Some of the protections that can be used to prevent more malicious integrity attacks include the use of Intrusion Detection Systems (IDSes), data encryption, and the use of access control through the NTFS file system.

The final piece of the CIA Triad is the *availability* of data. Just like the old question of whether a tree falling in the forest with no one around actually makes a sound, if your users cannot access their data when they need to, then any measures that protect that data's confidentiality and availability are hardly worthwhile. The recent spate of denial-of-service (DoS) attacks on the Internet have been designed to infringe on the availability of Internet-based Web services, sometimes affecting a company's network access altogether. Data availability can be affected by more than just network attackers and can affect system and network availability. Environmental factors such as adverse weather conditions or electrical problems, and natural disasters like fires and floods can prevent systems and networks from functioning. This is why backup and restore and disaster recovery planning should be included in any network security design plan. Many organizations are now considering the ever increasing influx of SPAM e-mail as a potential DoS attack.

Why Does Your Organization Need a Security Infrastructure?

As we have previously stated, though it might seem self-obvious, it's important to begin any security design process with one simple question: "Why?" Why has your organization hired or contracted with you to design their security infrastructure? What goals do they hope to achieve by implementing a security design framework? As you work through this book, always keep that fundamental "Why?" in the back of your mind, since a security design plan that does not meet an organization's requirements for securing its data and resources is hardly worth the paper it's written on.

Organizations will make an investment in network security to protect their data and resources, or assets, from anything that might damage those assets. A company's *assets* can include physical inventory such as server hardware and software, and intellectual property such as the source code to an application or a trade secret. Moving beyond that, most (if not all) companies would consider things such as their business reputation to be an asset as well. With so many choices in doing business today, many consumers base their business and purchases on their confidence level in a corporation, and a company's reputation being tarnished by a highly publicized security break-in can destroy that confidence and cost a company sales and customers.

It's relatively simple to assign a dollar value to a piece of equipment or real estate; any loss in this area is called a *quantitative* loss. Threats to things like intellectual property and reputation are far more difficult to nail down to a hard-and-fast number, so losses in this area are referred to as being *qualitative*. A network security design plan will use Risk Management (discussed later in this chapter) to assign priorities to different types of network threats, and use that prioritization to develop an effective and *cost*-effective security design for an organization. By combining an understanding of your company's current security procedures with knowledge of the types of network threats it might face, you can design a security framework that will meet your company's needs.

Analyzing Existing Security Policies and Procedures

Corporate security policies create a baseline for performing security-related duties in a systematic and consistent fashion based on your organization's information security requirements. In many cases, these policies will extend beyond the borders of the IT department and involve areas of Human Resource, Finance, and Legal departments attempting to address compliance and reporting issues specific to a given industry. Having well-developed security policies will also assist an organization in demonstrating its security consciousness to customers, stockholders, and the like. Security policies typically fall into one of three categories:

- **Physical Policies** While physical security can often be overlooked by IT professionals, these policies discuss security measures that can be implemented using physical controls such as door locks, controlled room access, and procedures for adding or removing equipment from a machine room or office.

- **Technical Policies** These are the kinds of policies that you will be most familiar with as a Windows administrator. Technical policies include security measures that protect data and resources at the operating system level, including security templates and NTFS permissions.

- **Administrative Policies** These are typically procedural measures that control facets of information security that can't be enforced through technical measures, such as a nondisclosure agreement.

When designing a plan for securing a Windows environment, your first step should be analyzing any existing security policies and procedures with an eye to how they can be improved (or, if necessary, replaced) to meet the security needs of your organization. You should keep in mind some common reasons why security policies either fail or are not implemented properly within an organization. If users are unaware of security policies, the odds that they will comply with them are slim indeed—a policy that no one knows about is no better than not having any security policy at all. Security policies also run the risk of becoming outdated or too difficult for an end user to understand; try to keep the technical jargon to a minimum when explaining your users' rights and responsibilities within your security design plan. You also need to work with your human resources, legal counsel, and compliance officers to ensure that the policies you draft are indeed enforceable. While creating and analyzing documentation might seem tedious, the existence of viable security policies can save both time and money when tracking down and addressing any security incidents that might occur on a corporate network.

Evaluating a company's existing security infrastructure will illustrate where any gaps or holes currently exist that need to be addressed by a new security design; it will help you determine how much actually needs to be changed or updated, rather than wholly reinventing the wheel. If the organization is already security-conscious, your security design might only require minimal updates to reflect new advances permitted by the latest security technologies. If there is no security infrastructure currently in place (or if the current security practices are not being enforced), however, you obviously have a whole different task ahead of you. This task includes securing the corporate network, and crafting procedures and policies that will be embraced by management and users alike.

Your evaluation of current security practices should extend not only to administrative policies issued by IT or Human Resources, but also any technical measures that are already in place or lacking. For example, do all users have administrative rights to their local workstations? This might require reexamination of policies to better secure the workstation environment. Are there measures in place that prevent users from downloading or installing unauthorized software? Developing an awareness of the security practices of your organization will help you determine the best way to design a sound security infrastructure.

Acceptable Use Policies

A common component of many enterprise security policies is an *Acceptable Use Policy*, often called an AUP. This means precisely what it sounds like—an AUP is a document that details the types of activity that are (and are not) permitted on a corporate network. Since many network security incidents arise from risks or situations created by internal employees, an AUP is crucial so that a corporation will know that a violation of network security has occurred, and what steps they should take to address the situation. (Consider the potential implications, for example, of an internal employee running a network scanner like Nmap to discover vulnerabilities on corporate machines, whether out of curiosity or maliciousness.) An AUP needs to address the rights and responsibilities of both employee and company in defining what type of network access is acceptable on a corporate network, and what steps the IT department will take to determine whether a violation of Acceptable Use has occurred.

The AUP is also an appropriate place to discuss what level of privacy an employee can expect on a corporate network. While many companies hold that "reasonable" personal use of resources like e-mail and Internet access are allowable, you need to specify whether things like network traffic and e-mail messages will be subject to monitoring. This is even more pertinent if your organization uses encryption to secure documents, since users need to understand what circumstances, if any, would require a member of management or IT to access their encrypted files or other personal encryption information. Consult a legal resource when creating or assessing an AUP, since privacy laws often vary from location to location.

Tip

Why is an Acceptable Use Policy important? By having an AUP as part of the hiring process and annual security awareness training, someone that commits a security breach cannot simply say they did not know about the policy. In fact, the AUP is a countermeasure that mitigates the vulnerability of a user not accepting responsibility for their actions. The AUP is the document that can provide the "Ignorance is No Excuse" warning to users of your network.

Privacy versus Security

According to the Microsoft Security Resource Kit, privacy can be best defined as "freedom from the intrusion of others in one's personal life or affairs." Privacy and security are related topics, but are not synonymous: information security is concerned with protecting sensitive information from anyone who doesn't have appropriate access to it, while privacy is more of a customer-centric concept concerned with meeting a person or organization's preferences for how information concerning them should be handled. Aside from the privacy concerns of employee information that we discussed in the last section, your company needs to be concerned about how it will handle and protect things like customer information and sales data. A common application of this is the disclaimer you'll see on many Web sites stating that lists of e-mail addresses will not be sold or distributed to other companies as marketing material, or options for consumers to opt out of receiving any directed marketing mailings. The terms under which your company will contact its customers need to be strictly defined and adhered to, if for no other reason than that it will improve your relationship with your customers. (You'll do far less business with those people who decide that any e-mail from you is SPAM, after all.)

From a legal standpoint, privacy concerns are some of the most highly visible within information security today. Laws as old as the U.S. Federal Privacy Act of 1974 limit how the government can use personal data and information. More recently, industry-specific measures such as HIPAA provide more stringent measures to control how your health and medical information can be processed, stored, or transmitted to prevent inadvertent or unauthorized disclosure or misuse.

Within private industry, organizations need to examine the privacy of their own information and assets, even if it's not mandated by legal regulations. Most companies, especially those that do business online, have created Privacy Statements that delineate what type of information a company will be collecting. Are you tracking IP addresses? Referring sites? Machine data? All of these things should be specified in a Privacy Statement. Moreover, the Privacy Statement should clearly define how a customer's personal information will be used, and what other organizations, if any, will have access to this information. Your company's Privacy Statement should also detail how users or consumers can opt out of having their personal information shared or even stored at all if they change their minds at a later date. Finally, you should detail the information security measures that will be used to protect customer data, and be sure that the systems you implement will be able to measure up to the standards that you've laid out.

As a final note when considering your company's privacy policy, remember that IT and security professionals themselves can sometimes introduce risks to the privacy of information because of their nearly unlimited access to network data and resources. While we would like to think that all IT professionals have integrity, security professionals themselves should be aware of and subject to privacy measures to ensure the integrity of customer data.

Security versus Usability

Of primary concern when analyzing security policies is the need to balance security with usability. If your security policies are so stringent that your users are not able to access their data, then you haven't really designed a functional security scheme. While we all want to design the most secure network environment possible, mandating measures like a 20-character password will, in most cases, simply lead to administrative overhead and user frustration as they continually forget their passwords or need to have them reset. (And such a measure could actually decrease security by encouraging the dreaded "Password on a yellow sticky note next to the monitor" phenomenon.) When surveying existing documentation (or creating your own), always keep this balance between security and usability in mind.

Designing a Framework for Implementing Security

Designing a secure network framework can be broken into four conceptual pieces:

- Attack Prevention
- Attack Detection
- Attack Isolation
- Attack Recovery

While the measures we'll be discussing in this book are specific to different aspects of the Windows and XenApp infrastructures, each topic will map back to one of these four key principles. This can include disabling unnecessary Windows services to prevent network attacks, installing an IDS to alert you of any suspicious network activity, or designing an Incident Response Plan to facilitate recovery from an attack. In this section, we'll take a broad look at topics relating to each of these four principles.

To adequately prevent attacks against your network, you'll first need to determine what form they might actually take. We'll look at the STRIDE model of classifying network attacks as a starting point for both attack prevention and detection. While the number of network attacks has grown exponentially in recent time, understanding how a specific threat is acting against your network will greatly assist you in acting to circumvent any damage. Another component of attack prevention that we'll discuss is Risk Management, where you prioritize your resources to create a secure yet cost-effective network structure. Later in this book, we'll look at Incident Response as a way to both detect and respond to any malicious activity on your network.

Predicting Threats to Your Network

Predicting network threats and analyzing the risks they present to your infrastructure is one of the cornerstones of the network security design process. Understanding the types of threats that your network will face will assist you in designing appropriate countermeasures, and in obtaining the necessary money and resources to create a secure network framework. Members of an organization's management structure will likely be resistant to spending money on a threat that they don't under-stand; this process will also help them understand the very real consequences of network threats, and to make informed decisions about what types of measures to implement. In this section we'll discuss some common network attacks that you will likely face when designing a secure XenApp network, and how each of these attacks can adversely affect your network.

Threats can typically be broken down into two distinct categories: Environmental and Human (shown in Figure 1.5). From the diagram, you can see that each category can be broken down further. This book addresses those threats that we can immediately work with. Unless you have some super powers, I doubt that you can control the weather. As for your system environment, that is where a Business Continuity Plan comes into play which is beyond the scope of this book. Even though we will only address Internal and External threats in this book, you need to be cognizant of the other types of threats.

Figure 1.5 Defining Threat Categories

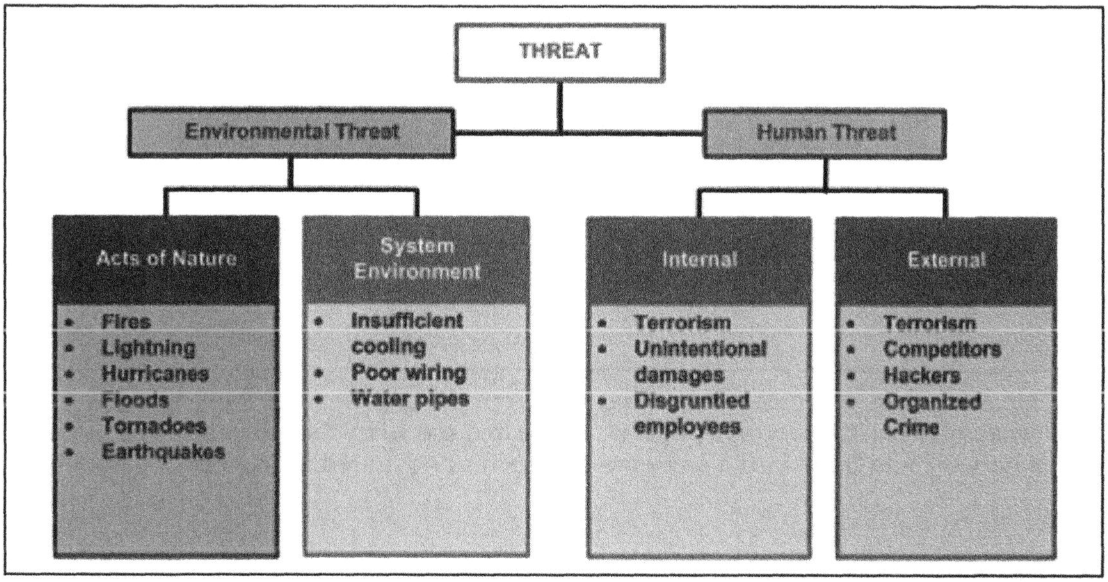

When classifying network threats, many developers and security analysts have taken to using a model called STRIDE, which is an acronym for:

- **Spoofing identity** These include attacks that involve illegally accessing and using account information that isn't yours, such as shoulder-surfing someone's password while he types it into his keyboard. This type of attack affects the confidentiality of data.

- **Tampering with data** These attacks involve a malicious modification of data, interfering with the integrity of an organization's data. The most common of these is a man-in-the-middle (MITM) attack, where a third party intercepts communications between two legitimate hosts and tampers with the information as it is sent back and forth. This is akin to sending an e-mail to Mary that says "The meeting is at 3 P.M.", but a malicious attacker intercepts and changes the message to "The meeting has been cancelled."

- **Repudiation** These threats occur when a user can perform a malicious action against a network resource and then deny that she did so, and the owners or administrators of the data have no way of proving otherwise. A Repudiation threat can attack any portion of the CIA triad.

- **Information Disclosure** This occurs when information is made available to individuals who should not have access to it. Information disclosure can occur through improperly applied network permissions that allow a user the ability to read a confidential file, or an intruder's ability to read data being transmitted between two networked computers. Information disclosure affects the confidentiality of your company's data and resources.

- **Denial of Service** So-called DoS attacks do not attempt to alter a company's data, but rather attack a network by denying access to valid users, by flooding a Web server with phony requests so that legitimate users cannot access it, for example. DoS attacks affect the availability of your organization's data and resources.

- **Elevation of Privilege** This type of attack takes place when an unprivileged, nonadministrative user gains administrative or "root level" access to an entire system, usually through a flaw in the system software. When this occurs, an attacker has the ability to alter or even destroy any data that he finds, since he is acting with administrative privileges. This type of threat affects all portions of the CIA triad, since the attacker can access, change, and remove any data that he sees fit.

When you are analyzing a potential network threat, try to remember the STRIDE acronym as a means of classifying and reacting to the threat. You can use the STRIDE model, not only with Windows and XenApp, but also throughout the life of your corporate network when designing and maintaining security policies and procedures.

Tip

Typical hackers download a scanning tool from the Internet and then choose a random Internet Protocol (IP) address range and see what they get back. For example, a hacker could download a freeware tool such as Advanced IP Scanner or Angry IP

Scanner, install and execute the tool, and then have a list of valid IP addresses from which they have a starting point for other more malicious activities. They look at the results from their scans to see if there are vulnerabilities that they have the tools or knowledge to exploit. They then use the tools or known techniques to break into the system and do what they want.

Recognizing Internal Security Threats

So, why is it so important to determine how an organization handles security for its internal users? Because in many ways, internal security threats from employees, contractors, or other sources can be even more damaging than external "hack attacks." This is because internal users have several factors working in their favor when they do damage against a network, whether unintentionally or maliciously. Internal users have far more opportunity to gain physical access to networking and computing equipment, even if it's just their personal workstation connected to the network LAN. Once an attacker gains physical access to a computer, most security safeguards become a simple matter to circumvent. If internal resources such as server rooms and wiring closets are not locked or secured in some way, the potential for damage increases exponentially. Additionally, if a company does not encrypt network traffic, it is a simple matter for an internal user to eavesdrop on network traffic to gain access to information that he should not actually have access to.

Moreover, internal users usually do not need to "break into" a network, *per se*, since they already have access via their username and password. This initial access to a corporate network gives any internal attackers a great advantage over their external counterparts, since the task of finding valid logon authentication to a network has already been handled for them by the network administrators. Especially if the attacker is someone with legitimate administrative privileges, it can be extremely difficult to determine if she is abusing her network credentials for illicit purposes.

Increasing Security Awareness

As a part of any security design plan, you should include measures that will provide security training for both IT and non-IT personnel within an organization. Since most people are resistant to change for its own sake, security awareness training is always helpful to bring people onboard with any new or changed security requirements or procedures. You might find that some users are not following security practices or introducing vulnerabilities because they do not know about their responsibilities in securing the corporate network. Users should be aware of security measures available to them such as file encryption, what makes a complex password better than a weak one, and the importance of physically securing resources like portable computers, PDAs, and the like. You should help your users understand when it is and is not appropriate to discuss their network log-on information, and that they should under no circumstances share their password with anyone, even someone from (or claiming to be from) IT. Security Awareness Training is perhaps the *only* measure that will help to address nontechnical attacks like social engineering, which rely on cooperation from unsuspecting users to gain access to a network.

TIP

When discussing information security a topic of discussion that usually comes up is that of change. Many people are resistant to change for a variety of reasons. As a security professional, you should be the one that openly embraces change and have the viewpoint that you will lead change (at least from a security standpoint) within your organization.

Recognizing External Threats

Now that we've discussed a model for classifying network threats, we can look at some of the more common attacks in more detail. While entire books can (and have been) be written solely discussing the kinds of threats that we'll be looking at in this section, we'll be giving you a "birds-eye" view of the kinds of attacks that your network security design will need to guard against.

Denial-of-Service Attacks

As we've already mentioned, the DoS attack (and its first cousin, the *Distributed* DoS attack) works to disrupt services on a network so that legitimate users cannot access resources they need. It should be noted that a DoS attack does not necessarily have to be initiated from an external source. Some examples include attempts to disrupt the connection between two specific machines, or more commonly, attempts to flood an entire network with traffic, thereby overloading the network and preventing legitimate traffic from being transmitted. There can also be instances where an illegitimate use of resources can result in denial of service. For example, if an intruder uses a vulnerability in your FTP server to upload and store illegal software, this can consume all available disk space on the FTP server and prevent legitimate users from storing their files. A DoS attack can effectively disable a single computer or an entire network.

A common venue of attack for DoS is against an organization's network bandwidth and connectivity; the goal of the attacker is to prevent other machines from communicating because of the traffic flood. An example of this type of attack is the "SYN flood" attack. In this type of attack, the attacker begins to establish a connection to the victim machine, but in such a way that the connection is never completed. Since even the most powerful server has only a certain amount of memory and processor cycles to devote to its workload, legitimate connection attempts can be denied while the victim machine is trying to complete these fake "half-open" connections. Another common DoS is the so-called "PING of Death," where an attacker sends so many PING requests to a target machine that it is again overloaded and unable to process legitimate network requests.

An intruder might also attempt to consume network resources in other ways, including generating a massive amount of e-mail messages, intentionally generating system errors that need to be included in Event Viewer logs, or misusing FTP directories or network shares to overload available disk space. Basically, anything that allows data, whether on a network cable or hard drive, to be written at will (without any type of control mechanism) can create a denial of service when a system's finite resources have been exhausted by the attacker.

Distributed Denial-of-Service Attacks

Distributed denial-of-service (DDoS) attacks are a relatively new development, made possible (and attractive to attackers) by the ever-expanding number of machines that are attached to the Internet. The first major wave of DDoS attacks on the Internet appeared in early 2000, and targeted such major e-commerce and news sites as   .

Yahoo!, eBay, Amazon, Datek, and CNN. In each case, the Web sites belonging to these companies were unreachable for several hours at a time, causing a severe disruption to their online presence and effectiveness. Many more DDoS attacks have occurred since then, affecting networks and Web sites large and small.

WARNING

While most publicity surrounding DDoS attacks has focused on Web servers as a target, remember that any computer attached to the Internet can fall victim to the effects of a DDoS attack. This can include everything from file servers or e-mail servers to your XenApp servers if directly attached to the Internet.

The DDoS attack begins with a human *Attacker* using a small number of computers, called *Masters*. The Master computers use network scanners to find as many weakly secured computers as they can, and use system vulnerabilities (usually well known ones) to install a small script or a service (referred to in the UNIX world as a *daemon*) onto the insecure computer. This machine has now become a *Zombie*, and can now be triggered by the Master computer to attack any computer or network attached to the Internet. Once the organizer of the DDoS attack has a sufficient number of Zombie machines under his control, he will use the Zombie-fied machines to send a stream of packets to a designated target computer or network, called the *Victim*. For most of the attacks, these packets are directed at the victim machine. Figure 1.6 provides a graphical illustration of the Master-Zombie-Victim relationship.

Figure 1.6 Illustration of a DDoS Attack

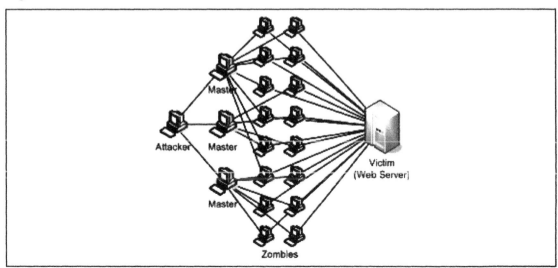

The distributed nature of the DDoS attack makes it extremely difficult to track down the person or persons who began it; the actual attacks are coming from Zombie machines, and the owners of these machines are often not even aware that their machines have been compromised. Making matters even more difficult, most network packets used in DDoS attacks use forged source addresses, which means that they are essentially lying about where the attack is coming from.

Viruses, Worms, and Trojan Horses

Viruses, trojans, and worms are quite possibly the most disruptive of all of the security threats that we'll be discussing in this section. These three types of threats, working alone or in combination, can alter or delete data files and executable programs on your network shares, flood e-mail servers and network connections with malicious traffic, and even create a "back door" into your systems that can allow a remote attacker to take over control of a computer entirely. While you'll often hear these three terms used interchangeably, each one is slightly different. A virus is a piece of code that will alter an existing file, and then use that alteration to recreate itself many times over. A worm simply makes copies of itself over and over again for the purpose of exhausting available system resources. A worm can target both hard drive space and processor cycles.

Trojan horses take their name from a Greek myth, in which attackers from Sparta infiltrated the Greek city of Troy by hiding inside a horse statue masquerading as a gift. When the Trojans brought the gift inside the city walls, they discovered too late that it was filled with Spartan soldiers who emerged from within the horse and took over the city. In similar fashion, a computer-based trojan will disguise itself as a friendly file, usually an e-mail attachment. This file, when executed, can damage computer data or install a "back door" into the operating system that will allow a remote attacker to take over the system entirely.

NOTE

For more information about computer viruses and other similar threats, check out www.symantec.com, www.mcafee.com, www.trendmicro.com, or www.-us-cert.gov for the latest virus threats and trends around the world.

Software Vulnerabilities

Some network attacks target vulnerabilities in the way that a software application or entire operating system has been programmed. For example, a buffer overflow attack occurs when a malicious user sends more data to a program than it knows how to handle. For example, you've all seen Web forms that ask you to fill in your personal information: first name, last name, telephone number, and so forth. A careless developer might program the "First Name" field to only be able to handle 10 characters; that is, a name that is 10 letters long. If the Web application does not check for buffer overflows, an attacker can input a long string of gibberish into the First Name field in an attempt to cause a buffer overflow error. At this point, the attacker could even embed the name of an executable file into that long string of text and actually pass commands to the system as if he or she were sitting at the server console itself. A similar software vulnerability is a *format string vulnerability* or *SQL injection attack* that would allow an attacker to insert random data into a file or database, once again including malicious code that can be executed against the server as if the attacker were sitting right in front of the keyboard.

Another attack that is specifically common to Web and FTP servers is a directory traversal vulnerability. This type of vulnerability allows a user to gain access to a directory on a server that he hasn't been specifically given permissions to, by virtue of having permissions to a parent or child directory. Say someone goes to the following URL: www.airplanes.com/biplanes/cessna/model1.html. He decides to manually change this URL (in other words, not following an <HREF> link on the site itself) to www.airplanes.com/biplanes/piper, to see if the directory structure holds any information there. If the Web site hasn't been properly patched and configured with the correct security settings, the user might find that he now has access to every single file in the piper/directory. Even worse, he can once again execute a command from the Web browser by changing the URL to something like www.airplanes.com/biplanes/piper/del%20*.*. ("%20" is used in HTML to represent a space, so that command would read "del *.*" on a regular command line.) Another common attack also occurred in NetMeeting and Windows Media Player some time ago, where an attacker could insert special characters during a file transfer that would allow him to browse an unsuspecting user's hard drive directory structure.

Notes from the Underground...

Blended Threats

As if it weren't hard enough to keep track of viruses, worms, and other similar attacks, the information security industry has coined a new term for a type of attack that blends the worst of both. Blended threats combine many of the characteristics of viruses, worms, Trojan horses, and attacks against software vulnerabilities to increase the rate at which they can spread and cause damage. If you've dealt with the fallout of threats like Code Red (which began circulating in 2001), Klez, and the like, you've already seen how insidious a blended threat can be.

Blended threats spread using multiple methods, usually beginning with a malicious e-mail attachment. Once the unsuspecting user launches the attachment, the now-infected machine will use a network-based attack to scan for vulnerabilities in other systems, including embedding code in HTML files on a Web server, sending a deluge of virus-infected e-mail from a compromised e-mail server, or altering files on an internal server's network shares. Even worse, these attacks are able to spread without any human intervention—they continuously scan the local network or the Internet for new systems to attack and infect.

The Nimda worm presents a perfect example of how a blended threat operates and spreads. Machines were initially compromised by Nimda through an e-mail attachment that exploited a software vulnerability in Microsoft Outlook and Outlook Express. This software vulnerability allowed the infection to spread without the user's

Continued

intervention, or even awareness. Once a desktop machine was infected, Nimda began to perform network scans to attack network shares and Web servers using yet another software vulnerability in an Internet Information Server.

The Internet Explorer vulnerability enabled Nimda to infect a Web server in such a way that any user who connected to the site would automatically have malicious code downloaded to his or her desktop, thus continuing the infection cycle. With so many venues to continue the spread of the virus, it's no wonder that Nimda caused worldwide havoc on many home and corporate networks.

The emergence of blended threats presents a huge challenge for Information Security professionals, since threats such as Nimda can now spread much more quickly than any of their nonblended predecessors. Without proper planning and monitoring, a network can become overloaded with a virus outbreak before an administrator is even aware of the problem. Moreover, since blended threats spread through methods other than just e-mail attachments, security professionals need to find new ways to secure other forms of network traffic such as Web server and file server traffic.

Nontechnical Attacks

A final category of attacks that we'll discuss here are those that use less technical means to circumvent network security. So-called social engineering attacks rely on an unsuspecting user's lack of security consciousness. In some cases, the attacker will rely on someone's goodwill, using a tactic like "We've really got to get this done and we don't have access to these files, can you help me?" (Most of us really want to be helpful to those around us.) Other social engineering attacks will use a more threat-based approach, insisting that the attacker is the secretary for Mr. Big-Shot VP who needs his password reset right away and heaven-help-you if you keep him waiting. This relies on the assumption that a show of authority will cause someone without adequate training to bypass security procedures to keep the "big-shot important user/client" happy. Because social engineering attacks are nontechnical in nature, the measures required to defend against them are more educational than any others are. It's critical to have well-understood security policies in place that apply to everyone, regardless of their position in your company. This will assist in preventing an attacker from circumventing security procedures because a help desk or other staff member is unaware of them.

Are You Owned?

The Overly Helpful Help Desk

I recall working for a company that had several satellite offices with several hundreds of users at each office. In an attempt to centralize help desk administration and to reduce the costs of password resets, the company selected to outsource its help desk. A secure

Continued

VPN link was established between the help desk vendor and the corporation and users could dial a local extension to be routed to the external help desk. The IT staff had incorporated the use of firewalls, network audits and scanning, IPsec, strong password enforcement, and so on. Yet, despite these measures they consistently received complaints that network data was being deleted at random. Initial investigation revealed that a manager was deleting the information, until it was learned that deleting the information negatively affected the manager in question. Through extensive research, it was learned that a disgruntled user figured out that he could call the help desk and request a password reset indicating he was his manager, and the help desk would reset the password to a corporate default, and the disgruntled employee had access to his manager's data. The manager trying to log on the next day simply thought he typed in his password wrong and got locked out and called to have his password reset. He didn't even correlate the events of the deleted data with having to change his password.

The problem was that the help desk had no way to verifying user authenticity, so the password was reset to the corporate default. The problem did not lie with the technical measures the IT staff had implemented, or the help desk, but rather with security policies and procedures that had NOT been implemented.

Eventually, the corporation established policies for the help desk and modified the way passwords were reset to creating a strong, random password and then automatically e-mailing the password to the user's e-mail address on record. Eventually, a password self-service portal was added so that users could only have their password reset based on a series of personal questions that the user previously answered.

Ultimately, the issue was the lack of clearly defined security policies and procedures.

What Motivates External Attackers?

Just as you need to know why a company is designing a security infrastructure, it's also helpful to know the reasons why total strangers seem compelled to make your life as a network administrator more difficult. Network attackers, usually referred to colloquially as hackers, attempt to break in to corporate networks for any number of reasons, and sometimes knowing the reason why they are doing so can assist you in defusing the threat and tracking down the perpetrator.

The most common, although perhaps not the most obvious, reason for attacking a company's network is to gain fame or notoriety. Whether it is someone seeking acceptance from an online hacker community, or someone who simply wants to see his or her name in the papers, attacks motivated in this manner tend to be extremely public in nature. A common attack in this category is Web site defacement, where an attacker will exploit a vulnerability in a company's Web server and change their default Web page to read something embarrassing or self-aggrandizing. Imagine if you went to the Web site of a company you were accustomed to dealing with and you were presented, not with the familiar home page, but a page containing offensive images or phrases like "The HAXOR Group OWNS This Site!" Companies that are the victims of these attacks find themselves facing public embarrassment and financial loss, while the perpetrators often brag about the successful attack or laugh at the news reports of the company's dismay.

Another common phenomenon is the hacker who breaks into networks for fun; they enjoy the challenge of defeating an "undefeatable" security system. This can be anyone from a college student attempting to flex his computing muscles against Internet-connected machines, to an internal employee who just wants to see what she can get away with on the office PC. In many cases, these attackers do not consider their actions unethical or immoral, their thinking being that "if the vulnerability hadn't been there in the first place, we wouldn't have been able to exploit it."

The last category of attackers that we will discuss (although this list is by no means complete) is those who are motivated by personal gain, either hacking for pay or as a means of exacting revenge. In the case of the former, this can range from simple criminal actions to attackers performing industrial espionage (trying to steal the secret formula from the database server) or even information warfare between governments. The "revenge" attacker is typically a former employee of a company, who might plant a "logic bomb" to damage networking resources after he or she has been fired or laid off.

Tip

A logic bomb is a type of attack, whether a virus, worm, DDoS, or trojan, that lies dormant until triggered by a specific event. This event is usually associated with a date, such as the now-famous Michelangelo e-mail virus that was triggered to be released on the date of the artist's birthday.

Implementing Risk Analysis

A favorite scenario many security professionals like to use is that the only way to have a truly secure computer is to unplug the network cable from the wall, remove the keyboard, mouse, and monitor, and dump the CPU in the middle of the ocean. While this is a somewhat sarcastic statement, the message is clear: no computer network will ever be completely free from security risks. When designing security for your network, therefore, a large part of your job will actually be a matter of *risk management*—deciding how to use finite resources to provide your company with the best security measures possible. When creating a *risk analysis* strategy, you should involve staff from areas other than IT, including your company's Legal and Finance departments, to assist you in assigning values to various projects and assets. Anyone who plays a leadership role in any project or product that your company is working on should have a say in the risk analysis process.

The first step in implementing a risk analysis strategy is assessing the value of your assets and resources. Some assets, such as physical servers, networking hardware, and cabling, are relatively simple to assign a value to, based on their purchase price minus any depreciation from the accountants. Other items will need to be valued according to the cost of producing them—the salaries of programmers during the development of a new software application, for example—or the cost to the company if something were lost. Assigning a concrete monetary value to something like a lost sales lead caused by an e-mail server outage can be difficult, but the risk analysis process cannot be successful without having this information available.

Next, you need to identify the potential risks to each asset in turn, including (but not limited to) the kinds of attacks that we've already discussed in this chapter. For each potential attack, you'll define the potential damage that could be done to each asset, again in monetary terms. To use our example of a lost sales lead resulting from an e-mail server outage, let's say that the company sales manager does some research and determines that your company loses about $1,000 an hour when the e-mail server is unavailable. Last year, the e-mail server was unavailable for 20 hours when it became overloaded with messages created by the various viruses; virus threats cost your company $20,000 last year. You can use this sort of equation to assign a value to most types of security risks faced by your company, allowing you to prioritize your budget and resources where they will do the most good.

Addressing Risks to the Corporate Network

Once you have created a prioritized list of risks to your network, as well as their associated costs, your next step will be to determine a course of action in handling each risk. When deciding how to address risks to your network, you typically have one of four options:

- **Avoidance** You can avoid a risk by changing the scope of the project so that the risk in question no longer applies, or change the features of the software to do the same. In most cases, this is not a viable option, since eliminating a network service like e-mail to avoid risks from viruses would usually not be seen as an appropriate measure. (Network services exist for a reason; your job as a security professional is to make those services as secure as possible.) One potential example of how avoidance would be a useful risk management tactic would be a company with a single server that acted as both a Web server and a database server housing confidential personnel records, with no interaction whatsoever between the Web site and personnel information. Purchasing a dedicated Web server and moving it to the DMZ or public network would in effect remove the personnel database from the Web server entirely. Having the employee database server on a private network segment with no contact to the Internet would be a way of avoiding Web–based attacks on personnel records.

- **Transference** You can transfer a risk by moving the responsibility to a third party. The most well-known example of this is purchasing some type of insurance—let's say flood insurance—for the contents of your server room. While the purchase of this insurance does not diminish the likelihood that a flood will occur in your server room, by purchasing insurance you have ensured that the monetary cost of the damage will be borne by the insurance company in return for your policy premiums. It's important to note that transference is not a 100–percent solution—in the flood example, your company will likely still incur some financial loss or decreased productivity in the time it takes you to restore your server room to working order, and flood insurance is not going to actually replace your data either. Like most risk management tactics, bringing the risk exposure down to zero in this way is usually an unattainable goal.

- **Mitigation** This is what most IT professionals think of when implementing a risk management solution. Mitigation involves taking some positive action to reduce the likelihood that an attack will occur, or reduce the potential damage that would be caused by an attack, without removing the resource entirely as is the case with avoidance. Patching servers, disabling unneeded services, and installing a firewall would be some solutions that would fall under the heading of risk mitigation.

- **Acceptance** After you have delineated all of the risks to your infrastructure that can be avoided, transferred, or mitigated, you are still left with a certain amount of risk that you won't be able to reduce any further without seriously impacting your business (taking an e-mail server offline as a means to combat viruses, for example). Your final option is one of acceptance, where you decide that the residual risks to your network have reached an acceptable level, and you choose to monitor the network for any signs of new or increased risks that might require more action later.

TIP

When determining the cost effectiveness of a safeguard, remember this formula: The total savings to your organization is the amount of money that the safeguard will be saving you, minus the cost of the safeguard itself.

Therefore, if you install a $25,000 firewall that you estimate will save you $100,000 from downtime due to hacker intrusions, the total net savings provided by the firewall is: $100,000 (savings) – $25,000 (cost of safeguard) = $75,000.

Analyzing Security Requirements for Different Types of Data

Once you've gone through the risk analysis process, you should have a good idea of what types of data are present on your network and how much the loss of each type of data will cost your organization, both in a quantitative and qualitative sense. At this point, it's often helpful to classify data into discrete categories to assist you in securing your information in an efficient manner. Many organizations use a four-tiered classification system that organizes data and resources into one of four categories:

- **Public** This might include informational items such as product listings on the corporate Web site and press releases issued by marketing or public relations. There is probably little risk associated with someone attempting to steal this data, since it is assumed to be common knowledge among a company's customers and competitors. However, the integrity of this data still needs to be maintained to retain consumer confidence and potential sales. (Imagine the impact if a press release were altered to read that your company suffered a 10-percent loss in sales, rather than posting a 20-percent growth.)

- **Private** This will include information that might be widely known within your company, but perhaps sufficiently sensitive that you do not want to share it with the world at large. Data contained on a corporate intranet might be included in this category, since it often includes contact information for specific personnel, as well as information concerning internal systems that might not be appropriate for release to the public.

- **Confidential** This is the kind of information (along with secret data) that most of us think of when we begin constructing a security plan. This can include information like customer financial records or corporate payroll information. The disclosure or alteration of data of this nature would almost certainly lead to real losses to the company, whether in terms of financial loss or reputation.

- **Secret** This is the most confidential classification of data and most often extends to intellectual property such as trade secrets, patent information, or upcoming products and ventures. The loss or defacement of secret data would be almost irreparable, since a trade secret that has been disclosed to the public or to competitors cannot simply be made secret again with the wave of a wand. Data at this level must be afforded the most stringent protection levels within your corporate network.

After you have classified your organization's data and resources, you can use this information to assign different security templates or policies to the different categories. This will increase the efficiency of your network security design, since you will be able to more easily assign similar or identical security measures to data that has similar security requirements. It will also save you from wasting time or effort assigning the same level of protection to, say, your company's softball schedule than you assign to more critical information such as sales or payroll data.

Defining Best Practices for Designing Your Security Framework

Are you feeling overwhelmed with the high level overview at this point? Before you can delve into the nuts and bolts of securing your XenApp environment, you must have a thorough understanding of basic information security principles. To assist you with evaluating your security needs, the following best practices can assist you:

- Don't start from scratch or reinvent processes others have already successfully created.

- Maintain open and productive communications with management and users.

- Attempt to ascertain what you don't know and determine how you will bridge this knowledge gap.

When drawing up even the most basic, foundational guidelines for your organization's security policy, you should never have to "start from scratch" or "reinvent the wheel." There are many examples of security polices relating to information security, and much of the groundwork for establishing a viable security policy that can be modified to meet the needs of your organization can be readily be found from a variety of sources. Organizations such as the American National Standards Institute (ANSI) (www.ansi.org), the International Organization for Standardization (ISO) (www.iso.org), and the SANS Institute (www.sans.org), are excellent resources.

An excellent starting point is the ISO 27001 and ISO 27002 series of information security standards published by ISO. ISO 27001 is titled "Information Technology – Security Techniques – Information Security Management Systems" and should be used in conjunction with ISO 27002. ISO 27001 covers certification requirements for organizations wishing to achieve an ISO level accreditation. ISO 27002, titled "Code of Practice for Information Security Management," lists security control objectives and recommends a range of specific security controls that, if implemented, will typically meet the certification requirements outlined in ISO 27001.

Structuring your security policy around the ISO 27002 standard will provide you with a comprehensive policy that should cover most of your organization's needs. The specifics of these ISO documents are available for purchase from the ISO Web site (www.iso.org). The sections covered by ISO 27002 are:

- Risk assessment

- Security policy – management direction

- Organization of information security – governance of information security

- Asset management – inventory and classification of information assets

- Human resources security – security aspects for employees joining, moving, and leaving an organization

- Physical and environmental security – protection of the computer facilities

- Communications and operations management – management of technical security controls in systems and networks

- Access control – restriction of access rights to networks, systems, applications, functions, and data

- Information systems acquisition, development, and maintenance – building security into applications

- Information security incident management – anticipating and responding appropriately to information security breaches

- Business continuity management – protecting, maintaining, and recovering business-critical processes and systems

- Compliance – ensuring conformance with information security policies, standards, laws, and regulations

The SANS Security Policy Project (www.sans.org) can also provide you with some very good information on establishing or revising information security policies. The point is you do not need to create this information by yourself.

When you are reviewing your organization's information security policies, you should seek participation from management, users, and those departments that will be affected by implementation of an information security policy. When you can prove the strategic benefits of having a sound information security framework, it will be easier for you to request the resources you need in order to implement your plan. You also want approval from your management so that the information security framework you introduce can be readily enforced.

Probably the worst thing you can do as a security administrator is to think that you know more than you actually do. This may sound alarming to some, but in many cases we are simply afraid to say "I don't know." For example, let's say you are responsible for implementing the security framework for just the XenApp environment within your organization. Your XenApp environment contains web servers, SQL servers, routers, and firewalls, but your primary area of expertise is Windows and XenApp. If you attempt to implement firewall policies without having a comprehensive understanding of how your specific firewalls work, you may end up doing more harm than good. It is at this point you should seek out assistance from others you trust. Our experience has shown that typically organizational management would rather pay less to supplement your knowledge and experience rather than face huge costs (maybe even in the form of fines and penalties) because their system was breached and vital data was compromised.

In order for many security policies to be properly accepted and enforced, your users need to be made aware of why information security policies exist in the first place. Being proactive with communications to an organization's users about InfoSec policies will ensure the successful implementation of those policies. Even though you can come up with a basic framework in a short period of time, you will find that as your security infrastructure progresses, new items will reveal themselves, requiring changes to your original plan. This is where you will fine-tune your security framework into detailed standards utilizing input from your employees, departments, management, and even customers.

Reviewing Compliancy

There are plenty of standards and regulations out there. If you are a publicly traded company in the United States, you must adhere to the *Sarbanes-Oxley Act of 2002* (SOX) mandates. If you are in the health care industry your network must comply with the *Health Insurance Portability and Accountability Act* (HIPAA) standards. The credit card industry banded together to develop the *Payment Card Industry* (PCI) *Data Security Standards* (DSS) to ensure that credit card customer information is adequately protected and to protect the industry.

The information security field has a number of laws and regulations to adhere to. However, as evidenced by the volume and continuing occurrence of data compromise and exposure, many organizations still fail to enforce adequate security measures.

The bottom line is that organizations need to secure and protect their networks. In some cases, weak network security may only affect the company. However, when the data on the corporate network contains personal information about patients, customers, or employees, a breach of security can have implications far beyond the company.

Citrix and HIPAA, Sarbanes-Oxley, FERPA

Application virtualization provided by Citrix products is functioning in all aspects of our information technology environment, including many organizations that are governed by federal and/or state guidelines. We will only cover the most well known to provide you with examples of how measures are being taken to secure information technology infrastructures.

The *Health Insurance Portability and Accountability Act* (HIPAA) was enacted by the U.S. Congress in 1996. This act requires the establishment of a national set of standards for electronic health care transactions and national identifiers for providers, health insurance plans, and employers.

The act also addresses the security and privacy of health data. The standards are meant to improve the efficiency and effectiveness of the nation's health care system by encouraging the widespread use of electronic data interchange.

The *Privacy Rule* of the act requires that reasonable steps must be taken by health care providers to ensure the confidentiality of communications with individuals. The Privacy Rule pertains to all Protected Health Information (PHI) including paper and electronic.

The *Security Rule* deals specifically with Electronic Protected Health Information (EPHI). It lays out three types of security safeguards required for compliance:

- Administrative Safeguards

- Physical Safeguards

- Technical Safeguards

For each of these types, the rule identifies various security standards, and for each standard, it names both required and addressable implementation specifications. Required specifications must be adopted and administered as dictated by the Rule. Addressable specifications are more flexible. Individual covered entities can evaluate their own situation and determine the best way to implement addressable specifications. The standards and specifications are as follows:

- **Administrative Safeguards** Policies and procedures designed to clearly show how the entity will comply with the act. These are your written documents providing direction for anyone using the information technology infrastructure, whether as an administrator or as a user.

■ **Physical Safeguards** Controlling physical access to protect against inappropriate access to protected data. Are the servers in a secured location?

■ **Technical Safeguards** Controlling access to computer systems and enabling covered entities to protect communications containing PHI transmitted electronically over open networks from being intercepted by anyone other than the intended recipient. Information systems housing PHI must be protected from intrusion. When information flows over open networks, some form of encryption must be utilized.

The *Family Educational Rights and Privacy Act* (FERPA) is a federal law that protects the privacy of student education records. This act applies to all schools and educational institutions that receive funds under an applicable program of the U.S. Department of Education.

The *Sarbanes-Oxley Act of 2002* (SOX or Sarbox) is a federal law that was enacted in response to a number of major corporate and accounting scandals including those affecting Enron, Tyco International, and others. These scandals, which cost investors billions of dollars when the share prices of the affected companies collapsed, shook public confidence in the nation's securities markets.

The legislation establishes new or enhanced standards for all U.S. public company boards, management, and public accounting firms. *It does not apply to privately held companies.*

NOTE

Following the guidelines in this book, such as implementing ICA encryption, IPsec, and network firewall configuration, should help you ensure that Citrix XenApp meets your requirements of protecting sensitive data.

FIPS 140-2, FIPS 201 and HSPD-12

The *Federal Information Processing Standard 140* (FIPS 140) is a U.S. federal government standard that details a benchmark for implementing cryptographic software. It provides best practices for using cryptographic algorithms, managing key elements and data buffers, and interacting with the operating system. An evaluation process that is administered by the National Institute of Standards and Technology's (NIST) National Voluntary Laboratory Accreditation Program (NVLAP) allows encryption product vendors to demonstrate the extent to which they comply with the standard, and thus, the trustworthiness of their implementation.

To facilitate implementing secure application server access and to meet the FIPS 140 requirements, XenApp products can use cryptographic modules that are FIPS 140-validated in Windows 32-bit implementation of secure Secure Sockets Layer/Transport Layer Security (SSL/TLS) connections.

The *Federal Information Processing Standard 201* (FIPS 201) is a U.S. federal government standard that was created in response to another federal directive, *Homeland Security Presidential Directive 12* (HSPD-12).

HSPD-12 is titled "Policy for a Common Identification Standard for Federal Employees and Contractors." This directive changed how federal agencies would identify their employees and how these employees would access data stored on federal information systems. The standard required the use of secure and reliable forms of identification for federal employees and contractors that meet these criteria:

- Is issued based on sound criteria for verifying an individual employee's identity

- Is strongly resistant to identity fraud, tampering, counterfeiting, and terrorist exploitation

- Can be rapidly authenticated electronically

- Is issued only by providers whose reliability has been established by an official accreditation process

FIPS 201 specifies the technical *Personal Identity Verification* (PIV, also known as a Smart Card) requirements for federal employees and contractors that satisfy the requirements of HSPD-12.

Smart cards must be personalized with identity information for the individual to whom the card is issued, in order to perform identity verification both by humans and automated systems. Humans can use the physical card for visual comparisons, whereas automated systems can use the electronically stored data on the card to conduct automated identity verification and to make use of a public key infrastructure to utilize data and e-mail encryption.

Explaining Security Technologies

There are a variety of methods available to improve the overall security posture of a Citrix XenApp environment, including the following:

- Using SSL encryption and utilizing digital certificates

- Using higher encryption algorithms such as TLS, FIPS, and AES

- Enforcing user information security awareness

- Establishing well defined information security policies and procedures

- Implementing multifactor authentication methods utilizing smart cards, tokens, and biometrics

If implementing just a single security technology will improve the overall state of your information security posture, then the proper implementation of several security technologies will enhance it that much more.

Digital Certificates

Public key infrastructure (PKI) is a security system that uses certificates as its basis. A certificate is a digital voucher containing the name of the account and a public key. The certificate can contain multiple names for the account, including the Active Directory ID, the UPN (where different), the e-mail account, and DNS names.

A certificate authority (CA) signs a digital certificate to attest that the account's private key is possessed by the account and is associated with the public key. The CA issues the certificate that includes the public and private encryption keys. This system is based on standard public key encryption, whereby either key can be used to encrypt, and the other key can be used to decrypt any message that the first key encrypted. Public keys are called such because they are available to the public to use when encrypting messages to be sent to the account (usually a user, but sometimes an application). The account can use the private key to decrypt the message. A second use for this system is to verifiably ensure to the public that a message sent is from the named account. This is called a digital signature. It is sent using the private key from the account, and the public, using the public key, can ensure that the message came from the named account.

The CA can be a body independent of your network such as VeriSign or Microsoft. Or you can host your own CA to provide the most flexibility and control over how you issue and control certificates for your internal users, partners, and external customers.

NOTE

XenApp fully supports the use of private certificates. If your organization opts to use its own certificate authority, you must ensure that the CA root certificates are installed on every device that will be PKI enabled.

CAs adhere to a structured hierarchy of trust to offer the best flexibility and security in a distributed service. If you understand how the DNS hierarchy works, it might help to think of CAs as having a similar structure with trust and delegation running from the root (the top) down to the intervening servers and finally to the end hosts.

With CAs, the top of the chain is the Root CA, which must be self-signed (there is no higher authority—much like a root DNS server). Any server that utilizes certificates from a CA (whether public or private) must have that Root CA's certificates installed locally and placed in the **Trusted Root Certification Authorities** store, as shown in Figure 1.7.

Figure 1.7 Viewing Trusted Root Certification Authorities

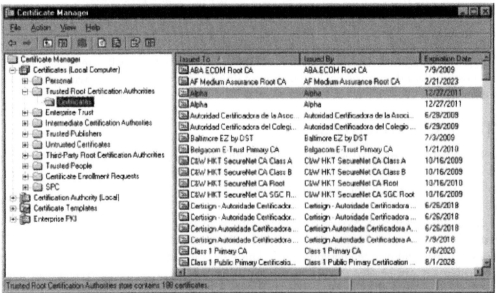

Below the Root CA you have subordinate CAs that obtain their certificate of trust from the Root CA and that can issue certificates to users and computers (as shown in Figure 1.8). The computer certificates can be for end services like IPsec, or they can be for a further subordinate CA. The final CA that issues users and computers with certificates is said to be the Issuing CA—although there's no reason why any CA shouldn't be an Issuing CA.

Figure 1.8 Viewing a Server Certificate

Cryptography

Cryptography is the process of taking *plain* text and then scrambling it into *cipher* text. As a part of the cryptographic process the form of the information can also be changed. Cryptography should be considered for data whenever that data is considered sensitive or has a high value. The implementation of cryptography provides a means to protect data against intentional and accidental compromise and/or alteration. Cryptography can be utilized for communications by encrypting the communication prior to transmission and decrypting it at receipt. It can also be used to provide data security by encrypting data prior to placement on a hard drive and decrypting it after retrieval.

> **NOTE**
>
> You should note that cryptographic methods that were once considered strong eventually succumb to *Moore's Law*. Moore's Law has plotted the pace of technology for more than 25 years. As the power of computing equipment has rapidly increased, so too has the potential to break cryptography that was once considered strong. With advances in hardware capabilities, coupled with the increased availability of cracking tools, some older encryption methods are becoming more vulnerable to attack than the newer forms of encryption.

The Internet and public links connecting different sites do not typically provide a secure means of communication between systems. Data that traverses over these links is subject to being read or altered by unauthorized personnel. The use of cryptography can provide a way to secure communications and data over otherwise insecure mediums.

There are several types of cryptographic methods available for use in a variety of ways:

- **Secret Key** Secret key encryption algorithms use a single secret key to encrypt and decrypt data. Types of secret key algorithms include:
  AesManaged
  DESCryptoServiceProvider
  HMACSHA1
  RC2CryptoServiceProvider
  RijndaelManaged
  TripleDESCryptoServiceProvider

- **Public Key** Public-key encryption uses a private key that must be kept secret from unauthorized users and a public key that can be made public to anyone. Types of public key algorithms include:
  DSACryptoServiceProvider
  RSACryptoServiceProvider
  ECDiffieHellman
  ECDiffieHellmanCng
  ECDiffieHellmanCngPublicKey
  ECDiffieHellmanKeyDerivationFunction
  ECDsaCng

NOTE

RSA allows both encryption and signing, but DSA can be used only for signing, and Diffie-Hellman can be used only for key generation. In general, public-key algorithms are more limited in their uses than private-key algorithms.

■ **Digital Signatures** Public-key algorithms can also be used to form digital signatures. Digital signatures authenticate the identity of a sender (if you trust the sender's public key) and help protect the integrity of data. Types of digital signatures include:

DSACryptoServiceProvider
RSACryptoServiceProvider
ECDsa (base class)
ECDsaCng

■ **Hash Values** Hash algorithms map binary values of an arbitrary length to smaller binary values of a fixed length, known as hash values. A hash value is a numerical representation of a piece of data. Types of has values include:

HMACSHA1
MACTripleDES.
MD5CryptoServiceProvider
RIPEMD160
SHA1Managed
SHA256Managed
SHA384Managed
SHA512Managed

■ **Key Exchange Algorithms** Are used to encrypt and decrypt exchange keys (symmetric session keys). Types of key exchange algorithms include:

KEA
Static Diffie-Helman
Elliptic Curve Diffie-Helman (ECDH)
PKCS

Windows 2003 makes use of what is referred to as a *cipher suite*. A cipher suite uses various protocols to create keys and encrypt information. Cipher suites available to Windows 2003 and XenApp are listed in Table 1.1. A cipher suite specifies one algorithm for each of the following tasks:

■ Key exchange

■ Bulk encryption

■ Message authentication

Table 1.1 Cipher Suites Available in Windows 2003

Type of Format	FIPS Enabled	Exchange	Encryption	Hash	Protocols
TLS_RSA_WITH_AES_128_CBC_SHA	Yes	RSA	AES	SHA1	TLS 1.0
TLS_RSA_WITH_AES_256_CBC_SHA	Yes	RSA	AES	SHA1	TLS 1.0
TLS_RSA_WITH_RC4_128_SHA	No	RSA	RC4	SHA1	TLS 1.0, SSL 3.0
TLS_RSA_WITH_3DES_EDE_CBC_SHA	Yes	RSA	3DES	SHA1	TLS 1.0, SSL 3.0
TLS_ECDHE_ECDSA_WITH_AES_128_CBC_SHA_P256	Yes	ECDH_P256	AES	SHA1	TLS 1.0
TLS_ECDHE_ECDSA_WITH_AES_128_CBC_SHA_P384	Yes	ECDH_P384	AES	SHA1	TLS 1.0
TLS_ECDHE_ECDSA_WITH_AES_128_CBC_SHA_P521	Yes	ECDH_P521	AES	SHA1	TLS 1.0
TLS_ECDHE_ECDSA_WITH_AES_256_CBC_SHA_P256	Yes	ECDH_P256	AES	SHA1	TLS 1.0
TLS_ECDHE_ECDSA_WITH_AES_256_CBC_SHA_P384	Yes	ECDH_P384	AES	SHA1	TLS 1.0
TLS_ECDHE_ECDSA_WITH_AES_256_CBC_SHA_P521	Yes	ECDH_P521	AES	SHA1	TLS 1.0
TLS_ECDHE_RSA_WITH_AES_128_CBC_SHA_P256	Yes	ECDH_P256	AES	SHA1	TLS 1.0
TLS_ECDHE_RSA_WITH_AES_128_CBC_SHA_P384	Yes	ECDH_P384	AES	SHA1	TLS 1.0
TLS_ECDHE_RSA_WITH_AES_128_CBC_SHA_P521	Yes	ECDH_P521	AES	SHA1	TLS 1.0
TLS_ECDHE_RSA_WITH_AES_256_CBC_SHA_P256	Yes	ECDH_P256	AES	SHA1	TLS 1.0
TLS_ECDHE_RSA_WITH_AES_256_CBC_SHA_P384	Yes	ECDH_P384	AES	SHA1	TLS 1.0
TLS_ECDHE_RSA_WITH_AES_256_CBC_SHA_P521	Yes	ECDH_P521	AES	SHA1	TLS 1.0
TLS_DHE_DSS_WITH_AES_128_CBC_SHA	Yes	DH	AES	SHA1	TLS 1.0
TLS_DHE_DSS_WITH_AES_256_CBC_SHA	Yes	DH	AES	SHA1	TLS 1.0
TLS_DHE_DSS_WITH_3DES_EDE_CBC_SHA	Yes	DH	3DES	SHA1	TLS 1.0, SSL 3.0

Continued

Table 1.1 Continued. Cipher Suites Available in Windows 2003

Type of Format	FIPS Enabled	Exchange	Encryption	Hash	Protocols
TLS_RSA_WITH_RC4_128_MD5	No	RSA	RC4	MD5	
	TLS 1.0, SSL 3.0				
SSL_CK_RC4_128_WITH_MD5	No	RSA	RC4	MD5	SSL 2.0
SSL_CK_DES_192_EDE3_CBC_WITH_MD5	No	RSA	3DES	MD5	SSL 2.0
TLS_RSA_WITH_NULL_MD5	No	RSA		MD5	TLS 1.0, SSL 3.0
TLS_RSA_WITH_NULL_SHA	No	RSA		SHA1	TLS 1.0

TIP

You can configure XenApp server, the Web Interface, and the Secure Gateway to use federal government-approved cryptography to protect "sensitive but unclassified" data.

Auditing and Vulnerability Assessments

Vulnerability assessments have become a critical component of many organizations' security infrastructures; the ability to perform a networkwide security snapshot supports a number of security vulnerability and administrative processes. When a new vulnerability is discovered, the network administrator can perform an assessment, discover which systems are vulnerable, and start the patch installation process. After the fixes are in place, another assessment can be run to verify that the vulnerabilities were actually resolved. This cycle of assess, patch, and reassess has become the standard method for many organizations to manage their security issues.

Many organizations have integrated vulnerability assessments into their system rollout process. Before a new server is installed, it first must go through a vulnerability assessment and pass with flying colors. This process is especially important for organizations that use a standard build image for each system; all too often, a new server can be imaged, configured, and installed without the administrator remembering to install the latest system patches. Additionally, many vulnerabilities can only be resolved through manual configuration changes; even an automated patch installation might not be enough to secure a newly imaged system. It's much easier to find these problems at build time when configuration changes are simple and risk-free than when that system is deployed in the field. We strongly recommend performing a vulnerability assessment against any new system before deploying it.

While many security solutions complicate system administration, vulnerability assessments can actually assist an administrator. Although the primary purpose of an assessment is to detect vulnerabilities, the assessment report can also be used as an inventory of the systems on the network and the services they expose. Since enumerating hosts and services is the first part of any vulnerability assessment, regular assessments can give you a current and very useful understanding of the services offered on your network. Assessments assist in crises: when a new worm is released, assessment reports are often used to generate task lists for the system administration staff, allowing them to prevent a worm outbreak before it reaches critical mass.

Assessment tools are also capable of detecting corporate policy violations; many tools will report peer-to-peer services, shared directories full of illegally shared copyrighted materials, and unauthorized remote access tools. If a long-time system administrator leaves the company, an assessment tool can be used to detect that a backdoor was left in the firewall. If bandwidth use suddenly spikes, a vulnerability assessment can be used to locate workstations that have installed file-sharing software.

One of the most important uses for vulnerability assessment data is event correlation; if an intrusion does occur, a recent assessment report allows the security administrator to determine how it occurred, and what other assets might have been compromised. If the intruder gained access to a network consisting of unpatched Web servers, it is safe to assume that he gained access to those systems as well.

Assessment Types

The term vulnerability assessment is used to refer to many different types and levels of service. A host assessment normally refers to a security analysis against a single system, from that system, often using specialized tools and an administrative user account. In contrast, a network assessment is used to test an entire network of systems at once.

Host Assessments

Host assessment tools were one of the first proactive security measures available to system administrators and are still in use today. These tools require that the assessment software be installed on each system you want to assess. This software can either be run stand-alone or be linked to a central system on the network. A host assessment looks for system-level vulnerabilities such as insecure file permissions, missing software patches, noncompliant security policies, and outright backdoors and Trojan horse installations.

The depth of the testing performed by host assessment tools makes it the preferred method of monitoring the security of critical systems. The downside of host assessments is that they require a set of specialized tools for the operating system and software packages being used, in addition to administrative access to each system that should be tested. Combined with the substantial time investment required to perform the testing and the limited scalability, host assessments are often reserved for a few critical systems.

The number of available and up-to-date host assessment solutions has been decreasing over the last few years. Tools like COPS and Tiger that were used religiously by system administrators just a few years ago have now fallen so far behind as to be nearly useless. Many of the stand-alone tools have been replaced by agent-based systems that use a centralized reporting and management system. This transition has been fueled by a demand for scalable systems that can be deployed across larger server farms with a minimum of administrative effort. At the time of this publication the only stand-alone host assessment tools used with any frequency are those targeting nontechnical home users and part-time administrators for small business systems.

Although stand-alone tools have started to decline, the number of "enterprise security management" systems that include a host assessment component is still increasing dramatically. The dual requirements of scalability and ease of deployment have resulted in host assessments becoming a component of larger management systems. A number of established software companies offer commercial products in this space, including, but not limited to, Internet Security System's System Scanner, Computer Associates eTrust Access Control product line, Symantec Network Access Control, and McAfee's ePolicy Orchestrator software.

Network Assessments

Network assessments have been around almost as long as host assessments, starting with the Security Administrator Tool for Analyzing Networks (SATAN), released by Dan Farmer and Wietse Venema in 1995. The Security Auditor's Research Assistant (SARA) evolved from SATAN and is still updated and available for free. SATAN provided a new perspective to administrators who were used to host assessment and hardening tools. Instead of analyzing the local system for problems, it allowed you to look for common problems on any system connected to the network. This opened the gates for a still-expanding market of both open-source and commercial network-based assessment systems.

A network vulnerability assessment locates all live systems on a network, determines what network services are in use, and then analyzes those services for potential vulnerabilities. Unlike the host assessment solutions, this process does not require any configuration changes on the systems being assessed. Network assessments can be both scalable and efficient in terms of administrative requirements and are the only feasible method of gauging the security of large, complex networks of heterogeneous systems.

Although network assessments are very effective for identifying vulnerabilities, they do suffer from certain limitations. These include not being able to detect certain types of backdoors, complications with firewalls, and the inability to test for certain vulnerabilities due to the testing process itself being dangerous. Network assessments can disrupt normal operations, interfere with many devices (especially printers), use large amounts of bandwidth, and create fill-up disks with log files on the systems being assessed. Additionally, many vulnerabilities are exploitable by an authorized but unprivileged user account and cannot be identified through a network assessment.

Automated Assessments

The first experience that many people have with vulnerability assessments is using a security consulting firm to provide a network audit. This type of audit is normally composed of both manual and automated components: the auditors will use automated tools for much of the initial legwork and follow it up with manual system inspection. While this process can provide thorough results, it is often much more expensive than simply using an automated assessment tool to perform the process in-house.

The need for automated assessment tools has resulted in a number of advanced solutions being developed. These solutions range from simple graphical user interface (GUI) software products to stand-alone appliances that are capable of being linked into massive distributed assessment architectures. Due to the overwhelming number of vulnerability tests needed to build even a simple tool, the commercial market is easily divided between a few well-funded independent products and literally hundreds of solutions built on the open-source Nessus Security Scanner. These automated assessment tools can be further broken into two types of products: those that are actually obtained, through either purchase or download, and those that are provided through a subscription service.

Stand-Alone versus Subscription

The stand-alone category of products includes most open-source projects and about half of the serious commercial contenders. Some examples include the Nessus Security Scanner, eEye's Retina, Tenable Security's Lightning Proxy, and Microsoft's Security Baseline Scanner. These products are either provided as a software package that is installed on a workstation, or a hardware appliance that you simply plug in and access over the network.

The subscription service solutions take a slightly different approach; instead of requiring the user to perform the actual installation and deployment, the vendor handles the basic configuration and simply provides a Web interface to the client. This is primarily used to offer assessments for Internet-facing assets (external assessments), but can also be combined with an appliance to provided assessments for an organization's internal network. Examples of products that are provided as a subscription service include Qualys' QualysGuard, Beyond Security's Automated Scan, and Digital Defense's Frontline product.

The advantages of using a stand-alone product are obvious: all of your data stays in-house and you decide exactly when, where, and how the product is used. One disadvantage, however, is that these products require the user to perform an update before every use to avoid an out-of-date vulnerability check set, potentially missing recent vulnerabilities. The advantages of a subscription service model are twofold: the updates are handled for you, and since the external assessment originates from the vendor's network, you are provided with a real-world view of how your network looks from the Internet.

The disadvantages to a subscription solution are the lack of control you have over the configuration of the device and the potential storage of vulnerability data on the vendor's systems. Some hybrid subscription service solutions have emerged that resolve both of these issues through leased appliances in conjunction with user-provided storage media for the assessment data.

Two Approaches

When performing an automated vulnerability assessment, the actual perspective of the test can have a huge impact on the depth and quality of the results. Essentially, there are two different approaches to vulnerability testing: administrative and outsider. Each has distinct advantages and disadvantages, such that many of the better assessment tools have migrated to a hybrid model that combines the best features of both approaches. Understanding these different approaches can provide insight into why two different assessment tools can provide such completely different results when used to test the same network.

Administrative Approach

The administrative approach performs the assessment from the perspective of a normal, authenticated system administrator. The assessment tool might require that it be launched by an authenticated administrative user or provided with a user account and password. These credentials can be used to detect missing patches, insecure configuration settings, and potentially vulnerable client-side software (such as e-mail clients and Web browsers).

This is a powerful approach for networks that consist of mostly Windows-based systems that all authenticate against the same domain. It combines much of the deep analysis of a host assessment with the network assessment's scalability advantages. Since almost all of the vulnerability tests are performed using either remote registry or remote file system access, there is little chance that an assessment tool using this method can adversely affect the tested systems. This allows assessments to be conducted during the day, while the systems are actively being used, without fear of disrupting a business activity.

The administrative approach is especially useful when trying to detect and resolve client-side vulnerabilities on a network of workstations. Many worms, trojans, and viruses propagate by exploiting vulnerabilities in e-mail clients and Web browser software. An assessment tool using this approach can access the registry of each system and determine whether the latest patches have been installed, whether the proper security settings have been applied, and often whether the system has already been successfully attacked. Client-side security is one of the most overlooked entry points on most corporate networks; there have been numerous cases of a network with a well-secured perimeter being overtaken by a network simply because a user visited the wrong Web site with an outdated Web browser.

Unfortunately, these products often have some severe limitations as well. Since the testing process uses the standard Windows administrative channels— namely, the NetBIOS services and an administrative user account—anything preventing this channel from being accessed will result in inaccurate scan results. Any system on the network that is configured with a different authentication source (running in stand-alone mode, on a different domain, or authenticating to a Novell server) will not be correctly assessed. Additionally, these products may have issues similar to the issues of host-based assessment tools, network devices, and UNIX-based servers. IP-enabled phone systems may also be completely missed or return incomplete results.

Network and host-based firewalls can also interfere with the assessment. This interference is a common occurrence when performing assessments against a system hosted on a different network segment, such as a demilitarized zone (DMZ) or external segment behind a dedicated firewall. Additionally, network devices, UNIX-based servers, and IP-enabled phone systems might also be either completely missed or have only minimal results returned. An example of this is a certain Windows-based commercial assessment tool that will report missing Internet Information Server (IIS) patches even when the Web server has not been enabled or configured. This type of testing is very helpful to verify a networkwide patch deployment, but should not be relied upon as the only method of security testing. Microsoft's Security Baseline Scanner is the best example of an assessment tool that uses this approach alone. Many of the commercial assessment tool offerings were originally based on this approach and have only recently started to integrate different techniques into their vulnerability tests.

The Outsider Approach

The outsider approach takes the perspective of the unauthenticated malicious intruder who is trying to break into the network. The assessment process is able to make decisions about the security of a system only through a combination of application fingerprinting, version identification, and actual exploitation attempts. Assessment tools built on this approach are often capable of detecting vulnerabilities across a much wider range of operating systems and devices than their administrative approach counterparts.

When conducting a large-scale assessment against a network consisting of many different operating systems and network devices, the outsider approach is the only technique that has a chance of returning accurate, consistent results about each discovered system. If a system is behind a firewall, only the exposed services will be tested, providing you with the same information that an intruder would see in a real-life attack. The reports provided by tools that use this hybrid approach are geared to prevent common attacks; this is in contrast to those tools using the administrative approach that often focus on missing patches and insecure configuration settings. In essence, the outsider approach presents a much more targeted list of problems for remediation, allowing the administrator to focus on the issues that would be the first choices for a potential intruder.

Although this approach is the only plausible method of conducting a vulnerability assessment on a heterogeneous network, it also suffers from a significant set of drawbacks. Many vulnerabilities simply cannot be tested without crashing the application, device, or operating system. The result is that any assessment tools that test for these types of vulnerabilities either provide an option for "intrusive" testing, or always trigger a warning when a potentially vulnerable service is discovered. Since the outsider approach can only detect what is visible from the point in the network where the assessment was launched, it might not report a vulnerable service bound to a different interface on the same system. This is an issue with reporting more than anything else, as someone reviewing the assessment report might not consider the network perspective when creating a list of remediation tasks for that system.

The Hybrid Approach

Over the last few years, more and more tools have switched to a hybrid approach for network assessments. They use administrative credentials when possible, but fall back to remote fingerprinting techniques if an account is either not available or not accepted on the tested system. The quality of these hybrid solutions varies greatly; the products that were originally designed with only the administrative approach in mind have a difficult time when administrative credentials are not available, whereas the products based on the outsider approach often contain glitches when using an administrative account for tests. It seems that the latter has better chances at overcoming its hurdles without requiring a rewrite. Overall, though, these products provide results that are often superior to those using a single approach. The Nessus Security Scanner and eEye's Retina product are examples of tools that use this approach.

One of the greatest advantages of tools using the outsider approach is that they are often able to determine whether a given vulnerability exists, regardless of whether a patch was applied. As many Windows network administrators know, installing an operating system patch does not actually guarantee that the vulnerability has been removed. A recent vulnerability in the Microsoft Windows Network Messenger service allowed a remote attacker to execute arbitrary code on a vulnerable system. Public exploits for the vulnerability started circulating, and companies were frantically trying to install the patch on all their internal workstations. Something that was overlooked was that for the patch to take effect, the system had to be rebooted after it was applied. Many sites used automated patch installation tools to update all their vulnerable systems, but completely forgot about the reboot requirement.

The result was that when an assessment was run using a tool that took the administrative approach, it reported the systems as patched. However, when an assessment was run using the Nessus Security Scanner, it reported these systems as vulnerable. The tool using the administrative approach simply checked the registry of each system to determine whether the patch had been applied, whereas the Nessus scan actually probed the vulnerability to determine if it was still vulnerable. Without this second assessment, the organization would have left hundreds of workstations exposed, even though the patches had been applied. The registry analysis used by many tools that take the administrative approach can miss vulnerabilities for a number of other reasons as well. The most common occurrence is when a hotfix has been applied to resolve a vulnerability, and then an older service pack is reapplied over the entire system. The changes installed by the hotfix were overwritten, but the registry entry stating that the patch was applied still exists. This problem primarily affects Windows operating systems; however, a number of commercial UNIX vendors have had similar issues with tracking installed patches and determining which ones still need to be applied.

Recently, many of the administrative and hybrid tools have developed new techniques for verifying that an installed patch actually exists. Shavlik Technology's HFNetChk Pro will actually check the last reboot time and compare it to the hotfix install date. The Nessus Security Scanner actually accesses the affected executables across the network and verifies the embedded version numbers.

The drawbacks to the hybrid approach are normally not apparent until the results of a few large scans are observed; because the administrative approach is used opportunistically, vulnerabilities that are reported on a system that accepts the provided user account might not be reported on a similar system that uses a different authentication realm. If the administrator does not realize that the other system might be vulnerable as well, it could lead to a false sense of security. These missed vulnerabilities can be difficult to track down and can fall under the radar of the administrator. Because there is a higher chance of these systems not being patched, the hybrid approach can actually result in more damage during an intrusion or worm outbreak. Although the administrative approach suffers from the same issue, tools using the administrative approach take it for granted that systems outside of the authentication realm will not be tested.

Realistic Expectations

When the first commercial vulnerability assessment tools started becoming popular, they were advertised as being able to magically identify every security hole on your network. A few years ago, this might have been close to the truth. The number of publicly documented vulnerabilities was still quite small, and tracking vulnerability information was an obscure hobby. These days, the scenario is much different, whereas there were a few hundred well-documented vulnerabilities before, there are literally thousands of them now, and they don't even begin to scratch the surface when it comes to the number of flaws that can be used to penetrate a corporate network.

In addition to the avalanche of vulnerabilities, the number and type of devices found on an average corporate network has exploded. Some of these devices will crash, misbehave, or slow to a crawl during a network vulnerability assessment. A vulnerability test designed for one system might cause another application or device to stop functioning altogether, annoying the users of those systems and potentially interrupting the work flow. Assessment tools have a tough job; they have to identify as many vulnerabilities as possible on systems that must be analyzed and categorized on the fly, without reporting false positives, and at the same time avoid crashing devices and applications that simply weren't designed with security in mind. Some tools fare better than others; however, all current assessment tools exhibit this problem in one form or another.

When someone first starts to use a vulnerability assessment system, he or she often notices that the results between subsequent scans can differ significantly. This issue is encountered more frequently on larger networks that are connected through slower links. There are quite a few different reasons for this, but the core issue is that unlike most software processes, remote vulnerability testing is more of an art form than a science. Many assessment tools define a hard timeout for establishing connections to a service or receiving the result of a query. If an extra second or two of latency occurs on the network, the test could miss a valid response. These types of timing issues are common among assessment tools; however, many other factors can play into the consistency of scan results.

Many network devices provide a Telnet console that allows an administrator to reconfigure the system remotely. These devices will often set a hard limit on the number of concurrent network connections allowed to this service. When a vulnerability assessment is launched, it might perform multiple tests on a given port at the same time; this can cause one check to receive a valid response, while another gets an error message indicating that all available connections are being used. If that second check was responsible for testing for a default password on this particular device, it might completely miss the vulnerability. If the same scan was run later, but the default password test ran before one of the others, it would accurately detect the vulnerability at the expense of the other tests. This type of timing problem is much more common on network devices and older UNIX systems than on most modern workstations and servers, but can ultimately lead to inconsistent assessment results.

Defining Authentication Models

Windows Server 2003 offers several different authentication types to meet the needs of a diverse user base. The default authentication protocol for a homogeneous Windows 2000 or later environment is Kerberos version 5. This protocol relies on a system of tickets to verify the identity of network users, services, and devices. For Web applications and users, you can rely on the standards-based encryption offered by the SSL/TLS security protocols as well as Microsoft Digest. To provide backward compatibility for earlier versions of Microsoft operating systems, Windows Server 2003 provides support for the NTLM protocol. In this section, we examine the various authentication options available to you as a Windows administrator.

There are three general ways (often called "factors") to authenticate a person. These are something you know, something you have, and something you are. An example of something you know is a password. This is something you recall from memory that (hopefully) only you would know. Something you have would be something you carry around with you that would help identify you. Some examples of this include a driver's license or some kind of a token such as a SecureID that would be needed to authenticate to the system. Something you are would be a feature you have that distinguishes you from everyone else in the world. Biometrics are often used to identify you by something you are. A fingerprint or hand reader can be used to determine who you are by scanning your hand. Other examples include voice recognition systems, facial recognition systems, and so forth.

How Does the System Authenticate a User?

Users are authenticated in Windows Server 2003 environments by first locating a domain controller and then using the proper authentication protocol. The process is completely transparent to the user. The only thing the user has to do is provide a username and password. Basically, what's happening here is that the users are proving to the system that they are who they say they are and that they should be allowed access to the system. The computer authenticates the user, or verifies his identity, and then builds an access token on the system that contains all the security identifiers (SIDs) that are associated with this user's account.

There are two ways that the computer can use to locate the domain controller: using the Windows 2003 Resolver and DNS or using the NetBIOS Resolver and NetBIOS name resolution. Windows 2000 systems and later will try the DNS Resolver first and will use the NetBIOS Resolver only if no domain controller can be located via DNS.

The Windows 2003 Resolver will query DNS for specific SRV resource records to locate the domain controller. The procedure is as follows:

1. The client computer queries the DNS for a list of domain controllers located within the DNS site. Domain controllers are identified in DNS as LDAP SVR records in:
   `_ldap.<sitename>._sites.dc_msdcs.<domain>`

2. The client computer then sends an LDAP UDP query to Port 389 on the domain controllers to identify which domain controllers are available.

3. The client computer uses the response it receives to the previous query to decide which domain controller is located closest. If no domain controllers respond, the client computer queries DNS for LDAP SRV records in: _ldap._tcp.dc_msdcs.<domain>

4. The client computer attempts to locate one of the domain controllers listed in the response to the previous query.

5. On locating a domain controller, the client computer sends it a log-on request.

Should the Windows 2003 Resolver be unable to locate a domain controller using DNS, the NetBIOS Resolver will attempt to locate one. The 1B record only contains the primary domain controller (PDC) for the domain. The 1C record contains a list of the (first 25 registered) DCs in the domain. This procedure is as follows:

1. The NetBIOS Resolver queries the NetBIOS interface for entries for the *Domainname <1B>* NetBIOS name that identifies the domain.

2. If the system is a WINS client, the WINS server is queried for *Domainname <1C>*, which provides a list of DCs in the domain.

3. The client computer then connects with one of the DCs in the list.

4. If the WINS server is not available or if there are no name registration records for *Domainname <1C>*, the client computer then broadcasts in an attempt to locate a DC.

Windows Server 2003 supports several network authentication protocols. The *key* protocols include Kerberos Version 5, NT LAN Manager (NTLM), Secure Socket Layer/Transport Layer Security (SSL/TLS), and .NET Passport Authentication. Table 1.2 provides a quick checklist of the protocols used in authentication and their purposes. The authentication protocol used will depend on the application requesting access to the resource.

Table 1.2 Authentication Protocols

Protocol	Description	Purpose
Kerberos version 5	A standard Internet protocol for authenticating users and systems. This is the primary authentication protocol used by Windows Server 2003.	Network authentication. Allows for the mutual authentication of both users and resources.
NT LAN Manager (NTLM)	NTLM is the primary NT authentication protocol.	Network authentication. Used to authenticate computers in Windows NT domains.
Secure Socket Layer/ Transport Layer Security (SSL/TLS)	This is the primary authentication protocol used when accessing secure web servers.	Network authentication. Based on X.509 public key certificates.

Continued

Table 1.2 Continued. Authentication Protocols

Protocol	Description	Purpose
.NET Passport Authentication	This protocol allows the .NET Passport authentication to be used for IIS 6.	Network authentication. Enables the user of Active Directory information in the authentication of Internet, intranet, and extranet users.
Microsoft Challenge Handshake Authentication Protocol Version 2 (MS-CHAP v2)	A Challenge Handshake-Authentication Protocol (CHAP) based on authentication providing mutual authentication.	Network and dialup authentication. Uses separate encryption keys for sending and receiving.
Extensible Authentication Protocol (EAP)	Designed as an extension to Point-to-Point Protocol (PPP), EAP provides greater extensibility and flexibility in the implementation of authentication methods for the PPP connection.	Network and dialup authentication. Provides support for additional authentication methods such as smart cards
Password Authentication Protocol (PAP)	A very simple, plain-text authentication protocol.	Network and dialup authentication. Sends passwords in clear text.
Extensible Authentication Protocol-Transport Level Security (EAP-TLS)	This protocol uses Transport Level Security (TLS) to provide authentication in establishing a PPP connection.	Network and dial-up authentication. Provides for the authentication over wireless connections.

Kerberos

Within a Windows Server 2003 domain, the primary authentication protocol is Kerberos version 5. Kerberos provides thorough authentication by verifying not only the identity of network users but also the validity of the network services themselves. This latter feature was designed to prevent users from attaching to "dummy" services created by malicious network attackers to trick users into revealing their passwords or other sensitive information. The process of verifying both the user *and* the service that the user is attempting to use is referred to as *mutual authentication*. Only network clients and servers that are running the Windows 2000, Windows Server 2003, or Windows XP Professional operating system will be able to use the Kerberos authentication protocol. When these operating systems are members of a domain, Kerberos will be enabled as their default authentication mechanism for domain-based resources. In a Windows 2000 or later Active Directory environment, pre–Windows 2000 computers that attempt to access a "Kerberized" resource will be directed to use NTLM authentication.

The Kerberos authentication mechanism relies on a *Key Distribution Center* (KDC) to issue *tickets* that allow client access to network resources. Each domain controller in a Windows Server 2003 domain functions as a KDC. Network clients use DNS to locate the nearest available KDC so that they can acquire a ticket. Kerberos tickets contain cryptographic information that confirms the user's identity to the requested service.

These tickets remain resident on the client computer system for a specific amount of time, usually 10 hours. This ticket lifetime keeps the Kerberos system from being overwhelmed, and is configurable by an administrator. If you set the threshold lower, you must ensure that your domain controllers can handle the additional load that will be placed on them. It is also important, however, not to set them too high. A ticket is good until it expires, which means that if it becomes compromised it will be valid until expiration.

Understanding the Kerberos Authentication Process

When a user enters his or her network credentials on a Kerberos-enabled system, the following steps take place. These transactions occur entirely behind the scenes. The user is only aware that he or she has entered the password or PIN number (if using a smart card) as part of a normal log-on process. The following steps occur in a single domain environment:

1. Using a smart card or a username/password combination, a user authenticates to the KDC. The KDC issues a *ticket-granting ticket* (TGT) to the client system. The client retains this TGT in memory until needed.

2. When the client attempts to access a network resource, it presents its TGT to the *ticket-granting service* (TGS) on the nearest available Windows Server 2003 KDC.

3. If the user is authorized to access the service that it is requesting, the TGS issues a *service ticket* to the client.

4. The client presents the service ticket to the requested network service. Through mutual authentication, the service ticket proves the identity of the user as well as the identity of the service.

5. The client retains this TGT in memory until needed or the TGT expires.

The Windows Server 2003 Kerberos authentication system can also interact with non-Microsoft Kerberos implementations such as UNIX-based Kerberos realms. In Kerberos, a realm is similar to the concept of a domain. This "realm trust" feature allows a client in a Kerberos realm to authenticate against Active Directory to access resources, and vice versa. This interoperability allows Windows Server 2003 domain controllers to provide authentication for client systems running other types of Kerberos, including clients that are running operating systems other than Windows. It also allows Windows-based clients to access resources within a non-Windows Kerberos realm.

Secure Sockets Layer/Transport Layer Security

Any time you visit a Web site that uses an https:// prefix instead of http://, you're seeing *Secure Sockets Layer* (SSL) encryption in action. SSL provides encryption for other protocols such as HTTP, ICA, LDAP, and IMAP, all of which operate at higher layers of the protocol stack. SSL provides three major functions in encrypting TCP/IP-based traffic:

- **Server Authentication** Allows a user to confirm that an Internet server is really the machine that it is claiming to be. It's difficult to think of anyone who wouldn't like the assurance of knowing that he or she is looking at the genuine Amazon.com site, and not a duplicate created by a hacker, before entering any credit card information.

- **Client Authentication** Allows a server to confirm a client's identity during the exchange of data. For example, this might be important for a bank that needs to transmit sensitive financial information to a server belonging to a subsidiary office. Combining server and client authentication provides a means of mutual authentication.

- **Encrypted Connections** Allow all data that is sent between a client and server to be encrypted and decrypted, allowing for a high degree of confidentiality. This function also allows both parties to confirm that the data was not altered during transmission.

Transport Layer Security (TLS) 1.0 is the latest, standardized version of the SSL 3.0 protocol. TLS is an open standard and like SSL, TLS provides server authentication, encryption of the data stream, and message integrity checks. TLS 1.0 was issued by the Internet Engineering Task Force (IETF) in January 1999, in document RFC 2246. Because TLS has been standardized, developers are encouraged to use TLS rather than SSL. Although their differences are minor, TLS 1.0 and SSL 3.0 are not interchangeable.

SSL and TLS can use a wide range of ciphers (authentication, encryption, and/or integrity mechanisms) to allow connections with a diverse client base. You can edit the registry in Windows Server 2003 to restrict the ciphers allowed. Within the registry editor on the server, browse to the following key: HKEY_LOCAL_MACHINE\SYSTEM\CurrentControlSet\Control\SecurityProviders\SCHANNEL\Ciphers, as shown in Figure 1.9. Each available cipher has two potential values:

- 0xffffffff (enabled)

- 0x0 (disabled)

Figure 1.9 Editing SSL/TLS Ciphers

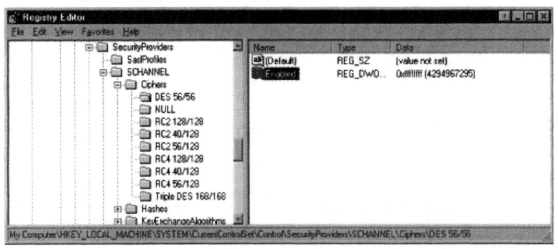

NT LAN Manager

Versions of Windows earlier than Windows 2000 used *NT LAN Manager* (NTLM) to provide network authentication. In a Windows Server 2003 environment, NTLM is used to communicate between two computers when one or both of them is running a pre-Windows 2000 operating system. NTLM will also be used by Windows Server 2003 computers that are not members of a domain. NTLM encrypts user log-on information by applying a mathematical function (or *hash*) to the user's password. A user's password isn't stored in the SAM or Active Directory database. Rather, the value of a hash that is generated when the user's account is first created or the user's password is changed, is stored. If the password is less than 15 characters long, two hashes are actually stored: an NT hash and a LM hash. The LM (or LAN Manager) hash is weak and can easily be broken by password crackers. Because of this it is recommended that you configure the **Network security: Do not store LAN Manager hash value on next password change** Group Policy setting.

During logon, the domain controller sends a challenge to the client. This is a simple string of characters that the client mathematically applies to the hash value of the user's password. The result of this mathematical algorithm is a new hash that is then transmitted to the domain controller. In this way, the user's password is never actually transmitted across the network.

The domain controller also has the hash for the user's password. Moreover, it knows the challenge it sent, so it is able to perform the same calculation. It compares the hash that it mathematically calculated with the one received from the client. If they match, logon is permitted.

The NTLM hash function only exists in Windows Server 2003 for backward compatibility with earlier operating systems. Windows Server 2003 domains support both NTLM and NTLM version 2. If your network environment is exclusively running Windows 2000 or later, you might want to consider standardizing on a stronger form of authentication such as Kerberos. Using NTLM is preferable to sending authentication information using no encryption whatsoever, but NTLM has several known vulnerabilities that do not make it the best choice for network authentication if your operating system supports more advanced schemes.

Digest Authentication

Microsoft provides *digest authentication* as a means of authenticating Web applications that are running on IIS. Digest authentication uses the *Digest Access Protocol*, which is a simple challenge-response mechanism for applications that are using HTTP or *Simple Authentication Security Layer* (SASL)-based communications. When Microsoft Digest authenticates a client, it creates a *session key* that is stored on the Web server and used to authenticate subsequent authentication requests without needing to contact a domain controller for each authentication request. Similar to NTLM, digest authentication sends user credentials across the network as an encrypted hash so that the actual password information cannot be extracted in case a malicious attacker is attempting to "sniff" the network connection.

Passport Authentication

Any business that wants to provide the convenience of single sign-on to its customers can license and use Microsoft Passport authentication. Passport authentication enables your company to provide a convenient means for customers to access and transact business on a given Web site. Sites that rely on Passport authentication use a centralized Passport server to authenticate users, rather than hosting and maintaining their own authentication systems. From a technical perspective, Passport authentication relies on standards-based Web technologies, including SSL, HTTP redirects, and cookies.

TIP

NTLM, Digest, and Passport authentication should not be used in a XenApp environment. Microsoft best practices dictate that Kerberos authentication should not be used for servers directly connected to the Internet.

Multifactor Authentication Models

No form of authentication is fool-proof. For example, there have been some cases where a biometric fingerprint scanner has been bypassed using a fingerprint from an authorized user. One problem with biometric authentication is if someone figures out a way to impersonate you, you can't change who you are. You can't easily replace your finger if your fingerprint is compromised. Passwords can be guessed and tokens can be stolen.

By using multifactor authentication, at least two forms of authentication are required before a person is properly authenticated. For example, you would require users to authenticate themselves by using something they know (by typing a password) and something they are (by placing their hand on a biometric scanner)—shown in Figure 1.10. The more factors that are required to identify a person generally make it harder to impersonate them. For secure systems, it is suggested that at least two factors should be used to authenticate a user before they are given access to the system. To do this authentication, secure remote systems such as Remote Authentication and Dial-in Service (RADIUS) or Terminal Access Controller Access Control System (TACACS) should use at least two factors for authentication as well.

Figure 1.10 Understanding Multifactor Authentication

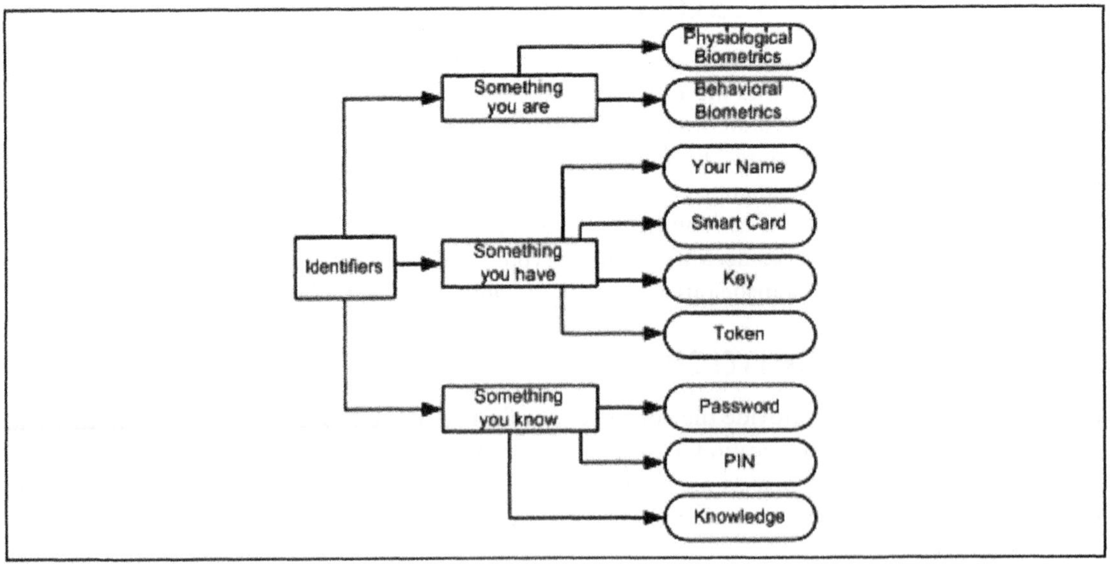

Passwords

Passwords are interesting beasts. Although they're one of the oldest ways to authenticate to computers, how they should be used is still debated today. Some security professionals feel strongly that complex passwords are important, while others feel that length is more important. Others say passwords should no longer be used but instead we should be using passphrases (which is basically using a phrase for a password). There are some great arguments for each of these systems, and you should select the ones that work best for your company.

Many security professionals will tell you that a good password should have random uppercase and lowercase letters, numbers, and symbols. While this does make for a good secure password, it also makes it hard to remember. Many times if a user cannot remember the password, they will end up writing it down on a Post-it note and placing it somewhere near the computer such as under the keyboard, in a drawer, or by sticking the Post-it note to the computer screen. This is like having the best lock on a door then putting the key on a nail in the middle of the door.

Other security professionals will argue that longer passwords are better than passwords that use a random complex string of characters. Mathematically, longer passwords make sense because the number of possible passwords increases exponentially as the length of the password increases. Because of this, some will argue that there should be no rules that require certain characters in a password; policies should only require long passwords. While advocates of this make good arguments, this system is not without problems. If an attacker can make some correct assumptions about what types of passwords a user will use, they can make them much easier to crack. For example, if an attacker assumes that the password will be composed of dictionary words that only use lowercase letters; this weakens a password's strength drastically.

Tools & Traps…

The Math of Password Complexity

One measure of password strength is the total possible combinations using your particular character set and length. Generally, the more possible combinations there are, the harder passwords are to crack. For example, you have 26 lowercase letters, 26 uppercase letters, and 10 numbers. This is a total of 62 total characters. Let's say you have a requirement that passwords must be at least 7 characters long, so for a 7-character password there would be $62^7 = 3,521,614,606,208$ possibilities. Note that the number of possibilities increases exponentially with the length. So, if your company required 8-character passwords, then that would be $62^8 = 218,340,105,584,896$ possibilities. On the other hand, if you left the length requirement at 7 characters and instead required that users also use symbols in their passwords, then that would add 32 characters to the equation. Now you have $94^7 = 64,847,759,419,264$, which is over three times less than if we had instead required the password to be longer.

A passphrase is basically a phrase used in lieu of a password. For example, the phrase "I went to the store at 9:52 and bought bread for $4.29" could be used as a password to log into an account. Advocates of this argue that they are much easier to remember and type (since it's generally easier for people to type words than individual letters) and can have complex characters in them. Generally, passphrases work very well if the phrase is chosen well. For example, the passphrase "thank you" is far less secure than the password above, because it is short and uses a limited number of characters.

WARNING

When enabled, password complexity will ensure that all users choose passwords with three different characters types, from the groups 'a–z', 'A–Z', '0–9' and special characters such as '@', '#', and '&'. However, if users are not educated and told how to choose complex passwords and are not used to doing so, most will struggle to choose a password that meets the complexity requirements. For this reason, complexity may need to be disabled within your environment, since its enablement might result in a huge increase in calls being logged with help desks, thus outweighing the benefits of more secure passwords.

Windows Password Policies

There are some things that you can do, and should do on a regular basis, to improve your password security. The following section highlights the recommended standards to use when maintaining and administering your passwords. Here are some basic rules for users to follow regarding passwords:

- **Change** The most important thing is to change your password periodically, because the longer a password is around the more susceptible it is to cracking.

- **Not in More Than One Place** A common mistake is to use the same password in multiple areas; this is a definite "no-no" as once a perpetrator obtains the password they will have multiple access to different places. Another thing to remember is when you use protocols that are in clear text, anyone can capture your password on the network, so protocols such as Post Office Protocol (POP) reveal the password to a network capture utility; therefore, it is imperative that these passwords be unique and used only in that one place.

- **Size** When it comes to passwords, the size is very important, because the longer the password, the more time it will take to crack it.

- **Creation** One technique for creating a password is to use a phrase or saying that you know well. A popular technique is the nursery rhyme, "Twinkle, Twinkle, Little Star, How I Wonder How You Are." In this technique we take the song, and the first letter of each word, and form our password. For example, Ttl*hIwhur!.

When Active Directory is installed and configured on a Windows Server 2003 server, default group policies are installed. The two group policies installed by default are the **Default Domain Policy** and the **Default Domain Controllers Policy**. The default policies should not be modified. If an existing policy requirement conflicts with the default policies, a separate policy should be configured instead of modifying the default policies.

The Default Domain Policy specifies settings that control the following security configurations:

- Password policy

- Account lockout policy

- Kerberos policy

Default Domain Policy controls security settings involving password and account policy settings, including Kerberos Policy. Figure 1.11 illustrates the password policy settings for the Windows Server 2003 Default Domain Policy. Table 1.3 lists each policy, with brief descriptions explaining the policy settings available.

Figure 1.11 Default Domain Policy: Password Policy Settings

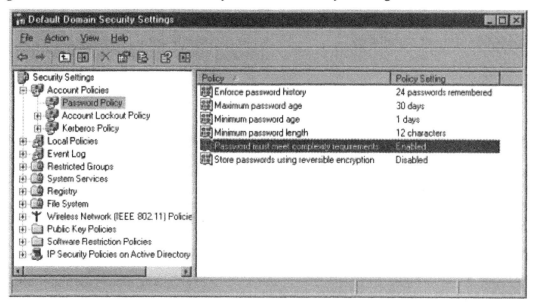

Table 1.3 Password Policies with Descriptions

Policy	Description
Enforce password history	Maintains a list of previously used passwords. Users must use a new password not currently residing on this list.
Maximum password age	Controls how long a user may use a given password before they are forced to change the password.
Minimum password age	Prevents users from circumventing the password history by repeatedly changing passwords during one session in an effort to use a preferred password.
Minimum password length	Forces users to use passwords of a specific minimum length to ensure greater security.
Password must meet complexity requirements	Forces users to use a combination of requirements to ensure greater security: capitals, lowercase letters, numbers, and special characters.
Password must meet complexity	Store passwords using reversible Stores a clear-text password (used by encryption CHAP in RRAS and Digest Authentication in IIS).

Best practice specifies a password history with a small maximum password age. Password complexity requirements with a minimum of eight characters in password length are the preferred settings for password length and complexity settings. Increasing password length in conjunction with enabling password complexity will greatly increase the level of security provided by Windows Server 2003. As is the case with any security setting, however, the design will ultimately be a tradeoff between the cost incurred by the increased level of support required to administer the tighter security and the cost of a security breach.

Smart Card

Smart cards, shown in Figure 1.12, provide a portable method of providing security on a network for tasks like client authentication and securing user data. Smart cards and smart card authentication are discussed in detail later in this book.

Using a smart card for network logons provides extremely strong authentication because it requires two factors: something the user knows (the PIN), and something the user has (the smart card itself). This system provides stronger authentication than a password alone, since a malicious user would need to have access to both the smart card and the PIN in order to impersonate a legitimate user. It's also difficult for an attacker to perform a smart card attack undetected, because the user would notice that his or her smart card was physically missing.

Figure 1.12 Authenticating Using Smart Cards

TIP

A drawback of smart cards is that if users leave their cards at home, they cannot log on. Also, every machine that users need to log on to must have a smart card reader attached. This can become expensive in a large environment.

Token

A security device or *token* is given to authorized users for them to use when authenticating to network resources. In order for them to log onto the network, the data (usually a changing number) generated by the token may be read by the user and then typed in as a password. Tokens may also plug directly into the computer via a USB port (samples are shown in Figure 1.13).

The numeric code that the user sees on the token is generated using an algorithm that exists in all tokens. The token also contains a clock and has a unique seed number. The current time and the unique seed are processed using the algorithm and produce the token code the user sees on the token.

This is normally done at least every minute which ensures that a unique code is generated that appears to be completely random. When the user connects to their system, they are prompted to enter in the token ID number that is generated. Since the server also knows the time and unique seed number of your token it can use the same algorithm to validate your token ID. The server also accounts for time discrepancies (typically a two- to three-minute window) of how long a token ID is valid. If an expired token ID is submitted, the system may check and recognize it as a valid token, but one that has expired, and prompt the user for the next token to ensure that the user is in actual possession of the token device. Using security tokens in addition to other authentication factors improves the overall security of your system by improving authenticity of your users.

Figure 1.13 Authenticating Using Secure Tokens

Biometrics

The word *biometrics* comes from the Greek words "bios," meaning life, and "metron," meaning measure. The use of biometrics in information technology authentication is quite literally, the measurement of a life indicator, or something you are. Biometric authentication mechanisms are based on either physical or behavioral traits; examples of various readers are shown in Figure 1.14. The concept behind biometric authentication is that it should be extremely hard to counterfeit a biometric trait. Examples of physical traits include fingerprints, eye retina, facial patterns, and hand measurements. Examples of behavioral traits include writing signatures, gaits, and typing patterns. Voice recognition is considered a combination of both physical and behavioral traits.

Figure 1.14 Authenticating Using Biometric Devices

Before a biometric authentication mechanism can be successful, a baseline of the biometric trait must first be taken to create a template, which can include several initial readings of the biometric trait. Each time the user authenticates using a biometric system, the biometric trait is read and compared to the template. The algorithm that analyzes the reading then matches a percentage of a matching pattern based off of the stored template. Many systems store each biometric reading to improve the accuracy of the authentication method so that a larger database of information can be validated against and ultimately improve the accuracy of the system.

Biometric systems are really only useful where there is some sort of oversight involved so that the authentication system cannot be compromised, such as a security guard monitoring the usage of the authentication mechanism.

Another concern with biometric authentication is that of user privacy. If a system contains biometric data of users and the system is compromised, a user cannot be issued a new fingerprint or other biometric trait. The answer to this has been the introduction of token biometric devices that have a biometric scanner as a part of the token device. These devices create the biometric template in the token and the biometric data is encrypted. The biometric data is never transferred from the token. Authentication is performed by the token and then the user is granted access to their information system. These devices are very simple to use and can connect to systems in a variety of ways including USB, RFID, and Bluetooth.

The performance of biometric systems is determined by the following items:

- **False Accept Rate (FAR), or fraud rate** What percentage of times an invalid user is accepted by the system.

- **False Rejection Rate (FRR) or insult rate** The percentage of times a valid user is rejected by the system

- **Failure to Enroll Rate (FTE or FER)** The percentage of times a failure of the biometric system to form a proper enrolment template for a valid user occurs

These rates must typically be less than or equal to 0.5 percent to be considered viable. However, the usage of biometric systems as an exclusive authentication mechanism is not realistic because not all people will be able to present the required biometric data. For example, amputees or individuals that have worn down their fingerprints over time or individuals with physical defects can preclude the use of a biometric authentication system for them. You must also consider any potential legal concerns regarding privacy that a biometric system may introduce.

TIP

Additional hardware and software must be purchased in order to use a biometric authentication system with XenApp.

Summary

All organizations should adopt a practice that is considered to be a minimally acceptable configuration practice for all systems. It is a key element of a security system and aids a security team's efforts in reducing the vulnerabilities on their systems and the overall risk to the organization.

In this chapter we covered the basic concepts of defining security. Security is simply the freedom from risk or danger. We expanded on that definition by defining risk as the potential loss resulting from the balance of threats, vulnerabilities, countermeasures, and value. Before you can define risk you must place a value on what it is that you want to secure. If there is no value, then ultimately there is no risk.

Understanding the security design process involves determining your organization's security needs and who and what you are securing your data against. One of the methods to assist with the design process is the CIA triad of confidentiality, integrity and availability. Before jumping feet first into a brand new security model, you should assess your current security policies and procedures and determine which ones meet the needs of your organization. If your security design requires modification, or if you are creating a new security design, you should make use of existing policies from standards organizations such as the ISO, ANSI, and the SANS Institute.

In order to design a security framework you should break up the process into four pieces: attack prevention, attack detection, attack isolation, and attack recovery. Understanding the types of threats that you may encounter will assist you in developing a framework to address these four areas. You should keep in mind that threats can be internal, external, malignant, malicious, human, and environmental. Some threats you cannot control. A threat that is often overlooked in the security framework is that of social engineering or nontechnical attacks which can be mitigated by having a proactive security awareness program. You have four choices when addressing risks to your network: avoidance, transference, mitigation, and acceptance.

Your organization may have to comply with various federal and/or state regulations such as HIPAA, SOX, and FERPA. Whether or not your organization has to meet required compliancy mandates, you should design a security framework that when implemented would meet or exceed the requirements. Standards such as FIPS 140-2, FIPS 201, and HSPD 12 provide specific details for security requirements that must be met by U.S. federal government computer systems.

There are a variety of methods available to improve the overall security posture, including using SSL encryption and utilizing digital certificates, using higher encryption algorithms such as TLS/FIPS/AES, enforcing user information security awareness, establishing well-defined information security policies and procedures, and implementing multifactor authentication methods utilizing smart cards, tokens, and biometrics. A security technology that is becoming more predominant in enterprise solutions is security auditing and vulnerability assessments. These tools will enable you to make the task of security management easier and more reliable.

The last thing we covered was the various authentication methods available such as Kerberos, SSL/TLS, NT Lan Manager, digest, passport, multifactor, token and biometrics. If your organization is using userid/passwords for authentication you should implement sound password policies that will prevent the compromise of user credentials.

Solutions Fast Track

Defining Security

☑ Security is the freedom from risk or danger.

☑ Risk is the potential loss resulting from the balance of threat, vulnerabilities, countermeasures, and value.

☑ There are three types of value: monetary, nuisance, and competitor.

☑ Threat is the who or what that can do harm if given the opportunity.

☑ A vulnerability is a weakness that allows a threat to be exploited. There are four types of vulnerabilities: technical, physical, operational, and personnel.

Understanding the Security Design Process

☑ The CIA Triad consists of confidentiality, integrity and availability. Understanding how these components interact will provide you with the proper balance of security in relation to productivity.

☑ When you are designing a plan for securing a Windows environment, your first step should be analyzing any existing security policies and procedures with an eye to how they can be improved (or, if necessary, replaced) to meet the security needs of your organization.

☑ Information security is concerned with protecting sensitive information from anyone who doesn't have appropriate access to it, while privacy is more of a customer-centric concept concerned with meeting a person or organization's preferences for how information concerning them should be handled.

☑ If your security policies are so stringent that your users are not able to access their data, then you haven't really designed a functional security scheme.

Designing a Framework for Implementing Security

☑ Designing a secure network framework can be broken into four conceptual pieces: attack prevention, attack detection, attack isolation, and attack recovery.

☑ Predicting network threats and analyzing the risks they present to your infrastructure is one of the cornerstones of the network security design process. Understanding the types of threats that your network will face will assist you in designing appropriate counter-measures and in obtaining the necessary money and resources to create a secure network framework.

☑ When classifying network threats, many developers and security analysts use the STRIDE model, which is an acronym for spoofing identity, tampering with data, repudiation, information disclosure, denial of service, and elevation of privilege.

☑ It is important for an organization to have well-defined procedures for identifying and then handling internal and external threats.

☑ The first step in implementing a risk analysis strategy is assessing the value of your assets and resources.

Reviewing Compliancy

☑ Some major compliancy initiatives include *Sarbanes-Oxley Act of 2002* (SOX), HIPAA, and *Family Educational Rights and Privacy Act* (FERPA).

☑ One of the requirements of HIPAA is to address security and privacy of health care patient information.

☑ FERPA protects the privacy of student education information.

☑ The Federal Information Processing Standard 140 (FIPS 140) is a U.S. federal government standard that details a benchmark for implementing cryptographic software.

☑ The Federal Information Processing Standard 201 (FIPS 201) is a U.S. federal government standard that details the usage of Personal Identity Verification, or Smart Cards, for all federal employees and contractors.

Explaining Security Technologies

☑ There are several security technologies available to XenApp, including using SSL encryption on digital certificates; using higher encryption algorithms, such as TLS, FIPS, and AES; enforcing user information security awareness; establishing well-defined information security policies and procedures; and implementing multifactor authentication methods utilizing smart cards, tokens, and biometrics.

☑ Public key infrastructure (PKI) is a security system that utilizes digital certificates. XenApp can utilize either public or private digital certificates.

☑ Cryptography is the process of taking plain text and then scrambling it into a cipher text. As a part of the cryptographic process the form of the information can also be changed. Cryptography should be considered for data whenever that data is considered sensitive or has a high value.

☑ Vulnerability assessments have become a critical component of many organizations' security infrastructures and have become integrated into their system rollout process. Before a new server is installed, it first must go through a vulnerability assessment and pass with flying colors. Additionally, when a new vulnerability is discovered, the network administrator can perform an assessment, discover which systems are vulnerable, and start the patch installation process.

Defining Authentication Models

☑ There are three general ways (often called "factors") to authenticate a person. These are something you know, something you have, and something you are.

☑ Within a Windows Server 2003 domain, the primary authentication protocol is Kerberos version 5. Kerberos provides thorough authentication by verifying not only the identity of network users but also the validity of the network services themselves.

☑ Other Windows authentication methods available include SSL/TLS, NT LAN Manager, digest authentication, passport authentication, and multifactor authentication.

☑ Windows password policies should follow these four basic rules: Change—change passwords on a regular basis; Not in More Than One Place— don't reuse passwords in multiple places; Size—the longer the password, the harder it is to break; and Creation— Do not use dictionary words; make use of pass phrases to create complex passwords.

☑ By using multifactor authentication, at least two forms of authentication are required before a person is properly authenticated. The more factors that are required to identify a person, the harder it is to impersonate a user.

☑ A security device or token is given to authorized users to use when authenticating to network resources. In order for them to log on to the network, the data (usually a changing number) generated by the token may be read by the user and then typed in as a password.

Frequently Asked Questions

Q: What is the definition for security?

A: Security is the freedom from risk or danger.

Q: What are the components of risk?

A: Threats, vulnerabilities, countermeasures, and value.

Q: What is the difference between malicious and malignant threats?

A: Malicious threats intend to do you harm. Malignant threats are threats that are always present.

Q: What is a threat?

A: The threat is essentially the *who* or *what* that can do you harm if given the opportunity. They cannot do you harm on their own. They require that you leave yourself vulnerable.

Q: What is a vulnerability?

A: Vulnerabilities are the weaknesses that allow the threat to exploit you.

Q: What is a countermeasure?

A: Countermeasures are the precautions that an organization takes to reduce risk.

Q: Why can't you realistically counter a threat?

A: Fundamentally, you cannot stop a hurricane, earthquake, flood, or other *what* threats. They will occur no matter what you do. At the same time, you cannot really counter a *who* threat because you cannot force people to do things according to your will all of the time.

Q: Why is it important to understand why we strive to optimize risk, rather than minimize risk?

A: It is impossible to remove all risks. Implementing more countermeasures to mitigate risks drives costs up past the value of the data you are protecting. This is why your goal is to optimize, not minimize, risk.

Q: What is the CIA Triad?

A: When securing data, a common phrase that you should be familiar with is CIA Triad, which stands for confidentiality, integrity, and availability.

Q: Why does your organization need a security infrastructure?

A: To adequately prevent attacks against your network.

Q: Why is it important to analyze existing security policies and procedures?

A: Because you should not waste time re-inventing processes that have already been created by others.

Q: What is probably the most important aspect of the acceptable use policy besides defining proper/improper network usage?

A: Enforces the "Ignorance is no excuse" axiom for users of your network.

Q: What is the definition of privacy?

A: Privacy is freedom from the intrusion of others in one's personal life or affairs.

Q: Why is security versus usability important?

A: You do not want to design a network so secure that no one can or will use it.

Q: What kind of threats are there?

A: Internal and External, Environmental and Human

Q: What is a nontechnical attack?

A: A contractor notices that a corporate user has his password written on a piece of paper taped in his office cube. The password is a strong password of 12 characters. The contractor writes the password down when the employee is away from his desk. The contractor did nothing more than collect and write down information.

Q: What are the minimum things that must be accomplished for a risk analysis?

A: You must assess the value of your assets and data, then identify potential risks that can cause loss of your assets or data.

Q: What do the federal compliancy regulations like HIPAA, SOX, and FERPA all have in common?

A: The requirement to protect data from unauthorized sources.

Q: What is a digital certificate?

A: A certificate is a digital voucher containing the name of an account and a public key.

Q: What is cryptography?

A: Cryptography is the process of taking *plain* text and then scrambling it into *cipher* text.

Q: What is the purpose of a vulnerability assessment?

A: When a new vulnerability is discovered, the network administrator can perform an assessment, discover which systems are vulnerable, and start the patch installation process. After the fixes are in place, another assessment can be run to verify that the vulnerabilities were actually resolved. A vulnerability assessment can also be used prior to placing a new server into a production environment.

Q: What are the two types of assessments?

A: Host and Network

Q: Should NT LAN Manager be used as an authentication method in a native Windows 2003 environment?

A: No. The LM (or LAN Manager) hash is weak and can easily be broken by password crackers.

Q: What is multifactor authentication?

A: Multifactor authentication requires at least two forms of authentication before a person is properly authenticated. Factors include something you know, something you are, and something you have or possess.

Q: What are four things a user can do to help ensure their password is not compromised?

A: Change passwords periodically, use longer "strong" passwords that use upper and lower case, numerals and special characters, do not "reuse" passwords for multiple applications, and try to use passphrases that are easy for the user to remember but do not contain any dictionary words.

Q: What are some good domain-based Windows password policies to consider?

A: Enforce password history, have a maximum password age, have a minimum password age, ensure passwords meet complexity requirements, and do not store passwords using reversible encryption.

Q: What is a smart card?

A: A smart card is a credit card-sized device that provides a portable method of providing security on a network for tasks like client authentication and securing user data.

Q: What is the purpose of a token?

A: A token is a security device that users can use when authenticating to network resources by entering in a number or code based on a mutual algorithm on the network and the token during a specific time period.

Q: What is the benefit of a biometric token over other biometric methods?

A: A biometric token does not transfer or release biometric data so that it makes it harder to compromise biometric data.

Chapter 2

Security Guidance for Operating Systems and Terminal Services

Solutions in this chapter:

- Windows 2003 Basics
- Windows 2003 Security Essentials
- Attacking Windows 2003
- Defending and Hardening Windows 2003
- Windows 2003 Terminal Services Basics
- Attacking Terminal Servers
- Defending Terminal Servers

☑ Summary

☑ Solutions Fast Track

☑ Frequently Asked Questions

Introduction

Windows 2003 has expanded capabilities arose from Microsoft's desire to develop their "Zero Admin Initiative," originally designed to improve interoperability, security, management, and ease of use both for system administrators and users. It incorporated a number of improvements to the former Windows Operating Systems, and these were made in areas such as Plug and Play, memory management, and kernel protection. System administrators and security professionals must be vigilant and aware of potential breach points to be successful in protecting systems using Windows 2003.

The core Windows 2003 operating system includes some vulnerabilities, however, as other components and additional services such as DNS and DHCP are added in the server platform to provide for the needs of users and network operations, and application-based services such as mail servers, news servers, and database servers are added, there is an accompanying increase in the number of security vulnerabilities and the amount of configuration that must be done to limit the potential areas of attack as the functions of the server are expanded. Some of these vulnerabilities are specific to the platform being used, and some are generic vulnerabilities that affect multiple operating systems and equipment vendors (such as SNMP concerns); in this chapter, the focus is specifically on the Windows 2003 conditions.

When starting to evaluate Windows 2003, it is good practice to first develop a basic understanding of what features of the operating system allow the administrator to *begin* to protect these resources; I discuss and consider this information in the section "Windows 2003 Basics." You'll see that there are some features that are conceptually shared with other operating systems, but that in Windows 2003 these may have unique configuration patterns or parameters that lead to exposure of resources or services to attack. Additionally, there is a need to understand where these features are likely to create holes or exposures that are undesirable and what can be done within the basic construction of Windows 2003 to provide the desired level of protection.

Following this discussion of the basics of Windows 2003, I proceed to a number of other topics. First among these will be learning about what security configurations and practices are available out of the box in the Windows 2003 platform. Some capabilities are provided in the initially installed software, and others may be added or specifically configured to lower vulnerability. The section titled "Windows 2003 Security Essentials" will explore and detail this information.

I then provide information about some other areas that will help you as an administrator and security provider to better understand and protect your systems from some common and uncommon attack sources. The section that follows, "Attacking Windows 2003," includes methods of enumeration and display and various attack Methods that you'll need to defend against in the Windows environment. At the conclusion of the discussions about the attack methods, the discussion focuses on methods of defense and hardening in the section "Defending and Hardening Windows 2003." This section details various methods and techniques that may be used to tighten security and reduce vulnerability in Windows 2003, and it reinforces some basic security principles. I point out and detail resources that will increase your chances of providing an environment that is as secure as possible and provides the level of protection that your operation requires.

I will then discuss Terminal Services and how it allows you to remotely execute applications on a Windows 2003–based server from a wide range of devices over virtually any type of network connection. In an article entitled "Terminal Server: The Day of Reckoning" (www.foundstone.com/knowledge/article-TermServer.html), Clinton Mugge and I stated, "The majority of our concerns, in most cases, are not a result of poor products but products being implemented poorly." I think we can all agree that if you hope to secure any system, you must first understand it. However, I feel like many Windows administrators, lacking a deep enough understanding of the system, are making the same security mistakes over and over—yet they still expect things to get better. "Doing the same thing over and over, but expecting different results" is actually a phrase I have heard used to define insanity!

One of these mistakes is remote administration—not the lack of it, rather the improper implementation of it. Some administrators lean too heavily on the extensive functionality of their Windows systems and forget about locking down the servers and implementing secure protocols or tunneling. Obviously, this isn't the best way to have a secure network.

Microsoft's security awareness is at an all time high, Bill Gates has stepped up to the plate, and as usual he is swinging for the fences. I have already seen a dramatic increase in security of Windows systems based on the implementation of Internet Connection Firewall, Windows Update, and Microsoft Security Baseline Analyzer. Microsoft is quickly stockpiling their security arsenal, and these tools are critical when attempting to tackle something as complex as securing a Terminal Server for multiuser access.

Windows 2003 Basics

Windows 2003 uses some common functionality and components that were available in both workstation (Windows 2000 Professional) and server (Windows 2000 Server) installations that can be used and configured in the workplace. The capability to create a basic security framework during the installation process exists in either implementation. In this section, an initial description of the basic features of Windows 2003 is examined, with a look at the basic construction of Windows 2003, the features that enable some protection of the operating system (OS) kernel from attack, and some first level actions that can be utilized to protect Windows 2003 equipment and data from compromise and attack.

Kernel Protection Mechanisms

Windows 2003 includes several changes that improve stability by providing improvements in these areas:

- **Kernel-mode write protection:** This capability prevents files in the kernel from being overwritten.

- **Windows file protection:** This has been enhanced to provide the capability to protect core operating system files from being overwritten by application installation programs and return the files to a stable version.

- **Driver signing:** A concept introduced in Windows 2003 and in Windows XP; it can be used to prohibit or prevent the installation of drivers that are untested and unproven on the platform.

The Windows 2003 model contains a number of subareas, which I describe briefly in this section to explain where the components are designed to operate, and the functions that are fulfilled through the design as it exists in Windows 2003. A basic diagram of the Windows 2000 kernel architecture is shown in Figure 2.1.

Figure 2.1 Windows 2003 Kernel Architecture

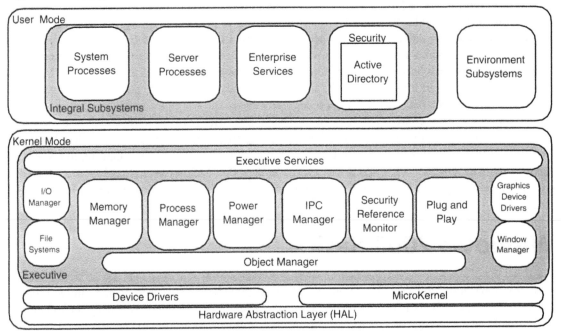

Like in Windows 2000, two distinct modes are detailed in the case of the Windows 2003 kernel. These are described as *user mode* and *kernel mode*. Operations that occur in user mode utilize software that is not granted full access to system resources. One significant change in the architecture involves the operation of Active Directory. Unlike Windows NT 4.0, the Active Directory operations occur in user mode, and operate under the umbrella of the security subsystem. In user mode, software is said to be in a *nonprivileged* state, and it cannot access system hardware directly. Applications designed for Windows 2003 run in user mode in protected spaces that are used only for the individual application. This same condition holds true for protected subsystems, such as those that are detailed in Figure 2.1 in the User Mode section. The Integral Subsystems section shows four services that provide the necessary interfaces for operating system functions such as network services and security. The Environment Subsystems include services that interface with application program interfaces (APIs) providing interoperability with applications written for other operating systems, such as POSIX, Win32, and OS/2. Generally, applications running in user mode that fail or crash will affect only the operation of that individual application, rather than affecting the operation of the Windows 2003 operating system.

Kernel mode allows software to access important system information and hardware directly. This mode consists of some specific architectural areas, which are divided into these four large areas:

- Executive
- Microkernel
- Device drivers
- Hardware Abstraction Layer (HAL)

The executive area is composed of system components that have a responsibility to provide services to other executive components and to the environment subsystems. This includes file management, input/output (I/O), resource management, interprocess communications, and virtual memory management duties. The microkernel is responsible for the microprocessor scheduling, multiprocessor synchronizing, and interrupt handling. Device drivers act as the interpreter for communication between requests for service and the hardware device, providing the ability to translate a job request into the specified action. The Hardware Abstraction Layer (HAL) allows compatibility with multiple processor platforms by isolating the Windows 2003 executive area from the hardware specific to the machine.

The important consideration when looking at the kernel construction and isolation mechanisms is to realize that the provision of security and stability of the operating system is partially controlled by the method that is used in applications and coding. If the user mode functions are utilized, in which the processes and applications are running in their own separate spaces, better protection is provided to the Windows 2003 operating system from attack by various outside control mechanisms.

Disk File System Basics and Recommendations

Windows 2003 provides backward compatibility to previous DOS and Windows implementations through the capability to utilize any of the file systems used in earlier versions. Windows 2003 does support Mount Points in a limited fashion, but foreign file systems are not supported in this mount system as they might be in the various 'Nix flavors. Windows 2003 still maintains the basic directory structure that has been present in all DOS-based and NT-based systems previously used. As I discuss the file system types and their benefits and drawbacks, you will see that you should use this backward-compatible capability only in rare circumstances because it eliminates the possibility of securing the data on the affected machine, or more specifically, the affected partition. The unsecured partition becomes an easy source of attack for anyone with interactive (local) access to the machine.

NTFS

NTFS (New Technology File System or NT File System, if you aren't that old) is used in all versions of the Windows platform, with version changes occurring in the file system as newer versions of the NT platform have been released. Windows 2003, in all versions, supports NTFS 5.2, which incorporates new features and functionality not available in previous NT-based implementations. It is important to understand that the implementation of NTFS 5.2 partitions is critical to the initial security configurations you must achieve to protect your systems running Windows 2003. NTFS 5.2 provides the capability to configure Discretionary Access Control List (DACL) settings to create the initial and basic access controls needed for security of resources.

NTFS was first developed in the early (NT 3.5 and later) versions of the NT platform. When originally created, it included some of the functions and capabilities that were developed in the high performance file system (HPFS) for OS2 that was being jointly developed by Microsoft, IBM, and others. As Microsoft broke away from that early development stage, the NTFS file system was created to provide a higher level of security and file system control. A number of enhancements to file structure and security mechanisms are available with the use of NTFS 5.2. Among them are the following:

- Smaller cluster sizes
- Compression

- Encryption
- Disk quotas
- Active Directory support

How are these new features important? Smaller cluster sizes, with their accompanying efficiencies in the use of disk space, also leave less slack space for use by attackers. Compression, although not directly a security benefit, does allow for more flexibility in storage of information on systems. Encryption, available on Windows 2003 systems utilizing the capabilities of NTFS 5.2, allows the user or administrator to activate the encryption mechanism to locally encrypt sensitive data and protect it more fully from attack. Disk quotas can be a useful tool in restricting access and storage on your systems by attackers, and Active Directory support enhances your ability to define access controls within the Windows 2003 environment.

FAT 32

File Allocation Table (FAT) 32 file systems is supported within Windows 2003 for backward compatibility with previous versions of Windows and DOS if that compatibility must be maintained on specific machines. The previously known limitations of FAT 32 file systems is still exist in the versions used in Windows 2003, and they should *never* be used in a Windows 2003 environment in a production system that is concerned with file-level security and the protection of data on the local machine. Neither format provides any local security capability, nor they further limit functionality due to the inability to compress and encrypt data on drives that are formatted with them. Data corruption and data loss are virtually ensured in the case of a FAT-formatted drive that is accessible interactively in the workplace.

Creating, Using, and Maintaining Users and Groups in Windows 2003

Users and groups are at the core of the capability to define DACLs within the Windows 2003 system. The ability to define users and groups and their levels of access allows administrators to define the types of access available and apply the access permissions to the resources they want to make available. Additionally, users and groups allow the administrator to apply these access levels either to the individual user or to a group of users with similar access needs. Two important divisions of account types need discussion at this time. In the next sections, I discuss and review some of the primary differences between Local and Domain accounts, and the appropriate uses for each type.

Local Accounts

Local accounts in Windows 2003 are employed in Windows 2003 installations when the server is not a domain controller (DC). Local accounts only allow resource access on the individual machine where they are created and configured; they allow administrators to control access to those resources and to be able to grant permission for a user or group to perform system tasks such as backup operations on the individual machine. Remember that the ability to control access in Windows 2003 depends on the choice of file system on the machine along with proper group assignments for the user accounts. FAT does not allow protection of local resources, whereas NTFS does. To work with users and groups on a local (either standalone or workgroup) machine, proceed to the Computer Management Microsoft Management Console (MMC) tool. To access this tool, choose **Start | Programs | Administrative Tools | Computer Management**. Expand the **Local Users and Groups** item, as shown in Figure 2.2.

Figure 2.2 Computer Management: Local Users and Groups

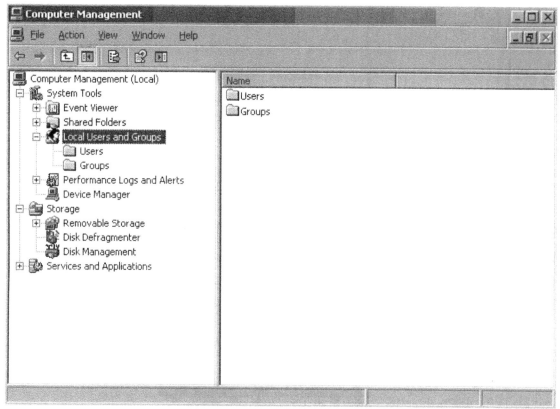

Expand the **Users** container, and you'll see something similar to what's shown in Figure 2.3.

Figure 2.3 The Windows 2003 Local Users Container

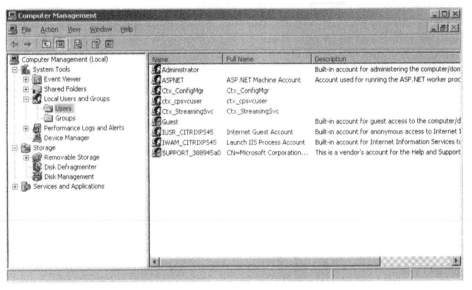

Notice in this default installation there are few accounts and those were created during the installation. These includes the Administrator and Guest account that are created in all Windows 2003 installations. As you can see, the Guest account is disabled; this occurs by default during the installation. The two additional accounts that are created by default during a Windows 2003 server installation are the IUSR_*computername* account and the IWAM_*computername* account, and these are created if you have installed Internet Information Services (IIS), to be used for anonymous connections to the Web server and File Transfer Protocol (FTP) server and for running out of process applications on the Web server.

Expand the **Groups** container, and you'll see something similar to what's shown in Figure 2.4.

Figure 2.4 The Windows 2003 Local Users Container

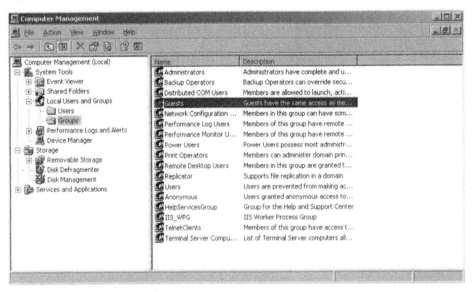

At the local level, the groups that are created in the default installation include Administrators, Backup Operators, Guests, Power Users, Print Operators, and Users. Additionally, in the default configuration, the Replicator group is added and used for file replication when the system is a member of a domain. In this level, the Users group has only basic access to the local machine and resources, and it is unable to install programs or drivers or to change configuration outside of their own local profile settings, which includes their desktop environment. Power Users have higher access, and Administrators have the ability to fully configure and manage the machine as they wish. Backup Operators are allowed to do the local backup and restore operations in the default configuration. (The Windows Internet Naming System [WINS] users group is not added by default; the WINS service must be present on the server before that group is added. None of these accounts has permission to perform any function or access any resource outside of the local machine).

Domain Accounts

In the case of a machine that is a member of an Active Directory domain, the administrator must create and manage domain accounts. There are significant differences in the portability of these accounts, their authentication methods, and the access that they can achieve throughout the enterprise. In this section, I take a quick look at the domain account structure and briefly describe some of the differences that need explanation in relation to the domain accounts and their functions (Active Directory is out of the scope of this book). While looking at domain accounts, it's important to understand that these accounts are created and maintained on domain controllers that replicate their content to each other. DCs that hold the domain account database do not use local accounts for their operation. As the DC is created, the tools for management of the user and group accounts switch from a local management console to a new tool, the Active Directory Users and Computers (ADUC) management console. From within this console, administrators are able to create, modify, and control user and group memberships. Figure 2.5 illustrates the ADUC console with the Users container open.

Figure 2.5 The Active Directory Users and Computers Console Showing the Users Container

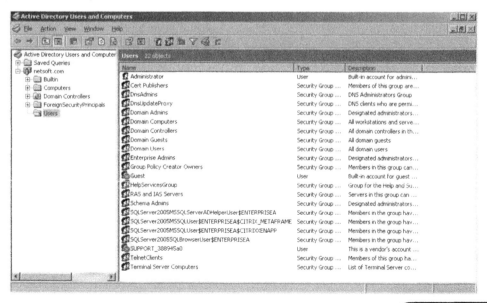

Note the significant difference in the number of default user accounts that are created as you create an Active Directory structure. This container contains not only the default users, but a number of domain-wide security groups that are used to maintain and manage the domain operations. Some new security groups are also created, which include Domain Computers, Domain Controllers, Enterprise Admins, Schema Admins, and Domain Admins, among others. All of these groups are used for domain-wide groupings that allow you to control or grant access to specific operations within the domain. Security groups also allow you to enforce group policy conditions, which I touch on later in this chapter and fully explore in Chapter 6. Figure 2.6 shows us the Built-in Groups that are created in an Active Directory domain.

Figure 2.6 Active Directory Users and Computers Console with Builtin Groups

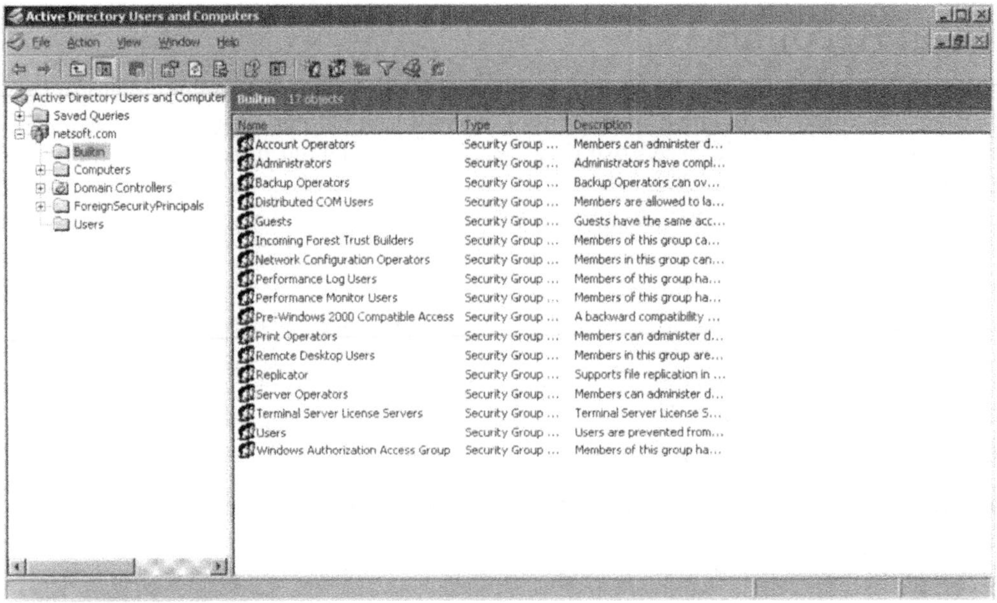

This collection of groups allows administrators to assign or delegate permission to work within specially defined areas of control to perform system-based tasks in the domain. These built-in groups provide the ability to delegate control. Notice in Figure 2.6 that there is a group called Pre-Windows 2000 Compatible Access. This group can lead to security difficulties, because it can contain the special group Everyone in its membership. When this is true, down-level machines (or attackers) may establish a *null* session connection with the use of a blank password for anonymous access. In this case, anonymous users (such as to a Web page) could potentially access and obtain control of your machine. This particular configuration requires much diligence as you prepare file and drive access control settings, but may be needed depending on your network's makeup.

There is a not significant difference in the sphere of influence of these groups in Windows 2000 and Windows 2003. Please remember that in NT 4.0, these groups had access only on machines that were either a PDC or BDC. In Windows 2003, these built-in groups have access and control over *any Windows 2003 machine that is a domain member*, even if it is not a domain controller. This is a change that you must be aware of as you assign membership to these groups. Now, what about the

"Everyone" group that is discussed all the time? Windows 2003 also has a number of groups that are not detailed here, but rather are present and utilized based on actions being performed. For instance, the Interactive group contains users who are allowed to log on locally to a machine. The Network group contains users that are allowed to connect from the Network. Membership in these groups is not assigned, but rather occurs during operation of the machine and network operations.

Windows 2003 Security Essentials

Once you have a basic understanding of the basics of Windows 2003, you can begin to learn about the basic security tools and settings that are available in the Windows 2003 platform. Many things can affect the level of security that is established on these systems depending on the path that is taken for installation and configuration. For instance, machines that are part of an upgrade process rather than clean installations will have a different, more vulnerable configuration than will a machine that is installed clean from the start.

What Is Vulnerable in Windows 2003?

A substantial number of vulnerabilities exist out of the box if basic configuration choices are not made properly when you install. In the subsections that follow, I point out some of the things that are vulnerable in these specific areas so that you can begin to see where the possible problems can occur. The goal in this area is to fully understand that the vulnerabilities exist out of the box but can be secured through proper configuration. You can eliminate much of the vulnerability by proper configuration and patching, which is discussed later in the chapter.

RUNAS Service

Microsoft introduced the RUNAS service in Windows 2003. This service allows the use of alternate credentials to perform system administrative tasks. It is a risk factor if administrative accounts and passwords are not properly controlled and secured. The Server service allows sharing of resources on the network and connection via named pipes connections. The Workstation service allows network connections to remote resources.

Files and Applications

Unlike in Windows 2000, Windows Server 2003 does not allow Everyone full control permissions to the root directory on each partition on the machine. In Windows 2000, the effect of this setting is to allow full control permissions to everyone (including anonymous access users through Web or FTP access), *unless* the underlying folders have had permissions set differently and inheritance blocked. From a security standpoint, it was a risk, however, Microsoft has significantly tightened this area of Operating System. Additionally, a major change is made to the DACL for the HKey Local Machine Registry key, where the permissions are changed to not allow certain users to change configurations that require a write operation on the Registry. For instance, the default in a clean NTFS 5.2 Windows 2003 installation would not allow users or power users to modify network settings on their network adaptors property sheet, because when these settings change they are recorded in the Registry, and this is not allowed.

NOTE

As with any installation of operating systems, it is always preferred to perform a clean install when possible. In the case of Windows 2003, an upgrade from a previous operating system will leave permissions in place that were established by the former operating system and will not include the more stringent protections afforded by the Windows 2003 operating system. Avoid upgrade installations if at all possible.

Accounts Data

Accounts data for accounts that are stored in the local machine's Security Accounts Manager (SAM) database is "secure" in the sense that the database is in use and therefore locked via a file locking mechanism while the operating system is running. However, someone could simply boot with a bootable floppy, copy the database from its default location, and use any number of tools to attack it. Additionally, if the attacker can physically access the machine, they can simply delete the SAM database. When the machine is rebooted, the administrator account is re-created with a blank password. (Of course, all of the other accounts are removed at the same time.) This information is also retrievable, of course, if backup media is not protected from theft or unauthorized use, since backup operations normally include the database information. Accounts data is vulnerable to attack when stored locally if the machines are not physically secure. A number of tools exist for breaching NTFS drives and retrieving data from them, which will be discussed in some of the later sections of this chapter. As some wise person stated before that if a bad guy has unrestricted physical access to your computer, it's not your computer anymore. That is absolutely the case in this instance; you must provide the basic physical security that is necessary in order to protect against this vulnerability. I discuss some ways to protect this data later in the chapter.

Providing Basic Security Levels in Windows 2003

Microsoft did provide administrators with a number of capabilities to provide basic security levels in Windows 2003. In the next sections, I discuss at a number of ways to measure and check security configurations to assure that they meet the standards defined in a security baseline analysis completed prior to implementation. I discuss security templates, including analysis, customization, and installing and verifying their function and settings. Following that, I discuss file system and disk configuration areas to see what must be done to provide basic levels of security to users and systems. At the end of this section, I cover the configuration of services and then configuration of local and network access controls.

NOTE

Creating a security baseline is very important when beginning to analyze the security of your operations. It is important to fully evaluate the characteristics and potential vulnerabilities of each portion of the system. This includes recording and knowing the basic settings of your operating system(s), network protocol(s), network devices, and applications related to security. Following that initial evaluation, appropriate adjustments can be made to the settings to more fully secure what you have.

Creating Security Templates

While preparing to provide security in the Windows 2003 environment, administrators can use several Microsoft-provided tools to get a more realistic view of the security levels established (or not established, as the case may be) in the configurations that have been created during or after setup. Microsoft provides a couple of tools within the MMC toolset that are very helpful in comparing various levels of security configuration and creating a security settings template and model that is acceptable and useful in a particular setting. In the following sections, I discuss the toolset and what can be done with it in the analysis arena, and then how to use the tool to configure machines appropriately to your needs.

Analyzing Security Policy Templates and Machine Security Configuration

One of the first functions that can be utilized within the Security Configuration And Analysis toolset is the capability to compare security settings among various templates with current machines, and with each other. This allows you to determine if the default configurations of the Microsoft supplied templates are valid for your needs, or whether a need exists to customize and apply your own templates. Figure 2.7 shows a custom Security Configuration management console that I use in the next sections to explain how the tool works. To create one, type **mmc** in the **Run** window, and add the Security Configuration and Analysis and Security Templates snap-ins to your console.

Figure 2.7 A Custom Security Configuration Management Console

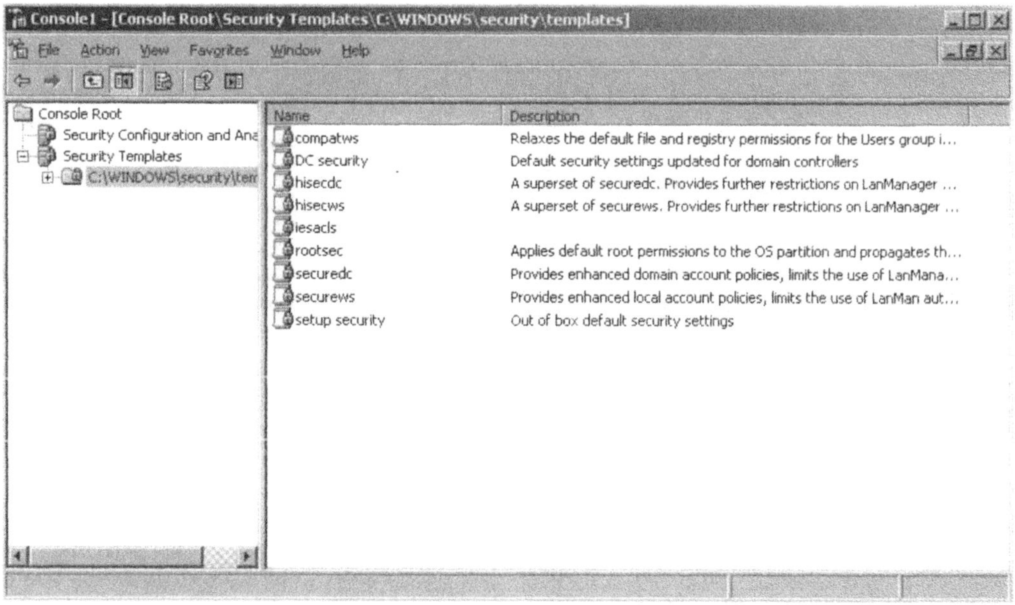

In the Figure 2.7 window, with the templates area expanded, you can see that a number of default templates are available for configuration of various levels of security. Table 2.1 gives a quick description of these templates.

Table 2.1 Default Templates Available for Various Security Levels

Template	Purpose
compawks	Relaxes the default file and registry permissions for the Users group in a manner that is consistent with the requirements of most non-certified applications. Normally the Power Users group should be used to run non-certified applications. See online help for further information.
DC security	Default security settings updated for domain controllers
hisecdc	A superset of securedc. Provides further restrictions on LanManager authentication and further requirements for the encryption and signing of secure channel and SMB data. In order to apply hisecdc to a DC, all of the DC's in all trusted or trusting domains must be running Windows 2000 or later. See online help for further info.
hisecws	A superset of securews. Provides further restrictions on LanManager auth and further requirements for the encryption and signing of secure channel and SMB data. In order to apply hisecws to a member, all DC's that contain accounts of all users that logon to the client must be running NT4 SP4 or higher. See online help for further info.
iesacls	
rootsec	Applies default root permissions to the OS partition and propagates them to child objects that are inheriting from the root. The propagation time depends on the number of unprotected child objects. See online help for further information.
securedc	Provides enhanced domain account policies, limits the use of LanManager authentication, and provides further restrictions on anonymous users. If a DC is configured with securedc, then a user with an account in that domain will not be able to connect to any member server from a LanMan only client. See online help for further info.
securews	Provides enhanced local account policies, limits the use of LanMan authentication, enables server-side SMB signing, and provides further restrictions on anonymous users. To apply to a domain member, all DC's that contain accounts of all users that logon to that member must be running NT4 SP4 or higher. See online help for further info.
Setup security	Out of box default security settings

Some of the templates involve assumptions about clean installs and that the settings match the settings that are configured during a clean installation, which we can compare to the setup security template. In the case of a machine that was not a clean installation, you need first to apply the *basic*** template that is applicable to your installation type (this is the equivalent of a clean install as far as the security templates are concerned) prior to installing the upgrade to the *secure*** templates (I discuss the process of template installation a little later in this section of the chapter). Before you can apply any templates, however, you need to analyze the current machine settings and compare them to the template you want to evaluate for improved security. Here are the steps to open a new database and then import a template for comparison to your system.

To Create a New Database and Important Template to Compare System Configurations:

1. Right-click the **Security Configuration and Analysis** scope item.

2. Click **Open Database…**.

3. Type a new database name, such as Secdatabase, and then click **Open**.

4. Select a security template to import, and then click **Open.**

5. Once you have opened the database, you can import any of the templates that you want to use for comparison. As shown in following figure, right-click the **Security Configuration and Analysis** item in the left-hand pane and then click on **Import Template…** item. Then import the **hisecdc** template for analysis, as shown in Figure 2.8.

Figure 2.8 Importing a Template for Comparison to Your System

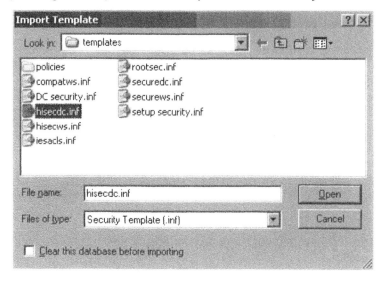

6. Having completed importing the chosen template for comparison, return to the Security Configuration and Analysis tool and choose **Analyze Computer Now…,** which is shown in Figure 2.9.

Figure 2.9 Analyze Computer against the Chosen Template

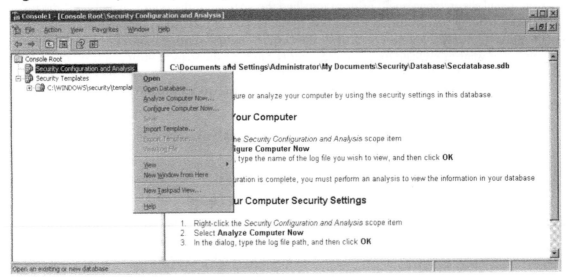

7. You will then be prompted to choose a path to generate an error log file to keep error logs (see Figure 2.10).

Figure 2.10 Choosing a path to keep Error log files

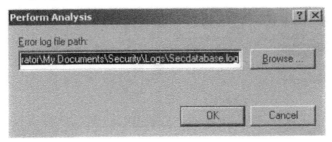

8. The system will now start analyzing the machine against the chosen template, as shown in the Figure 2.11.

Figure 2.11 Beginning the Analysis of the Machine against the Chosen Template

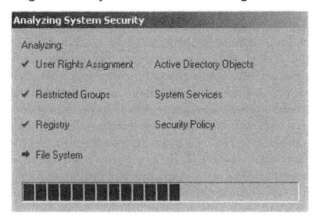

9. Now that you have successfully imported a template for comparison, you can begin to look at the areas that are different from your configuration. You may notice significant differences exist between the basic domain controller configuration and the **hisecdc** template in the area of Security options as shown in Figure 2.12. In just this one area, several values that are configurable are very different (denoted by the *x*) and are considerably weaker in the default configuration. Check marks appear where the configuration meets the conditions of the template. If you were to proceed through the various areas of comparison, you would find similar conditions and differences in each of the other areas.

Figure 2.12 Viewing the Initial Results of the Comparison between Template and Machine

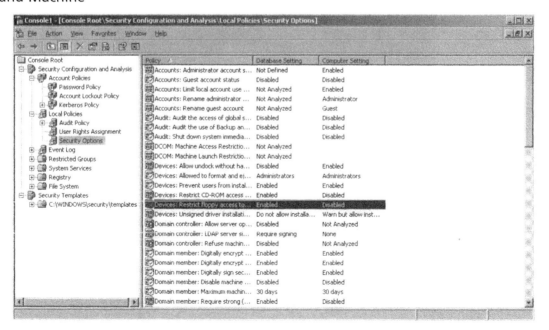

10. After you have had a chance to analyze the current and possible security settings and configurations available through the stock included templates, you may very well find that the stock settings do not give you the level of security that you want to use. In many cases, the *hisec*** templates are more restrictive than your climate will allow, and the basic templates are just not enough to keep you protected. For instance, if you apply the hardening principles to a machine that has extra services configured on it, such as Exchange 2000 or SQL 2000, you may find that there are unintended consequences to those applications and that you really need a custom configuration to allow for your particular needs. In that event, you can customize or build your own templates that contain the settings you need. To accomplish this, save any of the existing templates with a filename that you choose by highlighting the template name and choosing **Save As**. Using the Import Template procedure shown in the preceding section, you now import the new template and modify its content to suit your needs. Be sure to check the box **Define this policy in the database** for changes you want saved to the template. This is illustrated in Figure 2.13.

Figure 2.13 Customizing a Security Policy Template

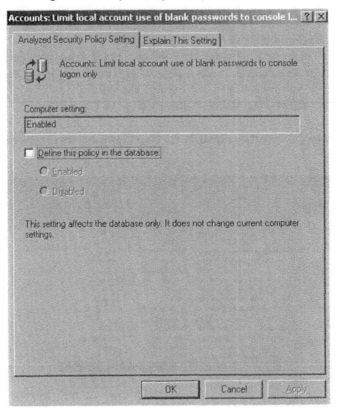

Changes to the database are saved when you select OK. After you have made changes to as many of the security settings that you need to change, you can proceed to the Installation and Checking Security Policy Templates section to apply the templates.

Installing and Checking Security Policy Templates

Following the creation and modification(s) of your security templates, the final step of the process is to install the security template and verify that the settings have been successfully implemented. To do this, you return to the Security Configuration and Analysis console, right-click the Security Configuration and Analysis object in the left-hand pane, and choose **Configure Computer Now...**, as shown in Figure 2.14.

Figure 2.14 The Security Configuration Console Configuration Choices Screen

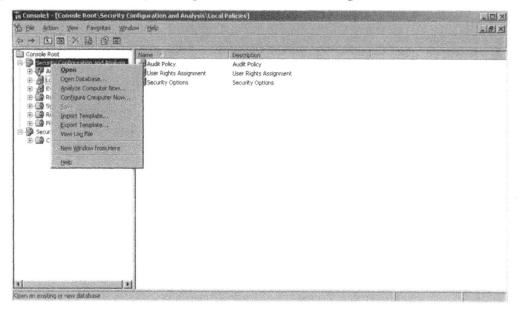

After making this selection, you're asked to verify the location of the log file that will be created, and then you are presented with the Configuring Computer Security screen shown in Figure 2.15.

Figure 2.15 Computer Configuration Progress Screen

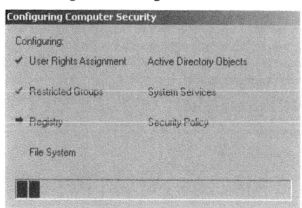

At this point, you're almost done. The last step in the process is to verify that the desired changes were actually made to the system you're working on. To accomplish this, follow the analysis steps you previously went through and compare the final result to the template you created and applied to the system.

Tools & Traps...

It's Not All Manual Configurations

All of the procedures detailed in this section allow the administrator to more fully secure the operating system environment. This detailed a manual procedure for illustration purposes, and an administrator could certainly copy the desired templates across a network connection and apply them in this manner. However, when using Active Directory, the administrator can distribute and install these templates via the Group Policy capabilities of Active Directory, thus saving much time and effort. The original construction of the custom templates must still be done in the manner detailed here.

One of the great things about these templates is that mistakes are relatively easy to fix. If it is discovered that the adjustments made are too rigid, another security template can always be imported and installed while working out the kinks. Be aware that this capability exists, but that the security template being applied must also define the settings changed in the previous template to remove them completely and return to a base setting.

Attacking Windows 2003

Windows 2003 has had lass numbers of attacks mounted against it as compare to Windows 2000. In this section, I show you some of the various methods that attackers use to discover and try to access Windows 2003 equipment and domains. I discuss methods that many attackers use to check systems for vulnerabilities and then discuss methods to make these attacks less profitable for the attackers and at the same time make your system more secure. I also show a pattern that has become pretty standard for detection of vulnerabilities. That standard takes a course that proceeds through a multistep process to identification and attack:

- Footprint potential victim systems
- Scan for entry points
- Enumerate possible entry points
- Get passwords
- Attack

Of course, although system administrators and security professionals follow this ordered type of methodology, the attacker is primarily interested in the quickest, easiest entry point. However, the result is generally the same if the work hasn't provided the ability to rebuff the initial efforts at discovery.

System Identification Methods

The first step to preparing for attempted access to a network is footprinting, which is simply the process used to begin to identify systems as potential targets to probe or eventually attack. This can involve a number of steps. For instance, in many cases attackers can simply find information about a company's systems through viewing its corporate Web site. Often, this will provide a picture of the overall business structure of the company, and it may follow that the IT department has closely followed that structure in developing their network structure. Certainly, it may indicate where certain components are likely to be geographically or physically located. Other publicly available resources may be utilized, such a telephone directories, search engines, financial information, and so on. I've found information in some cases when top-level people in the company have issued press releases detailing information that turned out to be useful in the evaluation of their structures. Often, a little social engineering with appropriate name dropping can reveal a lot about the organization that is being analyzed.

Once a decision is made that a particular organization is worthy of time and commitment, attackers begin working through the process to look for entry points. Initially, one may choose to scan the systems to begin to get a feel for what is available. A very quick GUI port scanner called SuperScan is available free from Foundstone, Inc. (www.foundstone.com/knowledge/free_tools.html). Scanline from Foundstone and a Win32 version of Nmap from eEye at www.eeye.com are command-line-oriented tools. These tools can be used to quickly check for response of an individual host or a range of addresses that may be in use by the subject network, and test for ports that are responsive. Other tools such as GFI's Network Security Scanner (www.gfi.com/lannetscan/index.html) allow not only scanning the network, but can begin to enumerate the hosts and obtain much more information about the systems being probed. This allows the refinement of the attack methodology to utilize the exposed interfaces and go after known vulnerabilities in these areas.

For instance, using Scanline, one could evaluate a range of addresses and return information about the remote systems, such as ports active on the remote systems:

```
C:\>sl -h-r 192.168.0.1-192.168.0.2
ScanLine (TM) 1.01
Copyright (c) Foundstone, Inc. 2002
http://www.foundstone.com

Scan of 2 IPs started at Sun May 18 06:41:39 2008
-------------------------------------------------------------------------
192.168.0.1
Hostname: ENTERPRISEA
Responded in 0 ms.
0 hops away
Responds with ICMP unreachable: Yes
TCP ports: 53 88 135 139 389 445 593 636 1025 1027 3268
UDP ports: 53 123 137 138 445 500 1434
```

```
-----------------------------------------------------------------------------
192.168.0.2
Hostname: Juliet.netsoft.com
Responded in 0ms.
0 hops away
Responds with ICMP unreachable: Yes
TCP ports: 80 135 139 445 1031 1494 3389
UDP ports: 123 137 138 445 500 1025
-----------------------------------------------------------------------------
Scan finished at Sun May 18 06:41:52 2008
```

Following this scanning visit and an indication of potential targets, you can then use this information to stop unnecessary services.

Remote Enumeration

Remote enumeration can often be accomplished with astonishing ease. Within the Windows environment, attackers can often locate potential targets through the use of simple commands at the command line, and they can establish communication with those targets through null session authentication. For instance, if default settings are in place on Windows 2003 machines allowing null session logons to be established with blank passwords, an attacker can establish that null session and then run tools such as Somarsoft's DumpSec (formerly DumpACL) to determine user names and SIDs with ease. Let's take a look at some of the methods used to accomplish entry to systems if they aren't secured with good practices.

NetBIOS

Enumerating existing Windows machines on a local wire is extremely easy if NetBIOS services are left running. Generally, this means that if a network is using File and Print Sharing and the normal use of Network Neighborhood or My Network Places, the chances are good that the capability exists to attack and enumerate your network. This is very simple if a single vulnerable system is available for connection. How easy is this? Just open a command window on any Windows machine with NetBIOS services enabled, and type the command **net view**. This will immediately deliver the machine names of any machines on the wire that have NetBIOS turned on. The output of that command might look like this:

```
Server Name          Remark
-----------------------------------------------------------------------------
\\ENTERPRISEA
\\JULIET
The command completed successfully.
```

Here are a few more steps in this basic enumeration procedure.

At the command prompt, type **net view /domain**, and you will enumerate the possible domains and workgroups on the network being probed. It might look like this:

```
Domain
-------------------------------------------------------------------------
NETSOFT
The command completed successfully.
```

Once the domain list is known, use the *nltest* tool from the Windows 2003 Resource Kit; enter **nltest /dclist:*domainname***, and get a list of the domain controller machines in the domain. Usual attack procedure would attack the domain controllers first, and then enumerate other hosts in the network, because the most valuable information (and highest level of control) can be obtained there. In this example, it would look like this:

```
C:\>nltest /dclist:netsoft
Get list of DCs in domain 'Netsoft' from '\\ENTERPRISEA'.
    enterprisea.netsoft.com [PDC] [DS] Site: Default-First-Site-Name
The command completed successfully
```

At this stage, prior to actually attacking the DC machines, further enumeration might be desirable to limit the effect of account lockout settings. A tool from the Razor Team at Bindview called *enum* can assist you in this part of your enumeration efforts. This tool can be found at http://razor. bindview.com, and it can easily give you information such as this:

```
C:\>enum -P 192.168.0.10
server: 192.168.0.10
setting up session... success.
password policy:
  min length: none
  min age: none
  max age: 42 days
  lockout threshold: none
  lockout duration: 30 mins
  lockout reset: 30 mins
cleaning up... success.
```

The information from *enum* in this case lets the attacker know that there is no restriction on failed attacks on passwords (*lockout threshold: none*) and that it can be continually worked on when performing that attack.

The process of enumeration provides a detailing of the currently active Windows systems, and allows quick checks for connectivity and security. Again at the command line, the attacker types a command to check for the ability to create a null session connection. If proceeding from the information gathered so far, the attacker would type the following command: **net use *machinename*\ ipc$ ""/u: ""** (substituting the appropriate machine name in the network being attacked) which would attempt a connection to the hidden remote logon share on the machine with a null password. If successful, this logon could be used to retrieve information using tools such as the DumpSec tool mentioned previously. The hacker can also use the normal TCP/IP **nbtstat** command as well. This will add to the information base by providing lists of services and names for the machines that have been identified. If the command **nbtstat –A 192.168.0.1** (substitute the IP address as appropriate to your environment) was entered in a command window, it would retrieve a full listing of names and NetBIOS service markers for services in use on the particular machine. This defines more information to use in a list of potential spots for entry to an unprotected or incorrectly configured system, and is illustrated here:

```
C:\>nbtstat -A 192.168.25.66

LAN:
Node IpAddress: [192.168.0.2] Scope Id: []
NetBIOS Remote Machine Name Table
Name                Type         Status
---------------------------------------------
ENTERPRISEA     <00>  UNIQUE      Registered
NETSOFT         <00>  GROUP       Registered
NETSOFT         <1C>  GROUP       Registered
ENTERPRISEA     <20>  UNIQUE      Registered
NETSOFT         <1B>  UNIQUE      Registered
NETSOFT         <1E>  GROUP       Registered
NETSOFT         <1D>  UNIQUE      Registered
..__MSBROWSE__.<01>  GROUP       Registered
MAC Address = 00-0C-29-DC-69-83
```

From this information, it is possible to see the currently logged on user, and information about the domain registration, services active on the machine, and even the Media Access Control (MAC) address. All of this information, together with the earlier enumerations, allows decisions about appropriate attack points and methodologies to be put to use.

SNMP

Simple Network Management Protocol (SNMP) is not installed by default in Windows 2003. However, many administrators install SNMP because they use other tools to centrally monitor and manage their systems, and they don't realize the level of information that can be obtained from systems configured to be SNMP agents. A major access point is created when SNMP is installed with no changes to the default configuration, because it is always set up with a default community string name of *PUBLIC*. If an attacker wants to retrieve information from systems identified through port scans of having UDP port 161 open, it is simple to use the Windows 2000 Resource Kit tool *snmputil* (SNMP Browse tool) to retrieve information from the machines that are configured with the defaults. To achieve the results desired, that attacker must know how to define Management Information Base (MIB) numbering and syntax. Although some effort is needed to understand the

MIB numbering system, it is relatively simple to retrieve information about the SNMP configured machine. This can include service information, version information, and other reportable information that may give attackers a method to breach the affected host. Some commercial tools allow the capability to query the machine via SNMP to retrieve user and group information as well as other configuration information that may prove valuable to an attacker. If you don't have the Windows Resource Kit at hand, you can download a significant number of the tools from Microsoft at www.reskit.com. Additionally, a small GUI SNMP query tool (*Snmputilg*) is available for people who are more comfortable with GUI tool rather than command line. As an example, I've run the command *snmputil walk 192.168.0.1 public 1* and displayed part of the output from the command below.

```
Variable = system.sysDescr.0
Value    = String Hardware: x86 Family 6 Model 15 Stepping 8 AT/AT COMPATIBLE -
Software: Windows Version 5.2 (Build 3790 Uniprocessor Free)

Variable = system.sysObjectID.0
Value    = ObjectID 1.3.6.1.4.1.311.1.1.3.1.3

Variable = system.sysUpTime.0
Value    = TimeTicks 45839

Variable = system.sysContact.0
Value    = String

Variable = system.sysName.0
Value    = String ENTERPRISEA

Variable = system.sysLocation.0
Value    = String

Variable = system.sysServices.0
Value    = Integer32 79
End of MIB subtree.
```

In short, SNMP can be used quite easily if not properly secured and configured to retrieve system information and potential attack areas. All of this work does not have to be done from the command line, however. A very good tool with a GUI interface is available from Solarwinds at www.solarwinds.net called IP Network Browser. This is included in each of their tool sets and is available as an evaluation download from their site. It enumerates the network, shares, and other information clearly and quickly, and it is worth looking at for your toolset. Figure 2.16 shows a sample of the output generated by this tool. As you can see, it enumerates a machine with SNMP installed and provides information on user accounts, shares, and much more.

Figure 2.16 Using IP Network Browser to Enumerate Using SNMP

Probing

When trying to enumerate, try to use various other methods to probe for information. For instance, port probing may reveal banner information about available services or platforms that also allow for creation of a plan and where or how to carry out connection attempts based on known vulnerabilities with those types of systems. For instance, a port probe of port 80 on a machine that has IIS 6.0 installed and running will return a banner that indicates to a the potential attacker that the Web server is IIS 6.0. This is a default banner setting that is hard-coded (although it can be modified and therefore may not be accurate always). Mail servers, FTP servers, and others return the same type of banner information, giving the attacker a leg up on knowing what and where to attack your system.

When probing for Windows 2003, the simplest scan is to check with a port scanner for TCP port 139 and 445. Responses from port 139 indicate only NT 4.0 or other downlevel systems. If both ports respond, the system is Windows 2000 or later. Of course, packet filters at the perimeter will distort this information. Here is an example using Scanline, which was used earlier in the chapter:

```
C:\>sl -c 500 -h -t 139,445 10.192.0.131-10.192.0.154

ScanLine (TM) 1.01

Copyright (c) Foundstone, Inc. 2002

http://www.foundstone.com
```

```
Scan of 24 IPs started at Thu Jan 09 22:30:05 2003
------------------------------------------------------------------
10.192.0.139
Responded in 10ms.
6 hops away
Responds with ICMP unreachable: No
TCP ports: 139 445
------------------------------------------------------------------
10.192.0.149
Responded in 10ms.
6 hops away
Responds with ICMP unreachable: No
TCP ports: 139 445
------------------------------------------------------------------

Scan finished at Thu Jan 09 22:30:08 2003
10 IPs and 20 ports scanned in 0 hours 0 mins 2.81 secs
```

Local Enumeration

If it is possible to achieve local access to a machine, it becomes a very simple matter to perform enumeration of the machine. Even in the case of proper NTFS restrictions on drives, folders, and files, it is possible to obtain significant information about the machine through an unsecured command prompt (cmd.exe in Windows 2003). For instance, with access to a machine interactively, an attacker can simply type **net localgroup administrators** at the command line and see the following:

```
C:\>net localgroup administrators
Alias name      administrators
Comment         Administrators have complete and unrestricted access to the
                computer/domain
Members

-------------------------------------------------------------------------
Joanna
Aaron
Jermie
Eric
NetSoft\Tariq Azad
NetSoft\Rahila
NetSoft\Naila
NetSoft\Afza
NetSoft\Khoula
```

```
NetSoft\Khalid
NetSoft\Shannon Forever
NetSoft\Angie
NetSoft\Megan
NetSoft\Maggie
NetSoft\Isabella
NetSoft\Kari
The command completed successfully.
```

As found in the remote enumeration section, the attacker then has a basis to begin to attack the system and find vulnerabilities. Remember that a single exposed and vulnerable host machine reduces security to the level of that point in the system.

Authentication Attack Methods

Once an attacker has succeeded in the enumeration process, the process switches from a pure discovery mode activity level to working with methods that can gain access to a vulnerable system. Remember that the attacker is looking for the easiest way in, so weaknesses detected on any machine in your system are fair game for the attacker who wants to penetrate your network. *Authentication attacks* can be mounted against vulnerable systems in a variety of ways. One of the simplest is to try a list of common passwords that are used during setup of systems. For instance, students of Microsoft's training classes formerly worked through their entire class sequence using the password "password" for administrator accounts. Up until last year, they were usually not told to not do this, so it has been quite rewarding to try that password in conjunction with a logon attempt. There are many others that are used routinely by services and applications that run as service accounts that are known passwords. If we can authenticate as administrator, it's all over; and if as a service, we still can often get what we want.

Password attacks can be mounted either via the network or against a database that we have recovered. Many tools exist on the Internet and from commercial sources that allow the recovery of SAM information. It is simple, for instance, to create a bootable Linux floppy and mount an NTFS file system from the resultant operating system. From here, it is a simple matter to copy the SAM directory from a locally accessible machine to other partitions, media, or the network. It is also relatively easy with the available tools to recover the hashed passwords from the Registry of remote machines. In either case, once the information is at hand, password attacks can be mounted using available tools.

There are a number of tools available for both types of attack. Two that come to mind that work very well are the well known L0phtCrack tools from @stake (www.@stake.com) and John the Ripper (www.openwall.com/john). These tools allow dictionary or brute force attacks against recovered databases and in some versions allow capture of SMB traffic on the network and then work to remove the hashes and decode the passwords for us. Again, once an attacker has access, the system is theirs, not yours.

Attacks Using Common and Known Vulnerabilities

It is a very wise security professional who subscribes to and reads mailing lists that report software bugs and vulnerabilities and patch availabilities and then make sure they apply the appropriate fixes to keep their systems secure. As has been reported many times, the Code Red virus could not have continued its unchecked proliferation had system operators and security professionals applied known fixes prior to its introduction. This is the case with many of the common attacks that are mounted. Unprotected resources running with unneeded services and unprotected passwords and file systems will always be subject to attack.

For example, it is very common for attacks to be mounted based on NetBIOS availability. These attacks are extremely easy to mount using common tools, and they yield a large amount of information to the attacker. Note that NetBIOS itself is not a vulnerability, and it continues to be needed in the Windows LAN environment. However, when NetBIOS traffic is unblocked or unchecked at the perimeter firewall, and is accompanied by poor password policies and protections, it becomes one of the most common sources of attack and one of the larger areas of potential breach of a system using Windows 2003. There have been numerous reports of common attacks against Windows 2000 IIS 6.0 servers, and other vulnerabilities continue to be discovered and patched.

Notes from the Underground...

Passwords, Passwords, Passwords

In our exploration of defense mechanisms, I have found that the easiest defense is most often the least used defense. Complex passwords, utilizing numbers, letters, upper and lower case, a minimum of eight characters, and special characters that are not repeated, that are changed regularly and not dictionary words severely limit the ability of attackers to gain access. However, it is also the case that if you don't do this on a single vulnerable machine, you have defeated the purpose of using complex passwords. Be vigilant in this, and it will save you lots of grief!

Defending and Hardening Windows 2003

Defending and hardening Windows 2003 requires that administrators make consistent, informed choices about the configuration of their systems and the need (or lack thereof) for extraneous local and network services. It is extremely easy to become complacent in these efforts, and also to succumb to the wealth of capabilities within the platform that are promoted very vigorously. However, if the Windows 2003 environment is viewed with the same eye to security and performance that is used with other operating systems, the process of defending becomes more manageable. Hardening Windows 2003 involves utilizing the knowledge that has been introduced in this chapter and the rest of this book with emphasis on areas that have helped to deter some of the basic attacks against the Windows 2003 platform. I draw heavily on my own experience, as you should. Additionally, it is appropriate to utilize tools that are based on the function of the machine, network, or enterprise that is being currently worked on. This often includes tools that are available from Microsoft, such as tools in the Support Tools set from the Windows 2003 Server CD, the Windows 2003 and Windows 2003 Resource Kit and its available tools, the IIS Lockdown tools, HFNetChk from Shavlik, the Microsoft Baseline Security Analysis tool, and resources such as the National Security Agency's recommended steps for hardening various systems. In the sections that follow, I compile a checklist of tasks and recommended steps for hardening Windows 2003 systems. Note that even with this checklist approach, and discussion of the types of action to take to minimize the risks involved, that ultimately the security of your system depends on your ability to react to problems that are occurring. You must detect problems that have occurred in the past, and proactively work to limit the ability of attackers both inside and outside your network from doing irreparable damage. This book is here to help, of course, but ultimately it's your job to get this done!

Evaluate Your Needs and Current Status

One of the most difficult tasks to undertake as security professionals is to perform accurate and honest evaluations of the needs of systems and users. Much like the purchaser of a new automobile, it is very tempting to operate our systems with all of the bells and whistles operating at full tilt. However, it is the rare system that truly needs to operate with all of the functionalities of the operating system and hardware engaged and available. In fact, much of the time those extra services are just idling along; and because they don't cause problems, they don't get much attention from us, making them easy targets for an attacker. You may want to consider tools, such as GFI's Network Security Scanner, eEye Digital Security (Retina), and Internet Security Systems (Security Scanner) to make the effort to do your evaluations honestly and completely. All of these tools can be extremely helpful as you evaluate your systems for vulnerability. The next few sections are important in the provision of security in your network and equipment. An appropriate part of the evaluation is to conduct the scanning of the equipment being evaluated to determine open ports and services that are running on them, to assist in the effort of securing them more fully.

Evaluating Services

Defense of systems and network will undoubtedly be simpler and less arduous if some initial time is spent in the evaluation stage to determine the actual services required in a particular operation. I've found that the time spent learning the functions of the various services that are provided in Windows 2003 has been repaid over and over by having that knowledge. It helps in both the evaluation section and the fact that having adequate knowledge of the interrelationships of the services and their dependencies helps so that you don't eliminate something that is critical and cause other problems. When making these choices, it is very helpful to consult resources such as the Windows 2003 Resource Kit for definitions and information regarding the individual services. A number of potential problems with default installations and services were detailed earlier, and if you follow the recommendations that have been set forth, you'll achieve a great deal toward securing your network.

Evaluating Access to Protocols

Discussion of protocols is always a problematic area, because most people tend to think of network protocols rather than service protocols when looking at controlling or securing systems. I believe it's a more important need to think along the lines of blocking access to particular protocols that allow penetration testing of the local and remote systems. It's pretty well understood, for instance, that there is a need to block ICMP traffic at the border of the network to block casual enumeration of the network. However, it is also important to remember to block or filter for other things. What are some of the areas to consider blocking in Windows 2000? Let's look at some of the things that might be a good choice to block or not allow:

- **SNMP:** This should be disabled if not being used.

- **Microsoft RAS Protocol:** Disable if no down-level RAS clients.

- **PPTP and L2TP:** Unneeded unless using VPN tunneling.

- **Unused network protocols:** Such as IPX/SPX, NetBeui, NetBIOS, AppleTalk

- **LDAP:** At the border, not internally; it's needed for Active Directory location services in an Active Directory domain.

- **Microsoft's File and Print Sharing:** On any machine not hosting shared resources.

Secure Your Equipment and OS

It should be something that doesn't need saying, but I'm going to reiterate a truism at this point. *It is absolutely of paramount importance that your systems be physically secured against unauthorized access.* Everything that is discussed throughout the book has to do with security. Yet, repeatedly as I visit or probe various networks and work sites I find that the equipment is not physically secured at all. Often, the doors are standing open and unlocked, cages are unsecured, or there is simply open air above and around the equipment that I can see. I've found network access points in hallways that were live on networks, and often unbelievable lackadaisical attitudes that permit us to just say to someone "I'm from IT, and will be working on this equipment for a while" and be allowed to do whatever I wish in the system with no challenge or questions raised at all. I've often wondered if people are as casual with their belongings that they perceive to be worth something as they are with the equipment and information that they are supposedly trying to protect. So, here are a few necessities before securing the OS:

- Secure the equipment from outside contact—that means from above, from below, from any side.

- Lock the doors, cages, and cabinets.

- Restrict access to equipment and network access points—and enforce and follow the restrictions.

- Train your users about appropriate access to said devices and storage facilities.

Now that that has been discussed, take a look through the next few sections and think about how you can sufficiently secure your systems against intentional or unintentional damage.

Applying Patches and Service Packs

Most of us are aware that the task of keeping track of patches and service packs is daunting, to say the least. In the current climate, it seems that there is a stream of new service packs and patches a number of times per week, and sometimes a number of times in a given day. What are we as administrators and security professionals supposed to do to try to keep up? I'd suggest that you should employ one of the tools available to scan your systems on a regular basis and identify needed patches and fixes, and make a continued and concentrated effort to keep up to date. It has been demonstrated quite often that many of the manifestations of viruses and Trojans are simply implementations by individuals creating havoc using known (and repairable) problems in various operating systems and applications. Of course, it is appropriate to issue the standard caveat at this time: *Do not apply patches and service packs to production machines until you have exercised the opportunity to test them on a parallel environment that is not part of your production network.* I'll take a quick look at a couple of these tools in the "Using Tools and Methodologies to Analyze Weaknesses and Configuration Changes" section a bit later in this part of the chapter.

Windows 2003 updates, service packs, and hotfixes can be obtained from the Microsoft updates site at http://v4.windowsupdate.microsoft.com/en/default.asp. Some critical hotfixes will be available earlier at the Microsoft Security site, www.microsoft.com/security, although they may not be available in all configurations prior to their introduction at the Windows Update site.

Security Templates

As was discussed in the "Windows 2003 Security Essentials" section, security templates are an excellent way to define the security environment for your Windows 2003 implementation. Take the time to explore the capabilities and configurable security settings within the templates. Basic settings are not the only ones that can be changed. We can use them to force and enforce services configurations, to protect our network connections, to define settings in the area of user rights assignments, set password and account and auditing policies, and many others. Don't be afraid to fully utilize their capabilities. This tool's content and ability to help secure your machines is often overlooked and unused, and it leads to much unnecessary work in repairing insecure systems.

Securing Access Control Methods

Working with access control methods, many environments will experience large swings in the complexity of configuration needs depending on the needs of the system that is to be secured.

In the case of the Windows 2003 workgroup configurations, the administrator must individually configure each of the machines to reflect the administrative and user needs of the company. This might include making decisions to not allow the users of the machine to have administrative privileges on their local machines, and instead delegating a person or two in the workplace to have knowledge of administrator name and passwords for local machines to perform administrative tasks as needed. The requirement to adequately analyze the base security of the machines and create appropriate templates and policies to achieve the security level that is desired still exists, regardless of the network design or distribution. Decisions also need to be made about the necessity for external access.

In an environment that utilizes Active Directory and Group Policy, the methods to secure access control change. In this case, the administrator is able to utilize the capabilities of Group Policy to distribute the policies over a larger area. Group policy provides the capability to deliver secure templates from a centrally controlled location to ensure that the base security settings are kept in place. Group policy is continually enforced in an Active Directory domain and keeps unintentional or malicious changes from being instituted on domain machines.

Windows 2003 also supports the capability to use third-party authenticators and certificates for verification and authentication operations. If your needs include a need for a higher level of authentication before access is granted, consider the use of smart cards, biometrics, and certificates as part of the process to help with your security efforts. Additionally, make sure to enable security auditing on all machines and regularly review the log files for this auditing. It will give you a quick and reliable heads-up about where and when someone is trying to attack your system.

File and Data Security Settings

I've mentioned a couple of times through the chapter that it is important to configure file and data security settings much more tightly than is done in the default configuration. When beginning to harden, it is important to accomplish this task early in the configuration process to ensure security. So, you are often told to change the defaults and never told what to change them to. Here are some recommendations for settings (as always, test these in your environment to see if they accomplish what you need to do):

- Add SYSTEM and Administrators to the DACL with Full Control (check all boxes)
- Add Authenticated Users with Read and Read and Execute
- Remove Everyone

With inheritance of permissions, this will not allow users to write content to any file or folder that they don't own or have other permissions defined on, but will allow them to run programs and read application information. These settings will have no effect on permissions if the Allow Inheritance Of Permissions box is unchecked on existing files or folders. When users have ownership of a folder (such as their home folders or their My Documents folder in their profiles), they automatically are granted full control as the owner, and so may write to those directories or create files within them. In general, these settings will limit much of the access to files and directories that should not have anonymous access to them.

Password Policies and Protections

Password policies are an area that is often treated too casually in network operations. In Windows 2003, it is extremely desirable to create and enforce strict password policies. Password attack tools are often free or available at low cost, and they allow an attacker to retrieve passwords for existing accounts or identify poor practices and vulnerabilities in a very short amount of time. Passwords should be changed at frequent intervals, should be a minimum of 8 characters (14 is preferred, since many password crackers can now retrieve 8-character passwords in a day or two), and should follow complexity rules. This means that the password should have letters, numbers, special characters, and upper/lower case in their construction. Passwords should not be names, parts of usernames, or common dictionary words or their derivatives. When trying to secure networks and resources, it is no longer an acceptable condition to accept insecure passwords or policies.

Windows 2003 allows us to configure these policies locally on workstations and standalone servers via the **Local Security Policy** management console in Administrative Tools. These locally created policies will apply to local accounts on the given machine only. If creating the policies in an Active Directory domain, the policies can be configured via the Domain Security Policy Group

Policy Object. If a member of the domain, the domain policies will override the machine policies if the user is authenticating with the domain.

Secure Network Communications

Windows 2003 has the capability to provide security in the connections it is involved with through the configuration of IPSec policies and security policies that can be configured through the Security Configuration and Analysis process discussed previously. The administrator can, for instance, require secure channel communications between machines, filter through the IPSec policies the protocols that are allowed to be used for communication, and require encryption of the data being transmitted. If that level of protection is not needed in a particular area, the administrator should at least use either security templates or Registry modifications to eliminate the use of null password connections and require valid credentials for connection.

Eliminating Unnecessary Components

One of the biggest challenges that we face when hardening Windows 2003 is making decisions about the elimination of unnecessary components from the systems. Many components are installed by default, and it has become apparent while working with Windows 2003 that it is increasingly necessary that the security professional and administrator be proactive in efforts when securing systems to eliminate unused applications and services. In this section, I touch on some of the areas that can be reduced or eliminated to make your system more secure.

Network Services

Hardening Windows 2003 network services requires that a good baseline evaluation of the systems involved is performed. When this is accomplished, it is possible that good decisions can be made, after the evaluation of required services and considering the needs of applications and users.

The first goal in most hardening scenarios involving Windows 2003 network services is to eliminate SMB/NetBIOS access and traffic on the wire. (Do not do this if you are running Windows clustering on the involved machines. Clustering requires NetBIOS resolution capability). If you want to totally eliminate the traffic, don't use the settings on the WINS tab in the network adaptor advanced properties section. Instead, open the Network Connections window, and then on the top file menu select **Advanced | Advanced Settings...** to reach the window shown in Figure 2.17. Uncheck the box for **File and Printer Sharing** (enabled by default) and you will shut down not only TCP ports 137, 138, 139 traffic but also TCP port 445 traffic, which carries the NetBT traffic for NetBIOS over TCP/IP. You've then stopped NetBIOS traffic from originating from your machine. (You must disable this on each adaptor that is configured.)

Figure 2.17 Disabling SMB and NetBIOS Traffic in Windows 2000

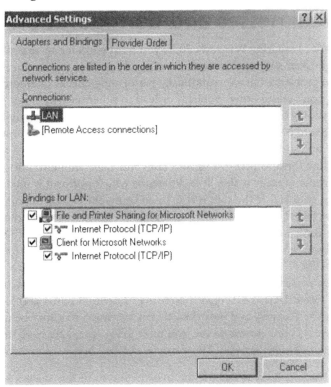

Hardening the network services area also requires that you exercise diligence and close down and eliminate services that are unused or unneeded from machines where they exist. In addition to file and print sharing, this means eliminating Telnet, SNMP, DHCP, FTP, WWW, NNTP, and other services from the system if they are not necessary. Don't be complacent here. It is much easier to install the component if needed than to recover from an attack if it is left in place.

Local Services

Consider eliminating unnecessary features from the local machine. This should include disabling floppy access and applying the same level of password policy and password complexity on the local machine as is required for network access. Services such as autologon should not be tolerated, and use of network monitoring agents and SNMP agents should be tightly controlled. Additionally, since most backup operations are conducted on a local level, be sure to split the capability of backup and restore operations to protect against theft of the local machine's data and identity. Consider eliminating the display of the last user name in the logon screen through the Local Security Policy snap-in for the Microsoft Management Console.

Using Tools and Methodologies to Analyze Weaknesses and Configuration Changes

To finish up your work of securing Windows 2003, you must continue to analyze and check for potential weaknesses in your systems. This includes not only performing routine, scheduled checks for vulnerabilities and problems, but also continually performing checks to ensure that the fixes and blockades you create don't create other problems or lead to other security holes. To do this, you need to employ tools that allow you to get good reports back about what is currently in place in your systems and what needs to be updated or changed to sufficiently protect your operations.

Tools for analysis and security configuration are numerous and are available for use both in GUI form and command-line form to perform various tasks and allow administrators to configure the security in their networks. It really makes little difference which platform is used for the configuration and analysis tasks, or whether the tool is text based or graphical. The important thing is to find tools that you are comfortable with, and then utilize them fully to verify the configurations you have established. Tools are available from Microsoft directly, and include HFNetChk for patch and service pack analysis and the Microsoft Baseline Security Analyzer, which I discuss in the "Hardening Windows 2003" section, and the IIS lockdown tool, Microsoft has a command-line version of HFNetChk available at the Microsoft Security site, which allows batch scheduling and outputs to log files if needed. GFI's LANguard Network Security Scanner also looks at patch level, but additionally scans the Registry and provides other information that may be useful in your efforts.

Regardless of the tools you choose to use, you must follow the same basic steps for analysis and verification of changes and configuration. These can be detailed briefly as follows:

- Perform a baseline analysis and use the information from this analysis as the basis for change—the Microsoft Baseline Analysis tool is a good place to start.

- Evaluate the potential risks involved in the problems that are uncovered in the Baseline analysis.

- Plan and *test* changes to the configuration that are proposed to eliminate holes and risks:

  1. Implement the changes on non-production equipment first.

  2. Implement on production equipment after verification.

- Perform a follow-up analysis to verify that the desired changes have been put in place.

- Schedule periodic re-evaluations and ensure that the system is still protected and solid.

Tracking and Applying Updates, Service Packs, and Patches

With all of the potential vulnerabilities that we have looked at throughout this chapter, applying updates, service packs, and patches is definitely an area that is crucial for your continued success in the hardening of Windows 2003 platform machines. You are very aware if you are working in the Infosec field that continued vigilance is absolutely a requirement for success in attempting to slow the flood of attackers. Be sure in your hardening efforts that you continue to stay on top of the large number of patches and repairs to keep your system as up to date as possible.

Again, there are many tools available to assist you in tracking the production and availability of updates, service packs, and patches. One of the freely available tools for analysis of domain or work-group machines in Windows NT, Windows 2000, Windows 2003 and Windows XP environments is the command-line hotfix checking tool HFNetChk, which is free from Microsoft on their security site. In the following example, I ran a quick scan with the tool against a test network and sent the output to a text file for further study. This tool is useful because the administrator has the ability to schedule a task calling this tool on a regular basis with an appropriate output to file. This allows for continued checking of the status of the checks with appropriate collection of the output files. The output from that test looked like this:

```
----------------------------
EXCELENT (192.168.25.77)
----------------------------

    * WINDOWS 2000 SP3
    Note                MS01-022    Q296441
    Note                MS02-008    Q318202
    Note                MS02-008    Q318203
    Note                MS02-008    Q317244
    Note                MS02-053    Q324096
    Patch NOT Found     MS02-055    Q323255
    Note                MS02-064    Q327522
    Note                MS02-065    Q329414
    Warning             MS02-070    309376

    * INTERNET EXPLORER 6 SP1
    Information
    All necessary hotfixes have been applied.
----------------------------
EXCW2KAS (192.168.25.66)
----------------------------

    * WINDOWS 2000 ADVANCED SERVER SP3
    Note                MS01-022    Q296441
    Note                MS02-008    Q318202
    Note                MS02-008    Q318203
    Note                MS02-008    Q317244
    Note                MS02-053    Q324096
    Warning             MS02-055    Q323255
    Note                MS02-064    Q327522
    Note                MS02-065    Q329414
    Warning             MS02-070    309376
    Patch NOT Found     MS02-071    328310
```

```
* INTERNET INFORMATION SERVICES 5.0
Information
All necessary hotfixes have been applied.

* INTERNET EXPLORER 6 SP1
Information
All necessary hotfixes have been applied.
```

This output noted that some patches were not found, and it included notes that can be referenced via the Technet site to determine if the patches are necessary or actually missing. This tool allows you to schedule the activity to scan individual machines, groups of machines, or domains as needed, and output the results to a log file for evaluation.

The Microsoft Baseline Security Analyzer (MBSA) tool also checks security conditions on Windows NT, Windows 2000, Windows 2003 and Windows XP. This tool runs with a graphical interface, and has the capability to check for vulnerabilities in Microsoft Office XP/2000, Internet Explorer, IIS, SQL, and the basic operating system and network components. This is an excellent tool to use for your initial evaluation, and is available on the Microsoft site at www.microsoft.com/security.

Security Checklist

This checklist is a compilation of items that should be considered and/or have their default configurations changed in order to secure your Windows 2003 platform systems. The initial portion of the checklist contains changes that should be made to both workstation and server platforms, and the following sections identify platform specific or configuration specific settings. This is a good base from which to begin your hardening process.

Windows 2003 System

- Use NTFS as the file system.
- Use dynamic disks.
- Rename the administrator account.
- Create a substitute administrator account that has no rights.
- Password protect the guest account.
- Create and maintain appropriate security templates.
- Create, maintain, and enforce strong password policies.
- Eliminate unnecessary protocols.
- Eliminate unnecessary services.
- Run and maintain anti-virus software.
- Create and maintain an up to date emergency repair disk.
- Install necessary service packs, updates, and patches—verify that they don't create other problems or exposures.

- Verify that outside vendor applications do not create breach conditions.

- Do not allow autologon.

- Require security screen (Ctrl+Alt+Del) logons.

- Use EFS to protect sensitive data.

- Do not allow users to administer their workstations.

- Do not allow general interactive logons.

- Physically secure the equipment.

- Verify specific service need. Eliminate unnecessary services.

- Modify the location and/or DACLs of the default FTP and WWW directories if used.

- Modify the membership of the pre-Windows 2000 compatible group as soon as possible.

Windows 2003 Terminal Services Basics

By default, Terminal Servers use the Remote Desktop Protocol (RDP) via Transmission Control Protocol (TCP) port 3389. Configured properly, each session is authenticated using Windows domain authentication and is bidirectionally encrypted with the 128-bit RC4 crypto algorithm. The kernel supports multiple users with graphical sessions that can simultaneously run any number of applications on a single server.

Windows Server 2003 comes preinstalled with a remote administration mode called Remote Desktop. If you require remote administration, you will need to enable Remote Desktop. This can be enabled on the Remote tab of the System Control Panel applet.

If you require application sharing for multiple simultaneous users, you need to install Terminal Services by choosing **Control Panel | Add or Remove Programs | Add/Remove Windows Components**.

NOTE

When you install Terminal Services on Windows Server 2003, all members of the local Users group will be added to the Remote Desktop Users group.

You will be prompted during installation to select default permissions for application compatibility, as shown in Figure 2.18. Your choices are as follows:

- Full Security
- Relaxed Security

Figure 2.18 Terminal Server Security

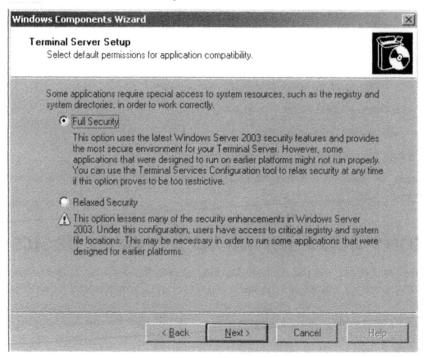

Full security implements all the latest and greatest Windows Server 2003 security features, and you should select it if possible. If you must select **Relaxed Security** due to legacy applications, understand that you are allowing users access to critical Windows components such as the Registry and system files. I think the choice here is obvious unless you like getting hacked.

WARNING

When you install Terminal Services on Windows Server 2003, your currently installed programs will no longer work in a TS session and will need to be reinstalled. All future applications for TS will need to be installed using Add Or Remove Programs in the Control Panel.

Terminal Server Clients

Terminal Services offers a wide range of options when it comes to selecting a client. Users can connect with their Windows 95 systems to a Terminal Server down the hall or across the Atlantic, harnessing the raw power of a 32-processor Windows 2000 Datacenter Server. Terminal Services clients even exist for the Linux, Mac, and the PocketPC. Although each client may look different, they all implement RDP in a similar manner, connecting to TCP port 3389 unless configured to do otherwise.

Windows Remote Desktop Client

Microsoft now offers a single client solution to connect to Terminal Services that will run on operating systems from Windows 95 to Windows XP. This is the client that I recommend because it forces 128-bit encryption and offers the ability to connect to ports other than 3389. To connect to an alternate port, just add it to the IP address separated with a colon: *10.1.1.1:9999.* This client is available on the Windows XP Professional CD and from Microsoft download site.

To install from the CD:

1. Insert the CD.

2. On the Welcome page, click **Perform Additional Tasks**.

3. Click **Set up Remote Desktop Connection**. Remote Desktop Connection runs on most of Microsoft's operating systems, including Windows 95/98/ME/NT 4, Windows 2000, and Windows XP.

Tools & Traps…

Starting the TS Client on Windows XP

There is no need to install this client on Windows XP; it comes standard. The application can be started from its elusive location, **Start | Programs | Accessories | Communications** or by simply executing **mstsc.exe** from the command line.

Windows XP and Windows Server 2003 allow you to connect directly to the console by using the following command:

```
mstsc /v:10.0.6.36 /console
```

Once you have entered a valid username and password, TS will tell you if another user is logged in to the console. If you select to connect anyway, the user session at the console will be ended, and any unsaved data will be lost.

TSAC (ActiveX)

Terminal Services Advanced Client (TSAC) is a Win32-based ActiveX control (COM object) that can be used to run Terminal Services inside Web browsers. Additionally, the ActiveX control and sample Web can be used by developers to create client-side applications that interact with applications running on a Terminal Server.

When users navigate to the Web page containing the TSAC, it is downloaded to the client computer. Once the Web page executes the control, users will receive a message asking whether they want to install and run the Terminal Services ActiveX Control If you click **Yes**, the TSAC executes on the client computer using Web page–defined parameters and connects to the Terminal Server on TCP 3389. The user will then be presented with a Windows logon screen (see Figure 2.19).

Figure 2.19 Connected to TS via TCP 3389 in Internet Explorer

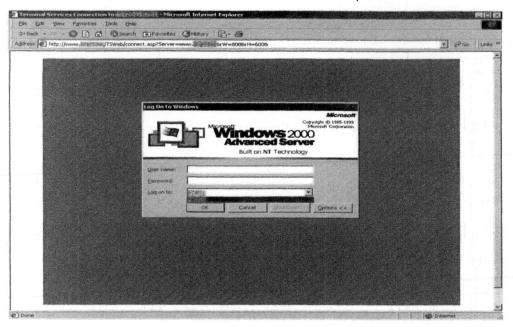

> **NOTE**
>
> A detailed tutorial by Thomas Shinder titled "Publishing Terminal Services and the TSAC Client" is available from www.isaserver.org/pages/article_p.asp?id=225.

Windows XP TSAC

Windows XP has an installable component set called Remote Desktop Web Connection, which is just a fancy name for the TSAC in an XP environment. The Remote Desktop Web Connection can be installed from the Add/Remove Windows Components Wizard in Add Or Remove Programs by adding IIS and the World Wide Web Service.

TSAC and Alternate Terminal Server Ports

TSAC in Windows XP offers the unique ability to modify the destination port for the ActiveX control. This is a wonderful new feature that allows the administrator to still use the functionality of TSAC, without removing the ability to implement an extra layer of security by modifying the TCP port of the destination Terminal Server.

Let's say you have a Terminal Server that is configured to listen on TCP port 19740, and you want TSAC clients to be able to connect to this server via the ActiveX control. You just need to make an addition to the connect.asp file located in the /TSWeb directory. Before the connect method in the CONNECT.ASP code, simply insert this line:

```
MsTsc.AdvancedSettings2.RDPPort = 19740
```

After the client acknowledges the updated ActiveX control download dialog, the Remote Desktop Web Connection will automatically connect on that port.

One word of caution: If you are using TSAC, I do not recommend running the IIS Web server on the same system as the Terminal Server. For security reasons, it is good practice to segregate applications on separate servers.

MMC Snap-in

Microsoft has included a snap-in to the Microsoft Management Console (MMC) to allow for managing multiple Terminal Servers from one place. The components of the MMC Snap-in are the following:

- A Mstsmmc.dll

- A console file called Tsmmc.msc

One problem with this MMC snap-in is it has no mechanism for one to specify an alternate connection port. Only Terminal Servers left at the default listening port of 3389 can be reached directly via this tool.

Regardless of that shortcoming, this tool can be quite useful if you have many servers that you normally connect to throughout the day—simply clicking each connection puts you right at the console. Figure 2.20 shows two servers that have been added to the MMC.

Figure 2.20 MMC Snap-In Viewing Multiple Servers

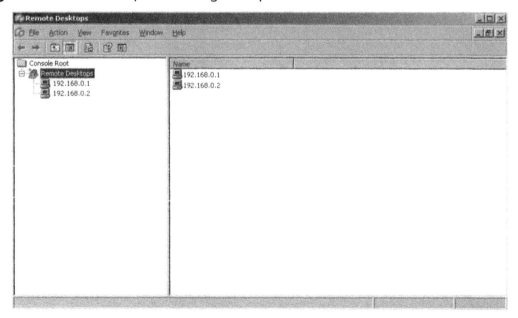

Using the *Rdesktop* Linux Client

Rdesktop is an open source client for Windows Terminal Services. It is capable of natively speaking RDP to achieve this task. *Rdesktop* currently runs on most Unix-based platforms with the X Window System.

Rdesktop was written by Matt Chapman and is free under the GNU General Public License (GPL). The *rdesktop* source code can be downloaded from www.rdesktop.org. Compile the source by running *make* on your platform to get the executable. Precompiled Linux binaries can also be downloaded from www.sourceforge.com.

Figure 2.21 shows Rdesktop starting the connection.

Figure 2.21 Connecting Using the Rdesktop Client

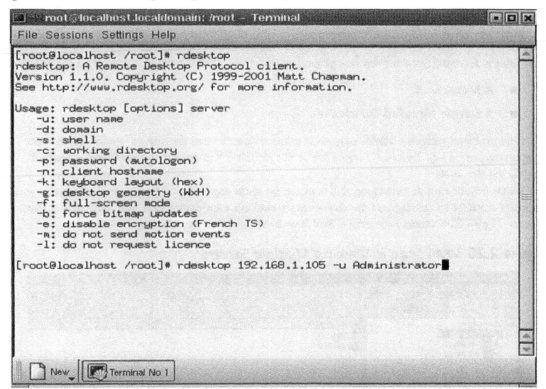

Once the server is specified, the application connects via TCP 3389 just like the Remote Desktop Connection client (see Figure 2.22).

Figure 2.22 The Rdesktop Connection in Action

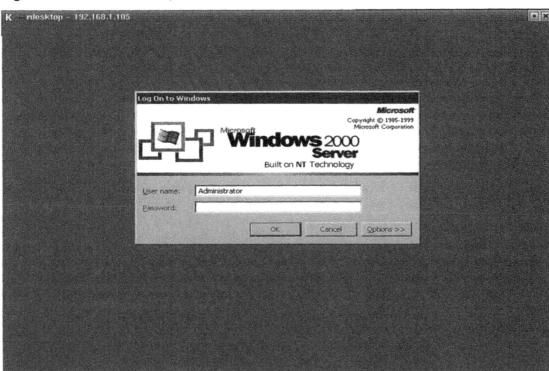

Macintosh Clients

There is even a Remote Desktop Connection client for Macs. You can download the client and detailed information from www.microsoft.com/mac/DOWNLOAD/MISC/RDC.asp.

Using Terminal Server Tools

Many tools are available to manage and secure the Terminal Servers in your network depending on your requirements. Some work only within a TS session, some are command-line applications, and some are GUI applications. The following categories are discussed in this section:

- Windows 2003 Terminal Server Commands
- Using TScmd.exe
- Terminal Server Manager
- Terminal Server Configuration
- Terminal Server Group Policies

Using Windows 2003 Terminal Server Commands

There are many command line tools available from Microsoft that are useful in a Terminal Server session. The following lists are some of the security-focused command-line tools from Microsoft. Each tool has a variety of uses; you should try all of them to find out which work best for you. Many of these tools exist on Windows XP and Windows Server 2003 as well:

- **Qwinsta.exe (query session)** This is useful to figure out who is connected and what their sessionids are in case you need to "look over their shoulders" for any reason using Shadow. This can also be used to monitor other Terminal Servers using the */server:server_ip* directive. Query Session is shown in Figure 2.23.

- **Shadow** This allows you to *monitor and control* other user sessions from your TS session. The ability to perform this action is determined by the setting with the highest precedence. The same applies regarding the Require Users Permission setting that determines if they will or will not be asked for permission to allow the shadowing. An interesting fact is that the Console can be shadowed and controlled on Windows XP and Windows Server 2003 but not on Windows 2000.

- **Query termserver** This command can only be used in a TS session. It is useful for attackers and administrators to find other Terminal Servers in the current domain.

- **TSDiscon and Reset Session** These commands are useful for attackers and administrators if they want to disconnect a session from a Terminal Server or reset the session (session will be terminated). They can be used locally and remotely. They requires the disconnect and reset permissions (respectively).

- **TSKill** This command can be very useful for an attacker when he hangs a process and needs to kill it. Conversely, an administrator can use this to kill suspect processes as well.

There are many more commands that can help your with administration of TS. For a complete reference, check out the Windows 2003 command reference from Microsoft.

Figure 2.23 Example of the Query Session Command

Using TSCmd.exe

A very useful command-line tool for administering TS is tscmd.exe from System Tools (www.systemtools. com/free_frame.htm). This tool allows remote configuration of Terminal Server user settings such as Remote Control and Allow Logon To Terminal Server. This tool can be used by attackers and defenders in their respective quests toward success. To use tscmd.exe, you will need a *net use* connection. What actions you can perform depends on the privileges of your connection.

Querying Logon Permissions with TSCmd.exe

Never underestimate the possibility of an administrator misconfiguration that allows logon access to a nonprivileged user. For example, if you connect with a *null session* you can enumerate users then try to find one with a weak password. Once you find an account with a weak password, you can use TSCmd.exe to query information about that user's TS logon rights. If TSCmd returns a **1**, you can connect. Figure 2.24 shows this process with captions to help you follow along.

Figure 2.24 TSCmd.exe + User Account * No Password = TSCompromise

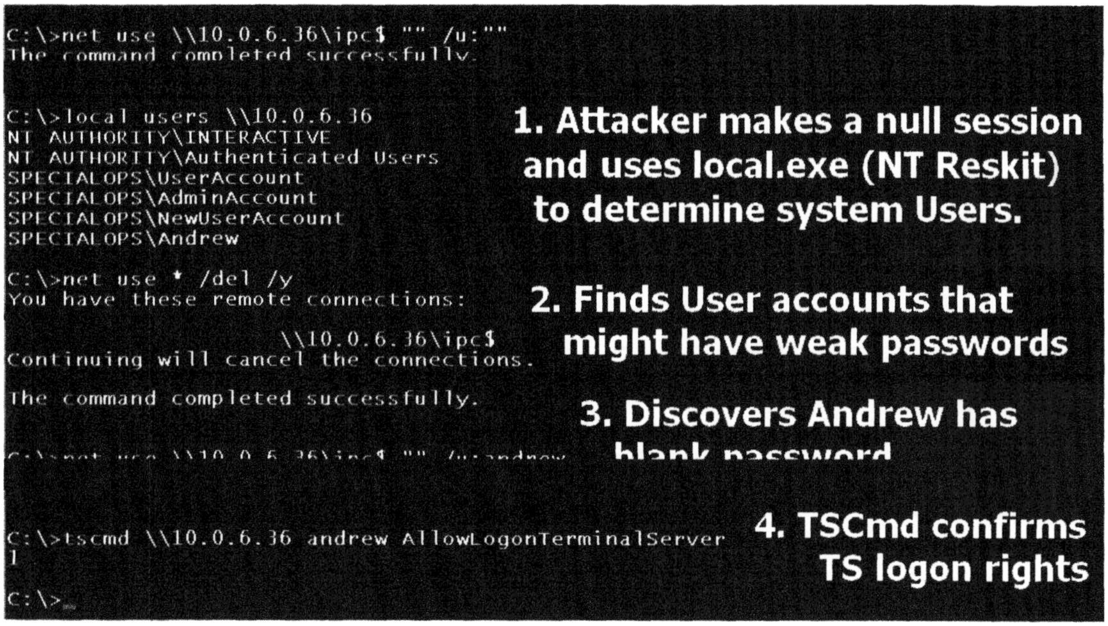

Modifying Settings with TSCmd.exe

You will probably need to have an administrative connection (*net use*) to the Terminal Server to modify the user settings. The syntax for using the tool to modify is as follows:

```
tscmd <Server> <User> <Setting> [New Value]
```

This tool is very useful if you have been disallowed access to a Terminal Server by another administrator or need to monitor what other administrators are doing without asking their permission. The following commands will help you regain access as well as obtain the ability to shadow (or interact with) a session of your choice without prompting for permission. This command gives TS logon access to the user *Joanna*.

```
tscmd.exe 10.1.1.202 Joanna AllowLogonTerminalServer 1
```

The next command is a bit more complex because there are five options for this setting. The options for ShadowingSettings are shown here:

- 0 = Disable shadowing
- 1 = Enable shadowing, allow input, notify user
- 2 = Enable shadowing, allow input, no user notification
- 3 = Enable shadowing, view only, notify user
- 4 = Enable shadowing, view only, no user notification

The following command will enable shadowing of *UserAccount* in view only mode, but it will not warn the TS user that someone is watching them. (Yes, they could identify using qwinsta.exe or query session.)

```
tscmd.exe 10.1.1.202 UserAccount ShadowingSettings 4
```

Since you can only remotely control a session from within another Terminal Services session, you will need to connect to the Terminal Server before you try to shadow. The next command shows the syntax for the *shadow* command:

```
C:\>shadow
Monitor another Terminal Services session.

SHADOW {sessionname | sessionid} [/SERVER:servername] [/V]
  sessionname          Identifies the session with name sessionname.
  sessionid            Identifies the session with ID sessionid.
  /SERVER:servername   The server containing the session (default is current).
  /V                   Display information about actions being performed.
```

For example, to shadow the rdp-tcp#2 session, you would type the following command:

```
C:\>shadow rdp-tcp#2
Your session may appear frozen while the remote control approval is being
negotiated.
Please wait...
```

NOTE

To end a remote control session, press **Ctrl** + the ∗ key on the numeric keypad. If you are using a laptop and do not have a numeric keypad, you may need to use **Ctrl+Fn+0** to simulate the escape sequence.

You can also use the *tscon* command from inside a TS session to connect to other user's session if the permissions are correct:

```
C:\>tscon
Attaches a user session to a terminal session.

TSCON {sessionid | sessionname} [/DEST:sessionname]
        [/PASSWORD:pw] [/V]
  sessionid            The ID of the session.
  sessionname          The name of the session.
  /DEST:sessionname    Connect the session to destination sessionname.
  /PASSWORD:pw         Password of user owning identified session.
  /V                   Displays information about the actions performed.
C:\>
```

Terminal Services Manager

Terminal Services Manager, shown in Figure 2.25, allows administrators to monitor the sessions, users, and processes of Terminal servers. Actions such as connecting to another user's session as well as disconnecting users can be performed here as well. Don't forget that the console can't connect to a session using Shadow; you need to be in a TS session.

Figure 2.25 Terminal Services Manager

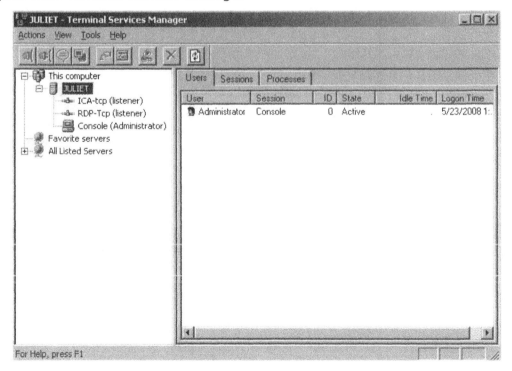

Terminal Services Configuration

Terminal Services Configuration Connections (TSCC) allows for configuring of server settings, as shown in Figure 2.26, and RDP-Tcp Properties, as shown in Figure 2.27. This tool is available in Windows 2000, Windows XP and Windows Server 2003. You should be sure to set the following basic settings in RDP-Tcp Properties:

- **General** Encryption Level: High

- **Logon Settings** Always prompt for a password

- **Network Adapter** Specify properties on an interface card basis

Figure 2.26 TSCC Can Configure Server Settings

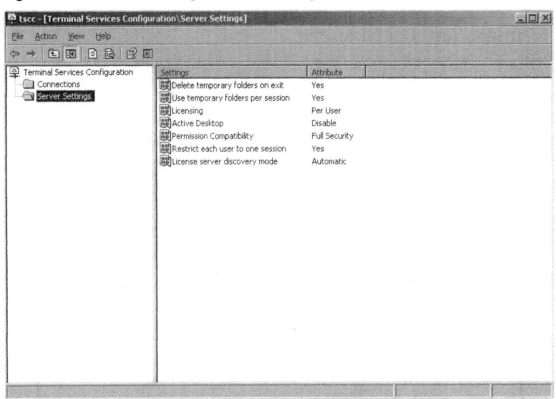

Figure 2.27 TSCC RDP-Tcp Properties Windows Server 2003

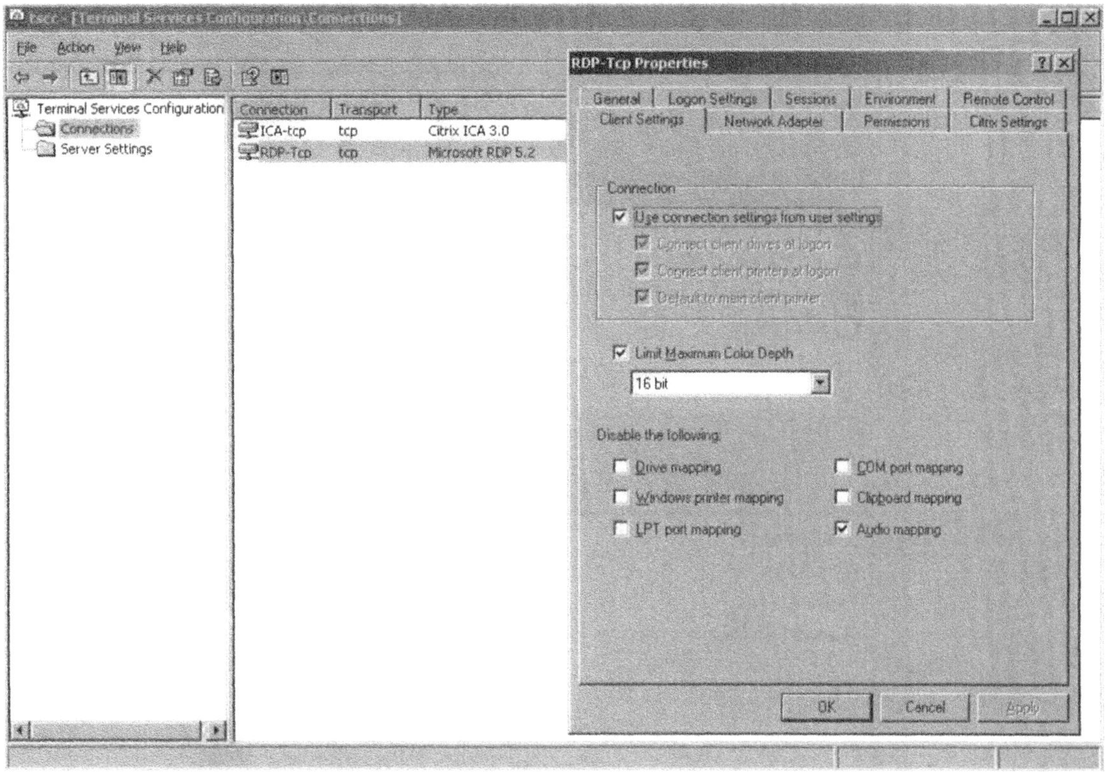

The RDP-Tcp properties have some minor differences between Windows 2000 and Windows XP/Server 2003, but all of them allows for connection permissions to be applied to users and groups. Figure 2.28 shows the permissions tab on a Windows 2003 Server.

Figure 2.28 Windows Server 2003 Permission Settings

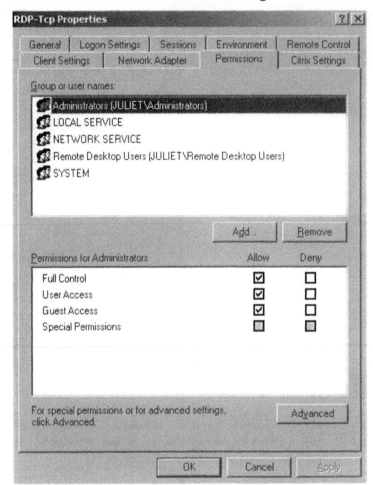

Attacking Terminal Servers

Organizations that use Windows 2000 and Windows 2003 as their production server operating system are likely to use Terminal Services for remote administration or as a jump point into their secured networks. If secured properly, it will serve them well for these purposes. However, if installed on an insecure system, it will assist hackers in their quests to attack other hosts or networks that may be protected by internal routers or firewalls. If an attacker is command-line challenged, she will now have a GUI where she can download and install the applications (automated vulnerability scanning tools and so on) of her choice.

Depending on the TS configuration, the compromise could be as simple as an attacker attempting to log on as Guest with no password. As shown later in this chapter, once an attacker has interactive access to his victim TS he can easily upload and execute a privilege escalation exploit to become an administrator. If the attacker is crafty, he will be able to do so without marking a single log with his real IP address. Once he *owns* the server, he will have a vantage point from which he can launch future attacks.

During an internal penetration test about a year ago, I was tasked with penetrating the highly secured administrative network from the user LAN. The steps that led to victory could have been performed using other techniques, but in this case compromising an IIS Web server on a dual-interfaced Terminal Server got the job done. Terminal Server really wasn't at fault here, but it certainly helped out my cause once I had used the Web server exploit to create my very own administrator account. For this reason, I consider TS a vulnerability catalyst for Window's servers.

Locating Terminal Servers

Finding Terminal Servers on an internal network is usually not very difficult. Even though the ability to relocate them to an alternate TCP port exists, most administrators do not take the time to make this configuration change.

Port Scanning

As you already know, TS runs on TCP 3389 by default. Any port scanner can be used to find TS running on this port. The following example shows a simple TCP port scan of a network segment to identify Terminal Servers running on port 3389:

```
C:\>fscan -q -p 3389 10.0.6.0-10.0.6.254
FScan v1.14 - Command line port scanner.
Copyright 2002 (c) by Foundstone, Inc.
http://www.foundstone.com

10.0.6.3          3389/tcp
10.0.6.8          3389/tcp
10.0.6.36         3389/tcp
10.0.6.38         3389/tcp
10.0.6.69         3389/tcp
10.0.6.80         3389/tcp
10.0.6.99         3389/tcp
10.0.6.240        3389/tcp
```

It appears I have found a TS-rich environment. If you are unsure of how many instances of Terminal Server exist in your network, I recommend that you perform some port scans to identify your exposure. Terminal Server can be configured to run on ports other than TCP 3389; so how can you determine where those servers are logically located?

Identifying Hidden Terminal Servers

When a server/workstation joins a domain, it registers itself with the Master Browser. Part of this registration includes the server type, which can be retrieved via the *NetServerEnum* function. Tim "Thor" Mullen created a tool called TSEnum.exe that uses this function to identify Terminal Servers in a domain. This tool will allow you to identify Terminal Servers even if they are running on alternate ports. It works best when authenticated to a domain, but it will sometimes work even if you have no domain credentials. Figure 2.29 shows TSEnum.exe locating a Terminal Server on my small test network.

Figure 2.29 TSEnum.exe Finding Terminal Servers

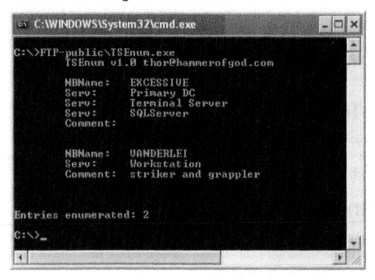

```
C:\>FTP-public\TSEnum.exe
        TSEnum v1.0 thor@hammerofgod.com

        NBName:     EXCESSIVE
        Serv:       Primary DC
        Serv:       Terminal Server
        Serv:       SQLServer
        Comment:


        NBName:     VANDERLEI
        Serv:       Workstation
        Comment:    striker and grappler


Entries enumerated: 2

C:\>_
```

Tools & Traps...

Terminal Services Server Advertisement

Trap: Q281307

In Windows XP, servers that are installed in Remote Administration mode do not advertise themselves as Terminal Services servers. So if you are using enumeration techniques such as tsenum.exe, be aware that some unpatched servers may not be visible. The take-home message here is: Never rely solely on one tool for enumeration activities.

Windows XP Terminal Services installed in Application Server mode and Microsoft Windows 2000 Terminal Services advertise themselves properly.

Finding Windows Servers with Access to Other Segments

Administrators frequently install multiple network cards (dual-NIC) on Windows servers connecting network segments to make their lives easier. This is never a good thing, but if the server has TS running it makes things much worse.

I recommend that you do not dual-NIC your servers. However, since they are out there, let's talk about way to find them. Once you find these servers, you can muster up a posse and find the culprit. Another option would be to remediate the exposure by physically disconnecting the server.

Using Windows Endpoints

The following steps describe a technique that I have used successfully to find dual-NICed Windows systems. Once I identified them, I used a port scanner to see if they are running Terminal Services.

1. Determine what network you are going to scan. For this example, let's assume that it is 10.0.6.0/24.

2. Port scan 10.0.6.0/24 for TCP 135 (Microsoft Remote Procedure Call [MSRPC]) and save the responding IP addresses in a file named **tcp135.txt**. This file will save you time in the next step.

3. Using a *for* loop in cmd.exe, process this list of IP addresses (tcp135.txt) with the Microsoft RPC Endpoint Mapper extraction tool, rpcdump.exe (http://razor.bindview.com), and save the output for analysis. This example will produce a listing of all RPC endpoints on each system in tcp135.txt, including IP addresses associated with each endpoint and save them in MSRPC.txt:

   ```
   C:\>for /F "delims=, tokens=1" %i IN (TS.txt) DO rpcdump %i >> MSRPC.txt
   ```

4. Parse the MSRPC.txt file for other RFC1918 IP address ranges using findstr.exe, qgrep.exe, or *grep* (if you use Cygwin). Your selection will depend on the networks that use in your organization. Obviously, if you are looking for servers with non-RFC1918 addresses, you will need to modify your approach. An example of how I parsed the data to look for servers with access to the 192.168.0.0/16 is shown here:

   ```
   C:\>qgrep -e "192.168." MSRPC.txt
   C:\>findstr "192.168." MSRPC.txt
   ```

5. Finally, use a port scanner with these hosts as the input to find out if they are running Terminal Services.

Enumerating Users and Logon Rights

If an attacker can port scan your server and identify Terminal Services running on TCP port 3389, he has all he needs to get started. Since we are discussing internal network security, it is likely the attacker will also have access to Windows Server Message Block/Common Internet File Services (SMB/CIFS) ports such as TCP 139 and 445. These ports will happily provide the attacker with the accounts on the server that have access via Terminal Services. The following example shows fscan.exe, local.exe, and tscmd.exe used together to enumerate which accounts on a server have access to log on to the target Terminal Server:

1. Scanning for Terminal Servers with SMB/CIFS.

   ```
   C:\>fscan -p 139,445,3389 10.0.6.1-10.0.6.254

   10.0.6.36          139/tcp
   10.0.6.36          445/tcp
   10.0.6.36         3389/tcp
   ```

2. Connecting with a "null session" to the identified server.

```
C:\>net use \\10.0.6.36\ipc$ "" /u:""
The command completed successfully.
```

3. Using Local.exe (Windows Resource Kit) to enumerate the members of the Administrators group. Local can be used to enumerate the members of any local group. If you need to enumerate the members of a global group, use Global.exe from the Windows Resource Kit.

```
C:\>local administrators \\10.0.6.36
NSOFTINC\JoannaQTPie
NSOFTINC\TariqAzad
```

4. Using Local.exe to enumerate the members of the Users group.

```
C:\>local users \\10.0.6.36
NT AUTHORITY\INTERACTIVE
NT AUTHORITY\Authenticated Users
NSOFTINC\UserAccount
NSOFTINC\AdminAccount
NSOFTINC\NewUserAccount
```

5. Using tscmd.exe (www.systemtools.com) to enumerate the AllowLogonTerminalServer right for each user identified in steps 3–4. If tscmd.exe's output is 1, logon is allowed; if it is 0, logon is not allowed.

```
C:\>tscmd 10.0.6.36 AdminAccount AllowLogonTerminalServer 1
C:\>tscmd 10.0.6.36 KevinSmith AllowLogonTerminalServer 1
C:\>tscmd 10.0.6.36 UserAccount AllowLogonTerminalServer 0
C:\>tscmd 10.0.6.36 NewUserAccount AllowLogonTerminalServer 1
```

Based on this example, the attacker has two administrator accounts that have the ability to access the Terminal Server as well as a nonadministrator account named NewUserAccount.

Manual Password Guessing via Terminal Server GUI

One should never underestimate the value of some good old guesswork. I have cracked many a password using only my creativity and patience. Not to mention that an attacker does not need to use complicated exploits and scripts if the server has a blank password on the Administrator account.

Automated Password Guessing via Windows (TCP 139,445)

A common step for an attacker who has access to TCP 139 or TCP 445 would be to enumerate users and then brute force the passwords for each account using a Windows brute force tool such as WinLHF. This example builds on the information gathered in the previous sections.

```
C:\>WinLHF.exe 10.0.6.36 -u NewUserAccount -p passwords.txt
WinLHF v1.0 - written by MattW  12-20-02
-------------------------------------------
Checking 10.0.6.36 for blank or easily guessable passwords.
10.0.6.36 responded to ICMP.. Checking for easy passwords...
Checking if IPC connection can be made..
Checking 10.0.6.36 :: pwd => NSOFTINC
C:\>
```

This attacker was able to guess the password for the NewUserAccount. Providing the account has Log On Locally, RDP-Tcp and Allow Logon To Terminal Server permissions, the attacker can now use the account to log on to the TS system. The only one of these three that is not default for users is the RDP-Tcp setting, however, if the server is in Application Server mode you will probably find that Users have been permitted.

Automated Password Guessing via TCP 3389

At the time of writing, I am only aware of two techniques that can be used to perform automated password guessing against a Terminal Server via TCP 3389:

- **TSGrinder** (www.hammerofgod.com) The TSGrinder tool was created by Thor from the Hammer of God Co-Op. It had some difficulties getting out of the starting gate, but hopes are high for this exciting new tool. Although it has been a long time coming, I am assured that not only will the tool be released, but it will be released as version 2; TSGrinder2. Based on Thor's other contributions to the security industry, this one should be worth the wait.

- **TScrack** (http://softlabs.spacebitch.com/tscrack or http://bogonel.mirror.spacebitch.com) TScrack is a password-testing tool that runs authentication attempts against a Terminal Server. See the Tools & Traps sidebar in this section for a detailed description of how TScrack works.

Tools & Traps...

Tool Analysis of TScrack against Windows 2000, Windows XP, and Windows 2003 Terminal Services

Joshua Leewarner
Sr. Security Consultant, Enterprise Risk Services, Deloitte & Touche, LLP

The Stage

With the present state of technology, a graphical systems interface poses a unique challenge to attackers. Text-based (or command-based) services such as Telnet, Secure Shell (SSH), and Hypertext Transfer Protocol (HTTP) can be attacked by the use of scripts and tools designed to submit arguments to valid interfaces. However, graphical interfaces require human intervention in order to make them work for the most part.

Windows Terminal Services is the quintessential example. There is no text interface, no means to submit commands to an active terminal session. Humans are required to click buttons and move the mouse just as they would from a computer console. Session traffic consists of relaying mouse clicks, keyboard strokes, and screen refresh information—all encrypted by default. In the vulnerability assessment world, about the most an assessor could do is detect or discover that Terminal Services is running at a specific IP address. Any further testing would require manually attempting passwords at the logon prompt, and depending on the machine policy, an attacker or assessor might be locked out after a predefined attempt limit is reached. In short, there has been no real way to mount efficient attacks against a sufficiently guarded Terminal Services interface.

The Actor

Enter TScrack, a new tool that uses a technology called *artificial neural networks* to actually "scrape" the Terminal Services login screen and enter password values submitted individually or obtained from an accompanying dictionary file. It is similar to the technology used in Optical Character Recognition (OCR), which improves over time as it is "taught" to recognize variations of the Terminal Services interface.

That being said, the name of the tool is somewhat misleading. TScrack is really not a session cracking or hijacking mechanism, but more along the lines of a password testing tool. That is, it runs authentication attempts against a Terminal Server and will only prove successful if the password is easily guessed or is a word in a commonly used dictionary (as opposed to a brute force program such as l0pht [www.atstake.com/research/lc] or John the Ripper [www.openwall.com/john]). The value of this tool is testing the strength of passwords used to protect terminal sessions.

Continued

TScrack is run from the command line on a Windows system, with the following available flags:

```
-h              Print usage help and exit
-V              Print version info and exit
-s              Print cipher strength info and exit
-b              Enable failed password beep
-t              Use two simultaneous connections
-N              Prevent System Log entries on targeted server
-f <number>     Wordlist entry to start cracking with
-l <user>       Account name to use, defaults to
                Administrator
-w <wordlist>   Wordlist to use; tscrack tries blank passes
                if omitted
-p <password>   Use <password> to logon instead of
                wordlist/blank pass
-D <domain>     Specify domain to attempt logon to
-F <delay>      Specifies the delay between session samples
                in milliseconds
-U              Uninstalls tscrack
```

There are a few notable features here.

■ The ability to use either a specified password to be attempted, or the inclusion of a text-file dictionary of words that can be attempted sequentially.

■ The ability to suppress log file entries in the Windows Event Viewer.

■ The ability to specify a Windows domain to attach to in the event there is more than one in particular environments.

■ The ability to initiate two sessions, which can split one dictionary file in order to double the rate of attempts per minute.

More information about the internals of TScrack can be found by reading the text file that accompanies the download. (See link at the end of this article.)

The single dependency for TScrack to run is the MSVBVM60.DLL library, the Visual Basic Virtual Machine file, normally located in %SYSTEMROOT%\System32. In Windows 2000/XP/.NET Server, it ships with the OS, but with different versions in each.

■ **Windows 2000** v6.0.84.95 (6.00.8495); May 1999

■ **Windows XP** v6.0.92.37 (6.00.9237); May 2001

■ **Windows 2003** v6.0.93.30 (6.00.9330); Sep 2001

Continued

There is a chance that the newer versions of this Dynamic Link Library (DLL) may not allow TScrack to operate on the newer Microsoft operating systems.

In sum, speed is the ultimate advantage of TScrack. It can make connections to a computer running Terminal Services at rates of 60 to 90 attempts per minute depending on network conditions. However slow it that may seem, it is still a big improvement over manual entry.

The Show

To prove the effectiveness of this tool, we performed a series of four tests consisting of using TScrack with the following information:

- A specific username and password
- A specific username and a dictionary file
- A specific username, dictionary file, and Windows logon banner
- A specific username, dictionary file, Windows logon banner, and encryption set to "high"

Because TScrack relies on a dictionary text file to complete dictionary-based attacks, we created a user account on a target machine running Windows 2000 Server. The user account was called "testing" with a password of "testing." We also created a sample file with 100 dictionary words, placing the word "testing" at the bottom the list as word number 100.

Here are the command lines used:

```
tscrack -N -1 testing -p testing 192.168.1.2
tscrack -N -1 testing -w 100words.txt 192.168.1.2
Result of test 1: SUCCESS in <2 seconds.
Result of test 1: SUCCESS in 97 seconds or 61.856 attempts /min.
Result of test 1: SUCCESS in 96 seconds or 62.500 attempts /min.
Result of test 1: SUCCESS in 99 seconds or 60.606 attempts /min.
```

As you can see in Figure 2.30, TScrack works as described; varying the components between two, three, and four tests resulted in minimal latency increase.

Continued

Figure 2.30 TScrack in Action

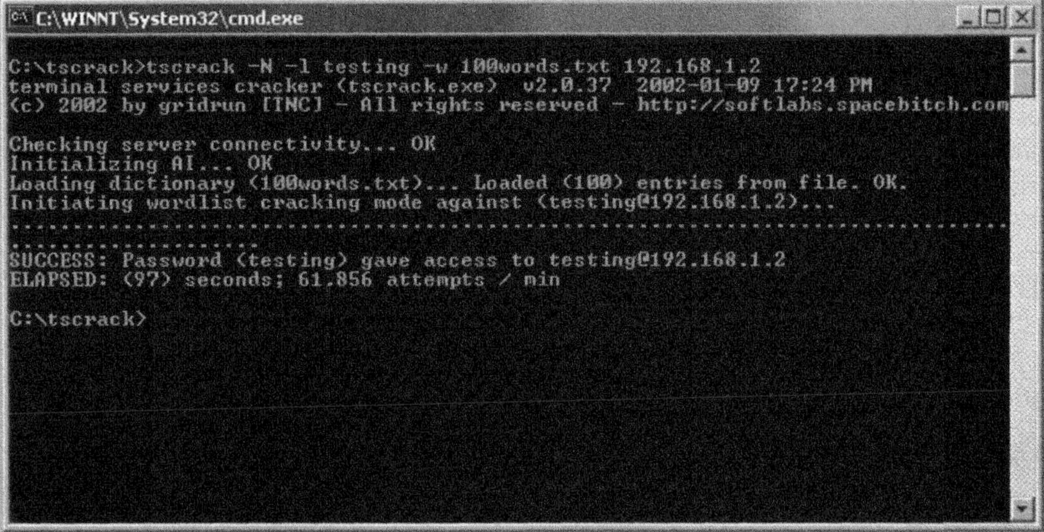

```
C:\WINNT\System32\cmd.exe                                            _|□|×

C:\tscrack>tscrack -N -l testing -w 100words.txt 192.168.1.2
terminal services cracker (tscrack.exe)  v2.0.37  2002-01-09 17:24 PM
(c) 2002 by gridrun [TNC] - All rights reserved - http://softlabs.spacebitch.com

Checking server connectivity... OK
Initializing AI... OK
Loading dictionary (100words.txt)... Loaded (100) entries from file. OK.
Initiating wordlist cracking mode against (testing@192.168.1.2)...
.........................................................................
.........
SUCCESS: Password (testing) gave access to testing@192.168.1.2
ELAPSED: (97) seconds; 61.856 attempts / min

C:\tscrack>
```

To prevent attacks from TScrack, choose sufficiently difficult-to-guess passwords. Your password policy may be enough to foil a tool that is designed to use only dictionary words and their variants. Additionally, consider changing the default TCP port from 3389 to make your Terminal Servers more obscure. Windows 2003 Server will introduce the ability to require smart-card authentication for Terminal Services sessions. Those with serious Terminal Services deployments may want to consider smart cards for added security.

The Curtain Call

- Find TScrack at http://softlabs.spacebitch.com/tscrack.
- Find the TScrack help file at http://ackers.org.uk/tscrack/tscrack.2.0.37.txt.
- Find out more about artificial neural networks at http://hem.hj. se/~de96klda/NeuralNetworks.htm.

Application Server Attacks

If you allow users to connect to your Terminal Server in Application Server mode, you should prepare for a server compromise. Unless you are obsessively vigilant, an attacker will be able to subvert your security controls and gain access to a cmd.exe shell. Once an attacker has access to this shell, he will most likely find success in a privilege escalation attack to achieve administrator access.

First, I discuss some ways your users may attempt to break out of applications to obtain access to the underlying Terminal Server. Next, I show how an attacker might escalate her privileges to become an administrator (or LocalSystem).

Breaking out of a Specified Internet Explorer Application

As an attacker, one useful technique to try if you find yourself stuck in an Internet Explorer (IE) application inside a TS session is to right-click on a link in IE then open the link in a new window. Once the new window opens, enter **c:** as the URL and you have just gained access to the file system. Next, browse to c:\winnt\system32\cmd.exe and obtain your very own command-line access (see Figure 2.31). Of course, this will not work if the permissions on that file/directory are set properly or right-click has been disabled on the Terminal Server.

Figure 2.31 Using IE to Access cmd.exe

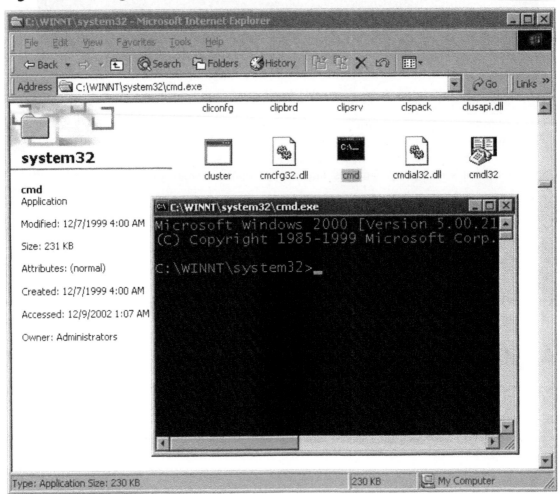

Using the Task Manager to Obtain a Shell

Another technique that has worked effectively to break out of a TS application is by using the default functionality of Windows as a weapon. When stuck in an application or restricted from cmd.exe, try using **Ctrl+Alt+End** to open Task Manager. If you are successful, click on the **New Task** button and then execute either cmd.exe or explorer.exe. This technique works as long as the administrator has not used the policy setting Disable Task Manager.

Using WinZip to Obtain a Shell

Another option for obtaining a shell is to use **Alt+Home** to open the Start menu and then open WinZip. Create a new Zip archive and copy cmd.exd into the .zip file (see Figure 2.32). Double-click on the file to run it. This technique will be defeated if WinZip is not on the system. Additionally, group policy settings can be used to disallow the Start menu.

Figure 2.32 Using WinZip to Get a Shell

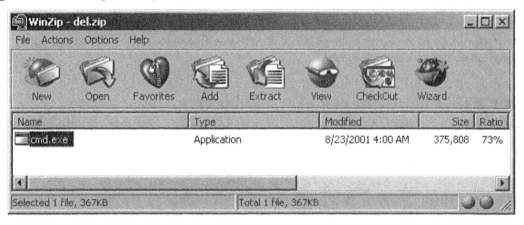

Privilege Escalation Attacks

Many exploits can be used to escalate a nonprivileged account to administrator or LocalSystem. In this section, I discuss two of these exploits (GetAd.exe and DebPloit [ERunAsX.exe]) to demonstrate the danger of allowing users to connect to a Terminal Server that does not have the current Microsoft-issued patches installed.

If you require Terminal Services' application sharing, the best way to secure yourself against these types of exploits is with vigilant patch management. All Terminal Servers in your environment should be kept up to date with the current Microsoft patches using http://windowsupdate.microsoft.com or a similar solution.

Running GetAd.exe

The Bugtraq ID for this vulnerability is 5927. It was discovered and published by Serus in Oct 09, 2002. This vulnerability affects Windows 2000 (including SP3). A nonprivileged local attacker can leverage the Winlogon NetDDE to obtain escalated privileges. This is performed by using a WM_COPYDATA message to send arbitrary code to NetDDE, which will be executed with Local System privileges when a second WM_TIMER message is sent. More information is available from www.microsoft.com/technet/security/topics/htshat.asp.

Running DebPloit Exploit in TS to Get Administrator

This privilege escalation attack was discovered on March 9, 2002 by Radim "EliCZ" Picha and is available from www.anticracking.sk/EliCZ/bugs.htm. The exploit works by impersonating the security context of smss.exe (SYSTEM) by using a duplicated handle, even from a TS session.

Windows 2000 Servers with SP3 are not vulnerable to this exploit. Additionally, servers that have implemented the specific Microsoft patch are not vulnerable. The patch, which can be downloaded from www.microsoft.com/technet/security/bulletin/MS02-024.asp, eliminates the vulnerability by implementing proper validation for requests to attach to the debugging system.

In the following example shown in Figure 2.33, I connect as the UserAccount and show that it is not in the Administrators group, then I run the exploit and tell it to execute the command *net localgroup administrators UserAccount /add*.

Figure 2.33 Demonstration of the ERunAsX Exploit

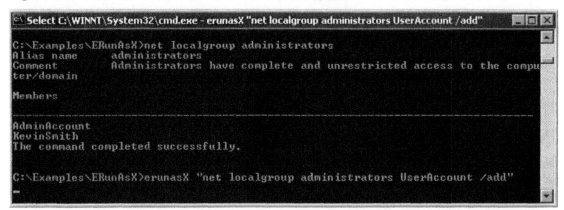

The window freezes, but if I open another cmd.exe on the TS (as shown in Figure 2.34) you can see that it was successful. You will need to log off the server then log on again to rebuild your token as an Administrator.

Figure 2.34 UserAccount has Successfully Escalated Privileges

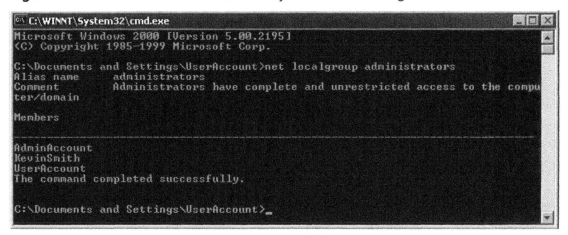

Regaining Logon Rights as an Administrator

If you are an administrator on a system, but you get the Logon Message shown in Figure 2.35 when you try to connect, that is because another administrator has removed your Allow Logon To Terminal Server.

Figure 2.35 No Permissions to Log On to Terminal Server

Since you are an administrator, you can solve this problem very easily using the technique shown here:

```
C:\>net use \\10.0.6.36\admin$ * /u:AdminAccount
Type the password for \\10.0.6.36\admin$:
The command completed successfully.
C:\>tscmd 10.0.6.36 AdminAccount AllowLogonTerminalServer 0
C:\>tscmd 10.0.6.36 AdminAccount AllowLogonTerminalServer 1

C:\>tscmd 10.0.6.36 AdminAccount AllowLogonTerminalServer 1
```

You now have the ability to log on to the Terminal Server again. What happens if another administrator or user modifies his permissions to disallow you to shadow them?

```
C:\>shadow RDP-Tcp#7 /SERVER:10.0.6.36 /V
Your session may appear frozen while the remote control approval is being
  negotiated.
Please wait...
Controlling session RDP-Tcp#7 remotely
Remote control failed. Error code 7051
Error [7051]: The requested session is not configured to allow remote
  control.
```

Simple, if you want to be able to shadow or interact with another user's session, even if you have been denied permission in the **Computer Management | User Properties | Remote Control** you can use TSCmd.exe to regain your privileges:

```
C:\>tscmd 10.0.6.36 AdminAccount ShadowingSettings 0
C:\>tscmd 10.0.6.36 AdminAccount ShadowingSettings 2

C:\>tscmd 10.0.6.36 AdminAccount ShadowingSettings 2
```

NOTE

Don't forget that to disconnect from a remote session you need to use **Ctrl+*** from the keypad. If you are on a Dell laptop like mine, you need to use **Ctrl+Fn+0** to simulate that command.

Maximizing Your SQL Compromise with Terminal Server

When performing a penetration test, if you find the very common SA blank password on a system you can easily use the XP_CmdShell extended stored procedure to add a user then make the user an administrator as shown here:

```
Xp_cmdshell 'net user hacker MyPassword /add'
Xp_cmdshell 'net localgroup administrators hacker /add'
```

Once the account is created, simply log on to Terminal Server and begin to copy your tools that will aid in furthering your network penetration.

Getting Your Tools for Further Attacks

One of the first things an attacker will do if he compromises a Terminal Server is copy his tools to the server so he can use them to pillage the server and use that information to attack other hosts and networks.

The default functionality of Windows Terminal Services allows users to cut and paste text and graphics between client and server using the shared clipboard. It does not transfer files by default in Windows 2000. Native TS file transfer is a handy feature; to add this functionality, Microsoft created a tool called File Copy. This tool implements the ability to copy, cut, and paste files to and from a Terminal Server via its Virtual Channel Architecture. So what would an experienced attacker do if he encountered a system that did not have RdpClip installed? He would install it on the TS using Internet Explorer from http://download.microsoft.com/download/win2000platform/rdpclip/1.0/NT5/EN-US/rdpclip_hotfix.exe.

If you are on an XP Terminal Server or a Windows Server 2003, you can cut and paste your files to the server by default. Additionally, Windows XP allows you to transfer files within a Remote Desktop Connection via sharing of local drives. This requires the client to configure the Remote Desktop Connection to *make local disk drives available in a session*. Once the connection is made, the folders will be available during the session via Explorer as *<drive_letter>*\ on tsclient. To reach these folders from the command line during your Windows XP Terminal Server session, you can type **\\tsclient\<drive_letter>**. For example, if you want your C drive, type **\\tsclient\C**. This will cause the Terminal Server to connect back to your local drive and allow for sharing of files and folders.

The Beauty of the GUI

During a penetration test a couple years back, I was able to gain administrative access to a Terminal Server on a network with a high level of Access Control Lists (ACLs). The problem was I could not connect back to my attack system to get tools to further my conquest. The network administrators had implemented ACLs that blocked my attempts at RDP (Virtual Channels), File Transfer Protocol (FTP), SMB, and Trivial File Transfer Protocol (TFTP). Some of the few outbound protocols that I had available were HTTP and Secure Sockets Layer (SSL). Why not use Web mail to help me out? I simply created an account on Hotmail, e-mailed my files to the account and used the victim Terminal Server to connect to my new Web mail account to grab my files.

NOTE

Another way to upload tools is to use netsend.exe to convert executables into an ASCII format, then just copy and paste them into Notepad on the server. Save them with an .exe extension.

Using Hacker Tools to Expand Influence from Terminal Server

Once you have taken control of a Terminal Server, there are a few things you should always do as quickly as possible. These steps are affectionately called *pillaging a server* and will probably get you domain access if you are lucky:

1. Run PWdump3 (www.polivec.com/pwdump3.html) to obtain the password hashes. Don't forget to copy the output file back to your attack server for cracking with John the Ripper. Since you are local, this attack will require you to use loopback as your address like this:

    ```
    pwdump3 \\127.0.0.1 outputFileName
    ```

2. Run LSAdump2.exe (razor.bindview.com) to dump the contents of the Local Security Authority (LSA) Secrets cache. Since you are in a Terminal Server session, it will not work like it does locally. I discovered that by using the scheduler and an escape character you can make it work in Terminal Server. Use the scheduler to run your command and have it save the output for you. This can be done with the *at* command or the *soon* command. If you use *soon*, be sure to add the */L* to make it delay past 60 seconds, otherwise you can end up scheduling the task to run tomorrow accidentally. In order to redirect the output in a scheduled command, you need to escape the > character by using the ^ character. Finally, since the scheduler runs with a path of %systemroot%, you need to copy the LSAdump2 files to %systemroot% or use the fully qualified path. In this example, I have the tools in the c:\temp directory. The command would look like this:

    ```
    Soon /L:61 c:\temp\lsadump2.exe ^> c:\temp\LSAout.txt
    ```

3. Review the output of LSAdump2, pay close attention to the last few lines. If you find a line that begins with _SC_, you are in luck because the name following it is a service name and the data across from it is its password in cleartext. You are not done yet, however; you still need the account that the service runs as if you want to use the password. I discovered a cool way to get this information using the NT Service Controller (sc.exe). The syntax is simple: *sc qc ServiceName*. If the username is a domain account (or a domain admin), you have just taken a simple compromise and made it a domain compromise. Connect to the domain controller and get those domain hashes.

Defending Terminal Servers

This book is focusing on Terminal Services in Internal network, and therefore, I will not talk about securing Terminal Services for the Internet. If you choose to run TS on the Internet, you will need to implement much stronger security mechanisms.

If you are new to Terminal Services, mind your step as you implement this application because it can easily amplify a small mistake on your end. Microsoft's new security slogan of "Get secure. Stay secure" is a great one. Build and secure your systems from the start, but don't stop there. Persistence is required in the process of staying secure. Without a secure initial implementation, vigilant patch application and regular security assessments, TS can easily become an enemy rather than a friend.

Unless secured properly, the increased functionality of Terminal Services will cause a decrease in overall security for the host operating system. Terminal Server is symbiotic with its operating system, and so a vulnerability in one will probably lead to a compromise of the other.

WARNING

It is critical that you secure the base operating system and provide adequate network protection for systems running Terminal Server. This information can be found in the respective chapters of this book.

Install Current Patches

This process has never been easier. Go to http://windowsupdate.microsoft.com and make sure your server is running the current vendor-issued patches. Additionally, Microsoft offers Software Update Services (SUS) for quick and reliable deployment of critical updates. You should use Microsoft Baseline Security Analyzer to verify patches.

Set Strong Windows Passwords

Any account that is permitted to access Terminal Server for remote administration must have a complex password that is a minimum of seven characters and includes three of the four subsets listed here

```
{a..z}
{A..Z}
{0..9}
{!@#$%^&*()_+-=[]{}\|;:'",<.>/?~`}
```

Even if this is a system used in Application Mode with users that log directly to an application, you need to force passwords of a reasonable complexity. If you have systems that are Internet facing, I recommend a minimum number of accounts be given access and they should be required to use 15+ character passwords. Use John the Ripper to test these passwords to ensure compliance. The other option is to use a dynamic password solution such as SecurID (www.rsasecurity.com).

Damage & Defense...

More on Windows Passwords

Having passwords that are easily guessed or cracked introduces a large security risk to critical assets. Complex passwords should contain a good mixture of upper/lower case letters, numbers, and symbols. Passwords should also not be based on dictionary words and should contain at least seven characters (the longer the better).

Windows NT/2000–downward compatibility for LanMan also complicates the issue. Windows LanManager (LanMan) passwords have a maximum length of 14 characters and are stored as two 7-character one-way hashes. This actually makes passwords more vulnerable because a brute force attack can be performed on each half of the password simultaneously.

Therefore, if I am cracking a LanMan hash of a password that is 8 characters long, it is broken into one 7-character hash and one 1-character hash. Obviously, cracking a 1-character hash (~3.5 million crack attempts per second) does not take long even if we consider all possible characters, and the 7-character portion can usually be cracked within hours.

Sometimes when users select an 8- to 11-character password, the smaller second half of the password (1 to 4 characters) actually decreases the strength of the first seven characters by assisting in the human guesswork of the longer portion. A good example of this is the password *laketahoe*—a password cracker might obtain *???????* *hoe*, and the attacker would likely guess the first half of the password. Because of this, the optimal password length for systems that save LanMan hashes is 7 or 14 characters, corresponding to the two 7-character hashes.

Windows 2003 systems allow passwords greater than 14 characters, allowing up to 127 characters total. A very interesting piece of research recently revealed if a password is fifteen characters or longer, Windows does not even store the LanMan hash correctly. This actually protects you from brute force attacks against the weak LanMan algorithm used in those hashes. If your password is 15 characters or longer, Windows stores the constant AAD3B435B51404EEAAD3B435B51404EE as your LanMan hash, which is equivalent to a null password. And since your password is obviously not null, attempts to crack that hash will fail.

Use High Encryption for Sessions in Windows 2003

Windows 2003 Terminal Services enables administrators to encrypt all or some of the data transmitted between the client and server with a key of up to 128-bit. On Windows 2003 Terminal Services, you should force the setting of High for all sessions. All Windows XP Professional sessions are protected bidirectionally with a 128-bit key. This is configured in the RDP-Tcp Connection settings of Terminal Services Configuration.

> **NOTE**
>
> Some clients, the PocketPC in particular, only support up to 56-bit encryption levels. If you plan to use the PocketPC Terminal Services client in your environment, you will not be able to force 128-bit encryption on participating servers. In these cases, I recommend a virtual private network (VPN) environment (oddly, the PocketPC does support 128-bit encryption for its VPN client) where you can first establish a strong tunnel from which one may then connect to a Medium or Low encryption Terminal Server.

Set Strongest Usable Terminal Server Permissions

Permissions for a particular action are critical when attempting to understand how to attack and defend your Terminal Servers. If applied, the permissions for TS actions are determined in order of precedence by the settings listed here:

1. Organizational Unit Group Policy takes the highest precedence

2. Domain Group Policy

3. Local Group Policy

4. RDP-Tcp Properties in TSCC

5. User Properties (specified on the Remote Desktop Connection [RDC] for Windows XP and Windows Server 2003)

So basically, if you want to control Terminal Services settings for local system administrators, you would need to set them at the Domain or OU.

The following four screenshots show your options for setting permissions. Figure 2.36 illustrates that Windows local group policies have precedence unless the Domain or OU specifies permissions.

Figure 2.36 Windows Local Group Policies

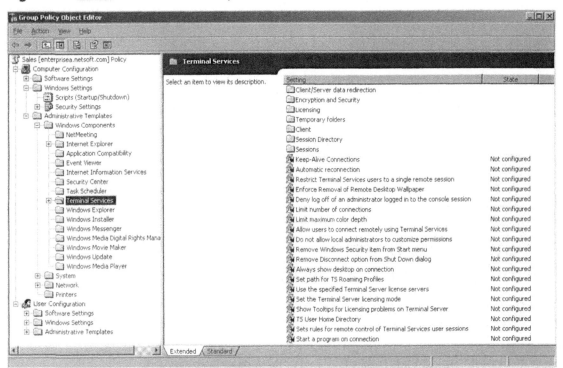

TSCC's RDP-Tcp Properties have precedence if local Group Policy is not configured (see Figure 2.37).

Figure 2.37 TSCC's RDP-Tcp Properties

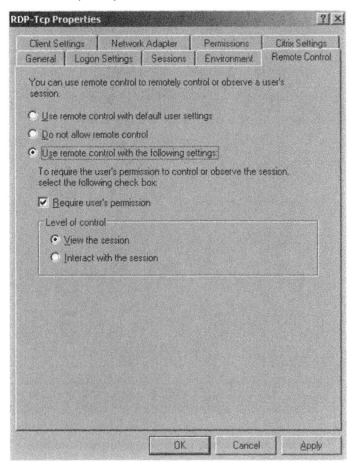

You can see in Figure 2.38 that user properties have the least clout when permission conflicts arise.

Figure 2.38 User Properties

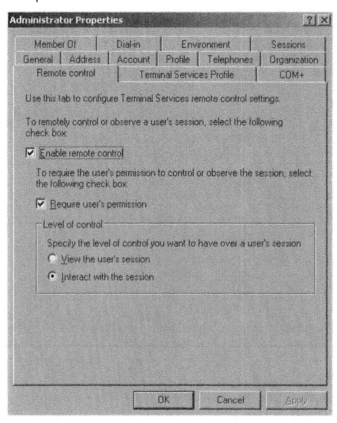

Windows Server 2003 shows permission inheritance information (see Figure 2.39).

Figure 2.39 Windows Server 2003

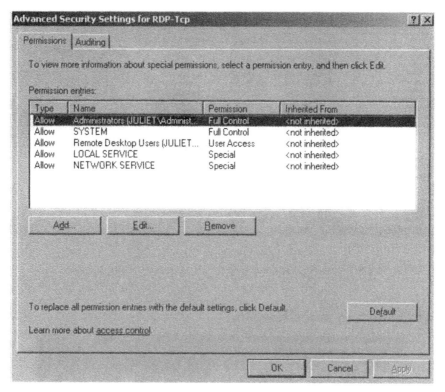

Terminal Server Group Policies

Group Policy can be applied to an OU, local computers, and even individual users to secure Terminal Services in your Windows architecture. Additionally, you can create group policy restrictions on Windows applications by choosing either **Run Only Allowed Windows Applications** or **Don't Run Specified Windows Applications**. You should use Active Directory Users and Computers to create a new OU and implement Group Policy to restrict the ability of users and administrators. Microsoft recommends these settings to lock down a Windows 2003 Terminal Server session on their Web site at http://support.microsoft.com/?kbid=278295.

I recommend that you use these settings as a baseline, then add or remove settings based on whether or not you allow users and administrators or just administrators. Some of the basics that can be disabled to increase security are the mapping of ports, printers, and drives. Randy Franklin Smith's article (the second part of four) gives recommendations for you to consider as well at www.windowsitsecurity.com/Articles/Index.cfm?ArticleID=19791.

Relocate Terminal Server to a Obscure Port

You can relocate Terminal Server to a new TCP port with a simple Registry modification. To do this, modify the PortNumber Value Name in the following key to a port of your liking (see Figure 2.40).

```
HKLM\System\CCS\Control\Terminal Server\WinStations\RDP-Tcp\PortNumber
```

Figure 2.40 Modifying Terminal Server's Listening Port

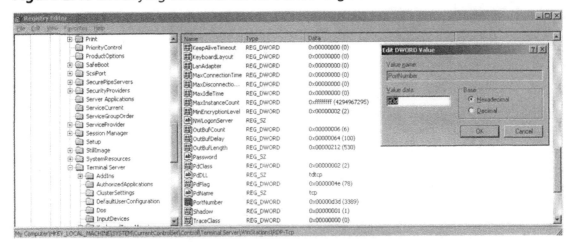

Figure 2.41 shows a screenshot of connecting to the server by using the new port.

Figure 2.41 Connecting to the New Port

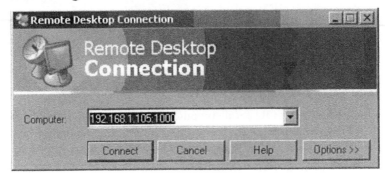

Implementing Basic Host-Level Security

If you are using Windows XP, Internet Connection Firewall is a great option to consider for host-level access control. If you are using Windows 2000, you can use IPSec filters to block access to dangerous ports. The following script should be modified based on your server's intended function:

```
@echo off
REM NSOFTINCIPSec.bat
REM you need to install IpSecPol,exe from the URL listed next
REMhttp://www.microsoft.com/windows2000/techinfo/reskit/tools/existing/ipsecpol-o.asp
```

```
REM This batch file uses ipsecpol.exe to block inbound services not required
REM ICMP will be blocked too
REM You should modify this based on the requirements of your TS

ipsecpol -x -w REG -p "SpecOps3389" -r "block139"   -n BLOCK -f *=0:139:TCP
ipsecpol -x -w REG -p "SpecOps3389" -r "block445"   -n BLOCK -f *=0:445:TCP
ipsecpol -x -w REG -p "SpecOps3389" -r "block1433"  -n BLOCK -f *=0:1433:TCP
ipsecpol -x -w REG -p "SpecOps3389" -r "block80"    -n BLOCK -f *=0:80:TCP
ipsecpol -x -w REG -p "SpecOps3389" -r "block443"   -n BLOCK -f *=0:443:TCP
ipsecpol -x -w REG -p "SpecOps3389" -r "blockUDP1434"  -n BLOCK -f *=0:1434:UDP
```

If still not convinced, use this script to implement IPSec filters and then scan the server with SL.exe (www.foundstone.com). If you specify the basic options, you should receive no reply from the host. This time use SL.exe with the –g option set to 88 (Kerberos) and scan again. You should be able to see all the ports that are blocked by IPSec filters.

How can you stop this? You need to set the *NoDefaultExempt* key. This can be configured by setting the *NoDefaultExempt Name Value* to *DWORD=1* in the Registry at HKLM\SYSTEM\CurrentControlSet\Services\IPSEC.

Use the Principle of Least Privilege

Users, services, and applications should have the minimum level of authorization necessary to perform their job functions. Do not give all Administrators access to all your Terminal Servers unless there is a valid business reason. The more people with access, the more likely you are to have a problem. Just like any system in your environment, you should treat access on a need-to-know basis.

You can use Active Directory to create security groups for your Terminal Services systems. Figure 2.42 shows two new groups that were created for Terminal Server access.

Figure 2.42 Using AD Security Groups

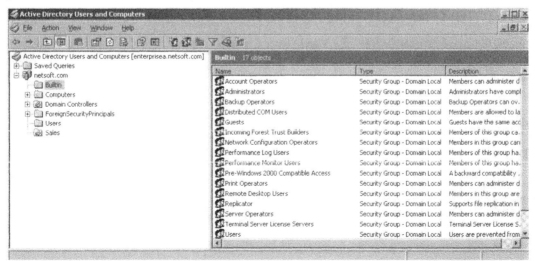

Set a Logon Banner

Going to **Local Computer Policy | Windows Settings | Security Settings | Local Policies | Security Options** will allow you to configure the following settings:

```
Message text for users attempting to log on
Message title for users attempting to log on
```

If configured, this "logon banner" can stop some older TS brute forcing tools. It may also provide some legal leverage should that be an issue. If you have PocketPC users connection to a Terminal Server with a Logon Banner configured, you may need to train your users to explicitly send an "ENTER" through to the server, as (depending on the length of the banner text) the PocketPC client software screen centering will only show the blank center of the logon banner—they will not know that they need to acknowledge the logon banner.

Increasing Security with Extreme Measures

If you are ultra paranoid, consider implementing a more robust encryption, authentication, IP address filtering, and logging solution. One option is to use Zebedee (www.winton.org.uk/zebedee) to tunnel Terminal Server traffic through a compressed and encrypted tunnel. A great article written about this topic is available from SecurityFocus at http://online.securityfocus.com/infocus/1629.

I have read articles about using Stunnel (www.stunnel.org) and IPSec tunnels to perform similar extraordinary measures, but I feel it is overkill for most situations. You should calculate your risk for a particular network, host, or data, then decide what fits your needs.

Remote Administration Mode Specific Defenses

If you are using the Terminal Server for remote administration, the biggest thing to worry about is limiting who has access to connect; do not give permissions to administrators that do not require access and be sure the ones that can connect have strong passwords. The easiest way to do this is by creating a Global Terminal Server group and making them local administrators on the Terminal Server.

Rename the Administrator

Rename the Administrator (RID = 500) and create a new administrator with a strong password and no privileges. Watch your logs to see if this user attempts to log on. If you see failed logons, investigate further. Don't forget to remove the description, otherwise an attacker can pretty easily figure out that you renamed the account.

Disable TSInternetUser and Remove Licensing Service

You can disable the TSInternetUser account when you are using Terminal Server for remote administration. This account allows anonymous access if Terminal Services Internet Connector Licensing is enabled. You should also be sure that Internet Connector Licensing is not enabled. To remove account permissions from some objects, Microsoft offers a security template (notssid.inf) in the %SystemRoot%\Security\Templates directory.

Application Server Mode Specific Defenses

Special care needs to be taken in Application Server mode since nonprivileged users have the ability to run code in the processor of the server. This is because most attacks against a Terminal Services application server will be privilege escalation attacks. When allowing nonprivileged users to connect to TS, precautions such as file and directory access control and auditing need to be carefully considered. Application mode also has the additional overhead of maintaining Terminal Server Licensing Servers to dole out application mode licenses to each console user. Application Server mode needs to be secured in the same way that you would secure a server that allowed users to log on locally.

File Security

Without NTFS, you don't have permissions or the ability to audit file accesses. Use them and use them well. They can be the last line of defense when a user is trying to do or see something they are not supposed to. For a more secure solution, separate the %systemroot% and required applications into different volumes. This will allow for easier securing of the file system. Be sure to verify permissions required for your Terminal Server. The first step is to remove all but SYSTEM and Administrators rights to c:\ and its subdirectories and then add the permissions back as needed to achieve functionality. Some common areas that require read and execute permissions are Windows system folder and Program Files (including subdirectories). Modify access is required for some applications as well as needed for Documents and Settings folders.

Disallow User Access to Shared Clipboard

I recommend that you limit the ability to use the Shared Clipboard feature to administrative accounts only. You can disable it via the TS Configuration Manager and remove virtual channels for users to restrict this functionality. I recommend that you add an Access Control Entry (ACE) that explicitly denies Everyone from Virtual Channels if this is a big concern to you.

Disallow Remote Control

Terminal Server features a Remote Control option to view or control other users sessions. Terminal Server nonprivileged users should not have access to this functionality. This access is controlled via the RDP-Tcp properties and should be disallowed for nonadministrators.

Specify an Initial Starting Program

The RDP-Tcp Properties can be set to automatically open a specified application when a user connects. The TS session will be restricted to only that application and will close if the user closes the application. The caveat is if the user can "break out" of the application the session will remain. Details on these techniques are listed in the "Attacking Terminal Servers" section of this chapter.

Restrict Application Usage

AppSec.exe is available in the Windows 2003 Resource Kit and can be used to specify what applications can be run in a TS session or which ones cannot be run. Only applications that are required by the TS users should be given access. If used properly, this tool can help keep users locked into a specific environment as well as reduce the risk of privilege escalation if they find a way to break-out of it. This tool, however, only limits applications by their filenames. So if you allow explorer.exe to run, any file renamed to explorer.exe will work.

Limit and Log Access from Older Clients

TSVer.exe is available in the Windows 2003 Resource Kit and can be used to restrict older versions of Terminal Server clients from making connections. Additionally, this tool will record an IP as well as a hostname to the system logs when attempted connections fail due to older versions. TSVer should be used to force users to use the current RDC client due to its 128-bit encryption requirements.

Case Study: Attacking Terminal Server

In this brief case study, I detail each successful step of my internal attack chronology from CorpLAN to FinanceLAN using Terminal Server as an integral part of the attack. The goal was to compromise the production MSSQL database in the FinanceLAN.

My first step was to attempt to enumerate the hosts in the FinanceLAN domain by using the *net view /domain:FinanceLAN* command. I was unable to see any hosts because there was a screening router in the way. So my other option was to attack the CorpLAN to find a server that would allow me to jump into the FinanceLAN.

Using the HSVAdmin.bat script, I was able to discover 24 out of 252 hosts with blank administrator passwords in the CorpLAN domain. Using these credentials, I was able to execute commands interactively on these hosts using a tool called psexec.exe (www.sysinternals.com/ntw2k/freeware/pstools.shtml).

```
NET USE \\VICTIMone\admin$ "" /u:VICTIMone\administrator

Psexec \\VICTIMone cmd.exe
```

This interactive access allowed me to view and enumerate the hosts in the FinanceLAN domain using *net view /domain*. Next, I used a tool (sqllhf.exe) that checked for blank SA (database administrator) passwords and found a host that contained a blank SA password. Using the xp_cmdshell stored procedure, I was able to execute commands on the server and add myself as an administrator. I connected to the Terminal Server with my new account and began to pillage the server for data to further my attack.

The next thing I did was use PWdump2 (http://razor.bindview.com). Using PWdump2 and administrative access, I was able to download a copy of the local SAM database (Windows password file). This password file was cracked, and the password for the administrator account was obtained. This password was 10 characters in length but of poor composition, containing only letters and numbers.

I determined that the local administrator account of this machine was the same password as the local administrator account on the FinanceLAN domain controller. With my newfound Domain Admin access, I used PWdump2 again, but this time to obtain all the domain hashes. Using a password cracker, I was able to completely crack all passwords in the FinanceLAN domain due to poor password length and complexity. I effectively had gained access to every machine in the FinanceLAN domain.

Using my newfound credentials, I proceeded to log into another host in the FinanceLAN domain via Terminal Server. Using MSSQL Enterprise manager, I connected to all the MSSQL servers in the FinanceLAN domain. Finally, I connected to the production MSSQL server and browsed the production databases. This signified the successful completion of my objective.

Security Checklist

Assessing the security of individual hosts can be very useful when trying to find vulnerabilities and configuration errors. A host assessment can uncover vulnerabilities that would never be found during a standard host and network assessment. This section is broken out into categories based on general and specific points of server inspection.

General Points of Server Inspection

- Using Ping, verify whether the host responds to an ICMP echo request.

- Perform a comprehensive TCP and UDP port scan of the host. This scan will provide you with the information you need to analyze the servers exposure level by reviewing its listening services and their business requirements. Additionally, this information will allow you to determine if host-level TCP/IP filtering is implemented.

- Verify that the server is not multipurposed (SQL and IIS, or DC and TS Application Server).

- Document all Administrative-level account names, including local and global groups.

- Run Microsoft Baseline Security Analyzer to identify missing patches and configuration errors.

- Use John the Ripper to crack/audit all Administrator accounts and passwords.

- Identify if services are running in the context of domain accounts. Use LSAdump.exe to dump the contents of the LSA Secrets Cache. This will need to be done locally or via the scheduler. Please refer to the "Using Hacker Tools to Expand Influence from Terminal Server" section for details. Review the output for _SC_ to find cleartext passwords for services. Then use the sc.exe command to determine the account name for the service like this: *sc qc ServiceName*. Services should not be run in the context of domain accounts.

- Verify if an OU been implemented and that it uses Group Policy to restrict the ability of users and administrators based on security requirements.

- Configure the RDP-Tcp Connection properties in Terminal Server Configuration based on required security level for the server.

- Implement an anti-virus solution.

**Customizing John the Ripper
to Audit Password Policy Compliance**

Use John the Ripper (www.openwall.com/john) by Solar Designer to verify that all rel-evant username/password combinations have a reasonably secure password and are compliant with the corporate password policy. John the Ripper can be customized to test only for passwords of a certain length and complexity; this will allow you to find policy violations. For example, if your user policy states that passwords must be 7 or more characters and contain at least 1 non-alphabet character, you can modify the *#incremental modes* section of the configuration file (John.ini for Win32 or John.conf for UNIX) to test all possible Alpha passwords with a length of 0 to 7. Then you need to run *john* using the *–incremental:Alpha* option.

Application Sharing Specifics

- Determine if file system permissions are appropriate for all nonprivileged users. For example, can users view or modify other users' data? Can a user access critical Windows system files?

- Determine if the Registry permissions are secured appropriately against attack from local users. Has access to Windows Registry tools such as regedit.exe and regedt32.exe been restricted?

- Use PWdump tools to obtain password hashes for all local accounts and then crack them using John the Ripper. Since any account could allow access to the Terminal Server, it is important to check all the passwords.

- If domain accounts are used on the system, use PWdump tools to obtain the password hashes for all relevant accounts and crack them, too.

Remote Administration Mode Specifics

- Verify whether the administrators have modified the listening TCP port to hide the Terminal Server from plain sight.

- Have they implemented a one-time password solution such as RSA's SecurID?

- Remove the TSInternetUser account and disable the Licensing service.

Windows XP Remote Desktop Specifics

- Identify and validate business need for each member or group in the Remote Desktop Users group available under Computer Management | Local Users and Groups | Groups. If members exist outside of the local system, these need to be validated as well. Remove accounts that do not require TS access.

- For all Remote Desktop Users, obtain password hashes using PWdump2 (razor.bindview. com) and crack them using John the Ripper. If possible, audit based on corporate password policy.

Summary

Windows 2003 presents some unique challenges to the security professional when it is used in the enterprise environment. Although very user friendly, it is subject to attack from many directions if administrators are not aware of the potential places for breach. During the course of the chapter, there have been opportunities to explore some of the default features of Windows 2003 and view how they operate out of the box as far as availability and security are concerned. The topics explored have revealed that there are some potential problems that exist in that out of the box configuration, such as permitting *null* passwords for authentication when using anonymous accounts for access. Tools are included and available with the operating system to better secure the default configurations according to your needs. These included Windows 2003 Support tools, and use of management consoles customized to perform necessary configuration tasks and apply security templates.

While working with the security templates, I included instruction that provided a framework to create a custom management console to view, analyze, and implement the features of security templates, which are used to create a custom and more secure configuration for Windows 2003 machines. In the basic setup, a strong template and an equally strong password policy puts you on the road to better security in your operation of Windows 2003 clients and servers.

I looked at some of the methods that attackers use to try to gain control of your systems and detailed the processes that an attacker can use to successfully abridge your system. There is a pattern that is used, and the chapter discussed the stages that occurred in this order:

- Footprint potential victim systems.
- Scan for entry points.
- Enumerate possible entry points.
- Get passwords.
- Attack.

At this point, following the path of an attacker, it was discovered that the basic operating system can be vulnerable if administrators leave some default conditions in place and services running that they don't need. Prime among these in the Windows environment is the use of NetBIOS functions for network browsing and file sharing, which exposes the network to attack. While looking particularly at the opportunities for attack that are present when enumerating a victim with NetBIOS running, attention was paid to the built in tools such as *Nbtstat* and *Net View* commands and *nltest* from the Resource Kit. Additionally, more information was found to be available by using SNMP tools such as *snmputil* or *snmputilg*, as well as tools like Scanline or Superscan for enumerating open ports.

The section includes discussion of methods to defend against the types of attack that were discussed earlier in the chapter. Among these, methods of physically securing equipment as well as the appropriate use of password policies and locally applied Registry and security templates were reviewed.

The majority of security concerns with Terminal Server are not a result of a poor product, but a product that is implemented poorly. Terminal Server is a catalyst for low- and medium-severity vulnerabilities, offering them a change to reach the big time. For example, a simple low- to medium-severity vulnerability such as a guessable user account/password combination can result in remote command execution if that user has Terminal Server logon rights.

If you are new to the Terminal Server world, I recommend that you start by using it as a remote administration tool only. Windows XP and Windows Server 2003 offer this in a service called Remote Desktop that comes installed by default; you just need to enable it. Thanks to their intuitive grouping of things like users with access to Terminal Services, these services are now very easy to manage. If you require application sharing on your internal network via Terminal Services, be ready for a steep road to the pinnacle of security competence. By allowing your potential enemy access to your server, you have dramatically increased your risk of compromise. If you must travel this road, I recommend that you use Windows Server 2003 because it offers the most secure solution for multiuser scenarios.

Whichever usage for Terminal Services you select, don't forget the fundamentals of security, such as principle of least privilege, defense in depth, and patch management. Terminal Server is an enabling technology. If left on your network insecurely, this door will swing both ways, allowing access to defenders as well as attackers.

Solutions Fast Track

Windows 2003 Basics

☑ Windows 2003 is based on an improved version of the Windows NT 4.0 kernel, which provides protection of the operating system through isolation of applications away from the operating system and hardware.

☑ Windows 2003 provides the capability to secure file systems and disk access through the use of the NTFS file system, but also allows for backward compatibility if needed by supporting FAT and FAT32 disk formatting.

☑ Windows 2003 uses local and domain-based user accounts and groups to begin the process of granting access to resources and authenticating users in either the workgroup or domain environment.

Windows 2003 Security Essentials

☑ Out of the box configurations are less secure if upgrade is used instead of a clean install.

☑ Microsoft provides the Security Configuration And Analysis snap-in for the management console to construct, analyze, and install custom security configurations.

☑ NTFS is the recommended file system to support DACL assignments that control access via both local and network access.

☑ Local security of resources is not possible unless NTFS is used in the formatting of the disk.

☑ Windows 2003 supports Encrypted File System in conjunction with NTFS formatting to further protect sensitive resources.

☑ File and directory access permissions should have the Everyone group removed to limit security vulnerability.

Attacking Windows 2000

- ☑ Attackers use a process that involves discovery, scanning, enumeration, and attack.

- ☑ Discovery may involve ping scanning or research via the Internet.

- ☑ Network scanning is used to discover open ports or available services.

- ☑ Enumeration can involve use of common tools if NetBIOS connectivity is possible, and it can lead to detection of vulnerable systems that are less difficult to connect to.

- ☑ Password cracking tools can be employed to try to gain access, particularly desirable to use the administrator account.

Defending and Hardening Windows 2003

- ☑ Start your defense of Windows 2003 with planning and evaluation of current risks.

- ☑ Track, test, and implement installation of service packs, patches, and updates.

- ☑ Use Security Baseline Analysis tools and patch and update checkers.

- ☑ Use strong password policies and implementation of security templates.

- ☑ Remove unnecessary services and network protocols.

- ☑ Restrict physical and network access to resources.

- ☑ Use NTFS file system.

- ☑ Use Dynamic Disks

- ☑ Use EFS.

Windows 2003 Terminal Services Basics

- ☑ By default, Terminal Servers use the Remote Desktop Protocol (RDP) via TCP port 3389. Configured properly, each session is authenticated using Windows domain authentication and is bidirectionally encrypted with the 128-bit RC4 crypto algorithm.

- ☑ Application Server mode for a Windows 2000 Server is used for application sharing; it facilitates concurrent sessions on individual desktops and environments that share the server's resources. Remote Administration mode for a Windows 2000 Server offers less overhead as well as dramatically increased security.

- ☑ Windows XP Professional comes with Remote Desktop (a scaled down version of Remote Administration mode) installed. It does not offer an application sharing mode.

- ☑ Security-focused command line tools available from Microsoft include qwinsta.exe (query session), shadow, query termserver , TSDiscon and reset session, and TSKill.

- ☑ Terminal Services Configuration Connections (TSCC) allows for configuring of server settings and RDP-Tcp Properties.

Attacking Terminal Servers

- ☑ Once an attacker has interactive access to his victim TS he can easily upload and execute a privilege escalation exploit to become an administrator.

- ☑ TSEnum.exe identifies Terminal Servers in a domain even if they are running on alternate ports. It will sometimes work even if you have no domain credentials.

- ☑ If you dual-NIC your servers to connect network segments (not recommended), attackers can use techniques to find them and then identify which ones are running Terminal Services.

- ☑ Fscan.exe, local.exe, and tscmd.exe can be used together to enumerate which accounts on a server have access to log on to the target Terminal Server.

- ☑ TSGrinder and TScrack can be used to perform automated password guessing against a Terminal Server via TCP 3389.

- ☑ If you allow users to connect to your Terminal Server in Application Server mode, an attacker may be able to subvert your security controls, gain access to a cmd.exe shell, then engage in a privilege escalation attack to achieve administrator access.

- ☑ The common SA blank password on a system allows an attacker to use the XP_CmdShell extended stored procedure to add a user, then make the user an administrator.

- ☑ In Windows 2003, the File Copy tool provides the ability to copy, cut, and paste files to and from a Terminal Server. Windows XP allows the transfer of files within a Remote Desktop Connection via sharing of local drives.

- ☑ An attacker with control of a Terminal Server can use techniques using the tools PWdump3 and LSAdump2 to gain domain access.

Defending Terminal Servers

- ☑ When not secured properly, the increased functionality of Terminal Services will cause a decrease in overall security for the host operating system. Vulnerability in one will probably lead to a compromise of the other.

- ☑ Install current patches and secure the operating system. Set strong Windows passwords and use a tool like John the Ripper to test these passwords.

- ☑ On Windows 2003 Terminal Services, force the setting of High encryption for all sessions.

- ☑ Set permissions and control Terminal Services settings for local system administrators by implementing Group Policy restrictions at the Domain or OU in Active Directory.

- ☑ Application Server mode needs to be secured in the same way that you would secure a server that allowed users to log on locally.

Frequently Asked Questions

Q: Why should I use NTFS to format my drives? Then I can't access it from a boot floppy!

A: NTFS should be used for that reason (to be more secure) and because it supports local security and encryption.

Q: Why should I be concerned about NetBIOS?

A: NetBIOS availability leads to much simpler methods of attack on your system, and should be disabled when possible and practical in your network.

Q: My users complain that they can't install applications like new screensavers and things that they've downloaded or brought from home. What should I tell them?

A: Be conciliatory, but firm. Security is designed that way in Windows 2003 to prevent users, viruses, and Trojan programs from modifying the system. This protects the operating system from breach.

Q: What tool do you recommend be used for baseline analysis?

A: I prefer the Baseline Analysis Tool from Microsoft for the initial analysis. After using this tool, you can proceed to evaluate and modify your security templates to begin to secure the machines and domain.

Q: If the server is running in Remote Administration mode, can I connect as a nonadministrative user?

A: Yes, but only if it has been configured to do so (Windows XP must be in the Remote Desktop Users group).

Q: Ctrl+Alt+Del doesn't work in a Terminal Server session—what can I do?

A: When in a TS session, you will need to use Ctrl+Alt+End to simulate a Ctrl+Alt+Del. Additionally, you can use Alt+(Page Up | Page Down) to switch applications and Alt+Del to right-click the active application's icon button.

Q: Does Windows XP Remote Desktop offer an application sharing mode like Windows 2000 Terminal Services?

A: No, if you require application sharing mode you should use Windows Server 2003 and add Terminal Services by using Control Panel | Add or Remove Programs | Add/Remove Windows.

Chapter 3

Terminal Services and XenApp Server Deployment

Solutions in this chapter:

- Introduction of Terminal Services and Citrix XenApp Server
- History of Terminal Services
- The Future and Beyond: Capabilities of Windows Server 2003 Terminal Services
- Limitations of Windows Server 2003 Terminal Services
- History of Citrix XenApp Server
- Understanding the XenApp Server Architecture
- The Future and Beyond: Capabilities of XenApp Server
- How XenApp Server Fills the Gaps in Terminal Services
- Planning for XenApp Server Deployment
- Platform Deployment Options
- Citrix XenApp Server Installation Process

☑ Summary

☑ Solutions Fast Track

☑ Frequently Asked Questions

Introduction of Terminal Services and Citrix XenApp Server

The concept of users sharing computing resources is not new. The practice of this computing model dates back to mainframes with green-screen terminals. While computing has evolved dramatically since those early days, the basic premise of "centralized" computing hasn't changed a great deal. Centralized or server-based computing originally sprang out of the need for many users to have access to very expensive computing resources without actually placing a computer on each user's desk. This was the right approach for the time due to two primary reasons. First, computers then cost hundreds of thousands, if not millions, of dollars to acquire and typically cost even more to maintain and operate. Second, computers were at best the size of large cars, so placing one on each user's desk would pose a serious space issue to any corporation. The benefits of centralized computing weren't as pronounced then as they are today. Centrally managed end-user devices weren't *an* option then, they were the *only* option. The ability to have a single point of update for applications and operating systems was the norm in the "good old days." Providing hundreds of users access to a new application was instantaneous—again, only one computer to "upgrade."

Popularity for centralized computing waned for several years as the advent of the personal computer (PC) allowed end users to have the power of the mainframe on the desktop without the expense of the mainframe. Individual PCs gave rise to the need for networking, so we began to tie PCs together to allow sharing of files and printers. Over time, our use of computers went from a centralized to a decentralized model as PCs were cheaper to maintain and purchase than mainframes and mini-computers. A host of new applications allowed for much greater range of computing uses, such as word processing, spreadsheets, and e-mail. We slowly moved from the point of placing computers on engineers' desktops to placing computers on everyone's desktop. We moved the majority of our computing power to the edge of the network, along with the majority of support issues. Anyone who has ever managed a network knows that purchasing the computer is the least expensive part of owning a computer. Maintenance, training, upgrades, viruses, and spyware all add up to the bulk of the cost over time for PC ownership. Several studies are available that indicate that the initial capital outlay for the purchase of new computing hardware and software only accounts for about 10 percent of the actual cost over a three-year period (then you get to start all over!). This process of suburban sprawl inside our networks continued unchecked for several years. With passage of time, IT personals then started moving towards putting all those applications and tools that users run on their desktops to the central computers to manage the applications centrally on controlled, reliable, enterprise-grade hardware to increase our uptime. We started creating highly available server "farms" to allow for reliable user connections instead of single points of failure. Thus the need of Terminal Services and Citirx server were born.

In this chapter, we look at the history of the Terminal Services and Citrix XenApp Server (Citrix Presentation Server 4.5) products. We also explore how the XenApp Server fill the gaps in Microsoft's Terminal Services technology, and why you might prefer to add XenApp to your Terminal Services environment. The discussion will then lead to installation of XenApp Server on Windows 2003 platform.

What Is Terminal Services?

"What is Terminal Services," you ask? For anyone who has used VNC, Timbuktu, PC Anywhere, Remotely Possible, X Windows, or even the new Remote Desktop for Microsoft Windows XP, you have some idea of what Terminal Services enables you to do. Terminal Services is the multiple simultaneous use of a Microsoft Windows computer remotely by the user population. This is the access of many users to a centrally located and managed server farm running the Microsoft Windows Server 2003 operating system. Each user's connection is "virtual" and remote. Whether users are accessing the terminal server from their local area network (LAN), or remotely from a Windows Mobile Powered handheld while waiting for a flight, it is all about access. Terminal Services allows users of virtually any device to be able to access the same applications and data from anywhere internal and external of the network, anytime.

All applications are installed on the terminal servers, creating a single easy to manage point of upgrade. All applications and code execute exclusively on the terminal servers, allowing devices to execute the latest and most feature-rich applications, even when the device would not natively support these applications. The terminal servers present the *interface* to the user's device. The end user interacts with this interface via his local keyboard and mouse, transmitting these signals to the terminal servers. This transfer of the *interface* of the application and the input from the user occurs via a presentation layer protocol. Presentation layer protocols exist at the presentation layer of the OSI model. Sandwiched logically between the application and the session layers, presentation layer protocols primarily perform the roles of translation and, to a lesser degree, encryption. To put this into perspective, presentation layer protocols allow computers to *understand* something that they cannot understand out-of-the-box. Logically, presentation layer protocols' primary functions are translation and encryption. Microsoft Terminal Services natively uses the Remote Desktop Protocol (RDP), and Citrix XenApp Server uses Independent Computing Architecture (ICA) as the presentation layer protocols of choice. The protocols and the software that is installed on the client devices act as the redirector that allows for translation and understanding of the Terminal Services *language*, whether ICA or RDP.

History of Terminal Services

Terminal Services began life as a concept created by Ed Iacobucci while working on the OS/2 project at IBM. After gaining no interest from IBM on including this technology in OS/2, Ed left to found Citrix Systems, Inc. Ed and his team at Citrix Systems had signed an agreement with Microsoft allowing Citrix to modify the code and create a multiuser version of Windows NT 3.*x*. This modification to the kernel became known as *MultiWin*, and Citrix Systems sold the solution as a product named WinFrame. WinFrame was in every sense a completely capable and functional Windows NT 3.*x* server. WinFrame could function in any capacity that a "standard" Windows NT 3.*x* server could. In addition, WinFrame could host multiple user sessions and allow users remote access to their applications and information.

The Dark Ages: The Birth of Windows NT 4.0 Terminal Server Edition

In February 1997, Microsoft informed Citrix that it would be pursuing its own version of WinFrame, which would be based around the Windows NT 4.0 platform. Both Microsoft and Citrix knew that the older file manager interface of Windows NT 3.*x* and WinFrame needed to be replaced with the current Windows 9*x* Explorer interface used in the recent release of Windows NT 4.0. Microsoft decided to consolidate the product offerings and base the next version on the Windows 9*x* Explorer interface. Many speculations exist as to why Microsoft chose to end the code-sharing agreement and pursue the centralized computing model directly. Some say that Microsoft perceived that the Windows NT kernel stood a good chance of becoming "fractured" into many camps, similar to the versions of UNIX, if Microsoft didn't maintain tight control over the source. Others claim that Microsoft wanted to have a "quick" entrance into the emerging centralized computing market space. Whatever the reasons, Microsoft chose to go it alone and announced Project Hydra, the codename for the upcoming release of Windows NT 4.0 Terminal Server Edition (TSE).

After several tenuous months, Microsoft and Citrix reached a new agreement. In August 1997, Microsoft agreed to license the MultiWin technology from Citrix for inclusion in Windows NT 4.0 Terminal Server Edition. While the core function of Terminal Services would now be under Microsoft's control, Citrix played and continues to play a large role in the product roadmap. As part of the agreement, Citrix would continue to have access to the source code. A new feature of the agreement was that Citrix would place developers onsite at Microsoft's campus in Redmond to work side by side with the terminal server development team. Citrix would retain rights to develop clients for all non-Microsoft Windows platforms. Additionally, Citrix would develop an add-on product, MetaFrame, which would provide ICA Services to Windows NT 4.0 TSE.

NOTE

The agreement that was reached in August 1997 has since expired. A new agreement was signed that continues the same kernel source-code sharing. The current agreement is set to expire in 2009, but conventional wisdom is that this also will be renewed. If you are wondering as to the "status" of the relationship between Microsoft and Citrix, ponder no more. Microsoft named Citrix Systems "Partner of the Year," Microsoft's highest partner award... so things must be pretty good.

In the summer of the following year, 1998, Microsoft released Windows NT 4.0 TSE. TSE was built on the MultiWin technology licensed from Citrix Systems through a collaborative development effort between Microsoft and Citrix. However, beyond that, several changes were made to licensing and connectivity to TSE. Since ICA Services were part of the Citrix solution, and the ICA protocol for client-server sessions was part of those services and not of the base terminal server product, Microsoft needed to develop its own presentation layer protocol for user sessions. Microsoft leveraged an existing technology that it had recently acquired in its product NetMeeting. NetMeeting contains a feature that allows users to "share" their desktop or applications with other users during the meeting. This capability is based on the T.120 or "T-Share" protocol. Microsoft adapted that presentation layer protocol for TSE and named it the Remote Desktop Protocol, or RDP.

RDP version 4.0 contained two pieces. First was the server-side component. The terminal server would run a *terminal server* service, similar to other services such as workstation, server, or messenger. This terminal server service basically listened to the network for incoming terminal server sessions, created the sessions, managed the sessions, and tore the sessions down on exit. The client-side component consisted of an RDP Client. Users could choose to install the RDP Client on a Windows

16- or 32-bit operating system to allow them to connect to the terminal server directly. RDP, being based on the T.120 protocol, requires TCP/IP as its transport protocol stack. RDP rides inside the payload section of a TCP packet. The list of initially supported clients was rather thin, no pun intended. With the release of TSE, Microsoft included client support for Win16, Win32, and WinCE operating systems. The WinCE client and support was originally only available from the manufacturer of the client device. Eventually, Microsoft would release an ActiveX-based plug-in for Internet Explorer 4.0 and higher and a client for the Apple MAC OS.

In addition to the *terminal server* service that ran on each TSE server, a new service was introduced to server-based computing by Microsoft known as the Terminal Server Licensing service. This service's job was to enforce Microsoft's license model for users connecting to terminal servers. The Terminal Server Licensing service maintained an Access or Jet Database on each terminal server to track the issuance of terminal server client access licenses, or TSCALs. The original implementation of this service had several flaws. The database and service were dependent on the version of the Microsoft Data Access Components (MDAC) that was installed on the terminal server. Occasionally, when you installed an application or upgraded the terminal server, it would "break" the database, causing the service to fail to start. Additionally, the database was maintained on *each* server and no mechanism existed to "reconcile" the issued licenses between the servers. The license issuance was based on the client's computer name or NetBIOS name. If the helpdesk rebuilt a user's computer, a *new* license would be issued and decremented from the total count available, without the original license ever being returned to the database. Due to these and other issues, many administrators chose to disable the Terminal Server Licensing service on the TSE servers and enforce the TSCAL requirements manually.

NOTE

Microsoft's TSCAL requirements are in addition to any Citrix licensing requirements. Both Microsoft and Citrix XenApp Server must be licensed correctly for user sessions to function. For a user session to be correctly licensed for a Citrix connection, several licensing requirements must be met. Microsoft will require a Client Access License and a Terminal Services Client Access License. These Microsoft licenses are in addition to the Citrix connection license consumed during the ICA session.

By many in the industry, especially those deploying the platform, TSE was viewed as a completely separate product offering from Microsoft with its own design considerations and support needs. Microsoft certainly viewed the platform as such. To that end, Microsoft created and maintained a separate Hardware Compatibility List (HCL) for TSE. In addition, Microsoft issued separate service packs and hotfixes specifically for TSE. Third-party vendors had a difficult time adapting to this new mainstream platform offering of terminal servers. Many applications that were developed to run correctly on Windows NT 4.0 Workstation or Server, failed outright to execute on the Windows NT 4.0 TSE platform. Many applications required modifications or tweaks to enable them to run correctly on TSE. With these kinds of disparities among versions of the same platform, one can see why support and design issues arose. Microsoft rose to the challenge.

The Renaissance: The Light of Windows 2000 Terminal Services

In December 1999, Microsoft released Windows 2000 to manufacturing. Some major steps in the right direction were made for the Terminal Services platform. The foremost change was the inclusion of Terminal Services into the Server product line. The perception of why Microsoft included Terminal Services in the platform is based on two lines of reasoning: 1) simplicity, allowing for the creation of a single kernel; and 2) administration, as Microsoft (as the rest of the server-based computing community already knew) discovered the invaluable benefit of remote administration. With this single change, Microsoft cemented the destiny of centralized computing. Now Terminal Services was part of the mainstream distribution of the platform available as a selectable service to install, similar to Windows Internet Naming Service (WINS) or Dynamic Host Configuration Protocol (DHCP). This allowed for the creation of a single HCL. A single service pack offering existed for servers built with Windows 2000 Server regardless if they were installed as file servers or terminal servers. Hotfixes, as is the nature of such updates, continued to be maintained somewhat separately based on the services installed on the server. In short, there were and continue to be hotfixes developed specifically for terminal servers that would not and most likely should not be applied to file servers, for example. The inclusion of this feature as a component allowed third-party integrators to more easily support their software on the platform, as the platform could then be viewed as one product instead of two separate products from the previous version.

NOTE

Unlike Microsoft Windows XP Professional, Windows 2000 Professional could not run the terminal server service or remote desktop function. A Windows 2000 Professional computer could only function as a client in the Terminal Services process and could not accept connections from other RDP clients. Windows XP Professional supports a single connection via Remote Desktop. Windows XP Home does not support this feature.

Another major change for Terminal Services under the Windows 2000 Server platform was the ability to select the role of the terminal server during the addition of this service. For the first time, administrators could choose between two modes of operation for their terminal servers, *Remote Administration* and *Application Server*. Remote Administration was a groundbreaking feature that included much of the benefit of Terminal Services' session speed and ubiquitous access simply scaled down to support only two simultaneous administrative sessions. For Windows administrators then and now, Remote Administration mode (or what has become known as Remote Desktop for Administration) is a lifesaver.

Remote Administration mode did not require any special or additional licensing to install and use. Microsoft *gave* us two free connections to the server for the purposes of remote administration. Application Server mode was reserved for true terminal servers (the focus of the remainder of this book). Application Server mode allowed for the unlimited connections (platform prohibiting) to the terminal server, and is the mode that all terminal servers are configured for today.

In addition to the change to the terminal server service, Microsoft heavily modified the Terminal Services Licensing (TSL) service. Gone are the days of being able to simply disable this service; as part of the new platform, Microsoft required the terminal server to be able to *talk* to a TSL server. Additionally, the TSL service no longer is installed and running on each terminal server, as with NT 4.0 TSE. Installation and configuration Terminal Server License Server is easy, as you can see in the following step y step procedure:

Configuring & Implementing...

Installing Terminal Server License Server

Here is a brief step-by-step exercise for installing Terminal Server License Server.

1. Click on Start menu, Control Panel and then double click on Add or Remove Programs.

2. In the Add or Remove Programs dialog box, click on Add/Remove Windows Components. On the Windows Components page of the Windows Components Wizard, scroll down and select Terminal Server Licensing in the Components section, and then click the **Next** button.

3. On the Terminal Server Licensing Setup page, specify the role of License Server and click on Your entire enterprise, as shown in Figure 3.1.
Click **Next** to continue.

4. Click **Finish**.

Figure 3.1 Terminal Server Licensing Setup

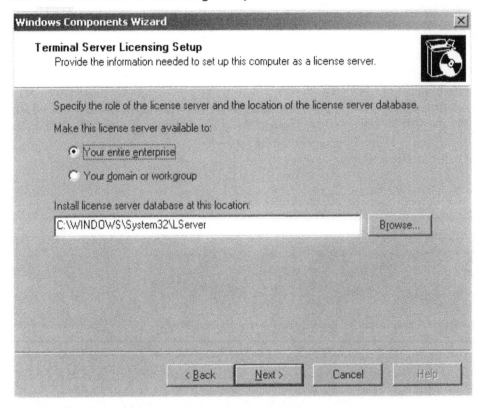

TSL is out of the scope of this book, but typically, one or two TSL servers will suffice for most organizations. The new TSL service allowed Microsoft to enforce the new licensing model. The basic premise of this new model was that clients that were equal to or greater than the terminal server platform would not be charged a TSCAL, but instead would be able to use the client operating system's built-in TSCAL. For all down-level clients or non-Microsoft clients, a TSCAL would be required and charged against the total TSCAL pool available from the TSL server. Table 3.1 demonstrates this licensing concept.

Table 3.1 Windows 2003 TSCAL Requirements

Terminal Server OS	Windows 2003 Pro or Newer[2]	Windows Pre-2003[3]	Non-Windows Clients[4]
Windows 2003 Server[1]	Built-in	TSCAL required	TSCAL required

[1] All versions of Windows 2003 Server, including Standard, Advanced, and Datacenter
[2] Includes all versions of Windows 2003, Windows XP Pro, and all versions of Windows Server 2003
[3] Includes all Windows platforms before Windows 2000 (Windows Me, Windows 9x, Windows 3.x, Windows CE, and Windows NT)
[4] Includes all non-Windows clients (MS-DOS, Mac OS, Linux, UNIX, etc.)

Improvements to the RDP protocol on the server side and client side were made to take advantage of the improvements to the server. Redirected printing (the ability to make use of client-based print resources while in the session) was added to the Terminal Services platform. Clipboard redirection, or the ability to cut, copy, and paste text between the local client and the Terminal Services sessions, was added. Shadowing (the ability to remotely control a session), disk bitmap caching for improved session speed and performance, and the RDP Advanced client were also included as updates for Windows 2000 Terminal Services. The RDP Advanced client was also known as the Terminal Services Advanced Client (TSAC). This specialized client was a plug-in created for Internet Explorer to allow users to browse a Web site to start a Terminal Services session.

The Future and Beyond: Capabilities of Windows Server 2003 Terminal Services

In March 2003, Microsoft released to manufacturing the current flagship for Terminal Services in the form of Windows Server 2003. Great advancements in security, scalability, and manageability were the bedrock of this release. With these improvements to the core platform, several major changes were made to the Terminal Services portion of that platform. Taking a queue from the Windows XP platform, Microsoft changed the name of Terminal Services to Remote Desktop—although most practitioners continue to refer to the feature set as Terminal Services. Remote Desktop is a feature available to all versions of Windows XP and Windows Server 2003, with a few minor differences.

On Windows XP Professional machines, Remote Desktop allows a single user to connect to the "console" of the target machine and assume control of it (similar to VNC or PC AnyWhere). The ideal is that a user could be away from his or her desktop and remotely access it via the Remote Desktop client on another machine, whether in the office or away. The capability to perform this function is already installed but disabled out-of-the-box for security reasons.

There are two modes in which Terminal Services can run:

■ **Remote Desktop for Administration** This mode is used for remote system administration and is available on all Windows Server Platforms. Additional licensing is not needed to use the Remote Desktop for administration, but only two connections are permitted to connect to the server at any given time.

■ **Terminal Services Role** This mode is designed for the sharing of either full remote desktop sessions or remote application windows with end-users for production use. The number of connections available for use is dependent upon the server hardware and the number of Terminal Services Client Access Licenses (TS CALs) available.

Remote Desktop is also installed out-of-the-box on Windows Server 2003, but is disabled. The primary difference on the server platform is that enabling Remote Desktop is functionally equivalent to Remote Administration mode in Windows 2000 Server. By enabling Remote Desktop on Windows Server 2003, an administrator is allowing two simultaneous remote connections to this server and one login at the console (where Windows XP only allows a single session to the console). Application Server mode, the mode typically associated with Terminal Services, requires a trip to **Add/Remove Programs** to install this additional functionality. Application Server mode is available on Windows Server 2003 editions, except for the Web edition, which is limited to the Remote Desktop for Administration mode. Enabling this feature is easy, as you can see in the following step-by-step procedure:

Configuring & Implementing...

Enabling Remote Administration Mode

To enable remote administration mode, follow these steps:

1. Click the **Start menu**, right click on **My Computer**, and then click **Properties**.
2. From the System Properties dialog box, click the **Remote** tab.
3. Click **Enable Remote Desktop on this Computer**, as shown in the Figure 3.2.

Figure 3.2 Enable Remote Desktop on this Computer

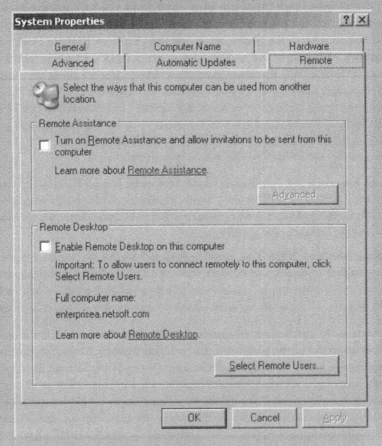

Continued

4. When the Remote Sessions dialog box appears, read the information concerning security and the requirement for a password on all accounts that will use Terminal Services, as shown in the Figure 3.3. Click **OK**.

5. Click OK to confirm your changes.

Figure 3.3 Remote Sessions

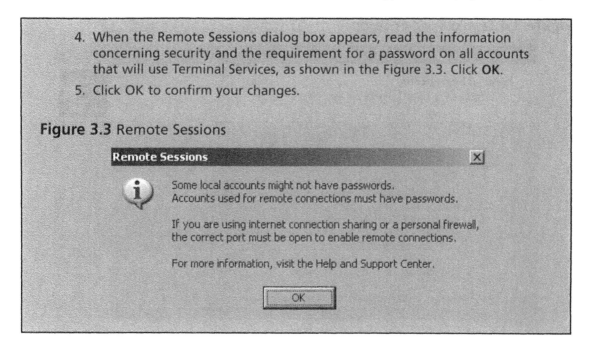

NOTE

The method described to enable Remote Desktop is similar to Remote Administration mode in Windows 2000 Server, and thus does *not* provide the full functionality of Application Server mode. Application Server mode can only be enabled through **Add/Remove Programs**, as explained in the follow exercise.

Installing Terminal Services

In this section we'll show you how to install Terminal Services.

1. Click the **Start** menu, **Control Panel** and then double click on **Add or Remove Programs**.

2. In the Add or Remove Programs dialog box, click **Add/Remove Windows Components**. On the Windows Components page of the Windows Components Wizard, scroll down and select **Terminal Services** in the Components section, and then click the **Next** button.

3. You will then receive the warning stating that you choose to install Terminal Server on this computer (see Figure 3.4). Click **Next** to continue.

Figure 3.4 Terminal Server Setup

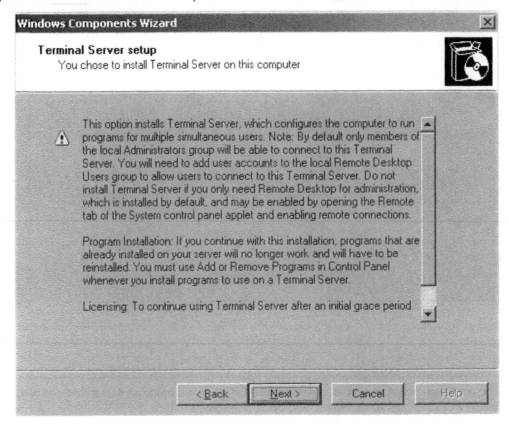

5. On **Terminal Server Setup** page, select **Full Security** as default permission for application compatibility (see Figure 3.5), and then click **Next**.

6. Select **Use these license Servers:** and then type in the license server name, and then click **Next**.

7. Select either **Per Device licensing mode** or **Per User licensing mode** (see Figure 3.6), and then click **Next.**

8. On Completing the Windows Components Wizard page, click Finish.

9. Click Yes to reboot your computer to finish the installation of Terminal Services.

Figure 3.5 Terminal Server Security mode

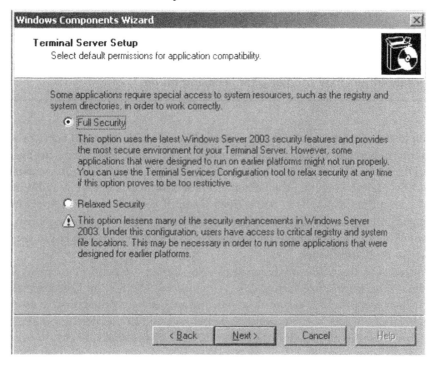

Figure 3.6 Terminal Server licensing mode

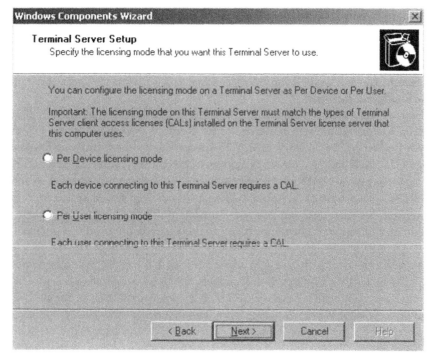

> **NOTE**
>
> Please confirm the licensing mode from your Citrix Administrator before you proceed with this section as some organizations may be prefer to use **Per Device licensing mode**, while others may use **Per User licensing mode**.

In addition to the installation differences between Windows 2000 Terminal Services and Windows Server 2003 Terminal Services, major changes occurred in TSL, and a new feature has been introduced called Session Directory. TSL became much easier to manage and understand. Quite simply, now everything is a TSCAL. No longer do the built-in licenses of Windows 2000 Pro and Windows XP Pro matter. All connections to Windows Server 2003 Terminal Services (when in Application Server mode) require and consume a TSCAL. The other big difference is that there are now two licensing modes to choose from on the terminal servers themselves. Now a terminal server can ask a TSL server for a per-device or a per-user license.

Session Directory is a new feature designed to allow for a more consistent experience when user devices disconnect from active Terminal Services sessions. The Session Directory stores session information, such as users, devices, terminal servers, and so forth in a "directory." If users want to disconnect and reconnect later, their session will be reconnected to the already running disconnected session based on the information the Session Directory maintains. There are some pretty steep requirements for implementing Session Directory, including the use of a load-balancer (either Windows Load Balancing Service (WLBS) or a third-party hardware load-balancer such as F5 Network's BigIP devices). Additionally, the Session Directory requires Enterprise or Datacenter editions of Windows Server 2003 on the terminal servers in order to function. The Session Directory itself can run on Windows Server 2003 Standard edition. Since Citrix XenApp Server already has this functionality and doesn't require the expense or complexity of hardware load-balancers and Windows Server 2003 Enterprise Edition, most production networks will opt not to install this feature. Instead, we will use load balancing as a function of Citrix XenApp Server Advanced and Enterprise Editions.

A new client has also been introduced to leverage the new server-side features' functionality. Remote Desktop Client (RDC) (the replacement for Remote Desktop Protocol Client (RDP Client)) is supported by Microsoft on Win32, Web Client (ActiveX for Internet Explorer), Mac OS X, and Windows CE, including the newer Windows CE .NET. Several third-party RDC clients are also available to allow Linux/UNIX distributions to connect directly to terminal servers without Citrix. These RDC clients were not created by Microsoft, nor are they supported. However, we've used various versions for years and they seem to function well, if not feature-complete. Citrix develops, maintains, and supports clients for many of the mainstream UNIX and Linux distributions.

Many improvements were made to RDC client versions 5.1 and 5.2 over the previous Windows 2000 version, RDP 5.0. RDC 5.1 ships with Windows XP and is preinstalled ready to use on every Windows XP machine, to include all editions. RDC 5.2 ships with Windows Server 2003 and is preinstalled on all versions of Windows Server 2003. The differences between RDC 5.1 and 5.2 are practically nonexistent, the one noticeable exception being the automatic reconnect feature of the RDC 5.2 client. Administrators wanting to use this feature might want to update the RDC client on their Windows 32-bit clients, from Windows NT 3.5*x* through Windows XP.

RDC 5.*x* also has improvements in color depth and performance optimization over the RDP 5.0 client of Windows 2000. RDC 5.*x* now supports True Color (24-bit) via the Terminal Services session. While this may seems like a trivial improvement on the surface, more and more developers are creating applications assuming that the target computer has the capability to "see" more than 256 colors (as we were restricted to in Terminal Services on Windows 2000 and Windows NT 4.0 Terminal Server Edition). Try running Publisher or Visio through a Terminal Services session at 256 colors, then increase to 24-bit, and you'll see the difference.

Microsoft has also included in the RDC 5.*x* interface the ability to "tweak" the performance characteristics of the client to allow users to optimize their Terminal Services session based on their network connection. This is a huge step forward for out-of-office and remote office users and a much-needed addition, albeit a feature that requires manual modification.

System configuration and automation has been greatly improved in Windows Server 2003 with the expansion of the Windows Management Interface (WMI) Providers. Currently, a great deal of the underlying functionality of Terminal Services has been exposed to various scripting languages that WMI and the Windows Script Host (WSH) support. In addition, Microsoft has exposed the Terminal Services attributes for user objects in Active Directory with this release. For the first time, administrators are able to create scripts to modify the Terminal Services properties for users' accounts with the need for third-party products.

Security of the Windows Server operating system has been improved. Out-of-the-box, Microsoft disables many unnecessary services that pose security issues to Terminal Services, such as Internet Information Services. Additionally, Microsoft has improved the security of Terminal Services itself. Windows Server 2003 now leverages a Remote Desktop Users built-in group to manage access rights to the terminal servers. Moreover, additional system rights are restricted based on membership in this group. No longer does every user account automatically have rights to access the terminal server remotely. RDC connections now default to 128-bit RC4 symmetric key for encryption of session information. This encryption setting can be adjusted on the connection properties or through group policy to allow for legacy clients, particularly older versions of Windows CE to connect to Windows Server 2003 terminal servers.

Microsoft also has included support for the Federal Information Processing Standard (FIPS), meeting both FIPS 140-1 (1994 revision) and FIPS 140-2 (2001 revision). FIPS is a security standard for cryptography that many governmental agencies (federal, state, and local) are required to meet. Broader support for the use of smart cards to authenticate to Terminal Services sessions has been introduced. The file system and registry have also been secured more tightly with this release. Microsoft has made extensive use of the Authenticated Users built-in group to assist in assigning NTFS permissions and Discretionary Access Control Lists (DACLs) to files, folders, objects, and registry keys. Microsoft's security initiative is certainly a step in the right direction for all parties concerned through decreased vulnerabilities, less administrative burden patching systems, and greater system uptime due to decreased patching. Currently, there are no service packs in release for Windows Server 2003, although there is a release candidate for Service Pack 1 for Windows Server 2003. This is quite a statement to make, considering that the platform is nearly two years old as of the writing of this book.

Limitations of Windows Server 2003 Terminal Services

Microsoft has truly brought a great platform to market with Windows Server 2003 Terminal Services. However, as with any product, there are certain limitations or situations in which Terminal Services by itself doesn't fit the bill.

The limitations can be broken down in a few key areas:

- Load balancing limitations
- Secure remote access solution
- Lack of an enterprise toolset for management
- Lack of a built-in application deployment solution
- Small list of supported clients
- Limited client-side functionality

Load Balancing Limitations

Microsoft has two options for load balancing in a Terminal Services environment. The first option is to implement the Windows Load Balancing Service (WLBS) that is now available in all versions of Windows Server 2003 (Windows 2000 Advanced and Datacenter Server previously had this feature). WLBS uses a *virtual IP* for the group of servers participating in the service. Up to 32 nodes may aggregate to form a single virtual IP that users can connect to for sessions. When a user session comes in, the servers that are part of the cluster (not true clustering) determine which server will service the incoming request. A user's session will continue to be serviced from that server until the session is terminated through a process known as *affinity*. If the user terminates his or her session, subsequent connections to the virtual IP will most likely redirect to one of the other available nodes. What then, are the true limitations of WLBS? First, it is a user-load based algorithm. As users start sessions, they are "loaded" onto the servers in the cluster "evenly," the old "one for me, one for you, one for me, and so on." If a user on ServerA launches a process that consumes a high percentage of the resources for an extended duration, WLBS is "unaware" of that situation and will continue to load users proportionally on the servers. This process continues despite the fact that ServerA may be nearing 100-percent resource utilization with 50 users, while ServerB and ServerC are at 30 percent with 50 users. WLBS would allow the 51st session to start on ServerA.

The second major limitation of WLBS is that it uses a "fabricated" Media Access Control (MAC) (hardware) address for the virtual IP. Certain enterprise switches do not allow a single MAC to be associated with more than one switch port at any time. The situation arises as follows:

1. ServerA boots to production with local IP 192.168.0.1 and converges in the WLBS cluster as NODE1 with virtual IP 192.168.0.100.
2. ServerA is plugged into switch port 1.
3. The switch "listens" to network traffic to allow it to build an Address Resolution Protocol (ARP) table (to know where to send packets).

4. The switch associates Port 1 with ServerA's real MAC and the virtual MAC from the convergence.

5. ServerB boots to production with local IP 192.168.0.2 and converges in the WLBS cluster as NODE2 with virtual IP 192.168.0.100.

6. ServerB is plugged into switch port 2.

7. The switch continues listening.

8. The switch associates port 2 with ServerB's real MAC and then associates the virtual MAC with port 2.

9. Since the virtual MAC isn't associated with both ports, only one of the servers will actually be able to respond.

Workarounds include updating switch code, trying various combinations of multicast and unicast with WLBS, statically entering the virtual MAC in the ARP table for each port necessary, or plugging all the servers that are "converging" into a hub and then uplinking that to the core switch. Beware of switch port flooding that can occur by allowing your switches to propagate the ARP broadcasts as a result of the convergence required for WLBS to function correctly.

Let's look at the second method of load balancing Windows Server 2003 Terminal Services without Citrix XenApp Server. This method of load balancing involves third-party hardware from vendors such as F5 Networks, Cisco, and Foundry Networks. Each of these vendors creates hardware that can more intelligently route incoming Terminal Services sessions (and other traffic types) to the least busy server. Some of the devices are more intelligent than others. Typically, the prospect of creating a redundant hardware solution just for Terminal Services is prohibitively expensive, often costing tens of thousands of dollars.

If your goal is to use the session directory feature of Windows Server 2003 Terminal Services, Microsoft recommends you implement one of the previously discussed technologies, WLBS or Hardware Load Balancers. XenApp Server's load balancing is far more dynamic and can direct user sessions based on a myriad of criteria. In addition to the standard user-load criteria that WLBS uses, XenApp Server can also load balance based on CPU utilization, memory utilization, time of day, and the subnet from which the client is establishing the session, just to name a few.

Secure Remote Access Solution

One of the biggest challenges that we face as administrators of Terminal Services solutions is providing users with secure remote access. Simply providing the user with remote access isn't enough these days. Access must be simple to use, adaptable to the user's connection, and totally secure for both the session data and the servers running the sessions. Various options exist to attempt to meet these needs. Virtual private networking (VPN), Remote Authentication Dial-In User Service (RADIUS), SecureID, and Server Publishing with ISA and Network Address Translation (NAT) are a few of the more popular methods to provide secure remote access to your Terminal Services deployment. Let us examine each of these options in more detail.

Server Publishing with Microsoft's ISA Server and NAT are very similar concepts as far as a remote access solution to Terminal Services is concerned. The idea is to place a device or service between the "outside" and the Terminal Services. This device or service will screen incoming requests specifically for the types of traffic you are expecting to receive on the terminal servers. While this goes a long way in helping to protect the servers from attack where system vulnerabilities or missing patches are concerned, the terminal servers are still exposed to the outside with only a username and password between the "bad guys" and your servers. If one of your users wants to access the terminal servers from a kiosk computer at the trade show, you may still be out of luck. Even if the kiosk computer has the RDP client, do they have the correct ports open to allow it to traffic out? Can you install a VPN client?

Virtual private networking is a popular method to allow users to gain remote access to the internal network. Depending on how they are implemented, VPN tunnels can provide secure access across virtually any connections. Issues with VPN solutions typically center on user configuration of the client-side piece to establish the tunnel, portability of the VPN solution from platform to platform, and split-tunneling. RADIUS and SecureID can provide an additional layer of security through confirmation that the device trying to establish the connection is legitimate. VPN client configuration can be challenging even for some of the best engineers in the business. Depending on which vendor you implement, the configuration and supportability can vary widely. Some VPN clients don't work well or reliably across digital subscriber lines (DSL). Some VPN clients don't work well with software that already exists on the client's computer. Some VPN solutions don't have client software for Mac OS X, Linux, and so forth. And of course, our personal favorite situation: you send a user home from work with the VPN client software, detailed directions on how to install and configure this software, and the next morning you arrive at your office with the user standing at your door with his computer in his hands explaining how *your* VPN client broke it and it won't boot.

The biggest problem from the standpoint of the VPN is that it allows any clients (that successfully connect) to bring all their problems to the corporate network. Split-tunneling is the capability for the VPN client to "interact" with other networks while in the active process of maintaining a VPN tunnel into your network. If split-tunneling is enabled, it allows the client that establishes the VPN tunnel to maintain connectivity with nonsecure networks, such as public LANs or the Internet. This exposes the private network to the possibility of attack via the client that establishes the VPN tunnel. Split-tunneling is a decidedly bad thing. To clarify, the possibility of split-tunneling can theoretically provide "bad guys" on the Internet the ability to route through the user's computer at home and into your production network. Viruses on home computers, spyware, unpatched operating systems, and more are now "on" your network attaching to your servers—hope you didn't have any plans for the weekend. One possible fix for this is to issue the user a company controlled device, something you can lock down with your own security measures. Secure Socket Layer (SSL)-based VPN with Client and Server certificates promises to help eliminate a good deal of these kinds of headaches, but it doesn't go very far in the portability category. Unless the user can "bring" her certificate to the device, she will not be able to establish a session.

We can see how secure remote access can be a real challenge. In later chapters, we will discuss in detail several methods of providing secure remote access to users leveraging a feature included in Citrix XenApp Server. This feature set includes Secure ICA, SSL Relay, Web Interface, and Secure Gateway. We will see how users can be anywhere they have an Internet connection and be able to securely and easily access their applications and data.

Lack of an Enterprise Toolset for Management

Windows Server 2003 has some tremendous centralized and remote management capabilities built in. From group policy to security templates, from Remote Desktop for Administration to WMI, the toolset is vast. However, there is a chink in the armor. There are several tools to do several jobs inside a Terminal Services-only world. No single toolset has been created by Microsoft to assist Terminal Services administrators in centrally managing their servers. In fact, the Terminal Services Manager tool found on every Windows NT 4.0, Windows 2000, and Windows Server 2003 is based (almost entirely) on the WinFrame Administrator (later MetaFrame) tool (MFADMIN.EXE). For those of you still running MetaFrame Presentation Server 1.0 or older, try launching the Terminal Services Manager and the Citrix Server Administrator and do your own comparison.

The point is that we have several tools that we have to master in order to perform our job as a terminal server admin without Citrix. A single framework for managing large-scale Terminal Services deployments is missing. Citrix XenApp Server provides that Enterprise Toolset through the existing Presentation Server Management Console and the Access Suite Management Console, both are part of the Citrix XenApp Server.

NOTE

The Presentation Server Management Console is the new name for the Citrix Management Console tool from MetaFrame Presentation Server 1.0.

Lack of Built-in Application Deployment Solution

Windows Server 2003 provides a good foundation for installing and managing software on servers, whether remote installation routines for application install, Group Policy based application package installs, or just the basic functionality that exists thanks to the Windows Installer Service 2.0. However, two major features are missing when it comes to enterprise-level application deployment.

The first issue relates to the ability to schedule the deployment and removal of applications or updates to servers centrally. Now before you drop us a note, yes, we have heard of Microsoft's SMS and the various other technologies that exist as third-party software to perform this function. However, there again, we are purchasing more software, creating more infrastructure, and creating more support burden to be able to perform this function. In addition, we may be involving more vendors to manage. In our efforts to reduce complexity, we inadvertently created more.

The second issue is the ability to create a package or modify an MSI. Some excellent products exist on the market today from InstallShield and Wise Solutions to allow developers and administrators alike to create and modify MSI packages. We strongly recommend both of these products to any Terminal Services administrator out there. However, we're looking, again, for something more "built in" to the product, which is where Installation Manager for Citrix XenApp Server comes in. Installation Manager provides a complete solution for packaging, distributing, and removing applications, hotfixes, service packs, and more, all integrated into the Presentation Server Management Console.

Small List of Supported Clients

While the majority of the computing ecosystem is a Windows 32-bit world, broader support for a heterogeneous client base is needed for a successful Terminal Services infrastructure. Currently, Microsoft supports the following list of RDC (and older RDP) clients:

- Win32

- WinCE (certain versions direct from Microsoft, others via OEM)

- Pocket PC (also known as Windows Mobile)

- Web Client (ActiveX plug-in for Win32 version of Internet Explorer)

- Mac OS X

The level of functionality varies widely based on the client version. Many advanced functions (such as drive, print, and com port redirection) exist only for the Win32 client. As administrators and enterprises embrace centralized computing, eventually the question arises as to how to continue to reduce costs and complexities. Replacing the Windows Desktop PC with a thin client or Windows-based terminal can provide substantial return on investments. Having greater feature set support on non-Win32 clients will become necessary.

Citrix XenApp Server has a very long list of supported clients, everything from Win32 to MS-DOS, from Mac System 7.1 to OS X, Windows CE, UNIX/Linux and OS/2, just to name a few. And for those hard-to-please operating systems, Citrix offers the Java client. To give you a glimpse into how long Citrix Systems has been building clients for their MultiWin technology, let's examine the MS-DOS client in more detail. What is the oldest version of MS-DOS supported with a Citrix Client? Give up? MS-DOS 3.3. How old is MS-DOS 3.3, you may ask? Well, let's answer that question with another question.

What was the largest physical or logical partition size that the file allocation table (FAT) version of MS-DOS 3.3 could support? Another stumper… the answer is 32 MB (no, that is not a typo, it is 32 MB). Remember the good ole days of 32 MB hard drives?

Limited Client-Side Functionality

While the RDC 5.*x* client has come a long way since its inception in 1998, several critical areas leave something to be desired when running a remote session via Terminal Services alone. Drive redirection, or the ability to access your local client drives inside the session, is only supported on the RDC client while running on Windows XP desktops. Citrix supports this functionality on all versions of Windows, Mac OS, and UNIX/Linux.

Printer redirection, or the ability to print to your (logically or physically) locally attached printers on the client device while in the session, is only supported on Windows XP desktops with the RDC client. Citrix supports all their clients with redirected printing, even MS-DOS and Windows CE (with some limitations of the client OS, of course).

The RDC client provides no mechanism for delivering role-based access to applications, data, and information. Additionally, there is no mechanism to integrate such access into the client's desktop to provide easy access to the Terminal Services infrastructure. If a user wants to execute a calculator installed on the terminal servers, he will have to navigate the desktop of the terminal server or adjust to the "window within Windows" phenomenon. RDC lacks a feature that Citrix leverages called *seamless windows*. This feature removes the "window-wrapper" around applications to allow the client to work within the application as if it were locally installed.

Administrators and users of server-based or centralized computing expect to be able to centralize nearly all of the applications that they use on a regular basis. As deployments of this technology increase, the integration of multimedia rich applications increases. Users expect to have the same experience use Flash and Shockwave animations through their Terminal Services session as they would if they executed the application locally on a fully functional desktop. Terminal Services is not optimized by default for such operations, nor does the RDC client offer such options. Citrix has created a series of technologies included in the XenApp Server platform that greatly enhance the multimedia experience through a XenApp Server session. Citrix refers to the various technologies as Speed Screen, which allows for better handling of multimedia through the session.

History of Citrix XenApp Server

Citrix XenApp Server (also known as Citrix Presentation Server 4.5) is the latest in a line of products from Citrix Systems. Citrix chose to re-brand the Presentation Server line in 2008, to go along with their new XenApp Server label. Building on the many versions of software before it, XenApp Server provides the latest enhancements and features for remote computing. XenApp Server is the third-party add-on for Microsoft's Windows Terminal Services, and it provides advanced remote access capabilities for system administrators. It interacts with the underlying architecture of Terminal Services to improve the remote application process.

Citrix has been a driving force behind Microsoft's development of remote access technologies. In the early years of server software development, remote access was a relatively low priority for Microsoft. In 1989, a small third-party company developed a remote access protocol named Independent Computing Architecture (ICA). In 1991, they shipped their first product called Citrix Multi-User.

The field was a fairly niche market, and so Citrix decided to be bold. In 1992, they worked out a licensing agreement with Microsoft for their NT Server software. Over the next few years, they modified the underlying operating system (OS), and in 1995, they released their own OS, Citrix WinFrame.

Based on the NT Server 3.51 OS, WinFrame was in fact an entirely individual system. It incorporated proprietary Citrix technology such as the ICA protocol. It also allowed multiuser remote access in a way that Microsoft had never addressed. WinFrame was an excellent product given the times and the hardware. It was relatively stable, and provided a new level of accessibility to remote users.

Microsoft was never one to ignore a good possibility, so when they released their NT4.0 server software, they also began the process of creating their own multiuser remote application software. When Citrix went back to negotiate the license rights for the NT4.0 server platform, they were told about Microsoft's own plans for remote access.

It was a difficult time for Citrix. Without the license to Microsoft's technology, they could not create a version of their ICA technology compatible with NT4.0. Moreover, with Microsoft having decided to release their own remote access platform, they would lose the advantage of being the primary player in the marketplace. After some intense negotiations, Citrix and Microsoft came up with a partnership for the marketing and development of the Citrix MultiWin technology.

Microsoft incorporated the MultiWin Citrix technology in its release of Windows NT4.0 Terminal Services Edition while Citrix retained the rights to their ICA architecture. In addition, in conjunction with the release of NT 4.0 TSE, Citrix released a new version of their technology known as Citrix MetaFrame 1.0. MetaFrame 1.0 was an add-on technology that expanded the reach of NT4.0 TSE. NT4.0 TSE used RDP as its client technology, and had many holes that prevented many administrators from using it exclusively.

Citrix soon released MetaFrame 1.8 and various upgrades for it. They eventually expanded their support for Windows 2000 Server, and in 2000, they released Citrix MetaFrame XP. Microsoft changed their Terminal Server technology to become a service, and continued adding features to it in an attempt to fill the gaps that remained in Terminal Services.

When Citrix renamed their MetaFrame 1.8 software to MetaFrame XP, they also decided to provide three different levels of the software so that administrators could purchase only the features they needed. And in 2002, Microsoft and Citrix signed a new licensing agreement that gave Citrix access to key underlying Windows software for the development of their next MetaFrame release, XenApp Server.

With the release of Windows Server 2003, Microsoft again expanded their remote access technology platform to try to fill the gaps in Terminal Services. Citrix continues to restructure and acquire more technologies that will position them as a valued add-on for Microsoft. The rest of this chapter deals with the features of XenApp Server (Citrix Presentation Server 4.5), and the advantages it gives you over using just Terminal Services.

Understanding the XenApp Server Architecture

Citrix XenApp Server uses server farms to organize and manage servers. This allows you to manage many settings as a unit, rather than apply them individually to each machine. Servers in a farm all connect to the same data store, and generally have some features in common that makes grouping them together logical. Farms also provide a method for application publishing. Publishing an application means to provide it to remote users from the server installation. Within the farm model are the two technologies that make the on-demand enterprise function: Independent Management Architecture (IMA) and Independent Computing Architecture (ICA).

XenApp Server Farms

Users and administrators alike quickly realize the value of a Citrix XenApp server in delivering applications for a variety of needs. However, it does not take long for one of these servers to reach its capacity. Administrators then bring other Citrix servers online to provide the needs for the new users. The problem seems to be solved, yet as new servers are added to the network, another issue arises: It becomes increasingly complex for users to determine which server to use. In addition, administrators are faced with having to install multiple servers with a variety of applications, configuring sessions and users, and managing them.

Server farms simplify these issues. When a server farm is constructed, administrators can manage the entire set of Citrix XenApp servers from a single point. Printer drivers and applications can be easily deployed to all the servers at once. Users can connect directly to applications, without needing to know the location of an individual server.

Citrix XenApp 4.5 Server —in particular, Enterprise version—was intended for a scalable server farm. Not only does it load balance user sessions across multiple servers and provide redundancy; it also provides easy administration capabilities. The first step toward installing a Citrix XenApp server farm involves understanding and designing one that will scale up with the network over time. Proper planning and project management can play a critical role in the success of your implementation. In addition, administrators must be capable of managing the farm after the installation to ensure that it remains reliable.

A server "farm" is typically a collection of servers that provide a similar service or function. The collection provides increased computing power over a single large system as well as a level of redundancy not usually available in any single PC-based server installation. The farm provides OS redundancy. Servers can provide processor, hard disk, power supply, and disk controller redundancy but very little in the operating system area. By farming like servers, even if the OS crashes, customers are still served. The customer might lose the current session when a server crashes, but he or she can immediately reconnect to another server and receive the same environment as before.

Windows 2003 Terminal Services can be placed into a physical farm and set to be accessed by methods such as Windows Load Balancing (WLB) or Domain Name Service (DNS) round robin. These methods are not truly load balanced, nor can the entire farm be managed as a single entity. WLB does not allow for all the metrics to be taken into consideration in determining the least busy server. DNS round robin will provide the address of a server that is offline, resulting in attempted connections to a server that is not available.

By adding Citrix XenApp Server to Windows 2003 Terminal Service, server farms can be managed from a single interface and provide redundancy and truer load-balancing services to users. XenApp Server also allows administrators to take advantage of features such as published applications, seamless Windows, multiple-platform clients, the Citrix Web Interface, and local drive and printer access. A single server farm can span an entire enterprise or can be broken up into smaller farms for localized management. This flexibility allows administrators to choose to centralize licensing and management by creating a single corporate farm or to distribute licensing and management to regional or departmental administrators.

Implementing a Server Farm

A well thought out design is key to a successful implementation. Before starting to build a new farm or upgrade an existing farm, take the time to document, evaluate, and design your new environment. Even though most deployments do not follow even the best plans to the letter, having a plan will ensure that your deployment does not stray too far from your intentions.

There are two basic approaches to designing your farm architecture. A single server farm centralizes functions and makes administration easier for a central IT group. Multiple farms can distribute the administrative load based on business or geographic needs. The next sections discuss the pros, cons, and concerns of each type of architecture.

A Single Server Farm

Creating a single farm carries many advantages, but it also presents some disadvantages. Based on your organization's needs, a single farm could be the best option. This architecture centralizes your management point and enables administrators to control the entire enterprise Citrix farm from a single console.

Advantages of a single Citrix server farm include the following:

- **Single point of administration** One Presentation Server Console can be used to administer the entire enterprise.

- **Pooled licenses** Your entire enterprise can use one pool of licenses. This is especially useful in "follow the sun" organizations in which, as users in one time zone log off, users in other time zones log on.

Disadvantages of a single Citrix server farm include:

- Increased Independent Management Architecture (IMA) traffic: A single farm with multiple sites must be set up into zones. Each zone has a data collector, and each data collector communicates all user logon, logoff, published application changes, and server load information to every other data collector in the farm. These communications can create a significant amount of WAN traffic.

- Replicated data stores: Citrix recommends having replicated data stores at each location to reduce latency and WAN traffic.

Multiple Server Farms

Multiple farms can be employed in both single- and multiple-site scenarios. Multiple farms can benefit a single site by providing departmentalized licensing and administration. The use of multiple farms also diversifies the fault vulnerability in the event of an IMA issue or data store corruption that would otherwise cause an interruption in service.

Multiple farms can also solve problems related to numerous Active Directory domains. Each domain could have its own Citrix farm, thus eliminating some of the trust issues associated with having a single farm span multiple domains.

Planning a Server Farm Project

The success of any Citrix XenApp Server farm depends heavily on a good project plan. Each step needs to be outlined, assigned, tracked, and refined throughout the life of the project. Be sure to include documentation in your project plan. Yes, most techies cringe at the thought of documentation, which is often out of date by the time it's printed and put in the binder, but it is a valuable tool to provide a baseline and insight into the thought processes of the planning and implementation teams. Most administrators do not fully appreciate the value of creating and maintaining good documentation until they inherit a legacy system containing a complicated setup with no documentation or even hand-scratched notes on how the system was installed, the application compatibility scripts that had to be written (much less what they do or why), or the system policies that were set or custom templates that were created. Now that we've described the nightmare, do everything possible to avoid passing this situation on to others.

Documentation doesn't take that long nor is it difficult to create. Simply sit down at the server with a laptop next to you and your favorite word processor open. Write down each step you take. Make screen shots of dialogs and insert them into the document. Copy and paste any scripts or policy templates that you modify or create, with a brief explanation of why the modifications were necessary.

Most technology projects follow the same process. First you have a business requirement that drives a vision. The vision gives rise to the method with which the company seeks to satisfy the business requirement with a process and/or technology change. This leads into the design stage. Design further leads to testing and development. Then you run a pilot and finally a full production deployment of the process and/or technology. At some point in the future, another business requirement could cause you to begin this process all over again, so it is somewhat circular in nature.

When you begin designing your Citrix environment—that is, the server and the network on which it will communicate—you should already have one or more business requirements and a vision that the Citrix server should satisfy. You should do your best to ensure that these business requirements are considered whenever you make a decision.

For example, if your business requirement is to eliminate viruses on the network and you discovered that they are being spread mainly through users bringing in diskettes from outside your network, you could deploy Citrix XenApp to control the spread of viruses—but that strategy would be successful only if you did not have diskette drives mapped to the Citrix XenApp sessions and/or if you replaced PCs with terminals that did not include diskette drives.

On the other hand, if your business requirement is to enable access to a SQL application on a global network on which slow, unreliable links are located in places such as Barrow, Alaska, and Moscow, Russia, you could deploy Citrix XenApp to provide a near-real-time access to the application. However, that would be successful only if you placed the Citrix XenApp server on the same subnet as the SQL server (or on a well-connected subnet in the same location, if the same subnet is not feasible) and if you provided dialup lines to back up those unreliable network links.

No matter what, you should always let the business requirement drive the technology vision. If you do, your project will be perceived as successful.

The IMA Data Store

The first component of the IMA is the data store. The data store is used to store information within the Citrix XenApp server farm that remains relatively static. Items such as published applications, administrator names and permissions, and server listings are among a few found in the data store. In earlier releases, these items were typically stored in the registry of each Citrix MetaFrame 1.8 server. With the new IMA, the ability to centrally manage and maintain this information became critical.

Based on standard database formats, the data store can reside on a Citrix XenApp server or on a dedicated host. A single data store is used for each individual server farm. Currently, three databases are supported for use with Citrix XenApp: Microsoft Access, Microsoft SQL, and Oracle. Table 3.2 describes each database format and situations in which each should be utilized.

Table 3.2 Data Store Usage

Scale	Servers	Applications	Databases
Small	1–50	1–100	MS Access, MS SQL, Oracle
Medium to large	51–100	100–1000	MS SQL, Oracle
Large to enterprise	100+	1000+	MS SQL, Oracle

Another factor to consider about the data store is the access mode. Citrix XenApp offers two modes of access to connect to the central database managing the data store for a farm: direct mode and indirect mode. In direct-mode access, servers located within the farm talk directly to the database hosting the data store. For example, if you set up a dedicated Microsoft SQL server to act as the data store, all servers communicate to the database using direct mode. Direct mode can also be used when databases are stored on the same server as Citrix XenApp. Direct mode is used primarily when Microsoft SQL or Oracle is used as the database product.

NOTE

Disk space requirements for the data store are approximately 20 MB for every 100 servers.

Indirect mode uses a Citrix XenApp server to communicate with the data store. This occurs when the IMA server requests access to the data store on behalf of another server. Indirect mode was designed to work around the limitations of Microsoft Access. When multiple users (or servers, in this case) try to access the same records, Microsoft Access has limited capability to prevent issues from arising. Indirect mode limits communication from multiple users by allowing a single server to communicate directly with the database on behalf of other servers. Indirect mode is most commonly used with data store implementations using Microsoft Access.

During installation of XenApp, you select the access mode you want.

NOTE

With the availability of three solutions for the data store, how do you tell which one best fits your environment? Microsoft Access was designed for very small server farms consisting of a few servers or very few published applications. Microsoft SQL and Oracle were designed for medium-sized to large enterprise server farms. SQL and Oracle are generally recommended, especially if you're using advanced tools such as Load Manager, Installation Manager, or Resource Manager.

When choosing between Microsoft SQL and Oracle, select the one your organization is most comfortable with. Both solutions provide scalability for large farms, but the staff at your organization might have no experience with one of the database formats. For example, if you primarily use Microsoft SQL within your organization, Oracle would probably not be the best choice.

Local Host Cache

The next component to consider is the *local host cache* (LHC). The LHC is a partial copy of the data store database that every XenApp server maintains locally to the server itself (hence the name). The partial local replica is maintained in MS Access format and is encrypted, similar to the information in the data store database. There are many reasons why a XenApp server would want to maintain a partial copy of the data store database locally; however, two reasons sum up most of the logic behind this decision. First, by maintaining a local partial replica of the data store database, the XenApp server could continue running based on the configuration that is last received from the data store. Therefore, in the event of failure of the server that houses the actual data store, the farm could continue functioning for up to 96 hours (based on a hard limit imposed by Citrix). The second reason is all about performance. Servers may need to frequently consult the information in the data store database. In a larger farm, this could lead to a bottleneck at the server housing the database. Therefore, with a partial replica being available locally, the IMA service can review those settings and synchronize in the background with the "master" copy of the data store. This provides much greater scalability and much less reliance on the server housing the data store database. By default, XenApp server maintains this database in the path C:\Program Files\Citrix\ Independent Management Architecture in a file named MF20.MDB.

IMA Zones

The next component associated with the IMA is a *zone*. Zones represent administrative boundaries for managing servers within a Citrix XenApp farm. Multiple zones are common in a single farm and are used to designate boundaries for servers within a farm. The most common boundary used with zones is geographic location. For example, you might have five servers in one location and three servers in another. The first location may participate in one zone while the other location is configured for another zone. Zones provide two primary functions:

- Efficiently manage data from all servers within a zone
- Distribute updates to servers in a timely manner

> **NOTE**
>
> By default, the TCP/IP subnet is used as the zone name. For example, a server with TCP/IP address of 10.9.4.2 with a mask of 255.255.255.0 would reside in zone 10.9.4.0.

The IMA Data Collector

Data collectors are another component of the IMA. The data collector serves a function similar to that of the data store. They are used to manage information that changes frequently, such as current sessions, active licenses, and server and application load values within a zone. For example, when the server load values change for a Citrix XenApp server, it notifies the data collector of this change. Similar to the ICA browser in older versions of Citrix MetaFrame, the data collector acts as the central point of information when clients connect to your server farm.

Every zone with a server farm consists of one data collector. Although multiple Citrix XenApp servers can be configured to operate in this role, only one can be active within a zone at any time.

To ensure this system operates correctly, an election process occurs. Based on a preset list of criteria, the election determines the most eligible server within the farm to take this role. An election starts if any of the following events occur:

- Zone configuration is modified.
- A server within the farm is started.
- The current data collector becomes unavailable.
- The QUERYDC utility is used to force an election.

If an election occurs, a set of criteria is used to determine which server will become the data collector. Any servers matching the first item are selected. If multiple servers match the first item, they are selected by the second item, and so forth. The criteria for selecting the data collector are:

1. What is the Citrix XenApp version? (Citrix XenApp always "beats" older versions.)
2. What is the current ranking as defined in the Presentation Server Console?
3. What host ID is randomly chosen at installation?

Although you cannot alter items 1 and 3, the preference can be modified to ensure that the designated servers win the election process. You have the option within the XenApp Server Console to designate the preference for data collectors. By default, the first server installed into the Citrix XenApp server farm is set to Most Preferred. All other servers are set to Default Preference.

Configuring & Implementing...

Setting Data Collector Preference

Follow these steps to set your Data Collector preferences:

1. Click on Start menu, All Programs > Citrix > Management Console and then click on the Presentation Server Console.
2. Right-click on Farm, and then click on Properties.
3. Click on **Zones**.
4. Expand the Zone on the right hand side.
5. Click on the Citrix Presentation server you would like to adjust the preference level on, and then click on **Set Election Preference ...**
6. Choose appropriate election preference settings as explained above.
7. Click **OK** and then click **OK** again.
8. Close the **Presentation Server Console** and reboot the server.

Bandwidth Requirements for a Server Farm

One of the key reasons for using zones is to manage the way that bandwidth is consumed within your Citrix XenApp server farm. The optimization of network bandwidth can be an ongoing effort. To manage the way in which your network links are affected by the use of Citrix XenApp, you must understand the normal bandwidth usage parameters.

In several scenarios, bandwidth utilization is key. For example, server-to-data-store communication must occur successfully for users to be able to locate resources throughout the farm. In addition, processes such as data collector elections must complete without latency, or your user base could be affected.

Server-to-Data-Store Communication

When a server starts and communicates with the server farm, it must query the data store to inquire about items such as published applications, other servers, and licenses. The amount of traffic generated by these updates is directly dependent on the amount of information included. As the number of servers or published applications increases within the farm, so does the traffic required to update a server. The following formula represents the amount of traffic associated with a server update at startup:

```
KB = 275 + (5 * Servers) + (0.5 * Apps) + (92 * Print Drivers)
```

For example, in a case in which you have a server farm with four servers, 12 published applications, and six print drivers, you would calculate the bandwidth used as follows:

KB = 275 + (5 * **4**) + (0.5 * **12**) + (92 * **6**)

KB = 275 + (**20**) + (**6**) + (**552**)

KB = 275 + (**578**)

KB = **853**

Data Collector Communication

Another item that can consume a fair bit of bandwidth for server farm communications is the data collector. Data collectors must manage updates between servers within a zone. Although they only send changes during a normal update process, at times complete updates are required. For example, if a new server comes online, a complete update must occur so that the server is aware of the information it requires. The following formula is used to calculate the bandwidth used for a complete data collector update to a server:

```
Bytes = 11000 + (1000 * Con) + (600 * Discon) + (350 * Apps)
```

In a case in which you have a server with 20 connected sessions, four disconnected sessions, and nine published applications, you would calculate the bandwidth used as shown here:

Bytes = 11,000 + (1,000 * **20**) + (600 * **4**) + (350 * **9**)

Bytes = 11,000 + (**20,000**) + (**2400**) + (**3150**)

Bytes = 11,000 + (**25,550**)

Bytes = **36,550**or **36.55 KB**

Listener Ports

One of the key components of terminal services and Citrix XenApp is the use of *listener ports*. Listener ports play a key role and must be carefully managed; without them, clients cannot access your terminal server. Listener ports work in cooperation with internal system components and client connections.

When a servers boots up, the terminal services components start the listener process. The listener service monitors for new client connections and manages the idle sessions. Once the listener service is operating, the session manager starts the idle ports to allow incoming connections.

Idle sessions start the core Windows process required for connecting clients. Once the process is completed, idle sessions wait for incoming connections. When a client connection is made, the idle session is turned over to the incoming client. The incoming client then continues the logon process and begins the session. Another idle process is then started and waits for new client connections. When each connection comes into the server, the server assigns it a session ID, and the connection is started.

> **NOTE**
>
> To add listener ports, you must modify the following registry key:
>   HKEY_LOCAL_MACHINE\System\CurrentControlSet\Control\Terminal Server\
> IdleWinStationPoolCount
>   Citrix recommends adding only what is necessary, because additional listener ports can degrade performance. Increase this counter from two to the number of listener ports needed.

Independent Management Architecture

IMA provides the basis for Citrix XenApp Server. It is a centralized management subsystem that allows you to define and control the elements of your server farm. XenApp servers communicate with each other using a newer framework service that Citrix introduced with Presentation Server 1.0 (also known as MetaFrame XP 1.0), Independent Management Architecture (IMA). IMA is described as a framework service due to the modular design the developers used to create the service. Each "module" or subsystem provides specific functionality within the farm. For instance, the Citrix Licensing subsystem assists in enforcing licensing, and the Program Neighborhood subsystem provides for application set enumeration based on user credentials (among other features). IMA is, in its simplest form, a collection of subsystems constituted by a series of DLLs and EXEs, tied to together under a single service. IMA could be considered the backbone of Citrix communication. IMA is also the name of the protocol used for this communication and occurs in two forms. Server-to-server communication occurs over TCP port 2512. When we as administrators open the Presentation Server Management Console (PMC) and "connect" to a particular server, the PMC-to-server communication occurs over TCP port 2513. In essence, it is the technology that allows you to group servers based on design decisions and not necessarily location.

Independent Computing Architecture

ICA is the communications protocol used by the ICA client software and the XenApp servers. It provides optimized transport of data between the devices, and can function even on low-bandwidth connections such as slow dial-up. ICA works by essentially piggybacking on top of other protocols such as TCP/IP. The TCP/IP header encapsulates the ICA packet, and on the receiving end, the ICA software handles the functions required. ICA can be run over several other protocols such as UDP and IPX/SPX.

At its heart, ICA intercepts and transports screens from the server that a published application runs on to the client PC. It then takes the user's return input and transmits it back to the server for processing. The data is transmitted on standard network protocols such as TCP between the client and the server.

On the client side, ICA intercepts user's interaction with the presented application and sends it back to the server. This includes mouse movement, clicks, typing, and anything that would cause a screen refresh. The ICA client is a minimal application, and requires few resources on a workstation to run. Citrix provides ICA clients for a variety of technology platforms.

The ICA client works by queuing and transmitting anything the user does to affect the state of the application. The transmission rate can be modified on the client side to happen with each mouse movement or keystroke, or to queue up a certain amount of data before sending. If you use the queue feature, be aware that it does impact the seamless feel of the session. Because the keystrokes and mouse movements are queued, the user will not have instant indication on the screen that they happened.

The ICA client also can cache frequently used graphics such as icons and menu items. This improves the client response because they do not have to be downloaded from the server each time they would occur. The client can simply call them from the cache. The size of the cache can be set by the administrator to limit the impact on local storage.

The Future and Beyond: Capabilities of XenApp Server

XenApp Server is a valuable extension for the Windows Terminal Services environment. Although Microsoft has improved on Terminal Services through various upgrades and hotfixes, it still lacks some of the enterprise functionality and ease of use that XenApp Server can provide. Here are some highlights of XenApp Server:

- Enterprise-level management and scalability

- Improved load-balancing criteria

- Published icons that link to server-side software

- Local application interaction with remote files

- Remote software updates and deployment

- Improved printer compatibility and creation

- Real-time monitoring of both XenApp Server and Terminal Services components in a single view

- Resource monitoring for historical data and reporting

Additionally, Citrix uses its own proprietary technology to improve the overall remote experience for users. Together with the Terminal Services architecture, XenApp Server can provide a complete end-to-end solution for almost any deployment.

XenApp Server Version Information

XenApp Server is packaged in three different versions. In theory, this allows administrators to purchase only the tools they require for their environment. In reality, many administrators simply purchase the highest tier to gain access to all of the application functionality. The decision about which version you will purchase is driven more by the feature set you require, and generally not the label. Table 3.3 lists the different XenApp Server editions.

Table 3.3 XenApp Server Versions

Version	Features
Standard Edition	Designed for the small farm environment, the Standard Edition provides many of the common features required by administrators.
Advanced Edition	Provides small and medium-sized installations with advanced scalability and manageability software such as workstation control, session reliability, and advanced Speedscreen acceleration techniques.
Enterprise Edition	Designed for the most demanding installations, Enterprise Edition gives administrators access to all of the tools Citrix provides. The most important improvements are the addition of Resource Management and Installation Management technologies.

Management and Monitoring

Citrix XenApp Server provides a significant level of management and monitoring capabilities for your remote application access. Within the Presentation Server Console (PSC) and Access Management Console (AMC) tool, administrators have access to almost every function of monitoring and reporting they might need. These tools allows for role definition, which gives users and groups limited rights within the CMC and AMC itself.

Management can be handled on an individual application level, individual server level, or by groups of applications and servers. You can perform hierarchal grouping to keep large environments organized into easily defined areas. You can also connect directly to your servers as either a remote user or a console user. The PSC and AMC give you total control over your XenApp Server architecture. For example, within these consoles, you could look up where a user is connected. Once you have him located, you could message that user to log off. If the user's session was hung, you could disconnect it and log it off yourself. You could even remote to that user's connection and shadow him to see what the problem was. These consoles would also warn you that a server is down, or that an application is exceeding the threshold levels you set for it.

If you have Citrix's Resource Manager software installed, the AMC can provide real-time status information on your servers and applications. Counters can be set that will alert the monitors in a variety of areas, and can provide paging and e-mail escalation of issues that occur in your farm. If configured correctly, Resource Manager can also provide statistical reporting on everything from individual user access to farm-wide application statistics. It can also provide real-time graphs and data about the current status of the farm.

Additionally, Citrix provides plug-ins for popular third-party monitoring programs such as Microsoft Operations Manager. This allows you to extend your monitoring to data center staff without the need to provide the AMC and the PSC. You can also use other third-party tools such as Crystal Reports to access the Citrix data and provide staff with precise reporting information.

Beyond the AMC/PSC and plug-ins, the Software Development Kit (SDK) from Citrix provides even more ideas for tools that you can deploy in your environment. In addition, several popular Web sites exist that have even more user-developed scripts and tools to give you more granular control over your servers and user community. Today, there is a wealth of resources available to Citrix administrators from both official and user-driven sources.

Application Publishing

Perhaps the key feature of XenApp server is the ability to publish applications to your user community. When an application is published on a XenApp server, it becomes available as an icon to the users and groups defined for it. This can be displayed as an application within a Web page, within users' client software, or even pushed to their desktop.

Application publishing opens up a whole new world for remote computing. Because you can provide a single point of access for all the remote applications, it creates the impression that they are local for the user. Remote and local apps can be blended on the same desktop, and can be managed through appropriate policies and groups. Applications can be launched from different servers without the users realizing that they are touching more than one machine. These multiple connections only consume a single Citrix license as long as the applications are in the same farm.

Along with application publishing, administrators can also load-balance their applications across multiple servers in the farm (or even multiple farms if architected correctly). With a load-balanced environment, administrators can plan for increases in user capacity, take servers out of the farm for upgrades and repairs without impacting the users, and provide fault tolerance in case of server failure.

Published applications are executed entirely at the server level, and the screen data is transmitted back to the clients. Other client components, referred to as *channels*, can also be enabled between the client and the server. Typical channels are local printers, sound, and COM or USB port mapping. With these channels, an administrator can create the illusion that the application is executing locally.

Printer Management

Printer management is also a key function of Citrix's toolset. Keeping track of print drivers in a remote environment is a headache for any administrator; drivers can cause hang-ups and crashes, and poorly implemented print strategies can consume both time and bandwidth. Citrix XenApp server gives you the ability to define specific driver mappings, push driver sets to servers that do not have them installed, and define settings for Citrix's Universal Print Driver (UPD). The UPD allows clients that connect with a printer that is not in the allowed list to use the universal driver instead. This driver gives a decent range of functionality to most printers commonly used by clients.

Printer mapping can be controlled in a number of other ways as well. It can be defined in individual user properties for their Terminal Services settings in Active Directory. It can also be defined on a per-connection basis on each server. In addition, using Citrix's policy management, an administrator can also define printer mapping for role-based users.

Within the PSC, it is possible to check each server and see what print drivers are installed. If one is missing, it can be pushed to that server in a relatively quick fashion. Your servers can also be set to propagate any and all print drivers amongst themselves without the need for you to constantly monitor them. Keep in mind, though, that if a rogue print driver gets in to this process, you could spread it to every server in your farm.

Deploying Service Packs and Hotfixes

Keeping your servers up to date is another problem farm administrators frequently face. With the constant stream of hotfixes coming from both Microsoft and Citrix, managing your patch levels and guaranteeing deployment is an important part of your day-to day-activities. Citrix tries to bridge that gap by providing packaging technology to administrators known as Installation Manager (IM).

IM allows administrators to package applications, registry changes, and even hotfixes for deployment. It can create entirely new packages, or use those already created by other install programs such as Windows Installer files with an MSI extension. These applications can be imported into the IM database and executed from a common share.

The benefit in using IM is control over the distribution process from the same tool as your administrative tasks. Servers can be grouped within the IM tool to provide managed distribution of applications. The distribution process can be scheduled to occur at specific times, allowing the gradual rollout of new software and patches. IM is a useful tool for Citrix administrators to keep servers up to date and in good order.

Security Improvements with XenApp Server

A significant advantage to using remote technology such as Presentation Server is that it provides an increased level of security for both users and administrators. Because of the way access is designed, both the server and client machines are safe from data interception both inside and outside your networks. Here are some features of XenApp security:

- **SecureICA** SecureICA allows you to encrypt the ICA transmissions between the client and server machines. Even if the encryption were broken, all the attacker would get is meaningless screen information.

- **Citrix Secured Sockets Layer (SSL) Relay** Usually used with smaller farms without the need for a demilitarized zone (DMZ). It does not provide end-to-end encryption between the servers and clients.

- **Citrix Secure Gateway** Using a gateway server provides complete encryption and firewall transversal. This is the most secure method for access with a public Internet site. It uses two-factor authentication and hides all internal IP address schemes from the user.

- **Virtual private network (VPN) solutions** A dedicated VPN solution is also a good way to provide security for your users. It provides a complete end-to-end tunnel between the user and server, and is the most secure method for access.

Because there is always an element of risk in allowing remote access, administrators should assess what their requirements are for security and plan appropriately. The best solution is always the one that limits exposure to risk from outside forces such as viruses and attackers. With good planning, a Citrix installation can be almost completely secure.

Beyond the security of the connection, there are other considerations for server administrators as well. By allowing or disallowing certain channels to connect, you can provide greater security to your network and servers. For instance, not allowing your users to map their local drives or clipboards will often prevent most virus attacks.

Still, for every feature you disallow, it becomes more of an inconvenience for your users. Often, administrators will be forced to choose between convenience and security. These choices are difficult, and need to be negotiated and explained to the user community.

How XenApp Server Fills the Gaps in Terminal Services

We've covered the basics of Microsoft Terminal Services and Citrix XenApp Server. They both offer an impressive feature set, and XenApp Server builds on top of the existing Terminal Services architecture. For some environments, Terminal Services alone might fill the needs for remote access. So why would you decide to choose XenApp Server over native Terminal Services?

The unfortunate fact is that Terminal Services has gaps. Despite years of design and upgrade, it still fails to perform some client-server tasks as well as XenApp can provide. For the rest of this chapter, we'll address where those gaps are and how XenApp Server fills them for you. We will then discuss the XenApp Server Installation.

Improvements in Terminal Services

Windows Server 2003 provides a number of improvements in Terminal Services capabilities over Server 2000. Microsoft has continued their commitment to improving the basic Terminal Services functionality, and with the improvements of Windows Server 2003, many administrators are considering only using Terminal Services. Citrix is a very useful product, but it is also an expensive one. When you consider licensing costs for Terminal Services Client Access Licenses (CALs), application licenses, and then XenApp license costs, it starts to add up to a lot of money.

The improvements that Windows Server 2003 provides lie chiefly in the area of its RDP client. The new RDP 5.2 protocol is thinner and now supports more virtual channels than ever before. RDP can now support clipboard, audio, printer, Component Object Model (COM), and Line Printer (LPT) mappings. It also provides full color depth to 24 bit at 1600×1200, and has clients across almost all platforms (Win32, Win16, DOS, Java, Macintosh, Linux, and others). Windows Server 2003 also supports technology such as smart cards for user authentication.

Windows Server 2003 also provides limited load-balancing capabilities and improved scalability. Load balancing in Windows Server 2003 is limited to node balancing only, which means that you can only balance the servers based on a narrow set of conditions and only with other comparable servers. Windows Server 2003 allows for more users per box than Server 2000 did, and gives remote management capabilities through the Windows Management Instrumentation (WMI) provider. New enhancements to roaming profiles, Group Policy Objects (GPOs), and application compatibility make Windows Server 2003 a valuable improvement over Windows 2000 Terminal Services.

So, Where Are the Gaps?

For all of the advances Windows Server 2003 has made, gaps do still exist. They are primarily in some client functionality, and more importantly with Terminal Services load balancing and application publishing processes. Citrix tries to fill these gaps to provide a reason for using their software.

Application-Level Improvements

Citrix has taken application publishing to a whole new level. With XenApp Server, administrators have the ability to create applications and publish them to specific groups or users. Although Terminal Services allows you to provide a simple redirect of the RDP client to specific applications on the terminal server, it does not provide direct application publishing. With XenApp Server, you gain the full capability of XenApps's publishing software.

Application publishing is an extremely valuable tool for administrators. When an application is published, your users are presented with an icon that corresponds to the program. That application is tied to an ICA file that contains the information needed for the client to connect to the application. This is everything from the security settings specified to the address information of the server that hosts the application.

Because application publishing gives your users a simple icon to launch a connection, it is much easier to integrate with their existing desktop. As mentioned before, you can provide this application to your users in several ways. Because the ICA client can integrate with your desktop, applications that are published to the users can be pushed to the desktop. This means that they will see an icon on the desktop that will appear to be a local application but will instead launch a remote connection.

Another method of providing applications is with the Citrix Program Neighborhood. The Program Neighborhood will display all of the icons published to a user in a single window, or separated into folders based on application groups. The administrator has complete control over the presentation of the applications, which require a single login for all applications to be displayed.

The third method is to use Citrix's Web technologies and provide the application icons through a Web interface. With Citrix's secure access technology and their Web interface software, you can design and present a Web page with all of your published applications. Users will see only the applications assigned to their ID, and those applications can again be grouped into folders by application suite.

Another advantage to application publishing in Citrix is the ability to use seamless windows. With a seamless window, there is nothing to indicate that the application is not running locally besides the small ICA icon in the taskbar. Users can interact with the application exactly as if it was running locally. They can maximize or minimize it, copy data to or from the application (assuming you have the clipboard channel enabled), and even use drag and drop to move data to and from the application.

Citrix Speedscreen

Both the RDP client and the ICA client use "thin" technology. This means that they are designed to be as streamlined as possible. The goal is to make the user feel like the application is actually being executed locally. This is relatively easy with simple applications, but applications that use many graphics (especially animated graphics) put a strain on the ICA channel. Not much compression can be done on these graphics to speed their presentation.

Citrix developed a proprietary technology called Speedscreen to help address this problem. It allows you to define some settings that improve the presentation speed of heavy graphics in applications. It is especially important with Internet browser applications. In XenApp Server (Presentation Server 4.5), Citrix has taken Speedscreen a step further.

The bane of Speedscreen has been streaming applications such as multimedia or flash animation. In XenApp Server, new virtual channels can be defined that allow you to stream the content untouched between the server and the client. This stream is outside the ICA channel, and can consume quite a bit of bandwidth.

Because the stream is being passed intact to the client, it does require that you have the appropriate codecs and client software installed to handle it. There is a significant trade-off here. The quality can be much better than accessing a streaming video that is being executed on the XenApp Server server itself. However, bandwidth concerns may make this an impossible choice.

XenApp Server also allows administrators the choice to use *lossy* compression, a JPEG-based compression scheme that can significantly reduce the size of graphics-laden material prior to transmission to the client. The client interpolates the missing data. In many situations, most clients will never know that lossy compression is being applied. It is not appropriate, however, for applications that require extremely accurate graphics representation.

Using this compression can speed up the client interaction significantly. Web pages with heavy graphics can load up to 10 times faster with compression enabled than without. Obviously, this solution would be less than ideal in situations where reference quality is needed for the graphics such as photo-editing, medical imaging, and so forth For instance, this author implemented a medical imaging package on a Citrix server for a radiology group. Although the images where huge and the load time was 10–15 seconds per image, it would not be appropriate to enable compression to speed up the connection. You wouldn't want your radiologist looking at anything but the highest quality pictures, would you?

Session Disconnections and Reliability

One of the drawbacks of allowing remote users access is the stability of the connection. When users connect to applications across a wide area network (WAN), latency and link reliability become a real concern. It doesn't do any good to provide all sorts of published applications if your users can't reliably access them. Moreover, when remote access is their only means of working, it becomes critical that their sessions are as reliable as possible.

Regardless of the steps you take, there will be hiccups in the connection. Unfortunately, RDP does not handle these hiccups particularly well. Sessions end up disconnected with no warning to the user, and information can be lost. When an RDP session drops to disconnect, it fades to a gray screen and attempts the reconnection process in the background. Citrix has implemented the auto-reconnect in a different fashion with the ICA client. There is no indication to the user that the link has failed, and to the user it looks like a seamless experience. When the session reconnects, it continues as if nothing happened.

Citrix also has implemented keep-alive technology between their clients and servers. A special keep-alive packet can be transmitted at a defined interval from the server to the client. This keep-alive packet does exactly what it says: it lets the client know that the link is still alive and well. By default, the packet is sent once every 60 seconds. This can be increased or decreased to meet your needs.

Configuring & Implementing...

Using the Keep-Alive Packet

The keep-alive settings can really improve the overall stability of your client sessions. If you maintain connections across a WAN, you will want to lower the default setting. Many administrators with high latency environments lower it to one second.

Yes, that does mean that a packet is sent every second to every client from each server to which they are connected. That might be a concern to your network team. However, the size of the packet is so small that the impact is nonexistent unless your network is already oversaturated. At one second, your disconnected sessions become much more manageable and can usually be traced to a significant network event.

Web Interface

As mentioned previously, Citrix provides a Web interface to their platform. This allows you to display a Web page to your users that contains icons for the applications published to their IDs. These applications can span the farm, or even multiple farms if configured correctly. The Web interface can be configured to run separately on a Web server in your DMZ, and secured with Citrix technologies such as Secure Gateway to provide complete encryption of the data between the client and server. Unfortunately, Terminal Services lacks these advanced features.

When users log in to the Web interface, they are presented with a page containing their application lists. This page can be customized if necessary, or can be left in the default state. Icons will be displayed in the Web interface in the same way they are shown in the Program Neighborhood, complete with folders.

When the user clicks on an icon, an ICA template file is generated and the Citrix client is called. The template file contains all the data required for the Citrix client to make the connection to the published application. This can include color depth, security settings, address schemes, and so forth. If you are using Web Interface and Secure Gateway, your gateway server(s) function as a tunnel through which all traffic flows. Using session tickets and security keys, the integrity of the information is maintained in a secure fashion.

Performance Issues

Microsoft has improved the speed of the RDP 5.2 client significantly. It is now on par with the speed of the ICA protocol, which is a big step forward. ICA maintains its advantage, however, in dealing with the virtual channels. Because of the advances that Citrix continues to make with the ICA protocol and related technologies, in many situations it could still be called "faster." For instance, with its new graphics acceleration and compression technology, pages can load up to 10 times faster in ICA than in RDP.

Printing through ICA using the universal client is usually going to be less bandwidth intensive than the local printer mapping method used by RDP. Because print jobs can cause significant bandwidth consumption, it is a good idea to pay attention to your users' printing habits. Citrix also allows you to engage bandwidth throttling for printers so that they do not lag the sessions of everyone else connected to the server.

As mentioned earlier, Speedscreen technology improves the performance of graphics-intensive applications and Web pages. By using Speedscreen's compression technology, application response can be significantly faster on an ICA connection as opposed to RDP. You can also use the streaming functionality to provide unaltered streams to your users.

Load Balancing

The last major improvement that Citrix provides over Terminal Services is the ability to load balance in a variety of ways. Microsoft's load-balancing technology is entirely dependent on node-to-node balancing. It is network-based only, and to be most effective requires the expensive Windows Server 2003 Enterprise Edition. It also is limited to 32 nodes at most. That is a lot of expense to achieve a limited load-balancing functionality.

Citrix handles load balancing differently than Microsoft does. Any application that is published to multiple servers can be load balanced between them, and the administrator can choose the method of load balancing. Default counters include CPU load, memory usage, and number of connected users. Far more granular counters can be set that allow you to customize load balancing on everything from an application level to a server utilization level.

When an application is load balanced and a user requests a session, XenApp Server will look at the current load information for every server defined as part of the load-balanced environment for that application. It will then assign the user to the server with the least utilization as defined by the load-balancing parameters. If a user launches additional applications, the load-balancing technology will try to provide them from the same server to prevent the need for multiple logins.

Because administrators have such advanced control over the load-balancing functionality, it is far easier to use than Microsoft's implementation. Even if you leave it at the default counters, it provides a level of load balancing that is tough to beat for the price. Citrix has a definite advantage when it comes to load-balanced servers and applications.

Planning for XenApp Server Deployment

Planning the deployment of Citrix XenApp Server is a very in-depth process. Since XenApp Server and the underlying Terminal Services platform will be required in many deployments to integrate into nearly every process an organization may have, careful consideration and forethought must be given as to how best to introduce the technology. As with any major initiative undertaken in our current information technology shops, much thought is given on how to provide the greatest chance for success of new deployments that leverage as many features of the new products being introduced as possible, while reducing risk to the current environment—and doing all this as inexpensively as possible. Careful planning is frequently the difference between a successful implementation and a failed deployment. Careful planning can be the difference between happy users and unhappy ones, as it can affect the performance of the overall network even if we are only conducting a project on one aspect of the network. This is a very serious issue.

Hardware Planning

Hardware planning is the process of selecting and testing the actual computer hardware from which our Windows Server 2003-based Citrix XenApp servers will operate. Hardware planning is a cyclical operation. Typically, the process involves selecting hardware that is compatible with the operating system, estimating the size of the servers required and then performing adequate load testing. Load testing, or stress testing, involves loading the server with sessions until a bottleneck is reached. Correct the bottleneck and then retest. Repeat this process as necessary until the desired number of connections per server is reached or you have exhausted the capacity of the hardware. The last step would be to plan for future growth, so scale your hardware with an eye on what would be expected of this solution six months, 12 months, and two years from today. We are going to look at hardware planning from an architect's viewpoint. We will look at the "big picture" pieces such as horizontal vs. vertical scaling and platform deployment options.

Horizontal vs. Vertical Scaling

The argument as to whether it is better to scale up or scale out our Citrix XenApp server farms is nearly as old as the concept of server-based computing itself. Scaling up is the process of servicing more user sessions on the same hardware or increasing session density within the server through internal upgrades, such as four processors instead of two. Scaling out is the process of servicing more user sessions by adding more physically or logically separate servers to accommodate an increase in user session load. For a given number of user sessions, is it better to service them on more "smaller" servers or fewer "larger" servers? The argument arose shortly after Citrix introduced the Load-Balancing Option License for WinFrame nearly a decade ago. Today, load balancing is built into all versions of Citrix XenApp Server except Standard (or "S"). We should consider the "type" of session that our users will leverage. Accessing the farm from an internal ICA thin client will require less resources and planning typically than external access.

The ability to service user session load across more servers, or scaling out, has its advantages. Lower user session density on a given server translates to less impacted user sessions in the event of hardware failure. This also allows for greater flexibility during hardware or software maintenance windows, again with fewer users impacted. However, there are disadvantages to scaling out.

More servers with lower user session densities mean more servers to license and maintain. More power requirements, more rack space, more components to replace when they fail, more Windows Server 2003 licenses to purchase—in general, just more to support and maintain. Increased cost in both hard and soft dollars, due to these factors, can make scaling out prohibitively expensive.

The flip side of higher user session densities on fewer, larger servers also has certain advantages. Less hardware to support and maintain, possibly less rack space, probably fewer Windows Server 2003 licenses to purchase, and overall, better utilization of software and hardware costs through the economies of scale.

The argument seems on the surface to be decidedly one-sided. Scaling up is the way to go, or so it seems. In the cruel, unforgiving reality of a production deployment, however, scaling out nearly always wins the day over scaling up. There are several reasons for this, but really none is "logically based." One would think that a four or quad processor server would be cheaper than two dual processor servers, when in fact that is usually not the case. A typical 2 U rack-mount Dual Xeon server with 4 GB of memory costs about 1/3 to 1/4 as much as a typical 4 U rack-mount Quad Xeon server with 8 GB of memory. Therefore, from a hardware standpoint, you can buy two to four times the number of dual processor servers as you can quad processor servers. For those of you who are interested, eight-way processor servers are even more skewed. Vendors produce even fewer eight-way servers than quads, so the economies of scale are even at a greater loss. Hopefully, money will not be the determining factor in the long run. A single eight-way processor server simply doesn't have the "oomph" that four dual-processor servers have.

The second issue with scaling up instead of out is due to design considerations within the operating system that is installed on the target hardware. Terminal Services' purpose in life is to "virtualize" a desktop computer for the remote user session. A typical desktop workstation contains a single processor, and hopefully enough memory for the operating system and an adequate amount of memory remaining for the applications that a single user would use. If the workstation processor becomes overwhelmed due to the demand the user places on the system, overall performance only affects the single user of that workstation. If we take the user desktop environment and "virtualize" it via a Terminal Services session, we can see how this can compound the problem. We can look further into this scaling discussion by comparing the differences in *roles* that can be placed on a given server. A typical terminal server will have many more active processes running in the operating system than the same server hardware functioning as a mail or database server. To expound upon this point further, consider a typical Windows Server 2003 in the role of domain controller running on a dual processor server with 4 GB of memory. The domain controller has roughly 30 processes actively competing for the hardware resources at any given time. That same server functioning as a terminal server may have thousands of processes competing for the resources at any given point. Now, one could argue that the single process, WINWORD.EXE, for a user executing Microsoft Word on a terminal server has far less impact on a server than the single process NETLOGON.EXE running on the domain controller to facilitate the authentication of the domain it services. Therein lays the crux of the matter. Typically, it is not the single process that causes the load on the terminal server, it is the juggling act that the operating system must maintain to service the user sessions as evenly and quickly as possible. Occasionally, however, that single process *may* impact the overall performance of all user sessions on the server if the process demands a disproportionate amount of system resources either through user action or faulty application design. The result is that during planning, we as architects must plan for normal load that a server would incur during typical operations. We must also plan for the occasions when abnormal load is introduced to the server or server farm.

NOTE

The ability to perform load balancing at the user session level is provided as a base function of the operating system in Windows Server 2003 called Windows Load Balancing Service (WLBS, previously known as Network Load Balancing). Citrix XenApp Server Advanced and Enterprise editions provide much greater control over load balancing through techniques Citrix developed years ago for larger WinFrame server farms. Today, larger Terminal Services implementations leverage the powerful load-balancing features of Citrix XenApp Server due primarily to the greater degree of control and lack of certain noted limitations of the WLBS.

To assist us in planning for and selecting the appropriate hardware for our Citrix XenApp Server farm, we must explore some of the possible bottlenecks that can occur in a typical XenApp Server deployment. The following list presents basic information for consideration and is not an exhaustive compilation of all potential scalability concerns for terminal servers. Primarily, the following list of bottlenecks is to aid in selecting a hardware platform through the basic components of that platform, namely central processing unit (CPU), memory, disks, network interface cards (NICs), and the limitations of the operating system. An exhaustive pilot should be conducted to determine the baseline for a given server platform prior to introducing that platform into production.

CPU performance obviously has the greatest impact on user perception of performance during periods of intense processor utilization on the server. When users start a session on a XenApp server, there is a great deal of processor time required to complete the authentication, apply the group policy objects, run the various login scripts, redirect the appropriate user devices (for example, drives and printers), and present the user session with the desktop or published application. Similarly, during logoff, the processor resources of the server are in greater demand than during a typical session. Periods of disproportionate logons or logoffs can cause a greater load on the servers than at other times. These periods of peak login/logoffs are typically associated with shift changes and start of the business day times. Additionally, lunch period and formalized break times can cause similar resource utilization issues, due to the frequency of logon and logoff operations. Multiple higher performance processors can assist with overcoming some of these issues. A solid recommendation would be to start with a server capable of dual processors and perform very detailed testing of your specific application needs to determine if scaling up to a quad processor server (or higher) will provide further benefit.

We must also consider the relationship between memory and disk subsystems on the server. A server can become memory bound through a variety of ways. If user session density is too high, available memory will be too low to adequately service the user sessions on the server. If flaws in applications, system drivers, or the operating system are present, these memory leaks can result in a similar memory-bound situation. Insufficient memory can masquerade as other system resource issues. If a server is low on available memory, the operating system will *swap* information from physical memory to virtual memory in the page file of the operating system. A memory-bound server in this case may actually report excessive disk times indirectly caused by the low system memory situation. Additionally, you will see this performance issue arise if the page file is not configured to be large enough, is placed on a volume with limited space, or on a volume that does not use the NT File System (NTFS). Memory minimums should be considered when detailing the specifications of the server platform for testing or building your production solutions. Consider the first 256 MB to 512 MB of the server's memory as reserved for the operating system. An average user session today using Microsoft Office 2003-based products, Internet Explorer, and a few line-of-business applications can easily consume 64 MB to 128 MB of memory. With that being said, consider any "special" applications that you know are greater consumers of memory in your environment and plan accordingly.

Disk subsystems can be a challenge to diagnose and overcome. Typically, disk utilization should be low on Citrix XenApp server. The logic behind such an assertion is that Citrix XenApp servers typically access application data across the network and really shouldn't "store" information locally. The use of the network file shares translates into lower disk times, typically, for the XenApp servers. We have several options when it comes to selecting the disk subsystem for our servers. We have Integrated Drive Electronics (IDE), Small Computer Systems Interface (SCSI), Boot from storage area network (SAN), and solid-state memory drives from which to choose. Which is the best option? Which solution will produce the best bang for the buck? Let's consider IDE-based systems. IDE drives are very inexpensive compared to the other solutions. They typically don't require expensive controllers to run them, and the new Serial Advanced Technology Attachment (ATA) devices are bursting at 150 MB throughput. IDE sounds good on the surface, but in reality, the Achilles heel of this platform is also what makes it so affordable. IDE (whether Parallel ATA or Serial ATA) on a Windows platform only supports multiple operations when they are spread across multiple channels. On a terminal server, there will undoubtedly be multiple simultaneous read and write operations, thus exposing this limitation, so… IDE is out as an option for most.

SCSI disks with a hardware Redundant Array of Inexpensive Disks (RAID) controller typically provide the best cost to benefit ratio. SCSI (especially RAID) controllers support the multiple input/output requests that characterize a terminal server. SCSI-based RAID drive sets provide a vast improvement over IDE and ATA drive sets. The RAID controller (not the CPU and IDE chipset) controls all the disk operations. The RAID card controls the drives via its own on-board CPU and memory. This allows the server CPU(s) to continue servicing requests without wasting time reading and writing to disk. Think of the RAID control as the "administrative assistant" to the CPU(s). In addition to the performance benefits gained through SCSI-based RAID controllers, there is the obvious fault tolerance benefits gained from creating RAID 1 Mirrored Sets or RAID 5 Fault Tolerance stripes.

Boot-from-SAN and solid-state memory drives can be excellent solutions to environment-specific needs. Boot-from-SAN allows you to leverage your considerable investment in your SAN and lower the cost per server (since there would be no local disks) for implementing your terminal servers. Boot-from-SAN may, however, prove slower than some of the newer faster SCSI RAID-based hard drives and can be prohibitively expensive if the SAN doesn't already exist.

Solid-state memory drives have come a long way since their inception a couple of decades ago. A few companies today make random access memory (RAM) drives that fit into most standard hot-plug device slots. These devices, while a little pricier than conventional disks, provide amazing throughput and make for great solutions to disk-bound servers. If you have servers that are disk-bound, a RAM drive can go a long way to improving performance by reducing and in some cases eliminating this bottleneck.

Network bottlenecks can occur anytime an application that is executed by Citrix XenApp Server doesn't actually exist on the server itself. For instance, Microsoft Word will typically install locally on the XenApp server, but the data normally exists somewhere else on the network. This is even truer for client server applications such as Peoplesoft or SAP. While the bandwidth used by the sessions the server is hosting is relatively low, the network requirements for those sessions will be substantially higher. There are several ways to address this issue: teamed cards to increase available bandwidth, co-location of the application and data on the Citrix XenApp server, and multihomed servers with network connects that separate session bandwidth from application bandwidth.

Teaming network cards for redundancy is almost always a good idea. This concept is covered in the next section, so we will wait until then to discuss that aspect in more detail. Teaming for increased bandwidth is really more what we are talking about in this section. By aggregating multiple network cards together, their "physical" bandwidth can be logically totaled to provide for more "pipe." Most network cards today support teaming (in various forms), and in some cases the ability to team dissimilar network cards (such as a 10/100Mbps card with a 1 Gbps card) if the need arises. We recommend that you always attempt to team identical cards to reduce the complexities and support-ability issues that could arise otherwise.

Placing the application and data on the Citrix XenApp server will certainly decrease the amount of traffic required to service the user request, thus eliminating the network as the potential bottle-neck. However, this action means we have indirectly created a single point of failure for access to this application. If the data is located on a single Presentation server, we will most likely not be able to "load balance" the application across the farm; therefore, this option isn't really a viable solution except in certain circumstances.

The last option of multihoming our XenApp server presents many opportunities to increase performance and in a more limited way to increase fault tolerance. The concept of multihoming servers of all kinds has been around the networking world nearly as long as the network itself! Multihomed servers presented solutions to allow for fault tolerance, increase bandwidth, and in some cases, "private" networks for backup and authentication services. However, historically, Citrix XenApp's ancestors had issues with multiple "paths" to a server. In the past, a Citrix server may inadvertently direct a user session to the "wrong" card in a multihomed server scenario, thus creating a denial of service. This problem has been long since fixed, so today we can discuss the benefit of multihoming our XenApp servers to improve quality of service (QoS). By multihoming our XenApp servers we can segment our session traffic from our data traffic (and possibly the authentication and backup traffic as well). Placing two "legs" or "routes" to the network also can provide some measure of fault tolerance for access to the specific XenApp server (although typically this is not as reliable or automatic as teaming). The situation arises due to the nature of application and network access. Let us consider the following scenario. Suppose we have a single XenApp server that has a single NIC for all user sessions and network data access. The server is servicing 50 user sessions. The applications are all well behaved with the exception of our in-house database system for order tracking. When the application running on the XenApp server (or client workstation) accesses the database for queries, large amounts of traffic are generated between the server and the database until the request is fulfilled. This translates into periods of slowness for the other user sessions on the server (even though the CPU, memory, and disk performance may be fine). Why? Because all the user sessions and the application data access are contending for the same network link. Consider separating the user sessions and database access onto two separate network cards.

Build In Redundancies

One of the many decisions that face Citrix architects is what types and how much redundancy to build into our production XenApp servers. The goals of redundancy are to improve uptime and availability of the system where the redundancies are implemented. Redundancy comes in two flavors: high availability and fault tolerance. High availability is concerned with the availability of the system regardless of the status of fault. Citrix XenApp Advanced and Enterprise editions include the feature of load balancing that provides high availability. A server that is servicing the user session may fail, but the user could simply reconnect and start a new session with limited downtime. Fault tolerance is the ability of a system to overcome the failure of any component of the system without a break in service occurring. Consider a set of hard drives connected to a RAID controller to provide redundancy. If a single disk fails, the remaining disks, through the controller, can provide the fault tolerance without interruption of service. If the controller to which the disks are attached fails, the system will fail. Thus, high availability is about minimizing the downtime associated with fault, and fault tolerance is about preventing the fault from occurring. The process of building in redundancies is the practice of selecting the appropriate components that are more likely to fail and balancing the cost of building in redundancies vs. the lost opportunity created when a non redundant component of the system fails. In simpler terms, is the cost of the lost productivity greater than the cost of the redundancies?

Building in these redundancies can be a slippery slope. Where to begin building them in is fairly easily, we will start with the physical hardware of the individual XenApp servers. The issue arises after we complete building the redundancies into the server and logically leave the server and touch the network. How far do we go toward creating a highly available and fault tolerant "system" depends entirely on how you define "system." Is the system the physical XenApp server hardware, the Citrix farm, or is it the entire local area network/wide area network (LAN/WAN) space in which our XenApp server farm will serve? This definition is up to you and your organization and typically correlates to the dependency on the solution in your environment. For the purposes of this chapter, we will look at the typical redundancies that we can build into our Citrix XenApp server's hardware to assist us in increasing server fault tolerance and availability.

Any typical XenApp server farm can benefit from the recommended hardware redundancies as outlined in Table 3.4.

Table 3.4 Recommended Hardware Redundancies

Redundancy	Recommendation	Benefit
RAID level	1	RAID 1 will provide mirror disk sets at a lower cost to implement than RAID 5. Additionally, some studies suggest that five to seven disks are required in a RAID 5 stripe before you will begin to regain the performance lost from the overhead of striping. Since our Citrix Presentation servers are typically smaller 1 or 2 U servers, the additional size and costs associated with RAID 5 typically fail to provide the return on the investment When creating a RAID 5 stripe, 1/n (where n is the number of drives) of the total capacity of the set will be lost to "overhead." In a mirrored set, a full 50 percent will be lost to overhead. Additionally, it is strongly discouraged to use the "built-in" RAID capability of the Windows platform. Although Windows Server 2003 supports creating "software-based" RAID arrays, the performance benefits and fault tolerance are substantially less than a true "hardware-based" solution. Final thoughts are that additional (thereby redundant) controller cards for the RAID drives may prove beneficial to eliminate the card as a single point of failure. A card with multiple "channels" is not sufficient, as the card itself may fail.

Continued

Table 3.4 Continued. Recommended Hardware Redundancies

Redundancy	Recommendation	Benefit
Network interface cards	TEAM	Teaming network cards provides benefits of both fault tolerance and increased network capacity through bandwidth aggregation. Teaming with two or more physically separate cards is recommended instead of teaming two ports on a multiple port card (as the card is still a single point of failure).
Power supplies	2 or more	Most servers in the class have the capabilities of redundant power supplies, and this should be leveraged. Additionally, uninterruptible power supplies or conditioned power should be considered.
Memory	Spare row	If your server hardware supports "spare row" memory, the additional expense of a "spare" piece of memory can provide greater server availability in the event of memory failure. The "spare row" memory stick will not be used until one of the regular sticks fails.

NOTE

The redundancies listed in Table 3.4 are based on a generic sampling of server hardware typically implemented in server farms as of the writing of this book. New technologies and hardware choices should be given consideration, as they may provide more redundant solutions at a lower cost. Additionally, some of these recommendations may not be available in all hardware platforms.

Server Virtualization

One of the most exciting new technologies to be introduced to server-based computing in the last few years is server virtualization. Server virtualization allows a *host* operating system to provide *guest* operating systems a completely virtualized hardware environment. For example, a single dual processor server running Windows Server 2003 as the host operating system could virtualize servers for Windows servers, Linux servers, or NetWare servers. By completely separating and virtualizing the hardware required by the guest operating system, server virtualization provides many benefits. While things would appear to be easier on the surface as far as the hardware planning for this environment, special consideration must be given to guarantee the resources needed by a particular guest operating system. The Datacenter and Enterprise Editions of Windows Server 2003 provide some of this functionality with the Resource Manager component CD that ships with the software. Additional third-party software is available to assist in "controlling" the virtualized environment; one product in particular called ArmTech is from Aurema (www.aurema.com). Aurema provides a specific toolset for "fair sharing" of resources, especially within a virtualized server context.

Server virtualization requires a special application to run on top of the host operating system. This software provides the management and hardware virtualization for the guest operating systems. Microsoft produces a relatively new offering known as Virtual Server 2005. Virtual Server 2005 is based on software created by Connectix (a company recently purchased by Microsoft) that allowed Macintosh and Windows users to virtualized x86 architecture operating systems. The biggest player in this space is definitely VMWare. VMWare offers a host of products for virtualization and management thereof, but the product that most closely relates to Microsoft's Virtual Server 2005 would be VMWare GSX Server. VMWare has been working on computer virtualization for quite some time and has developed a suite of products to aid in deploying and supporting this solution. One of our personal favorites is VMotion, which allows for uninterrupted transfer of guest operating systems from one host to another (very powerful stuff indeed!).

Server virtualization is definitely a situation when scaling up is the way to go. "Big Steel" is needed typically to see the return on investment from such a consolidation. The following would be a good list to start with and grow from there:

- Eight-way P4 2.8 GHz or faster

- 16 GB of RAM (the more the better, HOT ADD would useful)

- Multiple physical network cards (to allow for teaming or assigning to specific guest operating systems)

- RAID 1 for host operating system, separate RAID 5 stripe(s) for the guest operating systems

- Redundant power supplies

This setup would most likely support six or more (depending on applications) XenApp servers and would be excellent at consolidating the other pieces of the Citrix Access Suite, such as Web Interface, Secure Gateway, and the Secure Ticket Authority.

Platform Deployment Options

Now that we have a basis to assist in selecting our hardware, we will turn our attention to select the appropriate method to deploy the hardware and the operating system to support our Citrix XenApp Server. Platform deployment options include manual installation, unattended or scripted installs, server cloning, and a newer approach called server provisioning. Finally, we will discuss a mixed or hybrid approach that uses the best pieces of these various solutions. Selecting the best platform deployment option for your environment involves a detailed review of the requirements for each with special emphasis on the additional software and engineer expertise required. Most environments may lean heavily on one of the following solutions, but may ultimately be categorized as a hybrid due to the nuances required integrating into the existing networking environment.

Manual Installation

The manual installation method of platform deployment has been around as long as server deployments. It is the tried and true method that we have all used from time to time to build or rebuild servers—insert CD, follow on-screen instructions. Manual is a great option for building your first server in the farm, as the effort to build the first server using script typically isn't justified, as the scripts would require substantial changes in order to install member servers in the farm. The manual process would typically be used to build a dedicated data collector, for instance. While this option is the method we are most familiar with, there are certain advantages and disadvantages to using this for platform deployment.

The advantages include the following:

- No additional upfront investment in software or hardware.
- Little additional training required.
- Allows complete configuration of server hardware and operating system.

The disadvantages include the following:

- **Requires manual configuration:** All configuration and information is entered by hand, leaving room for human error.
- **Time-consuming:** This method requires the most effort on the part of the person doing the actual installation and offers no mechanism to deploy additional servers at an accelerated pace. If it takes eight hours to deploy one server, it will take 40 hours to deploy five servers.
- **Not scalable:** This method is scaled linearly. In other words, the more servers to build, the more effort required to build those servers.
- **Issues with consistency:** As this method relies heavily on repetitive human interaction with the installers and configuration tools, consistency of the configurations will undoubtedly become an issue.
- **Slow to recover a server:** Recovering a server would involve the same time-consuming steps that installing it would. Disaster recovery from tape may be faster than a manual rebuild, but that involves the additional expense of backup agents and tape media.
- **Slow to adapt:** Manual installation is slower to adapt to changes required in the environment. Every change, update, or patch would need to be applied to all servers by hand.

Recommended uses:

- Pilot or proof-of-concept environments.
- Labs or test servers.
- Initial builds for more advanced methods such as server cloning or server provisioning.

Unattended or Scripted Installs

Unattended or scripted installs offer some decided benefits over the manual installation option of platform deployment. Unattended installs have been supported for many years for both installation of Windows Server 2003 and for Citrix XenApp Server (and the previous incarnations thereof). Unattended or scripted installs are possible through two options provided by Citrix. The first option leverages a standard text file provided on the installation CD. Locate the installation media, browse the folders Support\Install, and locate a file named UnattendedTemplate.txt. This file can be edited with any standard text editor such as Notepad. This file provides full instructions *within* the file as to how to edit the file to accomplish the specific setup options, such as joining or creating a farm, adding a Web interface, selecting the version of XenApp Server, and so forth. It is important to note that not all options are required to have information entered. For instance, if you were editing the template file to allow for unattended installs to join an existing farm, you would not need to enter information in the create farm sections. Once the file has been edited, you can use it with a parser that Citrix also ships on the installation media in the same path as the UnattendedTemplate.txt called UNATTENDEDINSTALL.EXE. The UNATTENDEDINSTALL.EXE allows us to leverage the MSI package provided by Citrix and the unattended answer text file you just created to silently install XenApp Server. You can use the following command-line syntax to use it to install XenApp Server:

```
UNATTENDEDINSTALL.exe R:\XenAppServer\MPS.msi X:\YourAnswerFile.txt
```

R:\ is the path to the XenApp Server Install CD or the contents thereof.

X:\YourAnswerFile.Txt is the path and name of the unattended answer file we created by editing the template.

NOTE

The unattended answer file you create contains important information that most network administrators will want to keep secure. The file contains entries for the username and password for both farm creation and data store access. As there is no method to encrypt this information in a text file, you could optionally leave the entries blank. The file will still prove useful for installing XenApp Server; it will simply halt install and wait for input from the person executing the install for the "empty" answers.

When troubleshooting scripted installs, we recommend reviewing the following settings in the unattended answer file:
[Options]
RebootOnFinish=Yes
LogLevel=*v
LogFile=c:\msi.log
UILevel= BASIC_UI_NO_MODAL
In the OPTIONS section, the LogLevel=*v implies log everything and sets the level to verbose. More importantly is the path where the log is written in LogFile=C:\msi.log. Change this entry to an appropriate path based on your server's configuration, keeping in mind that some administrators choose to save these install logs to a common network share if you choose to install batches of server simultaneously.

The second unattended or scripting option involves using the command-line MSIEXEC.EXE to provide a "full string" of answers to the Windows Installer service as it reads and executes the directions in the MPS.MSI package. This is our personal favorite option, as it allows us to not have the bother of creating and maintaining an answer file. This syntax that we will review can also be leveraged to perform silent installs via group policy or Systems Management Server in the following section (in addition to the method described there).

The following list is the options that can be used as "switches" to perform a command-line install of XenApp server using the MSIEXEC.EXE (command-line Windows Installer Service). This example is of a server install that is joining a farm. It is important to keep in mind that as with the UnattendedTemplate.txt file from the previous section, not all options will be required.

```
msiexec /i mps.msi /qb- /l*v SOMELOG.log
INSTALLDIR="%systemdrive%\Program Files\Citrix\"
CTX_MF_FARM_SELECTION="Join" CTX_MF_JOIN_FARM_DB_CHOICE="Direct"
CTX_MF_ODBC_USER_NAME="sa" CTX_MF_ODBC_PASSWORD="pass1"
CTX_MF_ODBC_RE_ENTERED_PASSWORD="pass1" CTX_MF_NFUSE_DEF_WEB_PAGE="No"
CTX_MF_SHADOWING_CHOICE="Yes" CTX_MF_XML_PORT_NUMBER="80"
CTX_MF_XML_CHOICE="Separate" CTX_MF_SERVER_TYPE="e"
CTX_MF_SHADOW_PROHIBIT_NO_LOGGING="No"
CTX_MF_SHADOW_PROHIBIT_NO_NOTIFICATION="No"
CTX_MF_SHADOW_PROHIBIT_REMOTE_ICA="No" CTX_MF_LAUNCH_CLIENT_CD_WIZARD="No"
CTX_MF_SILENT_DSNFILE="PathtoDSN\MF20.DSN"
CTX_MF_CREATE_REMOTE_DESKTOP_USERS=CopyUsers CTX_MF_ADD_ANON_USERS=No
CTX_RDP_DISABLE_PROMPT_FOR_PASSWORD="Yes"
CTX_MF_TURN_FEATURE_RELEASE_ON="Yes" CTX_MF_REBOOT="Yes"
```

Let's exam what the various "switches" are doing in a method that's a little easier to understand. We will proceed "entry" by "entry" with the plain explanation of what is occurring in the preceding syntax.

- The Windows Installer Service (msiexec) is started and instructed to (/i) install MPS.MSI.

- During this install action, the service is to perform a quiet install (/qb-) and log (/l) everything verbosely (/l*v) to a file called somelog.log.

- XenApp Server will be installed (INSTALLDIR) to C:\Program Files\Citrix and will join the farm using a direct connection to the data store with the user sa and the password of pass1.

- Web Interface will not be the default Web site and shadowing will be enabled.

- The Citrix XML service will be installed separately from IIS and will use port 80.

- Shadowing will be allowed without logging or notification and will allow remote control of the session.

- The client CD wizard will not start at the end of installation.

- The installer can use the MF20.DSN from the path specified to find the data store so that it may read the information and join the farm defined therein.

- The members of the local users group on the target server will be copied into the built-in group remote desktop users (new security function with Terminal Services for Windows Server 2003).

- The anonymous accounts will not be created on the target server, thus prohibiting the use of anonymous connections to published applications on this particular server.

- As part of the new feature to support Microsoft's Remote Desktop Clients via Web Interface, the prompt for password feature will be disabled on the RDP-TCP connection.

- The feature release will be enabled and the server will reboot at the completion of the install.

Advantages:

- **Reduces time to production:** Once scripted, the deployment process is much faster, as the installers can simply read the answer or configuration files.

- **Tested, reliable, and scalable:** Many servers could be built simultaneously by a single person using the scripted method. Additionally, the resource executing the scripts could be a less-skilled resource than would be required for the manual install process.

- **Enforces best practices:** Since the "choices" based on best practices are incorporated into the scripts, best practices are easily enforced.

- **Repeatable:** The same scripts can be reused, and each reuse continues to return on the investment required to create them.

- **Portable between platforms:** With minor changes, typically, unattended installation scripts can be ported between various hardware platforms to allow for greater adaptability in the environment.

- **Possible hardware configuration support:** Typically can be used for hardware configuration as well, such as configuring the RAID controller settings.

Disadvantages:

- **Additional upfront time:** This method requires greater amounts of upfront time to plan and test the scripts.

- **Higher level of technical skill:** The person or team responsible for the creation and testing of these scripts will typically have a much higher level of skill with the hardware platform, operating system, and version of XenApp Server being deployed. Additionally, detailed knowledge of scripting languages will be required to create and maintain the scripts.

- **Server build time:** Although faster than the manual process, this method is typically slower than other options.

Recommended uses:

- Larger environments of 10 servers or more.

- Environments where server hardware is dissimilar.

- Already have staff highly skilled with scripting.

- Organizations that already have a standard scripted install for Windows 2003 (which could easily be modified).

- Server farms

- Inclusion into more advanced methods such as server provisioning.

Server Cloning

Server cloning was derived from a similar method used to "clone" workstations for deployment to users' desktops. The concept of cloning should be familiar to anyone who has ever used Symantec's

Ghost or PowerQuest's Drive Image. The principle is simple: you perform a manual install of the server (or workstation) and all the required software that an end user would need. Once the server is built and tested, you simply take a "snapshot" of the drive's contents to allow for easy duplication later. Server cloning is a widely used method, although with some supportability issues. The following steps should be taken prior to creating an image of Citrix XenApp server. Once these steps have been completed, the server cloning application can be utilized to create an image to be deployed:

1. A server installed as the first in a farm with an Access database cannot be cloned.

2. Do not use a server with an SSL certificate installed.

3. Select the **default zone name** during installation.

4. Delete the **wfcname.ini file** located on the root of the drive on which Citrix XenApp server was installed.

5. Stop the **Independent Management Architecture service** and set it to **manual startup**.

6. Delete the following **registry keys**:

   ```
   HKEY_LOCAL_MACHINE\Software\Citrix\IMA\Runtime\HostId
   HKEY_LOCAL_MACHINE\Software\Citrix\IMA\Runtime\ImaPort
   HKEY_LOCAL_MACHINE\Software\Citrix\IMA\Runtime\MasterRanking
   HKEY_LOCAL_MACHINE\Software\Citrix\IMA\Runtime\PSRequired
   HKEY_LOCAL_MACHINE\Software\Citrix\IMA\Runtime\RassPort
   HKEY_LOCAL_MACHINE\Software\Citrix\IMA\Runtime\ZoneName
   ```

The following steps should be taken to image a Citrix XenApp server server using cloning applications. Once these steps are completed, the server is ready to be utilized by users:

1. The **server name** and **SID** must be changed correctly to support operating system functions and Citrix XenApp. This is traditionally done by the cloning application.

2. Add the following **registry key** and set the **value** to the name of the XenApp server:

   ```
   HKEY_LOCAL_MACHINE\Software\Citrix\IMA\ServerHost
   ```

3. Edit the **wfcname.ini file** located on the root of the drive on which Citrix XenApp server is installed, and replace the **server name** with the new machine name.

4. Set the **Independent Management Architecture service** to start automatically.

5. Reboot the server to apply the changes and start **MetaFrame XP**.

Advantages:

- **Reduces time to production:** This method is the fastest of the options for platform deployment as outlined in this book. Servers can be "imaged" in a matter of minutes, depending on the methods used and the size of the image file(s).

- **Tested, reliable, and scalable:** Similar to the unattended or scripted option, server imaging provides a pre-tested highly scalable solution for deployment.

- **Enforces best practices:** Since the "choices" based on best practices are incorporated into the image, best practices are easily enforced.

- **Repeatable:** The same image can be "restored" an infinite number of times.

- **Typically faster to production:** Server cloning is typically faster than unattended or script-based installation due to less upfront time to develop the process.

Disadvantages:

- **Lack of portability:** The primary disadvantage of this method is the lack of real portability between server hardware platforms. Once an image of a server is "fixed," it is set at that point in time, with that specific configuration on a specific hardware platform. Restoring the image to a different hardware platform will typically meet with much lower success and a greater potential for problems to arise in the future.

- **Lack of support for hardware configuration:** Where the scripted install option provided some mechanism for configuration of the server's hardware, server cloning assumes that the hardware is identical and has been configured identically; for example, RAID controller type, RAID controller configuration, and RAID volume configuration.

- **Images are static:** Once configured, any updates, modifications, or changes to the image will typically require the recreation of the image. This will obviously require additionally time and introduces a new task commonly referred to as image maintenance.

- **Greater skill depth required:** A higher level of skill will be required, specifically with additional skills on cloning for those tasked with image creation and maintenance.

- **Additional cost:** Additional costs associated with the "cloning" software and the space required to maintain the image files for the various server platforms.

- **Lack of universal support:** Not all vendors support cloning. Citrix has had an off-again on-again stance to cloning XenApp servers, although the current position is that this method is supported. Microsoft doesn't support cloning Windows when applications are installed. This lack of support may be sufficient cause to investigate other methods of deploying servers.

Recommended uses:

- Larger environments of five servers or more.

- Environments where server hardware is identical.

- Already have staff highly skilled with cloning workstations.

- Environments in which the base image of the server would require little change over time.

- Inclusion into more advanced methods such as server provisioning.

Server Provisioning

Out of the need for a more complete and flexible solution for deploying server hardware (or redeploying as needed), many companies have recently started offering single-seat management solutions for hardware configuration and operating system deployment. These seemingly wondrous solutions fall into a space we typically call *server provisioning*. Some solutions are more complete than others are. Some solutions involve complete hardware configuration and management, operating system deployment and updates, and application deployment including beginning to end of life cycle management for our server solutions. Some vendors' solutions are designed only to provision the operating system and possibly install applications. The camps are fairly evenly divided between hardware vendor-specific and hardware vendor-independent. Microsoft provides solutions in server provisioning that are platform independent with products like Systems Management Server (SMS) and Remote Installation Services (RIS). Altiris originally started the whole "server provisioning" management software craze. The fine people at Altiris constructed the framework and toolset needed to allow us to automate nearly every piece in a server's life cycle. Various vendors (to include Hewlett-Packard and Dell) chose to leverage the Altiris platform instead of developing their own solution to assist in the deployment of their hardware. The benefits of these server provision solutions are too numerous to fully explore here. However, one of the major advantages of the vendor-based solution is that it allows a single seat for management of all your platforms, from Windows to Linux to NetWare. Table 3.5 lists the vendors and their solutions.

Table 3.5 Server Provisioning Vendor Solutions

Vendor	Server Provisioning Solution
Hewlett-Packard/Compaq	Rapid Deployment Pack (RDM) (based on Altiris product)
Dell	Dell OpenManage (Dell's newest products have snap-ins directly to Altiris' Deployment Server)
IBM	Remote Deployment Manager (RDM)

Advantages:

- Seamless integration with the vendor-specific hardware platform.

- Ability to use hardware-specific tools for scripting configurations of firmware, RAID controllers, and so forth.

- Pre-eXecution Environment (PXE) support to allow "diskless" booting to network resources for automation. Note: PXE requires support in both the NICs and the system's firmware. In same cases, system firmware can be "overcome" using PXE boot floppies.

- Single seat administration of the process to include reporting and asset tracking.

Disadvantages:

- **Lack of portability:** These solutions are typically tied to the specific vendor and are not portable from, say, IBM to HP platforms. This has changed a bit in recent history and some effort has been made to allow for better integration, but there is still a long way to go. For now, it would be best to assume that any solution you design using server provisioning will not be portable between vendors.

- **Cost:** Typically, servers that are managed using this solution require additional licensing for the management software. Additionally, the management solution normally requires some network file storage space and additionally some server resources.

- **Increased upfront time** A much greater amount of time will go into building the framework and setting up the mechanisms for hardware configuration and operating system deployment.

- **Expertise** There is a bit of a learning curve for people who are new to Altiris or IBM's RDM. The level of integration and capability comes at the price of a much deeper and broader skill set regarding hardware and scripting.

Recommended uses:

- Larger environments of 20 servers or more, or a blade-based server environment.

- Environments where there is a single server hardware vendor (or nearly).

- Already have staff highly skilled with automation scripting and server cloning.

- Environments that are trying to leverage a specific hardware vendor and maintain a single seat to management and deployment of server platforms.

Hybrid Approach

The hybrid approach allows you to combine the best from the previous four methods described, and is the method used by most real-life implementations. For instance, a hybrid approach would allow you to use a server cloning base image due to the very fast nature of deployment and combine that with an unattended/scripted installation method to update the server to the most current hotfixes, run a security identifier (SID) changing tool, and install a few pieces of software that may have "missed" inclusion in the base image. The hybrid approach offers the greatest flexibility for server deployments but also maintains the limitations of all the various methods (we are just choosing to ignore those limitations that apply to our environment).

Two possible submethods that exist under the hybrid approach (arguably, they could exist under scripting or server cloning) are System Preparation Tool (SYSPREP) and Remote Installation Services (RIS) based installs. Both of these techniques for installing a server operating system (or workstations for that matter) were developed by Microsoft and have been supported for some time. SYSPREP has been around since the days of NT 4.0, although not supported for servers until Windows 2000. RIS has existed since Windows 2000 Server and can be used to provide a variety of "clients" an unattended installation of the platform's operating system. We chose to place SYSPREP and RIS in the hybrid approach primarily because of the "blending" of techniques they employ.

SYSPREP, for instance, is a method of cloning a server after it has been built that also uses an answer file, thus blending the benefits of server cloning and unattended or scripted installations. SYSPREP is supported for Windows Server 2003 as a method of deploying the operating system fully configured with relevant service packs and hotfixes to the waiting hardware. Due to the cloning nature of the procedure, SYSPREPPED images are typically specific to the hardware platform at hand, therefore inheriting the limitations of the server cloning method. SYSPREP is, however, a very powerful method to assist in the automation of the operating system in a very fast and consistent manner. Due to the nature of the answer file that it employs, further automation of the image after "install" is a snap. This would allow inclusion of key elements such as installation of Citrix XenApp Server and various other applications or core tools needed on every XenApp server, such as backup agents or antivirus software.

RIS can be leveraged much in the same way as Altiris or the other server provisioning tools mentioned previously. Microsoft developed RIS to allow administrators to quickly and efficiently deploy the operating systems to new workstations as they were brought onto the network. Since its inception, RIS has been extended to include support for deploying servers. RIS supports the deployment of unattended installations and images similar to SYSPREP known as RIS-PREPPED images. In a typical deployment, RIS leverages the PXE feature of most modern computers' network cards to assign a DHCP address and "present" a menu of options or to execute a series of scripts. Since RIS can leverage unattended or "cloned" images, it provides a very flexible and fast method for deploying servers. More information on RIS and SYSPREP is available in the Windows Server 2003 documentation located on the installation media.

Advantages:

- **Greatest flexibility:** This method allows the use of any of the benefits of the other methods to include scripted installation, server cloning, and server provisioning.

- **Best of breed:** Allows for the selection of the key capabilities from each method to allow for better integration.

Disadvantages:

- Contains all limitations of previous methods.

- May increase complexity.

- May increase costs due to various pieces that may or may not be implemented.

Recommended uses:

- Environments of five servers or larger.

- Environments with highly skilled technical staff with depth of knowledge on the pros and cons of the various methods.

- Departments or divisions of an organization that deploy their own servers in separate locations with differing rules or practices.

Citrix XenApp Server Installation Process

At first glance, the installation process for XenApp Server (Citrix Presentation Server 4.5) looks very similar to previous releases. However, with further investigation, you will find that there is more under the hood than you initially thought. XenApp Server includes several new features, all of which should be included in your overall implementation strategy. In case you have not heard it enough, do not forget to plan your deployment! If you plan your deployment *before* putting that CD-ROM in the drive, you will save time and frustration and look like a genius to your coworkers, not to mention your boss! How can you prepare best prepare for an XenApp Server deployment? Here are a few tips:

- Make sure that your hardware meets or, more realistically, exceeds all the requirements.

- Check the Citrix Web site for Pre-installation Update Bulletins. Often, new information regarding operating system, hardware, and software configuration will become available after the initial release. Patches and hotfixes may be recommended or warned against, and work-arounds may be provided for various software installations.

■ After you build and configure your Windows Server 2003 and installing Terminal Services, download and apply any new Microsoft service packs and security updates prior to installing XenApp Server.

Configuring and Implementing...

Installing Service Packs and Updates

In multiuser environment, it is not a good idea to configure automatic updates on production servers. Service packs and updates should be reviewed and tested in a like environment before going live. Because keeping up with Microsoft security updates has become a major task, Microsoft has come up with two methods of staying current with updates: Software Update Server (SUS) and Windows Update Service (WUS). The Windows Update Service is included with Windows 2000, Windows XP, and Windows Server 2003 operating systems. It can be configured to download and automatically install updates, to download and hold until you have reviewed the updates, or not to download at all. This method works best for desktop operating systems. The newer method, SUS, is a free utility consisting of a client agent and server component that synchronizes with Microsoft daily to download updates. Once downloaded, an e-mail notification is sent to the administrator. SUS requires Windows 2000 or Windows Server 2003 running Internet Information Services (IIS). To find out more and download SUS, go to www.microsoft.com/windowsserversystem/sus/default.mspx.

■ Download and make ready any Citrix critical updates that may be needed after XenApp Server has been installed.

■ Make sure you understand what the installation will entail, what questions will be asked, and options from which you have to choose. Making these decisions on the fly could mean starting from scratch.

■ Drive remapping only works on new installations. If you plan to remap drives, do so before installing XenApp Server, any components or applications, and make sure the applications you plan to deploy are capable of running from the new drive letters.

As mentioned previously, Citrix has added a few brand new features in this release that require a bit more planning than before. You will want to be prepared so there will be no surprises. For those of you familiar with prior releases of XenApp Server, you will find that in addition to the usual installation choices including "View Installation Checklist," "Install or Upgrade" (now known as "Product Installation"), "Citrix on the Web," and "Browse CD," you are also given the opportunity to install the "Document Center." The Document Center is a handy online library that contains all the new Administration Guides for XenApp Server in portable document format (pdf). Adobe Acrobat Reader is necessary to view the documents and can be downloaded from www.adobe.com. The "Other Tools and Component" option no longer exists on the main screen, but the Console installations can be found when you drill down through Product Installations.

Under Product Installations, you will find yet another interesting addition: "Install XenApp Access Suite License Server." Citrix added the licensing server to simplify managing product licenses, which we all know is a nuisance. The licensing server is similar to the Windows Server 2003 licensing server in that it is a centralized location where you can manage and monitor licenses. It differs from Microsoft's version in that you can manage and monitor *all* the Access Suite products from the same location. The actual licensing process has changed as well and differs from prior versions, so be sure that you understand the new licensing features and requirements before diving in.

In this section, we will go over, in detail, the installation process for the new features and those that have not changed (for you newbies out there). If you followed along and built a test server, you may find it helpful to follow along in the step-by-step installation section in this chapter.

Citrix recommends the following sequence of steps to ensure that your XenApp Server and components run smoothly:

1. Planning for Home Folder and Terminal Server Profile

2. Analyze Hardware and Software Requirements

3. View installation checklist.

4. Remap the Server drives.

5. Install the Document Center.

6. Create the data store (unless using an Access database).

7. Install the license server.

8. Install XenApp servers.

Planning for Home Folder and Terminal Server Profile

As we begin to build or upgrade our XenApp server farm, several components exist outside the management boundary that is the farm. The external components are present to service the underlying functionality of the farm and the user sessions that the farm hosts.

The first external component to consider is home folder. Aside from the typical uses for a home folder, Terminal Services (and therefore XenApp Server) leverages the home folder to maintain per-user INI files. For instance, when running a session on the XenApp server, a user needs to "edit" an INI file that exists in the system paths (C:\Windows), Terminal Services will copy the original file to the user's home folder and allow the user to modify the home folder version instead of the shared C:\Windows version. Additionally, Terminal Services monitors the time stamps on the INI files to assist in determining if the user needs a newer copy of the file from the system paths in the event of a major system change, such as installing a new application to update the C:\Windows INI files. In addition, the per-user file repository, user home folders, obviously serve as the dumping ground for all user created files and are typically the target of many policies for redirecting content from the users' desktop and My Documents. Home folders come in two types, normal and Terminal Services. Normal home folders are like those we have always defined for user accounts in our NT or Active Directory domains. Terminal Services home folders allow administrators to specify an alternate folder structure that only applies when a user logs in to a Terminal Services session (and not at a workstation or desktop).

The second external component to consider is the user's profile. Before we delve into the types and strategies surrounding profiles, let's review what a profile is and what type of information it contains by default. A profile is the user side of the configuration of the computer's operating system, and to a lesser extent the applications that reside on the system. A profile contains two portions of information, a file and folder structure and a registry section. If we look at the %SYSTEMDRIVE%\Documents and Settings folder for a Windows Server 2003 computer, we can examine this structure in more detail. For instance, we see the All Users profile and the Default User's profile. The Default User's profile is the template from which a user's profile is built if at login time there is no local or network copy of a profile located for the user; for example, if this is the first time the user has logged on to this server and/or network. The All Users profile contains the shortcuts and information that is common to all users that log on to this specific server. We as administrators can simplify a user's experience by "modifying" the contents of the user's profile either by editing the Default User's profile prior to the user's profile being created, using Group Policy Objects to assist in the configuration, or writing some creative scripts to configure elements of the profile for the user in the background. Let's look specifically at the Administrator's profile on our test machine. The Administrator's profile functionally is no different from another nonprivileged user's profile. It contains similar file-based and registry-based information (Figure 3.7).

Figure 3.7 Administrator's Profile

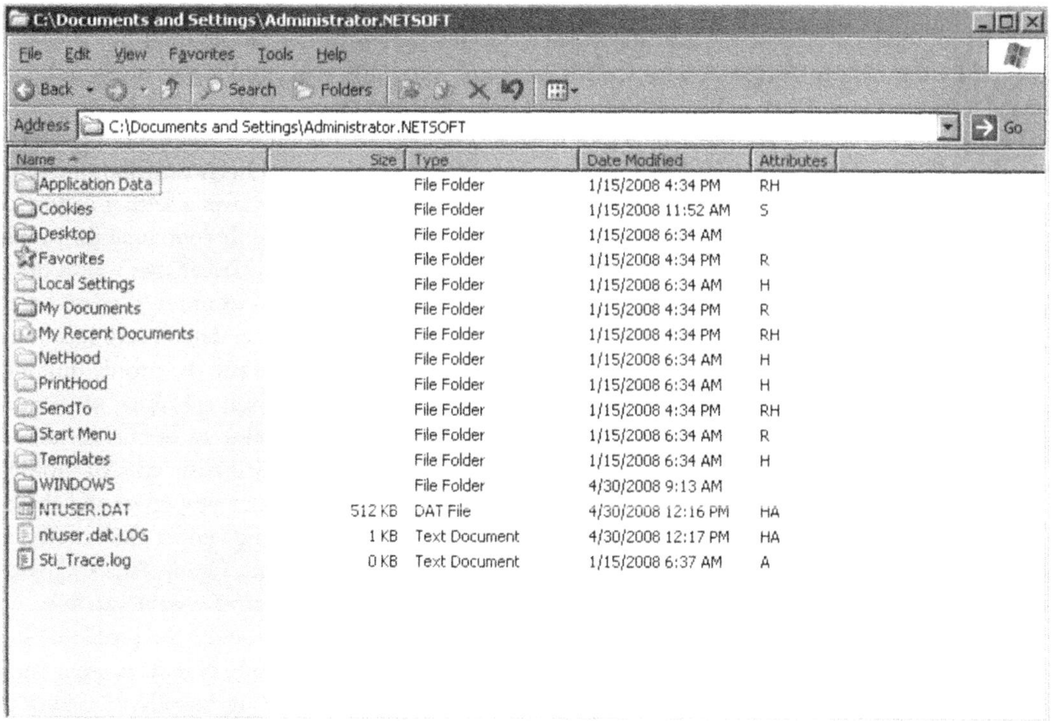

Everything you see as far as files and folders would be the file-based portion of the profile. For example, the folder Desktop would contain all the items that the administrator had placed on his or her desktop of this particular server. The file NTUSER.DAT is a very special file as it contains the registry-based portion. If this user were logged in, everything that is located in the Hive Key Current User (HKCU) section would be the result of information gathered from the NTUSER.DAT file and Group Policy Objects at that current point in time.

Profiles exist in three basic types. The first is a *local profile*. A local profile is a profile that exists only on the computers where a user logs in. Local profiles are beneficial because they are fast to load (as they are local to the server's hard drive). However, local profiles don't typically work well in a server-based computing environment because the settings and folder information found on server1 for userA don't necessarily exist on server2 for userA, resulting in a confused user. A good example of this would be Microsoft Word. If userA ran a session on server1 and set MS Word to "autosave" every five minutes and then later ran MS Word on server2, the user would expect that the auto-save feature would be enabled and set to five minutes. In fact, the setting may not be enabled. In a local profile scenario, userA has two profiles, one on server1 and one on server2, that have no way to synchronize. What we need is a profile that follows the user around no matter where he or she runs a session.

The profile that follows the user to the server he or she logs in to would be the second basic type of profile, the *roaming profile*. Roaming profiles are wonderful, as they allow userA to execute MS Word today on server1, and at logoff, userA's settings are copied to a network share point ready for later when userA runs a session on server2, thus allowing userA to "maintain" his or her configurations as he or she "roams" between servers. Roaming profiles have several administrative burdens. First, they tend to "grow" rapidly if not properly restricted. If we go back to our previous example of items on the user's desktop, if a user saves a 10 MB file to the desktop, then that is now part of the user's profile and must be written out to the network share every time the user logs out of the a session. In addition, every time the user starts a new session and his or her profile must be copied down locally, the 10 MB file comes with it. This can cause very long login and logoff times and dramatically increase network traffic with the result being unhappy users.

The second most common problem is profile "collisions" or corruption. Let's suppose that userA is running MS Word on server1 and MS Excel on server2 at the same time. UserA only has one profile available to him or her, so it is copied to both server1 and server2. If the user saves a setting or file to his or her profile on server1 and a different setting or file on server2, we have the potential for profile collisions. When userA ends his or her sessions on server1 and server2, the *last* server that writes the roaming profile out to the network share will be the copy retained. So, in this example, if userA saves a critical document to the desktop while on server1 and changes the MS Excel default save location (a registry-based change) while in session on server2, if server2 is the last to write the profile out, the user would potentially lose the critical document that was on the desktop of server1. What we need now is the ability to manipulate the profile to help minimize these profile collisions or corruptions.

This practice of minimizing profile corruption results in the third and final basic type of profile, the *hybrid profile*. Hybrid profiles are not "defined" anywhere in a user's account properties and there is no way to distinguish if a local or roaming profile is a hybrid without "digging" under the covers. Hybrid profiles are a culmination of techniques such as folder redirection with Group Policy Objects, login compatibility scripting to "correct" registry settings, and possibly a series of system variables resulting in multiple profile locations. Again, the goal of these practices is to reduce the profile collisions and corruption issues and present a more consistent user experience. Hybrid profiles are a fairly advanced topic and there is no "one right way" to implement them, as there are literally thousands of settings and files that may or may not need to be "redirected" based on your environments needs. The first place to start would be implementing a folder redirection policy in Active Directory.

Whether we choose to implement roaming or hybrid profiles, both types can be defined as either normal or Terminal Services profiles (similar to the concept of home folders). If you already implement some form of profile for your non-Terminal Services users, the concept of the Terminal Services profile allows you to maintain two separate profiles, one for "normal" desktop use, and one for "Terminal Services" use. The differences in the configuration of these folders exist in the account object inside Active Directory. By viewing the properties of any user account with Active Directory Users and Computers, we can see the two tabs that house the settings.

In Figure 3.8, we see the "normal" options for home folder and profile path.

Figure 3.8 Typical Options for Home Folder and Profile Path

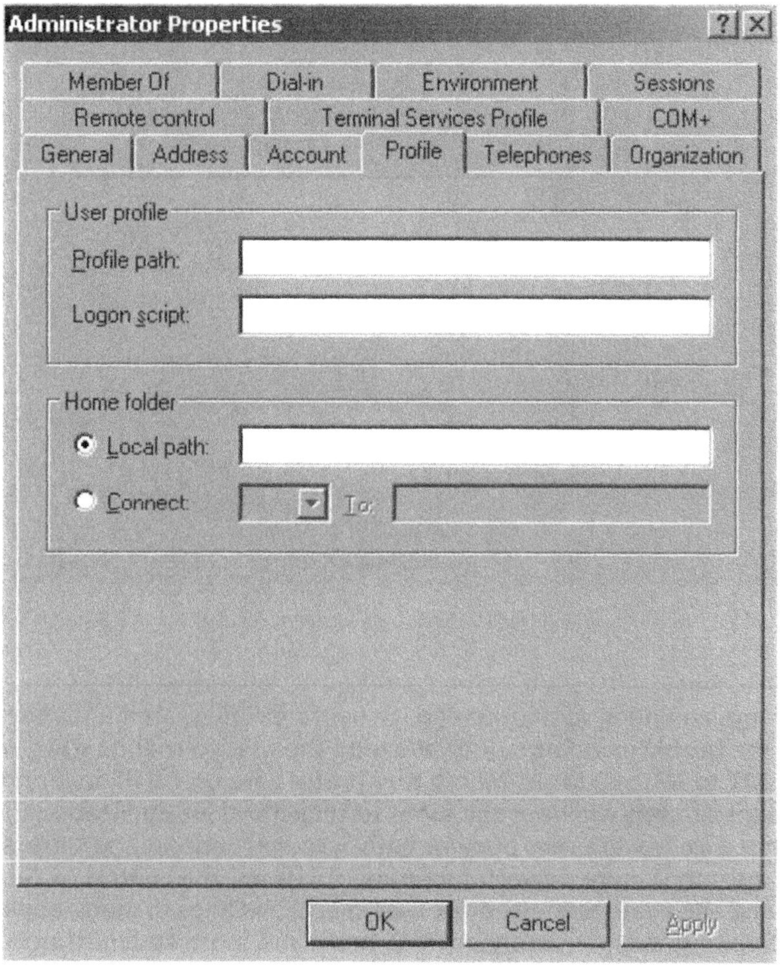

In Figure 3.9, we can see the Terminal Services specific versions for these two types.

Figure 3.9 Terminal Services Profile

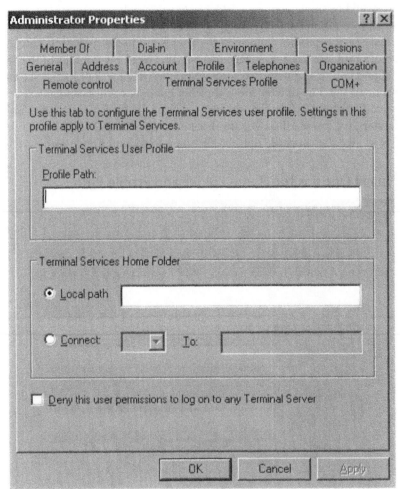

Analyze Hardware and Software Requirements

Citrix XenApp Server has no substantial hardware requirements beyond what Windows Server 2003 requires apart from some disk space requirements. The amount of hard drive space required to install XenApp Server depends on the version of XenApp Server and the amount of additional or optional components installed. Table 3.6 outlines the disk space requirements.

Table 3.6 Disk Space Requirements for Citrix XenApp Server

Component	Disk Space Requirement
Presentation Server, Enterprise Edition	400 MB
Access Suite Management Console (MMC snap-ins)	25 MB
Presentation Server Management Console	50 MB
Document Center	35 MB
Presentation Server Access Suite Licensing	30 MB

There are several software requirements for the installation of Citrix XenApp Server. These requirements depend on the component being installed. In general, you can install Citrix XenApp Server on computers running the Microsoft Windows Server 2003 family (with SP1 or SP2): Standard Edition, Enterprise Edition, and Datacenter Edition. As a general rule, the Setup will automatically install most non-Windows system components, such as the .NET Framework Version, Microsoft Visual J#, and Java Runtime Environment.

View Installation Checklist

Before beginning the installation process for XenApp server, insert the CD-ROM, and from the Autorun screen, select **View installation checklist** as shown in Figure 3.10.

Figure 3.10 XenApp Server Autorun Screen

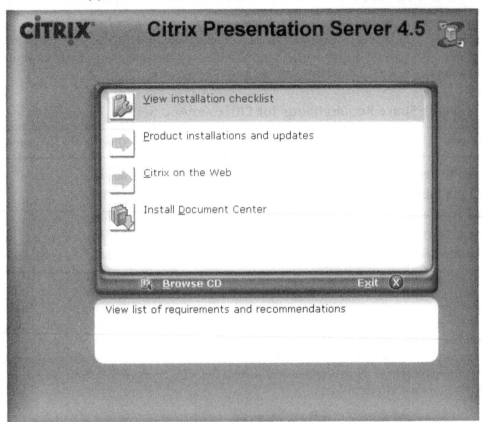

The pre-installation checklist is an actual checklist that Citrix provides that can be used online from the CD-ROM or printed out. It provides an easily accessible listing of basic information such as system requirements for each component and brief, step-by-step instructions for installing XenApp server and creating or joining a farm. Before we begin our installation, browse through the checklist to make sure that we met all prerequisite.

Remap the Server Drives

If you are unfamiliar with the concept, you may wonder what exactly "remap" means and why would you want to do it. The explanation lies on the client side. Users browsing My Computer from within a Citrix session will see server drives such as A:, C:, and D:. If they are on a machine with local drives (versus a thin client device with no drives), the local machine's drives will be mapped to V:, U:, and W:. This can be confusing for the user, and if the administrator has not locked down the server's drives, users could mistake them as their local drives and possibly cause damage to the server. For this reason, Citrix has provided a utility to reassign drive letters to the server drives, changing them to different letters and freeing up C: and D: for use on the client side.

Configuring and Implementing...

Remapping Server Drives

Remapping the server drives should be done before installing XenApp Server or any of the components. If you attempt to remap the drives after installation, the utility will let you, but Citrix warns that it can cause the server to be unstable and may render the operating system inoperable. You may also want to note that the drive remapping is permanent and the drives remain remapped even if XenApp Server is uninstalled.

Drive remapping should only be performed on a new installation. If you attempt to remap the drives on an existing server, you will be allowed to, but any existing applications will no longer work because the registry entries for the applications will still point to the original location. If you plan to remap your server drives, do so before installing XenApp Server or any applications. To remap the server drives, select **Remap drives** from the **Product installations and updates** menu. The utility opens, and next to the server's current drive designations, a drop-down box allows you to choose the first drive letter that will be used for the server's remapped drives. The default first letter is "M," but you can select other letters as long as they are not currently used. Once you have selected the first drive letter you will use, click **OK**. The utility makes the necessary changes and then prompts you to restart the server. Once the server restarts, the drives are reassigned.

Install the Document Center

The Document Center can be installed on any 32-bit Windows system and does not require XenApp Server. However, Adobe Acrobat Reader must be installed to read the documents, as they are in .pdf format. You can get a free version of Adobe Acrobat from the Adobe Systems Web site.

To install the Document Center, access the XenApp Server CD-ROM, and from the main menu, select **Install Document Center**. When the Welcome screen appears, click **Next** to continue. Select the destination folder where the Document Center will be installed and click **Next**. The documents will be copied to the folder specified and when completed, you will be informed that the installation was successful and prompted to click **Finish**. Once installed, you can locate the Document Center under **Start > All Programs > Citrix > Citrix Presentation Server > Documentation**. Double-click on **Document_Center.pdf** to access the Document Center main screen.

Create the Data Store

Each farm must have a data store to hold persistent information about the servers in the farm such as installed applications, configuration settings, and other information that remains fairly static. The data store uses a database to hold the information and Citrix has allowed for several mainstream database options.

Which database you choose will have a lot to do with your environment and the size of your farm. For instance, if your environment consists of only a few servers and there are no existing database servers or administrators, you have the option of using a Microsoft SQL Express 2005, which is included on the CD-ROM at no extra cost. Otherwise, your database options include Microsoft SQL Server, Oracle, and IBM DB2; all more robust and scalable databases that can be used for any size farm. In the following sections, we discuss installing Microsoft SQL Express 2005 with Service Pack 1. If you plan to use MS SQL, Oracle, or DB2, you will need to use your database management software to create the database the data store will use. In addition, remember that MS SQL and Oracle take considerable expertise to administer. If you do not currently have MS SQL or Oracle in your environment, you may want to consider using Access or Microsoft SQL Express 2005.

Unless you plan to use Microsoft Access for your data store, you will need to create the data store *prior* to beginning the XenApp Server installation. Then, during the installation, you will configure an Open Database Connectivity (ODBC) connection to the data store. If you use Microsoft Access, the data store database is created during the installation process.

Designing and Planning...

Data Store Considerations

Deciding which database you should use for the data store is an important decision. Before you decide, examine your current environment; how much do you expect it to expand in the next six months, in the next year to three years? Make sure the database you choose has the capability to sustain any future increase in servers, applications, and users. You may also want to keep in mind the expertise it requires to install and maintain these applications, as most higher end client/server database products require advanced knowledge to administer.

Installing Microsoft SQL Express 2005 Desktop Engine with Service Pack 1

As mentioned earlier, the Microsoft SQL Express 2005 Desktop Engine (MSDE) is included on the XenApp Server CD-ROM, and although you can download and install MSDE from Microsoft, Citrix recommends that you use the version with Service Pack 1 from the XenApp Server CD-ROM. MSDE must be installed on the first server that will run XenApp prior to installing XenApp software.

From the XenApp Server CD-ROM, there are two ways that you can install MSDE. The first method assumes that you have no other instances of MSDE running on the server and that you have opted to use the default instance name "CITRIX_METAFRAME" and password "citrix". If you cannot use the default values for instance name and password, you will need to run the MSDE setup from the command prompt. This method requires that you install XenApp Server manually, which we discuss later in this chapter.

NOTE

When you install MSDE with the default values, the default instance name is set to "CITRIX_METAFRAME" and the SA password to "citrix". Normally, this would be considered a security risk, but by default, SQL authentication is disabled so the SA password is not used. For security purposes, if SQL is enabled, you will want to create your own unique instance name and create a user account with appropriate administrator privileges.

To install MSDE with Service Pack 3 with the default values, browse to the \Support\MSDE folder on the XenApp Server CD-ROM. Double-click on **SetupSqlExpressForCPS.cmd** to launch setup. No other intervention is necessary to complete the install.

If you are required to specify the instance name and password, go to the command prompt and change to the \Support\SqlExpress_2005_SP1\SqlExpress folder on the XenApp Server CD-ROM. Place the server in Install mode by typing:

```
change user /install <ENTER>
```

Next, launch the setup program with the following parameters:

```
Setup.exe INSTANCENAME=<name> SAPWD=<password> <ENTER>
```

where <name> and <password> are the values you have selected for the instance name and password.

Once you have completed the installation, return to the command prompt and type:

```
change user /execute <ENTER>
```

NOTE

Placing the server in Install mode ensures that an application can be accessed by multiple users simultaneously. For applications to function, registry settings must be replicated to all users. There are two ways of placing the server into Install mode: using Add/Remove Programs to install an application, or using the commands just shown from the command line. The difference is that Add/Remove Programs creates a "shadow key" in the registry where changes to the HKEY_CURRENT_USER are monitored and propagated to each user.

Creating a Database with Microsoft SQL Server 2005

To create a database with Microsoft SQL Server 2005, follow these steps:

1. Open the SQL Server Management Studio.

2. Choose an appropriate selections under Server type:, Server name: and Authentication:, and then click Connect.

3. In the SQL Server Management Studio's left pane, expand the tree until you reach the folder level.

4. Right-click on Logins and then click on New Login....

5. A Login - New dialog box will appear with the General page selected. In the Login name box, enter a SQL Login name, and then click on SQL Server authentication. Enter a password and then confirm your password. Please make note of the SQL Server Login name and Password because you will need to enter this information during XenApp Server Installation and DSN creation. Uncheck the Enforce password policy check box, and then click on OK to create SQL user account.

6. Once you create the user account, the next step in the process is to create a database, and assign permissions to user. In the SQL Server Management Studio's left pane, expand the tree until you reach the Databases folder level.

7. Right-click on Databases and then click on New Database....

8. A New Database dialog box will appear with the General page selected. In the Database name box, enter a Database name, for example: citrixfarmdstore, and then assign an Owner by clicking on the browse button (...). Type in SQL Login name you specified in step 5, and then click on Check Names.

9. Click OK. Click OK again to create a data store database and assign an owner to the data store database.

10. In the SQL Server Management Studio's left pane, expand the tree until you reach the Security folder level.

11. Click on Logins folder, and then double click on an appropriate user on the right hand side.

12. In the Default database: area of the General page, change the Database from master to the Data Store database name you specified in step 8.

13. Click on the User Mapping page to make sure the user has db_owner permission on the datastore database.

14. Click OK and close the SQL Server Management Studio console.

Install the License Server

Since we are assuming that this is the first server in our server farm, we will begin our installation with the license server. Later, during the XenApp server installation, we will be prompted for the name of our license server, and since we have taken the time to plan our implementation, we *will* know its name. This is an excellent example of why the planning stage is so important!

Configuring & Implementing...

The License Server and Grace Periods

Citrix recommends that you install the license server prior to adding your first XenApp Server. This is an excellent recommendation because, as mentioned previously, you will be prompted for the license server name during the XenApp Server installation process, and because the XenApp Server will not accept user connections until it can contact a license server. Citrix provides a 96-hour initial grace period that will allow up to two users to connect while unable to connect to a license server. We recommend you use this period for testing your server before downloading license files. Coincidentally, XenApp Server licensing is not compatible with previous versions of Presentation Server 4.0, so you should not upgrade your licenses until you have upgraded or migrated to XenApp Server. Both versions can coexist in the same farm, but the licenses must be managed separately.

The license server can be installed on a server dedicated solely to licensing or share one with other applications. Whether you can use a shared server depends on the size of your farm. According to Citrix, the licensing server can co-reside if the number of machines connecting to the server is less than 50. For small environments of less than 50 servers, the licensing server can reside on the same server as XenApp server. Although Citrix allows the License Server to be installed on a Citrix XenApp Server, but it is not recommended to install the License Server with the XenApp Server as License Server requires a web Server component (Apache or IIS). XenApp Server (Application Server) should act only as a Terminal Server and not as a web Server and Terminal Server. A default installation of the license server also installs the License Management Console. To use the console, Microsoft IIS version 6.0 or later must be installed. If you do not choose to install IIS, you can use the License Administration Commands from the command prompt; however, you will not be able to generate licensing reports.

Installing Internet Information Server

To install Internet Information Server, follow these steps:

1. Click on Start menu, Control Panel and then double click on Add or Remove Programs.

2. In the **Add or Remove Programs** dialog box, click on **Add/Remove Windows Components.** On the Windows Components page of the **Windows Components Wizard**, highlight **Application Server** and click on **Details...**, as shown in Figure 3.11:

Figure 3.11 Windows Components

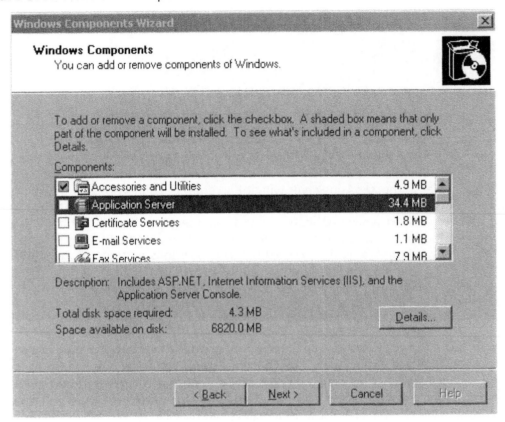

3. Next, from within the **Application Server** menu (see Figure 3.12), select **Internet Information Services (IIS)**. The **Enable network COM+ Access** will also be installed, as IIS and World Wide Web Services are dependent on this component.

Figure 3.12 Applications Server

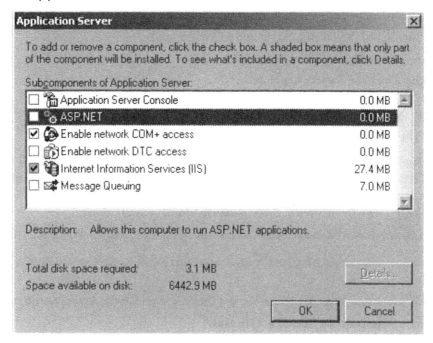

4. Click **OK** and then click **Next**. You will be prompted for the Windows Server 2003 source files. If you copied the \i386 folder to the server's hard disk or a network share, point the installation process to that folder. If not, insert the Windows Server 2003 CD-ROM.

5. Click **Finish**.

Once the installation completes, check the System Event Log for any problems or errors. Now we are ready to install the license server. The following information and procedure is defined only for information purposes. In reality, you do not have to follow this procedure every time when you build your XenApp Server environment. Once your License Server is up and running then you can just skip this section, and begin with installing and building Citrix XenApp Server for your environment. Please confirm from your Citrix Administrator before you proceed with this section.

Installing Citrix Access License Servers in a XenApp Environment

The following defines how to install Citrix Access license Servers in Citrix XenApp Server environment. Citrix has changed how it licenses their products. Each Citrix product in the Access Suite is centrally licensed through a Citrix License Server. To successfully install and configure Citrix License Server, you need to perform the following tasks:

1. Define the Server where you will be installing the Citrix License Server to.

2. Activate your Serial number and download a License file.

3. Install Citrix License Server.

4. Copy the license file to the folder on the License Server.

5. Verification of the License Server and Licenses.

6. Configure Delegated Administration.

7. Enable Licensing Report Logging.

Define the Server where you will be installing the Citrix License Server to

In your Windows environment, pick the Windows 2003 member Server where you will be installing the Citrix License Server. Make sure that your Server is build as per server build standards.

Activate your Serial number and download a License file

Here is a step by step procedure to activate and download Citrix License Server file:

1. Create an account on MyCitrix.com website, and logon to MyCitrix.com (www.mycitrix.com).

2. Click **Licensing** from the menu bar and then click on **Citrix Activation System.**

3. Click on **Activate or Allocate Licenses.**

4. Enter the serial number / license code for the XenApp Server. (Note: This can be in your connection license pack, in an email notification you received from Citrix, and/or from the Subscription Advantage Management-Renewal-Information system (SAMRI).

5. Enter the Country and State where your reseller is located and click **Search** to view a list of resellers.

6. Select your reseller and click **Continue.**

7. Click the radio button of the appropriate contact and click **Submit** to continue.

8. Enter the contact info for the location and person you wish Citrix to deliver the benefits associated with your Citrix Subscription Advantage License. Click **Submit** to continue.

9. You are now ready to generate the license file to be used on your Citrix License Server. Click **Continue.**

10. The next page prompts you to enter the NETBIOS name (hostname) of the Server you are installing the Citrix License Server to. **Important!** The hostname is case sensitive

11. Click on the **Start** menu, click **Run...,** type: **CMD** and then click **OK.**

12. Type "**hostname**" and hit the **Enter** key. Note the hostname on the piece of paper.

13. Click the **Hostname of your Citrix license Server** text box and type in the hostname.

14. Click the **Allocate** button to continue.

15. Confirm your license is correct and click **Confirm** to continue.

16. Click the **Download License File** button to download and save your license file.

NOTE

You have now successfully created your license file. You will need to keep this file handy as you will be copying it to the Citrix License Server in the following section.

Install Citrix License Server

The following defines how to install the Citrix License Server software.

1. Insert the **XenApp Server 4.5 Server** CD.

2. Click the **Product installations and updates** button.

3. Click the **Install Citrix Licensing** button to launch the setup program.

4. Read the license agreement. Scroll to the end of license agreement, and then click **I accept the license agreement** radio button. Click **Next**.

5. On the **Prerequisites Installation** page, click **Next**.

6. On the **Component Selection** page, make sure **Citrix Licensing** component is selected.

7. Click **Next**.

8. On the **Welcome to the Citrix Licensing Setup** page, click **Next**.

9. On the **Destination Folder** page, accept the default location and then click **Next**.

10. On the **Select Features** page, make sure that the **License Management Console** and the **License Server** is selected. Please note that Citrix does not require the License Management Console to be installed on same machine where you are installing the License Server as you can manage all licenses through the command-line utilities; however, you will lose the ability to generate licensing reports. Click **Next**.

11. On the **License Files Location** page, accept the default location of C:\Program Files\ Citrix\Licensing\MyFiles or enter the desired location. Click **Next**.

12. On the **Web Server Selection** page, make sure **Microsoft Internet Information Services (IIS)** is selected. Click **Next**.

13. On the **Restart Microsoft IIS Server** page, click **OK to restart Microsoft IIS Server** radio button and then click **Next**.

14. On the **Ready to Install the Application** page, click **Next** to install the Citrix License Server.

15. On the **Citrix Licensing has been successfully installed** page, click **Finish**.

16. Read the **Installation Summary** page, and verify that **Citrix Licensing** was installed successfully, and then click **Finish**.

Copy the license file to the folder on the License Server

Copy the license file you downloaded from MyCitrix.com to the directory you defined as the license file repository

Verification of the License Server and Licenses

Verify the license Server is running and licenses are being presented in the License Server Console. This is just a verification procedure to verify everything is working properly and that it sees your XenApp Server license.

1. Open Microsoft Internet Explorer and browse to http://license_server_name/lmc/index.jsp.

2. Enter your credentials to authenticate to the license Server. Use the name of the account you were logged in as while installing the Citrix License Server.

3. You are now presented with the **License Management Console** Welcome page. To view the current license usage and the licenses currently loaded click the **View Concurrent Usage Data** link.

4. Verify your license is listed. If it is not then click the **Refresh** link.

5. To view a complete list of all the licenses found click the **Complete Licenses Inventory** button.

6. Click to select the **Configuration** tab to view a list of the license files in use along with the date they were created. This tab allows selecting the **File Locations** and **Threshold Options** links to further configure the license Server.

Configure Delegated Administration

The License Management Console has the ability to delegate administration. You can delegate administration upon the following:

- **Current Usage**
- **Historical Usage**
- **Configuration**
- **User Administration**

The following details how to add and configure a new administrator.

1. Open Microsoft Internet Explorer and browse to http://license_server_name/lmc/index.jsp (This needs to be in all lowercase letters as it is case sensitive).

2. Enter your credentials to authenticate to the license Server. Use the name of the account you were logged in as while installing the Citrix License Server.

3. You are now presented with the License Management Console Welcome page. To view the current license usage and the licenses currently loaded click the **View Concurrent Usage Data** link.

4. On the User Administration page you have the ability to add a new User and/or change an existing user's access privileges. Click **Add New User** link to continue.

5. In the Add New User form enter the name of the account you wish to give access. This name is required to be entered in e format "Domain\username". You are also required to check to enable the checkbox(s) of the privileges you wish to grant to the new user. Click the **Submit** link when finished.

6. Once submitted you are brought back to the User Access page in which you will now see he new user you have added along with any existing users and their associated privileges.

Enable Licensing Report Logging

The report log contains historical data, such as the number of licenses used. The License Management Console requires the report log to generate licensing reports. In XenApp server, the default settings of the license Server do not create report logs. It is very important to archive the report log regularly to prevent them from growing to large, thus slowing the license Server down and causing unable to accept logins. Please keep in mind that the report log is not human readable, and it is meant for use with the License Management Console only.

The following details how to enable the Report Log in order to start collecting licensing historical data.

1. From the Welcome page click the **Configure License Server** link.

2. Click the **File Locations** link.

3. Click the **Change** link found in the Report Log section.

4. In the Report Log text box, enter the location you wish to store the report logs and any future backups. Once finished click the **Change** button to save your settings and continue. This adds the following line to the Add the following line to the Citrix.opt file: **REPORTLOG +"C:\Program Files\Citrix\Licensing\MyFiles\reportlog.rl"**

5. You will now see the path you specified in the previous step as the Report Log file location. It is recommended to backup your report log. To do this, click the **Backup** link.

6. Once you have backed up the report log you will see the "Last Backup" listed on the bottom of the File Locations page.

7. You have successfully installed and configured the Citrix License Server and are ready to continue with the project.

Installing XenApp Server

Finally, we come to a step to install the individual servers. We have installed the Document Center, created the data store, and installed the license Server; Now, we will install XenApp Server. The installation process is not different from previous releases, but as with other components, it is a good idea to become familiar with the process and the information you will need to complete it. Next, we will step through the process of installing XenApp Server and discuss in detail the information you will need and decisions you must make. Here is a step by step process to install XenApp Server (Platinum Edition):

1. Insert the XenApp Server 4.5 Server CD.

2. From the product CD-ROM Autorun screen, click on the **Product installations and updates** button.

3. Click on the **Install Citrix Presentation Server 4.5 and its components** button to launch the setup program.

4. Read the license agreement. Scroll to the end of license agreement, and then click **I accept the license agreement** radio button. Click **Next**.

5. Installation will now analyze the Server for the XenApp Server required components and will present you with a list of components that will be installed next, as shown in the Figure 3.13. On the **Prerequisites Installation** page, click **Next**.

Figure 3.13 Prerequisites Installation

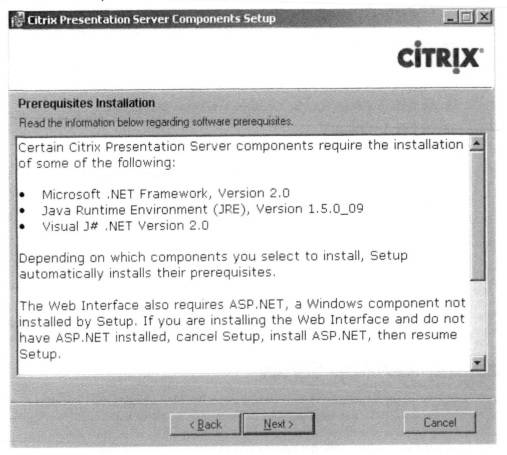

6. On **Component Selection** page, make sure **Citrix Licensing** is NOT selected, as we have already installed the License Server, as show in Figure 3.14. Click **Next**.

Figure 3.14 Component Selection

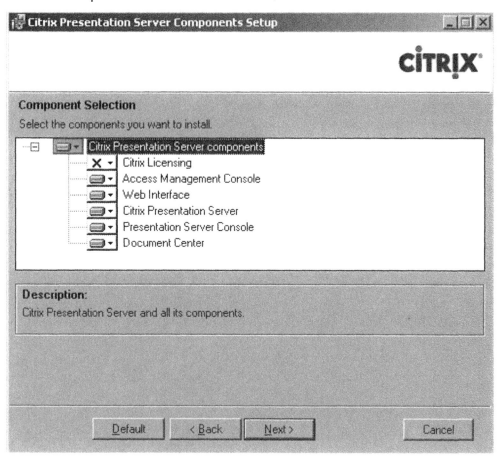

7. The next screen warns us that we did not elect to install a license server. Our options are to either have an existing license server or plan to install one later with the product CD-ROM. On the **Warning!** page, disregard this warning as we have installed a license Server and will be configuring XenApp Server to use it in a future step. Make sure **I already have a license server, or will use the product CD to install one later** is selected, as shown in Figure 3.15. Click **Next**.

Figure 3.15 Warning!

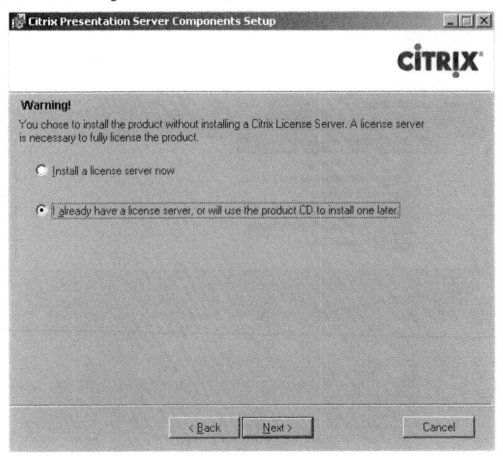

8. On the Welcome to the Citrix Access Management Console Installation page, click **Next**.

9. On the Component Selection page, you will be presented with the ability to select the components of the Citrix Access Management Console. These components include Diagnostic, Framework, Hotfix Management, Knowledge Base, Legacy Tools, Report Center, Web Interface, License Server Administration, Presentation Server Administration, and Presentation Server Reports. It is recommended to select the default of installing all components, as shown in Figure 3.16. Click **Next**.

Figure 3.16 Component Selection

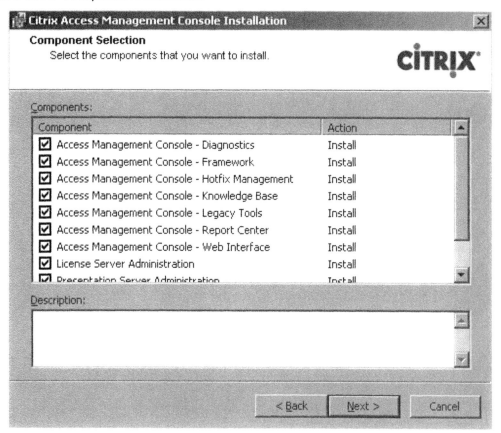

10. On the **Ready to Install** page, click **Next** to install the components of the Citrix Access Management Console.

11. On the **Installation Completed Successfully** page, click **Finish**.

12. On the **Welcome to the Citrix Web Interface Installation wizard** page, click **Next**.

13. On the **Common Components** page, specify a location to install common Web Interface components or select the default Destination Folder of **C:\Program Files\Citrix\Web Interface** and then click **Next**.

14. On the **Client** page, you will be promoted to either install the clients from the Components CD-ROM or do not install any client component. It is better not to install and distribute clients through the XenApp server as the clients on the Components CD-ROM might be older version. Please make sure **Don't install the Clients from the Components CD-ROM** is selected as shown in Figure 3.17. Click **Next**.

Figure 3.17 Clients

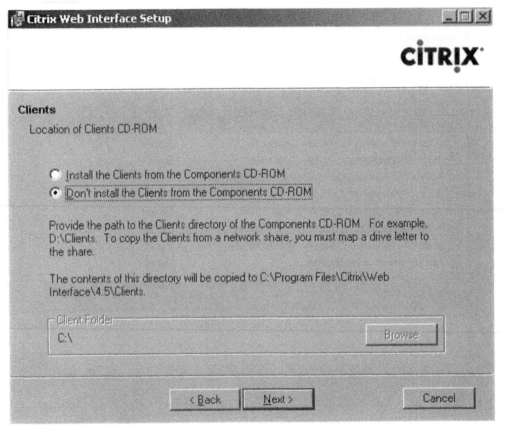

15.   On the **Ready to Install** page, click **Next.**

16.   On the **Citrix Web Interface has been successfully installed** page, click **Finish**.

17.   On the **Welcome to the Citrix Presentation Server for Windows Setup** page, click **Next**.

18.   You will then be presented with the Product Edition Selection page. If you are installing the Platinum Edition then you will not be presented with the Product Edition Selection page. On the other hand, if you are installing XenApp Server from the regular media, you will be presented with the Product Edition page. On the **Product Edition Selection** page, you are asked to select the product edition that you are licensed to run: Standard, Advanced, and Enterprise. If you are unsure of the edition you are licensed for, check your product documentation or check with your reseller. You do not want to install options that you will not be able to use. If you have a Standard Edition Licensing, you have just the basic XenApp Server and components. The Advanced Edition, designed for small to medium environments, includes load-balancing functionality. If your license entitles you to the Enterprise Edition, Load Balancing, Installation Manager, Resource Manager, and Network Manager are all included. This edition targets medium to large environments that

need a single point of control for resource monitoring, application packaging and delivery, and network monitoring. For our purposes here, we will select the **Enterprise Edition**, as shown in Figure 3.18. Click **Next**.

Figure 3.18 Product Edition Selection

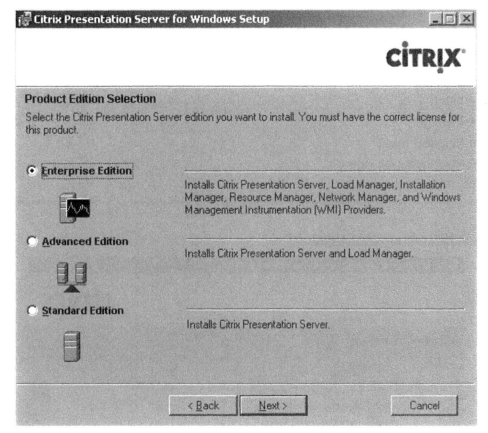

19. On the **Component Selection** page, select the components you will be installing. If you selected Enterprise Edition, you will see all the available components. If you selected another edition, you will only see those components included with the edition you selected. Please look at Table 3.7 to get details of components included in different edition of XenApp server. Citrix also includes a handy utility here that can check the disk space needed for the components you select. To see how much disk space you will need, click **Disk Cost**. I'd recommend removing the **Packager Component** and **Program Neighborhood Agent**. The Packager component should be installed only on the packager server. If this server is not a packager server, open the **Installation Manager** Key and click on **Packager** and then click on **X Entire feature will be unavailable**, as shown in Figure 3.19.

Table 3.7 Components Included with Each XenApp Server Edition

Components	Standard	Advanced	Enterprise
Management Console for XenApp Server	X	X	X
Installation Manager		X	
Installer Service			X
Packager			X
Resource Manager		X	
Load Manager	X	X	
Network Manager		X	
Program Neighborhood	X	X	X
Program Neighborhood Agent	X	X	X
WMI Providers			X

Figure 3.19 Component Selection

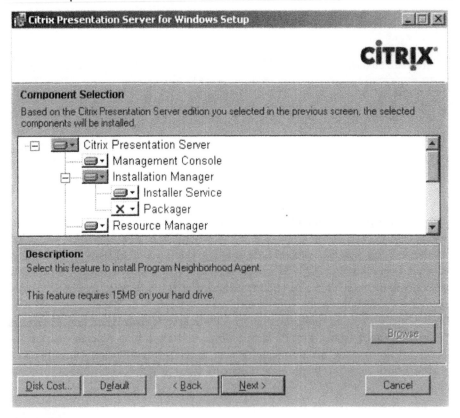

20. Depend on your environment; you may also want to disable the Program Neighborhood Agent client, as most people won't be using this client on the XenApp Server. Click on the **Program Neighborhood Agent** Key and then click on **X Entire feature will be unavailable**, as shown in Figure 3.20.

Figure 3.20 Component Selection

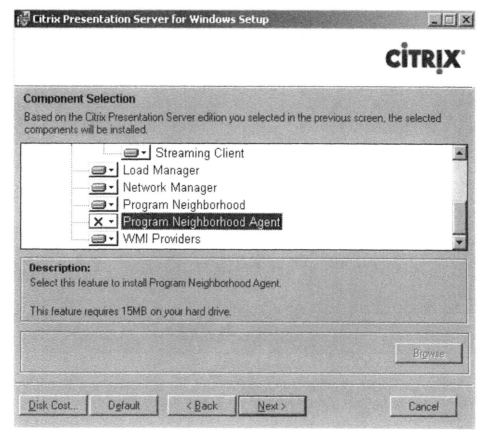

21. On the **Component Selection** page, you can also choose to install the Citrix XenApp Server to your chosen installation location or accept to the default location of C:\Program Files\Citrix. Click **Next**.

22. On the **Pass-through Authentication for the Pass-through Client** page, choose Yes to install the Pass-through Authentication for the Pass-through client or No to disable this component. Pass-Through Authentication allows the user's name and password to be passed from the local machine to the server. If you do not elect to install Pass-Through Authentication now and decide that you want this feature later on, you will need to reinstall the Pass-Through Client. Click to select the **Yes** radio button to give the end-users the ability to utilize Pass-Through authentication, as shown in Figure 3.21. Click **Next**.

Figure 3.21 Pass-through Authentication for the Pass-through Client

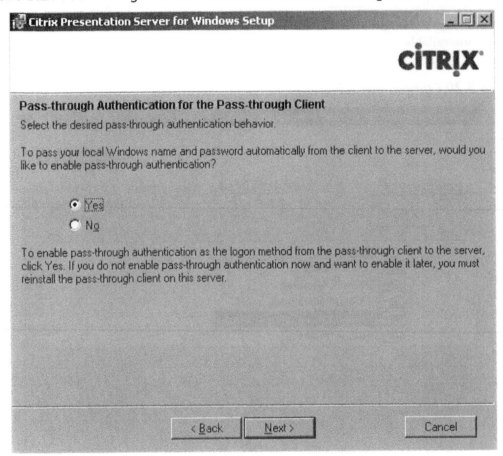

23. The next screen allows us to create a new farm or join an existing one. Because this is the first server in our farm, we will click on the **Create a new farm** radio button, and then click **Next.**

24. On the **Create a Server Farm** page (see Figure 3.22), enter a Server farm name in the **Farm name:** text box and select **Use the following database on a separate database server** to select an appropriate SQL database for the farm. You also have ability to select the Zone for the new Server. For the first Server in a farm, use the default zone name. When finished, click **Next**.

Figure 3.22 Create a Server Farm

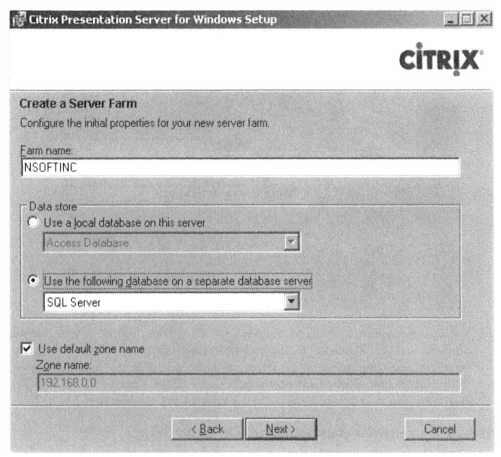

25. On the **Create a New Data Source to SQL Server** page (see Figure 3.23), enter a description in the **Description** text box and select the SQL Server from the **Server** drop down list. Click **Next**.

Figure 3.23 Create a New Data Source to SQL Server

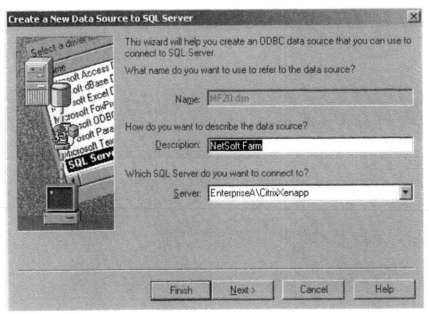

26. You are now prompted to select the authentication method. Depend on your environment, either choose With Windows NT authentication using the network login ID or With SQL Server authentication using a login ID and password entered by the user. Click to select the **With SQL Server authentication using a login ID and password entered by the user** radio button, as shown in Figure 3.24, and then click the **Next.**

Figure 3.24 Create a New Data Source to SQL Server

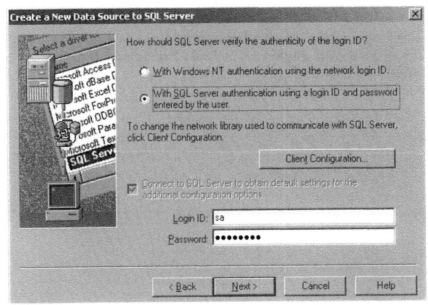

27. In **Create a New Data Source to SQL Server window** (see Figure 3.25), verify the
      data store database is selected as the default database and click **Next**. If it is not already
      selected then click to check the **Change the default database to** checkbox and select
      the XenApp Server data store database.

Figure 3.25 Create a New Data Source to SQL Server

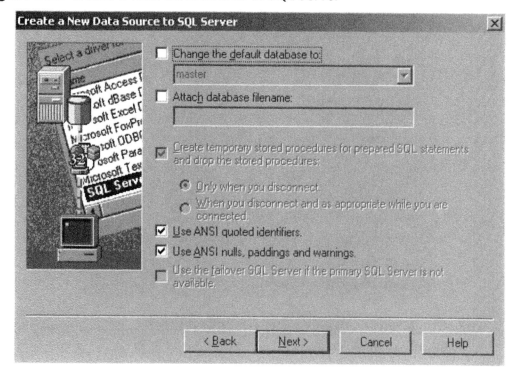

28. Click **Next** and then click **Finish**.

29. On the **ODBC Microsoft SQL Server Setup** page (see Figure 3.26), click the **Test
      Data Source...** button.

Figure 3.26 ODBC Microsoft SQL Server Setup

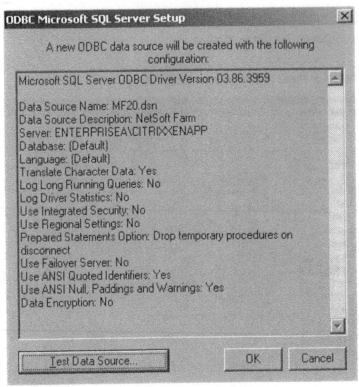

30.   Verify it reads **TESTS COMPLETED SUCCESSFULLY!**, as shown in Figure 3.27, and click **OK.** Click **OK** to continue.

Figure 3.27 SQL Server ODBC Data Source Test

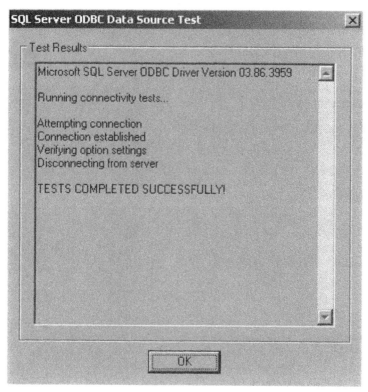

31. On the **Assign Farm Administrator Credentials** page, you are now prompted to enter a user account to assign Farm Administrator access. Use the default settings, and then click **Next**.

32. On the **Enable IMA Encryption** page, click **Next.**

33. On the **Citrix Licensing Settings** page (see Figure 3.28), we must provide the host name and port number for the licensing server, or we can choose to provide this information after completing the installation. Type in the license server name, choose an appropriate license server port, and then click **Next**.

Figure 3.28 Citrix Licensing Settings

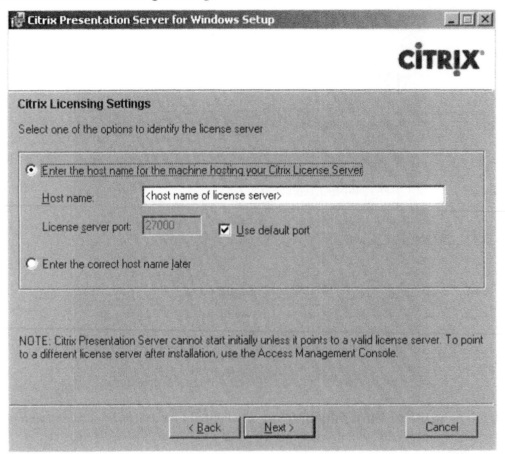

34.   Our next decision revolves around session shadowing. Shadowing is used to monitor users' sessions and, if needed, interact with their sessions. It is a handy tool for help desk personnel and others who need to actually see the users' sessions. However, in some secure environments, shadowing may not be permitted. You should check your company's policy and make sure you are compliant. During installation, we are given the option to prohibit shadowing. This option is permanent if configured during installation. Unless you are very sure that you do not want to allow shadowing, do not select this option. If you decide later not to allow shadowing, you can disable its use. Our other options with respect to shadowing are:

Prohibit remote control: This option prevents interacting with the user's session while shadowing.

Force a shadow acceptance popup: Users shadowed will receive a pop-up alert and must accept before shadowing is allowed.

Log all shadow connections: This option logs all shadowed connections to the Event Log.

On the **Configure shadowing** page (see Figure 3.29), accept the defaults settings, and click **Next**.

Figure 3.29 Configure Shadowing

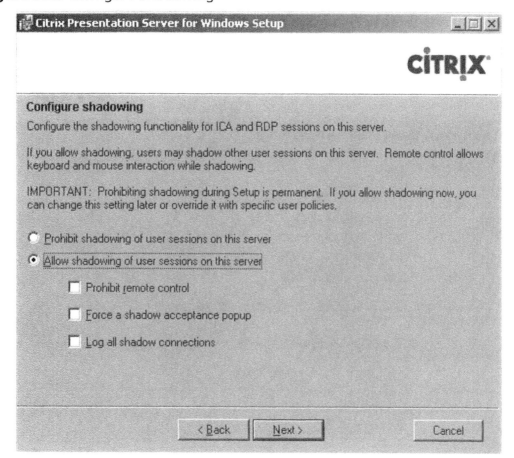

35.   Next, we must configure the port used by the XML service. The XML service provides the Web Interface and ICA-connected clients with the names of the published applications available in the farm. The default setting is to share port 80 with Internet Information Server and is necessary if sending data over HTTPS. If you do not intend to use HTTPS, select an unused port. If you are unsure of which ports are currently in use, type netstat –a at the command prompt. Be sure that all servers in a farm use the same port. On the **Configure Citrix XML Service Port** page, choose **Use a separate port**, and then enter the TCP/IP port that the Citrix XML Service will listen on and click **Next**. The default is port 80 and unless you have a reason for doing so, it is recommended that you stick with the default across all Servers in the farm.

36. On the **Add users to Remote Desktop Users group** page, you are required to add members in the Remote Desktop Users group in order to login. Of this page you are presented with the ability to have Presentation Server add the users group and/or anonymous users to the Remote Desktop Users group for you. Select the **Add the list of users from the Users group now**, and uncheck the **Add Anonymous users also** option to add only the authenticated users, as shown Figure 3.30. Click **Next**.

Figure 3.30 Add users to Remote Desktop Users group

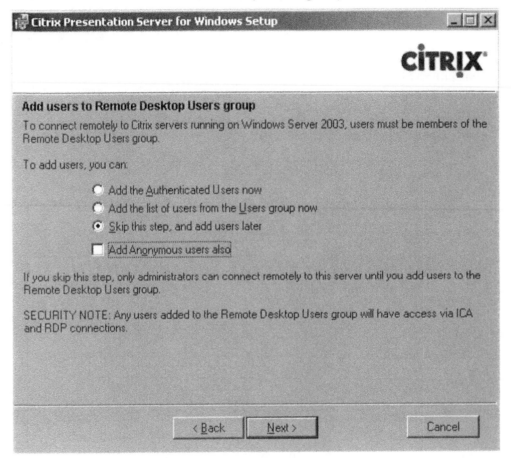

37. On the **Review your selections listed below** page, verify that the farm and installation settings are correct. Click **Finish**.

38. Uncheck the **View the Readme File** checkbox. Click **Close**.

39. On the **Welcome to the Management Console for Citrix Presentation Server 4.5 Installation Wizard** page, click **Next**.

40. On the **Ready to Install the Application** page, click **Next**.

41. On the **Management Console for Citrix Presentation Server 4.5 has been successfully installed** page, click <u>F</u>inish.

42. On the **Welcome to Citrix Presentation Server Document Center Setup** page, click **Next.**

43. On the **Destination Folder** page, accept the default location and then click **Next.**

44. Click <u>F</u>inish.

45. On the **Installation Summary** page, verify the desired components were installed successfully. Click <u>F</u>inish.

46. On the **Installer Information** page, click **Yes** to restart the Server and complete the installation. Once the server is rebooted, you can apply any Citrix XenApp updates that may be needed and begin testing your server.

Summary

In this chapter, we examined the history, features, and limitations of Terminal Services and Citrix XenApp server. We started with an introduction to Terminal Services, examining the logical basis of Terminal Services and how it works. We gained a basic understanding of presentation layer protocols and their critical role in the Terminal Services computing world. Next, we shifted our attention to the history of Terminal Services. We learned about MultiWin, the core technology built by Citrix Systems and licensed back to Microsoft for inclusion into what we use as Terminal Services today. We looked in greater detail at the features of Terminal Services in Windows Server 2003. Some of the most striking new features are the improvements made to RDP on the server side and the RDC client, such as the native ability to redirect client drives, printing, audio, and so forth. We discussed the changes made to Terminal Services because of the Microsoft security initiative, the result being increased uptime and a more secure platform out-of-the-box.

We then reviewed some of the major limitations of Terminal Services. We dug into the challenges of load balancing and reviewed the various ways of implementing the Microsoft recommended solutions. One of the major issues with a Terminal Services only solution centers on the lack of an enterprise-level toolset. Terminal Services has no centralized single seat toolset to assist in managing larger Terminal Services farms. We also looked at the client-side limitations such as limited client platform support. Additional client-side limitations include the lack of a consistent feature set across the Remote Desktop Connection Clients and the Remote Desktop Protocol Clients. This inconsistency in the feature set includes drive redirection and printer redirection, to name two. We also discussed desktop integration issues, such as the "window within Windows" and lack of role-based access to the Terminal Services farm and the applications it hosts. We closed with a review of multimedia support issues such as Flash animation and multiple monitor support and how it is lacking in the native Terminal Services solution and client.

We then discussed how Citrix XenApp Server 4.5 can "embrace and enhance" Windows Server 2003 Terminal Services to create a truly enterprise solution. Citrix XenApp Server is a technology platform that runs on Microsoft Windows Server 2003 servers with Terminal Services enabled. Microsoft and Citrix have a long history together and have co-developed much of the underlying technology that allows multiuser remote access to occur on Windows servers. For some administrators, Terminal Services alone will provide enough functionality for their environment. For more demanding installations, Citrix adds value with their XenApp Server 4.5 product. XenApp 4.5 addresses gaps that exist in Terminal Services. These gaps deal primarily with load balancing, client access methods, and application availability. Citrix expands on the very limited options Microsoft gives you in these areas to provide a more seamless experience for both users and administrators.

Beyond the gaps it fills, Citrix also provides some additional features that Terminal Services lacks. Depending on the version of XenApp you have installed, Citrix can provide everything from role management to advanced reporting and application packaging. By choosing the feature set that is right for you, you can add value to your Terminal Services environment without breaking the bank on Citrix.

We then looked into hardware planning with a detailed discussion of horizontal vs. vertical scaling. We looked at the traditional bottlenecks that terminal servers face to allow us to better understand when and how to scale up or out. We followed with a planning section on building redundancies into our server hardware. Next, we spent a great deal of time reviewing the architect-level concepts of platform deployment. We covered the "how am I going to deploy this hardware and software" question by examining the five different methods or approaches to platform deployment: manual installation, unattended or scripted installations, server cloning, server provisioning, and finally the hybrid approach. For each solution, we examined the pros and cons and looked at examples of the type and size of environment in which the given approach may work best. We also reviewed the basic concepts of farm design for Presentation Server. We looked at the components that exist outside the farm, such as licensing, home folders, and profiles, and reviewed the basic components that exist as part of the farm, such as the role of the data collector, the data store, and the local host cache.

The key to a successful installation and deployment is careful planning and methodical implementation. Preparation will save you time in the long run by avoiding common problems and known issues. In this chapter, we reviewed some of the planning steps and what items we should gather pre-installation. We also spent a good portion of this chapter explaining the installation of Citrix XenApp. XenApp (formerly known as Presentation Server) has a reputation for being complex and difficult to manage, and this is a *new* version with enough differences that beginning without finding out as much about it as possible and making a plan could end up in disaster. Use the Installation Checklist and check the Citrix Web site for new information or updates. If you have software that is known to be problematic, check the Citrix Support forums to see if anyone else out there has run into issues—they may have found the fix.

With any luck, this chapter provided enough information to help you perform the basics of creating a new XenApp farm. Depending on your environment, the process could be more or less complex. Each environment is unique and will have its own unique issues. Proper preparation and planning can help to avoid many of the common problems that arise, but others will require research and trial and error before they are resolved. Remember, practice makes perfect, and that goes for server builds as well. Find a way to perform test installations before doing a live installation.

Solutions Fast Track

Introduction of Terminal Services and Citrix XenApp Server

☑ Terminal Services and Citrix XenApp Server allows the multiple simultaneous use of a Microsoft Windows computer remotely by the user population. For anyone who has used VNC, Timbuktu, PC Anywhere, Remotely Possible, X Windows, or even the new Remote Desktop for Microsoft Windows XP, you have some idea of what Terminal Services and Citrix XenApp enables you to do.

☑ Terminal Services and Citrix XenApp Server allows users of virtually any device to be able to access the same applications and data from anywhere internal and external of the network, anytime.

History of Terminal Services

☑ Terminal Services began life as a concept created by Ed Iacobucci while working on the OS/2 project at IBM. After gaining no interest from IBM on including this technology in OS/2, Ed left to found Citrix Systems, Inc.

☑ Ed and his team at Citrix Systems had signed an agreement with Microsoft allowing Citrix to modify the code and create a multiuser version of Windows NT 3.x. This modification to the kernel became known as MultiWin, and Citrix Systems sold the solution as a product named WinFrame. WinFrame was in every sense a completely capable and functional Windows NT 3.x server. WinFrame could function in any capacity that a "standard" Windows NT 3.x server could. In addition, WinFrame could host multiple user sessions and allow users remote access to their applications and information.

☑ In February 1997, Microsoft informed Citrix that it would be pursuing its own version of WinFrame, which would be based around the Windows NT 4.0 platform.

☑ In August 1997, Microsoft agreed to license the MultiWin technology from Citrix for inclusion in Windows NT 4.0 Terminal Server Edition. The agreement that was reached in August 1997 has since expired. A new agreement was signed that continues the same kernel source-code sharing. The current agreement is set to expire in 2009.

The Future and Beyond: Capabilities of Windows Server 2003 Terminal Services

☑ Terminal Services in Windows 2003 provides great advancements in security, scalability, and manageability, as compare to Windows Server 2000 Terminal Services.

Limitations of Windows Server 2003 Terminal Services

☑ Microsoft Windows 2003 is a great remote access platform, however, as with any product, there are certain limitations or situations in which Terminal Services by itself doesn't fit the bill. The limitations can be broken down in a few key areas:

☑ Load balancing limitations

☑ Secure remote access solution

☑ Lack of an enterprise toolset for management

☑ Lack of a built-in application deployment solution

☑ Small list of supported clients

☑ Limited client-side functionality

History of Citrix XenApp Server

☑ Citrix developed their ICA technology in the early 1990s.

☑ Through a licensing agreement with Microsoft, Citrix released a stand-alone OS called Citrix WinFrame, which was based on NT 3.51.

☑ Starting with NT 4.0, Citrix became a technology that ran on top of Windows Terminal Services.

Understanding the XenApp Server Architecture

☑ XenApp is based on two core technologies known as ICA and IMA

☑ IMA is the underlying technology of the XenApp servers. It allows multiuser remote access to occur with all of Citrix's advanced features.

☑ ICA is the protocol technology that links together the client and the server. It uses virtual channels to improve the client's seamless experience.

The Future and Beyond: Capabilities of XenApp Server

☑ Advanced client connection options for mapping local resources.

☑ Administration through both a Java-based tool and an MMC snap-in.

☑ Advanced monitoring and reporting capabilities.

☑ Improved client printer experience with advanced printer mapping options.

How XenApp Server Fills the Gaps in Terminal Services

☑ Provides advanced load-balancing options over Microsoft's basic node balancing.

☑ Gives administrators more options to improve the speed of the client's experience.

☑ Has increased session reliability features to prevent remote users from being disconnected.

☑ Provides for published applications and access to them through a variety of methods, including Web-based access.

Planning for XenApp Server Deployment

☑ Planning the deployment of Citrix XenApp Server is a very in-depth process. Since XenApp Server and the underlying Terminal Services platform will be required in many deployments to integrate into nearly every process an organization may have, careful consideration and forethought must be given as to how best to introduce the technology.

☑ Careful planning is frequently the difference between a successful implementation and a failed deployment. Careful planning can be the difference between happy users and unhappy ones, as it can affect the performance of the overall network even if we are only conducting a project on one aspect of the network. Planning involves planning in different areas including:

☑ Hardware Planning

☑ Horizontal vs. Vertical Scaling

☑ Build In Redundancies

☑ Server Virtualization

Platform Deployment Options

☑ Platform deployment options include manual installation, unattended or scripted installs, server cloning, and a newer approach called server provisioning.

☑ Some organizations may want to use a mixed or hybrid approach that uses the best pieces of these various solutions. Selecting the best platform deployment option for your environment involves a detailed review of the requirements for each with special emphasis on the additional software and engineer expertise required. Most environments may lean heavily on one of these solutions, but may ultimately be categorized as a hybrid due to the nuances required integrating into the existing networking environment.

Citrix XenApp Server Installation Process

☑ Remember to remap the server drives prior to installing XenApp Server or components.

☑ Remapping the drives frees up the drive letters C: and D: for use by the client.

☑ Drive remapping is permanent and remains changed even if XenApp Server is uninstalled.

☑ Unless you plan to use MS Access, the data store must be created prior to installing your first server. You will be asked during the installation process for the name and location of the data store.

☑ A small farm of 50 or fewer servers can use MS Access or MSDE in indirect mode. Indirect mode refers the servers in the farm connecting to the data store installed on a XenApp Server that hosts the data store.

☑ Medium- to enterprise-level farms should have a dedicated server hosting the data store and use one of the true client/server database products supported, such as MS SQL Server, Oracle, or IBM DB2.

☑ Before deciding on a database to use for the data store, be sure your environment has the technical expertise to administer the database, and that the database you select will handle any expected growth in your environment.

☑ The licensing server can be run on a dedicated server, or it can share hardware with another XenApp Server. Citrix recommends a dedicated server if the number of servers in the farm exceeds 50.

☑ Ensure that IIS version 6 or later and ASP.net have been installed prior to installing the Web Interface.

☑ Configure the default URL for the login page to http://server name.

☑ Be sure you know the XML port that will be used and if the IIS service will share it.

☑ If using a dedicated database server, be prepared with the credentials necessary to access the database.

☑ Remember that Citrix provides a 96-hour grace period during which testing can be performed.

☑ Once the server has been tested, download the license files from http://mycitrix.com.

Frequently Asked Questions

Q: I am considering running Windows Server 2003 Terminal Services without using Citrix XenApp Server. Due to the lack of an enterprise management toolset, what would be the largest number of servers (thereby users) that you would recommend?

A: The answer to this question depends heavily on what types of users and applications you will be running. If the user population has similar needs as far as the application list, the servers could be built nearly identically, and therefore a larger farm of terminal servers without Citrix would be manageable. If your goal is to deploy a single application, the farm of terminal servers could be quite large to support this, upward of 10 to 20 servers, supporting 500 to 2000 user sessions. If the users have different application needs, this number would decrease sharply.

Q: Is there an updated RDC client for my Win16 users?

A: No. Microsoft hasn't created a newer version of the RDC client for Win16 platforms. However, users who still have the Win16 client from previous versions of Terminal Services will be able to connect to the new terminal servers (with decreased functionality).

Q: I have been around Terminal Services and Citrix for quite some time. There has always seemed to be a debate over whether to use dual processor or quad processor servers. Which is best for a Terminal Services implementation, with or without Citrix?

A: The answer to this question lies in whether the applications you are running on the terminal servers are multithreaded and behave well on the third and fourth processors of a quad. Typical applications found on users desktops and subsequently moved to the terminal servers do not scale well on the third and subsequent processors. The reason is simple: applications are written for workstations that at best have two processors. How many of your workstations in the past have been quads or eight-way processor machines? The real answer would be thorough testing of your application set to determine the benefits, if any, that advanced multiprocessor servers may bring.

Q: I keep reading about these license agreements between Microsoft and Citrix. When do they expire?

A: Citrix and Microsoft just announced that they renewed their deal through 2009.

Q: Will the Web Interface protect my servers from external hacking attempts?

A: Web interface alone will not, but you can add on other Citrix components such as Secure Gateway to provide the added security. If used in conjunction with a good firewall, you can isolate your servers from outside attacks.

Q: What if I don't use the new streaming technology in Citrix, and my users access a video stream?

A: Depending on the bandwidth, it's going to be really choppy. You are taking a data stream, converting it to ICA traffic, and then shoving it down the ICA pipe. Playback is seldom flawless and frequently unusable.

Q: I only have the Standard Edition of XenApp. Can I use the Web Interface?

A: Yes, Web Interface is included as part of the basic package. Other Citrix products may not work without Advanced or Enterprise Edition.

Q: I already use SMS to push my applications. What would I gain from using Citrix's Installation Manager?

A: Depending on how advanced your SMS infrastructure is, not much. Installation Manager does not have the full range of packaging options that SMS can provide, and the interface is not as easy to use. However, you do gain the benefit of having the data in the same management tool (the CMC) and you can use it to publish SMS-created packages that are in a .msi format.

Q: What exactly is "drive remapping" and why would I want to do this?

A: Drive remapping reassigns the drive letters used by the server. For instance, if your server drives are C: and D:, they could be remapped to M: and N:. If the server drives are not remapped, the local drives of users connecting to the XenApp servers will be remapped to U:,V:, and W: because C: and D: are taken by the server. Users often become confused by this and assume that C: and D: are their local drives. Remapping the server drives frees up C: and D: for use by the local drives.

Q: At what point should the drives be remapped?

A: Prior to installing XenApp Server or any of the components.

Q: What is the Document Center?

A: The Document Center is a new feature that creates a library of all the MetaFrame Access Suite guides, in .pdf format, in one central location where they can be easily accessed when needed. The Document Center can be installed on the server or workstation.

Q: What are the benefits of using Microsoft SQL Desktop Edition over using MS Access for the data store?

A: MSDE is a scaled-down version of Microsoft SQL Server and is included free on the XenApp Server CD-ROM. MSDE can be used in small server farms of 50 or fewer servers in indirect mode, just as MS Access, or in very small environments as a direct connection. MSDE support up to five concurrent connections, and since the servers do not all contact the data store at the same time, there is little risk that all five connections would be in use at the same time.

Q: What are the three editions of XenApp Server, and how do I know which edition I need?

A: The three editions are Standard, Advanced, and Enterprise. The Standard Edition is the core product, the administrative console and the Document Center. This edition is best for small environments with little need of centralized monitoring, unattended installations, or load balancing. The Advanced Edition is the core product and Load Management. Load Management manages the user load to servers and applications. The Advanced Edition is suitable for medium to large environments where users connect to multiple servers and a way to manage the load on each is needed. The Enterprise Edition includes all that the Standard and Advanced Editions have and adds Resource Manager, Network Manager, Installation Manager, and WMI Providers. This edition is suitable for large, enterprise environments where centralized monitoring and unattended installations are needed.

Q: What is the licensing server and where should it be installed?

A: The licensing server is a centralized licensing utility where all the Access Suite licenses can be managed.

Q: What information do I need to know to add a new XenApp Server to an existing farm?

A: You will need to know what type of database is being used for the data store, whether it is a local database (MS Access or MSDE) or one on a dedicated server (MS SQL Server, Oracle, or IBM DB2), and the host name of the server where the database resides. You will also need logon credentials to access the database.

Q: If during setup, I choose to prohibit shadowing, can I turn it on later?

A: No, the decision during setup is permanent. To turn it back on, you would need to reinstall the server.

Q: What if I decide after installing XenApp Server that I do not want to use the same port for IIS and the XML service?

A: The port can be changed post-installation. To change the port, go to the command prompt and type **ctxxmlss /u** to unload the XML service. Next, type **ctxxmlss /rxx**, where "xx" is the port you will use. When finished, restart the XML service.

Chapter 4

Understanding XenApp Security

Solutions in this chapter:

- Defining the XenApp Security Model
- Defining Types of Deployments
- Understanding Authentication Methods
- Encrypting XenApp

☑ Summary

☑ Solutions Fast Track

☑ Frequently Asked Questions

Introduction

Data security incidents and breaches into identity theft are now daily headlines. Until recently publicity regarding these breaches was more limited. In 2003, California was one of the first states to pass a law requiring companies to notify affected consumers regarding security breaches. Since then, many other states have passed similar legislation. These public notice requirements have heightened consumer and public awareness regarding data security breaches.

As a result of these many incidents, state and federal government agencies have created numerous policies that affect information security and the protection of data. Some of the most visible are the Sarbanes–Oxley Act of 2002, referred to as SOX, and the Health Insurance Portability and Accountability Act, referred to as HIPAA. Even though these policies identify what needs to be protected, they do not necessarily tell how to implement the protection. In some cases, administrators have found contradictory guidelines or guidelines that have caused a change in how information technology business is conducted. Additionally, some legislation only affects publicly held companies.

In many cases it is up to individual organizations to provide specifics for defining data security implementation. In this chapter, we hope to provide you with the information to take a manageable hold of your information security as it relates to XenApp.

The needs of your organization will dictate the optimal version of XenApp to use; for example, the requirements of your organization may dictate the need for session auditing, which only the Platinum Edition provides.

XenApp is offered in three versions:

- **Advanced Edition** This is the base version of XenApp that provides server-side application virtualization and application-based load management.

- **Enterprise Edition** In addition to the features of the Advanced Edition, the Enterprise Edition provides client-side application virtualization, application performance optimization, application compatibility optimization, and system monitoring and analysis.

- **Platinum Edition** This version includes all the features of the Enterprise Edition and provides additional features such as SmartAuditor session recording, application password policy control, universal SSL VPN with SmartAcess, application performance monitoring, and single sign-on application security.

Defining the XenApp Security Model

One of the first steps in securing your XenApp environment is to understand what we define as the *XenApp Security Model*. There has been some discussion on various forums and several documents have been prepared concerning how to secure Citrix XenApp Server. We will expand on that information and how it can be used to secure a XenApp environment. We have provided a culmination of these concepts into the XenApp Security Model. You can view the XenApp Security Model much like that of the *OSI Model*. The XenApp Security Model has six layers (see Figure 4.1).

Figure 4.1 The XenApp Security Model

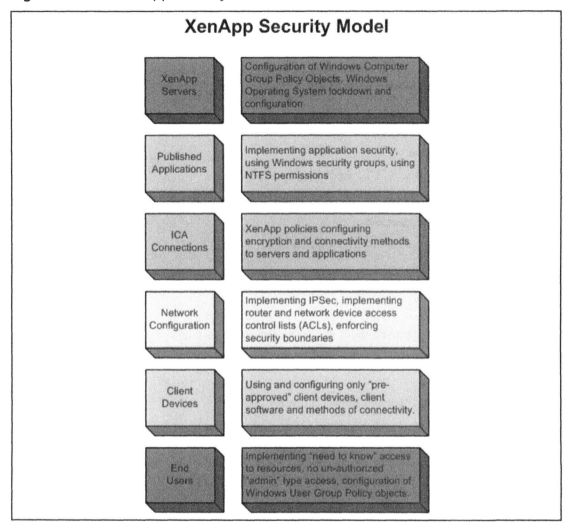

As a XenApp administrator, your job is mainly ensuring that applications and resources are published for your users. Your responsibility is not only protecting your users and their data from malicious external threats, but also from internal malicious threats AND protecting them from inadvertent mistakes they can potentially make in an unsecured XenApp environment. Keep in mind that no matter how hard you go about locking down any environment (not just XenApp), there may be that one user that is able to defeat the measures that have been put into place. At one time or another, you have probably encountered the user that insists on proving that they know more than you do. It is a challenge for them to overcome the measures you have put into place to protect the network. There are also users that may end up bypassing security mechanisms simply by accident rather than by design. Implementing security based on the XenApp Security Model will assist you in protecting your network from these different threats and different users. You must carefully review each level at which your environment provides information to the user. To assist you in defining policies for your XenApp network, security should be implemented in the following manner:

- **XenApp Servers**
    - Implementing *computer* group policy objects
    - Locking down the base operating system

- **Published Applications**
    - Implementing application security
    - Using Windows security groups
    - Implementing NTFS permissions on application executables

- **ICA Connection**
    - Security on the ICA connection
    - Encryption

- **Network Configuration**
    - Using Internet Protocol security (IPSec)
    - Router ACLs
    - Enforcing security boundaries

- **Client Devices**
    - Using only approved client devices to connect
    - Using only approved client software to connect

- **End Users**
    - Establishing a "need to know" access for users
    - Not allowing any unauthorized "admin" type access
    - Implementing *user* group policy objects

You need to consider all aspects of your environment. Does a user really need the capability to run CSCRIPT.exe or CMD.exe? Does a user need the capability to surf the Internet? For a multihomed server, does the ICA protocol need to be listening on every interface? Is the firewall team going to think kindly of you when you want to open up Transmission Control Protocol (TCP) port 1494? Do you want to have your payroll application published on a server that also has applications available to all employees in your company? When applying security in the XenApp environment and by using the XenApp Security Model presented here, you will be better prepared to address situations like these.

NOTE

The XenApp Model presented here may not cover all aspects for your particular network. The model is intended as a starting point to help assist you in addressing the security concerns of your environment. You may have to add or remove elements to best suit the needs of your organization.

Defining Farm Security and Farm Boundaries

XenApp networks range in size, both in number of users and geographical area. Some XenApp farms may only have one server with 10 to 20 users. Other farms may have several hundreds of servers globally dispersed with thousands of users. Regardless of what type of environment you have, you should clearly define your environment to assist you with applying the XenApp Security Model to your network. Many administrators already have this task completed in the form of a *network diagram*. You may think that this is an unnecessary task in providing security to your environment, but the saying "a picture is worth a thousand words" holds true in the world of information technology and information security. By having a quick glance view of your network boundaries and assets, you can quickly ascertain your "weak" points of security. We have seen that a network boundary diagram does not necessarily have to show every single device in your network, but it should show a logical definition of your network.

Our example in Figure 4.2 shows a single-forest, single-domain, two-site corporate network. The corporation has grouped its externally available assets into a demilitarized zone (DMZ). You will notice that there are firewalls between each segment. The diagram does not go into details as to the number of servers at each location or the type or even the layers of protection provided by the firewalls. For example, the firewall could be a combination of an actual firewall device and router ACLs defining access, but our diagram simply shows it as a boundary. So, what do we define as a boundary? In the simplest of definitions, a *boundary* can be defined any time data traverses a network device or leaves one logical network and enters another. Many corporations have multiple internal network devices that can bridge virtual LANs (VLANs) or provide redundancy, so would these be considered network boundaries? It is up to you, as the administrator, to determine how to best group these devices to come up with a workable network boundary diagram that you can use to assist you with identifying potential problems.

Once you have identified a workable network boundary diagram, simply add your XenApp components into the mix. In our example network, the corporation wants to make MS Office applications available to its users both internally and externally. The corporation uses smart card technology for internal authentication and wants to also use that same authentication mechanism for external users. The corporation is also concerned about the data because it contains sensitive information, so they want end-to-end encryption. The resulting XenApp farm boundary diagram is provided in Figure 4.3. The Web Interface server and a Secure Gateway server are placed in the corporate DMZ and the XenApp servers are placed at each site. The corporation decides that internally, the data is protected enough via Basic encryption provided by XenApp and that the encryption of the links between the sites and the corporate DMZ mitigates the need to further encrypt the data between the DMZ and the corporate sites. However, they do want external access encrypted to the maximum extent possible. How to go about configuring the scenario is explained in detail later in this chapter, but we have added it to our final XenApp network boundary diagram in Figure 4.3. From this diagram, the network administrator should be able to quickly ascertain where the potential for security risks lies.

WARNING

Having a network and farm boundary diagram can be extremely useful. But be careful as to the specific information that you place on the document. For example, do you want to include IP addresses for network devices and servers on a displayed diagram if your diagram is displayed where outside personnel, such as temporary contractors or consultants, could potentially see the information? The bottom line here is to assume that if you are advertising the information where someone can see it, then they can also remember that information for later use.

Figure 4.2 Defining Network Boundaries

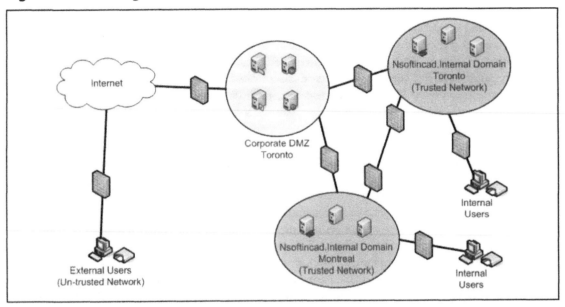

Figure 4.3 Defining XenApp Farm Boundaries

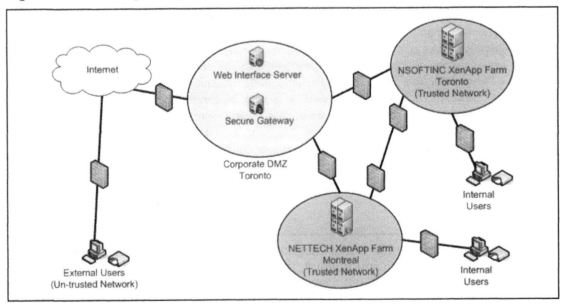

Defining XenApp Server Security

To protect vital information from unauthorized intruders, it is vital that you secure your network and computer assets. As computer and network systems have become more common, the need for security has grown exponentially. As an administrator, you must be careful to ensure that you take into account every option that can assist in securing the computing environment. Although Citrix XenApp provides several methods to ensure security of vital information, other products and solutions are used to protect data throughout a computing environment.

A critical component of XenApp security is the security of the underlying operating system (OS) platforms on which the XenApp software runs. If it is not possible to secure the OS, then XenApp itself cannot be secure. Even a securely configured operating system is vulnerable to the flaws of the programs and applications that run on it.

Introducing Microsoft Security Tools

The first level of the XenApp Security Model deals with the server itself. First and foremost, you need to have your Windows server properly configured and locked down. There are many ways that you can secure the base operating system. Microsoft has many freely available tools that can assist you with the security configuration of your servers and help you to maintain an effective security posture, such as:

- **Security Configuration and Analysis Tool** This is a Microsoft Management Console (MMC) snap-in that allows you to use default or custom configured templates so that you can analyze and configure security settings on a Windows 2003-based computer.

- **Microsoft Baseline Security Analyzer (MBSA)** This tool, shown in Figure 4.4, scans for missing security updates and common security settings that are configured incorrectly. Typically, this tool is used in conjunction with Microsoft Update or Windows Server Update Services.

- **Extended Security Update Inventory Tool** This tool is used to detect security bulletins not covered by the MBSA and future bulletins that are exceptions to the MBSA.

- **System Center Configuration Manager** This tool provides operating system and application deployment and configuration management. This is the latest version of Systems Management Server (SMS) 2003.

- **Microsoft Security Assessment Tool (MSAT)** This tool, shown in Figure 4.5, is designed to help you assess weaknesses in your information technology (IT) security environment. The tool provides detailed reporting and specific guidance to minimize risks it has identified.

- **Microsoft Update** (www.update.microsoft.com) This Microsoft Web site combines the features of Windows Update and Office Update into a single location that enables you to choose automatic or manual delivery and installation of high-priority updates.

- **Windows Server Update Services (WSUS)** This tool provides an automated way for keeping your Windows environment current with the latest updates and patches.

- **Microsoft Office Update** (www.officeupdate.com) This Microsoft Web site scans and updates Microsoft Office products.

- **IIS Lockdown Tool** This tool provides security configuration for Internet Information Servers (IIS) and can be used in conjunction with *URLScan* to provide multiple layers of protection against attackers.

- **UrlScan Tool** This tool helps prevent potentially harmful HTTP requests from reaching IIS Web servers.

- **EventCombMT** This multithreaded tool will parse event logs from many servers at the same time to assist you with finding specific event entries.

- **PortQry** This tool is a Transmission Control Protocol/Internet Protocol (TCP/IP) connectivity testing utility that can aid you in determining active TCP ports in use on a system.

- **Malicious Software Removal Tool** This tool checks a system for infections by specific, prevalent malicious software, to include *Blaster*, *Sasser*, and *Mydoom*. The tool can also assist in the removal of any discovered infections. Microsoft releases an updated version of this tool every month.

- **Port Reporter** This tool is a service that logs TCP and User Datagram Protocol (UDP) port activity.

Figure 4.4 Using the Microsoft Security Baseline Analyzer Tool (MBSA)

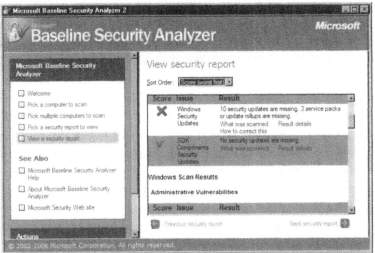

Figure 4.5 Using the Microsoft Security Assessment Tool (MSAT)

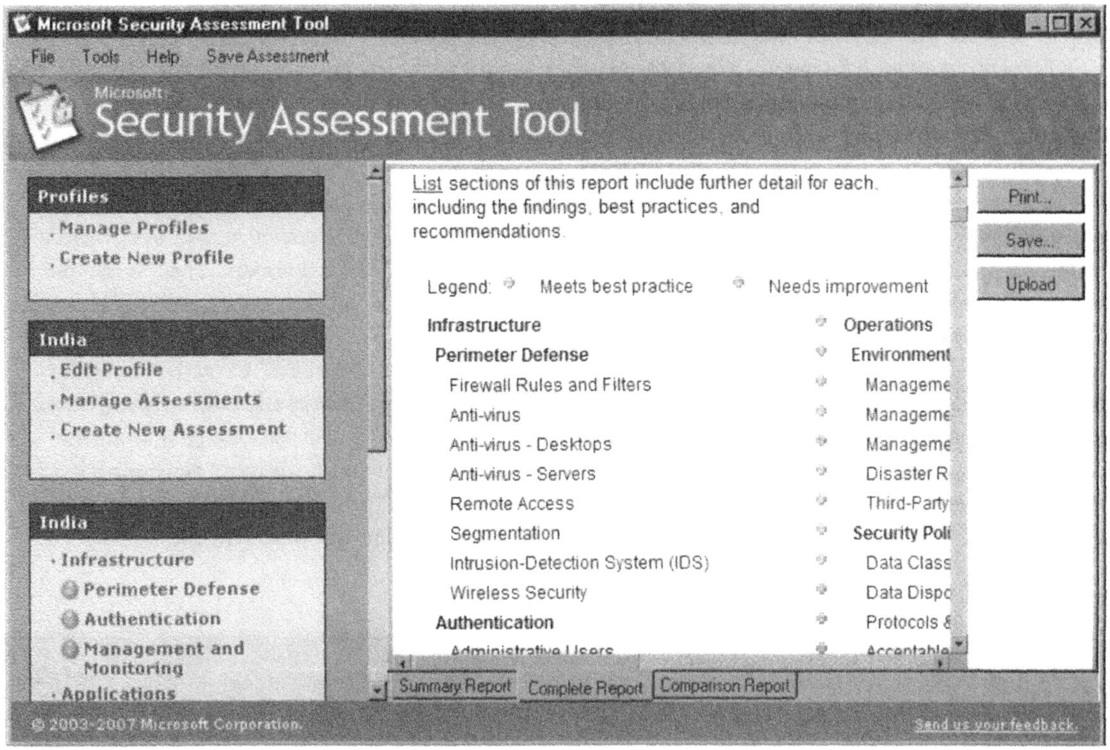

TIP

The servers used in our labs for this book were first locked down using the Windows Server 2003 Security guide and the tools listed above available from the Microsoft Web site, www.microsoft.com/security. The National Security Agency (NSA) also provides several documents that are publicly available from their Web site, www.nsa.gov/snac, to assist in the securing of other assets. As in any environment, you should first implement the recommended settings in a test environment before configuring a live production network.

Understanding Alternate Data Streams

Alternate Data Streams (ADS) is a virtually unknown compatibility feature of New Technology File System (NTFS) that can provide attackers with a method of hiding hacker tools, keyloggers, and so on, on a breached system and then will allow them execution without being detected. You need to be aware that an attacker does not play by any rules. Nothing is off limits when attempting to breach a system. In so doing, attackers have become very adept at hiding their tracks. Why does ADS exist? ADS capabilities were originally designed to allow for compatibility with the Macintosh Hierarchical

File System, HFS, where file information is sometimes inserted, or forked into separate resources. ADS is used for legitimate purposes by a variety of programs including the Windows operating system to store file attribute information and for temporary storage. Directories can also support ADS.

Typically the task of copying a root kit or other hacker tools can be tricky with the products that are installed in most environments, but an attacker that knows how to exploit ADS can be successful if proper security measures are not exercised. You should never underestimate the determination of someone that truly wants to breach your system.

A popular method that attackers use for covering their tracks on Windows-based systems is the use of ADS. The use of ADS provides the capability to store one file in another without outwardly changing the appearance, functionality, or size of the original file. The only modification is the file date, which can be changed by freely available utilities. In Figure 4.6 we have two programs listed, NOTEPAD.exe and BADPROGRAM.exe (a sample hacker tool). The figure illustrates the original states of the files. Then we insert the file BADPROGRAM.exe into NOTEPAD.exe by using the following command: **type c:\temp\badprogram.exe > c:\temp\notepad.exe:badprogram. exe**. Following along in the figure you will notice that the only thing that has changed about the original file NOTEPAD.exe is the file date. At first glance there is really no way to determine if a file is utilizing the ADS feature. Inspecting the file through a command prompt or Windows explorer does not give you any hint that the file has been modified other than the time stamp.

Figure 4.6 Using Alternate Data Streams

```
C:\Temp>dir
 Volume in drive C is Local
 Volume Serial Number is C8F1-834A

 Directory of C:\Temp

03/17/2008  11:58 AM    <DIR>          .
03/17/2008  11:58 AM    <DIR>          ..
03/17/2008  11:57 AM            16,384 BadProgram.exe
08/04/2004  06:00 AM            69,120 notepad.exe
               2 File(s)         85,504 bytes
               2 Dir(s)  26,484,039,680 bytes free

C:\Temp>type c:\temp\badprogram.exe > c:\temp\notepad.exe:badprogram.exe

C:\Temp>dir
 Volume in drive C is Local
 Volume Serial Number is C8F1-834A

 Directory of C:\Temp

03/17/2008  11:58 AM    <DIR>          .
03/17/2008  11:58 AM    <DIR>          ..
03/17/2008  11:57 AM            16,384 BadProgram.exe
03/17/2008  12:03 PM            69,120 notepad.exe
               2 File(s)         85,504 bytes
               2 Dir(s)  26,413,600,768 bytes free

C:\Temp>start c:\temp\notepad.exe:badprogram.exe

C:\Temp>_
```

The next line in the figure shows how the inserted program can be executed by entering: **start c:\temp\notepad.exe:badprogram.exe**. Running Task Manager now reveals that the file is using ADS as shown in Figure 4.7. Older versions of Windows did not show this and the issue of ADS was even more of a concern because damaging processes could then be executed without fear of detection. Only the most robust of intrusion detection systems will be able to identify and warn of files or processes initiated through an ADS. Moving an ADS to another system that supports ADS will keep the ADS file intact; however, if the file is moved to a system that does not support ADS, then the ADS is automatically destroyed.

Figure 4.7 File Using an Alternate Data Stream

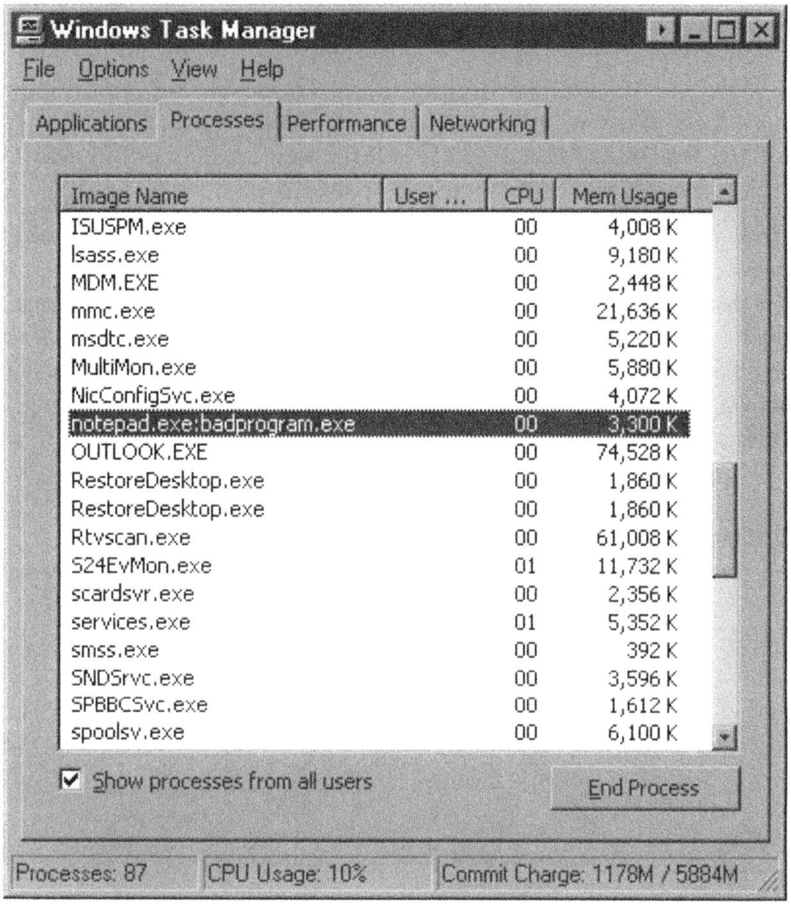

Understanding Security Configuration and Remediation

Security configuration and maintenance at the server level can be a very demanding and time consuming task, even for a small environment. Many organizations have adopted the Information Technology Infrastructure Library (ITIL) methodology for IT management. ITIL is a collection of guidelines and techniques for managing IT infrastructure, development, and operations, shown in Figure 4.8. ITIL covers areas such as configuration management, change management, and security. Implementation of this initiative can prove to be invaluable for your organization. To help implement some of the recommendations presented in ITIL there are many third-party tools that can assist with security configuration compliance scanning, security compliance remediation, configuration management, etc. We have listed just a few software packages and their descriptions that can support the parts of the ITIL methodology.

- *BladeLogic Operations Manager* performs, among other things, patch management, compliance measurement, enforcement, and reporting.

- *HP Data Center Automation Center* is a suite of products that can perform patching, configuration management, script execution, compliance assurance, incident resolution, change orchestration, and many other tasks in a standardized and documented manner to enforce ITIL and compliance.

- *BMC Performance Manager for Servers* provides server monitoring, process monitoring, log file monitoring, and Windows event log monitoring. (BMC has a product specifically for Citrix called *BMC Performance Manager for Citrix Presentation Server*, but this product deals primarily with Citrix performance monitoring and optimization.)

- *IBM Tivoli* products such as *Compliance Insight Manager* that provides effective, automated user activity monitoring through high-level dashboard and compliance reporting, *Risk Manager* that manages security incidents and vulnerabilities, *Security Compliance Manager* that identifies security vulnerabilities and security policy violations, *Security Information and Event Manager* that provides a centralized security and compliance management solution, and *Security Operations Manager* that is designed to improve security operations and information risk management.

Figure 4.8 Understanding the ITIL Methodology

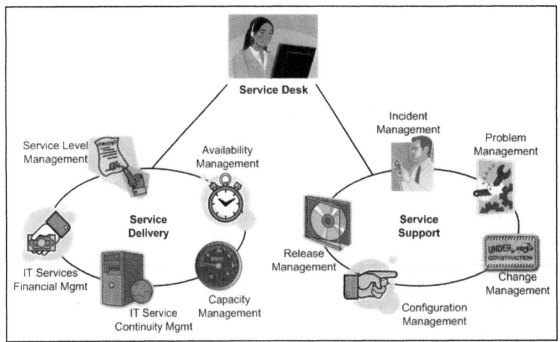

Using Windows Group Policy Objects

Your XenApp environment can be further configured by the use of *Group Policy Objects (GPOs)*, *Domain Security Policies*, and *NTFS permissions*. There are many different levels of the group policy object, but the basic details are shown in Figure 4.9. Group policies can be set by domain or be set locally on a server, or in some cases can be set in both places. Because of the flexibility offered with creating Windows GPOs, you could segregate your XenApp assets into their own Organizational Unit (OU) and apply specific GPOs that configure different aspects of your XenApp environment. You could have one GPO that deals specifically with server configuration settings for XenApp servers. Another GPO could be created to deal only with user level configuration settings on the server.

Your environment may already make use of default domain policies that apply to all servers. For example, settings such Server Message Block (SMB) timeouts, screensavers, and warning banners may apply to every server regardless of function, so be careful not to introduce a setting in a GPO that will adversely affect an unintended system. Terminal services settings in GPOs have been shown to affect both the RDP and ICA protocols, so having a separate GPO for remote administration and one for XenApp servers would be prudent. Can you imagine the result of having a single GPO for all of your terminal servers only to then have another administrator set the terminal services maximum connection time setting to three hours? This could prove disastrous if you are providing vital applications for users that stay logged on most of the day.

Figure 4.9 Using Window Group Policy Objects

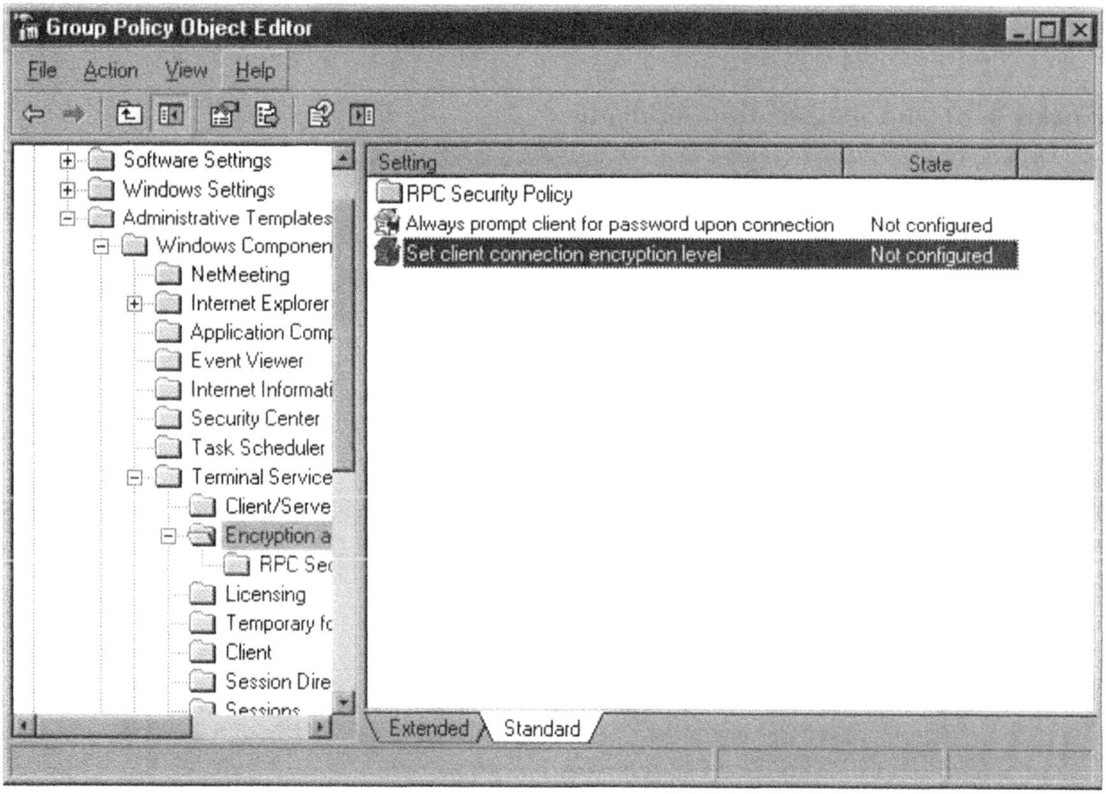

Using Windows Security Templates to Baseline Your System

As we have shown, Microsoft has many different solutions to assist you in securing your base operating system. But what happens if you have a customized set of security policies you would like to set that is beyond what is available through a GPO? The answer is Windows security templates. Security templates are not a new concept; they have been in existence since Windows NT. A *security template* allows you to configure security settings for different types of computers that you predetermine. You can view and configure existing Microsoft security templates through the MMC by selecting the **Security Templates** snap-in, shown in Figure 4.10.

WARNING

You can create a custom security template to be used in configuring your system. Keep in mind that designing a custom security template is just like making a change to your registry. If you make a mistake in the creation of a custom template, then you can adversely affect the performance and availability of your system once the custom template is deployed. Care and diligence should be exercised when creating a custom security template.

Figure 4.10 Utilizing Security Templates

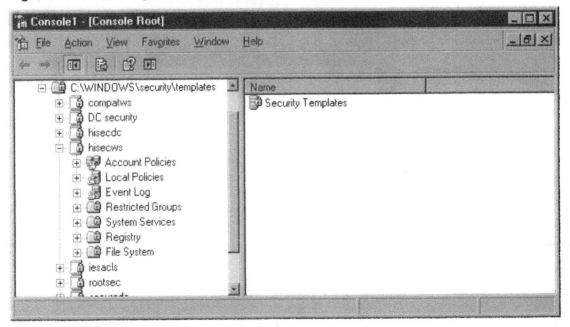

Upon configuration of a security template you can analyze your system utilizing the **Security Configuration and Analysis** MMC snap-in and your newly configured template. Using security templates in conjunction with the **Security Configuration Wizard** can provide you with an excellent way to configure your system and then to periodically check it for changes from its original security configuration.

Defining an Antivirus Solution

Your XenApp environment should also utilize *antivirus* software. By definition, a *virus* is a piece of computer code that produces unwanted results; it has the unique ability to replicate itself. A virus can perform an amazing array of damage, ranging from annoying messages and extensive resource utilization to destroying files and systems and causing massive outages. In addition, viruslike programs known as worms have become more prevalent due to their potential impact. The ability to protect computers against these types of attacks has become more a necessity than a luxury.

When considering antivirus software in your Citrix XenApp environment, you must take into account several factors. First, you must evaluate the various products along with feature sets to provide a solution to meet your organization's needs. It's very important to ensure that the software you select is supported in a Terminal Server and Citrix XenApp environment.

In addition to using antivirus software on your Citrix XenApp servers, you can use various products throughout the network to protect other resources available to a Citrix client, such as file servers, electronic mail, and Internet Web filtering. Limiting your user's capability to surf the Web or use e-mail can also reduce the risk of virus infection. When you use antivirus software on your Citrix XenApp server, you must carefully configure the application to minimize the impact to end users. Most antivirus solutions provide real-time scanning of file access, but you must carefully consider its impact on server performance. Carefully test how this software impacts the overall client experience to ensure that it's not causing more damage than good. In addition, active scanning can be performed to search the entire system for any virus. Although this is can be an effective tool, you should test the effect of implementing its use during peak production hours because it could cause severe performance degradation.

Last, antivirus software uses signatures to identify virus patterns while scanning. To ensure you are monitoring for the latest virus infections, you must periodically update the signatures from the manufacturer. Most software solutions available offer scheduled automatic updates. In addition, you can manually update the signature files if needed. It is recommended that you determine an acceptable interval for updating your antivirus signatures. You should check for new signatures at least once a week and install updates during nonpeak hours to minimize any user impact. In addition, if you become aware of any new virus infections, immediately check the vendor's web site for signature updates and information about the infection.

One of the most common threats today, virus attacks produce an astounding impact on organizations. With estimated damages being reported in the billions of dollars by various news sources, virus protection is a critical component to ensure that your networking environment is secure. Antivirus programs created by third–party software developers have become a huge part of any organization's security program.

Understanding Intrusion Detection

Another security measure you must consider is monitoring for intrusion. As hackers become more prevalent and savvy, you need additional tools to help protect your network environment. Intrusion detection is a strategy that any organization must consider.

Intrusion detection can be defined as the ability to monitor and react to computer misuse. Many hardware and software products on the market today provide various levels of intrusion detection. Some solutions use signatures to monitor for known attacks. Some platforms provide network monitoring; others are host-based systems. Some solutions react to particular alerts by shutting down services; others use a more passive approach. You must carefully select an intrusion detection strategy to ensure that your network resources remain secure from unwanted trespassers. Similar to virus protection, various locations and methods are appropriate to for intrusion detection. The most common use is to install an intrusion detection solution to monitor the access points from the Internet or outside world into your private networks. There are two main types of solutions: network-based and host-based. *Network-based* intrusion detection monitors network traffic for particular signs of malicious behavior. For example, if a user is continually trying to access a port known to be used with worms or Trojan horses, that could trigger an alert. *Host-based intrusion* detection programs are software products that are installed on your servers to monitor for suspicious behavior. This solution watches for viruslike activity so it can be stopped before it infects anything. It is critical to determine where you should monitor for intrusion and provide the appropriate solution to achieve these goals.

WARNING

The improper configuration of a host-based intrusion detection system can produce unwanted and adverse results. The worst can cause your XenApp server to be unavailable to your users. Care and diligence should be exercised when configuring a host-based intrusion detection policy for your environment.

Are You Owned?

Determining a Baseline for Your System

Having a comprehensive *baseline policy* is essential in the management of any system. Microsoft provides some good tools, such as Microsoft Baseline Security Analyzer, that you can use to evaluate your server for inconsistencies. Why is having a baseline important? A baseline serves as the starting point for measuring future changes to a system. The baseline indicates a state at a certain point in time; the result of changes made to a system (such as patches and hotfixes) can help determine from that point forward if

Continued

the overall performance and security health of the system is improving, staying even, or getting worse. Maintaining an effective baseline for your environment should be an essential part of your organization's *change management process*. A baseline can also be used to determine any unauthorized changes to your system.

Understanding Published Application Security

When XenApp is installed on a server with the default settings, it can allow XenApp users to run virtually any application they choose on the server. For security purposes it is necessary to limit the applications that a XenApp user can run on the server. Windows provides administrators the ability to control user access to applications in a number of ways. Group Policy can specify which applications are visible to a user. In addition, it can prevent users from launching applications through the Windows Explorer shell. However, users can launch hidden applications either by using the Run command or by launching an embedded object. Group Policies can affect a user's computer as well as their XenApp sessions if not created properly. The recommended approach to limiting access to applications is to implement Application Security policies, NTFS security, and XenApp application policies.

Understanding Application Security Policies

In Windows 2000, the Microsoft Application Security tool (APPSEC.exe) could allow an administrator to control access to each application/executable on the server. If configured properly, it could limit a user to accessing only specific applications via a XenApp ICA session. With Windows Server 2003, you now have *software restriction policies*, as shown in Figure 4.11, that can accomplish the same thing as APPSEC.exe and are much more flexible to use.

Figure 4.11 Using Software Restriction Policies

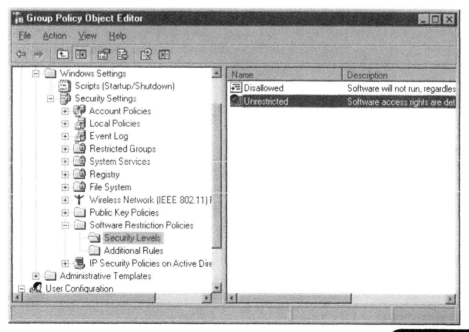

WARNING

Some people believe that providing access only to a single application (through published applications with XenApp) provides some measure of security. This is not the case. Even if you have configured only one application, such as NOTEPAD.exe, the unsecured environment can be breached. Any reasonably intelligent user will quickly learn that **Ctrl-Alt-Esc** will launch Windows Security in their session, which could potentially be a back door into your system.

When using software restriction policies, you can identify and specify the software that is allowed to run so that you can protect your XenApp environment from unauthorized programs and files. The basic configuration has two policies: *Unrestricted*, which allows access to software based on the access rights of the user and *Disallowed*, which prevents the execution of software regardless of user access rights. For your XenApp environment, you must select one of these policies as the default and then fine-tune the policy for your specific environment. To do this, you create exceptions to your default security level with rules. You may create rules such as the following:

- Hash rules
- Certificate rules
- Path rules
- Internet zone rules

A policy is made up of the default security level and all of the rules applied to a group policy object. You may apply the policy to specific computers or users. Implementing application security via the use of software restriction policies provides a number of ways to identify what software can be executed in your environment.

With software restriction policies, you can control which programs can run on your computer. You can permit users to only run certain file types. However, in large environments with several hundreds of servers and published resources, the administration of software restriction policies can prove to be arduous.

WARNING

Even though you can use software restriction policies to prevent the execution of specific files, Microsoft recommends that you do not use software restriction policies as a replacement for antivirus or antispyware software.

Explaining NTFS Permissions for Published Application Security

Another way to restrict applications that a user can access is to configure NTFS security on the application executables themselves. Using NTFS-level security pretty much ensures that the access restriction will not be circumvented. With NTFS security, no matter how the user accesses the server, the application will not run if the user does not have the proper NTFS rights to the application. The catch here, just like with using software restriction policies, is management of the security settings.

TIP

Some administrators find the maintenance of application security policies cumbersome and challenging. There are several third-party products that accomplish the same result, but have a much more robust user interface and are easy to use. One such product is Tricerat's Simplify Lockdown application that is part of Tricerat's Simplify Suite v4 server management tools for terminal server-based environments.

Defining XenApp Published Application Properties

You can define settings on each individual published application by selecting to modify the published application's properties, shown in Figure 4.12. You can select to have an application only be accessed via a particular encryption level, or to enable Secure Sockets Layer (SSL) and Transport Layer Security (TLS) protocols. You can choose the methods in which the application can be accessed, such as utilizing a Citrix Access Gateway which can be configured with its own security policies. You can place limits on the number of connections and even select to temporarily disable an application from being available if necessary.

Figure 4.12 Using XenApp Published Application Properties

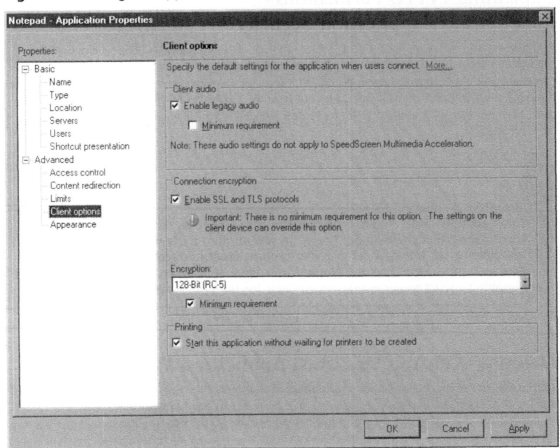

Notes from the Underground...

Who Wrecked My Server?

Having a system *audit policy* defined is a great place to start for tracking unusual events, because it can track account logons, account management changes, privilege use, etc. The Microsoft EventCombMT tool allows you to parse event logs from many servers at the same time to assist you with finding specific event entries, like repeated log-on failure events. Another tool is SmartAuditor, which is a new feature of Citrix XenApp Platinum Edition that uses policies to initiate recordings of user sessions. With SmartAuditor you can examine and monitor user activity.

Understanding ICA Connections

The ICA connection is the connection between the user and the XenApp server. Specifically, this is the *ICA protocol*. The ICA protocol can provide full client device mappings such as stereo, Component Object Model (COM) and printer mappings, and local drive remapping. What makes ICA so robust is its small size. The ICA protocol provides graphical and input information between the remote client and the XenApp server. Only screen updates and input are passed to lessen the bandwidth requirements to the client.

You can provide security on the ICA connection by:

■ Encrypting the connection.

■ Placing custom NTFS security on the protocol.

■ Limiting the number of connections that use that protocol.

■ Isolating the network card on which the protocol is bound on a multihomed server.

With Citrix Presentation Server 4.0 and earlier, you could configure the ICA protocol with the *Citrix Connection Configuration utility* (MFCFG.exe). On XenApp, the functionality of the Citrix Connection Configuration is added to the *Terminal Services Configuration utility* (TSCC.msc) as shown in Figure 4.13. Using this utility, you may lockdown specifics of the ICA protocol. Many features of the ICA connection are also configurable through the use of XenApp policies.

Figure 4.13 Using Terminal Services Configuration Utility

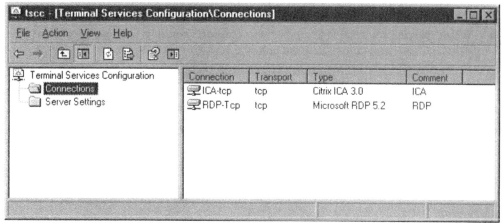

Understanding Network Configuration

Earlier in this chapter we defined the need for defining network boundaries and using a network diagram to assist in this task. Using a network diagram will help you in determining what needs to be secured and how you should go about securing it. Security at the network level for your XenApp environment can be accomplished by the following means:

- Implementation of IP security

- Implementation of router and network device *access control lists (ACLs)*

- Segregation of XenApp components based on role

- Disabling unused and unneeded ports, protocols, and services on the XenApp server

Internet Protocol security, or IPSec, is a framework of open standards for ensuring private, secure communications over IP networks, through the use of cryptographic security services. The following are Microsoft best practices for implementing IPSec:

- Establish an IPSec deployment plan.

- Create and test IPSec policies for each deployment scenario.

- Do not use preshared keys.

- Do not use Diffie–Hellman Group 1 (low).

- Use the Triple Data Encryption Standard (3DES) algorithm for stronger encryption.

- Create and assign a persistent IPSec policy for failsafe security.

- For computers connected to the Internet, do not send the name of the *certificate authority (CA)* with certificate requests.

- For computers connected to the Internet, do not use Kerberos as an authentication method.

- For computers that are connected to the Internet, do not allow unsecured communication.

- Restrict the use of administrative credentials in your organization.

- When applying the same IPSec policy to computers running different versions of the Windows operating system, test the policy thoroughly.

- Use the Windows Server 2003 IP Security Policy Management console (shown in Figure 4.14) to manage the IPSec policies that use the new features that are available only in the Windows Server 2003 family implementation of IPSec.

- Use Terminal Services to remotely manage and monitor IPSec on computers running different versions of the Windows operating system.

Figure 4.14 Using the IP Security Policy Management Console

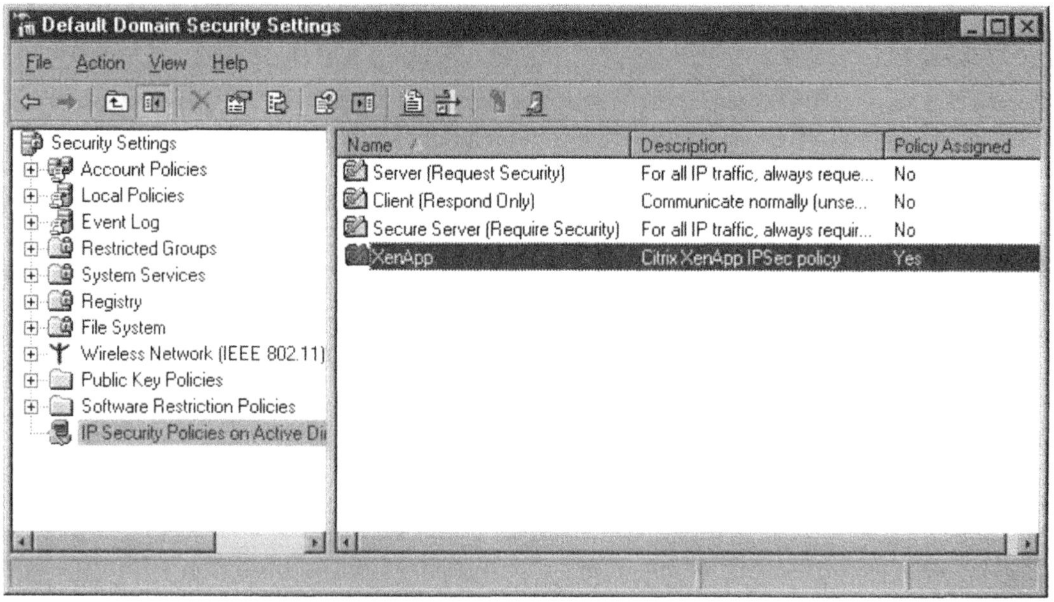

When connecting your computing resource to other networks such as the Internet, you must consider how you control access between your network and the others. In addition, some resources within your organization (such as human resources department computers that hold confidential personal information) need to be secured from internal intruders. A *firewall* is a common technique used to meet these requirements. A firewall is traditionally used to secure one set of network resource from another network. The most common implementation of firewalls today is organizations connecting their internal private networks to the Internet. A firewall allows administrators to restrict outside individuals' access to internal resources. Although many firewall products are on the market, a firewall is more a security strategy than a single product. The solution to fit your needs might be available in a single product, but many times multiple devices are required to completely secure a network. For example, many firewall implementations include items discussed earlier in this chapter, such as intrusion detection and IP security. As an administrator, you must select the options and product that best suit your environment's requirements. In order to utilize Citrix XenApp with firewalls, you must carefully consider who and what resources need to be available to external users. Whether it is you or another team that is responsible for your organization's firewall configuration, items discussed earlier in this chapter (network diagrams, PortQry, Port Reporter, etc.) will prove to be invaluable resources in the configuration.

WARNING

Incorrectly configuring IPSec policies can deny clients and other servers access to your system. You should have a thorough and complete understanding of your network environment before applying IPSec policies. Optimally, you should test IPSec policies in a test environment before applying on a production system.

Segregation of your XenApp resources is essential to a good security posture. By segregating your environment in this manner you can isolate potential problems to specific areas of your network instead of having the entire network affected. In Figure 4.15 we have placed our XenApp assets into a separate virtual LAN (VLAN) called XenApp. There are also VLANs defined for clients, web, production, and authentication. You can further secure the connectivity between servers with the implementation of IP Security policies, especially useful for protecting your XenApp license server. You should place any computer that is directly connected to the Internet in a DMZ and these servers should be stand-alone servers that are not part of a domain. Another way of providing additional security is by segregating traffic within your XenApp network by using multiple network cards in your servers. For example, you could have one network card that is used exclusively for private communication between XenApp resources and domain authentication, another card could be used for public communication between your XenApp resources and resources that are directly connected to the Internet, another network card could be used for conducting backups of your assets, and yet another card could be used for remote administration of your XenApp server. Establishing a multihomed server in this fashion requires the configuration of additional resources and potentially the configuration of a separate VLAN for each network card. However, by implementing a multihomed server in this fashion could provide increased performance by not overloading a single network card with multiple tasks.

TIP

In some configurations that make use of a multihomed server, you will find it necessary to ensure that the XenApp server communicates on the proper network card. To do this, you can use the command line **Altaddr** utility to configure the IMA and ICA Browser services to return the alternate/external IP address to the XenApp environment.

Figure 4.15 Segregating XenApp Assets

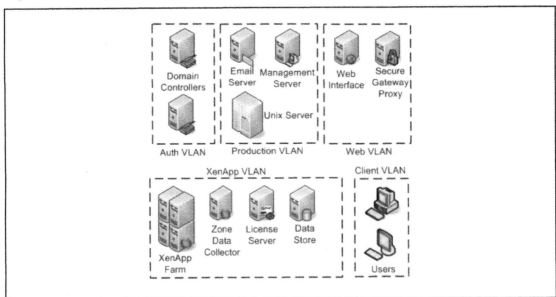

Earlier we discussed the use of security templates. The next step after configuring your system with a standardized security template is to use the new feature available in Windows 2003 Server SP1 called the *Security Configuration Wizard*, shown in Figure 4.16. This wizard is very easy to use and through a series of questions, you can quickly and easily disable unnecessary services, remove unwanted IIS virtual folders, block unused ports, configure audit settings, and lock down access to critical system files.

The Security Configuration Wizard (SCW) classifies servers based on roles. It will analyze your system and, based on the running services it finds, it will assign the server its appropriate role, like Web server or domain controller. SCW disables any services and ports not specifically tied to a defined role, which reduces the server's attack surface. Before running the wizard, you must first make sure that all applications are running correctly and are properly configured or you could inadvertently disable a needed service or port. The tool is quite granular in what you are allowed to select and you should make every effort to utilize this tool in the maintenance of your environment's security posture.

Figure 4.16 Using the Security Configuration Wizard

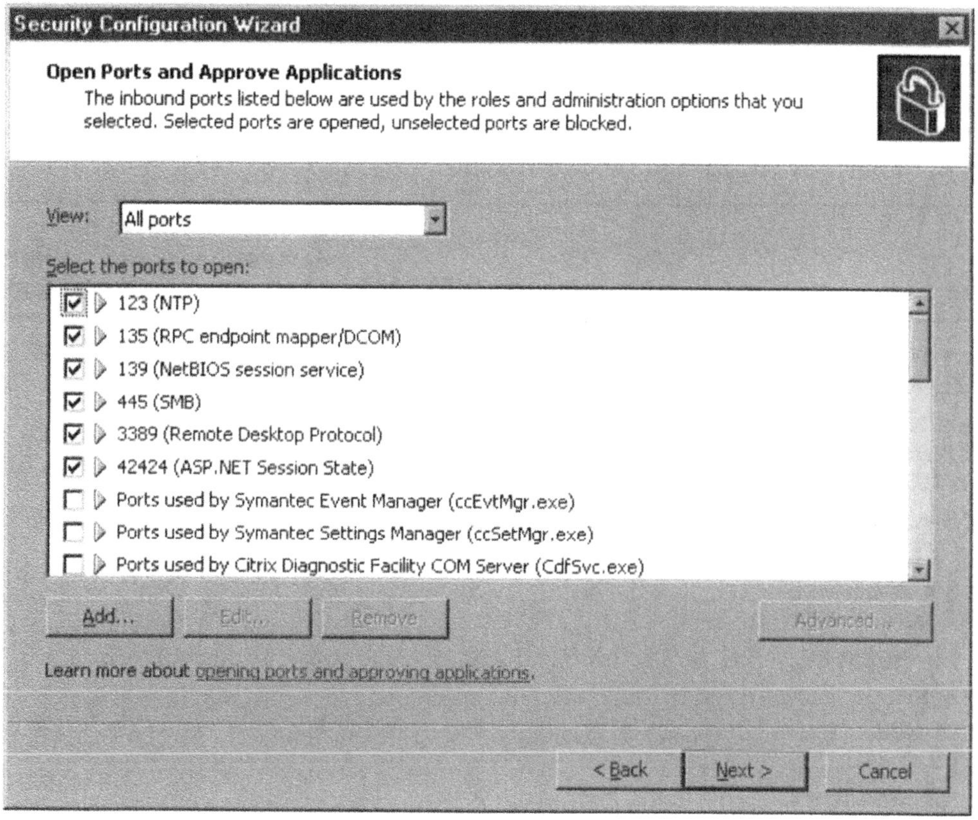

Understanding Client Devices

ICA Clients exchange information between a user's client device and the published application resources on XenApp. There are several versions of the Citrix client for a variety of platforms.

Your organizational policies should dictate what versions of the client software are acceptable, what devices on which they are permitted to run, and the specific configuration of the client software.

Something seemingly benign as a minor software version could potentially be used to an attacker's advantage. For example, *Citrix Security Bulletin CTX116227* states that, "Under some circumstances, the Citrix Presentation Server Client for Windows may leave residual credential information in the client process memory. This issue is present in all versions of the Citrix Presentation Server Client for Windows prior to version 10.200." Is this a major problem that is going to provide a likely avenue for an attacker to exploit? The real question is, do you want to give an attacker that opportunity regardless of how likely it is to happen?

ICA Client software is available for a range of different devices and platforms. Why should what kind of device or platform be of concern? Assume that a Citrix client is installed on a device for which your organization has not published any security lockdown policies, such as a *personal digital assistant (PDA)* that is running the Windows CE operating system. One of your users then connects to your corporate network via a public wireless link on a system that you have not locked down. The risk here is quite evident.

Different Citrix client versions also support different feature sets. You should be aware of what clients support multifactor authentication, certificate revocation checking, SSL/TLS, and so on, as shown in Table 4.1.

Table 4.1 Features Supported by Client Type

Feature	FIPS 140	TLS Support	3DES	AES	Certificate Revocation Checking	Smart Card Support	Kerberos Support
Program Neighborhood (Win32), version 10.x	X	X	X	X	X	X	X
Program Neighborhood Agent (Win32), version 10.x	X	X	X	X	X	X	
Web Client (Win31), version 10.x	X	X	X	X	X	X	X
Client for Windows CE WBT, version 10.x		X	X			X	
Client for Pocket PC, version 10.x		X	X			X	
Client of Java, version 9.x		X	X	X	X		X
Client for Macintosh, version 7.0		X	X				
Client for Macintosh, version 8.x		X	X			X	X

Continued

Table 4.1 Continued. Features Supported by Client Type

Feature	FIPS 140	TLS Support	3DES	AES	Certificate Revocation Checking	Smart Card Support	Kerberos Support
Client for Win16, version 6.20							
Client for Linux Version 10.x		X	X			X	
Client for UNIX (Sun Solaris), version 8.x		X	X			X	
Client for UNIX (IBM AIX), version 6.30		X	X			X	
Client for UNIX (SGI IRIX), version 6.30							
Client for UNIX (HP–UX), version 6.30		X	X				
Client for OS/2, version 6.012							

Understanding Users Rights, Responsibilities, and Permissions

Security is not just the responsibility of you as the administrator. It is a shared responsibility between you, your organization, anyone who uses the system, and anyone who is in the same physical location where a server or a client is located. This may sound extreme, but when it comes to security, it really is everyone's responsibility. Ever wonder why we have those *acceptable use policies* or the *warning banners* that precede a user logon? These are reminders to the users that security is serious business and must constantly be monitored. All users should be allowed the privilege of accessing the computing resources to which they are entitled as long as those purposes are consistent with your organization's mission.

With this in mind, there are responsibilities that accompany a user's privilege. Some basic user responsibilities include:

- Protecting their accounts, passwords, and data assigned to them to the best of their ability.
- Logging out of sessions when no longer active.
- Not introducing malicious code, viruses, or other harmful elements to the system.
- Using their access only for legal purposes.
- Not sharing their account information, passwords, or access codes with others.
- Reporting violations of policy to the proper personnel.

Just as users have their responsibilities, so do the administrators. As an administrator, you are also a user and are bound by the responsibilities above. In addition, some basic administrator responsibilities regarding users include:

- Ensuring that appropriate password policies are enforced.

- Ensuring that only authorized users are allowed access to the proper information.

- Providing a reliable and productive system.

- Providing a contingency plan in the event of service interruption.

- Providing reliable data backups in the event of disaster or data loss.

Of course there are many more items that can be added to these basic lists. It is the responsibility of your organization to identify what are the most important policies, and then to ensure that they are understood and adopted by all users.

Tip

Strong passwords should be used whenever possible. A strong password should be a completely random series of characters including upper and lower case letters, numbers, special characters, and even spaces. Many systems now support *passphrases*. A passphrase is simply a sentence that the user can easily remember. Microsoft has an excellent link regarding passwords and a strong password checker at www.microsoft.com/protect/yourself/password/create.mspx.

Tools & Traps...

Passwords – The Front Door to Your Network

Most security studies have shown that passwords are by far the number one security hole on most networks. Even networks that have policies in place to enforce strong passwords may have a test environment that overrides the default password policy simply for perceived ease of use.

Password crackers are easily attainable by a potential attacker. Tools such as *Cain and Able*, *John the Ripper*, *THC Hydra*, and *L0phtcrack* are just a few. As an administrator, you should make it a part of your routine security maintenance to run password cracking tools on your own environment to see what an attacker could potentially see. How many service accounts and passwords do you have in your network? Do you maintain separate accounts and passwords for Structured Query Language (SQL), e-mail services, and Web services? Right now, do you have a Windows Web server that has a configured IUSR account? When was the last time you changed that password? Give your network a password strength test. Do all of your passwords stand up to the latest brute force password cracking tools available? The results may surprise you.

Defining Types of Deployments

When designing a XenApp environment, the operational needs of your organization have to be weighed against the security requirements of your organization. Typically, deployments should be designed in such a way that they satisfy the requirements of the *CIA triad*, shown in Figure 4.17, dealing with information security. The CIA triad stands for confidentiality, integrity, and availability. It is a very good idea when designing a XenApp deployment that you remember these three concepts:

- **Confidentiality** Confidential or sensitive information must only be accessed, used, copied, or disclosed by personnel with the proper authorization and when they have a genuine need.

- **Integrity** This insures that data cannot by created, changed, copied, deleted, viewed or processed without proper authorization.

- **Availability** This means that the data, the systems used to process the data, and controls used to protect the data are all available and functioning when the data is needed.

Following these principles, any deployment you design should be a *secure deployment* where the threats and risks to your organization's information infrastructure have either been mitigated, eliminated, or accepted.

Figure 4.17 Defining Information Security Using the CIA Triad

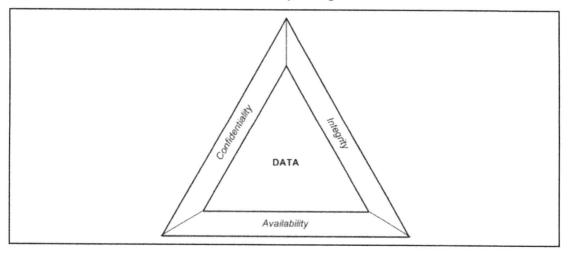

Internal Network (Intranet) Deployment Using SSL Relay

If your XenApp implementation does not require any external connectivity and will only be used by your internal users, you can opt to implement a standard XenApp deployment without the further need to encrypt your connections. However, if your organization's security requirements dictate the need to protect sensitive data from end to end, you will want to use the Internal Network (Intranet) Deployment using SSL Relay.

This deployment provides end-to-end encryption of the communication between the client and the server. Both SSL Relay and the appropriate server certificate must be installed and configured on each server within the server farm.

> **NOTE**
>
> If your public key infrastructure (PKI) employs the use of a third-party or intermediate certificate authority (CA), you will need to ensure that the appropriate CA root certificates are installed on each XenApp server and component utilizing SSL and every client that will initiate a session to your XenApp farm.

The SSL Relay operates as an intermediary component in the communications between the client and the XML Service on each XenApp server. The client authenticates the SSL Relay by checking the SSL Relay's server certificate against a list of trusted certificate authorities. After this authentication, the client and SSL Relay negotiate requests in encrypted form. The SSL Relay decrypts the requests and forwards the requests to the XenApp server. When returning the information to the client, the XenApp server sends all information through the SSL Relay, which encrypts the data and forwards it to the client to be decrypted.

Depending on your network configuration, there may or may not be a firewall involved in this deployment. In Figure 4.18, we have shown the deployment utilizing a firewall. Either with or without a firewall, the only traffic between client and server that is utilized is TCP 443. A comprehensive diagram of port traffic flow for this configuration is provided in Figure 4.22.

Figure 4.18 Internal Network Deployment Using SSL Relay

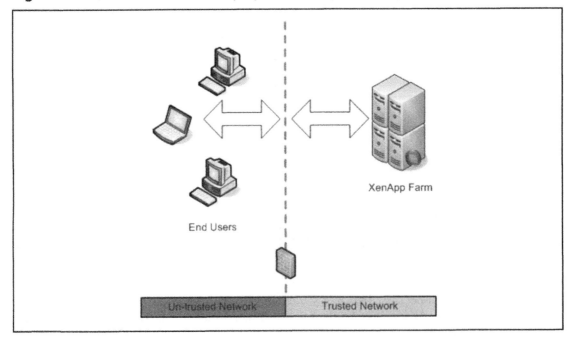

External Network Deployment (Single Hop)

If your XenApp implementation requires any sort of external connectivity, and you've just lost the fight with the firewall team asking them to punch a hole in the firewall to allow ICA traffic (TCP 1494) through, then you will need to look at the External Network Deployment (Single Hop). This deployment's data traffic flow goes from the XenApp server to the DMZ to the client, thus providing a single hop.

This deployment requires the use of a Web Interface server to be installed on a server running Internet Information Services (IIS) and a Secure Gateway server. Note that IIS does not need to be installed on the Secure Gateway server. A typical configuration of this type of deployment utilizes a firewall between the XenApp farm and the DMZ and a firewall between the DMZ and the client. In this type of deployment, it is possible to install the Web Interface and the Secure Gateway on a single machine; however, this configuration is not recommended for most environments.

The deployment in Figure 4.19 outlines the *parallel configuration* of the Single Hop deployment which utilizes a single DMZ. This configuration exposes both the Secure Gateway and the Web Interface to the Internet and requires that both servers have connectivity available to clients. The *inline configuration* of the Single Hop deployment places the Secure Gateway in front of the Web Interface causing only the Secure Gateway to be exposed to the Internet. However, by using the inline configuration of the Single Hop deployment, you are limited in your authentication methods. For example, when the Secure Gateway is placed in front of the Web Interface, smart card authentication is not supported.

Utilizing the parallel deployment provides for more authentication methods than are available utilizing the inline deployment. Figure 4.20 shows port traffic utilizing this configuration. You may further secure this configuration by configuring SSL Relay between the Web Interface and the XML service running on a XenApp server. To achieve FIPS 140 compliancy, you can secure the communication between the Secure Gateway and Citrix XenApp Server using IPsec policies.

Figure 4.19 External Network Deployment (Single Hop)

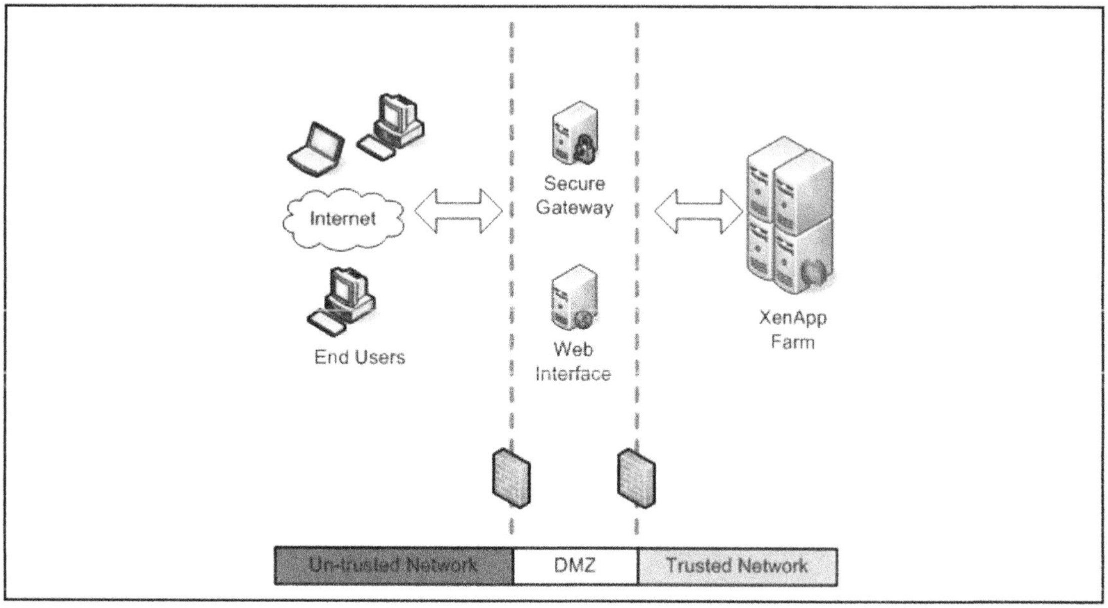

External Network Deployment (Double Hop)

The External Network Deployment (Double Hop) is shown in Figure 4.20 and makes use of two DMZs. Only the Secure Gateway is exposed to the Internet. If you choose not to expose your Web Interface to the Internet or your network configuration mandates the use of two DMZs, then this deployment is appropriate for your environment.

In this deployment the DMZ is divided into two segments or zones. The Secure Gateway is placed in the outward facing segment and the Web Interface and the Secure Gateway Proxy are placed in the second segment (or second hop).

This deployment requires the use of a Web Interface server to be installed on a server running Internet Information Services (IIS), a Secure Gateway server, and a Secure Gateway Proxy server. Note that IIS does not need to be installed on the Secure Gateway server or the Secure Gateway Proxy server. A typical configuration of this type of deployment utilizes a firewall between the XenApp farm and the first DMZ, a firewall between the first DMZ and the second DMZ and a firewall between the second DMZ and the client.

This configuration exposes only the Secure Gateway to the Internet. However, by using this deployment, you will not be able to utilize Smart Card authentication. Figure 4.24 provides a detailed examination of the ports used and their flow in this deployment. You may further secure this configuration by configuring SSL Relay between the Web Interface and the XML service running on a XenApp server. To achieve FIPS 140 compliancy, you can secure the communication between the Secure Gateway and Citrix XenApp Server using IPSec policies.

Figure 4.20 External Network Deployment (Double Hop)

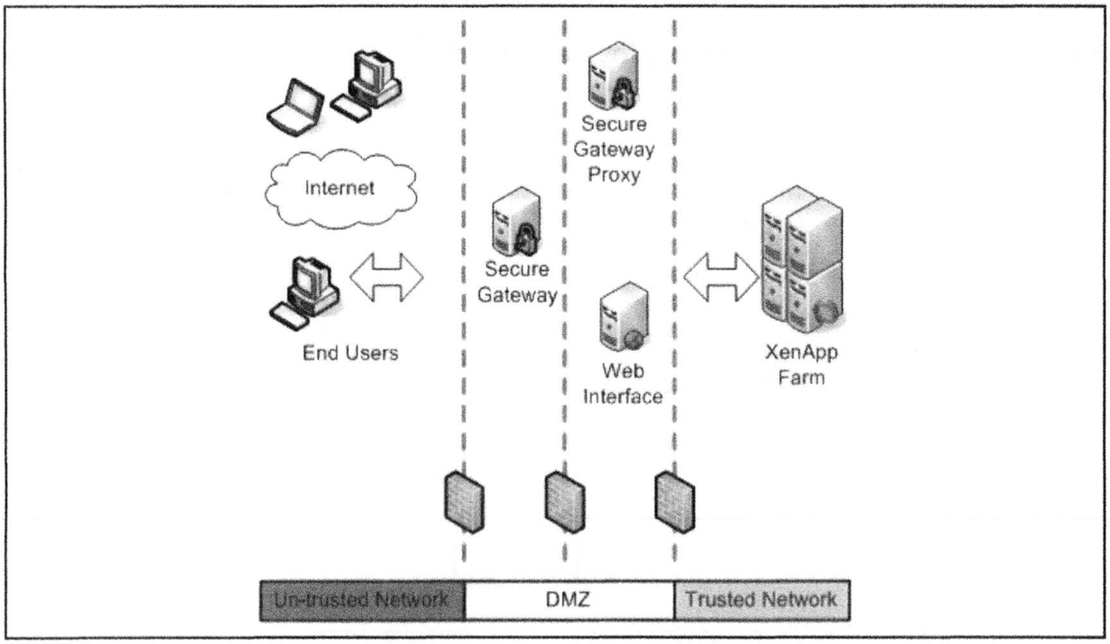

Web Interface with SSL Relay

If your XenApp implementation does not require any external connectivity and will only be used by your internal users, you can opt to implement a standard XenApp deployment without the further need to encrypt your connections. However, if your organization's security requirements dictate the need to protect sensitive data from end to end, you will want to use the Internal Network (Intranet) Deployment using SSL Relay.

This deployment provides end–to–end encryption of the communication between the client and the server. Both SSL Relay and the appropriate server certificate must be installed and configured on each server within the server farm.

The SSL Relay operates as an intermediary component in the communications between the client and the XML Service on each XenApp server. The client authenticates the SSL Relay by checking the SSL Relay's server certificate against a list of trusted certificate authorities. After this authentication, the client and SSL Relay negotiate requests in encrypted form. The SSL Relay decrypts the requests and forwards the requests to the XenApp server. When returning the information to the client, the XenApp server sends all information through the SSL Relay, which encrypts the data and forwards it to the client to be decrypted.

Depending on your network configuration, there may or may not be a firewall involved in this deployment. In Figure 4.21, we have shown the deployment utilizing a firewall. Either with or without a firewall, the only traffic between client and server that is utilized is TCP 443 (see Figures 4.22 to 4.24). A comprehensive diagram of port traffic flow for this configuration is provided in Figure 4.25.

Figure 4.21 Web Interface Using SSL Relay

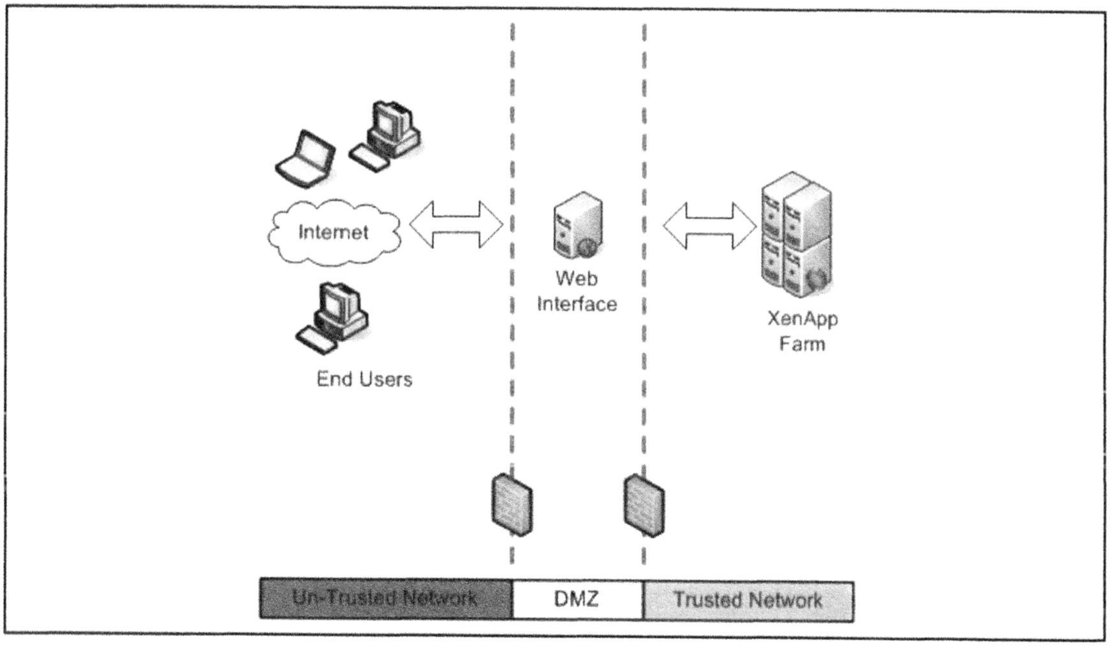

Figure 4.22 Understanding the SSL Relay Configuration

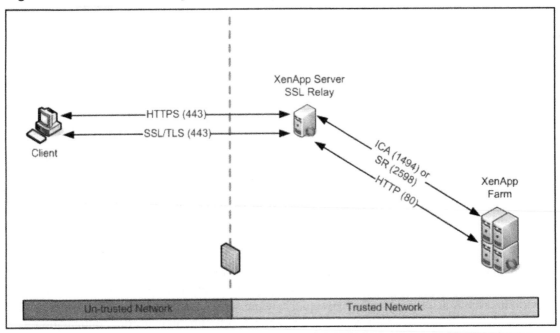

Figure 4.23 SSL Relay through a Web Interface and Secure Gateway

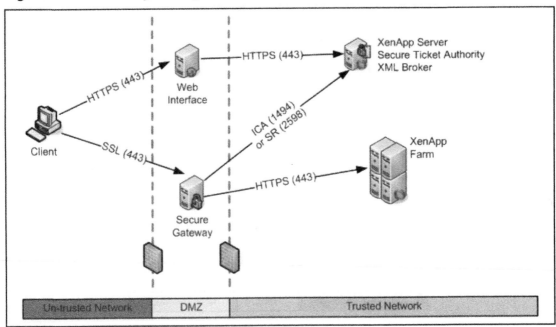

Figure 4.24 Understanding the Double–Hop Configuration

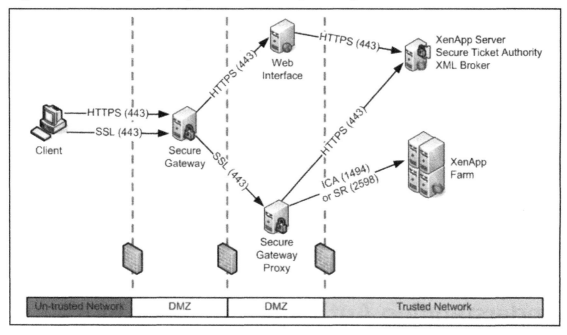

Figure 4.25 Understanding the SSL Relay Configuration with Web Interface

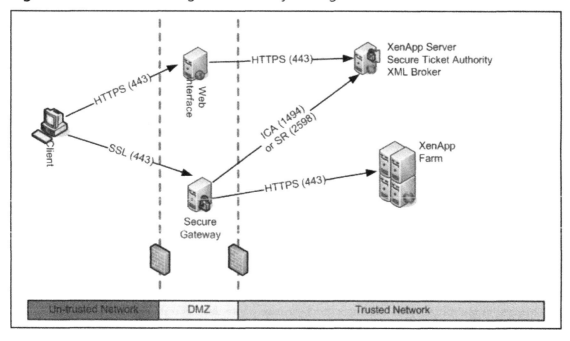

Understanding Wireless LANs (WLANs)

The mobile Internet is a trend that is now a common part of the workplace. People want to access the Internet from any location, using any device and without needing any wires. Once users are connected to the Internet, it is not a far leap to want to access and run applications. Now with the user of broadband wireless internet and the increased memory and processing power of PDAs, users can essentially have a usable workstation right in their pocket.

As the world continues to move further through the information age, businesses are turning more to technology to gain a competitive advantage in their respective industries. Every day, businesses make strategic decisions based on information that is as up to date as they can obtain. It follows that the ability of an organization to send and receive information and thus act on that information faster than its competitors gives it a distinct advantage over competition. Until now, no one has been able to collect and act on information in a real-time manner.

One of the biggest concerns facing network administrators in implementing a WLAN is data security. In a wired environment, the lack of access to the physical wire can prevent someone from wandering into your building and connecting to your internal network. In a WLAN scenario, it is impossible for the AP to know if the person operating the wireless device is sitting inside your building, passing time in your lobby, or seated in a parked car just outside your office.

Understanding Authentication Methods

Citrix XenApp provides a variety of authentication methods to use. Explicit authentication using the traditional user name and password combination where the user is prompted to enter their information, pass-through authentication where the existing log-on credentials of the current logged on session are passed to the XenApp session, authentication methods utilizing Kerberos, Smart cards, biometrics

Understanding Explicit Authentication

Explicit authentication is simply forcing the user to enter their userid and password. Explicit authentication is an option on XenApp clients and the Web Interface.

Understanding Kerberos Authentication

Kerberos, version 5, is an industry standard security protocol that Windows Server 2003 uses as the default authentication service. It is used to handle authentication in Windows Server 2003 trust relationships, and is the primary security protocol for authentication within domains. Kerberos uses mutual authentication to verify the identity of a user or computer, and the network service being accessed. Each side proves to the other that they are who they claim to be. Kerberos does this through the use of tickets.

Kerberos authentication can only be used by network clients and servers running Windows 2000, Windows Server 2003, or Windows XP Professional; any Windows 9x or NT clients that attempt to access a Kerberos secured resource will use NTLM authentication instead.

Kerberos authentication relies on a Key Distribution Center (KDC) to issue tickets to enable client access to specific network resources. Each domain controller (DC) in a Windows Server 2003 domain functions as a KDC, which creates fault tolerance in the event that a DC becomes unavailable.

Network clients will use Domain Name Service (DNS) to locate the nearest available KDC; once they've located the KDC they will provide a passphrase in order to acquire a ticket. Kerberos tickets contain an encrypted password that confirms the user's identity to the requested service. These tickets will remain active on a client computer system for a configurable amount of time, usually 8 or 10 hours. The longevity of these tickets allows Kerberos to provide single sign-on capabilities, where the authentication process as a whole becomes transparent to the users once they've initially entered their log-on credentials.

These steps occur completely behind the scenes; the users are only aware that they've entered their password or Personal Identification Number (PIN) number as part of a normal log-on process. The Kerberos process is shown in Figure 4.26.

1. Using a smart card or a username/password combination, a user authenticates to the KDC. The KDC issues a ticket-granting ticket (TGT) to the client system. The client retains this TGT in memory until needed.

2. When the client attempts to access a network resource, it presents its TGT to the ticket-granting service (TGS) on the nearest available Windows Server 2003 KDC.

3. If the user is authorized to access the service that it is requesting, the TGS issues a service ticket to the client.

4. The client presents the service ticket to the requested network service. Through mutual authentication, the service ticket will prove the identity of the user and the identity of the service.

Figure 4.26 Understanding How Kerberos Works

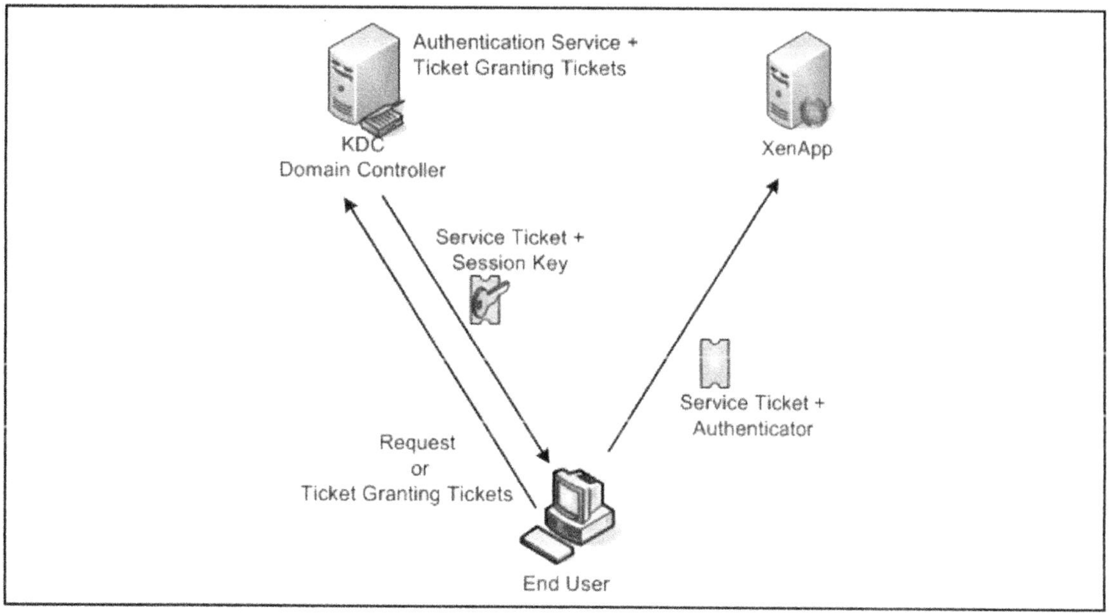

WARNING

Kerberos authentication relies on timestamps to function properly. As such, all clients that are running the Kerberos client must synchronize their time settings with a common time server. If the time on a network client is more than five minutes slow or fast compared to the KDC, Kerberos authentication will fail.

Kerberos is supported in the XenApp environment, but there are specific requirements that must be met before it will work successfully. Requirements for Kerberos Support with XenApp:

- XenApp on Windows 2003

- ICA Client, version 8.x or higher

- Client\Server connections must be in same domain or have trusts between domains.

- Servers must be "**trusted for delegation**" (must be configured through **AD Users and Computers management tool**).

- SSPI requires the XML Service, DNS service address resolution to be enabled for the server farm, or reverse DNS resolution to be enabled for an AD domain.

Because of the security complexities required of many XenApp environments, even though you may want to implement a Kerberos authentication scheme, you may not be able to do so because of your specific configuration. Kerberos will not work in any of the following conditions:

- Within your terminal services configuration if you have **Use standard Windows authentication** enabled, or **Always use the following log-on information** is completed, or the **Always prompt for password** option is checked

- Your configuration utilized connections through the Secure Gateway

- If the XenApp server is configured to *require* smart card logon.

- If the user account requires a *smart card* for interactive logon.

Understanding Multifactor Authentication

An authentication factor is a piece of information and process used to authenticate a person's identity for security purposes. Two-factor authentication (2FA), shown in Figure 4.27, is an authentication mechanism based on two pieces of information: something you have, such as a smart card, token id, etc. and something you know, such as a PIN. When presented with a log-on option, the user must provide both pieces of the authentication mechanism or they will be denied access to the system. There is another factor of authentication providing multifactor authentication based on something a person is or does, such as a biometric recognition. Citrix XenApp natively supports 2FA and can support 3FA with third-party add-on products.

Figure 4.27 Understanding Multifactor Authentication

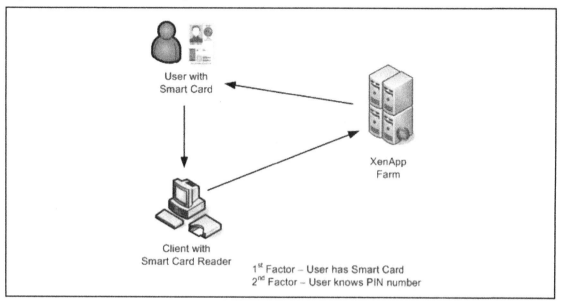

Understanding Pass-Through Authentication

Pass-through authentication allows the user's name and password to be passed from the local machine to the server. If you do not elect to install Pass–through authentication during the initial installation of XenApp server and decide that you want the feature later on, you will need to reinstall the pass–through client. However, the use of pass-through credentials may be contrary to your organization's security policies unless pass–through authentication is used in conjunction with other technologies, such as smart cards, that can provide multifactor authentication. Pass-through authentication can be enabled on the Citrix client as shown in Figure 4.28.

Figure 4.28 Enabling Pass-Through Authentication

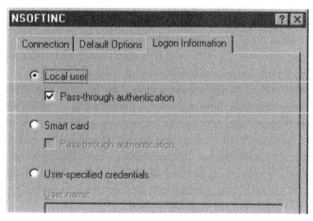

Encrypting XenApp

In addition to the numerous security solutions and products available on the market today, XenApp provides built-in capability to help secure server and client communications from intruders. Using a standard technology known as *encryption*, server-to-server and client/server communication can be protected against intruders. Understanding how encryption works and where to apply it is important to ensure proper implementation of a secure server farm. Once you understand how encryption is used, you can properly set up the products and add-ons provided for XenApp.

Understanding Encryption

Encryption is the process of converting data into nonreadable text, also referred to as *ciphertext*. Ciphertext is used for transmitting confidential data. Once the data has arrived at its destination, it is then reconverted into the original data through a process known as *decryption*.

Various types of data encryption are available on the market today. Each type provides both benefits and disadvantages, including categories such as strength of security, ease of use, and standardization. The effectiveness of any security algorithm is found in its strength and the keys used to secure it. Weaker security algorithms are more easily cracked; however, if implemented properly, these options can still provide very effective solutions.

Encryption techniques are based on using keys similar to keys for your home or car. Using a key to open your car door is a method that identifies you as someone authorized to use the car. Whoever has possession of this key is able to access the car. Based on mathematical algorithms, encryption keys work the same way. If you have the correct key, you can encrypt or decrypt the data from ciphertext.

Symmetric Key Encryption

Primarily two forms of encryption are in use today. The most common form of encryption uses the *symmetric algorithm*. This method requires that each individual or device that accesses this encrypted data possess a copy of the key. Commonly referred to as *shared-key encryption* because it uses a single key for encryption and decryption, this is a relatively simple encryption technology to implement, but it might not provide the best security.

One common issue with symmetric encryption algorithms is the way the keys are transported to other users. If this type of key is obtained by an unauthorized user (such as during the encryption setup process), that unauthorized user can then easily decrypt that data, resulting in loss of data integrity. Most solutions that use symmetric keys to encrypt data also provide additional secure methods by which to negotiate and transport these keys to ensure that they are secured.

Another issue associated with symmetric keys is managing multiple identities. If you want to communicate securely using symmetric keys without all users having access to all data, you must maintain different keys for different data sets. For example, Jane at Company A wants to send data to Bill at Company B. Jane must configure communications to Bill using Key 1, and Bill must use the same key. Jane also wants to communicate with Bob at Company X. To communicate with Bob, Jane must use a different key; therefore, Key 2 is created. As the number of companies or individuals grows, so does the number of keys required to maintain communications among them. Now imagine using this technology on an enterprise scale with hundreds or thousands of sites.

A common symmetric algorithm implementation used today is the Digital Encryption Standard, or DES. Based on a fixed 56-bit symmetric key, this algorithm creates a single key based on a binary number used to encrypt and decrypt data. Using a block cipher methodology, it uses 64-byte blocks to randomly populate a key. Currently in use by organizations such as the National Security Agency (NSA), DES offers 72 quadrillion possible encryption keys at this point. In addition, developers have created a stronger version of DES, known as Triple DES, or 3DES, because it uses the DES key by encrypting, decrypting, and encrypting again to ensure data is secure. Figure 4.29 shows an example of symmetric key processing.

Figure 4.29 Symmetric Key Encryption

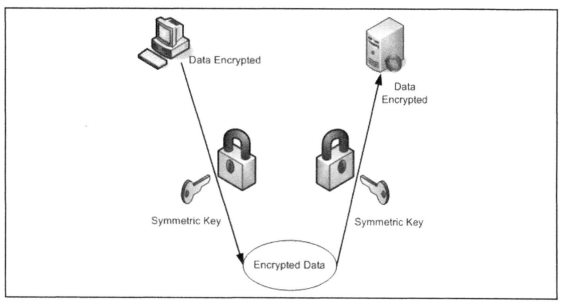

Asymmetric Key Encryption

The second method of encryption uses an asymmetrical algorithm and is commonly known as *public key encryption*. Although similar to the symmetric algorithm, this technology uses two keys to encrypt data. The first key is held privately in a secure location for the receiver to decrypt data sent to him. This validates that the receiver is authentic. The second key is freely published, is used to encrypt the data, and is commonly posted in public locations. This allows anyone to send the data, but only the holder of the private key is authorized to receive and decrypt the data. Even the public key originally used to encrypt the message cannot be used to decrypt it. This encryption technique allows you to send the public key over insecure channels and still maintain the integrity of encrypted data.

Therefore, if Tom wants to send encrypted data to Jim, he uses Jim's public key to encrypt it. Once the data is transferred to Jim, he uses his private key to decrypt the data. This methodology ensures that only Jim can access the data. Created by and named for Ron Rivest, Adi Shamir, and Leonard Adleman, the Rivest–Shamir–Adleman (RSA) data encryption standard is the most commonly used asymmetric algorithm. It uses prime numbers to randomly generate public and private keys. A common application using RSA encryption includes Pretty Good Privacy (PGP) and Novell NetWare for a secure client-to-server communications channel. Similar to RSA, Diffie-Hellman is another common algorithm. Primarily used to transfer symmetric keys securely, Diffie–Hellman provides another form of asymmetric keys. A common example of asymmetric key encryption is using PGP to digitally sign e-mail communications. If you use a PGP signature, recipients of your messages can ensure that your e-mails are authentic. Figure 4.30 shows an example of how asymmetric keys work.

Figure 4.30 Asymmetric Key Encryption

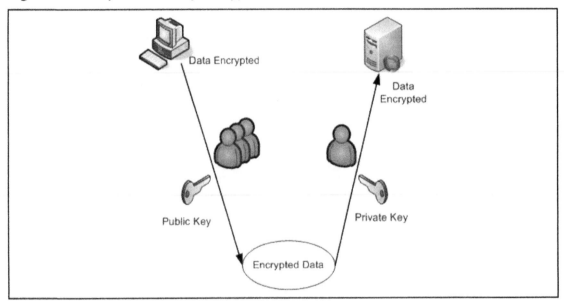

NOTE

When you are implementing encryption within your XenApp farm, it is critical to correctly identify the encryption strength to use and where it will be configured. All encryption strengths, with the exception of basic, use 128-bit strength for the log-on process. Afterward, they revert to the selected option, such as 56-bit. You might ask, "Why not just use 128-bit encryption if it's the best?" Unfortunately, the stronger the encryption algorithm, the more performance overhead is required on the server and client communications. For example, 128-bit encryption will not function properly when you use a 33.6Kbps modem connection to access a XenApp. In the same manner, client performance degrades faster over inconsistent network links when you use higher strength encryption algorithms. Carefully test each option to ensure it suits your environment; it can have a major impact on the performance of your server farm if not optimized properly.

Secure Sockets Layer (SSL)

Secure Sockets Layer (SSL) was created to encrypt data transmitted between a client computer and a Web server. Traditionally, Web traffic is transmitted in cleartext, potentially providing network intruders with sensitive data. Netscape developed SSL to provide a secure communications method by which to converse across the Internet. Based on RSA public/private key technology using digital certificates, SSL has become the standard for secure communication across the World Wide Web and can be used to complement your security strategy for your XenApp farm.

SSL is classified as a transport layer security protocol, since it secures not only the information generated at the application layer, but at the transport layer as well. It is considered a secure protocol by providing the mechanisms for supporting the basic elements of secure communications, namely confidentiality, integrity, and authentication.

Authentication ensures that the information received is indeed from the individual believed to be the sender. Integrity guarantees that the message received is the same message that was sent, while confidentiality protects data from inspection by unintended recipients.

SSL protects information passed by application protocols such as File Transfer Protocol (FTP), Hypertext Transfer Protocol (HTTP), and Network News Transfer Protocol (NNTP). An application must be explicitly designed to support SSL's security features. Unlike Layer 3 protocols, it is not transparent to application layer processes.

SSL uses several protocols to provide security and reliable communications between client and server SSL-enabled applications. Specifically, the handshake protocol negotiates levels and types of encryption, and sets up the secure session. These include SSL protocol version (2.0 or 3.0), authentication algorithms, encryption algorithms, and the method used to generate a shared secret or session key.

SSL uses a record protocol to exchange the actual data. A shared session key encrypts data passing between SSL applications. The data is decrypted on the receiving end by the same shared session key. Data integrity and authentication mechanisms are employed to ensure that accurate data is sent to, and received by, legitimate parties to the conversation. SSL uses an alert protocol to convey information about error conditions during the conversation. It is also used by SSL hosts to terminate a session.

SSL is used to confirm the identity of a server or a client machine and then encrypt all traffic between the two devices. For example, when you process a credit card transaction through a Web site, you want to ensure the identity of the receiver. SSL allows digital signatures to be used and are verified by a trusted certificate authority (CA). When you connect to a Web site using SSL, a certificate is processed, validating that the Web site is authentic. If it isn't, an error is issued, allowing you to determine whether to continue. As the process is completed, all traffic between your client and the Web site is encrypted to ensure that someone else cannot monitor the data flow.

SSL can be very useful when you're trying to secure a Web Interface server. Using SSL allows you to first confirm that your Web site is authentic to users. In addition, traffic such as authentication will not be sent in cleartext, increasing your security risk. To use SSL with Web sites, you connect using Secure Hypertext Transfer Protocol (HTTPS) instead of HTTP. Once this is configured, you no longer have to use standard HTTP services—you can rely solely on HTTPS to ensure that your site is secured.

How a Secure Channel is Established

To understand how a secure channel is formed, let's examine how an SSL client establishes a session with an SSL Web server:

1. A URL is entered into a Web browser using HTTPS rather than HTTP as the protocol. SSL uses TCP Port 443 rather than Port 80. The HTTPS entry requests the client to access the correct port on the target SSL Web server.

2. The SSL client sends a client Hello message. This message contains information about the encryption protocols it supports, what version of SSL it is using, what key lengths it supports, what hashing algorithms to use, and what key exchange mechanisms it supports. The SSL client also sends a challenge message to the SSL server. The challenge message will later confirm the identity of the SSL-enabled server.

3. The server then sends the client a Hello message. After examining methods supported by the client, the server returns to the client a list of mutually supported encryption methods, hash algorithms, key lengths, and key exchange mechanisms. The client will use the values returned by the server. The server also sends its public key, which has been signed by a mutually trusted authority (a digital certificate of authenticity).

4. The client then verifies the certificate sent by the server. After verifying the server certificate, the client sends a master key message. The message includes a list of security methodologies employed by the client and the session key. The session key is encrypted with the server's public key (which the server sent earlier in the server Hello message).

5. The client sends a client finished message indicating that all communications from this point forward are secure.

Almost all messages to this point have been sent in cleartext, implying that anyone listening in on the conversation would be able to read all parts of the exchange. This is not a problem, since no information other than the session key is secret. Moreover, the session key is safe because it is encrypted with the server's public key. Only the server is able to decrypt the session key by using its private key. The next series of events takes place in a secure context.

6. The server sends a server verify message to the SSL client. This message verifies that the server is indeed the server with which the client wishes to communicate. The server verify message contains the challenge message the client sent earlier in the conversation. The server encrypts the challenge message with the session key. Only the legitimate server has access to the session key. When the client decrypts the challenge message encrypted with the session key, and it matches that sent in the challenge, then the server has verified itself as the legitimate partner in the communication.

7. The last message used to set up the secure SSL channel is the server finish message. The SSL server sends this message to the SSL client informing of its readiness to participate in data transmission using the shared session key. The SSL session setup is complete, and data passes through a secure SSL channel.

The setup procedure is dependent on several security technologies, including public key encryption, symmetric encryption, asymmetric encryption, message hashing, and certificates. In the following sections, we define these terms and see how SSL uses them to create a secure channel.

Transport Layer Security (TLS)

Transport Layer Security (TLS) is the latest, standardized version of the SSL protocol. TLS is an open standard and like SSL, TLS provides server authentication, encryption of the data stream, and message integrity checks. Although their differences are minor, TLS 1.0 and SSL 3.0 are not interchangeable. If the same protocol is not supported by both parties, the parties must negotiate a common protocol to communicate successfully. The primary goal of the TLS Protocol is to provide privacy and data integrity between two communicating applications. The protocol is composed of two layers: the *TLS Record Protocol* and the *TLS Handshake Protocol*. At the lowest level, layered on top of some reliable transport protocol, like TCP, is the TLS Record Protocol. The TLS Record Protocol provides connection security that has two basic properties: privacy and reliability.

The TLS Record Protocol is used for encapsulation of various higher level protocols. One such encapsulated protocol, the TLS Handshake Protocol, allows the server and client to authenticate each other and to negotiate an encryption algorithm and cryptographic keys before the application protocol transmits or receives its first byte of data. The TLS Handshake Protocol provides connection security that has three basic properties:

- The peer's identity can be authenticated using asymmetric, or public key cryptography.

- The negotiation of a shared secret is secure: the negotiated secret is unavailable to eavesdroppers, and for any authenticated connection the secret cannot be obtained, even by an attacker who can place himself in the middle of the connection.

- The negotiation is reliable: no attacker can modify the negotiation communication without being detected by the parties to the communication.

One advantage of TLS is that it is application protocol independent. Higher level protocols can layer on top of the TLS Protocol transparently. The TLS standard, however, does not specify how protocols add security with TLS; the decisions on how to initiate TLS handshaking and how to interpret the authentication certificates exchanged are left up to the judgment of the designers and implementors of protocols which run on top of TLS.

Advanced Encryption Standard (AES)

The Advanced Encryption Standard (AES) is a Federal Information Processing Standard (FIPS), specifically FIPS Publication 197, that specifies a cryptographic algorithm that can be used to protect electronic data for use by the United States Government to protect sensitive, unclassified information. The AES algorithm is a symmetric block cipher that can encrypt and decrypt information. The AES algorithm is capable of using cryptographic keys of 128, 192, and 256 bits to encrypt and decrypt data in blocks of 128 bits.

In addition to the increased security that comes with larger key sizes, AES can encrypt data much faster than Triple-DES, a DES enhancement that essentially encrypts a message or document three times. It is based on the Rijndael algorithm, named for Belgian researchers Vincent Rijmen and Joan Daemen, who developed it.

NOTE

The following Citrix clients support the AES cipher for connections using TLS: Win32 10.x, Linux x86 10.x, and Java 9.x. You should check the Citrix Web site at www.citrix.com for the latest list of ICA clients that support AES and TLS. Remove hyperlink for Web site?

FIPS 140-2

Federal Information Processing Standard 140 (FIPS 140) is a U.S. federal government standard that details a benchmark for implementing cryptographic software. It provides best practices for using cryptographic algorithms, managing key elements and data buffers, and interacting with the operating system. An evaluation process that is administered by the National Institute of Standards and Technology's (NIST) National Voluntary Laboratory Accreditation Program (NVLAP) allows encryption product vendors to demonstrate the extent to which they comply with the standard, and thus, the trustworthiness of their implementation.

To facilitate implementing secure application server access and to meet the FIPS 140 requirements, XenApp products can use cryptographic modules that are FIPS 140-validated in Windows 32-bit implementation of secure SSL/TLS connections.

The following XenApp components can use cryptographic modules that are FIPS 140-validated:

- Citrix Clients for 32-bit Windows (including Program Neighborhood, Program Neighborhood Agent, and the Web Client)
- Secure Gateway
- XenApp
- Citrix SSL Relay
- Web Interface

When using the client and server components listed above with the SSL/TLS connection enabled, the cryptographic modules that are used are FIPS-140 validated.

Encryption Strength Options

Another important factor in implementing encryption strategies is defining the strength of your solution. In addition to the encryption techniques used, the key length is a major factor in determining the strength of any algorithm. For example, 16 bits in a key provide 65,536 possible key combinations. As the number of bits increases, so does the number of key variations. When you factor the computing power of today's computers, the ability to try every combination of larger keys, such as 128 bits, can take a few years to complete.

XenApp has five encryption levels from which to select:

- Basic
- 128-bit login only
- 40-bit
- 56-bit
- 128-bit

Each option provides 128-bit encryption for the log-on process, and then the selected key strength is used to secure the remainder of ICA traffic throughout the session. Once a session has been established, all traffic, with the exception of a small encryption header, will be secured. This traffic includes items such as:

- Keystrokes
- GUI information
- Mouse data
- Client drive data
- Client printer data

Where Can You Use Encryption?

Using a combination of symmetric and asymmetric key technologies, XenApp provides a comprehensive encryption solution to ensure secure communications. First, XenApp uses RC5, a fast block cipher developed for RSA security, as the symmetric key technology to encrypt all ICA traffic between clients and servers. To exchange these keys securely, XenApp has implemented the Diffie-Hellman asymmetric key algorithm. When an ICA client session is initiated, a unique public/private key pair is generated and passed through the communications channel. Once communication is established, these key pairs are used to arrive at the same RC5 symmetric key. Using a 1024-bit symmetric key, the client then begins processing ICA traffic and log-on information. Figure 4.31 illustrates how each of the encryption technologies is used to provide a complete solution. The communications path for initiating a connection via the Web Interface to a XenApp farm is shown.

Figure 4.31 Encryption Technologies at Work

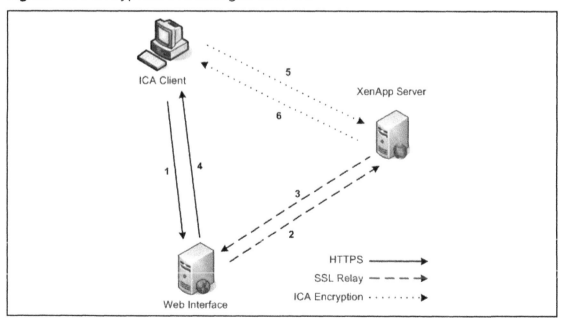

1. Client connects to the Web Interface using HTTPS.
2. The Web Interface server validates the user and requests available applications using SSL Relay service to encrypt traffic to the XenApp server.

3. XenApp returns published applications available for this user.

4. The Web Interface server provides a Web page using HTTPS with available applications.

5. ICA client connects directly to the XenApp server providing published applications.

6. A communications channel is opened using ICA encryption, and the client session begins.

Encrypting Server, Published Application, and Client Communications

XenApp offers multiple encryption techniques providing flexibility in managing secure sessions. As discussed within this chapter, encryption is a key component ensuring secure communications between the XenApp farm and the ICA client. There are several ways to configure encryption:

- Encrypting traffic at the server level

- Setting encryption for each published application

- Setting encryption on an individual client basis

You must understand how each option affects the overall environment and how the options can be used together successfully. The first option is encrypting traffic for all connections coming into the server. When you select this option, all ICA sessions initiated to the configured server encrypt data to the specified strength. This option mandates that each server must be configured independently, requiring administrators to touch each server any time this setting must be modified. For larger server farms, this requirement can be very prohibitive. To adjust the encryption properties for each server, use the XenApp Connection Configuration administration tool, as defined later within this book. The advantage to this approach is that all ICA connections communicating with this configuration are encrypted, whether through any published application or a custom ICA connection.

The next option involves setting encryption options per published application. The primary advantage of using this method is that it applies to all servers using the published application. Any user connecting through this application will use the specified encryption level across all servers in the XenApp farm. Another advantage is that you can specify different levels of encryption for each published application. For example, if a user connects to a financial application, you might require him to use 128-bit encryption. At the same time, other users connect to a word processing tool over slow network links. For these connections, you may opt to force users to use only 40-bit encryption. To configure published application encryption, you can select the encryption strength when the application is created.

If the settings were managed at the server level, as described in the last section, you would have to separate the user connections by server or configure each client independently to allow this to work. By configuring encryption for each published application, you can easily manage multiple encryption levels simultaneously, without the users knowing the difference. The third option involves specifying an encryption level for the ICA client device. By default, the ICA client attempts to use whatever encryption strength is requested by the server. You can configure the ICA client to use different encryption strengths if the server or published application allows it. For example, if the server connection encryption strength is set to 56-bit, the ICA client cannot connect unless it is using 56-bit or higher. If you're connecting as an administrator to your XenApp farm across the Internet, you might prefer to use 128-bit encryption to ensure that traffic is secured.

Using HTTPS

Encrypting the ICA client traffic secures the session information, but you must also consider accessing published applications via the Web Interface. By default, standard Web browsing with HTTP access from client devices accessing via the Web Interface transmit data in cleartext. If you want to ensure that your communications are completely secure, you must consider using SSL on the Web server hosting the Web Interface. SSL is an industry-standard encryption technology that is application independent and works well with Web-based solutions. By configuring your Web server to support SSL technology in the form of HTTPS, client to Web server communication will now be secure. Once a server certificate is installed, the Web site can digitally sign and encrypt packets as they are sent between the client device and the Web server.

ICA Encryption (Secure ICA)

Secure ICA is the oldest method for securing communications between XenApp Servers and clients. Back in the days of WinFrame, Secure ICA was considered an additional feature pack that would be purchased from Citrix and then licensed on your WinFrame servers to allow the administrator or users to secure the connection. Today, this functionality is built in to the product although not enabled by default. The current implementation of Secure ICA is simply referred to as Encryption in the XenApp suite. Secure ICA is the legacy name, but we will continue to use it here to allow us to better differentiate the concepts. The use of the legacy name will be helpful, as we will be discussing and comparing several types of encryption in this section.

> **NOTE**
>
> Secure ICA uses symmetric key algorithms based on the work by [OR of] Ron Rivest. The algorithms used today are RC5 (meaning either Ron's Code or Rivest Cipher, and this being the fifth derivation thereof). Symmetric algorithms are also known as "shared" key algorithms and are designed for speed of use. For more information, visit Ron's homepage at http://theory.lcs.mit.edu/~rivest/.

To implement Secure ICA, we must first understand how it works. Secure ICA is a feature of XenApp server and client that allows for complete encryption of all data flowing through ICA packets between the client and server. Traffic such as screen updates, mouse movements, keyboard input, and print jobs that are redirected to the client's printers can all be encrypted. Secure ICA does not encrypt other types of data (such as Web browsing, unless it occurs within an ICA session). Secure ICA supports 40-, 56-, and 128-bit encryption settings, plus an option for 128-bit at log-in time only and then drops to 40-bit for the rest of the session.

NOTE

The requirements governing the use of encryption change on a regular basis. Today, the United States government has "relaxed" the restrictions of the use of 128-bit encryption continuously from outside the United States and its territories. However, prior to implementing an encryption-based solution for remote access security, check with all governmental parties involved, as several nations prohibit the use of encryption (France). Moreover, it is illegal to "export" the encryption to certain countries, especially those considered enemies of the State (Libya, North Korea, etc.).

The impact of choosing to encrypt data on modern servers and clients is negligible. Provided the server and the client have enough horsepower to perform the encryption and decryption necessary, this can be a very easy solution to securing access to XenApp. Typically, only legacy hardware or low-end thin clients will notice a difference in performance between a Secure ICA versus standard ICA session. Secure ICA can be enabled at various locations in the XenApp toolset, at the network interface level, at the published application level, or via XenApp policies. Alternatively, clients can request that connections to servers or published applications be encrypted at a higher level, regardless of settings on the server.

NOTE

A user may ask for a session to be encrypted or ask for a higher level of encryption for an already encrypted session. However, if the server's connection or published applications require a minimum level, then the user will not be allowed to connect at a lower level of encryption.

Secure ICA can be implemented internally to your network or externally. It uses the same Transmission Control Protocol (TCP) port, 1494, as a non-encrypted ICA session. In many early solutions (prior to Secure Gateway or Access Gateway), many administrators would opt to use Secure ICA to encrypt their otherwise open solutions of network address translator (NAT)/PAT and proxy servers. Prior to Web Interface and XenApp server policy, some administrators chose to implement multihomed servers to allow for control of when and how to encrypt data.

In this scenario, sessions originating from the production network would not be required to use encryption. External (nontrusted) network users would be denied connections if they didn't connect using encryption. As previously mentioned, Secure ICA can be required on the network interface (via the XenApp Connection Configuration utility), on a published application by published application basis, or via XenApp policy. Published applications and XenApp policy are "automatic" in allowing clients to connect with no changes required on the client end. If we configure XenApp policies to require encryption, then any connection created (except those already published applications with encryption or policies requiring encryption) will require a setting adjustment on the client. Let us begin by looking at the client side. Remember, a client can request encryption at any point (even if it isn't required from the server side). For clients to request encryption, they will have to change the configuration of their application sets or their custom connections.

Using the SSL Relay Service

Another security issue to consider is the way in which traffic is passed between the Web Interface server and the XML service on XenApp. In a process that is similar to standard Web traffic, data is transmitted in cleartext. This becomes a security concern when traffic between the Web Interface server and the XenApp farm is insecure. For example, many organizations will place a Web Interface server in the DMZ, or demilitarized zone, while maintaining a XenApp server farm in a more secure network. In the event XenApp is not located in a secure network environment, the use of the SSL Relay service will help to mitigate the security concern for unencrypted traffic. Although the password is slightly encrypted, it does not provide a secure alternative to the encryption methods discussed in this chapter. To assist you with this problem, Citrix has developed the SSL Relay service. This service allows you to configure all traffic passing between Web Interface servers and a XenApp server to use SSL encryption.

Secure Gateway

Another methodology developed by Citrix allows the tunneling of all ICA client traffic using industry-standard security protocols such as Secure Sockets Layer (SSL) or Transport Layer Security (TLS). Citrix has developed a solution known as Secure Gateway that encrypts all XenApp client traffic such as ICA packets via industry-standard Internet encryption protocols to simplify the management of a secure infrastructure throughout your network. For example, by deploying a Secure Gateway in the corporate DMZ, the firewalls protecting your network from the Internet must only be configured to allow SSL packets to the Secure Gateway server from any ICA client. The Secure Gateway server will manage the connectivity and encryption across the public Internet and mask the XenApp farm. Not only does this provide a simplified security solution, it hides the server farm from potential intruders on the Internet. Although this offers security to the ICA clients, once the traffic passes through the Secure Gateway it is no longer encrypted. It is recommended to use one of the many other encryption techniques for the TCP\IP packets from the Secure Gateway to the XenApp farm.

The Secure Gateway is made up of the following components:

- **Secure Gateway Server** Central server that acts as "gateway" to the XenApp farm. The Secure Gateway Server acts as the middleman and validates the ticket provided by the STA.

- **Secure Ticket Authority (STA)** Creates a ticket for each session offering a more secure access methodology. With Citrix XenApp Server 4.5, the STA is handled by the XML service on the XenApp Server.

- **Citrix XML Service** Provides the interface between a XenApp server and the Web Interface server.

- **XenApp Farm** XenApp server farm provides published applications via the ICA Client.

The typical Secure Gateway sequence, shown in Figure 4.32, follows:

1. A remote user launches a Web browser and connects to a Web Interface server on port 80 (HTTP) or port 443 (HTTPS). The Web Interface portal requires the user to authenticate using valid user credentials.

2. The Web Interface uses the user credentials to contact the Citrix XML Service, on port 80, running on a XenApp server and obtains a list of applications that the user is authorized to access. The Web Interface populates the Web portal page with the list of published applications

that the user is authorized to access. The communications so far are the normal sequence of events that occur when a Web Interface server is deployed to provide ICA client users with access to published applications.

3. When the user clicks on a link for a published application, the Web Interface sends the IP address for the requested XenApp server to the STA, also located on a XenApp server, and requests a Secure Gateway ticket for the user. The STA saves the IP address and issues the requested Secure Gateway ticket to the Web Interface.

4. The Web Interface generates an ICA file containing the ticket issued by the STA, and then sends it to the client browser. Note that the ICA file generated by Web Interface contains only the IP address of the Secure Gateway server. The address of the XenApp server(s) that the ICA client eventually connects to is not exposed.

5. The browser passes the ICA file to the ICA client, which launches an SSL connection to the Secure Gateway server. Initial SSL handshaking is performed to establish the identity of the Secure Gateway server.

6. The Secure Gateway server accepts the ticket from the ICA client and uses information contained in the Secure Gateway ticket to identify and contact the STA for ticket validation. If the STA is able to validate the ticket, it returns the IP address of the XenApp server on which the requested application resides. If the ticket is invalid or has expired, the STA informs the Secure Gateway server, and an error message is displayed on the ICA client device.

7. On receipt of the IP address for the XenApp server, the Secure Gateway server establishes an ICA connection to the XenApp server. After the ICA connection is established, the Secure Gateway server monitors ICA data flowing through the connection, and encrypts and decrypts client-server communications.

Figure 4.32 How the Secure Gateway Works

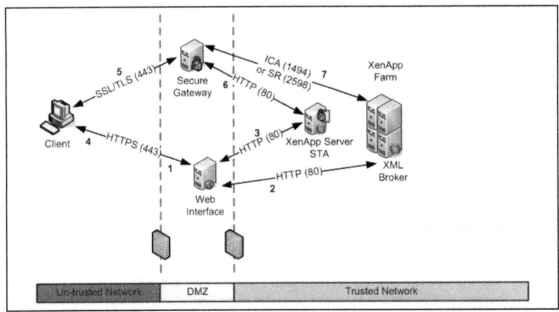

Clients that Can Support Encryption

To use encryption technologies, the ICA client software must be able to negotiate encrypted sessions. To accomplish this task, you must run a minimum version of 6.01 of the Citrix ICA client software. Additional enhancements continue to be released and it is recommended to use the Citrix ICA client version 10.x or higher. Using the client upgrade database can relieve the administrative overhead of managing client versions because the database can be used to deploy the version you want to use. For more information about the client upgrade database, download the Citrix Administration Guide available at http://www.citrix.com/.

Explaining IMA Encryption

A new feature included with XenApp is IMA encryption. This feature utilized the AES encryption algorithm previously discussed in this chapter to protect sensitive data in the IMA data store. IMA encryption is a farm–wide setting that applies to all XenApp servers once it is enabled. Therefore, once you enable IMA encryption, you must ensure that it is enabled on every XenApp server in your farm.

TIP

In environments that have a requirement for increased security, the IMA encryption feature should be utilized to protect sensitive data in the IMA data store. It is much easier to enable IMA encryption during your initial installation of XenApp than after you already have your farm installed and configured.

To enable IMA encryption, you must generate a key which is then used by all servers in your XenApp farm. You can specify the key before or during your setup. IMA encryption consists of the following components:

- **CTXKEYTOOL** This command line program is also known as the IMA encryption utility. You use this tool to manage and generate key files.
- **Key File** The key file contains the encryption key used to encrypt sensitive IMA data.
- **Key** Using the CTXKEYTOOL, you load the key you created during setup that is saved in the key file.

When using IMA encryption, Citrix recommends that you keep a backup of the farm key in a safe and secure location.

Summary

Maintaining the security of any system is not an easy task. Much thought and consideration must be given to the benefits of having a secure system weighed against the productive ability to use that system. When applying security measures to your system you must keep in mind that the system exists for one purpose and that it is to be used by clients that need to be productive. If you fail to take into account the parts of the CIA triad outlining the confidentiality, integrity, and availability of a system, then you will most certainly be looking for a new job. You can make your system so secure that not even you can use it. The XenApp Security Model is provided as a tool to assist you in completing the task of securing your system while at the same time maintaining the availability and performance level required by your organization. The model breaks down XenApp security into individual components, each with its own set of resources which you can use to make your XenApp environment more secure.

As an administrator it is your job to know and understand your network, to know which authentication mechanisms are the most appropriate for your organization, and to know which deployments will provide the best security while providing optimal availability. Make use of the resources that are readily available to you that can make your job easier. Microsoft has numerous tools available that can be used in assisting you to harden the underlying Windows 2003 server operating system on which XenApp is installed. Perhaps the best tool (probably the most dangerous in the hands of the inexperienced) is the Security Configuration Wizard that you can use to quickly and easily disable unnecessary services, remove unwanted IIS virtual folders, block unused ports, configure audit settings, and lock down access to critical system files. Other resources should be fully investigated and researched to see if they will be a good fit in your environment.

Understanding the IT methodology presented in ITIL can help you establish a firm security posture by making use of the processes and procedures it outlines. The ITIL concept is only briefly discussed in this book but contains volumes of information that is continually updated. It would be in your best interest to learn more about this methodology. Implementation of third-party products that support the ITIL approach by providing services such as automated patch management, compliance measurement, configuration management, compliance assurance, and remediation will help to make your job easier as a XenApp administrator.

Solutions Fast Track

Defining the XenApp Security Model

☑ The Citrix XenApp model consists of the following six layers: XenApp Servers (implementing computer group policy objects, locking down the base operating system), Published Applications (implementing application security, using Windows security groups, implementing NTFS permissions on application executables), ICA Connection (security on the ICA connection, encryption), Network Configuration (using IPSec, router ACLs, enforcing security boundaries), Client Devices (using only approved client devices to connect, using only approved client software to connect), End Users (establishing a "need to know" user access, no unauthorized "admin" type access, implementing user group policy objects).

☑ Defining farm and network security boundaries can assist you in using many of the security tools provided by Microsoft and other vendors to help you successfully secure your XenApp server.

☑ You should adopt and follow security guidance provided by trusted and established resources such as Microsoft, the National Security Agency, the SANS Institute, and others. In addition, adopting sound information technology methodologies such as ITIL will greatly improve your overall security posture and organizational productivity.

Understanding Types of Deployments

☑ Using the XenApp Security Model as a guide, you can determine the best type of deployment for your organization and best approach to secure that deployment. Insuring that your deployment follows the principles of the CIA triad of confidentiality, integrity, and availability will provide you with the proper balance of security in relation to productivity.

☑ There are several types of XenApp deployments that you can implement. The most common is Internal Deployment using SSL Relay; External Deployment using only a Web Interface server and a Secure Gateway server; External Deployment using a Web Interface server, Secure Gateway proxy, and a Secure Gateway server; External Deployment using SSL Relay with a Web Interface server; and deployments using a combination of all methods.

☑ Employing the use of IP Security policies can provide greater security to your deployments by restricting access to defined ports.

Authentication Methods

☑ Kerberos is supported in the XenApp environment, but there are specific requirements that must be met before it will work successfully. Requirements for Kerberos Support with XenApp are the following: XenApp on Windows 2003, ICA Client Version 8.x or higher, client\server connections must be in same domain or have trusts between domains, servers must be "trusted for delegation," SSPI requires the XML Service, DNS service address resolution to be enabled for the server farm, or reverse DNS resolution to be enabled for an AD domain. Microsoft best practices recommend not using Kerberos for authentication via the Internet.

☑ An authentication factor is a piece of information and process used to authenticate a person's identity for security purposes. Two-factor authentication (2FA) is an authentication mechanism based on two pieces of information: something you have, such as a smart card or token id, and something you know, such as a Personal Identification Number (PIN). XenApp fully supports the implementation of 2FA authentication mechanisms.

☑ You can optimize your XenApp environment by utilizing multihomed servers to segregate server functions, such as dedicating a single NIC for private traffic for server-to-server communication between XenApp resources and domain controllers, and by having another network card configured for communicating with DMZ components such as the Web Interface or the Secure Gateway.

Encrypting XenApp Server

☑ Citrix XenApp provides built-in capability to help secure server and client communications from intruders. By implementing the use of various encryption technologies available to XenApp, you can provide secure server-to-server and secure client/server communication that can be protected against intruders.

☑ Citrix XenApp offers multiple encryption techniques providing flexibility in managing secure sessions. Encryption is a key component ensuring secure communications between the XenApp farm and the ICA client. There are several ways to configure encryption: encrypting traffic at the server level, setting encryption for each published application, and setting encryption on an individual client basis. Citrix XenApp fully supports encryption standards such as FIPS140-2 and AES.

☑ A new feature included with XenApp is IMA encryption that utilizes AES encryption to protect sensitive data in the IMA data store.

Frequently Asked Questions

Q: Why is XenApp security broken down by the XenApp Security Model?

A: Implementing security based on the XenApp Security Model will assist you in protecting your network from different threats and different users.

Q: What are the components of the XenApp Security Model?

A: Servers, Published Applications, ICA connections, network configuration, client devices, end users.

Q: How can creating a Farm Boundary or network diagram assist you?

A: A "picture is worth a thousand words" and by having a quick glance view of your network boundaries and assets, you can quickly ascertain your "weak" points of security.

Q: What are some resources available to assist in server security hardening?

A: Microsoft tools such as Security Configuration and Analysis Tool, Baseline Security Analyzer, Security Assessment Tool, IIS Lockdown Tool, Security Configuration Wizard, Security Templates, Group Policy Objects.

Q: What is ITIL?

A: ITIL stands for Information Technology Infrastructure Library which is a methodology for IT management that covers areas such as configuration management, change management and security configuration and remediation.

Q: What are the different types of XenApp Server deployments?

A: Internal with SSL Relay, External (single-hop), External (double-hop), External with SSL Relay, and Combination Deployment

Q: What is the CIA triad?

A: The CIA triad stands for confidentiality, integrity, and availability.

Q: Which deployment(s) can provide end-to-end 128-bit encryption?

A: Internal SSL Relay, External deployments using Secure Gateway, or a Citrix Access Gateway used in conjunction with SSL Relay

Q: Are the Secure Gateway or SSL Relay features configured by default installation?

A: No. SSL Relay, though installed on the XenApp server, is not configured by default. Secure Gateway is a separate product that must be installed and configured separately from XenApp server.

Q: Can smart card authentication be utilized in a double-hop deployment?

A: No. Citrix does not support smart card authentication for this type of deployment or for a single-hop deployment where the Secure Gateway is placed in front of the Web Interface.

Q: Does XenApp support the use of Smart Cards?

A: Yes. Smart Card authentication is supported in most types of XenApp deployments.

Q: Should you use Kerberos authentication for any XenApp component that will be connected to the Internet?

A: No. Microsoft best practices recommend that for computers connected to the Internet, do not use Kerberos as an authentication method.

Q: What is the definition of two-factor authentication?

A: Two-factor authentication consists of something you have (like a smart card) and something you know (like a PIN).

Q: Does XenApp support the use of biometric devices to provide multifactor authentication?

A: Yes, but to enable authentication mechanisms utilizing biometric devices requires the installation of third-party software.

Q: What is the benefit of AES encryption?

A: In addition to the increased security that comes with larger key sizes, AES can encrypt data much faster than Triple-DES.

Q: Which XenApp components are FIPS-140 compliant?

A: Citrix Clients for 32-bit Windows (including Program Neighborhood, Program Neighborhood Agent, and the Web Client), Secure Gateway, XenApp, Citrix SSL Relay, Web Interface, Citrix Access Gateway, and Citrix NetScaler.

Q: If a user creates a custom ICA connection and configures the session to be encrypted at a lower level than what XenApp policies have already applied, will the user be able to initiate the session?

A: No. If a XenApp policy has defined a minimum encryption level, then the user will not be allowed to connect at a lower level of encryption.

Q: What is the difference between symmetric and asymmetric encryption?

A: Symmetric encryption requires that each individual or device that accesses encrypted data possess a copy of a key, commonly referred to as shared-key encryption. Asymmetric encryption uses two keys to encrypt data and is known as *public key encryption*.

Q: What is the command line tool used for creating and managing keys enabling IMA encryption?

A: The command line tool is CTXKEYTOOL.

Chapter 5

Security Guidance for Citrix XenApp Server

Solutions in this chapter:

- Deployment Considerations

- Maintaining Software Integrity

- Configuring XenApp Components

- Securing Your XenApp Farm

- Securing the Data Store

- Monitoring Your XenApp Farm

☑ Summary

☑ Solutions Fast Track

☑ Frequently Asked Questions

Introduction

Whenever you're connecting a computer to the Internet, that computer is open to sabotage. Worms and viruses can destroy entire systems, from the operating system right down to the hardware. Intruders can access servers on the Internet and obtain the passwords for administrative functions, using them later to wreak havoc on the system. Bored or unskilled programming students, also known as *script kiddies*, can download complex scripts from a hacker's Web site and test them on any vulnerable server just to see what happens.

Among many of the destructive attacks that can take place is the theft of confidential data. This activity is especially sensitive in the areas of e-commerce and financial systems; the theft of confidential data can destroy a company's competitive edge. Even a Citrix XenApp server, whose traffic consists mainly of graphics transmitted to clients and keyboard and mouse clicks received from clients, can be preyed upon by a saboteur.

To protect vital information from unauthorized intruders, it is vital that you secure your network and computer assets. As computer and network systems have become more common, the need for security has grown exponentially. As an administrator, you must ensure that you take into account every option that can assist in securing the computing environment. Your first step in following the XenApp Security Model defined in Chapter 4 is to secure the XenApp server and its base operating system.

Deployment Considerations

Planning the deployment of Citrix XenApp is a very in-depth process. Since XenApp and the underlying Terminal Services platform will be required in many deployments to integrate into nearly every process an organization may have, careful consideration and forethought must be given as to how best to introduce the technology. As with any major initiative undertaken in our current information technology shops, much thought is given on how to provide the greatest chance for success of new deployments that leverage as many features of the new products being introduced as possible, while reducing risk to the current environment—and doing all this as inexpensively as possible. Careful planning is frequently the difference between a successful implementation and a failed deployment. Careful planning can be the difference between happy users and unhappy ones, as it can affect the performance of the overall network even if we are only conducting a project on one aspect of the network. This is a very serious issue.

When considering your XenApp environment and the different deployment scenarios, you must look at the various tasks that must be considered in order to minimize risks to your deployment and your existing environment, while allowing for easy expansion and growth in the future. You must consider areas such as hardware planning, operating system platform deployment options, and concepts regarding your XenApp farm design and the components required that will help in fulfilling your organization's mission.

Even in the smallest of businesses, there are those who make the decisions and those who follow them (even if they make no sense). This command structure becomes more complex as the business gets larger. Staff will be assigned to different departments, which fall under the jurisdiction of people in other departments, who answer to divisions of management, who ultimately answer to senior management. In some cases, the company may be further broken into branch offices or divisions that reside in different geographic locations, or are separated for business, political, or security reasons.

Because the structure and chain of command of a business will vary from others, it is important to understand the administrative model being used in your network environment. An administrative model describes the organization of a company, and shows how it is managed. As is seen in a company's organizational chart, an administrative model is a logical structure. In other words, it doesn't tell you where the vice president's office is located, only that he or she answers to the president of the company.

Once your environment has been assessed and fully documented, the actual XenApp farm design can now be developed. You should by now have sufficient data relating to your organization to start putting together designs that are appropriate for the organization and meet any requirements to which you must adhere. During the initial stages of a XenApp infrastructure design, you should identify the administrative model that will be implemented. This can only be done when the current model has been assessed, the service and data administrators have been identified, and those sections of the organization requiring isolation and/or autonomy have been identified. These factors, together, will determine the best XenApp solution for your organization.

This book attempts to provide guidance not just on how to deploy your XenApp solution, but rather how to deploy it with security in mind. There are numerous books and documents from Citrix and others that will tell you the best practices for deploying XenApp in an Active Directory environment. In this book, we will explain items for you to consider regarding a secure XenApp deployment.

Notes from the Underground...

Are You the Weakest Link in Your Deployment?

Are you under-designing your system where you are the one that is creating a denial-of-service because you failed to plan properly? With the introduction of XenApp, Citrix has come a very long way from the day of the WinFrame product. You now have options such as CPU management, memory optimization, and application isolation to make your environment more productive to your users.

But what if you design a new deployment or upgrade an existing environment and have a new application to deliver to your users that you design based solely on "paper" metrics without actually testing how the application will react in a "real world" scenario? As you probably already know, not all applications and environments behave in the way they are described on vendor Web sites and marketing documents. Therefore it would be wise for you to develop your own scalability matrix based on your existing environment with a factor that allows for growth over time.

A single XenApp server on a 2–CPU host can provide a lot of functionality to your users, but what happens when your user base grows and you are not prepared? What if you are tasked with adding a CPU intensive application that consumes 20% CPU utilization per user and you have 50 users and only four XenApp servers? The bottom line is to pre-plan and to expect the unexpected so when your manager asks if you can handle a new graphic or CPU intensive application, you can provide the correct answer with exactly what you will need to accomplish the task.

Active Directory

As anyone familiar with networking knows, a network can be comprised of a vast number of elements, including user accounts, file servers, volumes, fax servers, printers, applications, databases, and other shared resources. Because the number of objects making up a network increases as an organization grows, finding and managing these accounts and resources becomes harder as the network gets bigger. To make a monolithic enterprise network more manageable, directory services are used to store a collection of information about users and resources, so they are organized and accessible across the network.

A directory allows accounts and resources to be organized in a logical, hierarchical fashion so that information can be found easily. By searching the directory, users can find the resources they need, and administrators are able to control and configure accounts and resources easily and effectively. Keeping this information in a centralized location ensures that users and administrators don't have to waste time looking at what's available on each server; they only have to refer to the directory.

Any directory is a structured source of information, consisting of objects and their attributes. Those who have access to the directory can look up an object, and then view its attributes. If they have sufficient rights (as in the case of an administrator), the object can be modified. These attributes can be used to provide information that's accessible to users, or control security at a granular level.

Because a user can access account information from anywhere on the network, directory services allow a user to log on to multiple servers using a single logon. A single logon is an important feature to directory services, because without it, a user must log on to each server that provides needed resources. This is common on Windows NT networks, where the administrator must create a different account on each server the user needs to access. The user then needs to log on to each server individually. This is significantly different from the way Windows 2000/2003's directory services works, where a user logs on to the network once and can use any of the resources to which he or she has been given access.

Sophisticated directory services gives administrators the ability to organize information, control security, and manage users and resources anywhere on the network. Information resides in a central repository that's replicated to different servers on the network. It allows the data to be accessed when needed and saves the administrator from having to visit each server to manage accounts. This lowers the amount of work needed to manage the network, while providing granular control over rights and permissions. The administrator only needs to modify a user account or other object once, and these security changes are replicated throughout the network.

Because the components making up Active Directory can be broken down into logical and physical elements, the logical components in Active Directory allow you to organize resources, so their layout in the directory reflects the logical structure of your company. By separating the logical and physical components of a network, users are better able to find resources, and administrators can more effectively manage them. This concept holds true with XenApp since it is installed in an Active Directory environment.

Let's look at the logical components in an Active Directory environment:

- Domains
- Domain Trees
- Forests
- Organizational Units (OUs)
- Objects

Domains

Since the days of Windows NT, domains have been a cornerstone of a Microsoft network. A domain is a logical grouping of network elements, consisting of computers, users, printers, and other components that make up the network and allow people to perform their jobs. Because domains group these objects in a single unit, the domain acts as an administrative boundary within which you can control security on users and computers. In Windows Server 2003, a domain also shares a common directory database, security policies, and, if other domains exist in the network, relationships with other domains. They are important logical components of a network, because everything is built upon or resides within the domain structure.

In serving as an administrative boundary, each domain uses its own security policies. Group Policies can be applied at a domain level, so that any users and computers within that domain are affected by it. This allows you to control access to resources, password policies, and other configurations to everyone within the domain. These security settings and policies affect only the domain, and won't be applied to other domains in the network. If large groups of users need different policies, you can either create multiple domains or apply settings in other ways (such as by using organizational units, which we'll discuss later).

When a domain is created, a DNS domain name is assigned to identify it. DNS is the Domain Name System, which is used on the Internet and other TCP/IP networks for resolving IP addresses to user–friendly names. As we'll discuss later in this chapter, because an Active Directory domain is integrated with DNS, this allows users, computers, applications, and other elements of the network to easily find domain controllers and other resources on the network.

Active Directory resides on domain controllers, which are used to manage AD and control access to network resources. To ensure that each domain controller has an identical copy of the directory database, Active Directory information is replicated to every DC within a domain. Each domain uses its own directory database. Because the information isn't replicated to other domains, this makes the domain a boundary for replication as well as for administration and security.

Domain Tree

Although domains serve as administrative boundaries, this does not mean that you will only encounter environments that have a single domain. A *domain tree* consists of Parent and Child Domains in a contiguous namespace. Many organizations have established multiple domains for some of the following reasons:

- To decentralize administration
- To control replication
- To use different security settings and policies for each domain

When a child domain is created, a two–way transitive trust relationship between the parent and child domains is automatically created. A trust relationship allows pass–through authentication, so users who are authenticated in a trusted domain can use resources in a trusting domain. Because the trust between a parent and child domain is bidirectional, this means that both domains trust each other, so users in either domain can access resources in the other (assuming, of course, that the users have the proper permissions for those resources).

The other feature of the trust relationship between parent and child domains is that they are transitive. A transitive relationship means that pass–through authentication is transferred across all domains that trust one another. For example, in Figure 5.1, Domain A has a two-way transitive trust with Domain B, so both trust each other. Domain B has a two–way transitive trust with Domain C, so they also trust each other, but there is no trust relationship between Domain A and Domain C. With the two–way transitive trust, Domain C will trust Domain A (and vice versa) because both trust Domain B. This will allow users in each of the domains to access resources from the other domains. Trusts can also be manually set up between domains so that they are one–way and non–transitive, but by default, transitive bidirectional trusts are used in domain trees and forests. These trusts are also implicit, meaning that they exist by default when you create the domains, unlike explicit trusts that must be created manually.

Figure 5.1 Adjoining Domains in a Domain Tree Use Two–Way Transitive Trust

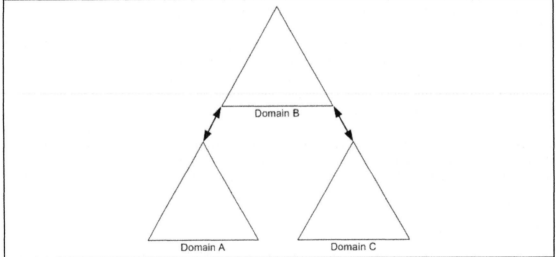

Forests

Just as domains can be interconnected into trees, trees can be interconnected into forests. As is the case with domain trees, domains in the same forests use two–way transitive trusts between the roots of all domain trees in the forest (that is, the top level domain in each tree) to allow pass–through authentication, so users can access resources in domains throughout the forest. As shown in Figure 5.2, although trees require a contiguous namespace, a *forest* can be made up of multiple trees that use different naming schemes. This allows your domains to share resources across the network, even though they don't share a contiguous namespace.

Every Active Directory structure has a forest, even if it consists only of a single domain. When the first Windows 2003 domain controller is installed on a network, you create the first domain that's also called the forest root domain. Additional domains can then be created that are part of this forest, or multiple forests can be created. This allows you to control which trees are connected and can share resources with one another (within the same forest), and which are separated so that users can't search other domains.

Figure 5.2 A Forest with Multiple Domain Trees

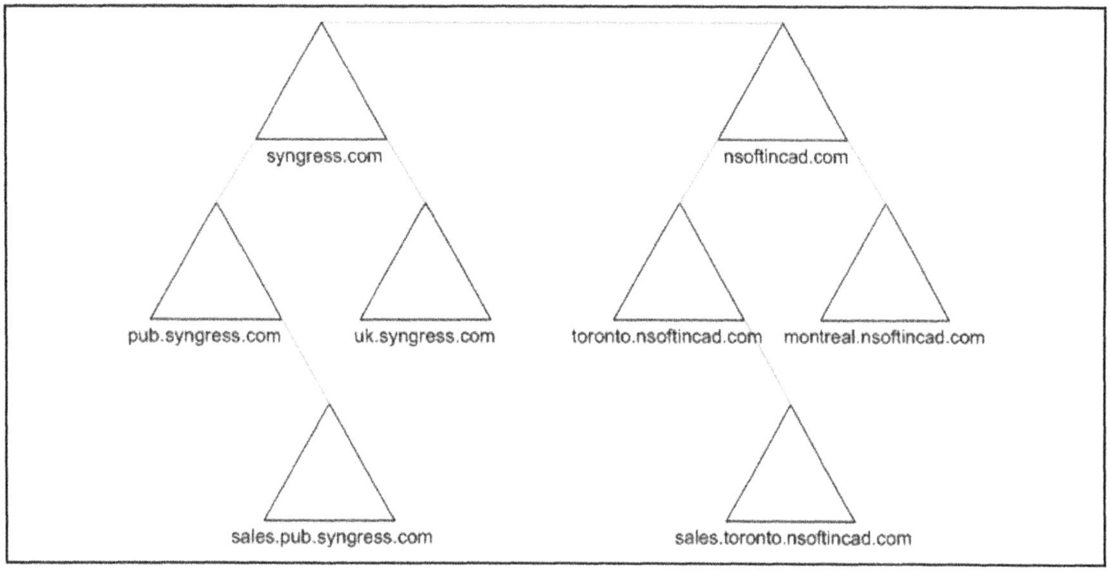

Organizational Units

To organize Active Directory objects within this single domain, organizational units can be used. *Organizational units (OUs)* are containers that allow you to store users, computers, groups, and other OUs. By placing objects in different organizational units, you can design the layout of Active Directory to take the same shape as your company's logical structure, without creating separate domains. As shown in Figure 5.3, you can create OUs for different areas of your business, such as departments, functions, or locations. The users, computers, and groups relating to each area can then be stored inside the OU, so that you can find and manage them as a single unit.

Organizational units are the smallest Active Directory unit to which you can delegate administrative authority. When you delegate authority, you give specific users or groups the ability to manage the users and resources in an OU. For example, you can give the manager of a department the ability to administer users within that department, thereby alleviating the need for you (the network administrator) to do it.

Figure 5.3 Organization Units Can Contain Other Active Directory Objects

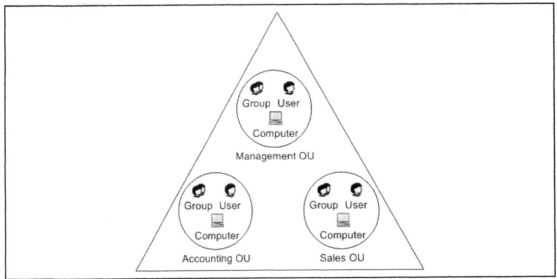

Protecting Your Active Directory Data

Active Directory can be installed on Microsoft Windows Server 2003, Standard Edition; Windows Server 2003, Enterprise Edition; and Windows Server 2003, Datacenter Edition. When a server is configured to be a DC on any of these editions, a writable copy of the directory is stored on the server's hard disk. Because any file can be damaged, destroyed, or compromised (such as in the case of a hacking attempt or virus), you should take steps to ensure that the directory is safe on your server(s).

If only one DC is used, then only one NTDS.DIT file will exist, meaning there is only one copy of the directory for that domain. Failure of this server or damage to the NTDS.DIT file will disable the network. Users will be unable to log on, computers will be unable to access needed information from the directory, and any configurations on your network could be lost. Rather than hoping that nothing ever happens to your one DC, it is wise to use multiple DCs on your network.

If more than one DC exists in a domain, any updates to the NTDS.DIT will be replicated to other DCs. This will allow multiple copies of the directory to exist on the network, providing a level of fault tolerance if one server fails. If one fails, another can continue authenticating users, supplying services, and providing access to resources.

Because of the importance of the NTDS.DIT file, the drive on which it is stored must be formatted in NTFS format. NTFS is a file format that allows the best possible level of protection, allowing you to set permissions on who can access the directory and NTDS.DIT file locally and across the network. Such permissions cannot be set on hard disks that are formatted as FAT16 or FAT32. Limiting the access to this file lessens the chance that someone might accidentally or maliciously damage or delete the data source.

It is also important to remember that any measures you take to protect Active Directory from harm do not negate the need to perform regular backups. When backups are performed, the data on a computer is copied to other media (such as a tape, CD, or DVD), which can then be stored in another location. Should any problem occur, you can restore any files that were damaged or lost.

Implementing Active Directory Security Groups

A security group is a collection of users who have specific rights and permissions to resources. Although both can be applied to a group account, rights and permissions are different from one another. Rights are assigned to users and groups, and control the actions a user or member of a group can take. In Windows Server 2003, rights are also sometimes called privileges. Permissions are used to control access to resources. When permissions are assigned to a group, it determines what the members of the group can do with a particular resource.

Security groups are able to obtain such access because they are given a SID when the group account is first created. Because it has a SID, it can be part of a DACL, which lists the permissions users and groups have to a resource. When the user logs on, an access token is created that includes their SID and those of any groups of which they're a part. When they try to access a resource, this access token is compared to the DACL to see what permissions should be given to the user. It is through this process and the use of groups that the user obtains more (and in some cases, less) access than has been explicitly given to his or her account.

Scope is the range that a group will extend over a domain, tree, and forest. The scope is used to determine the level of security that will apply to a group, which users can be added to its membership, and the resources that they will have permission to access. Active Directory provides three different scopes for groups:

- **Universal** Universal groups can contain groups from other domains. Universal groups are stored in the Active Directory global catalog. Universal groups can be used for assigning permissions to resources in any domain.

- **Domain Global** Global groups have a narrower scope than universal groups. A global group can contain accounts and groups from the domain in which it is created, and be assigned permissions to resources in any domain in a tree or forest. Because it only applies to the domain in which it's created, this type of group is commonly used to organize accounts that have similar access requirements.

- **Domain Local** Domain local groups also have a scope that extends to the local domain, and are used to assign permissions to local resources. The difference between domain local and global groups is that user accounts, global groups, and universal groups from any domain can be added to a domain local group. Because of its limited scope, however, members can only be assigned permissions within the domain in which this group is created.

NOTE

Citrix recommends that you use *domain global groups* for user access to XenApp resources.

Best Practices

Citrix recommends the following for configuration of server farms with Active Directory:

- All servers should reside in the same domain
- A XenApp farm domain should have no trust relationships with non–Active Directory domains
- Do not mix different release versions of Citrix Presentation Server with Citrix XenApp in the same XenApp farm
- XenApp farms should be in a single Active Directory forest

Of course Citrix only offers these as recommendations, not requirements, and the particular circumstances of your organization may force you to use other configurations. If that is the case, you should keep in mind that those configurations can affect user authentication and access to published resources and applications for both users and administrators alike.

When defining domain trusts keep in mind that published resources available through XenApp are only available to users who can access every server that hosts that resource. If you have several servers on which the same resource is published and you have different security access to those servers, you could in effect deny access to that resource for some users.

NOTE

To help prevent the issue of having accounts that do *not* have the required access to published resources, XenApp will automatically remove users from the authorized users of a published resource if the accounts fail authentication through the local domain or through trust–based routing.

Forest Trusts

With Windows Server 2003, Microsoft fully advocates the forest as the administrative or security boundary. This change brings about the need to connect forests in certain design scenarios. The mechanisms used for connecting forests in Windows Server 2003 are trusts and metadirectories.

Trust relationships allow users hosted by one forest to access resources located in a separate, external forest. This is a new feature for Windows Server 2003, extending the external trust capabilities that were introduced in Windows 2000 Server. Windows 2000 Server only provided nontransitive trusts between two domains in separate forests; the new forest trust capabilities for Windows Server 2003 provide transitive trusts between entire forests via the root domains of each forest. With the new forest trust capabilities, it is possible for implicit trusts to exist between forests. In other words, if Forest A trusts Forest B, and Forest B trusts Forest C, Forest A will trust Forest C through an implied trust, as shown in Figure 5.4.

Figure 5.4 Implied Trusts Between Forests

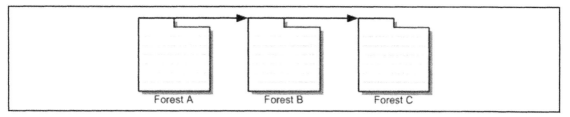

Forest A   Forest B   Forest C

Windows Server 2003 forest trusts provide the following:

■ A reduction in the number of necessary external trusts, providing simplified management of resources across Windows Server 2003 forests

■ Two–way trust relationships with every domain in each forest

■ User principal name (UPN) authentication across two forests

■ Availability of Kerberos V5 and NTLM authentication protocols, providing improved interforest authorization data trustworthiness

■ Flexibility of administration—administrative tasks can be unique to each forest

The world of information technology views security with a much greater awareness than it did in the not–so–distant past. To most administrators and engineers today, the thought of an external organization gaining access to internal company resources is a scary proposition. Fortunately, Microsoft introduces the authentication firewall with Windows Server 2003. The authentication firewall places a special security ID (SID) on incoming authentication requests that pass through the authentication firewall. This special SID, called the other organization SID, triggers a special allowed–to–authenticate check on authentication requests in an effort to control access to internal forest resources for external users. This added authentication check helps lock down the forest from unwanted external requests; it also helps prevent denial–of–service (DoS) attacks against your organization's domain controllers.

To create a forest trust between Windows Server 2003 forests, it is necessary to change the forest functional level to .NET native functionality. This eliminates the possibility of running any non–Windows Server 2003 domain controllers in either forest. Furthermore, to establish the trust between forests, the operators must be part of the Enterprise Administrators groups for each forest.

Products like Microsoft Identity Integration Server (formally known as Microsoft Metadirectory Services) provide metadirectory connectivity that facilitates simplified management of disparate systems. Metadirectory services provide synchronization for the following types of information:

■ Public Folders

■ Directory Objects

■ Global Address Lists (GALs)

Microsoft provides for full or partial synchronization between the following directory products using Microsoft Identity Integration Server:

- Active Directory
- Active Directory Application Mode
- Attribute value–pair text files
- Delimited text files
- Directory Services Markup Language
- Fixed–width text files
- GALs (Exchange)
- LDAP Directory Interchange Format
- Lotus Notes/Domino 4.6 and 5.0
- Microsoft Windows NT 4 domains
- Microsoft Exchange 5.5 bridgeheads
- Microsoft Exchange 5.5, 2000, and 2003
- Microsoft SQL 7 and 2000 databases
- Novell eDirectory v8.6.2 and v8.7
- Oracle 8i and 9i databases

Trust-Based Routing

Citrix defines *trust–based routing* as allowing servers to be members of a server farm even if the servers belong to domains that do not trust each other. Even though you cannot configure resources to be published to users that do not have permissions on servers where the application is published, it is still possible that a user could initiate a request that would require an authentication request by a server where the user has no access rights. Trust–based routing allows the user's authentication to be transparently passed to another XenApp server where the user does have access rights.

Trust–based routing applies to the following operations:

- Authenticating a Citrix administrator to the Presentation Server Console
- Refreshing the display or launching an application in Program Neighborhood or Web Interface
- Enumerating users and groups in the console
- Resolving users and groups into distinguished account names when you add users or groups to a published application, add users to a printer autocreation list, or define new Citrix administrators

NOTE

The XenApp data store is the central repository of all trust data for XenApp servers in your farm. If a XenApp server initiates a request on a domain that it does not trust, the XenApp server queries the data store on which servers can authenticate the request and then forwards the request to that server.

Maintaining Software Integrity

A critical component of Citrix XenApp security is the security of the operating system platforms on which the XenApp software runs. If it is not possible to secure the operating system, then XenApp itself cannot be secure. Even a securely configured operating system is vulnerable to the flaws of the programs and applications that run on it.

You should ensure that Citrix XenApp software runs only on approved operating systems as defined by your organization's security policies. Installing XenApp on a Windows 2003 server with only service pack 1 installed, when the rest of your environment is at service pack 2, could potentially cause problems. Your organization's local security policies should dictate minimum configurations needed for any operating environment that is produced. Introducing a lower level patched server that is missing important security updates creates a new and unnecessary vulnerability into your environment.

TIP

We have had the opportunity to talk to several administrators and engineers that support Citrix environments and a common topic of discussion relates to Citrix support and the need to have a paid support contract to address really serious issues. If for whatever reasons, your organization does not see the need to have a paid support contract with Citrix—do not let that stop you from seeking support from numerous Citrix professionals, administrators, and engineers that routinely offer advice and troubleshooting through the Citrix Support forums at no charge. You can access the support forums at http://support.citrix.com/forums. Additionally, Citrix has recently introduced a new vehicle for providing information through various Citrix blogs. You can access the Citrix blogs at http://community.citrix.com/blogs/.

Using a Supported Software Version

The integrity of the Citrix XenApp software executables and data files is crucial to the optimal and correct operation of all applications using XenApp. To protect the XenApp environment, you should ensure that the XenApp version is a Citrix Systems supported product version. Citrix Systems supported product versions are those that continue to receive security updates by Citrix in response to the discovery of vulnerabilities.

Keeping your servers up to date with the various patches and hotfixes is a problem all administrators face. With the constant stream of hotfixes coming from both Microsoft and Citrix, managing your patch levels and guaranteeing deployment is an important part of your day-to-day activities. Security updates and hotfixes can be of concern to many. It is for this reason that you should have at your disposal the use of a test environment. With the availability of virtual server tools (like XenServer, Microsoft Virtual Server, and VMWare) there should be no reason why you are not able to first test out security patches and hotfixes before implementing into a production environment. If you have not done so already, you should sign up to receive e-mail notifications regarding newly released Citrix product hotfixes and security patches. You can receive these notifications through the Citrix Knowledge Center's e-mail alert system accessed through your *MyCitrix* account.

NOTE

If you are a XenApp administrator that does not handle Citrix product licensing, support contracts, or subscription advantage renewals for your organization, you may not have a MyCitrix account. In order to get a MyCitrix account, simply go to the Citrix Web site, www.citrix.com, and look for the MyCitrix link and register as a new user, or have your organization's primary Citrix administrator create an account for you.

Something that is often overlooked in a network environment is the use of outdated software. If your environment is currently running Citrix products that have reached or will soon reach end of life, then an appropriate migration plan should be implemented for either removing or upgrading the Citrix products in question. Typically this migration plan should be implemented prior to the date Citrix drops security patch support. Many times we have heard the phrase, "If it ain't broke, don't fix it." Maintaining this mentality could potentially cause problems. Vendors routinely update the life cycles for their products as to patch maintenance, security vulnerabilities, and support. Maintaining a product that is no longer supported by a vendor is just bad practice. Your organization's security policies should prevent the installation and/or continued use of outdated products. Like most respected hardware and software vendors, Citrix maintains a matrix of life–cycle support for all of its products available on the Citrix Web site at www.citrix.com.

Citrix defines a product's progress through three distinct lifecycle phases:

- **Mainstream Maintenance Phase** begins on the General Availability date of a product release and transitions to the next phase on the End of Maintenance date.

- **Extended Maintenance Phase** begins on the End of Maintenance date and transitions to the next phase on the End of Life date.

- **End of Life Phase** begins on the End of Life date Platinum Edition.

Citrix will announce additions and changes to product life cycles through the Citrix Web site. The definitions for life cycle dates defined by Citrix are:

- **General Availability (GA)** is the date that signifies a new product release may be ordered and fulfilled.

- **Notice of Status Change (NSC)** is the date on which Citrix publicly communicates the specific dates for a product's End of Sales (EOS), End of Maintenance (EOM), and End of Support/Life (EOS/L).

- **End of Sales (EOS)** is the date that a specific software or appliance release will no longer be available for purchase.

- **End of Maintenance (EOM)** is the date that signifies a specific product release will have no further code level maintenance other than security related updates.

- **End of Life (EOL)** is the date on which security related hot fixes, technical support, and product download(s) will no longer be available.

Understanding Citrix Service Accounts

Service accounts defined for access to XenApp servers, shown in Table 5.1, allow various interactions with associated applications, services, user sessions, and external supporting systems. These interactions can be relatively benign, such as access to availability information, or quite powerful, such as reconfiguration, redeployment of applications, or even the installation and deletion of user applications. All accounts, not just service accounts, must be carefully scrutinized to ensure that privileges assigned are those that are genuinely needed.

Table 5.1 XenApp Service Accounts and Default Permissions

Account Name	Permissions	Notes
NT AUTHORITY\ LocalService	Minimal	Default Windows account
NT AUTHORITY\ NetworkService	Minimal, network resources	Default Windows account
NT AUTHORITY\System	Administrator	Default Windows account
Ctx_CpsvcUser	Domain or local user	Acts as a power user
Ctx_StreamingSvc	Domain or local user	Acts as a user
Ctx_ConfigMgr	Domain or local user	Acts as a power user
Ctx_CpuUser	Domain or local user	Acts as a user

One setting that should be enabled is the **Strengthen default permissions of internal system objects** found under **Computer Configuration | Windows Settings | Security Settings | Local Policies | Security Options**. This security setting (which can be configured through a GPO or locally) determines the strength of the default discretionary access control list (DACL) for objects. Active Directory maintains a global list of shared system resources, such as DOS device names, mutexes, and semaphores. In this way, objects can be located and shared among processes. Each type of object is created with a default DACL that specifies who can access the objects and what permissions are granted. If this policy is enabled, the default DACL is stronger, allowing users who are not administrators to read shared objects but not allowing these users to modify shared objects that they did not create.

Tip

CtxCpsvc10.exe is a command line tool that re–creates (if deleted) the Ctx_CpsvcUser account and checks and assigns all required access permissions. This tool is available for free from the Citrix Web site www.citrix.com.

During installation of XenApp several service accounts may be created depending on the version of XenApp being installed and the hardware configuration of the server on which XenApp is being installed. Typical service accounts that are created:

- **Ctx_CpsvcUser** Used with the Citrix Print Manager Service to handle the creation of printers and driver usage within ICA sessions.

- **Ctx_ConfigMgr** Used to run the Configuration Manager for the Web Interface. Allows you to copy the Web interface configuration from one server to another.

- **Ctx_StreamingSvc** Used in Enterprise and Platinum versions to manage the Citrix Streaming Client when streaming applications.

- **Ctx_CpuUser** Used for multiple processors and CPU rebalancing. This account is only created when multiple CPUs exist on the system.

By default, these accounts have only the necessary permissions, group memberships, and rights needed to perform those functions as shown in Table 5.2. Each of these accounts has their password dynamically assigned at installation time, so there is no default. If you have a requirement to periodically change these service account passwords, you may do so without any adverse affects to your environment.

Table 5.2 Rights Assigned to the XenApp Service Accounts

Rights	Local Service	Network Service	Ctx_ CpsvcUser	Ctx_ ConfigMgr	Ctx_ CpuUser	Ctx_ StreamingSvc
Change the system time	X					
Generate security audits	X	X				
Increase quotas	X	X				
Load and unload device drivers			X			
Log on as a batch job	X	X	X	X	X	X

Continued

Table 5.2 Continued. Rights Assigned to the XenApp Service Accounts

Rights	Local Service	Network Service	Ctx_ CpsvcUser	Ctx_ ConfigMgr	Ctx_ CpuUser	Ctx_ StreamingSvc
Log on as a service		X	X	X	X	X
Replace a process level token	X	X				X
Restore files and directories						X
Debug programs					X	
Increase scheduling priority					X	

WARNING

Any deviation from the default set of permissions and rights for the purpose of hardening or locking down the server may result in undesirable effects (that is, printers may not autocreate in an ICA session or certain reporting components of the Access Suite Console may not function properly).

Securing Java Client on XenApp Servers

Some XenApp components require the use of the Java runtime environment (JRE). Regardless of which version of Java is installed on your XenApp server you should be aware that having Java installed on your system can potentially introduce multiple vulnerabilities to your system, which can be exploited by malicious people to bypass certain security restrictions, manipulate data, disclose sensitive/system information, or potentially compromise a vulnerable system.

In order to address this issue, you should use the latest patched level of whichever version of the JRE is installed. To determine the latest Java version you should check the Sun Microsystems web site www.java.com.

Defining Multiple Services on Host Systems

The installation of Citrix XenApp on a server can introduce additional vulnerabilities and resource requirements to the server. Additionally, the XenApp farm frequently offers services to clients that are members of a different audience than other services. Since it is a best security practice to separate or partition services offered to different audiences, any XenApp server should be installed on a server dedicated to its support and offering as few services as possible to other clients. For this reason, XenApp should not be installed on a server that also provides Web services (other than Web Interface and Citrix Secure Gateway), directory services including a Windows domain controller, directory naming services, database server, and so forth.

Here is a listing of potential server roles that may exist in your environment:

- **Domain controller** This role is used for authentication and installs Active Directory on the server.

- **File server** This role is used to provide access to files stored on the server.

- **Print server** This role is used to provide network printing functionality.

- **DHCP server** This role allocates IP addresses and provides configuration information to clients.

- **DNS server** This role resolves IP addresses to domain names (and vice versa).

- **WINS server** This role resolves IP addresses to NetBIOS names (and vice versa).

- **Mail server** This role provides e-mail services.

- **Application server** This role makes distributed applications and Web applications available to clients.

- **Terminal server** This role provides Terminal Services for clients to access applications running on the server.

- **Remote access/VPN server** This role provides remote access to machines through dial-up connections and virtual private networks (VPNs).

- **Streaming media server** This role provides Windows Media Services so that clients can access streaming audio and video.

Understanding Anonymous Accounts

When XenApp is installed a special group named Anonymous is created which by default contains 15 user accounts with account names in the form AnonXXX, where XXX is a number from 000 to 014. These anonymous users have guest permissions and differ from other user accounts in that they have a default 10-minute idle time before being logged off. XenApp administrators may create more than the default 15 anonymous accounts by following the guidelines in the most recent Administrator's Guide.

Anonymous accounts have the following attributes:

- Ten minute idle time-out

- No password is required

- Logged off on broken connection

- User cannot change password

NOTE

The Anonymous user idle time can be changed by modifying the idle time setting within the property of the user account.

Anonymous accounts can be used in marquee type environments or whenever the above restrictions will not affect user productivity. When a user starts an anonymous application, the XenApp server does not require an explicit user name and password to log the user on to the server, but selects a user from a pool of anonymous users who are not currently logged on. If none of your published resources are utilizing anonymous accounts then you should delete the individual anonymous user accounts and the Anonymous user group as well. If at a later time you need these accounts and groups, you can re-create them manually.

Configuring XenApp Components

XenApp has many components and services that perform a variety of functions. Many of these components and services can be configured individually to meet the needs of an organization's security requirements and if a service or component is not being used at all, then it should be either disabled or not installed. A listing of the most common XenApp services include:

- **Citrix ActiveSync Service** Installed with R01 and supports ActiveSync in ICA sessions.

- **Citrix ADF Installer Service** Used by Installation Manager in Enterprise and Platinum versions to install packages onto Presentation Servers.

- **Citrix Client Network** Handles the mapping of client drives and peripherals within ICA sessions.

- **Citrix CPU Utilization Mgmt/CPU Rebalancer** Enhances resource management across multiple CPUs.

- **Citrix CPU Utilization Mgmt/Resource Mgmt** Used in Enterprise and Platinum versions to manage resource consumption.

- **Citrix Diagnostic Facility COM Server** Manages Diagnostic Facility tracing when used to diagnose problems with the Citrix Server.

- **Citrix Encryption Service** Handles encryption between the client device and the Citrix Server.

- **Citrix Health Monitoring and Recovery** Provides health monitoring and recovery services in the event problems occur.

- **Citrix Independent Management Architecture** Provides management services within the Citrix farm.

- **Citrix License Management Console** Provides the Web-based interface for licensing administration (License server only).

- **Citrix Licensing WMI** Provides information and notification regarding licensing events on the license server (License server only).

- **Citrix MFCOM Service** Provides COM services which allow remote connections of the management consoles.

- **Citrix Print Manager Service** Handles the creation of printers and driver usage within Citrix sessions.

- **Citrix Resource Manager Mail** Used in Enterprise and Platinum versions to send e-mail alerts when thresholds in the server farm have been exceeded.

- **Citrix Services Manager** Allows the components of Presentation Server to interface with the operating system.

- **Citrix SMA Service** Monitors the event log and Citrix WMI to raise alerts in the Access Management Console.

- **Citrix Streaming Service** Used in Enterprise and Platinum versions to manage the Citrix Streaming Client when streaming applications.

- **Citrix Virtual Memory Optimization** Used in Enterprise and Platinum versions to rebase .dlls in order to free up server memory.

- **Citrix WMI Service** Used to provide the Citrix WMI classes for information and management purposes.

- **Citrix XTE Server** Handles SSL Relay and Session Reliability functionality.

- **Citrix Licensing** Handles allocation of licenses on the license server (License server only).

All binary files, objects, and applications installed by Citrix XenApp that are not actively used should be removed from the system. Optimally, you should not even install the components you know you will not be using.

Aside from the administrative overhead in maintaining unused software, unnecessary vulnerabilities associated with them could remain. You should take precautions to remove any objects or components that are no longer required.

XenApp has the following components that can be installed:

- **Management Console** (This component is also known as the Presentation Server Console.) This is the interface that lets you create policies, configure printing, configure zones, create isolation environments, and perform specific tasks with Citrix management tools, such as Resource Manager and Installation Manager. To administer your farm, you must install this component on at least one server in your farm or one remote computer. It is recommended that you do not install the Management Console on a XenApp server functioning as a data collector.

- **Installation Manager** (Enterprise Edition only.) Provides centralized, farm–wide installation capabilities such as support for unattended installs, packager rollback, scheduled package delivery, and MSI support.

- **Resource Manager** (Enterprise Edition only.) Provides customizable metrics and reporting, real-time graphs and alerts, and capacity planning for server farm resources.

- **Application Streaming** Provides application streaming to servers and desktops. This component includes the Streaming Client subfeature.

- **Load Manager** (Advanced and Enterprise Editions.) Provides load balancing of user connections across servers to more effectively use server resources.

- **Network Manager** (Enterprise Edition only.) Provides the ability to administer server farms through the native management consoles of leading network management solutions.

- **Program Neighborhood** Installs a pass-through client on the server. If you do not select either Program Neighborhood or Program Neighborhood Agent, Program Neighborhood Agent is installed by default.

- **WMI Providers** (Enterprise Edition only.) Installs WMI providers. Windows Management Instrumentation (WMI) is the standard management infrastructure included as part of Windows Server 2003. The WMI Provider for XenApp supplies information about servers and server farms.

- **Citrix Web Interface** Installed as a Web site on IIS that allows users to connect to published applications via a Web page.

- **Citrix Secure Gateway** Installed on a server that allows for encrypted sessions of published applications accessed via the Citrix Web Interface.

Understanding and Using XenApp Policies

Administrators can create policies and configure them to meet the needs of the users they support. Policies and the rules they contain can be made to support end users based on their geographic location, job function, and the method by which they connect to the network. Citrix policies can even be used cooperatively with Windows Group Policy to secure end-user connections via encryption and deny drive mapping, for example. More specific instructions for creating, applying, and maintaining XenApp policies is covered in Chapter 6.

Understanding XenApp Shadowing

The XenApp shadowing utility provides the ability to remotely control, monitor, and interact with another user's session. During a shadow session, the session being monitored is displayed in the shadower's session window. The monitored session can be viewed only, or the shadower can interact with the monitored session, depending on the configuration. When the session is placed in interactive mode, all keyboard and mouse strokes are passed to the monitored session.

Shadowing is one of the most powerful tools available on the XenApp server; as is always the case with such tools, it has the potential for misuse. The power of these tools lies in their ability to spy on users without their permission, which can be considered an intrusion of privacy and could have legal consequences. For these reasons, you should make careful selection of the user base that will be given Shadowing rights, and you should configure shadowing according to your company policy.

> **WARNING**
>
> By default, a user who is being shadowed is prompted with a popup window telling them that \\server\user is requesting to control their session remotely and giving them the option to allow or refuse the shadow session. This notification can be disabled in the connection profiles or in the individual user profile. Before disabling this notification, be sure that you have the authority to do so and have obtained the necessary waiver(s) from your users. Many companies now require, at every initial server logon, a popup with some type of legal disclaimer and privacy waiver. This could also suffice for monitoring purposes, depending on the wording. Consult with your attorney before attempting to conduct any "covert" monitoring. Failure to do so could have serious legal ramifications. For all these reasons, many companies have decided not to allow any sort of shadowing.

Cshadow.exe is a command line executable that acts as the shadowing engine for all XenApp shadow utilities. It's located in C:\Program Files\Citrix\System32 and is invoked anytime a shadow session is launched. As an added measure of security, it is suggested that you apply appropriate NTFS permissions to the Cshadow.exe executable.

Configuring Shadowing

XenApp shadowing (as well as Terminal Services remote control) can be configured in a variety of ways. Some of the most common are:

- Configuration during installation
- User account properties
- Windows group policy
- Terminal Services Configuration Tool
- Editing Registry
- Creating a XenApp Policy

Because shadowing can be configured in a variety of ways, you should keep in mind that you can potentially create conflicting settings just like you can with Windows Group Policy objects and the other ways you can configure Windows settings. Because of this, you should understand the order of priority for the settings you choose. Only XenApp policies are controlled by the IMA service—all other settings are controlled by the Windows registry. When two policies contradict one another the most restrictive policy wins.

Determining which method is best for you is dependent on your environment and any security requirements your organization may have.

Keep in mind that the settings you can change control the amount of interaction you can have with the session being shadowed. The settings that can be modified are:

- **Shadowing is enabled: input ON, notify ON** This setting enables shadowing and gives the shadower input; in other words, it gives the user the ability to move stuff around within the shadowee's session and sends a message to the user being shadowed, requesting permission to shadow his or her session.

- **Shadowing is enabled: input OFF, notify ON** This setting enables shadowing and gives the shadower view–only rights to the shadowee's session. This setting also requests permission from the user before you can shadow his or her session.

- **Shadowing is disabled** This setting disables shadowing altogether.

NOTE

As you might have noticed in the first two options, notify is always ON; there is no option for notify OFF. Notify OFF translates to shadowing a user session without the user's permission—it would be like spying on the user. The reason you don't see notify OFF is that when you installed XenApp, you explicitly selected the option to always request permission before shadowing a user session. Had you selected the option to not notify the user prior to your shadowing a session, the options would be different—you would be given the option of notify OFF in some of these settings.

Configuring During Installation

During initial installation you have the option of either allowing or prohibiting shadowing, as shown in Figure 5.5. If you select to allow shadowing, you have three options you may select:

- **Prohibit remote control** Allows only the viewing of a user session, no interaction is allowed.

- **Force a shadow acceptance popup** Displays a popup message in a user's session asking the user permission for the session to be shadowed.

- **Log all shadow connections** Logs all shadow connections to the event log.

If the option to allow shadowing is selected, the options to configure shadowing may be configured at a later time.

Figure 5.5 Enabling Shadowing During Installation

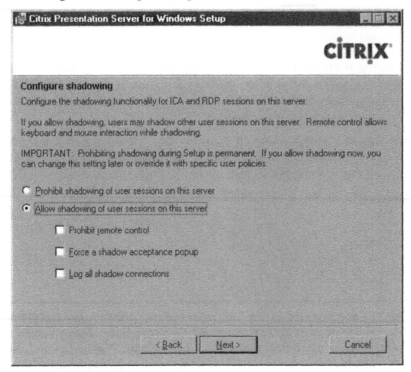

NOTE

One very important point that you need to keep in mind is that if during setup you explicitly selected not to allow any kind of shadowing, this setting cannot be changed unless you reinstall XenApp. This is done as a security measure so that security policies cannot be inadvertently or intentionally overridden.

Creating XenApp Shadowing Policies

To create a XenApp policy that controls shadowing, you must create a policy using the Citrix Presentation Server Console. (The specific steps required to create and assign a XenApp policy are covered in more detail in Chapter 6.)

XenApp policy settings for Shadowing are found under the User Workspace folder when configuring a policy as shown in Figure 5.6. The settings you can use are:

- **Not Configured** Defers to lower-priority policies.

- **Disabled** Turns off shadowing

- **Enabled** Turns on shadowing policy and allows the same shadowing options as during initial installation.

Figure 5.6 Configuring a Shadow Policy

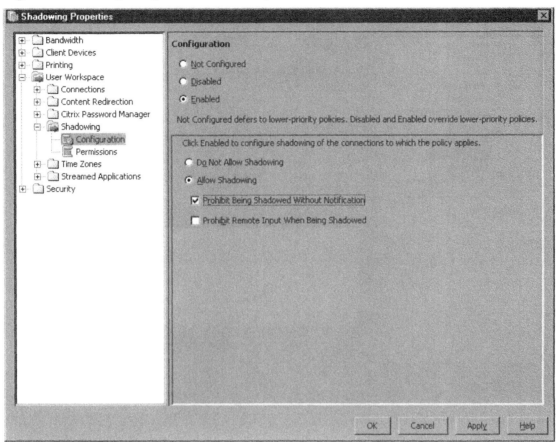

After creating a XenApp shadow policy, you must then assign permissions to that policy, shown in Figure 5.7. For shadowing, it is recommended that you create specific security groups that offer different levels of shadowing functionality. For example, a XenApp Administrator group could be given remote input capability, while a Help Desk group may only be given a view capability without being able to provide input. Additionally, you may have a need to provide shadowing without notifying a user that they are being shadowed, such as being a part of an investigation in misuse of corporate resources. When assigning permissions to a policy, you should only assign permissions to a security group and never to a specific user account.

Figure 5.7 Configuring Shadow Policy Permissions

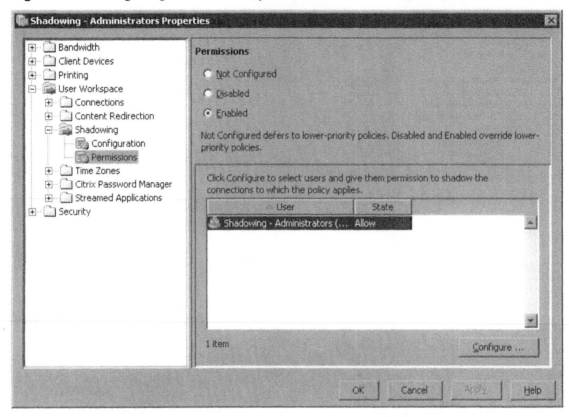

The last item you must do is then apply the policy. As shown in Chapter 6, you can filter the policy based on:

■   Access Control

■   Client IP Address

■   Client Name

■   Servers

■   Users

Shadowing through Group Policy Objects

Like many other Windows settings for Terminal Services, remote control (shadowing) settings can be configured through Group Policy as shown in Figure 5.8. To configure remote control in a Group Policy Object (GPO) in Active Directory, you need to navigate to **Computer Configuration | Administrative Templates | Windows Components | Terminal Services**. In the Terminal

Services folder you'll find the option, **Sets rules for remote control of Terminal Services user session**. (The same policy exists in the User Configuration tree. Whether you want to use the Computer Configuration or User Configuration depends on how you choose to apply your policy.) Again, here you have the ability to enable or disable remote control, specify notification, and specify what level of control is allowed for the session.

Figure 5.8 Configuring Shadowing via Group Policy

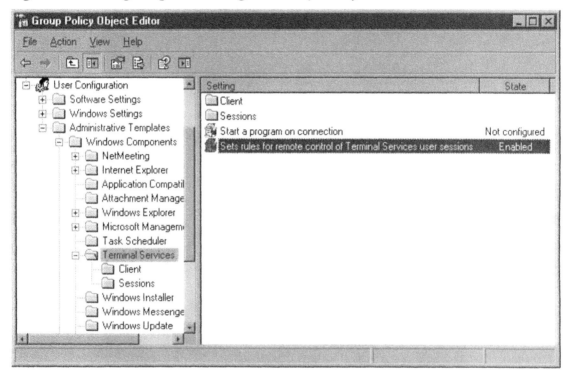

Using the Terminal Services Configuration Tool

The Terminal Services Configuration tool is another option where shadowing can be configured, as shown in Figure 5.9. Keep in mind that you can configure shadowing for ICA connections and remote control for RDP connections. To configure shadowing using the Terminal Services Configuration tool:

1. Go to **Administrative Tools | Terminal Services Configuration | ICA–tcp | Properties | Remote Control**.

2. Select the options you want to configure and click **OK** to apply.

Figure 5.9 Configuring Shadowing via the Terminal Services Configuration Tool

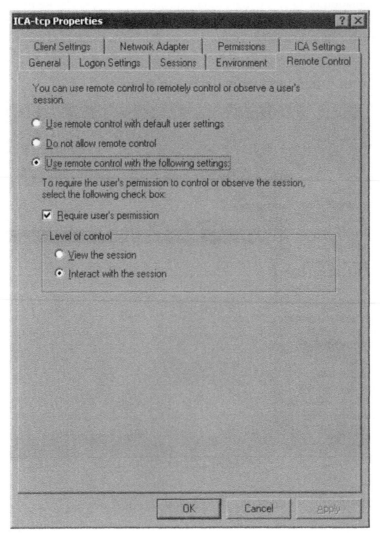

Editing the Registry

It is also possible to manually edit the connection level settings that configure shadowing, as shown in Figure 5.10. The registry key that controls XenApp shadowing is HKLM\SYSTEM\Current ControlSet\Control\Terminal Server\WinStations\ICA–tcp\Shadow and the registry key that controls Windows remote control is HKLM\SYSTEM\CurrentControlSet\Control\Terminal Server\WinStations\RDP–Tcp\Shadow. Configuring shadowing in this way prevents you from having centralized control of your farm environment and is not recommended.

WARNING

If you decide to edit the registry manually, you should keep in mind the Microsoft warning that states, "Using Registry Editor incorrectly can cause serious, system-wide problems that may require you to re-install Windows to correct them. Microsoft cannot guarantee that any problems resulting from the use of Registry Editor can be solved. Use this tool at your own risk."

Figure 5.10 Configuring Shadowing by Using the Registry

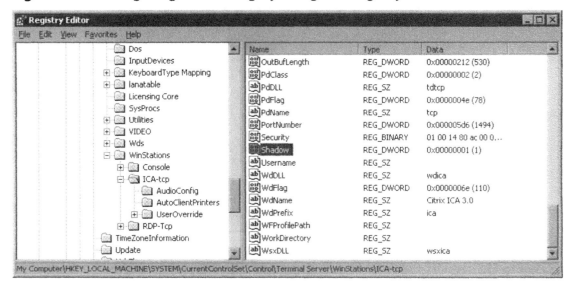

Controlling through User Account Properties

You can configure shadowing settings at the user account level through the Active Directory Users and Computer snap-in as shown in Figure 5.11.

On the Remote Control tab, you have the ability to enable or disable remote control, specify notification, and specify what level of control is allowed for the session. By default, in Active Directory, the user account is configured to *enable remote control*, *require user's permissions*, and *interact with the session*. Settings configured here will apply to all terminal services sessions whether RDP or ICA.

Figure 5.11 Configuring Shadowing through User Account Properties

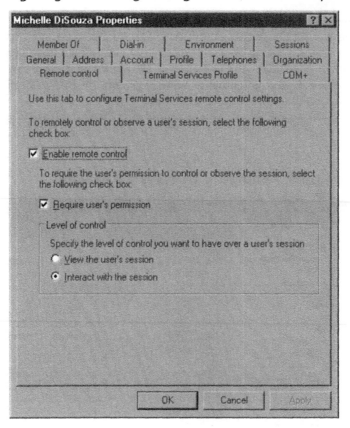

Configuring Shadow Auditing and Logging

If your situation requires that you have to enable shadowing at any level it is recommended that you also enable shadow auditing and logging so that you can track who is performing shadowing and who is being shadowed. This information is recorded in the Windows event log as shown in Figure 5.12.

Figure 5.12 Event Log Shadow Entry

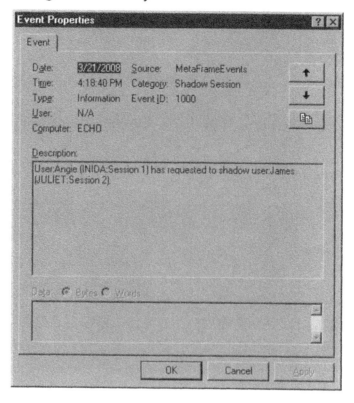

To enable Shadow Logging, you must select the option to Log Shadowing Sessions under the Shadow Logging section of the XenApp farm or server properties as shown in Figure 5.13.

Figure 5.13 Enabling Shadow Logging

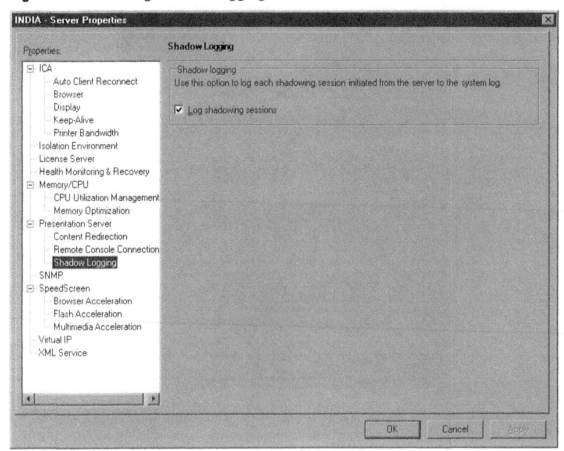

If you have multiple XenApp shadow policies defined you should also consider configuring the option to merge multiple shadow policies, as shown in Figure 5.14. This allows the farm to merge shadowers in XenApp shadowing policies. The resultant policy applies to merged policies without taking into consideration the prospective priorities of each policy.

Figure 5.14 Merging Multiple Shadow Policies

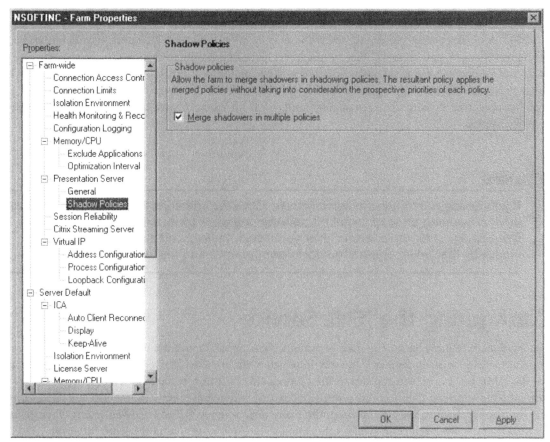

Understanding Drive Remapping

Default drive mappings for client sessions are shown in Table 5.3. Client drives C and D are renamed V and U, because the server drives use the letters C and D.

XenApp gives you the ability to remap your server drives to make drive access more familiar to

Table 5.3 Default Client Drive Remappings

Logical Drive Letter	Drive Letter in ICA Sessions
A	A
B	B
C	V
D	U

users that are saving data to their local systems. For example, during installation you could opt to change the default server drives from C and D, and instead use letters such as M and N. In doing this, the original lower drive letters become available for assignment during client drive mapping, ultimately making the use of client drives easier to understand for your end users.

How does server drive remapping affect the security of your system? There has been considerable debate in various forums as to whether or not server drive remapping presents any security concerns. Some administrators have noted unusual problems with applications installed on servers that have drives remapped. Since drive remapping could potentially cause a denial of service to a particular published application on a server with drive remapping configured, our recommendation is to *not* perform server drive remapping.

WARNING

If you decide to remap your server drives, Citrix recommends that you perform server drive remapping prior to installing XenApp and prior to installing any applications. Remapping server drive letters after you install XenApp can cause unstable performance by the server, operating system components, and installed applications.

Configuring the XML Service

The XML Service provides the interface between a XenApp server and the Web Interface server. Another security issue to consider is the way in which traffic is passed between the Web Interface server and the XML service on XenApp servers. In a process that is similar to standard Web traffic, data is transmitted in cleartext. This becomes a security concern when traffic between the Web Interface server and the XenApp farm is insecure. For example, many organizations will place a Web Interface server in the DMZ, or demilitarized zone, while maintaining a XenApp farm in a more secure network.

The XML Service can run by itself or as a component of Internet Information Services (IIS). If XML is shared with IIS, XenApp will configure your server appropriately. If you have XML configured to share its port with IIS, then you should configure IIS to use HTTPS traffic only.

TIP

If you need to modify the XML port after initial installation of XenApp, you can use the CTXXMLSS.EXE command line utility to register, unregister and modify the XML service. The syntax for the CTXXMLSS utility:
CTXXMLSS [switches] [/Rnnnn] [/Knnn] [/U] [/?]
Parameters
/Rnnnn – Registers the service on port number nnnn
/Knnn – Keep–Alive nnn seconds (default 9)
/U – Unregisters the service
/? (help) – Displays the syntax for the utility and information about the utilities options.

You also have the option to configure the XML Service to trust requests, as shown in Figure 5.15. Reasons that this feature is enabled are:

- So that users can move from one client device to another and reconnect to their applications where they initially left them. This process is known as SmoothRoaming.

- To use pass-through authentication or smart cards for connecting to sessions through the Citrix Web Interface.

- To access applications through the Citrix Access Gateway or Citrix NetScaler.

If you decide to have the XML Service trust requests, you should utilize IPSec, firewall access control lists, and other means to ensure that XML requests are only received by authorized services.

Figure 5.15 Configuring the XML Service

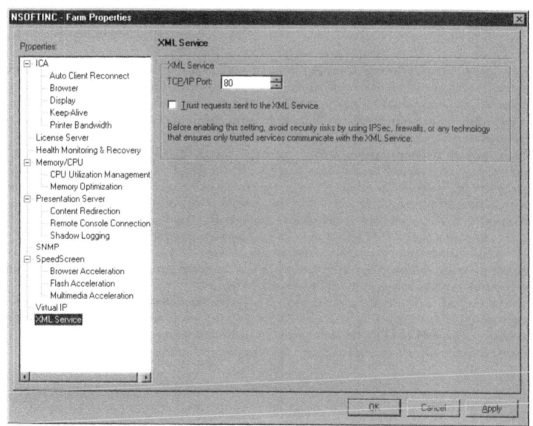

Configuring Session Reliability (XTE Service)

Session Reliability is available with the Advanced, Enterprise, and Platinum Editions of XenApp. This feature allows a user's applications to remain open even if they lose network connectivity.

Users continue to see the application they are using until network connectivity resumes. This feature uses the Common Gateway Protocol (CGP) on TCP port 2598.

If your clients are operating on a network with drastic changes in bandwidth or network reliability problems, Session Reliability can be configured to keep the application window available to the client while the ICA software is attempting to restore connectivity behind the scenes. To keep users from continuing to click links or type text while the connection is being restored; the user's display freezes and the mouse pointer becomes an hourglass icon until the application connection is restored.

NOTE

You can use Session Reliability in conjunction with SSL.

By default, Session Reliability is enabled at the server farm level as shown in Figure 5.16. You can customize the settings for this feature by selecting the server farm's **Properties** page in the Access Management Console and modifying the Session Reliability settings. You can edit the port on which XenApp listens for session reliability traffic and edit the amount of time Session Reliability keeps an interrupted session connected.

The **Seconds to keep sessions active** option has a default of 180 seconds, or three minutes. Even though you can extend the amount of time Session Reliability keeps a session open, you should be aware that this feature is designed as a convenience to the user and does not prompt the user for reauthentication. If you extend the amount of time a session is kept open to longer time periods, you could possibly create an unneeded vulnerability on your system. For example, a user could walk away from the client device potentially leaving the session accessible to unauthorized users.

If you do not want users to be able to reconnect to interrupted sessions without having to reauthenticate, use the Auto Client Reconnect feature. You can configure Auto Client Reconnect to prompt users to reauthenticate when reconnecting to interrupted sessions.

If you use both Session Reliability and Auto Client Reconnect, the two features work in conjunction with one another. Session Reliability disconnects the user session after the amount of time you specify in **Seconds to keep sessions active**. After that, the settings you configure for Auto Client Reconnect take effect, attempting to reconnect the user to the disconnected session.

NOTE

If you enable session reliability, then ICA traffic uses the Common Gateway Protocol which uses TCP port 2598 by default. Just like ICA (TCP 1494) traffic, the port is used for inbound sessions to your XenApp server, and a dynamically created port is used for outbound sessions. Your firewall configuration should allow internal inbound traffic only for ports 1494 and 2598.

Figure 5.16 Configuring Session Reliability

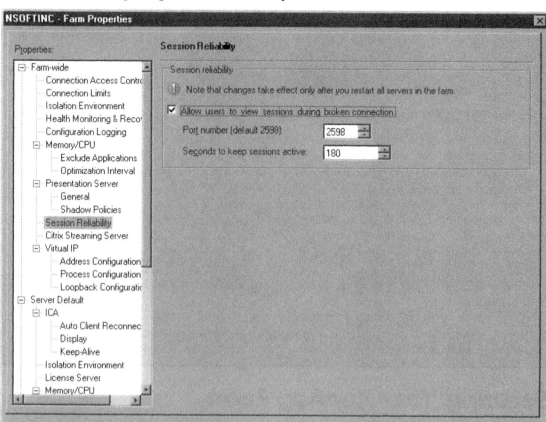

Understanding MFCOM

MFCOM is a programming interface for assisting you with the management of your farm servers and their components. The configuration options available through the various XenApp administration consoles are available through the MFCOM interface. You have the capability to create tools to perform and automate tasks that are specific to your own environment. MFCOM works in conjunction with Visual Basic or .NET to communicate with the XenApp environment through the MFCOM interface.

From this description, you should see that MFCOM left un-secured provides yet another avenue for authorized changes to your XenApp environment. As stated previously in this chapter, if you will not make use of this service, then it should be disabled. If you do have a need for the capabilities provided by using MFCOM, then you should take appropriate measures to lockdown the components that utilize MFCOM. You can use NTFS permissions to restrict access to VB and .NET executables that are used to utilize the functionality of MFCOM. In addition, if you are running the Platinum version of XenApp, you should enable configuration logging of your XenApp environment, which is covered later in this chapter.

Tools & Traps...

How MFCOM Can Be Used Against You

So you've decided to automate various tasks in your XenApp environment to assist you with copying Published Applications or modify printer mappings. By doing so, you've eliminated some mundane administrative processing time. You've followed the best practices of locking down your XenApp environment and do not have any management consoles installed on servers that publish applications and content. All is well.

One of your users has just completed a VB scripting class and just happens to have been a Citrix administrator at his last job. This user happens to have enough knowledge to write scripts that can utilize MFCOM and can then execute these scripts on one of your XenApp servers because he has figured out a gap in your security and can access Windows explorer on the XenApp server and can run CScript.exe and WScript.exe unrestricted.

Even though the management tools are not on the XenApp server, this user now has the capability to possibly perform configuration changes to your XenApp environment by utilizing MFCOM.

Securing Your XenApp Farm

The only truly secure network is one that is totally inaccessible. We've all heard that line before! Security is always a trade–off between usability and protection. When planning security, you need to find an acceptable balance between the need to secure your network and the need for users to be able to perform their jobs.

In creating a security plan, it is important to realize that the network environment will never be completely secure. The goal is to make it difficult for intruders to obtain unauthorized access, so it isn't worth their time to try or continue attempting to gain access. It is also critical to protect servers from potential disasters and to have methods to restore systems if they become compromised.

A good security plan considers the needs of a company and tries to balance it with their capabilities and current technology. As you'll see in the sections that follow, this means identifying the minimum security requirements for an organization, choosing an operating system, and identifying the configurations necessary to meet these needs. To develop a security plan, you must identify the risks that potentially threaten a network, determine what countermeasures are available to deal with them, figure out what you can afford financially, and implement the countermeasures that are feasible.

Planning for Farm Security

Planning an effective security strategy for your XenApp farm requires an understanding of the roles that different servers play on the network and the security needs of different types of servers based on the security requirements of your organization. Securing the servers is an important part of any network administrator's job.

Before you can begin implementing security measures, you need to know what needs protecting. For this reason, the security planning process involves considerable analysis. You need to determine which risks could threaten a company, what impact these threats would have on the company, the assets that the company needs to function, and what can be done to minimize or remove a potential threat.

The following are the main types of threats:

- Environmental threats, such as natural and man-made disasters
- Deliberate threats, where a threat was intentionally caused
- Accidental threats, where a threat was unintentionally caused

Environmental threats can be natural disasters, such as storms, floods, fires, earthquakes, tornadoes, and other acts of nature. When dealing with this type of disaster, it is important to analyze the entire company's risks, considering any branch offices located in different areas that may be prone to different natural disasters.

Human intervention can create problems as devastating as any natural disaster. Man-made disasters can also occur when someone creates an event that has an adverse impact on the company's environment. For example, faulty wiring can cause a fire or power outage. In the same way, a company could be impacted by equipment failures, such as the air conditioning breaking down in the server room, a critical system failing, or any number of other problems.

The deliberate threat type is one that results from malicious persons or programs, and they can include potential risks such as hackers, viruses, Trojan horses, and various other attacks that can damage data and equipment or disrupt services. This type of threat can also include disgruntled employees who have authorized access to such assets and have the ability to harm the company from within.

Many times, internal risks are not malicious in nature, but accidental. Employees can accidentally delete a file, modify information with erroneous data, or make other mistakes that cause some form of loss. Because people are fallible by nature, this type of risk is one of the most common.

Each business must identify the risks it may be in danger of confronting and determine what assets will be affected by a potential problem, including:

- **Hardware** Servers, workstations, hubs, printers, and other equipment.
- **Software** Commercial software (off the shelf) and in-house software.
- **Data** Documents, databases, and other files needed by the business.
- **Personnel** Employees who perform necessary tasks in the company.
- **Sundry equipment** Office supplies, furniture, tools, and other assets needed for the business to function properly.
- **Facilities** The physical building and its components.

When identifying minimum security requirements, it is important to determine the value and importance of assets, so you know which are vital to the company's ability to function. You can then prioritize risk, so that you can protect the most important assets of the company and implement security measures to prevent or minimize potential threats.

Determining the value and importance of assets can be achieved in a number of ways. Keeping an inventory of assets owned by the company will allow you to identify the equipment, software, and other property owned by the company.

To determine the importance of data and other assets, and thereby determine what is vital to secure, you can meet with department heads. Doing so will help you to identify the data and resources that are necessary for people in each department to perform their jobs.

In addition to interviewing different members of an organization, review the corporate policies for specifications of minimum security requirements. For example, a company may have a security policy stating that all data is to be stored in specific folders on the server, and that the IT staff is required to back up this data nightly. Such policies may not only provide insight on what is to be protected, but also what procedures must be followed to provide this protection.

Companies may also be required to protect specific assets by law or to adhere to certain certification standards. For example, hospitals are required to provide a reasonable level of security to protect patient records. If such requirements are not met, an organization can be subject to legal action.

Securing Your XenApp Server

There are several steps you can take to secure your XenApp server. Citrix best practices recommend the following:

- If not using the File Type Association feature (client to server redirection) you should ensure that there are no file types associated with any published applications.

- If not using command line parameters for published applications you should ensure that the wildcard ("%*") is not present in the "Location" field of the published application path.

- For deployments that require either File Type Association or published application parameters you should consider making published application names unpredictable. This can help to prevent an attacker guessing such a name.

- Any XenApp deployment that is accessible from an untrusted network should implement strong authentication.

- Ensure that XenApp is not deployed directly onto an untrusted network.

- Ensure that applications available to users connecting to XenApp are correctly configured, in order to prevent access to inappropriate functionality.

- Ensure that XenApp machines are configured to allow only published applications to be launched.

Additionally, the following areas should also be considered:

- Apply NTFS permissions to Windows and XenApp system files
- Remove admin tools from servers that publish content
- Implement use of Windows Group Policy Objects
- Use the Security Configuration Wizard
- Implement IP Security using IPSec
- Keep your server and software patched

Securing Client Server Communication

The primary methods of securing remote access to our XenApp Servers:

- Secure ICA (ICA Encryption)

- Secure Socket Layer Relay (SSL Relay)

- Virtual private networking (VPN)

- Citrix Secure Gateway (CSG)

- Citrix Access Gateway or Citrix NetScaler

Each of these solutions has its benefits and disadvantages to deploying the solution. From Chapter 4 we know that Secure ICA is the oldest method of securing communications between Citrix client and server. Also from Chapter 4, we know that Secure Sockets Layer (SSL) was created to encrypt data transmitted between a client computer and a Web server, and that Citrix leverages the use of SSL through the implementation of the Citrix Secure Gateway, the Citrix Access Gateway and the Citrix NetScaler device, which are covered later in this book.

TIP

For maximum protection of users' credentials and sessions, use SSL encryption for all communication between clients and the XenApp server farm.

Configuring ICA Encryption

From Chapter 4, we gave you a general overview of what encryption technology can do and when to use it; the next step is to secure your XenApp farm using encryption. Several products and techniques ensure that your environment is secured. The first step to configuring encryption options is to understand the various techniques and how they apply to your environment. Encryption can be applied at several different levels using XenApp policies.

Perhaps the simplest way of enabling encryption for your XenApp server is by creating various encryption policies and applying them to individual servers. The nice thing about enabling encryption in this way is that even if you publish a resource and set the encryption to basic and you have a server encryption policy set to RC5 (128–bit), the policy enabled on your server takes precedence. If needed, you could make a different policy for each encryption requirement you have. Configuration is completed with the following steps:

1. Open the **Citrix Presentation Server Console** by selecting **Start | Programs | Citrix | Management Consoles | Presentation Server Console**.

2. Right-click **Policies** and select **Create Policy**.

3. Type an appropriate name for your policy, such as **Encryption – RC5 (128–bit)**. You may also want to add a description of the policy. For this book, we created a policy for each

encryption option. If required by your configuration, you can configure your policy specific to a connection type, such as **WAN**, **Satellite**, or **Dial–up**. Click **OK** to save your policy.

4. Now that your policy has been created, you must configure it. Double-click on the name of the policy created in step 3. Select the **Security** folder, expand it, and then select **SecureICA encryption**, as shown in Figure 5.17.

Figure 5.17 Configuring an Encryption Policy

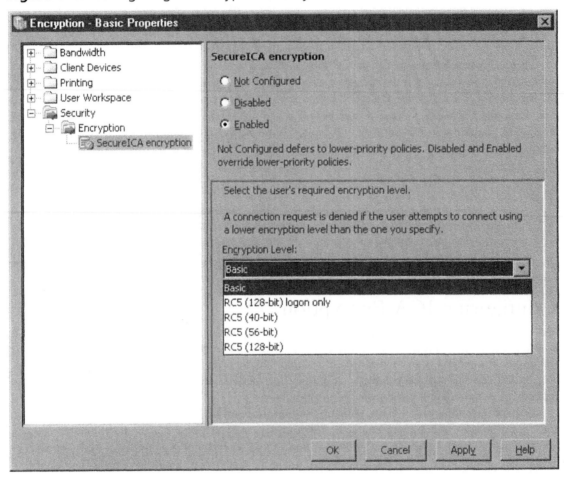

5. To enable an encryption level, you must select **Enabled** and then select one of the available encryption levels, which are: **Basic**, **RC5 (128–bit) logon only**, **RC5 (40–bit)**, **RC5 (56–bit)**, **and RC5 (128–bit)**. To enforce no encryption, you must select **Disabled**.

6. Once you have made the appropriate changes to the encryption policy, click **OK**.

7. Now you must apply the encryption policy. Highlight the newly created policy and select **Apply this policy to**.

8. As Figure 5.18 shows, there are several ways in which to apply the encryption policy. We have seen that in most environments, encryption is applied at the server level (much like the way you could configure ICA encryption in Presentation Server 4.0 from the Citrix Connection Configuration Utility). However, your encryption policy can be filtered like any other XenApp policy. For our policy, select **Servers**, check **Filter based on servers**, then select the servers to which you want this encryption policy to apply.

Figure 5.18 Configuring Several Encryption Policies

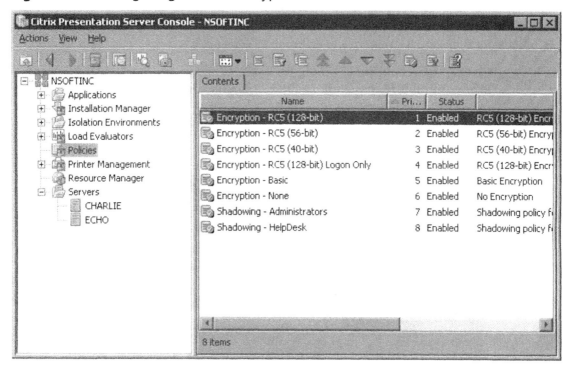

9. When that's done, select **Apply** and **OK** to finish configuring the SSL Relay service. The SSL Relay service will not be activated until after the server has been rebooted.

NOTE

Keep in mind that different requirements may have you provide different encryption settings dependent upon specific criteria. For example, let's say you have MS Word published to all users in your network and you do not have encryption configured on a per server basis. However, you do want to encrypt *any* data coming from corporate executives, so you opt to create encryption policies filtered by user.

Configuring SSL Relay

Communication between the Web Interface server and XenApp server farm is not encrypted. In addition, the SSL TCP port can be used for client-to-server communication instead of TCP port 1494 to pass through a firewall. The SSL Relay service has been designed to address both these issues. To use the SSL Relay service, you must first obtain a server certificate from a trusted authority such as www.verisign.com. Once you receive the certificate and install it on your XenApp server, the XenApp server will automatically locate and prompt for validation of the certificate. In addition to configuring the XenApp servers, you must also configure your Web Interface server to support SSL. Information to configure SSL technology within Microsoft Internet Information Server is available online at www.microsoft.com.

To configure the SSL Relay service, complete the following tasks:

1. Open the **Citrix SSL Relay Configuration Tool** by selecting **Start | All Programs | Citrix | Administration Tools | Citrix SSL Relay Configuration Tool**.

2. Verify that a certificate is displayed with the server name, as shown in Figure 5.19.

Figure 5.19 Configuring SSL Relay Credentials

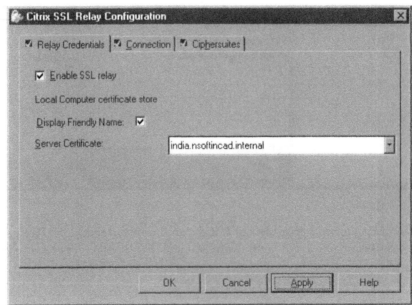

3. Select **Enable SSL Relay**.

4. Next, select the **Connection** tab, as shown in Figure 5.20. Insert the TCP/IP address of each XenApp server to which this server will communicate if it has not already been populated. Specify the port for each server on which the XML service is running. You can opt to use SSLv3 or TLSv1.

Figure 5.20 Configuring SSL Relay Connections

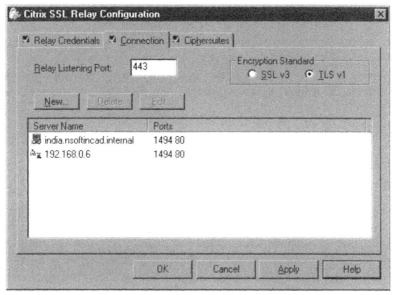

5. Select the **Ciphersuites** tab to configure the algorithms to accept from the Web server, as shown in Figure 5.21. This allows you to further define the encryption methodologies used with the SSL Relay service. Ciphersuites define the parameters by which secure communication will occur, such as encryption type and authentication mode. By default, all options should already be selected.

Figure 5.21 Configuring the Ciphersuites

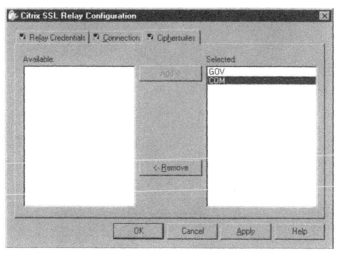

6. When that's done, select **Apply** and **OK** to finish configuring the SSL Relay service. The SSL Relay service will not be activated until after the server has been rebooted.

Using Virtual Private Networking to Secure XenApp Sessions

The VPN initially appears to present the "simplest" solution for providing users' remote access to your XenApp farms. However, this perception can be deceiving. VPN access to production networks brings with it a series of issues, some of which are specific to XenApp servers, and others that are more generic.

Let us first examine the primary security issues surrounding VPN as a method of accessing your XenApp farms:

- Split–tunneling
- Client is "part of the network"
- Worm/virus propagation

Split-tunneling is a concept in virtual private networking whereby the end device establishes the tunnel to your corporate network and is able to gain access to resources outside your corporate network. In simpler terms, the external computer has simultaneous access to corporate resources and public resources. This presents serious security issues, especially in situations where a client's computing device could have been turned into a "zombie" and some external "bad guy" has leveraged your user's computer as a free ticket into the corporate network. Fortunately, split-tunneling can be disabled in most cases. However, disabling it means that the user's access outside the tunnel disappears, and all requests are sent through the tunnel to include print requests, web browsing, e-mail, and so forth, much of which may be unserviceable by the corporate network. Figure 5.22 demonstrates the concept of split-tunneling.

Figure 5.22 Effects of Split-Tunneling in VPN Access

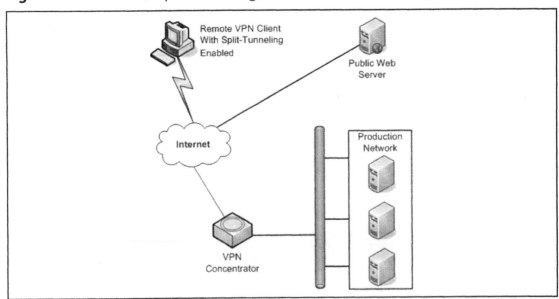

The last couple of security concerns for using VPN access as a remote access solution to XenApp servers are based on the following simple statement, "Clients are part of the corporate network." Once a VPN tunnel is established, virtually it is as if the remote computer were actually on your corporate network, bringing with it all of the issues and concerns that exist from supporting workstations. In our corporate networks, we spend a great deal of time securing, protecting, updating, and disinfecting our workstations through a host of services and software. While these devices are not "easy" to support and manage, they are typically within our "sphere of power" and are controllable to some extent. Computing devices in users' homes or remote trusted networks are typically outside of our management scope. The unpatched vulnerabilities, viruses, and worms that they bring to our production network the instant they establish the tunnel should be of paramount concern to all network administrators.

This last concern alone had nearly halted the adoption of VPN solutions in many environments. The recent advent of SSL-based VPNs and newer "hybrid" VPNs are taking some of the sting out of VPN solutions.

Configuring the Secure Ticket Authority (STA)

In XenApp deployments that will utilize Citrix Secure Gateway (CSG), you must also configure at least one XenApp server to be an STA server. The CSG server does not perform authentication of incoming requests, it only defers authentication to an application enumeration server and uses the STA to guarantee that each user is authenticated. Application enumeration servers request tickets only for users who are already authenticated to the Web Interface. If users have a valid STA ticket, the gateway assumes that they passed the authentication checks at the Web Interface and should be allowed access.

This design allows the Citrix Secure Gateway server to inherit whatever authentication methods are in place on your Web server. For example, if your Web Interface server is protected with RSA SecurID, by design only SecurID-authenticated users can traverse the secure gateway server.

Since the STA shares its port with the XML service, no additional configuration must be performed on a XenApp server, but there are changes to the STA configuration that will make it more secure:

- Configure the STA to utilize SSL to prevent an attacker from intercepting the ticket as it travels from server to client

- Reduce the ticket time-to-live as much as possible to reduce the amount of time an attacker would have to transfer the ticket from one machine to another

- Use IPSec if the STA is configured on a XenApp server on which IIS is also installed and is sharing its port with the XML service

To configure specific settings for the STA, you must edit the CtxSta.config file typically found in the directory C:\Program Files\Citrix\System32. The contents of the CtxSta.config file are shown in Figure 5.23. An explanation of the settings in this file is described in Table 5.4.

Figure 5.23 Editing the CtxSta.config File

```
[GlobalConfig]
UID=STAA28FD497153B
TicketVersion=10
TicketTimeout=100000
MaxTickets=100000
LogLevel=0
MaxLogCount=10
MaxLogSize=20
LogDir=C:\Program Files\Citrix\system32\
; Allowed Client IP addresses
; To change, substitute * with client IP addresses. Use ";" to seperate IP
addresses/address ranges.
; To specify a range of IPs always use StartIP-EndIP.
; For example, AllowedClientIPList=192.168.1.1;10.8.1.12-10.8.1.18;123.1.2.3
AllowedClientIPList=192.168.1.50-75,
; SSL only mode
; If set to on, only requests sent through HTTPS are accepted
SSLOnly=off
```

Table 5.4 CtxSta.config File Settings

Setting	Description	Recommended Setting
UID	Unique identifier for the STA	Set by XenApp
TicketVersion	Version of the STA	Set by XenApp
TicketTimeout	Ticket timeout setting in milliseconds	No more than 10000 (100 seconds)
MaxTickets	Maximum number of tickets that can assigned	10000
LogLevel	Level of logging, 0 – minimal, 1 – XXX, 2 – XXX, 3	3 – Enables full logging of all STA traffic and errors
MaxLogCount	The number of STA logs that are maintained	At least 30 (this would be 30 days of logs)
MaxLogSize	The maximum size of the STA log	At least 20
LogDir	The directory where the STA log is maintained	Should be placed on a separate partition from system files and should configured to only be modified by system auditors

Continued

Table 5.4 Continued. CtxSta.config File Settings

Setting	Description	Recommended Setting
AllowedClient IPList	The list of IP addresses that are "trusted" by the STA	All IP addresses that will communicate with the STA
SSLOnly	Enable SSL encryption for the STA	On

TIP

If you are securing communications between the Secure Gateway and the STA, ensure that you install a server certificate on the server running the STA and implement SSL Relay. In most cases, internally generated certificates are used for this purpose.

Configuring Smart Card Authentication

Your users can access their published applications by authenticating with smart cards rather than typing in passwords. This feature will work with smart card-aware applications such as Microsoft Outlook. Configuring the Web Interface and ICA clients to utilize smart card authentication is covered later in this book. XenApp fully supports the usage of Smart Cards for authentication to your environment. In XenApp, smart cards can be used to:

■ Authenticate users to networks and computers

■ Secure channel communications over a network

■ Use digital signatures for signing content

To configure your XenApp server to use Smart Cards, you should first consult the Smart Card vendor configuration instructions. Typically, the following components are required for a XenApp server to utilize Smart Cards:

■ PC/SC software

■ Cryptographic Service Provider (CSP) software

■ Certificate Revocation Checking (CRL) software (optional)

NOTE

You do not need to attach the smart card reader to your server during CSP software installation if you can install the smart card reader driver portion separately from the CSP portion.

The server configuration involving the use of Smart Cards is totally dependent on the vendor instructions regarding the Smart Card software you need to have installed. Smart Card authentication can be controlled by domain policy and configured on ICA clients, and also on the Web Interface (if that component is utilized.)

Configuring Kerberos

Kerberos, a network authentication protocol included in the Microsoft Windows operating systems, can now be used in conjunction with Security Support Provider Interface (SSPI) to provide pass-through authentication with secret key cryptography and data integrity. When using Kerberos, the client does not need to handle the password and it is not sent over the network. This greatly reduces the risk of Trojan horse attacks on the client to access user's passwords.

NOTE

Microsoft Kerberos authentication must be working correctly in order for XenApp to work successfully with Kerberos. Recommended Kerberos policy settings are shown in Figure 5.24.

Figure 5.24 Configuring Kerberos

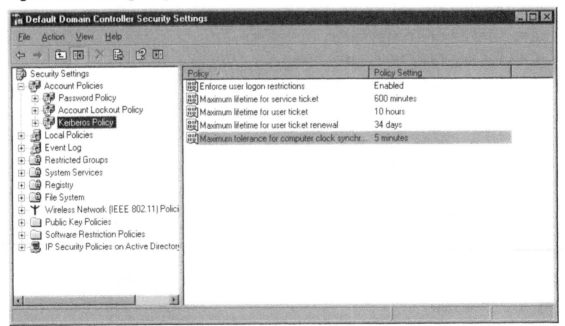

Using XenApp and Kerberos without Pass–Through

Users log on with Kerberos Authentication only. If user authentication fails (for any reason) the user will be prompted for credentials. This is supported with Web Interface or Program Neighborhood Custom ICA Connections only, other connections will result in being prompted for credentials. The WFCLIENT.INI file in Citrix\ICA Client Directory on each client device you do not want pass-through to be enabled must have the following configuration settings:

```
SSPIENABLE=On
UseSSPIOnly=On
```

Using XenApp and Kerberos with Pass-Through

Client attempts to use Kerberos Authentication first and uses Pass–through authentication if Kerberos fails. You must use Kerberos with Pass Through if you want to use Kerberos authentication with the PNAgent or Program Neighborhood Application Sets. The WFCLIENT.INI file in Citrix\ICA Client Directory on each client device must have the following configuration settings:

```
SSPIENABLE=Off
UseSSPIOnly=On
```

> **NOTE**
>
> By default the Citrix client is not configured for Kerberos Authentication. Kerberos Authentication is available with or without Pass–Through.

Configuring Automatic Client Reconnection

The Auto Client Reconnect feature allows XenApp clients to detect broken connections and automatically reconnect users to disconnected sessions. When a client detects a disconnection of a session, it attempts to reconnect the user to the session until there is a successful reconnection or the user cancels the reconnection attempt.

By default, Auto Client Reconnect is enabled at the server farm level, and user reauthentication is not required (see Figure 5.25). You can customize the settings for this feature at the farm level and for individual servers. To do this, select ICA on the corresponding farm or server Properties page in the Access Management Console and modify the Auto Client Reconnect settings as appropriate.

When a user initially logs on to a server farm, XenApp encrypts and stores the user credentials in memory, and creates and sends a cookie containing the encryption key to the client. The client submits the key to the server for reconnection. The server decrypts the credentials and submits them to Windows logon for authentication.

Cookies are not used if you select **Require user authentication**. Selecting this option displays a dialog box to users requesting credentials when the client is attempting to reconnect automatically. Use the Access Management Console to enable **Require user authentication**.

If the option to **Reconnect automatically** is selected, you also have the option to **Log automatic reconnection attempts** to the event log. This setting should be checked if you use the **Reconnect automatically** option.

Figure 5.25 Configuring Automatic Client Reconnection

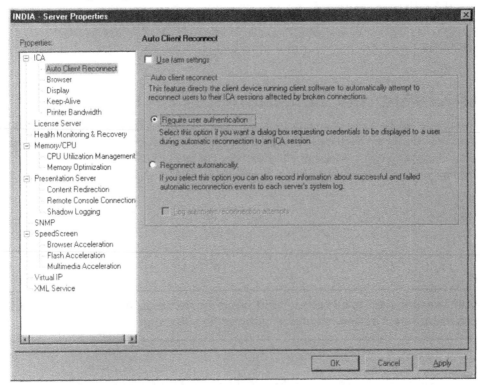

Configuring the SNMP Service

The Simple Network Management Protocol provides a way to gather statistical information. An SNMP management system makes requests of an SNMP agent, and the information is stored in a Management Information Base (MIB). The MIB is a database that holds information about a networked computer (for example, how much hard disk space is available). The SNMP agent software is installed as a Windows Component and runs as a service.

The Simple Network Management Protocol is not a utility in and of itself. Rather, it is a protocol used to communicate status messages from devices distributed throughout the network to machines configured to receive these status messages. Machines that report their status run SNMP *Agent* software, and machines that receive the status messages run SNMP *Management* software. One way to remember how this works is to think of the agent software as the "secret agent" that gets information about a network device, and then reports the information to his "manager" at headquarters.

While the name of the protocol itself would lead you to believe that the primary function is to allow you to "manage" objects on the network, management in this context is more related to monitoring rather than actually effecting any changes to the devices themselves. Administrators typically think of managing something as taking an active role in configuring or changing the behavior of a device, so don't let the name of the protocol fool you.

SNMP allows you to audit the activities of servers, workstations, routers, bridges, intelligent hubs, and just about any network-connected device that supports the installation of agent software. The agent software available with the Windows 2003 implementation allows to you monitor several Windows 2003 server operating system parameters, the DHCP service, the WINS service, the Internet Information Services, QoS Admission Control Services, and so on.

In order for agent software to collect information regarding a particular service, a *Management Information Base (MIB)* must be created.

The agent is responsible for reporting the information gathered by the MIB. However, agents rarely volunteer information spontaneously. Rather, the agent must be queried by an SNMP management system before it gives up its knowledge.

There is an exception to this: a "trap" message. A trap message is sent spontaneously by an agent to the SNMP Management System for which it has been configured to send. For example, we could set a trap message to indicate that the World Wide Web service is hung. We would then configure the agent to send a trap message to the IP address of our computer running the SNMP Management software so that we can quickly handle this catastrophic event.

SNMP messages themselves are sent to UDP Port 161 for typical GET and SET type messages, and UDP Port 162 for trap messages.

The SNMP Agent Tab (shown in Figure 5.26) is for descriptive purposes only. SNMP Management Systems can obtain information about a contact person and location from information provided here. Also, information about what type of system the agent is running on is indicated by the selections made in the Service frame area.

Figure 5.26 Configuring SNMP Agent Tab

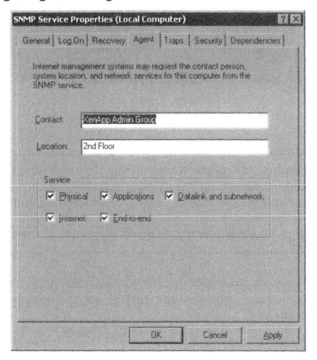

Click the Traps tab and you see what appears in Figure 5.27. If you want the agent to initiate a trap message, you need to make the agent part of a community that the agent and the SNMP Management software have in common. The community name can be anything you like, and it is not related to domain names, usernames, or any other security principle you might think of in Windows 2003.

Figure 5.27 Configuring SNMP Traps Tab

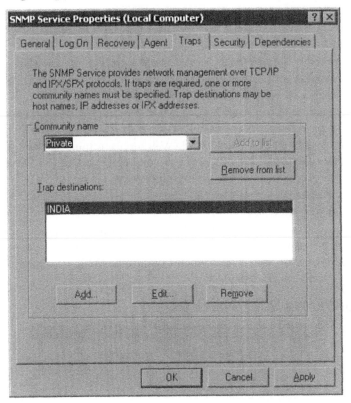

NOTE

The community name does represent a somewhat primitive degree of security, because only machines from the same community can communicate with the agent. Microsoft documentation states that you should make your community name hard to guess. However, since the community name is transmitted in clear text, it really doesn't make much of a difference how difficult it is to guess the name of the community.

After configuring at least one community membership, you then need to enter the IP addresses or host names of the machines that will receive the trap message. You do so by clicking **Add** under the **Trap destinations** text box.

Now click the **Security** tab and see what appears in Figure 5.28. On the Security tab, you can configure some basic security parameters for the SNMP agent. In the "Accepted community names" frame, you can add new communities that the agent can report to, and define the level of permissions for Management Station access to the agent and MIBs.

Figure 5.28 Configuring SNMP Security Tab

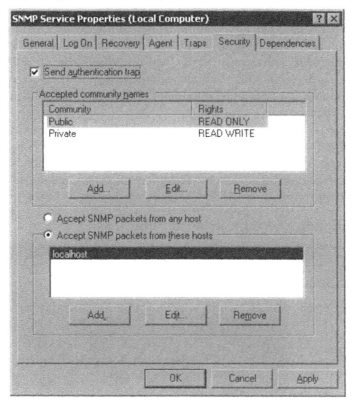

You see the **SNMP Service Configuration** dialog box, which appears after clicking **Edit** in the **Accepted community names** frame.

- **None** means no permissions.

- **Notify** means only traps will be sent to the Management Station, and that the Management Station cannot make SNMP requests.

- **Read Only** allows the Management Station to read the values of the information provided by the MIBs.

- **Read Write** and **Read Create** do the same thing, which is to allow a SET command to be sent to the agent.

WARNING

By default, when SNMP Agents and Management Stations communicate, their messages are sent over the wire in clear text. IPSec can offer an appropriate solution to provide security for these processes.

The Windows SNMP service has many read/write privileges by default; however, you must give read/create permissions to the SNMP service for administrative tasks, such as logoff and disconnect through Network Manager. If you use Network Manager or other SNMP management software for monitoring the server only (and not remote management), Citrix recommends that the privileges be read only. As stated earlier, if no SNMP consoles are used, then do not install SNMP components on the server.

If you are utilizing SNMP, you should configure the SNMP community and designated management consoles to prevent unauthorized access by configuring SNMP agents to accept traps from known SNMP consoles only. You can also configure the SNMP settings within XenApp on the Farm or server level as shown in Figure 5.29. You can select to send session traps to a selected SNMP agent on all farm servers and then specify which SNMP agent session traps you want to enable.

Figure 5.29 Configuring XenApp SNMP Settings

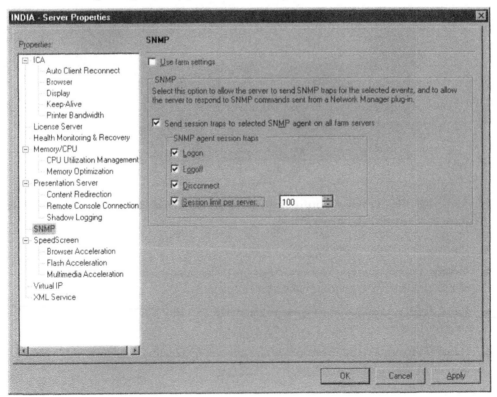

Configuring Network Firewalls

One of the biggest challenges faced by many XenApp administrators is how to provide remote access to the farm resources without compromising the security of the network. Additionally, such access needs to be easy to use, very secure, and provide as close to local area network (LAN) performance as possible. Fortunately, Citrix has always been a company that produces products with a single goal in mind—access. Over the years, Presentation Server (and most recently, XenApp) has become a highly secure solution for allowing remote and mobile access to your company's internal network.

There are several methods of providing secure access to your remote and mobile users. As you investigate the complexities of leading user sessions through a firewall you will see how the methods of access you choose to implement will impact the firewall, the XenApp servers, and ultimately the users themselves as they attempt to make use of the solutions you provide them. Some of the methods that are available for allowing XenApp traffic to traverse firewalls include:

- Network Address Translation (NAT)
- Port Address Translation (PAT)
- Proxy servers
- HyperText Transfer Protocol (HTTP)
- SSL Relay
- Citrix Secure Gateway
- Citrix NetScaler
- Citrix Access Gateway

Configuring IMA and IMA Encryption

Independent Management Architecture (IMA) is the underlying architecture used in XenApp for configuring, monitoring, and operating all Presentation Server functions. The IMA data store stores all Presentation Server configurations.

A new feature included with XenApp is IMA encryption. This feature utilizes the AES encryption algorithm previously discussed in this book to protect sensitive data in the IMA data store.

IMA encryption is a farm–wide setting that applies to all XenApp servers once it is enabled. Therefore, once you enable IMA encryption, you must ensure that it is enabled on every XenApp server in your farm. To provide a more secure IMA environment, it is recommended that you utilize the IMA encryption feature to protect the sensitive data in the IMA data store.

To enable IMA encryption, you must generate a key which is then used by all servers in your XenApp farm. You can specify the key before or during your setup. IMA encryption consists of the following components:

- **CTXKEYTOOL** This command line program is also known as the IMA encryption utility. You use this tool to manage and generate key files.
- **Key File** The key file contains the encryption key used to encrypt sensitive IMA data.
- **Key** Using the CTXKEYTOOL, you load the key you created during setup that is saved in the key file.

When using IMA encryption, Citrix recommends that you keep a backup of the farm key in a safe and secure location. The process of using IMA encryption includes:

- Generate a key file
- Make the key file accessible to each server in the farm, or put it on a shared network location
- Load the key on to the server from the key file
- Enable IMA encryption

The Citrix documentation provided for XenApp, specifically the Administrator's Guide, gives the step-by-step process on how to generate the IMA encryption key.

Securing the Data Store

All XenApp servers within a farm all share a common repository for configuration known as the *data store*. The data store provides a repository of persistent farm information for all servers to reference. The data store retains information that does not change frequently, including the following:

- Published application configurations
- Servers in the farm
- Citrix administrators
- Trust relationships

The data store is a standard database format. The servers that are members of the given farm, which this specific data store defines, perform read/write operations against this data store database based on the configuration we enter as administrators into the Presentation Server Management Console and the server-to-server communication associated with the Independent Management Architecture service. There are two types of data store databases: local databases and network databases. At the time of creation of a new farm, the "type" of database must be considered, as it will impact the design, scalability, and cost of the server farm. The local data store databases consist of two formats, either MS Access or Microsoft SQL Desktop Engine (MSDE). The network data store databases can leverage MS SQL, Oracle, or IBM's DB2. Each type, local or network, has its benefits and disadvantages. Let's outline some of the facts and best practices around these two types to allow us to make the best design decisions for our environment.

Local data store databases:

- No additional costs associated with database software, database servers, or database client software to load
- Good for farms of up to 40 servers (we recommend no more than five servers in a farm with Access or MSDE)

Network data store databases:

- Additional cost for database server and licenses
- More flexible, as the database is separate from a Presentation Server in the farm

- More scalable through database replication
- More fault tolerant through database clustering
- Good for larger farms (five servers and larger)

Data store connections come in two flavors, direct and indirect. Depending on the type of data store database you select, you will have options here. Indirect connections are required for servers that are members of the farm where a local data store database (MS Access or MSDE) is used. Why, you may ask? Since the database exists on the first Citrix server in the farm, all servers must communicate indirectly via the IMA service to gain information from the database. In other words, if Server1 were the first server in the farm, it would maintain the MS Access database. If Server2, a member of the same farm, needs to gain access to the farm database, the IMA service on Server2 communicates with the IMA service on Server1, and then the IMA service on Server1 fulfills the request for Server2 and returns the results via IMA (thus indirectly). As you can see, Server1 is the single point of failure and a major scalability concern. Thus, most architects agree that a direct connection method is the best in terms of scalability and fault tolerance. A direct connection requires each Presentation Server to maintain its own connection to the data store; therefore, it will require all the necessary database client software (such as the MDAC, Oracle client, or DB2). Additionally, licensing will need to be maintained for each server that will connect.

The next component to consider is the *local host cache* (LHC). The LHC is a partial copy of the data store database that every XenApp maintains locally to the server itself (hence the name). The partial local replica is maintained in MS Access format and is encrypted, similar to the information in the data store database. There are many reasons why a XenApp server would want to maintain a partial copy of the data store database locally; however, two reasons sum up most of the logic behind this decision. First, by maintaining a local partial replica of the data store database, the XenApp server could continue running based on the configuration that is last received from the data store. Therefore, in the event of failure of the server that houses the actual data store, the farm could continue functioning for up to 96 hours (based on a hard limit imposed by Citrix).

The second reason is all about performance. Servers may need to frequently consult the information in the data store database. In a larger farm, this could lead to a bottleneck at the server housing the database. Therefore, with a partial replica being available locally, the IMA service can review those settings and synchronize in the background with the "master" copy of the data store. This provides much greater scalability and much less reliance on the server housing the data store database. By default, XenApp maintains this database in the path C:\Program Files\Citrix\Independent Management Architecture in a file named MF20.MDB.

With the exception of indexes, all information in the data store is in binary format. No meaningful queries can be executed directly against the data store. Neither Citrix administrators nor users can directly query or change information in the data store.

The risk of compromising sensitive data from the data store is low. Opening the database natively does not reveal much useful information and even with the Citrix SDK it is not possible to directly access the database. However, it is possible that someone with database administration rights could delete key portions of the database. While your environment should be designed so that the database is backed up and could be restored in case of a loss, this is still a risk that needs to be mitigated.

One of the most important aspects of securing your server farm is protecting the data store. This involves not only protecting the data in the data store database but also restricting who can access it. In general:

■   Users who access your farm's servers do not require and should not be granted any access to the data store.

■   When the data store connection is a direct one (that is, no intermediary server is used), all of the servers in the server farm share a single user account and password for accessing the data store. Select a password that is not easy to deduce. Keep the user name and password secure and give it to administrators only to install Presentation Server.

More specific Citrix recommendations for securing the data store vary depending on the database you use for the data store. The following sections discuss security measures to consider for each of the database products Presentation Server supports.

WARNING

If the user account for direct mode access to the database is changed at a later time, the Citrix IMA Service fails to start on all servers configured with that account.
To reconfigure the Citrix IMA Service password, use the **dsmaint config** command on each affected server. For information about the **dsmaint config** command, refer to the XenApp Administrator's Guide.

MS Access Database Data Store

If you use a Microsoft Access database as your XenApp data store the default password must be changed. During the installation of the first XenApp server in a new farm that is utilizing an Access database as the data store, a database is created with the default username of "citrix" and the default password of "citrix." The credentials should be changed by using the dsmaint config command. Additionally, NTFS permissions should be set to prevent unauthorized user access and modification to the database.

SQL Express Data Store

This type of database is most appropriate for small to medium-sized farms and can be administered using standard Microsoft SQL Server tools. When using SQL Server 2005 Express Edition SP1, first install it and then create an instance. Then run the Citrix Presentation Server Setup. The database is stored on the first server in the farm.

NOTE

The security recommendations listed for a SQL 2005 database can also be applied to a SQL Express data base.

DBMS Data Store (IBM DB2)

If you utilize a data store that is hosted on IBM DB2, you need to grant the DB2 user account used for the XenApp farm the following permissions:

- Connect database
- Create tables
- Register functions to execute to database manager's process
- Create schemas implicitly

NOTE

DB2Admin account permissions are not needed for data store access.

DBMS Data Store (SQL)

The user account that is used to access the data store on Microsoft SQL Server has *public* and *db_owner* roles on the server and database. System administrator account credentials are not needed for data store access; do not use a system administrator account because this poses an additional security risk.

If the Microsoft SQL Server is configured for mixed mode security, meaning that you can use either Microsoft SQL Server authentication or Windows authentication, you may want to create a Microsoft SQL Server user account for the sole purpose of accessing the data store. Because this Microsoft SQL Server user account would access only the data store, there is no risk of compromising a Windows domain if the user's password is compromised.

Multifaceted SQL Server Security

Security in SQL Server 2005 is multifaceted, and it can seem impossibly complicated. SQL Server 2005 security starts at the ground level and builds upon itself. This section discusses producing the foundations required to begin thinking in a natively secure manner, upon which the rest of the security principles in this book can be built. This section also starts you on the learning curve required to implement SQL Server 2005 security by providing a guide in your journey into SQL Server 2005 security.

Security: Why Worry About It?

In February 2000, the company RealNames informed its customers that its database had been broken into and that information including credit card numbers had been taken. The thought of being the person in charge of security on that database is enough to make anyone break into a cold sweat. How exactly do you go to your boss and tell him that the database that fuels your company and holds your customer's information has been broken into?

Then there were the W32.CBlade and W32.Digispid worms. These worms attacked SQL Servers using the SA account and a blank password. The fact that either of these two worms could get into systems spoke volumes about the security of the databases they were attacking. The one positive aspect was that when the SQL Slammer worm hit in 2003, IT security professionals had some knowledge of how databases are attacked by worms. Even more fortunate was that even though the Slammer worm was one of the most aggressive worms to date, it was dedicated to creating a denial-of-service (DoS) type attack where the goal was to flood the Internet with traffic, versus a database breach.

In 2001, the World Economic Forum had a database breach. Some of the information from this breach ended up on a Swiss newspaper's Web site. The data taken included Bill Gate's e-mail address, PepsiCo Beverages CEO Peter Thompson's credit card number, and Jeff Bezos's home phone number. Additionally, some 800,000 pages of data from people like Bill Clinton, Vladimir Putin, and Yassir Arafat were accessed using the passwords acquired when the database was breached.

Other companies whose databases were breached were PetCo.com and Guess, both of which fell victim to SQL Injection attacks on their Web sites. The attack on Guess netted the attackers an unknown quantity of credit card numbers. PetCo.com's Web site was later detected to have the same vulnerability. This vulnerability was detected by someone randomly checking sites for this issue, and would have provided about 500,000 credit card numbers to anyone less honest who discovered this vulnerability.

Information is money. Other than credit card numbers, there are people willing to pay for phone numbers, e-mail addresses, physical addresses, client information, social security information, and just about every other form of client or personal information available. With this as a driving force, people looking to make money see databases as a bank vault full of money. Just as banks build their buildings with plans on how to secure their vault, you need to protect your information in your databases the same way.

Now that the Sarbanes Oxley (SOX), Gramm-Leach-Biley Act (GLBA), Health Insurance Portability and Privacy Act (HIPAA), Basel II, Code of Federal Regulation (CFR) Part 11, and the Japan Privacy Law (J-SOX) regulations are becoming the model for governments, private companies, and public companies across the globe, more and more companies are being affected even if these regulations do not apply directly to them. These regulations do not state what needs to be done in crystal clear terms. They hold you liable for the security of your information, but leave it up to you on how to interpret what they are saying.

It seems that in all of the preceding cases, there were security precautions that could have been taken to prevent the breaches. In most cases, applying the best practices of securing a SQL Server would prevent breaches from ever happening. It is just a matter of knowing what to secure, which is where this book comes in.

The Principle of Least Access

The principle of least access is a simple way to make databases more secure. Whenever you are presented with a choice of how to configure permissions, choose the method that provides the least access to the database. This goes for everything at every level. If you are asking yourself, "Do I need to install this feature?" the answer is either a definite yes or a definite no. If you are thinking maybe, possibly, "well, we might…", do not install it. If you think that this person might need access to a specific extended stored procedure, then they do get access. This also applies to the level of service accounts that run your SQL services. Start with the most secure setting, and only open it past that point of what you need it to do.

This is now a constant in the world of SQL Server 2005. By default, Microsoft has made things secure for when you start working in SQL Server 2005. But in order for it to work, it means resisting the urge to make sure everything works as it should by turning on everything and giving everyone owner permissions. Yes, it can be annoying when someone keeps coming back to your desk because they need more access to get their job done, but in order to offset this, keep in mind the person in charge of the RealNames database and how his day was when it was announced publicly that the database had been hacked.

Installing SQL Server

Let's start from the point of installing SQL Server 2005. From the time you put the disk into the machine, think security. At the beginning you will be asked what you want to install. There is the database engine itself, which is only installed when you are going to be immediately housing SQL Server 2005 databases on that server. Next there is the analysis services engine, which is the OLAP/data cubes portion of SQL Server 2005. This should only be installed if you are going to be immediately using OLAP cubes on the server. Additionally, there is Reporting Services, Integration Services, and Notification Services. Reporting Services is SQL Server 2005's Web-based reporting engine. Integration Services lets you design and deploy SSIS packages, the replacement for DTS. Notification Services provides the engine for keeping people notified. The same principle applies to these—install them only if you are going to use them immediately. Documents and samples is the last optional choice in installing SQL Server 2005, and is also the easiest to decide on whether to install or not. If you are installing on a development box, it is usually a good choice to choose to install both of these. For installation to any other server, never install the Documents and Samples. These are meant for learning, and although they have been reviewed to make sure that they follow Microsoft's best practices, they provide no benefits when installed to a production environment.

One note at this point has to do with the experience I had installing SQL Server. Many times I have installed SQL Server, adding in extra components because I was told that they would be needed next week, next month, or immediately. Although in every case the person who told me had the best of intentions, about 50 percent of the time they were never used. In the case where they have not been used, you end up having to make sure that they are configured correctly and patched, and they cause general overhead. During a security audit, they have been rightly referred to as a *security violation*. From this, a policy change has been made that states that no SQL Server 2005 components will be installed until they are required. Once they are no longer required, they are to be completely removed. Keep this in mind as you install components, and try to install them only when you know they will be used.

Best Practices for Installing SQL Server According to Microsoft

- Install only those components that you will use immediately. Microsoft recommends that you create a list of components that you will be using, and only enable those. If the need arises, you can install the additional components at that time. The components in a SQL Server installation are the Database Engine, Analysis Services Engine, Reporting Services, Integration Services, Notification Services, and Documents and Samples.

■ Enable only the optional features you will use, and review optional feature usage before doing an in-place upgrade and disable unneeded features. Microsoft recommends that you create a list of the optional features that you will use, and only turn those on. If this is an existing SQL Server that is being upgraded, they recommend creating the same list, and disabling any optional features not on the list. These optional features are CLR Integration, OLE Automation, remote use of a dedicated administrator connection, Database Mail and SQL Mail, OpenRowset and OpenDataSource functions, SQL Server Web Assistant, and xp_cmdshell availability.

■ Develop a policy with respect to permitted network connectivity choices and for the usage of optional features. Microsoft recommends defining policies that would be company wide on Connectivity Choices and the use of optional features. They also recommend using SQL Server Surface Area Configuration to standardize this policy and documenting exceptions to the policy on a per-instance basis.

■ Turn off unneeded services by setting the service to either Manual startup or Disabled. Microsoft recommends going into the service management area and setting all services that you will not be using to be disabled or manual. These services include SQL Server Active Directory Helper, SQL Server Agent, SQL Server FullText Search, SQL Server Browser, and SQL Server VSS Writer.

■ Choose the service account with the last privilege possible. Microsoft recommends that the account you choose to run each of the SQL Services as should have the least possible level of privilege. You could use a domain user, local user, network service account, local system account, a local user that is an administrator, or a domain user who is a domain admin.

■ Use a separate specific user account or domain account that has no special privileges for SQL Server Services. Microsoft recommends using a separate account for each SQL Service. This account should be a specific user or domain account rather than a shared account. It is also recommended that this account not be granted any special privileges, but if special privileges are required, manage those through the SQL Server-supplied group account.

■ Always use Windows Authentication Mode if possible. Microsoft recommends using the Windows Authentication versus the Mixed Mode authentication. They recommend the mixed mode Authentication only for legacy application and non-Windows users.

■ Do not expose a server that is running SQL Server to the public Internet. Microsoft recommends that any servers that are running SQL Server not be exposed to the Internet.

Services Off by Default

In SQL Server 2005, during installation, most services are turned off by default. You are provided with the option of turning each one on at installation. After installation, you can also choose to turn services on SQL Server on or off individually. The SQL Server 2005 services that can be turned off are the Database Engine, Analysis Services, Reporting Services, SQL Server Agent, FullText Search, Integration Services, and SQL Browser. It is highly recommended to turn off all of the services that you can. After installation, you can turn them off by going to the Surface Area Configuration

Manager for Services and Connections, while during the installation process, leaving the services you do not need unchecked will prevent them from being installed.

The best way to determine if you need to have each of these services running is to determine what each service does. If you do not use these features at the present time, it is safe to disable that service.

The database engine itself is the engine that stores SQL Server database files. In most installations this service is being used; however, if you were only using SQL Analysis Services on a server, it would then be safe to disable the Database Engine.

Analysis Services is the OLAP and data mining service used in cubes that make up the base for Business Intelligence applications. If you are not using OLAP cubes or data mining, you can safely disable these services.

Reporting Services is the Web-based application for creating and viewing reports. When using Reporting Services, it uses a SQL Server 2005 database to store its configuration, which requires that the Database Engine be enabled. If you are not utilizing Reporting Services 2005, it is best to disable this service.

The SQL Server agent is used to run jobs inside SQL Server. Two types of jobs are *maintenance jobs* and *custom jobs*. Maintenance jobs do things like back up your database at a particular time each day, whereas custom jobs can execute anything from T-SQL statements to things like SSIS packages. If you do not have reoccurring processes that you have scheduled through the SQL Agent, it is safe to disable this service.

The FullText Search service is disabled by default in most installations. The FullText Search is used when you need to go beyond the normal equal or like comparisons to things like finding two words near one another or some sort of fuzzy matching. If you currently do not use these features, FullText Search should be disabled.

Integration Services is the SQL Server 2005 upgrade to Data Transformation Services. It is a platform that allows ETL processes and other more complex processes to be stored as a process and scheduled in SQL Agent or executed manually. If you do not do any ETL processes, you most likely can disable this service.

For SQL Browser, this is required only when you are attempting to connect to named SQL Server instances that use dynamic port assignments. Named instances tend to be used only when you have more than one instance of SQL Server running on a server, or with things like clustering. If you are in charge of installing SQL Server and you have installed only one instance on each server, or if you have installed multiple instances but specified the Transmission Control Protocol/Internet Protocol (TCP/IP) port assignment, it is recommended that you disable the Browser Service.

As an additional note, if you are installing a named instance of SQL Server, it is definitely more secure to use a static TCP/IP port, as this will allow you to use the browser service. Earlier in the section, the SQL Slammer Worm was mentioned. The mechanism that was exploited was the SQL Server 2000 browser engine. Although the browser service has been updated for SQL Server 2005, this shows you how an apparently rather safe choice can be used in a malicious way to compromise security on your server.

SQL Server Surface Area

SQL Server is a feature-rich product, with many options when it comes to processing data. It is great having all these options available, but it can also mean vulnerability. Resist the urge to enable a service "just in case" you'll need it further down the road. Enable only services that are going to be used immediately, because each service and feature that is enabled increases the surface area available for an intruder to attack.

What Is Surface Area?

Surface area is defined as the parts of an application or server exposed to attack—some examples would be interfaces or enabled services. It can also be defined as everything that can be seen from the network on the SQL Server.

To help minimize the surface area exposed to attack, SQL Server 2005 now ships with many of its services and features disabled. As a rule of thumb, all services not being used should be disabled to reduce the server's vulnerability. This is not only true with SQL Server, but also with the operating system. Services that are not being used (Internet Information Service, for example) should be disabled to minimize the risk of someone taking advantage and gaining control of the server.

Many of the features in SQL Server 2005 are disabled by default. This is part of Microsoft's new "trustworthy computing initiative." The idea is the installation is secure by default. It is still recommended to check a new installation and make sure all the services and features not being used are disabled.

It's much better to evaluate the security risk on the SQL Server installation than to respond to a security breach on the SQL Server. A security breach can result in the destruction of data, lost revenue, and information becoming public that shouldn't. If your security is compromised, and sensitive information is accessed by intruders, this could do irreparable harm to your business.

The Surface Area Configuration Tool

In the following section, we will discuss in detail each of the features of the Surface Area Configuration tool. Familiarize yourself with the features and options; they may come in handy when your boss or client asks you to perform a specific configuration task.

The Surface Area Configuration Tool GUI

SQL Server 2005 ships with a Surface Area Configuration tool. This tool allows the balance between enabled services and features to be controlled on the SQL Server installation. Administrative rights are needed in order to run the SQL Server Configuration tool.

The Surface Area Configuration tool can be used to start, stop, enable, and disable the various services and features associated with SQL Server. The SQL Configuration tool can be run against a local or remote machine.

Roles

Roles in SQL Server 2005 are a lot like groups in Windows. Their primary use is to allow an easy method of assigning permissions to a group of users. Roles can have built-in (predefined by SQL Server 2005) or user-defined permissions, and exist at both the server and database level. Most built-in roles cannot be modified, with the exception of the public role at the database level.

At the server level, roles are usually granted to give users some sort of SQL Server 2005 administration permissions. At the database level, roles have two purposes: to allow administration of the database, or to grant specific data or structure permissions inside that database. A role is used to grant certain permissions to SQL logins, SQL roles, Windows logins, or Windows groups. It's important to note that roles can be given other roles as well, making it possible to create roles which group other roles.

Using Roles

Roles can make your life easier when applying SQL Server 2005 security. Imagine you are told that eight logins are going to need select access to 133 tables, and write access to another 30 tables, and that they will need these first thing in the morning when the new project kicks off. You look in the database, searching for ways to make this task easier, only to find these tables are spread around and cover parts of many schemas. Sounds like you'll be working late, doesn't it? Well...maybe not. Rather than going through each of those eight logins and scrolling through the list clicking the 163 check-boxes necessary to give these users the permissions they require, you could create a user-defined role, click those checkboxes once rather than eight times, and give those eight users that role. With such simplicity, you might even get home in time to catch the end of the big game.

In addition to the role I talked about creating earlier, which would be a database-level user-defined role, there are a few other types of roles: application roles and server- and database-level predefined roles.

Role Types

Roles can exist at either the server level or the database level, and fall into a few different types. These role types are user-defined standard roles, user-defined application roles, and fixed server and fixed database roles. The fixed roles are normally used to give members administrative capabilities, and depending on the level, they either affect all databases for server-level roles, or just the single database for database-level roles. The fixed roles are called fixed because other than the public database-level role, they cannot have their rights modified.

User-Defined Standard Roles

User-defined standard roles are like the role that was added in the preceding example, called TheNewRole. These roles are used for grouping together permissions so each user does not have to be individually given permissions to the objects. These roles are created by the SQL Server 2005 administrator. The best way to think of these in categories is to imagine a company with a database. You have sales people, administrators, accounting folks, IT personnel, and all kinds of other groups. If I was administering SQL Server 2005 for this company, I would create a role for many of these groups. I would give the accounting people select, insert, and update on financial data. The personnel people would get select, insert, and update on the employee records. This is the typical use of user-defined standard roles.

In general, user-defined roles are underutilized. I can't even begin to count how many times I have come across SQL Server 2005 instances which were perfect opportunities for utilizing roles, yet all the permissions were set individually on the login and object level. By taking a few moments and classifying your objects with even a finer grain than I've just listed, you can begin to take advantage of the benefits of user-defined standard roles.

Let's take a look at a theoretical ordering system's database. Very typical classes of data exist in this theoretical ordering system, such as customers, orders, items, and inventory. You have set up a role called customer. Of course, the role grants access to the customer table, but also the pr_addnewcustomer user-defined stored procedure that adds new customers, along with the pr_getcustomerlist and the pr_getcustomerdetails procedures, and a couple customer-level views. This role is then given to the customer service people, customer service supervisors, and the quality control department, who all access the theoretical database's customer data. Now someone creates a new procedure called pr_getcustomerorders that all those same customer service people must be able to access. Because you granted each of these groups the role, you are only able to add execute permission to the new procedure to your customer role, and everyone in those groups inherits that new grant. Without utilizing roles, you must grant individual permission to this new procedure to the customer service employees, the customer service supervisors, and the quality control department individually. If you add this up each time this happens for each of the groups over each of the databases you run on SQL Server 2005, you're looking at a whole lot of work time.

User-Defined Application Roles

User-defined application roles are very similar to user-defined standard roles except that the roles are password protected and assigned to applications rather than users. Application roles can be used to allow access to specific data based on the application connecting to the database. Application roles cannot be granted to members, but are instead instantiated by the application that has connected to the database. The application inherits the role permissions by connecting to the database using standard Windows or SQL-level login credentials, and then executing the sp_setapprole stored procedure with a password known only to the application. The connection at this point gains its permissions from the application role. Because these are database-only permissions, any cross-database references will only work if objects that the application is attempting to access in the other database can be accessed using guest permissions. The sp_unsetapprole procedure is used by the application to deactivate the application role. When this procedure is executed, the application connection permissions revert to the previous security context.

Predefined Database Roles

SQL Server 2005 comes with certain predefined, or fixed, database-level roles. In general, these roles are used to define the administrative privilege of each user at the database level. Predefined roles cannot be changed with the exception of the public role. Predefined database roles also cannot be dropped and exist on every database in SQL Server 2005.

The public role is the default role for all database users. This role is inherited when the user is given permission to access the database.

Two other fixed database roles are db_accessadmin, which gives its members the ability to add or remove logins in the database, and the db_backupoperator role, which gives its members the ability to back up a database. These roles are often given to the team or project leader in development projects. This allows them to add the users who need to perform the development, and perform backups at key intervals during development. Of course, the team leader does not have the same permissions on the production server. One rule I always follow is to have production servers tightly locked down, but have development servers remain secure, but not so locked down as to prevent users from doing what they need to on a day-to-day basis.

The next four roles all have to do with data access on the server. These roles are db_datareader, db_datawriter, db_denydatareader, and db_denydatawriter. These roles are the most often used roles in SQL Server 2005 installations. Their reader roles are fairly self-explanatory in that the data reader roles give their members the ability to read all data in user-defined tables for the database, whereas the db_denydatareader denies read access to all data in user-defined tables for the database. The write roles are fairly simple in that the db_datawrite role permits its members to perform inserts, updates, and deletes on any user-defined table in the database, while the db_denydatawriter role cannot perform any inserts, updates, or deletes on any user-defined table in the database.

The db_ddladmin role allows users to perform tasks related to the data definition language (DDL) in the current database. Members of this role are limited in that they cannot perform the grant, revoke, or deny data definition language commands, but they can execute all other DDL commands.

The db_securityadmin is for members who need to maintain all aspects of security on a particular database. This role allows its members to work with database roles, manager permissions, and object ownership. Finally, there is the db_owner role. This gives its members complete control over a database. They can perform maintenance, manage all aspects of the database's security, change settings for the database, and perform all administrative tasks on the database.

To grant the fixed database roles to a login, you would use the sp_addrolemember to grant SQL logins, SQL Roles, Windows users, or Windows groups membership. To check the membership of a fixed database role, use the sp_helprolemember system-stored procedure.

Fixed Server Roles

Fixed server roles cannot be dropped and so exist at the server level in SQL Server 2005. Fixed server roles include bulkadmin, dbcreator, diskadmin, processadmin, securityadmin, serveradmin, setupadmin, and sysadmin. Each of these roles has a specific purpose, but in general these tasks allow their members to perform administrative or maintenance duties at the server level.

The role bulkadmin gives administers bulk copy and other bulk operations. The role dbcreator allows its members to create, alter, or drop databases. The diskadmin role allows its members to work with the actual files on the disk—for instance, it could manage filegroups. Processadmins have the ability to manage SQL Server 2005 processes—for example, they can use the KILL command to terminate a session. Any members of the securityadmin role can alter, create, or delete any login. Serveradmin can change SQL Server 2005 settings, shut down SQL Server 2005, and alter the state, resources, or endpoint of SQL Server 2005. The setupadmin role allows members to add, change, or delete any linked server. The final role, sysadmin, can do anything on the server. These roles were listed in order of increasing power. Each should truly only be given to members of the database management team, with the possible exception of bulkadmin. If you have a particular group or individual (outside of the people who administer SQL Server 2005) whom you trust in performing bulkadmin duties, by all means add them as members of the bulkadmin role. Any other roles delegate a lot of power, and thus should be treated with caution.

Understanding the SQL Server Authentication Modes

SQL Server is capable of validating two types of logins:

- Windows logins
- SQL Server logins

A Windows login can be a domain user account or a local user account on the computer on which SQL Server is running. SQL Server logins are those that exist only within SQL Server. SQL Server is responsible for keeping track of the login information, to include the password. The SQL Server login is a legacy holdover from earlier versions of SQL Server, as the preferred type of login is a Windows-based one. Windows logins generally are considered more secure. However, SQL

Server logins aren't going away any time soon. They are used too extensively by third-party products and in situations where a client isn't on the same domain as the SQL Server being connected to (for instance, a Web server that is set up to service the Internet).

In order to accommodate these two types of logins, SQL Server can be configured in one of two authentication modes. The first is Windows-only mode. When SQL Server is configured in this mode, it will only accept Windows-based logins. Even if SQL Server is aware of a SQL Server login, it will not accept the login. This goes for all SQL Server logins, to include the sa account. The second mode is what is commonly known as mixed mode. This is where SQL Server will accept both Windows logins and SQL Server logins. There is not a mode where only SQL Server logins are accepted. Although this could be accomplished by removing all Windows-based logins (both users and groups), this is not generally recommended.

Best Practices According to Microsoft

Microsoft's recommendations with respect to SQL Server Authentication Mode are:

- Use Windows-only authentication whenever possible.
- Only drop back to Mixed Mode due to applications that don't support Windows authentication or users coming from a non-Windows environment.
- Regardless of which authentication mode you select, secure the sa account with a strong password. Under *no* circumstances should you ever leave the SA password blank.
- If Mixed Mode is selected, use Windows logins to manage SQL Server.
- Rename the sa account so it cannot be targeted for a brute force password attack.

Some Independent Advice

Although I aim for Windows-only authentication as my authentication mode of choice on my SQL Servers, there are certain cases where I must plan for Mixed Mode. These usually involve what are known as untrusted clients. The term trust here refers to a Windows domain trust, either a transitive trust between Windows domains in the same forest (or domains in forests that have a forest-level trust) or two domains for which there is an external trust relationship. Therefore, a server sitting in a workgroup for security reasons would meet the criteria of an untrusted client. It has no way of connecting to SQL Server via an accepted Windows account. Examples of such servers might include:

- Web servers sitting in the Demilitarized Zone (DMZ) providing services to Internet-based users.
- Servers that contain potentially sensitive configuration information such as the router configurations for the network.

- Servers that run a building's access control system.

Ensure that you plan for these types of clients when selecting your authentication mode. Whenever possible, try to isolate applications requiring SQL Server logins to a particular set of SQL Servers running in Mixed Mode while configuring the remainder of your SQL Server for Windows-only authentication.

Security must be maintained at every level in an enterprise solution. Each of these three major SQL Server 2005 services (Reporting, Analysis, and Integration) handles security differently in terms of authenticating user accounts, authorizing access to various processing and rendering components, and connecting to the underlying data store. After reading this section, you will have gained the essential knowledge to protect your systems and data from unauthorized access.

For Reporting Services, we'll cover role-based security and how to secure reporting resources and define tasks that a user may perform. We'll also cover other techniques for securing reports, including data filtering and data hiding.

For Analysis Services, we'll review how Analysis Services applications are secured. For Integration Services, we'll review how Integration Services "packages" are secured using package-level properties, database roles, operating system permissions, and digital signatures.

You'll also learn that the default security settings can work well under certain circumstances, but there's never one single "best way" for all situations and that understanding the fundamentals is critical to designing a customized solution for your specific environment.

Understanding Granular Access

In security there are the 3 A's: Authentication, Authorization, and Accounting (or Auditing). Thus far in this section, we've talked about the first A, Authentication. It naturally follows that we should now begin our discussion on the second A, Authorization. Once a login has been authenticated, SQL Server is not done. It must determine what rights that login has—that's authorization.

SQL Server 2005 has a robust security model that allows for very customizable rights, especially when compared to its predecessors. For instance, in SQL Server 2000, server administration type functionality was rolled up into predefined fixed server roles. If a particular fixed server role (let's use serveradmin) had the permission you wanted to assign someone (such as giving a junior DBA the ability to execute SHUTDOWN on the SQL Server) but the fixed server role had more permissions than what you wanted to give out, there was no recourse. Either you didn't assign the permission or you lived with the fact that the role gave more permission than you wanted to be given out. In SQL Server 2005 this is no longer an issue. The granularity of permissions has been greatly increased, leading to the concept called Granular Access. That means that if you want that junior DBA to have SHUTDOWN permissions but nothing else that a serveradmin role has, you can simply assign the SHUTDOWN permission. However, in order to understand Granular Access, we must first start with the concept of principals.

Principals

In SQL Server 2005, a principal is a server login, a database user, or a role. Server logins can be Windows users, Windows security groups, or SQL Server logins. In previous versions of SQL Server the terms logins and users were used, but users was used to mean domain user, database user, a user of the SQL Server, and so on, and this could lead to confusion, especially if the context wasn't clear. In order to try and remediate that issue, Microsoft introduced the terms server principals for logins and server-level roles and database principals for database users and database-level roles (including application roles).

Principals are the "who" when we grant access. For instance, if we're talking about granting execute rights against a particular stored procedure, we have to define who is getting those rights. That's what the principal is for. Now that we know the who, we have to understand what we are assigning rights to. Those are *securables*.

Securables

Securables are simply any resource within SQL Server, to include the server itself, which can be assigned access. Some of these securables are containers that can contain other securables. These container securables are called *scopes*. The entire set of securables is a hierarchical structure that allows us to assign permissions at the correct level to grant the access needed and no more, in keeping with the Principle of Least Privilege.

If you are familiar with Active Directory, think along the lines of organizational units (OUs). Domains contain OUs. OUs can be assigned permissions, and this is often a way to delegate certain administrative tasks within Active Directory (such as the ability to reset user passwords). OUs can also contain objects such as user, computer, and group accounts, each of which can have their own set of security permissions assigned. Unless inheritance is intentionally broken on these objects, the actual permissions on them are a superset combining the permissions assigned at the OU level as well as the permissions assigned directly against the object. Securables work in a similar fashion.

The scopes within SQL Server are:

- Server
- Database
- Schema

Each of these scopes has its own set of securables. The Server securables are small in number:

- Database
- Endpoint
- Login
- Remote Binding
- Route

Note that the Database securable, one of the three scopes, is in the list of the Server securables. Therefore, permissions assigned at the server level (which are applicable to databases) are applied to each database. If we look at the Database scope, we have quite a few more securables. Some of the securables of interest to the discussion at hand are:

- User
- Role

- Application Role
- Schema

This doesn't represent the whole list of the securables in the Database scope. However, it gives us the ability to see the effect permissions assigned at the Database scope level can have. Note that just as the Database scope is a securable in the Server scope, the Schema scope is a securable within the Database scope. As a result, we can clearly see a hierarchy, even among the scopes that go from Server to Database to Schema.

Permissions

The securables represent what resources we can assign access to within SQL Server. However, in order to understand granular access, we must understand what permissions we can assign and what those permissions do. With SQL Server 2005 we have the following new set of permissions:

- CONTROL
- ALTER
- ALTER ANY
- TAKE OWNERSHIP
- IMPERSONATE
- CREATE
- VIEW DEFINITION
- BACKUP (or DUMP)
- RESTORE (or LOAD)

If you aren't familiar with the permissions from earlier versions of SQL Server, they are:

- SELECT
- INSERT
- UPDATE
- DELETE
- REFERENCES
- EXECUTE

Let's take a look at the new permissions in more detail.

Control

Control is a permission that conveys all the benefits of ownership over a securable without actually taking ownership of the object. SQL Server resources like databases and schemas can have only one owner, but there are situations where you want ownership like rights given to multiple users. In this case, CONTROL is the appropriate permission to use.

Having CONTROL permissions means having all permissions over a given securable. It also means having the ability to assign permissions against that securable. Not only that, but given the hierarchical structure of securables, having CONTROL on a particular scope means having CONTROL access on any securables that are below that scope. For instance, having CONTROL access over a database means having CONTROL access over all securables inside that database.

Alter

Although ALTER has been around in previous versions of SQL Server, what it applies to has been greatly expanded. ALTER gives the ability to change the properties, with the exception of changing the securable's owner, on a securable. If assigned to a scope, such as ALTER SCHEMA, it gives the ability to CREATE, ALTER, or DROP any securables under that securable. In the case of ALTER SCHEMA, this would be any table, view, stored procedure, function, or other securables within the schema.

Alter Any

ALTER ANY can apply either to server- or database-level securable. It does not apply to schema-level securables because the ALTER (without the ANY) already conveys the same rights. For instance, giving a principal ALTER TABLE rights gives that principal the ability to alter any table. The ALTER ANY permissions gives the ability to alter the properties of any securable of that type within the scope. For instance, ALTER ANY DATABASE gives the ability to change the properties of any database on the server. This allows access to be given across a given securable type without having to worry about reassigning permissions every time a new securable of that type is added.

Take Ownership

This permission allows the principal to take ownership of the securable. This permission doesn't change the ownership; however, the principal will have the ability to take ownership so long as it has this permission.

Impersonate

IMPERSONATE gives the ability to act as another login or user. If a principal is granted the right to impersonate another principal, it can switch its execution context to the other principal. This is similar to using Run As at the operating system level. Previous versions of SQL Server allowed a member of the sysadmin fixed server role to change execution context using the SETUSER command. However, other principals were not capable of changing context. In SQL Server 2005 any principal has the ability, if granted IMPERSONATE permissions, to change execution context.

Create

Like ALTER, CREATE has been around in previous versions of SQL Server. Also like ALTER, what it applies to has been expanded to include server- and database-level securables. Previously it applied only to schema-level securables such as tables, views, and stored procedures. For instance, the ability to create an endpoint can be granted using this permission.

View Definition

The VIEW DEFINITION permission was added to SQL Server 2005 because the newest version of SQL Server locks down the definition of objects like stored procedures and views. Previous versions of SQL Server had an information disclosure issue where any user with access to a database had the ability to view the definitions of any of the database objects. Even though these definitions could be encrypted, the majority of the time they aren't. As a result, SQL Server 2005 solves this issue by not allowing a principal to see an object's definition unless explicitly granted otherwise.

Is this permission very useful given that database administrators should already have the ability to view the definitions anyway? Yes, because there are cases where non-DBAs need the ability to see the definitions. For instance, in the development environment, QA personnel may need the ability to see object definitions to ensure design patterns and best practices are being followed. In a production environment auditors may need to check definitions to ensure that no unauthorized changes have occurred.

Backup

This permission is self explanatory. It gives a principal the ability to back up a database or log (each is a different permission). The fixed database role db_backupoperator has the ability to do both. There may be cases where you want to grant access only to one and not both. This permission gives such a capability, but it is likely a rare situation that you would use it.

Restore

Like BACKUP, this grants specific access to restore databases. By default, none of the fixed database roles short of db_owner have the ability to execute a restore statement. Though the RESTORE command is something most DBAs hold close to the vest, like the BACKUP permission, there may be cases where you want to assign it without giving out db_owner. As a result, it has been added to the permissions list for SQL Server 2005.

Managing Granular Access

We've talked about principals, securables, and the permissions themselves. Now let's talk about some best practices with respect to managing them. First and foremost, never forget the Principle of Least Privilege. Because of the potential complexities with SQL Server 2005's granular access model, it's very easy to take shortcuts, like giving CONTROL over a schema when a principal only needs CREATE permissions for stored procedures. This is an exaggerated example, but it illustrates the point that it is very easy to grant more rights than is absolutely necessary. A small weakness in a security model is usually an audit point at best, an exploited vulnerability at worst. Therefore, honor the Principle of Least Privilege.

Second, try to avoid assigning permissions to individual users (people). Seek to use Windows groups and SQL Server roles as the principals. The reason for this is that you have to assign permissions only once. Consider if there are two auditors in your organization. You grant the VIEW DEFINITION permission to both of these auditors as individuals. As your company expands, two more auditors are hired. Because the permissions were granted to individuals, you're now faced with reassigning permissions for these new auditors. Another example is when a user changes roles in the organization.

For instance, a user transfers from Accounts Payable to Capital Markets. The two departments share some of the same databases but the permissions are different. If permissions are done on a person-by-person basis, this will be a tedious change for the database administrator. If, however, permissions were assigned to user-defined database roles, it's a simple matter of taking the user's database principal out of the role for Accounts Payable and putting that principal in the role for Capital Markets.

Finally, develop a plan when it comes to managing permissions. When permissions are managed on an ad hoc basis, permissions tend to become duplicated and/or violations of the Principle of Least Privilege begin to occur. By developing a plan (and having it reviewed) you can think about the possible scenarios and insure you've covered them with your security plan. As a result, you can also minimize permission duplication and you can ensure that no person has more permissions than he or she should.

Understanding Implied Permissions

Given the hierarchical nature of the securables, it is very easy to forget what a particular permission at a particular scope gives access to down the hierarchy. For instance CONTROL DATABASE gives permission to do anything to any securable within the Database scope (and as a result, any Schema scope, too). These kinds of permissions are called implied permissions and they can lead to violations of the Principle of Least Privilege.

Microsoft has foreseen this issue and provided a function called *dbo.ImplyingPermissions* to be able to trace what higher level permissions grant an implied permission to perform that action. For instance, if we're interested in what permissions grant the equivalent of CREATE TABLE, we would use *dbo. ImplyingPermissions* to determine that. Unfortunately, *dbo.ImplyingPermissions* is not created automatically in SQL Server 2005. You'll have to copy the source code for it from the Books Online topic Covering/Implied Permissions. However, if you have any question about what permissions might imply a certain lower-level permission, it's a good idea to do so on a development or nonproduction SQL Server.

Assigning Permissions

When it comes to SQL Server, there are three actions with respect to permissions to understand:

- GRANT
- DENY
- REVOKE

Let's look at each one. To give a principal access, we GRANT the permission. GRANT is therefore a synonym for assign. To prevent a principal from having access, things are bit more complicated. This is because, by default, if no permissions are defined, no access is granted. Therefore, if there are no GRANT permissions, a principal will not have access. However, if a security principal has received access due to its membership in a role and that permission cannot be removed (for instance, there are other members of the role who should have that level of access), the only option is to use DENY. DENY blocks access. It'll trump any GRANTs that are in place. If you're familiar with NTFS file system security, it's the same idea. As with the file system, the use of DENY should be rare. It's a solution when nothing else works. Otherwise, seek to remove the GRANT. If GRANT permits access and DENY blocks access, what does REVOKE do? Quite simply, REVOKE removes whatever has been set, whether it be a GRANT or DENY. Think of REVOKE as undo. It undoes what has been done, regardless of what it is.

When it comes to assigning permissions, there are two more terms to become familiar with. They are *grantee* and *grantor*. The grantee is the security principal to which the permission is assigned. The grantor is the security principal assigning the access. The grantor is there for audit purposes. It allows us to see who assigned a permission. If the permission was set incorrectly, we know who to go speak with. This is great in theory, but falls short in practice. Unfortunately, when permissions are assigned, it is usually a DBA who is a member of the sysadmin fixed server role doing the task. In this case, server-level securables will show the grantor as sa and database or schema-level securables will show the grantor as dbo. The DBA's actual login won't be shown as the grantor.

Now that we've discussed the actions around assigning permissions and the concept of grantee vs. grantor, let's step through how to assign permissions using SQL Server Management Studio:

1. In Object Explorer, locate the object to assign permissions against in the hierarchy. Some objects may be under the Programmability or Security folders.

2. Right-click the object and choose **Properties** from the pop-up menu.

3. Click on the **Permissions** page under Select a Page.

4. If the security principal isn't present in the list, click the **Add** button (otherwise go to step 6).

5. Enter the name of the security principal to manage permissions on in the **Enter the object names to select** text box for the **Select Logins/Users or Roles** dialog window and click **OK**.

6. On the **Security** page, modify the permissions for that security principal as necessary and click **OK**.

Configuring & Implementing...

Managing Permissions through T-SQL

Permissions can be managed through T-SQL via the GRANT, REVOKE, and DENY statements. If you are quickly trying to lock down or manage access to your SQL Server, the GUI is probably the quickest way to do so. However, if you're managing source code, the permissions for objects should be included with the object definitions themselves. For instance, the code that defines a stored procedure should include the GRANT EXECUTE statements for the appropriate security principals. In this way, the proper permissions for the objects are maintained with the source code in your code repository system.

DBMS Data Store (Oracle)

If the data store is hosted on Oracle, give the Oracle user account used for the server farm "connect" and "resource" permissions only. System administrator (system or sys) account permissions are not needed for data store access.

Implementing basic Oracle security involves the easiest fixes that give you optimal results. The idea here is to get your database to a reasonably secure state without much effort or risk. The most egregious problems luckily are the easiest to fix. These fixes will block the most common attacks and the reconnaissance leading up to attacks. Install the latest patchset, set a listener password, and change default passwords and you are halfway there!

You can use this list as a guide to implementing basic Oracle security:

- Install the latest patchset (A patchset includes security fixes from CPUs released since the previous patchset so this is a good first step when you are getting started with security.)

- Restrict access to configuration files (Examples of these files are listener.ora, sqlnet.ora, tnsnames.ora, and control files)

- Only the Oracle user on the host should have access; remove all access from other users

---

NOTE

If you have local users on the host, they can have their own copy of tnsnames.ora and client software. This allows you to lock them out of the server's copy thus reducing risk.

- Turn off unneeded services, e.g. ext proc, http server

- Unnecessary services are unnecessary risks. Also, services that are not used tend to be the least secure because no one is paying attention to them.

- Assign a password to the listener and lock down access to it according to your database security policy

- Lock accounts that are not in use

- Revoke permissions to PUBLIC that are not explicitly required

- To start, ensure PUBLIC is not a member of any role.

- PUBLIC should generally not have DDL access, but this varies based on each database's requirements

- Remove unneeded permissions to roles and to users

- Change default passwords

- Remove access to Oracle executables

- Only the Oracle user should have read, write and execute permissions to most executables.

- You may want to leave on read and execute permissions on some executables such as sqlplus, but do so only for the DBA group, not for everyone.

- Remove all access to executables that are not in use, even from Oracle

- Often extproc and other Oracle features are not used, so turn off all access to them as well.

- Implement minimal permissions to important directories such as audit_dest_dir and user_dump_dest.

- Remove all access to datafiles and redo logs from users other than Oracle

- Set minimal permissions on backups and exports

- Set umask appropriately

- Error and trace logs should only be accessible to database administrators

Implementing Oracle Best Practices

Best Practices reflect proven security processes in real world environments. These steps enhance Basic Security by making it even more difficult for an attacker to penetrate your system, help track user activity, and implement processes that make security inherently better:

- Consider locking out accounts with too many failed login attempts. Be careful with this one though. If a middle tier application server uses a pool of connections all logged in as "bob" and then bob gets locked out, your system effectively goes down.

- This also includes using a password verification function to validate adequate password complexity. Be careful with this one, too, for two reasons. First, requiring new passwords to be complex does not imply old ones must be.

- Use the password strength tools to find easily guessed passwords.

- Turn off access to OS resources

- Packages such as UTL_FILE, UTL_HTTP, UTL_TCP, UTL_UDP and UTL_SMTP give access to the host's operating system including the file system and network. An attacker can use UTL_SMTP for example to send himself an email with data.

- Encrypt data at rest

- Audit privileged users and known attack patterns

- Separation of duties: An auditor should monitor privileged users such as DBAs, and DBAs should not have access to the audit trail. A third party should verify this process is in place to ensure, for example, that the auditor is a different person from the DBA. (A relatively new Oracle feature called Data Vault helps to implement this requirement)

- Install all CPUs and security alerts

- Because CPUs are released quarterly, you will need a predefined testing and deployment process in place to be able to keep up the pace. Use as much automation as possible to speed this process along. CPU release dates are available a year in advance and the effort to evaluate them, to test them, and to deploy them is predictable. This enables you to plan resources (people, hardware, software) effectively and schedule time for this effort.

Locking Down Your Database

Lock Down is the final stage of database security. Beyond best practices, these steps go the extra mile to monitor the most remote threats and to prevent even accidentally revealing private data. The steps here are advanced, they require training and research, and they will generally affect your operating environment. Expect significant lead time before being able to deploy them:

- Don't permit direct access to host, even for DBAs, unless necessary. Monitor all activity where the client is local to the server. This follows the standard secure practice of "least privileges." Most DBA activity can be done via a remote client and does not require local access. Local access implies access to the file system which is more permissive than is necessary for most tasks. An operating system administrator can perform many of the tasks necessary, and to prevent his/her access to the data, use encryption.

- Oracle Advanced Security (OAS) encrypts data at rest and in transit thus maintaining confidentiality and integrity of your data.

- Build on your Best Practice auditing. Include suspicious activity, access to sensitive data and access to the auditing tool. Activity monitoring at this level requires a commitment to analyze its results. Suspicious activity, for example, may or may not be a problem. You will need to implement a workflow where someone investigates and acknowledges security alerts. Expect advanced auditing of this type to generate a significant volume of results. Plan storage space accordingly.

- Restrict access to individual records within tables.

- Virtual Private Databases and Label Security are technologies related to access control on a row-by-row basis. You set access privileges to particular rows or to rows meeting a rule that you define. Using technologies built into the database is more secure than doing so at the application layer.

- Use centralized authentication.

- Separate the data from the mechanism of accessing the data, i.e. use LDAP, Kerberos, or some other authentication process that integrates with Oracle.

- Storing passwords in clear text in application server configuration files is a common security problem which can be solved by using centralized authentication.

- Single Sign On (SSO) features are very often linked to centralized authentication. This will help you detect the real user behind an Oracle connection.

- Seeing only a connection pool's proxy user is often a problem in database auditing.

- Hire third-party personnel to try to break into your systems. Some organizations choose to have specially trained internal staff for this and some of them outsource. Either way, you cannot be sure your security posture is working unless you test it.

- Review error logs daily for anomalies.

■ Configure the listener to validate hosts that attempt to access the database. Generally, the client machines which are allowed to access a database are known in advance so disallow all others.

■ Generate strong cryptographic hashes of the executables and other static files on the host, especially those belonging to Oracle. Periodically verify that the hashes have not changed.

Monitoring Your XenApp Farm

A new feature available with the release of XenApp is the ability to log configuration changes to your XenApp environment called Configuration Logging. This feature allows for the generation of reports that can assist you in determining what changes have been made to your environment, who made them, and when they were made. This is especially useful when your XenApp environment consists of several XenApp administrators that have the capability to make configuration changes to your environment. The use of this feature can also serve as a useful troubleshooting tool by tracking configuration changes.

When this feature is configured, all administrative changes initiated from the Access Management Console, the Presentation Server Console, some command-line utilities, and tools custom built with the Citrix SDKs create log entries in a central Configuration Logging database.

Planning for Logging

Before you enable the Configuration Logging feature, Citrix recommends that you decide the following:

■ Determine the level of security and control you need over the configuration logs.

■ Determine how strictly you want to log tasks.

Enable Configuration Logging

To enable Configuration Logging for your XenApp environment, you must do the following:

■ Set up the Configuration Logging database

■ Define the Configuration Logging database access permissions

■ Configure the Configuration Logging database connection

■ Test the connection to the Configuration Logging database

■ Set the Configuration Logging properties

■ Delegate administrative permissions, if needed

To setup the Configuration Logging, you must first set up the Configuration Logging Database as shown in Figure 5.30. The Configuration Logging feature supports Microsoft SQL Server 2000 and 2005 and Oracle Version 9.2 and 10.2 databases. The Configuration Logging database must be set up before Configuration Logging can be enabled. Only one Configuration Logging database is supported per server farm, regardless of how many domains are in the farm. When the Configuration Logging database is set up, you also must ensure that the appropriate database permissions are provided for XenApp so that it can create the database tables and stored procedures (preceded by "CtxLog_AdminTask_") needed for Configuration Logging. To do this, create a database user who has the connect and resource roles and unlimited tablespace system privilege for Oracle; this is used to provide XenApp full access.

The exact steps to create and configure a Configuration Logging database are outlined in the Citrix Administrator's Guide.

Figure 5.30 Setting Up Configuration Logging

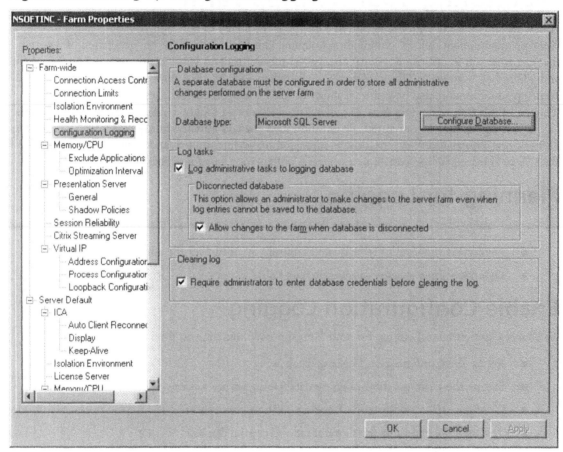

To configure the specifics of Configuration Logging data under the **Log tasks** section:

- **Log administrative tasks to logging database** Select this check box to enable the Configuration Logging feature.

- **Allow changes to the farm when database is disconnected** This check box is selected by default; however, when the database is disconnected, log entries resulting from administrative actions are lost.

- **Clearing log** This check box requires that XenApp administrators enter their login credentials before they can clear a configuration logging database.

Using Configuration Logging and Creating Reports

After the Configuration Logging feature has been enabled, it runs in the background and monitors your XenApp environment for administrative changes. If configuration changes are detected, these changes are written to the Configuration Log database. Configuration Logging reports can be created to help you with displaying configuration changes to your XenApp environment.

You can view Configuration Logging reports at the farm level.

1. In the Access Management Console, select the **Report Center** node in the scope pane and select **Configuration Logging Report** to display a report, as shown in Figure 5.31.

Figure 5.31 Creating a Configuration Logging Report

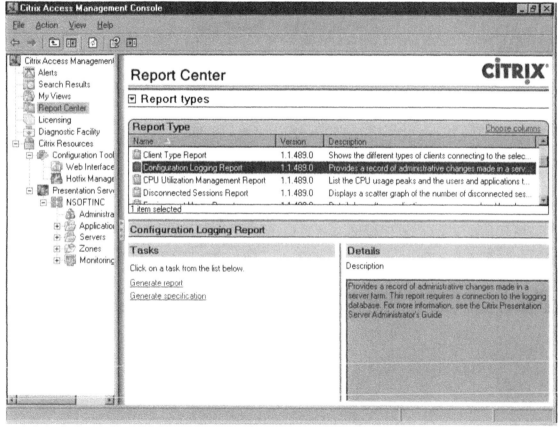

2. Select to generate a report or generate a specification.

3. A final report will be displayed based on whatever specification you define, as shown in Figure 5.32.

Figure 5.32 Displayed a Configuration Logging Report

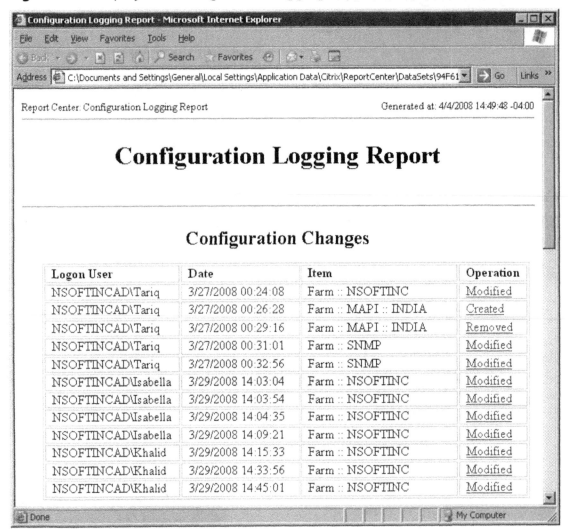

Summary

In this chapter, we explored the various deployment considerations of a Windows Active Directory and how that design can impact your XenApp environment. We started with the basic components of the Active Directory design, which includes: Domains, Domain Trees, Forests, and Organizational Units. We explained the process of protecting your Active Directory data and also ensuring that valid backups are being performed in your environment. We explained the differences between the various groups contained in Active Directory with domain global groups being the best suited for your XenApp security needs. We learned about the Active Directory best practices as defined by Microsoft and were given an examination into the workings of Forest Trusts and Trust Based Routing.

We continued with an examination of how maintaining software integrity of a XenApp environment affects the overall security of your environment. We learned that only supported XenApp products should be used. We gained an understanding of the various XenApp service accounts, how to secure a Java JRE environment on your XenApp server, and why running multiple service hosts on a XenApp server could open your environment to unnecessary vulnerabilities.

We learned about the various components that comprise a XenApp server and how you can best optimize the usage of XenApp policies in addition to gaining a better understanding of how to configure and secure XenApp shadowing using a variety of methods. We also covered security concerns of server drive remappings, and how to configure the XML and XTE (session reliability) services. Additionally, we explained how the MFCOM component could be used maliciously in your XenApp environment.

We looked in greater detail at how to secure your XenApp farm by planning for security and then applying that plan to secure your environment. We discussed how you could secure client-server communication and how to secure communications between your clients and your XenApp servers using XenApp encryption policies. We also discussed the configuration of SSL Relay, IMA Encryption, and the effects of using a VPN connection to connect to XenApp resources. We reviewed the configuration of the Secure Ticket Authority, authentication using Smart Cards, configuring Kerberos, configuring automatic client reconnection, and how to configure SNMP in a secure environment.

Finally, we reviewed some of the ways of locking down and securing various forms of the XenApp data store as well as the basic setup of the XenApp Configuration Logging feature and how to produce reports using that tool to determine changes to your system.

Solutions Fast Track

Deployment Considerations

☑ Planning the deployment of Citrix XenApp is a very in depth process. Since XenApp and the underlying Terminal Services platform will be required in many deployments to integrate into nearly every process an organization may have, careful consideration and forethought must be given as to how best to introduce the technology.

☑ Citrix recommends the following for configuration of server farms with Active Directory:

☑ All servers should reside in the same domain

☑ A XenApp farm domain should have no trust relationships with non-Active Directory domains

☑ Do not mix different release versions of Citrix Presentation Server with Citrix XenApp in the same XenApp farm

☑ XenApp farms should be in a single Active Directory forest

☑ Citrix defines trust-based routing as allowing servers to be members of a server farm even if the servers belong to domains that do not trust each other. Even though you cannot configure resources to be published to users that do not have permissions on servers where the application is published, it is still possible that a user could initiate a request that would require an authentication request by a server where the user has no access rights. Trust-based routing allows the user's authentication to be transparently passed to another XenApp server where the user does have access rights.

Maintaining Software Integrity

☑ The integrity of the Citrix XenApp software executables and data files is crucial to the optimal and correct operation of all applications using XenApp. To protect the XenApp environment, you should ensure that the XenApp version is a Citrix Systems supported product version. Citrix Systems supported product versions are those that continue to receive security updates by Citrix in response to the discovery of vulnerabilities.

☑ Service accounts defined for access to XenApp servers allow various interactions with associated applications, services, user sessions, and external supporting systems. These interactions can be relatively benign, such as access to availability information, or quite powerful, such as reconfiguration, redeployment of applications, or even the installation and deletion of user applications. All accounts, not just service accounts, must be carefully scrutinized to ensure that privileges assigned are those that are genuinely needed.

☑ Since it is a best security practice to separate or partition services offered to different audiences, any XenApp server should be installed on a server dedicated to its support and offering as few services as possible to other clients.

Configuring XenApp Components

☑ XenApp has many components and services that perform a variety of functions. Many of these components and services can be configured individually to meet the needs of an organization's security requirements and if a service or component is not being used at all, then it should be either disabled or not installed.

☑ The XenApp shadowing utility provides the ability to remotely control, monitor, and interact with another user's session. During a shadow session, the session being monitored is displayed in the shadower's session window. The monitored session can be viewed only, or the shadower can interact with the monitored session, depending on the configuration. When the session is placed in interactive mode, all keyboard and mouse strokes are passed to the monitored session.

☑ The XML Service provides the interface between a XenApp server and the Web Interface server. Another security issue to consider is the way in which traffic is passed between the Web Interface server and the XML service on XenApp servers. In a process that is similar to standard Web traffic, data is transmitted in cleartext. This becomes a security concern when traffic between the Web Interface server and the XenApp farm is insecure. For example, many organizations will place a Web Interface server in the DMZ, or demilitarized zone, while maintaining a XenApp farm in a more secure network.

☑ MFCOM is a programming interface for assisting you with the management of your farm servers and their components. The configuration options available through the various XenApp administration consoles are available through the MFCOM interface. You have the capability to create tools to perform and automate tasks that are specific to your own environment. MFCOM works in conjunction with Visual Basic or .NET to communicate with the XenApp environment through the MFCOM interface.

Securing Your XenApp Farm

☑ Planning an effective security strategy for your XenApp farm requires an understanding of the roles that different servers play on the network and the security needs of different types of servers based on the security requirements of your organization. Securing the servers is an important part of any network administrator's job.

☑ Perhaps the simplest way of enabling encryption for your XenApp server is by creating various encryption policies and applying them to individual servers.

☑ In XenApp deployments that will utilize Citrix Secure Gateway (CSG), you must also configure at least one XenApp server to be an STA server. The CSG server does not perform authentication of incoming requests, it only defers authentication to an application enumeration server and uses the STA to guarantee that each user is authenticated. Application enumeration servers request tickets only for users who are already authenticated to the Web Interface. If users have a valid STA ticket, the gateway assumes that they passed the authentication checks at the Web Interface and should be allowed access.

☑ The Auto Client Reconnect feature allows XenApp clients to detect broken connections and automatically reconnect users to disconnected sessions. When a client detects a disconnection of a session, it attempts to reconnect the user to the session until there is a successful reconnection or the user cancels the reconnection attempt.

☑ A new feature included with XenApp is IMA encryption that utilizes AES encryption to protect sensitive data in the IMA data store.

Securing the Data Store

☑ XenApp servers within a farm all share a common repository for configuration known as the *data store*. The data store provides a repository of persistent farm information for all servers to reference. The data store retains information that does not change frequently, including the following:

☑ Published application configurations

☑ Servers in the farm

☑ Citrix administrators

☑ Trust relationships

☑ If you use a Microsoft Access database as your XenApp data store the default password must be changed.

☑ This type of database is most appropriate for small to medium-sized farms and can be administered using standard Microsoft SQL Server tools. When using SQL Server 2005 Express Edition SP1, first install it and then create an instance. Then run the Citrix Presentation Server Setup. The database is stored on the first server in the farm.

☑ Security in SQL Server 2005 is multifaceted, and it can seem impossibly complicated. SQL Server 2005 security starts at the ground level and builds upon itself.

Monitoring Your XenApp Farm

☑ A new feature available with the release of XenApp is the ability to log configuration changes to your XenApp environment. This feature allows for the generation of reports that can assist you in determining what changes have been made to your environment, who made them, and when they were made.

☑ Before you enable the Configuration Logging feature, Citrix recommends that you decide the following:

☑ Determine the level of security and control you need over the configuration logs.

☑ Determine how strictly you want to log tasks.

☑ After the Configuration Logging feature has been enabled, it runs in the background and monitors your XenApp environment for administrative changes. If configuration changes are detected, these changes are written to the Configuration Log database. Configuration Logging reports can be created to help you with displaying configuration changes to your XenApp environment.

Frequently Asked Questions

Q: What file contains the Active Directory information?

A: NTDS.dit

Q: What is the smallest Active Directory unit to which you can delegate administrative authority?

A: Organizational Unit (OU)

Q: What is Trust Based Routing?

A: Allowing servers to be members of a server farm even if the servers belong to domains that do not trust each other.

Q: How many product lifecycle phases has Citrix defined?

A: Three: Mainstream Maintenance Phase, Extended Maintenance Phase, End of Life Phase

Q: What are the four service accounts that can be created by a XenApp installation?

A: Ctx_CpsvcUser, Ctx_ConfigMgr, Ctx_StreamingSvc, Ctx_CpuUser

Q: By default, how many anonymous accounts are created during a default installation of XenApp?

A: 15 user accounts are created with account names in the form AnonXXX, where XXX is a number from 000 to 014.

Q: What XenApp service handles SSL Relay and Session Reliability functionality?

A: Citrix XTE Server

Q: What are the most common ways that XenApp shadowing can be configured?

A: Configuration during installation, user account properties, Windows group policy, Terminal Services Configuration Tool, editing the registry, and creating a XenApp Policy.

Q: What is the default port used by the XML service?

A: TCP port 80

Q: What are the primary methods of securing remote access to XenApp?

A: Secure ICA (ICA Encryption), Secure Socket Layer Relay (SSL Relay), Virtual private networking (VPN), Citrix Secure Gateway (CSG), Citrix Access Gateway or Citrix NetScaler

Q: What is perhaps the simplest way of enabling encryption for a XenApp server?

A: Creating various encryption policies and applying them to individual servers.

Q: How can traffic between the XenApp servers and the Web Interface server be secured?

A: By implementing the use of SSL Relay.

Q: If you implement the Citrix Secure Gateway solution, what is the minimum number of XenApp servers that must act as a Secure Ticket Authority?

A: One

Q: What feature is used to encrypt and protect sensitive data in the XenApp data store?

A: IMA Encryption

Q: What is the common repository for configuration information that all XenApp servers within a farm all share called?

A: The data store

Q: What types of databases can be used as a XenApp data store?

A: MS Access, MS SQL Express, IBM DB2, Oracle, and MS SQL Server

Q: What is the default user id and password used for a MS Access data store?

A: citrix / citrix

Q: A new feature available with XenApp that has the ability to log configuration changes to your XenApp environment is called?

A: Configuration Logging.

Q: To enable Configuration Logging for your XenApp environment, what must you do?

A: Set up the Configuration Logging database, define the Configuration Logging database access permissions, configure the Configuration Logging database connection, test the connection to the Configuration Logging database, set the Configuration Logging properties, delegate administrative permissions.

Q: What reports can be created to help you in displaying configuration changes to your XenApp environment?

A: Configuration Logging reports.

Chapter 6

Policies and Procedures for Securing XenApp

Solutions in this chapter:

- Windows Server 2003 Group Policy
- Planning a Group Policy Strategy
- Configuring Group Policy with the Group Policy Management Console
- Configuring XenApp Policies
- Using Policies to Make XenApp More Secure

☑ Summary

☑ Solutions Fast Track

☑ Frequently Asked Questions

Introduction

The successful implementation of an efficient, easy to use, and easy to manage XenApp farm does not simply rely on a correctly installed terminal server. The associated infrastructure (Active Directory, domain security and network topology) plays an undeniably essential role in supporting users, application access, and performance and reliability—all factors that determine whether XenApp farm is living up to its potential.

To illustrate this point, think about these questions. How do you ensure that confidential documents used by one group of users you support are printed only on the printers at that group's location? How do you ensure that remote users connecting from a hotel's unsecured Internet connection are adequately protected from a hacker snooping around for information? How do you ensure that those same remote users are not passing viruses to your network over the Web Interface connection from the PC they are using at the local Internet café? The answers to these questions can all be supplied via the appropriate application of a combination of Windows group policies and XenApp policies.

The goal of this chapter is to familiarize you with both Windows and XenApp policies and show you how you can configure them to work together to ensure seamless, reliable, and secure access for your users to their applications via their Citrix connections no matter where they are and how they connect.

Windows Server 2003 Group Policy

Some of us who are familiar with group policies in Windows 2000 will appreciate the enhancements introduced in Windows Server 2003 Group Policy; others who have been frustrated by Windows 2000 Group Policy will be pleasantly surprised. Although it brings with it more than 200 policy settings, Window Server 2003 Group Policy also brings with it an easier to understand management interface in the form of the Group Policy Management Console (GPMC), and modeling and testing features that allow administrators to more accurately and effectively plan domain and security policies before implementing them.

Administrators are now able to affect policies that fit their particular situations more closely and avoid more of the mistakes that result from poorly configured group policy objects (GPOs). Microsoft's new unified Group Policy model makes it possible to view and manage all GPOs across a domain, organizational unit (OU), or site, and for the first time gives administrators the "big picture" view of the networks they manage. Coupled with Windows Management Instrumentation filters, administrators can see how GPOs affect different machines based on their individual hardware and software characteristics. In addition, Windows Server 2003 Group Policy enhancements support group policy changes in the entire Windows 2000 family of operating systems, Windows XP, and Windows Server 2003 platforms.

For example, it is now possible to see how a GPO that requires machines to perform an antivirus update and scan may require more memory or simply not work for remote laptop users versus desktop users in the office on a Windows network. You could also predict how older machines with slower processors are affected versus the newer, faster machines that an IT staff rolled out (Figure 6.1). The benefit to an IT staff in the time and cost savings that Windows Server 2003 Group Policy provides is more than just an abstract factor. Knowing how a policy affects different machines on a network beforehand or as it is happening allows an IT staff to quickly identify and implement remedies to the issues that arise. This in turn translates to less downtime and increased productivity.

Figure 6.1 Different Windows Server 2003 Policies for Different OUs

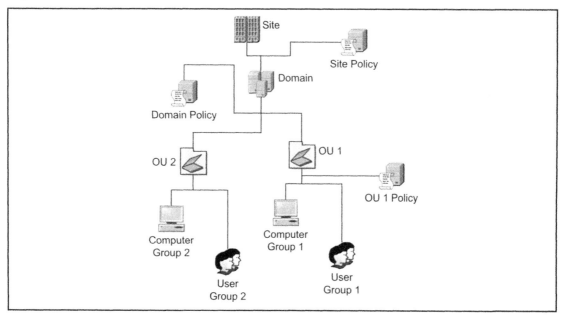

One of the primary aims of group policy was the enforcement of a consistent security stance within an organization's network. Most IT professionals know the concept of a rigidly enforced security policy across an enterprise is a fallacy. Operational demands and changing business rules and roles have made the "one solution fits all situations" paradigm outdated and a rather foolish proposition. The flexibility required of systems that support business of any kind continues to grow. Multiple GPOs must apply to individual user and computer groups, OUs, and domains. Administrators must meet the demands of in-house and remote users, customers and partners. Windows Server 2003 Group Policy goes further to aid administrators in this constantly evolving endeavor via the Administrative Templates node of the Group Policy snap-in.

The new Group Policy features also allow for backup and restore of GPOs. If an administrator has backed up his GPOs, he can restore them to user and computer groups, domains, OUs, or sites should his new GPOs produce an undesired effect.

You can use Group Policy to accomplish the following tasks, among others:

- **Assign scripts** You can specify scripts that will run at login, logoff, startup, shutdown, and other times.

- **Manage applications** You can designate applications that will be installed on, updated on, or removed from computers.

- **Redirect folders** You can specify alternate locations for system folders, such as My Documents, My Pictures, and others.

■ **Change Registry settings** You can designate a set of Registry settings that will be applied to the local computer when a user logs on.

Gaining a full understanding of how Group Policy can impact the network requires a full understanding of the terminology and concepts.

NOTE

Windows 2003 includes over 200 policy settings.

Terminology and Concepts

You will encounter a number of terms, acronyms, and jargon when designing and implementing a group policy in your organization. When we refer to Group Policy, we are actually talking about the superset of all the individual components that make up the larger whole. You will find policy elements that affect only users or computers, policies that are set at the workstation level or applied to an OU in Active Directory, and ways to apply basic security to policies. Let's review the basic terms used as the foundation of building Group Policy.

Local and NonLocal Policies

Group Policy allows you to set policies that will impact resources connecting to a specific computer or interacting with the entire directory. The terms local policy and non-local policy identify where the group policy settings originate. A local policy is stored on a specific computer (a workstation or a member server) and applies only to activities on that computer. For example, a local policy only affects a user object when the user logs on interactively on the server, either at the console or via terminal services. Local policies can also affect the way a user object accesses data from the specific server across the network. Generally, local policies should only be used on workstations; however, there are a few situations where local policies on a server would make sense.

Non-local policies are applied primarily to group objects. These policies affect objects in the directory and are enacted when the object is active in the network. If a non-local policy affects a user object, its effect is applied every time that user object logs on, no matter what PC is used as the logon console. Group policies can apply to any of the following:

■ A local computer

■ An entire site

- A domain

- A specific OU

Group policies can be filtered through security settings, much like NTFS file and folder permissions control access to data on a server volume. As you will see shortly, there is a specific order in which policies are applied if local and group policies differ in a specific area, but the best practice for policies in general is to apply the policies at the group level, not at the local level.

User and Computer Policies

As you might have guessed, some policies apply to user accounts, and other policies apply to computer accounts. You can only apply policies to user and computer objects, not security groups or other objects (however, policies can be filtered by security groups by setting the security group Access Control Entry on the GPO). These two types of policy application work as follows:

- User policies affect how user accounts interact with the network and are applied when a user logs on to the network.

- Computer policies affect how computer objects interact with the network and only apply to those computers that participate in the Active Directory.

You configure each of these types of policies in separate areas in the GPO Editor. User and computer policies are divided into three groups: Software Settings, Windows Settings, and Administrative Templates.

Software Settings

The primary use of this setting is to install, update, or remove software on computers on the network. The Software Installation node is located in this group, and other policy groups can be added in this area by other applications.

Software policies set in this area under Computer Configuration apply to all users who log on to the computer where the policy applies. This policy setting could be used to designate a specific computer on the network where a particular application should be installed, no matter who logs on to the computer. Software policies set in this area under User Configuration apply to all computers that a particular user logs on to. This setting is useful if a particular user has a specific application that he or she needs to use, no matter where that user uses a computer in the organization. The policies can be set so that if an application is installed on a computer this way, only the user to whom the policy is applied is able to see or run the application.

Windows Settings

Policies applying to scripts, security, folder redirection, and Remote Installation Services, among others, are located in this area. There are significant differences between these policy settings depending on whether they are applied in the Computer Configuration or User Configuration node. Table 6.1 details some of the policy groups and whether they are applied to user or computer settings.

Table 6.1 Group Policies for Windows Settings

Policy	Location	Description
Scripts	Computer Configuration	Specifies startup and shutdown scripts to be run on the computer.
Scripts	User Configuration	Specifies startup and shutdown scripts to be run by users.
Account policies	Computer Configuration\ Security Settings	Contains policies related to password and account lockout settings.
Folder redirection	User Configuration\Security Settings	Contains policies to redirect certain user folders such as; Application Data, My Documents, and Start Menu, to alternate locations.
Internet Explorer maintenance	User Configuration\Security Settings	Contains settings to modify defaults for IE, such as user interface settings, favorites, connection settings, and security zone settings.
Public Key policies	Computer Configuration\ Security Settings	Contains policies related to system-level public key activities, such as Encrypted File System, Enterprise Trust, Autoenrollment settings, and Automatic Certificate Request settings.
Public Key policies	User Configuration\Security Settings	Contains policies related to user-level public key activities, such as Enterprise Trust and Autoenrollment settings.

Administrative Templates

Policy settings that appear in the Administrative Templates node of the GPO Editor contain Registry settings to achieve each of the settings contained in the hierarchy. Policies for user configuration are placed in the HKEY_CURRENT_USER (HKCU) area of the Registry, while those for computer configurations are placed in the HKEY_LOCAL_MACHINE (HKLM) area.

Administrative templates contain settings for Windows components such as NetMeeting, Internet Explorer, Terminal Services, Windows Media Player, and Windows update, to name a few. Other components common to both user and computer configurations include settings for user profiles, script execution, and group policy.

While the different policy settings between user and computer configurations are too numerous to list here, there are some key components available for the user configuration. These include the Start Menu, Taskbar, Desktop, Control Panel, and Shared folder settings.

Group Policy Objects

All group policy information is stored in Active Directory in GPOs. You can apply these objects at the site, domain, or OU level within the directory. Since the GPO is an object in the directory, you can set security permissions on the objects to determine who will access the policy settings stored in the GPO.

Because GPOs can impact a large portion of the directory, you should update GPOs infrequently. Each GPO update must propagate across the entire directory to take effect, and this could be a time consuming process if the directory structure is very large. You should also restrict the number of individuals who make changes to GPOs that can impact the entire organization. Otherwise, you can run into the situation where two administrators make contradictory changes to a GPO in different locations of the tree, and the changes propagate differently around the tree, potentially causing problems until the directory has completely updated the GPO changes.

Scope and Application Order of Policies

A single object in the network can be subject to multiple policy settings, depending on how Group Policy is configured on the local machine and in the directory. Active Directory processes policy settings in a specific manner when an object connects to the network. Knowing this process will help you troubleshoot problems with policy settings as they arise.

Local, Site, Domain, OU

Group Policy settings are applied in the following order:

1. **Local settings** Each computer has its own local GPO, and these settings are applied before any others. There is only one local GPO per computer.

2. **Site settings** Group policies associated with the site in Active Directory are processed next. The system administrator can set a specific order in which the site policies are to be applied, if more than one policy is defined.

3. **Domain settings** Group policies associated with a domain object follow the completion of the site settings. If multiple domains are involved, the administrator can set the order of preference in which those settings will be applied.

4. **OU settings** Group policies associated with an OU are applied last in the processing order, but the processing starts with the OU highest in the directory structure. The remaining OU GPOs will be processed in descending order until the OU that contains the directory object is reached. If multiple policy settings are applied for a particular OU, the administrator can set the order in which the settings are applied.

Figure 6.2 details the order in which multiple policies are applied when a user object logs on to the domain. In the diagram, the user object exists in the OU 4 OU, which is in the OU 3 OU of Domain 1 of Site. When the user logs on, the local policy of the computer is applied, followed by any GPOs attached to Site, then Domain 1, then OU 3, and finally OU 4.

Figure 6.2 Processing Policy Settings at User Logon

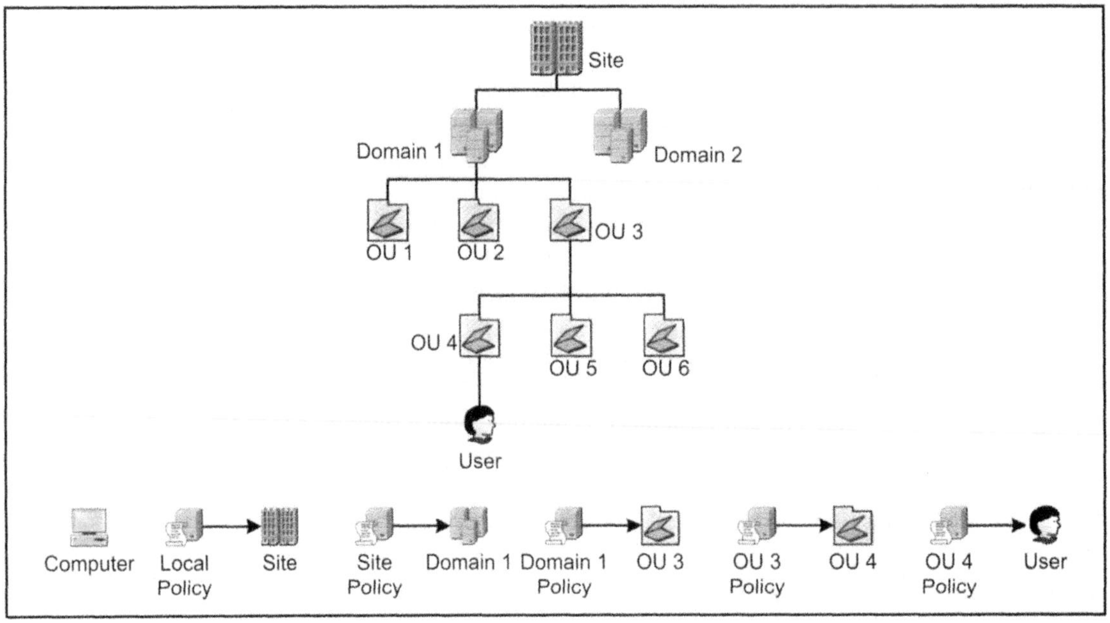

Understanding Policy Inheritance

We saw in Figure 6.2 that when the user logged on, policies from the Site, Domain, and OUs were applied to the user object. The example indicated that any policies associated with OU 3 would be applied before the policies in OU 4. Through policy inheritance, the policies in OU 3 will apply to all objects in OU 3, OU 4, OU 5, and OU 6, even if no specific policies are assigned to OU4, OU5, or OU6.

Objects in child containers generally inherit policies from the parent containers within a domain. If a policy setting is enabled in OU 3 and that same policy setting is not configured in OU 4, then objects in OU 4 inherit the policy setting from OU 3. If a policy setting is disabled in OU 3 but that same policy setting is enabled in OU 4, then the policy setting is enabled in OU 4, as the GPO for OU 4 overrides policy settings from OU 3. This is the way it works by default.

However, administrators can block inheritance on group policy settings at the OU level. If you want to start with a clean slate at a particular OU, you can use the Block Policy Inheritance setting at that OU, and only the settings in the GPO for that OU will apply to objects in the OU. Blocking policy inheritance does not impact local computer policy settings, only Active Directory group policy settings.

In addition, policies set at a higher container can be marked as No Override, which prevents any lower container settings from changing the policy settings of the higher container. Going back to Figure 6.2, if the GPO for OU 3 is marked for No Override, and a policy setting in the GPO for OU 4 conflicts with a setting from OU 3, the setting in OU 4 will not take effect. You cannot block a policy that is set to No Override.

You should use great care in using the Block Policy Inheritance and No Override settings when configuring Group Policy. Changing the default way in which policy is applied can complicate troubleshooting of policy settings if problems are encountered.

Filtering Scope by Security Group Membership

As mentioned, you can further control which policies are applied to which objects by filtering policy application by security group membership. Similar to setting permissions on files and folders with NTFS security settings, you can set security on a GPO so that only certain groups can see the GPO, which means that only those groups will have the policies applied.

Looking back at Figure 6.2, the diagram assumes that there is no security filter on the GPOs at any level. Now let's suppose that the user object is a member of the Accounting group, and that the GPO in OU 4 has security permissions set. If the security permissions on the GPO in OU 4 do not give members of the Accounting group access to read the GPO, then the user will not have the GPO settings for OU 4 applied when he or she logs on.

If you find yourself needing to filter GPO settings based on group membership, you might need to set multiple GPOs on a container and adjust the security settings accordingly. Again, adding a number of GPOs to a container increases the complexity of the policy setting process, which can cause complications for troubleshooting.

Planning a Group Policy Strategy

You must consider a number of factors when planning the group policy strategy for your organization. Some of these factors include size of the organization, geography of the organization, structure of the organization, and so on. More importantly, you must determine the effective policy settings you want to have for each object in the directory.

One way to test your policy plan is to create the policies and then log on with user accounts from different locations of the directory and see how the policies impact the user experience. This is time consuming, cumbersome, and has a definite impact on the production network. Fortunately, Microsoft provides a way for evaluating the proposed policy environment without impacting the production system.

Using RSoP Planning Mode

The **Resultant Set of Policy** (RSoP) tool, included with Windows Server 2003, has a special planning mode that system administrators can use to evaluate the design of the group policy within the directory. The planning mode of RSoP can simulate a number of situations where group policy settings can be affected by a number of factors, including slow network links.

Opening RSoP in Planning Mode

To use RSoP in planning mode, you will need to run the **Resultant Set of Policy Wizard** from inside the Microsoft Management Console (MMC). You can follow these steps to open RSoP in planning mode to collect information for an RSoP report.

1. Open Microsoft Management Console (MMC) and add the RSoP snap-in.

   - Select **File | Add/Remove Snap-in**.

   - Click **Add**.

   - Select **Resultant Set of Policy** from the list.

   - Click **Add**, and then click **Close**.

   - Click **OK**.

2. Right-click on **Resultant Set of Policy** and select **Generate RSoP Data**.

3. Click **Next** in the Resultant Set of Policy Wizard window.

4. Click the **Planning Mode** option button, and click **Next**.

The RSoP wizard will walk you through the steps of gathering the data that can be collected and included in the RSoP report. On each page, there is a **Skip to the final page of this wizard without collecting additional data** check box. If you select the check box, only the data specified up to that point in the wizard will be included in the RSoP query. All other settings will take their default values.

The first page of the wizard collects user and computer information on which the query will run. This is the only data that is required in the wizard, as all subsequent pages can be skipped by clicking the **Skip to the final page of this wizard without collecting additional data** check box. On this page, you must select a specific user or user container, and a specific computer or computer container. You can use the **Browse** buttons to search for a user or computer or the parent container, or you can enter the information directly into the fields. After the information for the user and computer selections is complete, the **Next** button will enable and you can move to the next page of the wizard.

The next page of the wizard allows you to specify any advanced simulation options. On this page, you can specify the report to simulate a slow network connection and loopback processing options, if any. You can also specify which site's policies to test, if there are multiple sites available.

If you specified a specific user or computer in the initial page of the wizard, the next page of the wizard will allow you to specify an alternate location for the object or objects specified. Changing the location of the object will let you test what changes would occur if you moved the object to a different location in the directory. If you only select containers in the initial page, this page will not display.

The next page of the wizard identifies the security groups for the user object selected. If a specific user is selected in the first page of the wizard, the security groups for that user are displayed. If a user container is specified, the Authenticated Users and Everyone groups are listed as defaults. You can add user groups to the list or remove groups from the list to see what changes will occur as a result.

The next page of the wizard identifies the security groups for the computer object selected. As with the user selection in the previous page, you can specify which security groups to use when running the query.

The next options page of the wizard allows you to select the Windows Management Instrumentation (WMI) filters to use on the user object or container in the query. The default selection is for all linked WMI filters, or you can select only specific WMI filters.

The last options page of the wizard selects the WMI filters for the computer object or container. As on the previous page, you can accept the default selection of all WMI filters, or you can specify which filters to use.

After you complete all the pages of the wizard, or if you select the option to skip the remaining information pages, a summary page will display the options that will be used when running the query. Figure 6.3 shows the summary page and the information specified for a sample query. In this window, you can choose to gather extended error information or select a different DC to process the simulation. Clicking **Next** will start the query based on the information listed in this page.

Figure 6.3 Reviewing the Settings of the RSoP Query Prior to Execution

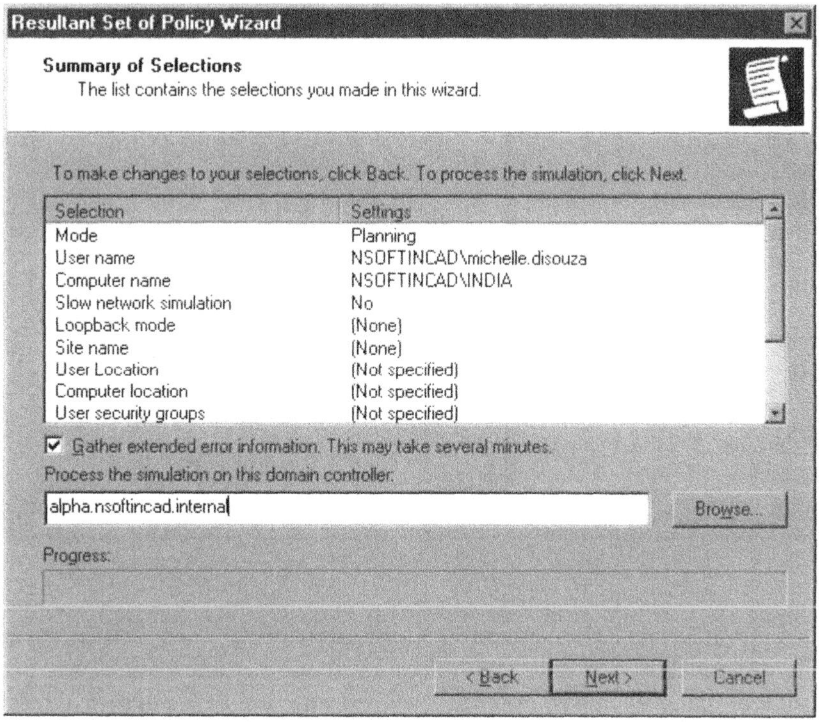

When the query has completed (which might take several minutes depending on the size and configuration of your environment), the wizard's finish page will display. Clicking **Finish** will close the wizard and return you to the MMC to review the RSoP report.

Reviewing RSoP Results

The results of the RSoP query displayed in the MMC will look similar to the Group Policy Object Editor window, with a few important differences. Figure 6.4 shows the RSoP results window in the MMC. This particular query was run on the user *michelle.disouza* and the *Computers* container. When looking at the policy settings in the window, you only see the policies that will be in effect for the user when logged on to a computer in that particular container. You will also only be able to view the policy settings in this interface. You will not be able to change any policy.

Figure 6.4 Reviewing the RSoP Planning Results

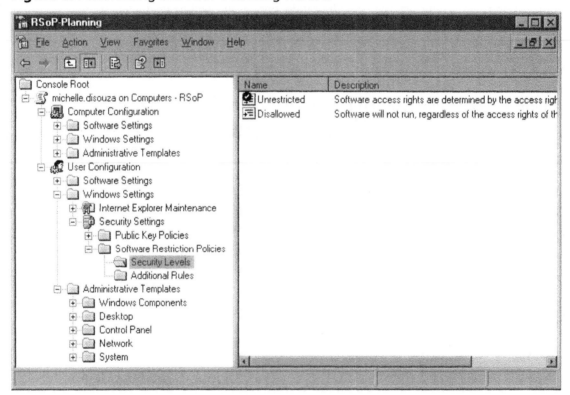

When you right-click either the **Computer Configuration** or **User Configuration** node in the tree and select **Properties**, you will find information about the policies that were processed to generate the results found in the report. You can select to view all GPOs and their filtering status to see which GPOs were processed and which were not, and why not if they were not. You can display revision information to see how many times a particular GPO has been modified, and you can display scope information that tells where the GPO resides. If you click the **Security** button, you can see the security permissions set for the GPO.

If you open a policy setting, you can view the properties of that policy setting. Figure 6.5 shows the properties of the setting selected in Figure 6.4. As shown in the figure, the option to set this particular setting as default is grayed out, because no changes can be made in this interface. If you click on the **Precedence** tab, you will see a list of GPOs where this particular policy is set, including the order in which this policy was processed.

Figure 6.5 Viewing the Properties of a Policy Setting in the RSoP Report

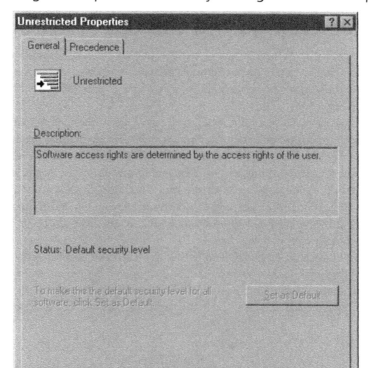

You can run an additional query on a different set of user and computer objects from this interface by right-clicking on the RSoP result object in the left pane, **michelle.disouza on Computers – RSoP** in this instance, and selecting **Change Query**. If you go in and make group policy changes that would impact the results of the query and want to see how those changes actually affect the system, you can right-click the RSoP result object and select **Refresh Query**. This second option will rerun the query with the same options.

TIP

By using the RSoP, you can cut down on the number of redundant policies that are being applied in your environment. The RSoP can also be used as a troubleshooting tool to determine if you do have contradictory policies in place.

Strategy for Configuring the User Environment

When setting group policy at the user level, you are creating an environment that will follow the user around the network. No matter what computer the user logs on to, the group policy settings inherited by that user will apply. This section covers some of the "shoulds" and "should nots" related to the user environment.

One policy setting that will follow the user around no matter where he or she logs on is *roaming profiles*. Enabling roaming profiles for a user community will store all the user settings on a server rather than on the local computers. When a user logs on, all of his or her profile settings (Desktop items, My Documents, Registry settings, etc.) will be pulled off the server, ensuring that the user has the same environment on each computer he or she uses. This approach has many advantages, but it has disadvantages as well. Some profile settings are hardware-dependent, and if the computers used by the user do not have the same hardware, the user could encounter difficulty upon logon (video cards can be especially problematic in this regard).

The vast majority of other group policy settings that you can apply to users in the directory have little chance of causing conflict with other settings on the local computer. Logon and logoff scripts, application settings, folder redirection, and environment configurations can help to standardize the user's computing experience across multiple machines, which can, in turn, ease the support burden on your IT staff.

Are You Owned?

Letting That One Client Through: Configuring GPOs in Mixed Environments

Many organizations still use multiple operating systems on client machines. It should be noted that Microsoft's WMI features have only begun to mature, and client support for WMI only exists on Windows XP. Therefore, note that when configuring WMI filters for GPOs, Windows 2000 and earlier clients will ignore the WMI filter and the GPO will always apply regardless.

Strategy for Configuring the Computer Environment

When setting policy for the computer environment, the settings applied will impact every user who logs on to the computer. Unlike user settings, there are two places where computer policy is applied. The first is the local policy set at the computer each time it boots. These settings are applied first, and any subsequent policy that conflicts with the local settings will override the local settings. However, computer policy can also be set in Active Directory. These settings follow the same rules as user settings in terms of priority order. Any computer policies set at the site level will be overwritten by additional policy settings at the domain or OU level when the settings conflict.

One case where computer policy overrides user policy is when a GPO containing computer settings is configured to operate in *loopback mode*. Loopback mode is a special setting that is only used in cases where a very specific set of policies needs to be applied in a controlled environment. Loopback mode allows administrators to apply group policy based on the computer at which the user is logging on. In other words, this setting is used if a particular user should have different policies applied, depending on where he or she logs on. When loopback processing is enabled, the computer policies set for the system override any user policy settings applied during logon.

Loopback operates in two modes—*replace* and *merge*. When loopback is enabled, one of these two modes must be selected. Replace mode will eradicate any user policy settings applied at logon and only retain the computer policy settings. Merge mode will allow user settings that do not conflict with computer settings to be applied. If there is a conflict between the two, the computer settings override the user settings.

The philosophy of "less is more" applies directly to the approach for setting computer policy in the domain. In general, you should try to have only one set of policies apply to computers. If you do have cases where you need different policy settings to apply to different sets of computers within the organization, set up the separate policy objects, but restrict access to those objects so that only the systems that need to be affected by the object will process the settings.

Run an RSoP Planning Query

This following procedure walks you through the process of generating an RSoP planning report based on changing a user object from one OU to another. For this example, we will use the user object for Robert Smith, which exists in the Marketing OU, and build an RSoP report showing the policy settings that would apply to the object if it were moved into the Accounting OU. As long as you have appropriate permissions to run an RSoP query on a system, you should be able to emulate the steps in this example on a system to which you have access, as you will not be changing any settings on the system in the process.

1. Open an MMC window and load the RSoP snap-in (see the steps outlined earlier in this section if needed).

2. Right-click the **Resultant Set of Policy** object in the console tree, and select **Generate RSoP Data**.

3. In the Resultant Set of Policy Wizard, click **Next**.

4. Select the **Planning Mode** option button, and click **Next**.

5. In the **User and Computer Selection** window, select the **User** option button, and click the **Browse** button in the **User information** frame.

6. In the **Select User** dialog box, choose a user object and click **OK**.

7. In the **User and Computer Selection** window, click the **Computer** option button, and click the **Browse** button in the **Computer information** frame.

8. In the **Select Computer** dialog box, choose a computer object and click **OK**.

9. The **User and Computer Selection** window should now appear as in Figure 6.6. Click Next.

Figure 6.6 Specifying the User and Computer Objects in the RSoP Wizard

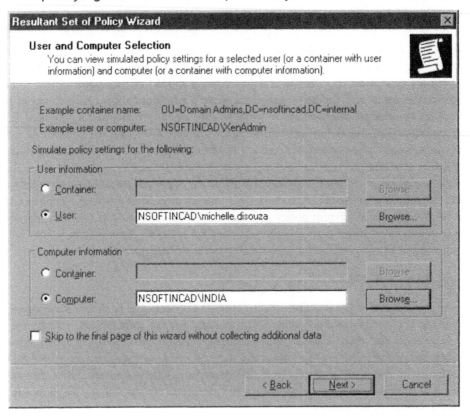

10. In the **Advanced Simulation Options** page, select the appropriate site from the **Site** drop-down list, shown in Figure 6.7, and click **Next**.

Figure 6.7 Specifying the User and Computer Objects in the RSoP Wizard

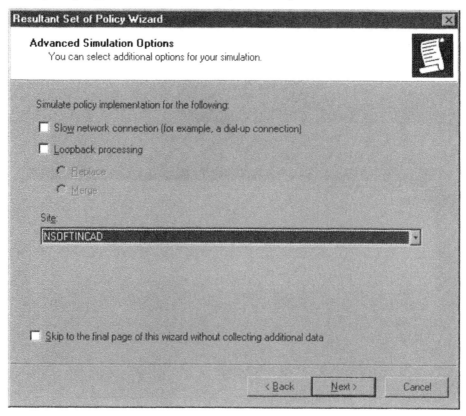

11. In the **Alternate Active Directory Paths** page, change the location for the user and computer objects. When the new locations have been selected, click **Next**.

12. In the **User Security Groups** page, change the security groups to match those of the new location. Select the groups that the user would no longer belong to, and click **Remove**.

13. To add new security groups to the query, click the **Add** button and select the appropriate groups. Click **Next**.

14. In the **Computer Security Groups** page, you can leave the security group setting as it is, or you can change group assignments by using the **Add** and **Remove** buttons. Figure 6.8 shows the settings used for this query. When complete, click **Next**.

Figure 6.8 Selecting Computer Security Group Settings

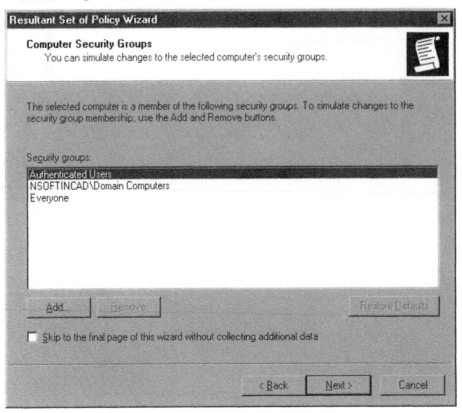

15. In the **WMI Filters for Users** page, select the **All linked filters** option button to include all WMI filters in the query, as shown in Figure 6.9, or select the **Only these filters** option button to specify which filters to use. When finished, click **Next**.

Figure 6.9 Selecting WMI Filters for Users

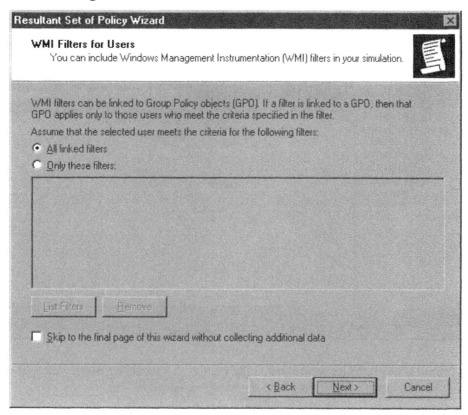

16. In the WMI Filters for Computers page, select the **All linked filters** option button to include all WMI filters in the query, or select the **Only these filters** option button to specify which filters to use. When finished, click **Next**.

17. Review the selections made in the Summary of Selections page, and click **Next** to start the query.

18. When the query has completed, click the **Finish** button to close the wizard and view the RSoP report, shown in Figure 6.10.

Figure 6.10 Viewing the RSoP Report

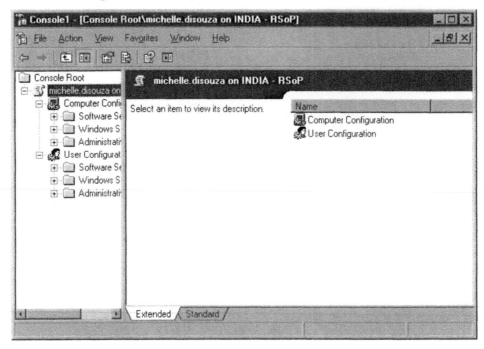

19. Browse through the report looking at the policies that would be enabled for user michelle. disouza on computer INDIA. Close the MMC when done.

Applying Group Policy Best Practices

If you have been reading straight through this chapter, you've seen that there are a vast number of ways that group policy can be implemented in an Active Directory environment. How should you approach a group policy implementation in your environment? This section covers some of the best practices related to implementing group policy.

- **The fewer, the better** Keep the number of policies defined as small as possible. Why fewer? Not so much for processing issues, but rather for administrative overhead. A smaller number of policy objects means fewer places for you to look for problems or conflicts when troubleshooting group policy issues.

- **Avoid conflicting policies whenever possible** Although you can set up a lower-level policy to override a higher-level one, you should avoid doing this unless necessary. Again, simplicity should be the rule.

- **Filter out unnecessary settings** If you set up a policy object that only contains user policy settings, set the properties on the object so that only the user configuration portion is processed. This will help cut down on unnecessary processing time.

- **Avoid nonstandard group policy processing whenever possible** Even though you can use Block Policy Inheritance, No Override, and loopback processing options, you should only do so for special cases. Because each of these options alters the standard way in which policy is applied, they can cause confusion when attempting to troubleshoot policy problems.

■ **Keep policy objects contained within the domain** It is possible to link a container to a GPO that resides in another domain, but it is unwise to do so. Pulling a GPO from a different domain slows the processing of policy settings at logon time.

■ **Use WMI filters sparingly** This suggestion relates to processing time. The more WMI filters there are to process, the longer it takes to apply policy at logon.

■ **Keep policy object names unique** If you name each policy object to describe its function, this should not be a difficult practice to adopt. Even though the directory can support multiple GPOs with the same name, it could get very, very confusing for you when trying to troubleshoot a policy problem.

■ **Link policies to a container only once** You can link the same GPO to a container more than once, but you shouldn't. The system will attempt to process each policy linked to a container, and even if there are different options set on each instance of the policy link, it can still yield unexpected results.

Configuring Group Policy with the Group Policy Management Console

Group Policy is a feature used in Windows to enhance and control users' desktops and computers. It is enabled by the Windows Active Directory Service and can also be used with XenApp servers installed as member servers. The procedures for using group policies are the same on either platform, so any procedures we discuss in this section can be used in any configuration of the two.

Group Policy was designed and is used by administrators to help centralize administration of user desktop configurations, reduce user support requirements, and enhance the security of network systems. It handles these tasks by allowing the administrator(s) to customize and control users' access to registry-based settings, security settings, and software installation and maintenance. They can automate many tasks using logon, logoff, startup, and shutdown scripts, and OS installation and Internet Explorer maintenance. User data files and folders can be redirected from the user's hard drive to network drives, where backups can be performed or preconfigured desktop displays can be pushed to new users. All these options are available, with different levels of access and control provided to different users and locations, depending on the requirements. This flexibility enables programmers to have virtually complete access to their desktops and all kinds of applications, while restricting data entry staff to only the few applications they need to perform their job.

The features and controls provided by Group Policy become even more valuable to XenApp administrators when you realize that your server becomes the users' desktop machines when they are using a thin client, Terminal Services client, or ICA client connection. How many times have your users broken their desktop machines through ignorance or misuse? We don't really want them doing that to our servers, do we? This is where group policies come into play.

We do not try to go into a detailed discussion of all the finer aspects and programming issues of Group Policy in this chapter. That topic could make up an entire book in itself. Instead, we focus on how to get started with group policies, how they can improve the user's experience with XenApp, and how they can benefit you, the XenApp administrator. From there, you should be able to develop your own policies and apply them in a manner consistent with your environment.

NOTE

The Group Policy Management Console installation file, **gpmc.msi** can be downloaded from the Microsoft download site www.microsoft.com/downloads free of charge.

Features of the GPMC

As in Windows 2000, Windows Server 2003 Group Policy allows an administrator to configure groups of computers or users in a domain, site, or OU. Administrators would typically have read and write access to the domain system volume (Sysvol) folder to make configuration changes to user and computer accounts in a domain. Administrators use a combination of Active Directory administration tools, the Windows Server 2003 Group Policy Management Console (GPMC), and the Group Policy Object Editor to deploy and manage group policy. The GPMC includes the following features:

- **Integrated MMC Snap-In** The new MMC snap-in provides a view of an enterprise from a policy management perspective. The user interface displays GPOs and associated links in a way that makes more sense to the administrator. All administrative features such as user and computer administration, site and OU administration are integrated into the new console so we no longer have to switch to other consoles to perform the various operations involved in Windows domain management.

- **GPMC Reporting** A rich HTML-based reporting environment for GPOs and their policy settings is included.

- **Group Policy Results and Modeling** This feature allows administrators to readily see Resultant Set of Policy (RSoP) data. RSoP makes it easy for an administrator to determine the resulting set of policies for a given user or computer in both actual and "what-if" scenarios. In the GPMC, Group Policy Results displays the result of a query made directly against a computer/user. Group Policy Modeling enables what-if simulation of user/computer scenarios and can be an important tool when planning changes to a Group Policy implementation. Group Policy Modeling requires a Windows Server 2003 domain controller.

- **Support for Backup, Staging, and Testing Group Policy Objects** Using this feature, administrators can maintain GPO templates—versions of GPOs for different configurations, such as highly managed desktops, laptops, Terminal Services on Windows Server 2003, and so on. Administrators can use backup, copying, and importing features with GPOs to deploy configurations rapidly throughout an organization.

- **Enhanced User Interface in the Group Policy Object Editor** Policy settings are more easily understood, managed, and verified with Web-view integration in the Group

Policy Object Editor. Clicking a policy displays text that explains its function. The operating systems that support the policy are displayed via a new **Supported On** tag.

- **Scriptable Interfaces** Operations such as backup, restore, import, copy, and reporting on GPOs can be performed via Windows scripts, which lets administrators customize and automate management. However, don't get too happy; it is not yet possible to script individual policy settings within a GPO using the scriptable interfaces.

- **Support for Cross-Forest Trusts** Administrators can manage group policy for multiple domains and sites within a given forest, all in a simplified user interface with drag-and-drop support. Cross-forest trust enables administrators to manage group policy across multiple forests from one console.

The Group Policy Management Console provides a more complete view of the operating system, computer, software, and user configurations across a domain, OU, or site. The GPMC, shown in Figure 6.11, includes all the functionality of the following administration tools in one management console:

- Active Directory Users and Computers

- Active Directory Sites and Services

- Resultant Set of Policy MMC snap-in

- ACL Editor

- Delegation Wizard

Figure 6.11 The GPMC

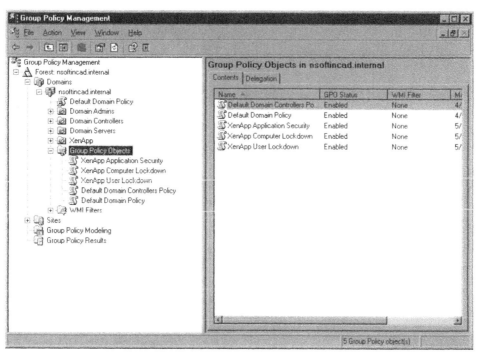

Installing the GPMC

The GPMC is a downloadable product from the Microsoft Downloads Web site. It does not come on the Windows Server 2003 CD. To install the GPMC:

1. Double-click the **gpmc.msi** package, and click **Next** (Figure 6.12).

Figure 6.12 GPMC Installation

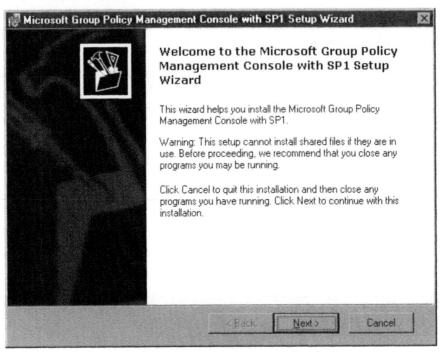

2. Agree to the End User License Agreement (EULA), and click **Next** (Figure 6.13).

Figure 6.13 Policy Management Console License Agreement

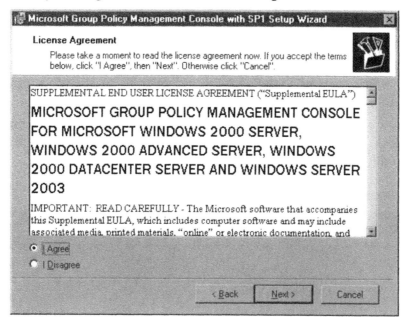

3. Click **Finish** to complete the installation (Figure 6.14).

Figure 6.14 Group Policy Finish

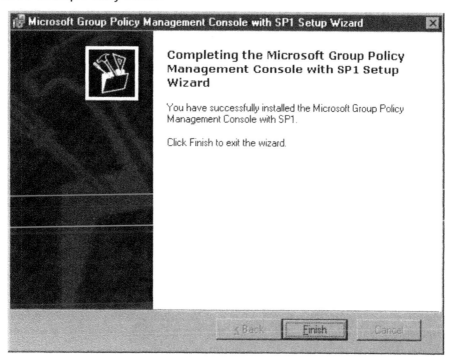

Upon completion of the installation, the Group Policy tab that appeared on the Property pages of sites, domains, and OUs in the Active Directory snap-ins is updated to provide a direct link to GPMC. The functionality that previously existed on the original Group Policy tab is no longer available, since all functionality for managing Group Policy is available through GPMC.

To open the GPMC snap-in directly, use either of the following methods:

■ Click the **Group Policy Management** shortcut in the **Administrative Tools** folder on the Start menu or in the Control Panel (Figure 6.15).

■ Create a custom MMC console. Click **Start**, **Run**, type **MMC**, and click **OK**. Point to **File**, click **Add/Remove Snap-in**, click **Add**, highlight **Group Policy Management**, click **Add**, click **Close**, and then click **OK**.

Figure 6.15 Accessing the GPMC

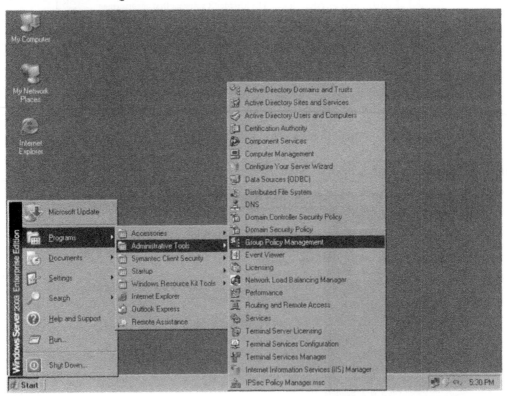

To repair or remove GPMC, use **Add or Remove Programs** in Control Panel. Alternatively, run the gpmc.msi package, select the appropriate option, and click **Finish**.

Using the GPMC

As mentioned previously, the GPMC takes the place of the administration tools usually used to manage computers and users in a Windows Server 2003 domain. Administrator can use the GPMC for the same tasks that previously required a combination of tools to perform.

Now, let's turn our attention to the components (referred to as *nodes*) and their relevance to managing XenApp in a Windows 2003 Terminal Services environment (Figure 6.16).

Figure 6.16 GPMC Components

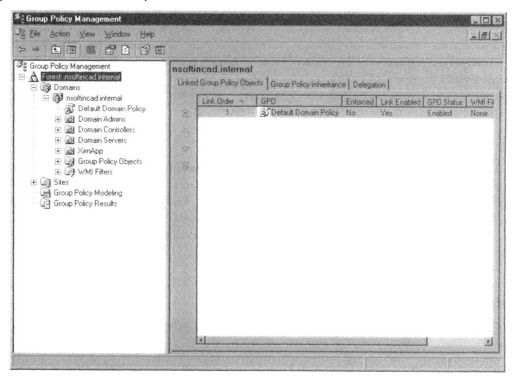

The Domains Node

The Domains node contains all the domains within an Active Directory forest. Domains nodes are identified by their DNS domain names. Administrators can choose which domains to display by right-clicking the Domains node and selecting the **Show Domains** menu option. Group policies that are meant to affect individual domains should be created at this level. Domain user accounts with Terminal Services access are frequently used to grant access to specific applications in a XenApp environment. Group policies that affect domains and the inheritance of these policies play an important part in configuring the environment appropriately.

The Sites Node

The Sites node contains all the sites within an Active Directory forest. As with domains, administrators can choose the sites they see by right-clicking the node and selecting the **Show Sites** menu option. No sites are displayed by default. Group policies intended to affect individual sites should be created here.

The Group Policy Modeling Node

This node is a new and powerful management feature that allows administrators to simulate policy settings applied to users and computers before actually applying the policies. This "what if" tool makes it possible to see via the **Resultant Set of Policy (RSoP)—Planning Mode**, a new feature in Windows Server 2003, what effect a policy or policies would have on any users and computers in a forest. This node only works if at least one domain controller is a Windows Server 2003 server, as the service that actually performs the simulation only exists on Windows Server 2003 domain controllers. Each policy simulation is displayed as a subnode of the Group Policy Modeling node.

Policy modeling comes in handy when first designing a XenApp infrastructure or when making changes to security settings that may affect access to applications. The ability to try the policies first, before implementing them, helps the administrator to avoid crucial mistakes. For example, in designing policies for remote XenApp users as opposed to local users, an administrator may need to make provisions for bandwidth differences or security levels between the two groups. Modeling allows the administrator to see what settings would work.

The Group Policy Results Node

Instead of showing you the **Resultant Set of Policy** for a simulation, the Group Policy Results node allows you to see the effect of policies that have actually been applied to computer and users accounts in a forest (referred to as the RSoP—Logging Mode). The results here are obtained via queries performed on the user or computer account and are displayed as subnodes in the GPMC (Figure 6.17). Group Policy Results information can only be obtained from computers running Windows XP or Windows Server 2003.

Figure 6.17 Group Policy Results

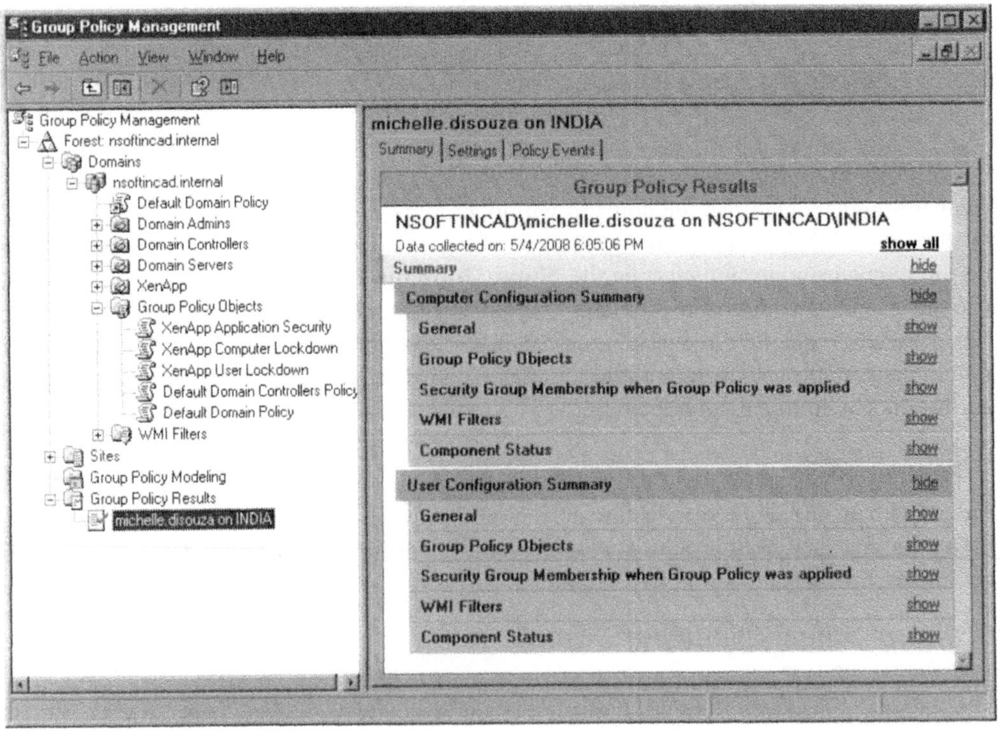

As with Group Policy Modeling, the ability to see the effect of a policy or set of policies provides administrators a roadmap of what's going on and what policy affects what user or computer in what way. For example, in troubleshooting connectivity problems, the RSoP would help to point an administrator in the right direction to identify the problem and come up with a viable solution.

Creating and Editing Group Policy Objects with the GPMC

The main purpose of the GPMC is to allow administrators to more easily create, implement, and manage GPOs in an Active Directory forest. The process of creating a GPO and applying it to a set of users or computers is called "scoping the GPO." Effectively scoping a GPO depends on three factors:

- The domain, site, or OU where the GPO is created and linked
- The security filtering configured on the GPO
- The Windows Management Instrumentation filter configured on the GPO

Let's follow the process of creating and applying a GPO: Right-click a domain or OU displayed in the GPMC and select **Create and Link a GPO Here...**(Figure 6.18). It's that simple!

Figure 6.18 Creating a GPO

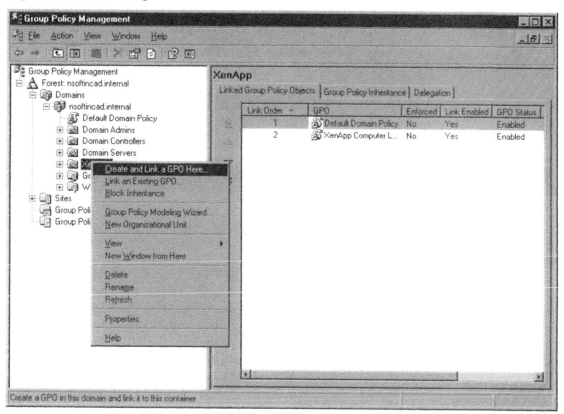

After a GPO is created and linked to a site, domain, or OU, it is referred to as the GPO's Scope of Management (SOM). When a GPO is created, it has no settings defined. GPOs are configured by using the Group Policy Object Editor. The GPO Editor can be accessed by right-clicking a GPO and selecting **Edit**. Figure 6.19 shows the details and settings that can be configured in a GPO.

Figure 6.19 Editing a GPO

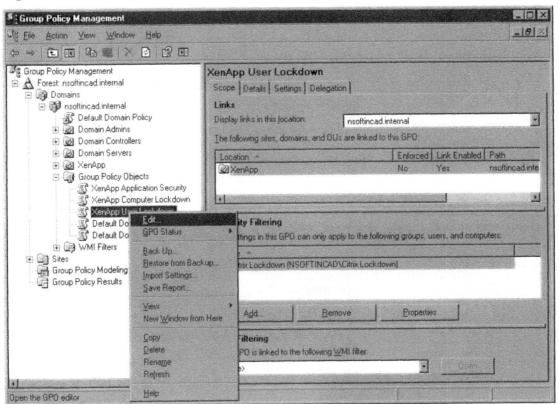

Once the GPO is created, configured, and linked to a SOM (a domain, site, or OU), it can be tweaked to have the desired effect on the SOM. This can be accomplished either by security filtering or WMI filtering, or a combination of both.

Security filtering involves setting the permissions on a GPO for a user, a user group, or a computer. The Windows Authenticated Users group—which usually contains all domain users and computers—has the default permissions of Read and Apply Group Policy for any GPO that is created and linked to the SOM they are in. However, users, groups, or computers that are normally a part of the Authenticated Users group can be excluded from the effects of a GPO by removing those permissions from them. Figure 6.20 shows the Security filter of an OU GPO.

Figure 6.20 Security Filter on a GPO

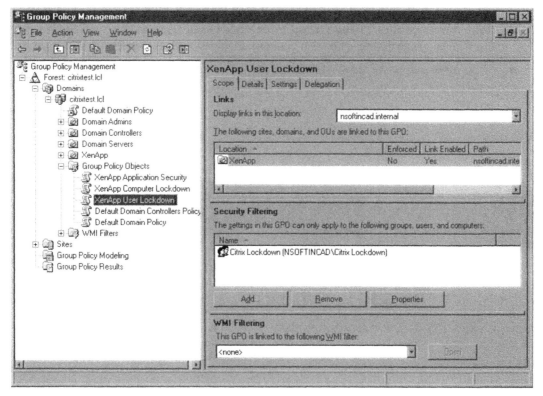

WMI filtering, however, involves using the attributes of a computer to determine application of the GPO. WMI filters are queries that search for specific attributes of a computer (hard disk space, memory, operating system version, etc.). The query information is returned as true or false responses for particular properties of the target computers. It is important to note that a WMI filter is a separate object from a GPO in Active Directory. They can be linked, however, and this is where filtering comes in. If an administrator attempts to apply a GPO that is linked to a WMI filter, the queries contained in the filter are run. If the queries return true responses, the GPO is successfully applied. If not, the GPO has no effect on the computer.

Policy Design Considerations

As alluded to in the preceding sidebar, not everything configured in a Windows Server 2003 infrastructure works for every client. Many of the features of Windows Server 2003 Group Policy are not compatible with Windows 2000 and earlier clients. A compromise in design of a XenApp infrastructure using Windows Server 2003 that supports clients running various versions of Windows must be reached that has the most backward compatibility possible. The following tips will be useful in planning a design:

- **Create a test group that accurately represents your client base.** This give you the ability to test your deployment as any good IT professional would.

- **Take full advantage of the Group Policy Modeling feature.** The ability to see what can happen beforehand is a gift that administrators seldom have—use it wisely.

- **If possible, separate down-level clients from up-to-date clients.** Creating a separate policy for each group may bridge the gap and give you the control and security you need.

Tools & Traps...

Making Your Life Easier when Configuring GPOs

It is a good practice to separate distinct functional groups in Active Directory into OUs. User accounts and computers should be in separate OUs. For example, Executive Management at your company should be in their own OU, separate from Engineering, and so on. Their computers should also be in their own OU. This allows for more granular control. You can apply or disable GPOs to specific groups and not have to worry about exceptions to the GPO. If you take the time to design a hierarchy that makes sense with regard to your business, managing and troubleshooting Active Directory and GPOs will be much less complex.

We have found that for a Citrix environment it is easier to have at least two distinct XenApp OUs. One for computer configuration and one for user configuration and to use these OUs specifically for your XenApp environment.

GPO Elements of Special Importance

Since we've familiarized ourselves with Group Policy and how to navigate within the GPMC, let us now look at some GPO elements of special importance to deploying and administering a XenApp environment.

So, we've built and configured our servers and set up a farm. How then do we get the Citrix client software to our end users without having to track each of them down and install the software? The answer is very simple. Use group policy to install the software on the end-users' machines when they log on to the domain. The second question arises: How do we accomplish that? The answer is Group Policy Software Installation (Figure 6.21).

Figure 6.21 Group Policy Software Installation Node

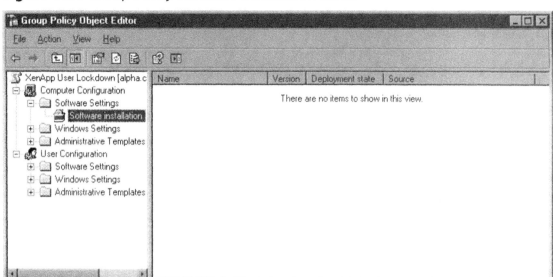

The Group Policy Software Installation node enables administrators to install and manage software across the enterprise. Administrators can specify the method of installation, the installation targets, and the parameters for the installation. Once an installation package has been created, the Winlogon service controls deployment of the application. Applications within the Group Policy Software Installation node can be managed in one of two modes: assigned or published. An assigned application is one that is installed when the computer starts up or when the user logs in to the domain. Once the application is installed, the end -user accesses the software and the installation is completed. A published application is one in which the application appears in the Add/Remove Program dialog box and the end user is able to install it from there. The Group Policy Software Installation node is reached by editing a GPO.

There are two Software Installation assignments, a per-computer assignment and a per-user assignment. The Software Installation node under the Computer Configuration GPO node is used to deploy software that is necessary for every computer in your enterprise. The software to be installed under this node is always installed in Assigned mode (Figure 6.22). Once a machine starts up on the domain, the software is installed and is available to any user that logs on to the machine. Assigned software can also be assigned to a specific end user so that when that person logs on to a computer, the software is installed even if the user logs on to different computers. The software installation follows the user. As with the computer assignment, the software installation isn't finalized until end-users launch the application.

Figure 6.22 The Software Installation Method Window

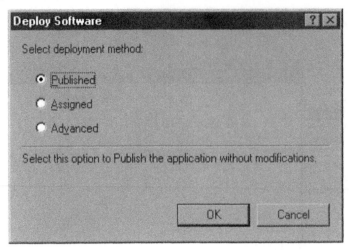

Published applications can only be installed for end users (Figure 6.23) in the User Configuration node. Published applications are meant to service the end users managed by a particular GPO. The users choose whether they want the application installed. When users log in to their computers, the published application is available for installation via the Add/Remove Programs window. The software becomes installed when the user selects to perform the installation in the Add/Remove Programs window, or opens a file that is native to the application such as a .doc file for Microsoft Word.

Figure 6.23 The Published Application Installation Method

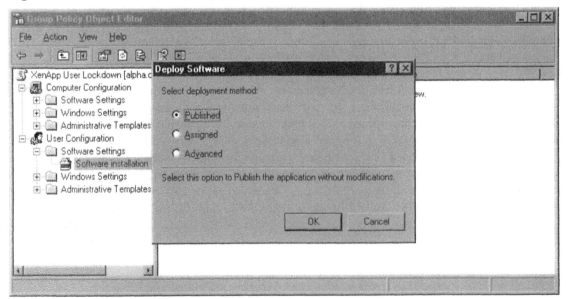

It is important for software installations of either kind to access installation packages that are located on a network share that is available to the intended target. Let us now look at creating an assigned and a published software installation.

Creating an Assigned Software Package Installation in the Computer Configuration Node

1. Right-click the **Software Installation node** under the **Computer Configuration node** and select **New Package** as shown in Figure 6.24.

Figure 6.24 Creating a New Installation Package

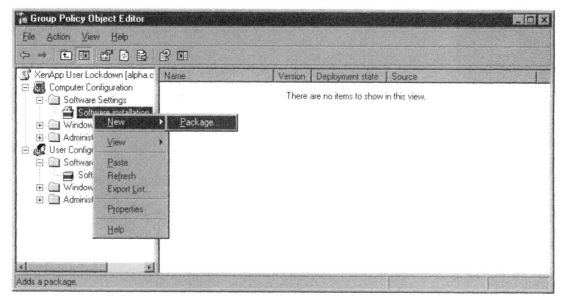

2. Browse to the network share in which the desired software installation package is stored and select the package as shown in Figure 6.25.

Figure 6.25 Selecting Installation Package

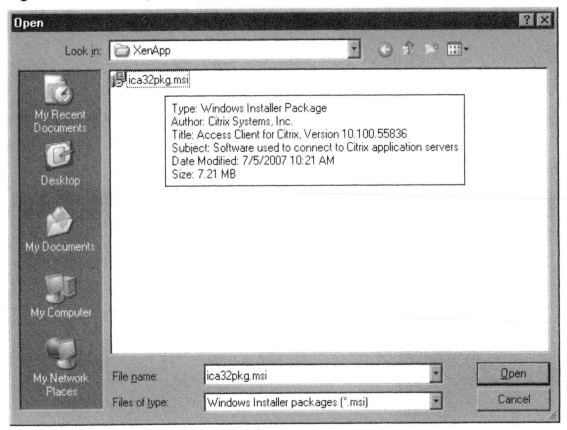

3.   Click **OK** on the **Deployment Method** window that appears.

4.   Click **OK** on the next window that displays the package properties to accept the defaults. A software installation package has been created. The same process is followed for the published software installation package

Configuring XenApp Policies

Now that we've seen what can be done to facilitate users and computers from a Windows standpoint, we are ready to delve into the added flexibility and robustness provided by XenApp for clients.

As in earlier Citrix versions, administrators are able to configure policies for users and user groups. XenApp allows creation and configuration of user and user group policies, and allows administrators to create and configure policies based on server groups, IP addresses, and client names.

At the heart of it, XenApp policies define connection settings. The capabilities provided by XenApp allow an administrator to define the policies for and servers, client machines, and IP addresses he wishes. A single policy can contain multiple rules that apply different settings to all of these entities in one shot.

Creating and Configuring Policies

Administrators can create policies and configure them to meet the needs of the users they support. Policies and the rules they contain can be made to support end users based on their geographic location, job function, and the method by which they connect to the network. XenApp policies can even be used cooperatively with Windows Group Policy to secure end-user connections via encryption and deny drive mapping, for example.

Since in most scenarios it usually makes sense to use uniform criteria in designing Windows and XenApp policies, the procedures used for creating a policy are:

- Creating the policy.

- Configuring the policy rules.

- Assigning the policy to user accounts, servers, or client machines.

- Prioritizing the policies.

To configure a policy:

1. Launch the Presentation Server console and locate the Policies node.
2. Right-click the **Policies** node and select **Create Policy**.
3. Type a name for the policy and click **OK**. You have just created a XenApp policy.

WARNING

An unconfigured policy does not turn the policy off, but defers it to a lower priority policy.

Once a policy is created, it must be configured and assigned to servers, users, or client machines. A policy is inactive unless its rules have been configured and it has been assigned to an object on your network. Policies take effect once a user logs in and remain in effect for the duration of the ICA session. We mentioned earlier that a policy can contain many rules. These rules determine what happens at the user, server, or client machine level once an ICA session has been established. Policy rules exist in three states: enabled, disabled, and not configured. By default, all policy rules are not configured. All rules that are not configured are ignored when users log on to the server, so a rule only has functionality when it is enabled or disabled. Disabled rules effectively turn off or turn on a feature or setting for a user. For example, if the rule **Turn off auto client** update is enabled, the Citrix ICA client software on a connecting client machine will not be updated to the newest available version when a user logs in to the XenApp farm using that client machine (Figure 6.26).

TIP

Policies are essentially rules that contain settings.

Creating a XenApp Policy

The steps to create a XenApp policy are as follows:

1.   Open the **Citrix Presentation Server Console** by selecting **Start** | **Programs** | **Citrix** | **Management Consoles** | **Presentation Server Console**.

2.   Right-click **Policies** and select **Create Policy**, as shown in Figure 6.26.

Figure 6.26 Creating a XenApp Policy

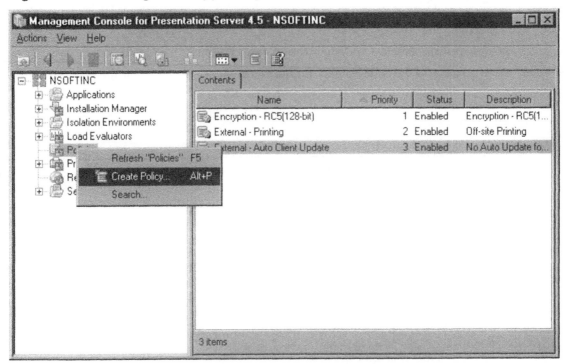

3.   Type an appropriate name for your policy, in this case we are going to create a policy for basic encryption so our policy name is **Encryption – Basic**. You may also want to add a description of the policy. If required by your configuration, you can configure your policy specific to a connection type, such as **WAN**, **Satellite**, or **Dial–up**. Click **OK** to save your policy, as shown in Figure 6.27.

Figure 6.27 Naming a Policy

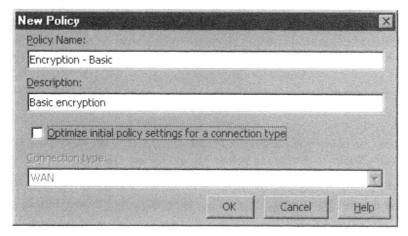

4. Now that your policy has been created, you must configure it. Double click on the name of the policy created in step 3. Following along with creating a basic encryption policy, select the **Security** folder, expand it, and then select **SecureICA encryption**, as shown in Figure 6.28.

Figure 6.28 Configuring an Enabled Policy

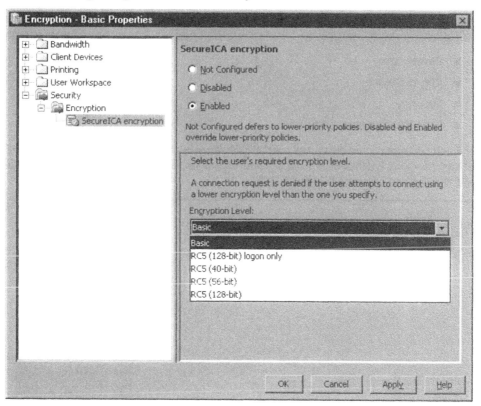

TIP

Enabled rules allow administrators to turn a feature on or off when someone logs in to the XenApp farm, and to configure the extent or support an activated feature provides.

5. To enable the policy, you must select **Enabled** and then select one of the available options, in this case **Basic**. To disable the policy, you must select **Disabled**.

6. Once you have made the appropriate changes to the XenApp policy, click **OK**.

7. To have the policy go into effect you must apply the policy (covered in the next section).

NOTE

It is important to note that entire policies can be disabled, and then none of the rules contained in the policy has any effect. Policy rules can be configured for all of the following main features in XenApp via the policy's Properties dialog window:

- Bandwidth
- Client Devices
- Security
- User Workspace

Each of these main features contains subnodes that allow configuration of options ranging from a user's audio and visual settings to the level of encryption used during the sessions (Figure 6.29).

Figure 6.29 A Main Policy Rule and Its Subnodes

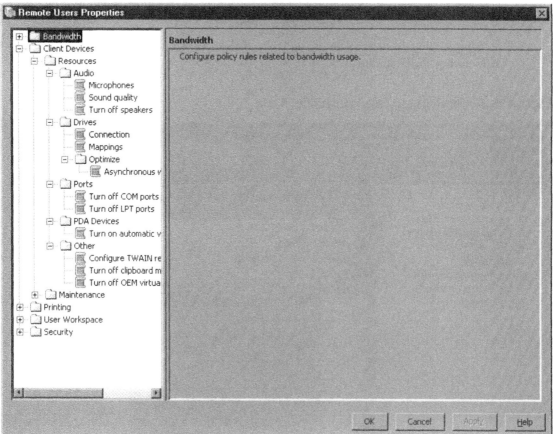

Applying Policy Filters

The next step in using XenApp policies is the assignment of a policy to a server, user or user group, or client machine. This is done by configuring a *policy filter*. A policy filter simply says that a certain policy is to be applied to client machines, users or certain user groups, servers they log in to, and the range of IP addresses from which they access the XenApp farm. For example, a policy can be created for remote users in Cleveland who connect from the 172.16.1.0 IP address range, while a second policy can be applied to remote users from Cleveland who connect from the 192.168.1.0 IP address range. Policies are not applied to any users, client machines, servers or groups by default when they are created. They must be applied to at least one object for the policy to take effect. The following steps demonstrate how to apply a policy to a user group, a server, an IP range, or specific client names.

1. Right-click the policy, or select the policy and click the **Actions** menu, and select **Apply this policy to** (Figure 6.30).

Figure 6.30 Applying a XenApp Policy Filter

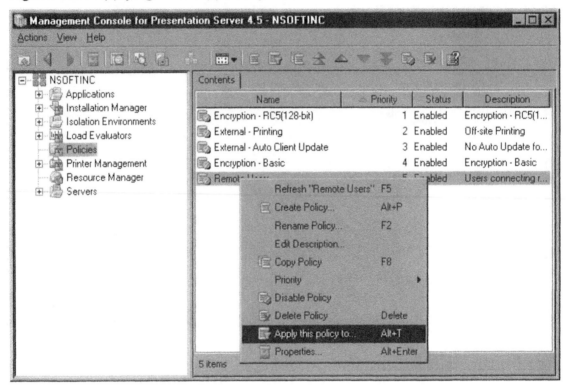

2. When the Policy Filters window appears, select **Client IP Address** to apply the policy to a specific IP or IP range (Figure 6.31), **Client Name** to apply the policy to specific client machines, **Servers** to apply a policy to a server or group of servers, or **Users** to apply the policy to a specific Windows domain user or user group.

Figure 6.31 Policy Filters

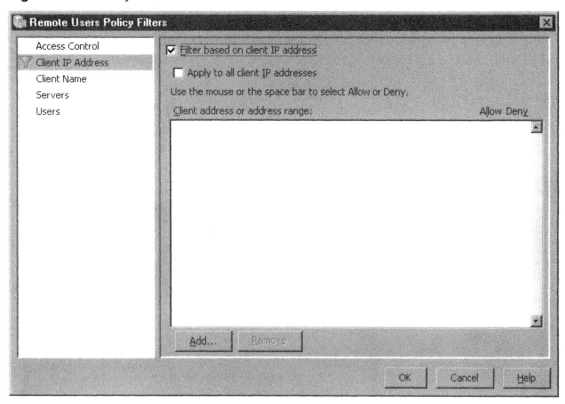

WARNING

There is no hierarchical grouping of XenApp policies – so naming conventions should be descriptive.

Policies can have exceptions. For example, you may wish that all employees except executives are never able to save data to their local hard drives. To accomplish this, you must first create and apply a policy that prevents mapping of local drives to all users. Then, another policy must be created that allows mapping of local drives. This policy is assigned to the Executives domain user group. You would then give this new policy precedence over the original policy. This is known as *prioritizing policies*.

Prioritizing policies sets the order of application or validity of one policy over another. When policy A has higher priority over policy B, policy A's rules are enforced on its target users, servers, or client machines. As mentioned previously, prioritizing policies is a great way to set up exceptions for special access to resources. All newly created policies have the lowest priority by default. A policy with a priority number of 1 has the highest priority. The larger the priority number, the lower the policy's priority. When a user logs in to a XenApp farm, the enabled policies that match that user's policy filter are evaluated. The highest priority policy is assessed and applied first, then the next highest policy, and so on. Policy rules that are configured as disabled take precedence over similarly ranked policies that have the same rule configured as enabled. To prioritize policies:

1. Locate the policies in the **Policies** node.

2. Right-click the policy you want to set priority for and select the **Priority** option.

3. If you want to assign the highest priority to the policy, select **Make Highest Priority**; if not, select **Increase Priority** to specify the priority you want to assign (Figure 6.32).

Figure 6.32 Setting Policy Priority

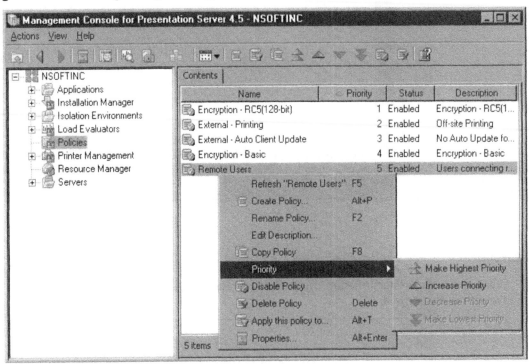

Using Policies to Make XenApp More Secure

It is extremely important after all the hard work has been done to be sure that the policies created in Active Directory and in XenApp work to support your decided security and functionality stance. Designing policies that conflict with each other could result in the thin-client infrastructure failing to get up and running. If your infrastructure is already supporting clients, new policies that conflict with your strategy could quickly bring things to a halt. That being said, here are some points to remember:

- Microsoft Group Policy settings can override XenApp policy rules for connections. If the Group Policy security settings are more restrictive than the XenApp policy rules, Microsoft wins!

- Good Active Directory design makes it easier to apply sound XenApp policy rules. This seems obvious, but still bears mentioning.

- Make sure that policy inheritance is appropriately set on each GPO. You don't want to end up thinking that a policy setting applies, only to find out the hard way that it doesn't.

- Make use of the XenApp policy search tool. This tool is XenApp's equivalent of the Microsoft GPMC RSoP tool. It will calculate the resultant effect of multiple policies on the objects to which they are applied.

- Collaborate, compare, and contrast. Match the Microsoft RSoP with the MetaFrame Resultant Policy view. Make sure that both XenApp and Windows policies address the issue the same way.

WARNING

When users log on to the server farm, XenApp policies are applied. Other Windows settings may over ride XenApp policies.

Windows Policies to Secure XenApp

These are policies that can be configured via Windows Group Policy Objects. When creating user accounts that will be accessing XenApp resources, you should place these user accounts into their own OU which you can then lock down with settings specific to Terminal Services and XenApp. You should do the same thing for your XenApp servers that are serving resources to users by placing them into their own OU. Our recommendation is to have a user OU labeled *XenApp Users* and a computer OU labeled *XenApp Servers*.

Computer Policies

These policies are only applied to computer objects that are placed into a "locked down" XenApp server OU. These settings are system wide, affecting all users. Table 6.2 provides a listing of the suggested computer settings for a secure XenApp server.

Table 6.2 Group Policies for Computer Configuration

Policy	Setting	Description
Windows Settings\Security Settings\Local Policies\ Security Options		
Devices: Restrict CD-ROM access to locally logged-on user only	Enabled	Allows only users who log on to the console of the XenApp Server access to the CD-ROM drive. It is recommended that you enable this policy to prevent users from remotely accessing programs or data on a CD-ROM.
Devices: Restrict floppy access to locally logged-on user only	Enabled	Allows only users who log on to the console of the XenApp Server access to the floppy disk drive. It is recommended that you to enable this policy to prevent users from remotely accessing programs or data on a floppy disk.
Interactive logon: Do not display last user name	Enabled	Policy prevents the displaying of the last logged on user.
Windows Settings\Security Settings\System Services		
Help and Support	Disabled	This policy disables Help and Support Center service. It prevents users from starting the new Windows Help and Support Center application. This policy does not disable the old help files (such as the *.chm) or Help in other applications. It is recommended that you disable this service to prevent users from starting other applications or viewing system information about the XenApp Server. Disabling this service might cause issues with other programs and services that depend on this service.
Administrative Templates\ Windows Components\ NetMeeting		
Disable remote Desktop Sharing	Enabled	

Continued

Table 6.2 Continued. Group Policies for Computer Configuration

Policy	Setting	Description
Administrative Templates\ Windows Components\ Application Compatibility		
Prevent access to 16-bit applications	Enabled	This policy prevents the MS DOS subsystem (ntvdm.exe) from running for the user. This setting affects the starting of all 16-bit applications in the operating system. By default, the MS DOS subsystem runs for all users. Many MS DOS applications are not Terminal Server friendly and can cause high CPU utilization due to constant polling of the keyboard. It is recommended that you enable this policy to prevent the 16-bit command interpreter, Command.com, from executing.
Administrative Templates\ Windows Components\ Terminal Services		
Restrict Terminal Services users to a single remote session	Enabled	This policy can prevent a single user from creating multiple sessions on the Terminal Server using a single user account.
Remove Disconnect option from Shut Down dialog box	Enabled	This policy removes the disconnect option from the Shut Down Windows dialog box. It does not prevent users from disconnecting session to the Terminal Server. Use this policy if you do not want users to easily disconnect from their session and you have not removed the Shut Down Windows dialog box.
Administrative Templates\ Windows Components\ Terminal Services\Client		
Do not allow passwords to be saved	Enabled	Controls whether passwords can be saved on this computer from Terminal Services clients. If you enable this setting the password saving checkbox in Terminal Services clients will be disabled and users will no longer be able to save passwords. When a user opens an RDP file using the Terminal Services client and saves his settings, any password that previously existed in the RDP file will be deleted. If you disable this setting or leave it not configured, the user will be able to save passwords using the Terminal Services client.

Continued

Table 6.2 Continued. Group Policies for Computer Configuration

Policy	Setting	Description
Administrative Templates\ Windows Components\ Terminal Services\Client/ Server data redirection		
Do not allow drive redirection	Enabled	By default, Terminal Server maps client drives automatically upon connection. It is recommended that you enable this policy to prevent users from having easy access to applications on their local computer.
Administrative Templates\ Windows Components\ Terminal Services\ Encryption and Security		
Set client encryption level	See Description	Specifies whether to enforce an encryption level for all data sent between the client and the server during the Terminal Services session. If the status is set to Enabled, encryption for all connections to the server is set to the level you specify. The following encryption levels are available. High: All data sent between the client and the server is protected by encryption based on the server's maximum key strength. Clients that do not support this level of encryption cannot connect. Client compatible: All data sent between the client and the server is protected by encryption based on the maximum key strength supported by the client. Low: All data sent from the client to the server is protected by encryption based on the maximum key strength supported by the client. If the status is set to Disabled or Not Configured, the encryption level is not enforced through Group Policy. However, administrators can set the encryption level on the server using the Terminal Services Configuration tool.

Continued

Table 6.2 Continued. Group Policies for Computer Configuration

Policy	Setting	Description
Administrative Templates\ Windows Components\ Terminal Services\Encryption and Security\RPC Security Policy		
Secure Server (Require Security)	Enabled	Specifies whether a Terminal Server requires secure RPC communication with all clients or allows unsecured communication. You can use this setting to strengthen the security of RPC communication with clients by allowing only authenticated and encrypted requests. If the status is set to Enabled, the Terminal Server accepts requests from RPC clients that support secure requests, and does not allow unsecured communication with untrusted clients. If the status is set to Disabled, the Terminal Server always requests security for all RPC traffic. However, unsecured communication is allowed for RPC clients that do not respond to the request. If the status is set to Not Configured, unsecured communication is allowed. Note: The RPC interface is used for administering and configuring Terminal Services.
Administrative Templates\ Windows Components\ Terminal Services\Sessions		
Set time limit for disconnected sessions	Enabled	By default, Terminal Server allows users to disconnect from a session and keep all of their applications active for an unlimited amount of time. This policy specifies a time limit for disconnected Terminal Server sessions to remain active. Use this policy if you do not want disconnected sessions to remain active for a long time on the Terminal Server.

Continued

www.syngress.com

Table 6.2 Continued. Group Policies for Computer Configuration

Policy	Setting	Description
Administrative Templates\ Windows Components\ Terminal Services\ Temporary Folders		
Do not use temp folders per session Properties	Enabled	Specifies whether to prevent Terminal Services from creating session-specific temporary folders. You can use this setting to disable the creation of separate temporary folders on a remote computer for each session. By default, Terminal Services creates a separate temporary folder for each active session that a user maintains on a remote computer. Unless otherwise specified, these temporary folders are in %USERPROFILE%\Local Settings\Temp\ <sessionID>. If the status is set to Enabled, per-session temporary folders are not created. Instead, users' temporary files are stored in a common Temp directory for each user on the server (by default, %USERPROFILE%\Local Settings\Temp). If the status is set to Disabled, per-session temporary folders are always created, even if the administrator specifies otherwise in the Terminal Services Configuration tool. If the status is set to Not Configured, per-session temporary folders are created unless otherwise specified by the server administrator.
Administrative Templates\ Windows Components\ Windows Installer		
Disable Microsoft Windows Installer	Enabled - Always	If this is set for non-managed applications only, the Windows Installer still functions for applications that are published or assigned by means of group policies. If this is set to Always, Windows Installer is completely disabled. This may be beneficial if some published or assigned applications are not wanted on Terminal Server. Disabling Windows Installer does not prevent installation of applications by means of other setup programs or methods. It is recommended that applications be installed and configured prior to enabling this policy. After the policy is enabled, administrators cannot install applications that use Windows Installer.

Continued

Table 6.2 Continued. Group Policies for Computer Configuration

Policy	Setting	Description
Administrative Templates\ System\Group Policy		
User Group Policy loopback processing mode	Enabled	If the Terminal Server computer object is placed in the locked down OU, and the user account is not, loopback processing applies the restrictive user configuration policies to all users on the Terminal Server. If this policy is enabled, all users, including administrators, logging on to the Terminal Server are affected by the restrictive user configuration policies, regardless of where the user account is located. Two modes are available. Merge mode first applies to the user's own GPO, then to the locked down policy. The lockdown policy takes precedence over the user's GPO. Replace mode just uses the locked down policy and not the user's own GPO. This policy is intended for restrictions based on computers instead of the user account.
If this policy is disabled, and the Terminal Server computer object is placed in the locked down OU, only the computer configuration policies is applied to the Terminal Server. Each user account must be placed into the OU to have user configuration restriction placed on that user.		

Continued

Table 6.2 Continued. Group Policies for Computer Configuration

Policy	Setting	Description
Administrative Templates\ System\User Profiles		
Delete cached copies of roaming profiles	Enabled	Determines whether the system saves a copy of a user's roaming profile on the local computer's hard drive when the user logs off. This setting, and related settings in this folder, together describe a strategy for managing user profiles residing on remote servers. In particular, they tell the system how to respond when a remote profile is slow to load. Roaming profiles reside on a network server. By default, when users with roaming profiles log off, the system also saves a copy of their roaming profile on the hard drive of the computer they are using in case the server that stores the roaming profile is unavailable when the user logs on again. The local copy is also used when the remote copy of the roaming user profile is slow to load. If you enable this setting, any local copies of the user's roaming profile are deleted when the user logs off. The roaming profile still remains on the network server that stores it. Important: Do not enable this setting if you are using the slow link detection feature of Windows 2000 Professional and Windows XP Professional. To respond to a slow link, the system requires a local copy of the user's roaming profile.

User Policies

These policies are only applied to user accounts that are placed into a "locked down" XenApp user OU. If loopback processing is used, all user accounts that log on to computers that are in the locked down OU also have these restriction applied. Table 6.3 provides a listing of the suggested user settings for a secure XenApp server.

Notes from the Underground...

Don't Give a User Access to Something That They Do Not Need!

In many Citrix environments, we have seen that administrators are not fully aware of the numerous ways in which a user can gain access to parts of a XenApp server that they should not have access. Specifically, think about what a user could potentially do by just having access to a command prompt on one of your XenApp servers. By default without any sort of lockdown, a user could execute a published application as simple as Notepad and by executing the Help feature, could then use the option of Jump to URL and execute any number of executables on the XenApp server.

Table 6.3 Group Policies for User Configuration

Policy	Setting	Description
Windows Settings\ Folder Redirection		
Application Data, Desktop, My Documents, Start Menu	* See Note 1	If the policy to restrict access to local drives is enabled (below), the users need folder redirection if they do not want to see messages saying that they have restricted access. If a roaming profile server is not available, local shares can be used. Create a master folder for all of the user data (such as D:\userdata). Create four sub folders, one for each folder type (such as AppData, Desktop, MyDocs, and Start). Share each of the sub folders and set the share permissions for the "everyone" group to "change". Set each path to its corresponding share. The Start Menu can be configured differently. It can be shared across all users. Place links to applications in here. Change the share permissions for the "everyone" group to "read". You should manually create the "Programs\Startup" folder under the shared Startup folder (D:\userdata\ Start\Programs\Startup).

Continued

Table 6.3 Continued. Group Policies for User Configuration

Policy	Setting	Description
Administrative Templates\ Windows Components\ Internet Explorer		
Search: Disable Find Files via F3 within the browser	Enabled	This policy disables the use of the F3 key to search in Microsoft® Internet Explorer and Windows Explorer. Users cannot press F3 to search the Internet (from Internet Explorer) or to search the hard disk (from Windows Explorer). If the user presses F3, a prompt appears that informs the user that this feature has been disabled. This policy can prevent a user form easily searching for applications on the hard disk. It is recommended that you enable this policy to prevent users from searching for applications on hard drive or browsing the Internet.
Administrative Templates\ Windows Components\ Internet Explorer\ Browser menus		
Disable Context menu	Enabled	This policy prevents the shortcut menu from appearing when users click the right mouse button while using the browser. It is recommended that you enable this policy to prevent users from using the shortcut menu as an alternate method of running commands.
Hide Favorites menu	Enabled	This policy prevents users from adding, removing, or editing the list of Favorite links. If you enable this policy, the Favorites menu is removed from the interface and the Favorites button on the browser toolbar appears dimmed. Use this policy if you want to remove the Favorites menu from Windows Explorer and do not want to give users easy access to Internet Explorer.

Continued

Table 6.3 Continued. Group Policies for User Configuration

Policy	Setting	Description
Administrative Templates\ Windows Components\ Terminal Services\ Sessions		
Allow reconnection from original client only	Enabled	Specifies whether to allow users to reconnect to a disconnected Terminal Services session using a computer other than the original client computer. You can use this setting to prevent Terminal Services users from reconnecting to the disconnected session using a computer other than the client computer from which they originally created the session. By default, Terminal Services allows users to reconnect to disconnected sessions from any client computer. If the status is set to Enabled, users can reconnect to disconnected sessions only from the original client computer. If a user attempts to connect to the disconnected session from another computer, a new session is created instead. If the status is set to Disabled, users can always connect to the disconnected session from any computer. If the status is set to Not Configured, session reconnection from the original client computer is not specified at the Group Policy level. Important: This option is only supported for Citrix ICA clients that provide a serial number when connecting; this setting is ignored if the user is connecting with a Windows client. Also note that this setting appears in both Computer Configuration and User Configuration. If both settings are configured, the Computer Configuration setting overrides.

Continued

Table 6.3 Continued. Group Policies for User Configuration

Policy	Setting	Description
Administrative Templates\ Windows Components\ Windows Explorer		
Removes the Folder Options menu item from the Tools menu	Enabled	Removes the Folder Options item from all Windows Explorer menus and removes the Folder Options item from Control Panel. As a result, users cannot use the Folder Options dialog box. It is recommended that you enable this policy to prevent users from configuring many properties of Windows Explorer, such as Active Desktop, Web view, Offline Files, hidden system files, and file types.
Remove File menu from Windows Explorer	Enabled	This policy removes the File menu from My Computer and Windows Explorer. It does not prevent users from using other methods to perform tasks available on the File menu. It is recommended that you enable this policy to remove easy access to tasks such as "New," "Open With," and shell extensions for some applications. Enabling this policy also prevents easy creation of shortcuts to executables.
Remove Map Network Drive and Disconnect Network Drive	Enabled	This policy prevents users from connecting and disconnect to shares with Windows Explorer. It does not prevent mapping and disconnecting drives from other applications or the run command. It is recommended that you enable this policy to remove easy access to browsing the domain from Windows Explorer. If mapped drives are necessary, they can be mapped from a logon script.
Remove Search button from Windows Explorer	Enabled	It is recommended that you enable this policy to prevent users from searching for applications from Windows Explorer. This policy does not prevent search routines in other applications or the Start Menu.

Continued

Table 6.3 Continued. Group Policies for User Configuration

Policy	Setting	Description
Remove Security Tab	Enabled	This policy removes the Security tab from Windows Explorer. If users can open the Properties dialog box for file system objects, including folders, files, shortcuts, and drives, they cannot access the Security tab. It is recommended that you enable this policy to prevent users from changing the security settings or viewing a list of all users who have access to the object.
Remove Windows Explorer's default context menu	Enabled	This setting removes the shortcut menu from Windows Explorer. It is recommended that you enable this policy to prevent easy access to applications that place hooks into the shortcut menu. This policy does not remove other methods of accessing applications on the shortcut menu, such as using shortcut hotkeys.
Hides the Manage item on the Windows Explorer shortcut menu	Enabled	This policy removes the Manage option from Windows Explorer or My Computer. The Manage option opens the Computer Management MMC snap-in (compmgmt.msc). Items like Event Viewer, System Information, and Disk Administrator can be accessed from Computer Management. This policy does not restrict access to these tasks from other methods such as Control Panel and the run command. It is recommended that you enable this policy to remove easy access to system information about the Terminal Server.

Continued

Table 6.3 Continued. Group Policies for User Configuration

Policy	Setting	Description
Hide these specified drives in My Computer	Enabled	This policy only removes the icons from My Computer, Windows Explorer, and the standard file dialog box. It does not prevent users from access these drives by using other means such as the command prompt. The policy only allows you to hide drives A through D. It is recommended that you enable this policy to hide the floppy disk drive, the CD-ROM drive, and the operating system partition. A partition for public data can be configured to be the only drive viewable to the users. If required, NTFS permissions can be used to restrict access to this partition. You should restrict at least drives A, B, C and D or create a custom policy. *See Note 2.
Prevent access to drives from My Computer	Enabled	This policy prevents access to drives A through D with My Computer, Windows Explorer and the standard file dialog box. This policy does not prevent access from programs that do not use the common dialog boxes. The users can still start applications that reside on the restricted drives. It is recommended that you enable this policy to restrict file browsing of system partitions. You should restrict at least drives A, B, C and D or create a custom policy. *See Note 2.
Remove Hardware tab	Enabled	This policy removes the Hardware tab from Mouse, Keyboard, and Sounds and Audio Devices in Control Panel. It also removes the Hardware tab from the Properties dialog box for all local drives, including hard drives, floppy disk drives, and CD-ROM drives. It is recommended that you enable this policy to prevent users from using the Hardware tab to view the device list or device properties.
Remove Order Prints from Picture Tasks	Enabled	It is recommended that you enable this policy to remove the "Order Prints Online from Picture Tasks" link in the My Pictures folder.

Continued

Table 6.3 Continued. Group Policies for User Configuration

Policy	Setting	Description
Remove Publish to Web from File and Folders Tasks	Enabled	This policy setting removes Publish this file to the Web, Publish this folder to the Web, and Publish the selected items to the Web from File and Folder tasks in Window Explorer. It is recommended that you enable this policy to prevent users from publishing files or folders to a Web page.
No "Computers Near Me" in My Network Places	Enabled	This policy removes computers in the user's domain from lists of network resources in Windows Explorer and My Network Places. It does not prevent users from connecting to other computers by other methods, such as the command prompt or the Map Network Drive dialog box. It is recommended that you enable this policy to remove easy access to browsing the domain.
No "Entire Network" in My Network Places	Enabled	This policy removes all computers outside of the user's local domain from lists of network resources in Windows Explorer and My Network Places. It does not prevent users from connecting to other computers by other methods, such as command prompt or the Map Network Drive dialog box. It is recommended that you enable this policy to remove easy access to browsing the network.
Turn off Windows+X hotkeys	Enabled	This policy turns off Windows+X hotkeys. Keyboards with a Windows logo key provide users with shortcuts to common shell features. For example, pressing the keyboard sequence Windows+R opens the Run dialog box; pressing the Windows+E starts Windows Explorer. It is recommended that you enable this policy to prevent users from starting applications with the Windows logo hotkey.

Continued

Table 6.3 Continued. Group Policies for User Configuration

Policy	Setting	Description
Turn on Classic Shell	Enabled	This policy allows you to remove the Active Desktop and Web view features. If you enable this setting, it disables the Active Desktop and Web view. Also, users cannot configure their system to open items by single-clicking (such as in Mouse in Control Panel). As a result, the user interface looks and operates like the interface for Windows NT 4.0, and users cannot restore the new features. It is recommended that you enable this policy to remove Folder Tasks. Some Folder Task, such as for the My Music folder can start Internet Explorer.
Turn off shell protocol protected mode	Enabled	This policy setting allows you to configure the amount of functionality that the shell protocol can have. When using the full functionality of this protocol, applications can open folders and launch files. The protected mode reduces the functionality of this protocol allowing applications to only open a limited set of folders. Applications are not able to open files with this protocol when it is in the protected mode. It is recommended to leave this protocol in the protected mode to increase the security of Windows. If you enable this policy setting the protocol is fully enabled, allowing the opening of folders and files. If you disable this policy setting the protocol is in the protected mode, allowing applications to only open a limited set of folders. If you do not configure this policy setting the protocol is in the protected mode, allowing applications to only open a limited set of folders.

Continued

Table 6.3 Continued. Group Policies for User Configuration

Policy	Setting	Description
Administrative Templates\ Windows Components\ Windows Explorer\ Common Open File Dialog		
Hide the common dialog places bar	Enabled	This policy removes the shortcut bar from the Common Open File dialog box. This feature was originally added in Windows 2000, so disabling it makes it look as it did in Windows NT 4.0 and earlier. These policies affect only programs that use the common dialog box. It is recommended that you enable this policy to remove easy access to browsing the network or the local computer.
Items displayed in Places Bar	Enabled	This policy allows you to replace the Place Bar items in the Common Open File dialog box with predefined entries. To view this bar, start Notepad, select File, and then click Open.
Administrative Templates\ Windows Components\ Task Scheduler		
Hide Property Pages	Enabled	It is recommended that you enable this policy to prevent users from viewing and changing the properties of an existing task.
Prohibit Task Deletion	Enabled	This policy prevents administrators from deleting tasks from the Scheduled Tasks folder. This does not prevent administrators from deleting tasks with the AT command, or from a remote computer.
Prevent Task Run or End	Enabled	This policy prevents administrators from starting and stopping tasks.
Prohibit New Task Creation	Enabled	It is recommended that you enable this policy to prevent users from creating new scheduled tasks and browsing for applications. This does not prevent administrators from creating new tasks with the AT command, or from a remote computer.

Continued

Table 6.3 Continued. Group Policies for User Configuration

Policy	Setting	Description
Administrative Templates\ Windows Components\ Windows Messenger		
Do not allow Windows Messenger to be run	Enabled	This policy disables Windows Messenger for the user. It is recommended that you enable this policy to prevent users from receiving links or files from other Windows Messenger users.
Administrative Templates\ Windows Components\ Windows Update		
Remove access to use all Windows Update features	Enabled	This policy removes access to Windows Update. If you enable this setting, all Windows Update features are removed. This includes blocking access to the Microsoft Windows Update Web site, from the Windows Update hyperlink on the Start menu, and also on the Tools menu in Internet Explorer. Windows automatic updating is also disabled; you are neither notified about critical updates nor do you receive critical updates from Windows Update. This setting also prevents Device Manager from automatically installing driver updates from the Windows Update Web site. This policy can be used to prevent changes to the Terminal Server while it is production. If you disable Windows Update, you should schedule periodic checks to ensure Windows has latest critical updates.

Continued

Table 6.3 Continued. Group Policies for User Configuration

Policy	Setting	Description
Do not display 'Install Updates and Shut Down' option in Shut Down	Enabled	This policy setting allows you to manage whether the 'Install Updates and Shut Down' option is displayed in the Shut Down Windows dialog box. If you enable this policy setting, 'Install Updates and Shut Down' will not appear as a choice in the Shut Down Windows dialog box, even if updates are available for installation when the user selects the Shut Down option in the Start menu. If you disable or do not configure this policy setting, the 'Install Updates and Shut Down' option will be available in the Shut Down Windows dialog box if updates are available when the user selects the Shut Down option in the Start menu.
Administrative Templates\ Start Menu & Taskbar		
Remove links and access to Windows Update	Enabled	This policy removes links and access to the Windows Update Web site. The Windows Update Web site is only available for administrators. It is recommended that you enable this policy to remove easy access to Internet Explorer for users.
Remove common program groups from Start Menu	Enabled	This policy removes shortcuts to programs from the all users' profile. Only the Start Menu in the user's profile or the redirected Start Menu is available. It is recommended that you enable this policy to remove easy access to built-in applications like games, calculator, and media player.
Remove pinned programs list from Start Menu	Enabled	This policy removes the Pinned Programs list from the new Start Menu. It also removes the default links to Internet Explorer and Outlook Express if they are pinned, and it prevents users from pinning any new programs to the Start Menu. The Frequently Used Programs list is not affected.

Continued

Table 6.3 Continued. Group Policies for User Configuration

Policy	Setting	Description
Remove programs on Settings menu	Enabled	This policy removes Control Panel, Printers, and Network Connections from Settings on the Classic Start menu, My Computer and Windows Explorer. It also prevents the programs represented by these folders (such as Control.exe) from running. However, users can still start Control Panel items by using other methods, such as right-clicking the desktop to open Display Properties or right-clicking My Computer to open System Properties. It is recommended that you enable this policy to prevent easy access to viewing or changing system settings.
Remove Network Connections from Start Menu	Enabled	This policy prevents the Network Connections folder from opening. The policy also removes Network Connections from Settings on Start Menu. Network Connections still appears in Control Panel and in Windows Explorer, but if users try to start it, a message appears explaining that a setting prevents the action. It is recommended that you enable this policy to prevent users from creating new connections such as VPN or Dial-up.
Remove the Search menu from Start Menu	Enabled	This policy removes the search function from the Start menu. This setting removes Search from the Start menu and from the shortcut menu that appears when you right-click Start Menu. Also, the system does not respond when users press Windows+F or the F3 key. In Windows Explorer, the search item still appears on the Standard buttons toolbar, but the system does not respond when the user presses CTRL+F. Also, Search does not appear in the shortcut menu when you right-click an icon representing a drive or a folder. This setting affects the specified user inter-face elements only. It does not affect Internet Explorer and does not prevent the user from using other methods to search. It is recommended that you enable this policy to prevent users from easily searching for applications that they are not assigned to them

Continued

Table 6.3 Continued. Group Policies for User Configuration

Policy	Setting	Description
Remove Drag-and-Drop shortcut menus on Start Menu	Enabled	This policy prevents users from using the drag-and-drop method to reorder or remove items on the Start menu. This setting does not prevent users from using other methods of customizing the Start menu or performing the tasks available from the shortcut menus. It is recommended that you enable this policy to remove shortcut menus from the Start menu, including tasks such as creating a new shortcut.
Remove Favorites menu from Start Menu	Enabled	This policy prevents users from adding the Favorites menu to the Start menu or the Classic Start menu. Use this policy if you do not want users to execute Internet Explorer.
Remove Help menu from Start Menu	Enabled	This policy removes the Help link from the Start menu. This setting only affects the Start menu. To disable the new Help and Support application disable the service in Computer Configuration (See Restricted Computer Policies). It is recommended that you enable this policy to prevent users from easily viewing System Information about the Terminal Server.
Remove Run menu from Start Menu	Enabled	It is highly recommended that you enable this policy to prevent users from attempting to execute any application. This is very critical for locking down the Terminal Server. Enabling this removes the Run command from the Start menu, New Task from Task Manager, and users are blocked from entering a UNC path, local drive, and local folders into the Internet Explorer address bar. Also, users with extended keyboards can no longer display the Run dialog box by pressing Windows+R.
Remove My Network Place icon from Start Menu	Enabled	This policy removes the My Network Places icon from the Start menu. It is recommended that you enable this policy to prevent easy access to browsing the network.

Continued

Table 6.3 Continued. Group Policies for User Configuration

Policy	Setting	Description
Add Logoff to Start Menu	Enabled	It is recommended that you enable this policy to make it easy for users to log off of their Terminal Server sessions. This policy adds the "Log Off <user name>" item to the Start menu and prevents users from removing it. This setting affects the Start menu only. It does not affect the Log Off item on the Windows Security dialog box that appears when you press CTRL+ALT+DEL or CTRL+ALT+END from a Terminal Server client.
Remove and prevent access to Shut Down command	Enabled	This policy removes the ability for the user to open the Shutdown dialog box from the Start menu and from the Windows Security dialog box (CTRL+ALT+DEL). This policy does not prevent users from running programs to shut down Windows. It is recommended that you enable this policy help remove confusion from the users and prevent administrators from shutting down the system while it is in production.
Prevent changes to Taskbar and Start Menu settings	Enabled	This policy prevents customization of the taskbar and the Start menu. It can simplify the desktop by adhering to the configuration set by the administrator. It is recommended that you enable this policy to restrict the ability to add other applications to the start menu by browsing or typing the location of an application.
Remove access to the shortcut menus for the taskbar	Enabled	This policy removes the right-click menu on the taskbar. This setting does not prevent users from using other methods to issue the commands that appear on this menu. It is recommended that you enable this policy to prevent potential access to files and applications by starting Windows Explorer or Search.

Continued

Table 6.3 Continued. Group Policies for User Configuration

Policy	Setting	Description
Force Classic Start Menu	Enabled	This policy effects the presentation of the Start menu. The Classic Start menu in Windows 2000 allows users to begin common tasks, while the new Start menu consolidates common items onto one menu. When the Classic Start menu is used, the following icons are placed on the desktop: My Documents, My Pictures, My Music, My Computer, and My Network Places. The new Start menu starts them directly. Disabling the new Start menu removes Printers and Faxes. From Printers and Faxes, users can view Server Properties to see where the Spool folder is installed.
Administrative Templates\Desktop		
Remove Properties from My Documents shortcut menu	Enabled	This setting hides Properties for the shortcut menu on My Documents. It is recommended that you enable this policy if shortcut menus are not disabled and you do not want the users to easily view or edit the location of their My Document folder.
Remove Properties from My Computer shortcut menu	Enabled	This setting hides Properties on the shortcut menu for My Computer. It is recommended that you enable this policy if shortcut menus are not disabled and you do not want the users to easily view configuration information about the Terminal Server.
Remove Properties from Recycle Bin shortcut menu	Enabled	This policy removes the Properties option from the Recycle Bin shortcut menu. It is recommended that you enable this policy if shortcut menus are not disabled and you do not want the users to easily view or change Recycle Bin settings.

Continued

Table 6.3 Continued. Group Policies for User Configuration

Policy	Setting	Description
Hide My Network Places icon on desktop	Enabled	It is recommended that you enable this policy to remove easy access to browsing the network for applications. This setting only affects the desktop icon. It does not prevent users from connecting to the network or browsing for shared computers on the network with other methods.
Hide Internet Explorer Icon on the desktop	Enabled	This policy removes the Internet Explorer icon from the desktop. This setting does not prevent the user from starting Internet Explorer by using other methods.
Prohibit user from changing My Documents path	Enabled	This policy restricts the My Documents location to the designated location. It is recommended that you enable this policy to prevent browsing for applications.
Hide and disable all items on the desktop	Enabled	This policy removes icons, shortcuts, and other default and user-defined items from the desktop, including Briefcase, Recycle Bin, My Computer, and My Network Places. Removing icons and shortcuts does not prevent the user from using another method to start the programs or opening the items they represent. User can still save and open items on the desktop by using the Common File dialog box or Windows Explorer. The items; however, are not displayed on the desktop.
Remove My Documents icon on the desktop	Enabled	This policy removes most occurrences of the My Documents icon. It does not prevent the user from using other methods to gain access to the contents of the My Documents folder.
Remove My Computer icon on the desktop	Enabled	This policy hides My Computer from the desktop and from the new Start menu. It also hides links to My Computer in the Web view of all Explorer windows, and it hides My Computer in the Explorer folder tree pane. If the user navigates into My Computer by using the Up icon while this setting is enabled, they view an empty My Computer folder. It is recommended that you enable this policy to present users with a simpler desktop environment and remove easy access to Computer Management and System Properties by no longer allowing right-clicking of the icon.

Continued

Table 6.3 Continued. Group Policies for User Configuration

Policy	Setting	Description
Administrative Templates\ Control Panel		
Prohibit access to the Control Panel	Enabled	This policy removes access to Control Panel and disables all Control Panel programs. It also prevents Control.exe, the program file for Control Panel, from starting. It is recommended that you enable this setting to prevent users from viewing configuration information about the Terminal Server.
Administrative Templates\ Control Panel\ Add or Remove Programs		
Remove Add or Remove Programs	Enabled	This policy removes Add or Remove Programs from Control Panel and removes the Add or Remove Programs item from menus. If access to Control Panel is prohibited, this policy can be used to remove the links to Add or Remove Programs from places like My Computer. The link then displays an access denied message if clicked. This setting does not prevent users from using other tools and methods to install or uninstall programs. It is recommended that you enable this policy to prevent users to viewing Terminal Server configuration information.

Continued

Table 6.3 Continued. Group Policies for User Configuration

Policy	Setting	Description
Administrative Templates\ Control Panel\ Printers		
Prevent addition of printers	Enabled	This policy prevents users from using familiar methods to add local and network printers. It is recommended that you enable this policy to prevent users from browsing the network or searching the active directory for printers. This policy does not prevent the auto-creation of Terminal Server redirected printers, nor does it prevent users from running other programs to add printers.
Administrative Templates\System		
Prevent access to the command prompt	Enabled	This policy prevents users from running the interactive command prompt Cmd.exe. From the command prompt users can start applications. This setting also determines whether batch files (.cmd and .bat) can run on the computer. Set "Disable the command prompt script processing also" to No.
Prevent access to registry editing tools	Enabled	This policy restricts users from changing registry settings by disabling Regedit.exe. It is recommended that you enable this policy to prevent users from changing their shell to the command prompt or bypassing several other policies. This policy does not prevent other applications for editing the registry.
Run only allowed Windows applications	Enabled	It is recommended that you enable this policy to restrict users to only run programs that are added to the List of Allowed Applications. This setting only prevents users from running programs that are started by Windows Explorer. It does not prevent users from running programs such as Task Manager, which can be started by a system process. Also, if users have access to the command prompt, Cmd.exe, this setting does not prevent them from starting programs from the command window that they are not permitted to start by using Windows Explorer. You will need to define a list of authorized applications.

Continued

Table 6.3 Continued. Group Policies for User Configuration

Policy	Setting	Description
Restrict these programs from being launched from help	Enabled	Allows you to restrict programs from being run from online Help. If you enable this setting, you can prevent programs that you specify from being allowed to be run from Help. When you enable this setting, enter the list of the programs you want to restrict. Enter the file name of the executable for each application, separated by commas. If you disable or do not configure this setting, users will be able to run applications from online Help. Note: You can also restrict users from running applications by using the Software Restriction settings available in Computer Configuration\Security Settings. Note: This setting is available under Computer Configuration and User Configuration. If both are set, the list of programs specified in each of these will be restricted.
Administrative Templates\ System\Internet Communication Management		
Restrict Internet Communication	Enabled	Specifies whether Windows can access the Internet to accomplish tasks that require Internet resources. If this setting is enabled, all of the policy settings listed in the "Internet Communication settings" section will be set to enabled. If this setting is disabled, all of the policy settings listed in the 'Internet Communication settings' section will be set to disabled. If this setting is not configured, all of the policy settings in the 'Internet Communication settings' section will be set to not configured.

Continued

Table 6.3 Continued. Group Policies for User Configuration

Policy	Setting	Description
Administrative Templates\System\ CTRL+ALT+DEL Options		
Remove Task Manager	Enabled	This policy prevents users from starting Task Manager. It is recommended that you enable this policy to prevent users from using task manager to start and stop programs; monitor the performance of the Terminal Server; and find the executable names for applications.
Remove Lock Computer	Enabled	This policy prevents users from locking their sessions. Users can still disconnect and log off. While locked, the desktop can not be used. Only the user who locked the system or the system administrator can unlock it.
Administrative Templates\System\ Scripts		
Run legacy logon scripts hidden	Enabled	This policy hides the instructions in logon scripts written for Windows NT 4.0 and earlier. It is recommended that you enable this policy to prevent users from viewing or interrupting logon scripts written for Windows NT 4.0 and earlier.

NOTE

Note 1: Basic redirection and create a folder for each user under the root path. On the Settings tab, enable grant the user exclusive rights. Enable move contents of folder to new location. Set the policy removal to redirect the folder back to the local user profile location when policy is removed.

NOTE

Note 2: The mask for determining disk drives to be hidden in a GPO is determined by bits. The low order (right most) bit is drive A: while the 26th bit is Drive Z: To hide a drive, turn on its' bit. If your not happy working in Hex, add these decimal number to hide the drive(s):

A: 1, B: 2, C: 4, D: 8, E: 16, F: 32, G: 64, H: 128, I: 256, J: 512, K: 1024, L: 2048, M: 4096, N: 8192, O: 16384, P: 32768, Q: 65536, R: 131072, S: 262144, T: 524288, U: 1048576, V: 2097152, W: 4194304, X: 8388608, Y: 16777216, Z: 33554432, ALL: 67108863.

Desktop restrictions can be implemented by editing the following Explorer values in the registry: (all values default to 0)

HKEY_CURRENT_USER\Software\Microsoft\Windows\CurrentVersion\Policies\Explorer.

Software restriction policies are a feature in Microsoft Windows XP and Windows Server 2003. This important feature provides administrators with a policy-driven mechanism for identifying software programs running on computers in a domain, and it controls the ability of those programs to execute. This is probably the single best item you can implement in your XenApp environment and by enabling and configuring software restriction policies, you can actually eliminate some of the policy settings presented above. Policies can be used to block malicious scripts, help lock down a computer, or prevent unwanted applications from running.

For additional information about Software Restriction Policies, see the Microsoft whitepaper, "Using Software Restriction Policies to Protect Against Unauthorized Software," available from the Microsoft web site www.microsoft.com.

TIP

XenApp has a new Windows group policy template **icaclient.adm** that can be found on the XenApp installation CD. This template provides several settings that can be configured via a Group Policy Object.

The user is reminded that this list is not all inclusive and that the requirements of your organization may require different settings from what is provided here. With this list, we are providing you with a starting point of the settings that are available for configuration, and it is up to you to implement the best configuration for your organization. You can also create custom GPO templates and incorporate specific XenApp settings and configure those settings via group policy.

XenApp Policies to Secure XenApp

These are policies that can be configured via the Presentation Server Console. It is recommended to use XenApp policies AFTER you have configured user and computer GPOs specific to XenApp. The reason for this is that for each setting in XenApp requires its own separate policy where a XenApp

Windows GPO can contain many settings. The management of several policies and their priorities could become cumbersome for some administrators.

First you need to decide the criteria on which to base your policies. You may need to create a policy based on user job function, connection type, client device, or geographic location, or you may want to use the same criteria that you use for your Windows Active Directory group policies. XenApp policies can be created that affect the following areas of XenApp:

- Bandwidth
- Client Devices
- Printing
- User Workspace
- Security

Each policy you create exists as a separate object in the IMA data store. You create a policy and the edit its properties as described earlier in this chapter. Theoretically, there is no limit to the number of policy objects you can create in your farm. But remember that just by creating a policy does not automatically apply the policy. You have to apply (or "filter") the policy based on:

- Access Control
- Client IP Address
- Client Name
- Servers
- Users

Policy rules have three states: *enabled*, *disabled*, or *not configured*. By default, all rules are *not configured*. All rules that are not configured are ignored when users log on to the server, so the rule comes into play only when the state is enabled or disabled.

TIP

Except for the Session Printer policy (which is applied when users connect), policies are applied when users log on. Therefore, policies remain in effect for the length of the session, and changes you make do not affect users who are already logged on. The changes take effect the next time users log on.

Currently, the management of XenApp policies is limited because you cannot organize policies by folder or functional area – they exist at a single level. Because of this, you can end up having over a hundred policies to handle different scenarios in your environment.

Table 6.4 list those XenApp policies can be configured that directly affect the security of the XenApp server.

Table 6.4 XenApp Policies

Policy	Setting	Description
Client Devices folder\ Resources folder\ Drives folder		
Connection	Enabled	By default, all client drives are mapped when a user logs on and users can save files to all their client drives. To prevent users from saving files to one or more client drives, set the rule to Enabled and select the drives that you want to prevent users from accessing. Turn off Floppy disk drives. Prevents users from accessing their floppy disk drives, such as drive A. Turn off Hard drives. Prevents users from accessing any of their hard drives, such as drive C. Turn off CD-ROM drives. Prevents users from accessing any of their CD-ROM drives. Turn off Remote drives. Prevents users from accessing any mapped network drives, such as remote drives located under "My Network Places" in Windows Explorer.Disabling this rule causes the default of access to all drives to override the same rule in lower priority policies. Note: This rule does not turn drive mapping on for users. Use the Connection rule to stop or start mapping drives automatically when users log on.
Mappings	Enabled	By default, all drives are Mapped when a user logs on. If you want to stop drives from being mapped when the user logs on; for example, to prevent users from saving files to their local drive, you can set the following rule.

Continued

Table 6.4 Continued. XenApp Policies

Policy	Setting	Description
User Workspace folder\Connections folder		
Limit total concurrent sessions	Enabled	Starting with XenApp, the Citrix Connection Configuration tool is no longer supported. Instead, the configuration of connection settings to your server farm is done through the Microsoft Management Console (MMC) using Terminal Services Configuration. You can restrict the number of concurrent connections (ICA sessions) that users can have in the server farm. This reduces the number of ICA connection licenses in use and conserves resources. You restrict concurrent connections using policies. The setting for the least connections overrides any other setting.
User Workspace folder\Shadowing folder		
Configuration	Enabled	Covered in Chapter 4.
Permissions	Enabled	Covered in Chapter 4.
Security folder\ Encryption folder		
Secure ICA encryption	Enabled	Covered in Chapter 4.

Summary

In this chapter, we covered both Windows Server 2003 Group Policy and XenApp policy. We saw that Windows Server 2003 Group Policy is a more mature, robust offering that adds over 200 policy settings that affect an end-user's entire experience in a Windows Active Directory domain. We discussed the new Group Policy Management Console (GPMC) and the strength and integrity it brings to Active Directory forest management. We examined the features in the GPMC and saw how they are used. We looked at installing the GPMC and examined GPOs, and looked at the different management features on the GPO. We briefly discussed design considerations for Group Policy.

We also discussed XenApp policies and their uses. We looked at creating policies, configuring the rules within the policies, and applying policy filters. We also discussed the rules that govern MetaFrame policies and how they are applied and affect the users, servers, client machines, and IP address ranges to which they are applied. We talked about policy prioritization and creating exceptions to policies by changing priority between two conflicting policies.

We briefly discussed some tips for designing XenApp and Windows policies so that they complement each other and the built-in tools that can help accomplish this. Finally, we provided Windows and XenApp policy settings that should be reviewed and enabled in any environment where security is of a concern.

Solutions Fast Track

Windows Server 2003 Group Policy

☑ Includes over 200 policy settings.

☑ Introduces more mature WMI features that enable administrators to manage different computer hardware more appropriately.

☑ New management model enables cross-forest policy management.

Planning a Group Policy Strategy

☑ You must consider a number of factors when planning the group policy strategy for your organization. Some of these factors include size of the organization, geography of the organization, structure of the organization, and so on.

☑ The Resultant Set of Policy (RSoP) tool, included with Windows Server 2003, has a special planning mode that system administrators can use to evaluate the design of the group policy within the directory. The planning mode of RSoP can simulate a number of situations where group policy settings can be affected by a number of factors.

☑ There are a vast number of ways that group policy can be implemented in an Active Directory environment.

Configuring Group Policy with the Group Policy Management Console

- ☑ Integrates all Group Policy Management and domain administrative tools into one MMC.
- ☑ Enables administrators to model policy changes and see results in a test scenario before actually applying them.
- ☑ Enables the configuration of policies to match users and their functions and to match the types of client computers they use.
- ☑ Windows Server 2003 WMI filters are not supported in Windows 2000 and earlier operating systems.
- ☑ The RSoP and Group Policy Modeling tools can be used to ensure that policies have the desired effect.
- ☑ GPOs can be configured to deploy client software on a per-user or per-machine basis.

Configuring XenApp Policies

- ☑ XenApp policies can be applied to users and user groups, servers, client machines, and IP address ranges.
- ☑ Policies take effect at login and are active for the duration of the ICA connection.
- ☑ Polices exist in three states: enabled, disabled, and not configured.
- ☑ A Citrix policy's power lies in its rules that affect every facet of an ICA session, from desktop appearance to security and encryption.
- ☑ Policies can be prioritized so that exceptions to one policy can be enforced by another higher priority policy.

Using Policies to Make XenApp More Secure

- ☑ Designing policies that conflict with each other could result in your XenApp infrastructure failing to get up and running.
- ☑ If your infrastructure is already supporting clients, new policies that conflict with your strategy could quickly bring things to a halt.
- ☑ Good Active Directory design makes it easier to apply sound XenApp policy rules. This seems obvious, but still bears mentioning.
- ☑ Microsoft Group Policy settings can override XenApp policy rules for connections. If the Group Policy security settings are more restrictive than the XenApp policy rules, then the most restrictive policy wins.

Frequently Asked Questions

Q: Why can't I employ different group policies to distinguish between Windows 2000 laptops and Windows 2000 desktop computers?

A: Windows Server 2003 WMI filters are not supported on Windows 2000.

Q: Why can't I use the Group Policy Modeling feature on Windows 2003 servers in my Windows 2000 domain?

A: Group Policy Modeling requires that a domain has at least one Windows Server 2003 domain controller.

Q: Why are my clients trying to update their ICA client software even though the auto client update policy is not configured?

A: That's exactly the problem. An unconfigured policy does not turn the policy off, but defers it to a lower priority policy. To stop the clients from trying to update the Turn off client, auto update policy must be enabled.

Q: What is the RSoP tool?

A. Resultant Set of Policy Wizard that can be used to assist administrators in planning ane evaluating group policy within their Active Directory.

Q: Can WMI filters be configured for GPOs that support Windows 2000 clients?

A: No, Windows 2000 and earlier clients will ignore the WMI filter and the GPO will always apply regardless.

Q: Why should you limit the number of group policy objects?

A: The main reason is for ease of administration - NOT because of logon delay times!

Q: How can I ensure that my XenApp policy, not the Microsoft policy, is controlling my security settings?

A. Make the XenApp policy the most restrictive policy. This may mean relaxing Microsoft security, so do this with care.

Q: I have configured the policy to auto-create client printers on login but my printers are not added. What is wrong?

A: The Printer driver rule may be disabled in a higher ranked policy. Disabled policies and rules take precedence over lower ranked policies and rules. Enabling the rule in a higher ranked policy should solve the problem.

Q: Why does a particular application keep getting installed on every computer one of my users logs in to?

A: The application was configured for installation and assigned to that user's account, so it will follow the user and be installed on every computer he logs on to that does not already have the application.

Q: If a Microsoft Group Policy settings and a XenApp policy setting contradict each other, which one will apply?

A: The most restrictive policy wins.

Q: What tools can assist you with managing XenApp policies?

A: XenApp policy search tool (available with the Presentation Server Console) is used much like the Microsoft RSoP tool.

Q: What two Windows GPOs can be created to ease policy management of XenApp servers?

A: A computer configuration GPO, such as XenApp Servers and a user configuration GPO, such as XenApp Users.

Chapter 7

Locking Down Your XenApp Server

Solutions in this chapter:

- Protecting Your Server (and Its Parts)
- Protecting Your Data
- Planning Physical Security
- Security Measures and Objectives

☑ Summary

☑ Solutions Fast Track

☑ Frequently Asked Questions

Introduction

To protect assets from risks that were identified as possible threats to a business, countermeasures must be implemented. Servers will need certain configurations to provide security, and plans must be put into practice. Compare the risks faced by an organization with an operating system's features to find support that will address certain threats. Configuring the server to use these services or tools can assist in dealing with potential problems. For example, installing AD and using domain controllers on a network can heighten security and provide the ability to control user access and security across the network. In the same way, configuring a file server to use EFS so that data on the server's hard disk is encrypted can augment file security. Using security features in an operating system allows you to minimize many potential threats.

Protecting Your Server (and Its Parts)

As we have said many times in this book that your job as a XenApp administrator is to not only make applications and resources available to your users, but to do so securely while still maintaining a productive environment that is usable. There are many tools and resources available to assist you in completing the task of protecting your server. However, sometimes the most obvious things are often overlooked. For example, let's say that an industrious employee can quickly reboot one of your XenApp servers and change the BIOS configuration to boot from a USB device that they connect to the server, or even a CD that has "questionable" content on it. Sound bizarre? Perhaps, but how long would that employee need to compromise the system if he were to have physical access to one of your servers? What could he do? Your job as security administrators is to think about situations just like this one, and in this section, we will cover some of the ways you can protect your server (and its parts.)

System BIOS Lockdown

You can adopt the best security policies and implement the latest software and you can still have a security incident. Without adequately ensuring the physical integrity of your servers, you could be easily compromised by an insider, like coworker, contractor, visitor or even a friend. Therefore, you must ensure that even the most mundane ways of gaining access to your systems is thoroughly considered.

All your security measures are useless if an attacker can gain physical access to your system. What would happen if an attacker were to gain access to one of your servers, could he then take a bootable CD and reboot your server and have it boot from the CD because your BIOS setting allows for that – or worse yet, your BIOS is not protected.

To prevent this, use the system BIOS to disable boot devices other than the hard disk (or, if that's not possible, select the hard disk as the first boot device). For computers located in hard-to-protect public areas, consider removing floppy and CD/DVD drives, and disabling or removing USB and FireWire ports, to prevent people from booting the PC with a Linux disc, IPod or flash memory USB drive.

Password protect your system BIOS. Most types of BIOS let you create a user password that must be entered to permit the system to start up. If your BIOS supports it, an administrative password will prevent attackers from changing BIOS settings (including the boot password).

You should have this password stored in a secure location in case you need to make changes to the system later. Keep in mind that just because you password protect your system BIOS you will thwart an attackers efforts. Some systems accept *master* passwords, lists of which appear on the Internet. By entering particular key combinations an attacker may be able to sidestep BIOS password security on certain systems.

Additionally, anyone with the opportunity to open the system's case can clear the passwords by moving a jumper on the motherboard, or by disconnecting the battery that powers the BIOS settings' memory chip. If you're worried about that happening, get a lock for the case itself and have the server in a locked server cabinet.

USB Blockers

USB blockers can be installed to minimize the security risks imposed by using portable storage media and portable devices in your enterprise, such as:

- Memory sticks
- Jump drive
- Personal Digital Assistants (PDAs)
- Cell Phones
- MP3 Players
- Digital Cameras
- Scanners
- Hard disk drives
- CD/DVD
- Printers

By using these devices, data can be retrieved and often changed while bypassing established security guidelines. Of course, this frequently causes irritation to administrators. Because of that, enterprises are threatened not only of the danger of the data theft and integrity compromise, but also of the intentional or unintentional "import" of viruses, Trojan horses and other damaging software.

Most USB blockers are built up on the Windows Device Manager and can be configured to prevent new or unknown devices from being accessible. These blockers are typically installed as a software component within the Windows operating system and can then be configured via Windows Group Policy.

Alarms

You can utilize XenApp Resource Manager with or without the summary database to establish a means of producing alarms based on metrics you configure and want to monitor.

The first step is to establish the metrics that you want to track. This process is easier than establishing the thresholds for those metrics; in short, this initial step is more art than science.

However, you can leverage Resource Manager and/or Performance Monitor in the creation of this baseline to allow you to more accurately establish the metrics and their thresholds that you will track.

Each metric has both yellow and red thresholds as configured on the right. Yellow represents the warning state, meaning something is slightly out of ordinary but not considered catastrophic yet. Red is reserved for those metrics that indicate a severe state that will need immediate attention. As we have stated several times, choosing the correct values to enter into the Threshold Configuration is definitely a challenge that we all face. The reality is that no two Presentation Server environments are identical; every environment has its own specific server hardware, operating systems, applications, and so on. Add to that the nuisance of differences in patch levels, software configuration, and usage patterns within various applications and you can quickly see why this will present a "tweaking" exercise for your environment. As a general rule of thumb, however, you can use the Visual Threshold Configuration window to get good idea of what your current environment looks like so you can make a more educated guess as to the values to enter.

Configuring alerts is a two-step process. Step one is to configure the individual metrics you want to be alerted on and the method to be alerted with. The second step is to enable alerting and configure the alerting methods. Alerts can be sent to e-mails, SNMP traps, or Short Message Service (SMS) pages. The Alerts tab of a given metric's properties allows for the configuration of these options. Basically, enable the way you want to be alerted when that particular metric enters an alert state, such as the transition to red. As a best practice, it is considered good etiquette to notify that the alert state is over by sending confirmation of the transition back to a green state.

Intrusion Detection Systems

"Danger! Will Robinson! Intruder Alert!" When we heard that ominous announcement emanating from a robot as it twisted and turned with arms thrashing and head spinning, we sat galvanized to our televisions waiting for the intruder to reveal itself. Would this be the end of Will Robinson as we knew him?

All right, this might be a bit dramatic for a prelude to a discussion of intrusion detection, but with most security administrators, when a beeper goes off there is a moment of anxiety. Is this the big one? Did they get in? Do they own my network? Do they own my data?

These and many other questions flood the mind of the well-prepared security administrator. Conversely, the ill-prepared security administrator, being totally unaware of the intrusion, experiences little anxiety. For him, the anxiety comes later.

Okay, so how can a security-minded administrator protect his network from intrusions? The answer to that question is quite simple, with an intrusion detection system.

NOTE

Intrusion detection works in conjunction with firewalls in various ways. One of the ways is to use intrusion detection is to test your firewall rules to make sure they are working properly. One of the other ways is to use intrusion detection and firewalls to set rules for a firewall.

What Is an Intrusion?

Borrowing from the law enforcement community, crime prevention specialists use a model called the "Crime Triangle" to explain that certain criteria must exist before a crime can occur. We can adapt this same triangle to network security: the same three criteria must exist before a network security breach can take place. The three "legs" or points of the triangle are shown in Figure 7.1.

Figure 7.1 All Three Legs of the Triangle Must Exist for a Network Intrusion to Occur

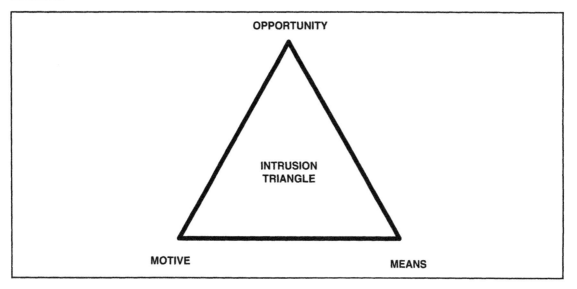

Let's look at each point individually:

- **Motive** An intruder must have a reason to want to breach the security of your network (even if the reason is "just for fun"); otherwise, he/she won't bother.

- **Means** An intruder must have the ability (either the programming knowledge, or, in the case of "script kiddies," the intrusion software written by others), or he/she won't be able to breach your security.

- **Opportunity** An intruder must have the chance to enter the network, either because of flaws in your security plan, holes in a software program that open an avenue of access, or physical proximity to network components; if there is no opportunity to intrude, the would-be hacker will go elsewhere.

If you think about the three-point intrusion criteria for a moment, you'll see that there is really only one leg of the triangle over which you, as the network administrator or security specialist, have any control. It is unlikely that you can do much to remove the intruder's motive. The motive is likely to be built into the type of data you have on the network or even the personality of the intruder him/herself. It is also not possible for you to prevent the intruder from having or obtaining the means to breach your security. Programming knowledge is freely available, and there are many experienced hackers out there who are more than happy to help out less sophisticated ones. The one thing that you can affect is the opportunity afforded the hacker.

What Is Intrusion Detection?

Webster's dictionary defines an intrusion as "the act of thrusting in, or of entering into a place or state without invitation, right, or welcome." When we speak of intrusion detection, we are referring to the act of detecting an unauthorized intrusion by a *computer* on a *network*. This unauthorized access, or intrusion, is an attempt to compromise, or otherwise do harm, to other network devices.

An intrusion detection system (IDS) is the high-tech equivalent of a burglar alarm—a burglar alarm configured to monitor access points, hostile activities, and known intruders. The simplest way to define an IDS might be to describe it as a specialized tool that knows how to read and interpret the contents of log files from routers, firewalls, servers, and other network devices. Furthermore, an IDS often stores a database of known attack signatures and can compare patterns of activity, traffic, or behavior it sees in the logs it is monitoring against those signatures to recognize when a close match between a signature and current or recent behavior occurs. At that point, the IDS can issue alarms or alerts, take various kinds of automatic action ranging from shutting down Internet links or specific servers to launching backtraces, and make other active attempts to identify attackers and actively collect evidence of their nefarious activities.

By analogy, an IDS does for a network what an antivirus software package does for files that enter a system: It inspects the contents of network traffic to look for and deflect possible attacks, just as an antivirus software package inspects the contents of incoming files, e-mail attachments, active Web content, and so forth to look for virus signatures (patterns that match known malware) or for possible malicious actions (patterns of behavior that are at least suspicious, if not downright unacceptable).

To be more specific, intrusion detection means detecting unauthorized use of or attacks on a system or network. An IDS is designed and used to detect and then to deflect or deter (if possible) such attacks or unauthorized use of systems, networks, and related resources. Like firewalls, IDSes can be software based or can combine hardware and software (in the form of preinstalled and preconfigured stand-alone IDS devices). Often, IDS software runs on the same devices or servers where firewalls, proxies, or other boundary services operate; an IDS *not* running on the same device or server where the firewall or other services are installed will monitor those devices closely and carefully. Although such devices tend to operate at network peripheries, IDSes can detect and deal with insider attacks as well as external attacks.

IDSes vary according to a number of criteria. By explaining those criteria, we can explain what kinds of IDSes you are likely to encounter and how they do their jobs. First and foremost, it is possible to distinguish IDSes by the kinds of activities, traffic, transactions, or systems they monitor. IDSes can be divided into network-based, host-based, and distributed. IDSes that monitor network backbones and look for attack signatures are called *network-based IDSes*, whereas those that operate on hosts defend and monitor the operating and file systems for signs of intrusion and are called *host-based IDSes*. Groups of IDSes functioning as remote sensors and reporting to a central management station are known as Distributed IDS (DIDS).

In practice, most commercial environments use some combination of network, and host, and/or application-based IDS systems to observe what is happening on the network while also monitoring key hosts and applications more closely. IDSes can also be distinguished by their differing approaches to event analysis. Some IDSes primarily use a technique called *signature detection*. This resembles the way many antivirus programs use virus signatures to recognize and block infected files, programs, or active Web content from entering a computer system, except that it uses a database of traffic or activity patterns related to known attacks, called *attack signatures*. Indeed, signature detection is the most widely used approach in commercial IDS technology today. Another approach is called *anomaly detection*. It uses rules or predefined concepts about "normal" and "abnormal" system activity (called *heuristics*) to distinguish anomalies from normal system behavior and to monitor, report on, or block anomalies as they occur. Some anomaly detection IDSes implement user profiles. These profiles are baselines of normal activity and can be constructed using statistical sampling, rule-base approach or neural networks.

Literally hundreds of vendors offer various forms of commercial IDS implementations. Most effective solutions combine network- and host-based IDS implementations. Likewise, the majority of implementations are primarily signature based, with only limited anomaly-based detection capabilities present in certain specific products or solutions. Finally, most modern IDSes include some limited automatic response capabilities, but these usually concentrate on automated traffic filtering, blocking, or disconnects as a last resort. Although some systems claim to be able to launch counterstrikes against attacks, best practices indicate that automated identification and backtrace facilities are the most useful aspects that such facilities provide and are therefore those most likely to be used.

IDSes are classified by their functionality and are loosely grouped into the following three main categories:

- Network-Based Intrusion Detection System (NIDS)
- Host-Based Intrusion Detection System (HIDS)
- Distributed Intrusion Detection System (DIDS)

Network IDS

The NIDS derives its name from the fact that it monitors the entire network. More accurately, it monitors an entire network segment. Normally, a computer network interface card (NIC) operates in nonpromiscuous mode. In this mode of operation, only packets destined for the NICs specific media access control (MAC) address are forwarded up the stack for analysis. The NIDS must operate in promiscuous mode to monitor network traffic not destined for its own MAC address. In promiscuous mode, the NIDS can eavesdrop on all communications on the network segment. Operation in promiscuous mode is necessary to protect your network. However, in view of emerging privacy regulations, monitoring network communications is a responsibility that must be considered carefully.

In Figure 7.2, we see a network using three NIDS. The units have been placed on strategic network segments and can monitor network traffic for all devices on the segment. This configuration represents a standard perimeter security network topology where the screened subnets on the DMZ housing the public servers are protected by NIDS. When a public server is compromised on a screened subnet, the server can become a launching platform for additional exploits. Careful monitoring is necessary to prevent further damage.

The internal host systems inside the firewall are protected by an additional NIDS to mitigate exposure to internal compromise. The use of multiple NIDS within a network is an example of a defense-in-depth security architecture.

Figure 7.2 NIDS Network

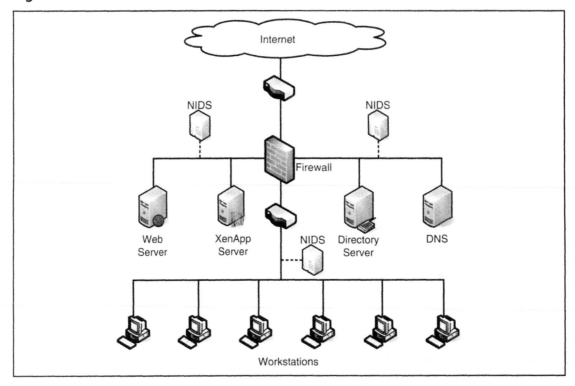

Host-Based IDS

HIDS differ from NIDS in two ways. HIDS protects only the host system on which it resides, and its network card operates in nonpromiscuous mode. Nonpromiscuous mode of operation can be an advantage in some cases, because not all NICs are capable of promiscuous mode. In addition, promiscuous mode can be CPU intensive for a slow host machine. HIDS can be run directly on the firewall as well, to help keep the firewall secure.

Another advantage of HIDS is the ability to tailor the ruleset to a specific need. For example, there is no need to interrogate multiple rules designed to detect DNS exploits on a host that is not running Domain Name Services. Consequently, the reduction in the number of pertinent rules enhances performance and reduces processor overhead.

Figure 7.3 depicts a network using HIDS on specific servers and host computers. As previously mentioned, the ruleset for the HIDS on the mail server is customized to protect it from mail server exploits, while the Web server rules are tailored for Web exploits. During installation, individual host machines can be configured with a common set of rules. New rules can be loaded periodically to account for new vulnerabilities.

Figure 7.3 HIDS Network

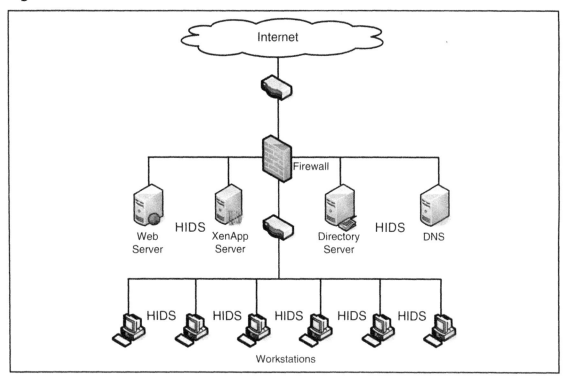

Distributed IDS

The standard DIDS functions in a Manager/Probe architecture. NIDS detection sensors are remotely located and report to a centralized management station. Attack logs are periodically uploaded to the management station and can be stored in a central database; new attack signatures can be downloaded to the sensors on an as-needed basis. The rules for each sensor can be tailored to meet its individual needs. Alerts can be forwarded to a messaging system located on the management station and used to notify the IDS administrator.

In Figure 7.4, we see a DIDS system comprised of four sensors and a centralized management station. Sensors NIDS 1 and NIDS 2 are operating in stealth promiscuous mode and are protecting the public servers. Sensors NIDS 3 and NIDS 4 are protecting the host systems in the trusted computing base. The DIDS are on the outside of the firewall, usually on the DMZ or outside.

The network transactions between sensor and manager can be on a private network, as depicted, or the network traffic can use the existing infrastructure. When using the existing network for management data, the additional security afforded by encryption, or VPN technology, is highly recommended.

Figure 7.4 DIDS Network

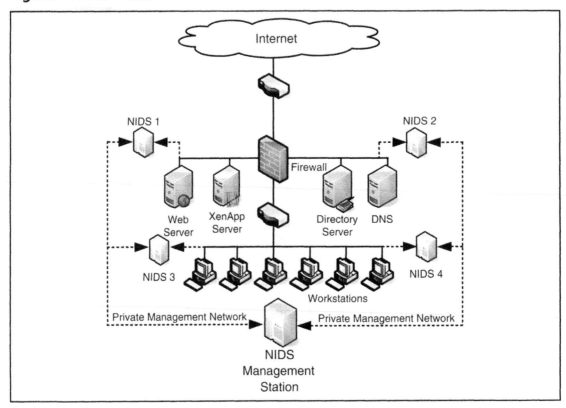

In a DIDS, complexity abounds. The scope and functionality varies greatly from manufacturer to manufacturer, and the definition blurs accordingly. In a DIDS, the individual sensors can be NIDS, HIDS, or a combination of both. The sensor can function in promiscuous mode or nonpromiscuous mode. However, in all cases, the DIDS' single defining feature requires that the distributed sensors report to a centralized management station.

Why Are Intrusion Detection Systems Important?

Everyone is familiar with the oft-used saying, "What you don't know can't hurt you." However, anyone who has ever bought a used automobile has learned, first hand, the absurdity of this statement. In the world of network security, the ability to know when an intruder is engaged in reconnaissance, or other malicious activity, can mean the difference between being compromised and not being compromised. In addition, in some environments, what you don't know can directly affect employment—yours.

IDSes can detect ICMP and other types of network reconnaissance scans that might indicate an impending attack. In addition, the IDS can alert the admin of a successful compromise, which allows him the opportunity to implement mitigating actions before further damage is caused.

IDSes provide the security administrator with a window into the inner workings of the network, analogous to an x-ray or a blood test in the medical field. The ability to analyze the internal network traffic and to determine the existence of network viruses and worms is not altogether different from techniques used by the medical profession. The similarity of network viruses and worms to their biological counterparts has resulted in their medical monikers. IDSes provide the microscope necessary to detect these invaders. Without the aid of intrusion detection, a security administrator is vulnerable to exploits and will become aware of the presence of exploits only after a system crashes or a database is corrupted.

Why Are Attackers Interested in Me?

"The Attack of the Zombies"—sounds a lot like an old B-grade movie, doesn't it? Unfortunately, in this case, it is not cinema magic. Zombie attacks are real and cost corporations and consumers billions. Zombies are computerized soldiers under the control of nefarious hackers, and in the process of performing distributed denial-of-service (DDoS) attacks, they blindly carry out the will of their masters.

In February 2000, a major DDoS attack blocked access to eBay, Amazon.com, AOL-TimeWarner, CNN, Dell Computers, Excite, Yahoo!, and other e-commerce giants. The damage done by this DDoS ranged from slowdown to complete system outages. The U.S. Attorney General instructed the FBI to launch a criminal investigation. This historical attack was perpetrated by a large group of compromised computers operating in concert.

The lesson to be learned from this event is that no network is too small to be left unprotected. If a hacker can use your computer, he will. The main purpose of the CodeRed exploit was to perform a DDoS on the White House Web site. It failed, due only to the author's oversight in using a hard-coded IP address instead of Domain Name Services. The exploit compromised over a million computers, ranging from corporate networks to home users.

In light of the recent virus activity, the growth of the information security industry, and taking into account government-sponsored hacking, the use of an IDS such can prove crucial in the protection of the world's network infrastructure.

Where Does an IDS Fit with the Rest of My Security Plan?

IDSes are a great addition to a network's defense-in-depth architecture. They can be used to identify vulnerabilities and weaknesses in your perimeter protection devices; for example, firewalls and routers. The firewall rules and router access lists can be verified regularly for functionality. In the event these devices are reconfigured, the IDS can provide auditing for change management control.

IDS logs can be used to enforce security policy and are a great source of forensic evidence. Inline IDSes can halt active attacks on your network while alerting administrators to their presence.

Properly placed IDSes can alert you to the presence of internal attacks. Industry analysis of percentages varies. However, the consensus is that the majority of attacks occur from within.

An IDS can detect failed administrator login attempts and recognize password-guessing programs. Configured with the proper ruleset, it can monitor critical application access and immediately notify the system administrator of possible breaches in security.

Doesn't My Firewall Serve as an IDS?

At this point, you may hazard the question, "doesn't my firewall serve as an IDS?" Absolutely Not! Having said that, we shall try to stop the deluge of scorn from firewall administrators who might take exception to the statement. Admittedly, a firewall can be configured to detect certain types of intrusions, such as an attempt to access the Trojan backdoor SubSeven's port 27374. In addition, it could be configured to generate an alert for any attempt to penetrate your network. In the strictest sense this would be an IDS function.

However, it is asking enough of the technology to simply determine what should and shouldn't be allowed into or out of your network without expecting it to analyze the internal contents of every packet. Even a proxy firewall is not designed to examine the contents of all packets; the function would be enormously CPU intensive. Nevertheless, a firewall should be an integral part of your defense-in-depth, with its main function being a gatekeeper and a filter (see Table 7.1).

Table 7.1 Comparing Firewalls and IDS

Functionality	Firewall	IDS
Detects unauthorized and malicious access by a computer	Yes	
	Yes	
Uses signatures to identify malicious intrusions	No	Yes
Defines borders on a trusted network from an untrusted network	Yes	No
Enforces Network Security Policies	Yes	Yes
Can detect failed administrator login attempts and recognize password-guessing programs	No	Yes
Used to identify vulnerabilities and weaknesses in your perimeter protection	No	Yes
Defines network traffic flow	Yes	No
Detects Trojan horses and Backdoors	No	Yes

Firewalls and IDS do both enforce network policy, but how they implement it is completely different. An IDS is a reconnaissance system: It collects information and will notify you of what it's found. An IDS can find any type of packet it's designed to find by a defined signature.

A firewall, on the other hand, is a like a dragon protecting the castle. It keeps out the untrusted network traffic, and only allows in what it has defined as being acceptable. For example, if an attacker has managed to compromise a Web server and uses it to store contraband (for example, pornographic materials, pirated software), your firewall will not detect this. However, if your Web server is being used for inappropriate content, this can be discovered through your IDS.

Both firewall logs and IDS logs can provide you with information to help with computer forensics or any incident handling efforts. If a system is compromised, you will have some logs on what has been going on—through both the firewall and the IDS.

What makes an IDS necessary for a defense in depth is that it can be used to identify vulnerabilities and weaknesses in your perimeter protection devices; in other words, firewalls and routers. Firewall rules and router access lists can be verified regularly for functionality. You can set up various IDS signatures to test your firewall to make sure it's not letting some undesired network traffic through the filter.

Where Else Should I Be Looking for Intrusions?

When computers that have been otherwise stable and functioning properly begin to perform erratically and periodically hang or show the Blue Screen of Death, a watchful security administrator should consider the possibility of a *buffer overflow attack*.

Buffer overflow attacks represent a large percentage of today's computer exploits. Failure of programmers to check input code has led to some of the most destructive and costly vulnerabilities to date.

Exploits that are designed to overflow buffers are usually operating system (OS) and application software specific. Without going into detail, the input to the application software is manipulated in such a manner as to cause a system error or "smash the stack" as it is referred to by some security professionals. At this point in the exploit, malicious code is inserted into the computer's process stack and the hacker gains control of the system.

In some cases, for the exploit to be successful, the payload, or malicious code, must access OS functions located at specific memory addresses. If the application is running on an OS other than that for which the exploit was designed, the results of overflowing the buffer will be simply a system crash and not a compromise; the system will appear to be unstable with frequent resets. Interestingly, in this situation the definition of the exploit changes from a system compromise to a DoS attack.

IDSes can alert you to buffer overflow attacks. Snort has a large arsenal of rules designed to detect these attacks; the following are just a few:

- Red Hat lprd overflow
- Linux samba overflow
- IMAP login overflow
- Linux mountd overflow

Using an IDS to Monitor My Company Policy

In today's litigious society, given the enormous legal interest in subjects such as downstream litigation and intellectual property rights, it would be prudent to consider monitoring for compliance with your company's security policy. Major motion picture companies have employed law firms specializing in Internet theft of intellectual property. Recently, many companies were sued because their employees illegally downloaded the motion picture *Spiderman*. Some of the employees involved were not aware that their computers were taking part in a crime. Nevertheless, the fines for damages were stiff—up to $100,000 in some cases.

Many file-sharing programs, such as Kazaa and Gnutella, are often used to share content that is federally prohibited. Computers are networked with computers in other countries that have differing laws. In the United States, the possession of child pornography is a federal offense. One is liable under the law simply for possessing it and can be held accountable whether one deliberately downloaded the content or not.

Protecting Your Data

Regardless of how hard administrators work to protect their networks and systems from disaster, sometimes the worst occurs. Servers are subject to hardware failure due to age, overuse, or defects, data loss from hack attacks, and even natural disasters such as fire or flood that can destroy both the data and the systems themselves. Effectively implementing the plans and procedures for protecting corporate data is an important part of every network administrator's job.

Considerations for Disaster Recovery and Business Continuity

Powerful Earthquake Triggers Tsunami in Pacific. Hurricane Katrina Makes Landfall in the Gulf Coast. Avalanche Buries Highway in Denver. Tornado Touches Down in Georgia. These headlines not only have caught the attention of people around the world, they have had a significant effect on IT professionals as well. As technology continues to become more integral to corporate operations at every level of the organization, the job of IT has expanded to become almost all-encompassing. These days, it's difficult to find corners of a company that technology does not touch. As a result, the need to plan for potential disruptions to technology services has increased exponentially. Business continuity and disaster recovery (BC/DR) plans were certainly put to the test by many financial firms after the terrorist attacks in the United States on September 11, 2001; but even seven years later, there are many firms that still do not have any type of business continuity or disaster recovery plan in place. It seems insane not to have such a plan in place, but statistics show that many companies don't even have solid data backup plans in place. Given the enormous cost of failure, why are many companies behind the curve? The answers are surprisingly simple. Lack of time and resources. Lack of a sense of urgency. Lack of a process for developing and maintaining a plan.

A study released by Harris Interactive, Inc. in September 2006 indicated that 39% of CIOs who participated in the survey lacked confidence in their disaster readiness. There's good news and bad news here. The bad news, clearly, is the fairly high lack of confidence in disaster plans in firms with revenues of $500M or more annually. The good news is that only 24% of CIOs in 2004 felt their disaster plans were inadequate. Although the increase in lack of confidence may appear to be a negative, it also highlights the increasing awareness of the need for comprehensive disaster readiness and a more complete understanding of what that entails. Back in 2000, some companies might have thought a "good" disaster readiness plan was having off-site backups. After the terror attacks, bombings, anthrax incidents, hurricanes, and floods that hit the United States (and other major incidents worldwide) since that time, most IT professionals now understand that off-site backups are just a small part of an overall strategy for disaster recovery.

In today's environment, no company can afford to ignore the need for BC/DR planning, regardless of the company size, revenues, or number of staff. The statistics on the failure rate of companies after a disaster are alarming and alone should serve as a wake-up call for IT professionals and corporate executives. Granted, the cost of planning must be proportionate to the cost of failure, which we'll address throughout this book.

Let's face it—very few of us want to spend the day thinking about all the horrible things that can happen in the world and to our company. It's not a cheery subject, one that most of us would rather avoid—which also helps explain the glaring lack of BC/DR plans in many small and medium companies (and a share of large companies as well). Stockholders of publicly held companies are increasingly demanding well-thought-out BC/DR plans internally as well as from key vendors, but in the absence of this pressure, many companies expend their time and resources elsewhere. Business continuity and disaster recovery planning projects have to compete with other urgent projects for IT dollars. Unless you can create a clear, coherent, and compelling business case for BC/DR, you may find strong executive resistance at worst or apathy at best.

You may wonder why you should have to champion this cause and push for some sort of budget or authorization to create such a plan. The truth is that you shouldn't, but since a disaster will probably have a disproportionately high impact on the IT department, it's very much in your own self-interest to try to get the OK to move forward with a planning project.

Business Continuity and Disaster Recovery Defined

Let's first take a moment to define *business continuity* and *disaster recovery*. These two labels often are used interchangeably, and though there are overlapping elements, they are not one and the same. *Business continuity planning* (BCP) is a methodology used to create and validate a plan for maintaining continuous business operations before, during, and after disasters and disruptive events. In the late 1990s, BCP came to the forefront as businesses tried to assess the likelihood of business systems failure on or after January 1, 2000 (the now infamous "Y2K" issue). BCP has to do with managing the operational elements that allow a business to function normally in order to generate revenues. It is often a concept that is used in evaluating various technology strategies. For example, some companies cannot tolerate any downtime. These include financial institutions, credit card processing companies and perhaps some high volume online retailers. They may decide that the cost for fully redundant systems is a worthwhile investment because the cost of downtime for even five or ten minutes could cost millions of dollars. These companies require their businesses run continuously, and their overall operational plans reflect this priority. Business continuity has to do with keeping the company running, regardless of the potential risk, threat, or cause of an outage.

Continuous availability is a subset of business continuity. It's also known as a zero-downtime requirement, and is extremely expensive to plan and implement. For some companies, it may be well worth the investment because the cost of downtime outweighs the cost of implementing continuous availability measures. Other companies have a greater tolerance for business disruption. A brick-and-mortar retailer, for example, doesn't necessarily care if the systems are down overnight or during nonbusiness hours. Although it may be an inconvenience, a retailer might also be able to tolerate critical system outages during business hours. Granted, every business that relies on technology wants to avoid having to conduct business without that technology. Every business that relies on technology will be inconvenienced and disrupted to some degree to have to conduct business without that technology. The key driver for business continuity planning is how much of a disruption to your business is tolerable and what are you able and willing to spend to avoid disruption. If money were no issue, every business using technology would probably elect to implement fully redundant, zerodowntime systems. But money *is* an issue. A small retailer or even a small online company can ill afford to spend a million dollars on fully redundant systems when their revenue stream for the year is $5 to $10 million. The cost of a business disruption for a company of that size might be $25,000 or even $100,000 and would not justify a million dollar investment. On the other hand, a million dollar investment in fully redundant systems for a company doing $5 billion annually might be worth it, especially if the cost of a single disruption would cost more than $1 million. As previously mentioned, your BC/DR plan must be appropriate to your organization's size, budget, and other constraints. In later chapters, we'll look at how to assess the cost of disruption to your operations so you can determine the optimal mitigation strategies.

Disaster recovery is part of business continuity, and deals with the immediate impact of an event. Recovering from a server outage, security breach, or hurricane all fall into this category. Disaster recovery usually has several discreet steps in the planning stages, though those steps blur quickly during implementation because the situation during a crisis is almost never exactly to plan. Disaster recovery involves stopping the effects of the disaster as quickly as possible and addressing the immediate aftermath. This might include shutting down systems that have been breached, evaluating which systems are impacted by a flood or earthquake, and determining the best way to proceed. At some point during disaster recovery, business continuity activities begin to overlap, as shown in Figure 7.8. Where to set up temporary systems, how to procure replacement systems or parts, how to set up security in a new location—all are questions that relate both to disaster recovery and business continuity, but which are primarily focused on continuing business operations. Figure 7.5 shows the cycle of planning, implementation, and assessment that is part of the ongoing BC/DR maintenance cycle.

The details of BC/DR are quite vast and are beyond the scope of this book, but we briefly mention these methodologies here because they are vital in the overall security health of your environment.

Figure 7.5 Business Continuity and Disaster Recovery Planning, Implementation, and Revision Cycle

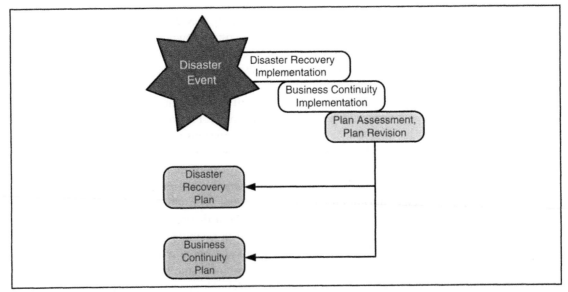

Understanding Disaster Recovery

A disaster occurs when events make continuing normal business functions impossible, and can result in some form of loss. These losses can include human life, data, equipment, money, property, or any number of other assets. Because the potential effects of a disaster can be both catastrophic and diverse, it is important to identify the types of disasters that can affect your company and implement measures to deal with them accordingly.

Disasters can result from a wide variety of sources. When people think of disasters, they generally think of storms, floods, fires, earthquakes, tornadoes, or other naturally occurring events. However, other environmental and naturally occurring threats exist. These include (but are not limited to) the following:

- Inadequate security in a building or area

- Poor air quality and temperature control in the server room

- Outdated software

- Aging equipment

Beyond these, disasters can also result from human involvement, where the deliberate or accidental actions of a person or group cause some form of damage. A hacker can gain access to sensitive information, viruses might infect a network and corrupt data, or disgruntled employees can damage equipment or sabotage data. Whatever the source, the resulting disaster has the potential to cause massive damage to a company.

Disaster recovery is the process of recognizing which threats have the potential to escalate into a disaster, and then taking steps to prevent or minimize their impact. In doing so, the most mission-critical systems of a company can be restored immediately or within a short period of time after a disaster occurs. This means that while the company might suffer some loss, it won't be crippled by it.

To understand how disaster recovery works, consider a common scenario: as network administrator, you have determined that viruses are a likely threat to your company. If one infected the network, data could be corrupted and systems could be disabled. To deal with this potential threat effectively, you can install antivirus software to prevent viruses from infecting the network, and you can perform backups regularly. You could develop and distribute a procedure to be followed as a matter of policy if a new virus does infect the network. You might check the vendor's Web site for new antivirus signature files and information about the virus, and restore backed-up data and system files to return them to a previous, uninfected state. In doing these tasks, you look at the cause and effect of a potential threat that is likely to affect your company, and then devise a solution to prevent and/or recover from it. That is what disaster recovery focuses on achieving.

The key to disaster recovery is being prepared. You will rarely know ahead of time exactly where and when a disaster will occur. Some disasters are more unexpected than others. Although we knew that there might be repercussions from the "Y2K bug" on a certain date, and that preparations needed to be completed by January 1, 2000, no one could have foreseen the events of September 11, 2001. In the same light, you know that your Windows software will cease to function on a particular date if you don't activate the product, but it is nearly impossible to determine when a hard disk will fail, viruses will infect systems, or when the next lightning storm will adversely affect your network. By establishing plans and procedures and having tools and technologies in place before the disaster occurs, your company will be better able to recover from a disaster and resume normal business practices quickly.

Understanding the Components of Disaster Recovery

Just as no single manual can cover every piece of hardware and software installed on a computer, no single plan or utility can adequately protect or restore a business after a disaster. Because disasters can have far-reaching effects and can affect a wide variety of systems, many components are involved in the recovery of systems and the organization as a whole. These include policies and procedures for dealing with individual systems and elements of a business. Some specific documents that should be developed as part of your overall recovery policy include the following:

- Business Continuity Plans (Disaster recovery plans are actually a part of the BCP, but the BCP is listed here to show the relationship between the two documents.)
- Disaster Recovery Plans
- Backup Plans
- System Recovery Plans
- Hardware Recovery Plans

Using Disaster Recovery Best Practices

As with many issues faced by network administrators, certain practices have proven successful in the field and can save valuable time when problems arise. There is no need to completely "reinvent the wheel." Instead, you can learn from the experiences of others who have survived the types of disasters to which your own company is vulnerable. By having disaster recovery components in place beforehand, you will be able to access them quickly when needed. In a disaster, every minute saved beforehand is one that won't be wasted later.

Passwords are a common security mechanism, and are often the sole method of controlling access to computers and networks. Passwords should be used on all accounts, especially administrative accounts that have the capability to modify other accounts and system settings. Passwords are also used on password-protected documents, which require that a password be entered before a person can read or modify the document. Following a disaster, these accounts and documents might be necessary to fix problems, but they won't be accessible if the people who need them don't know the required passwords.

For this reason, a list of important passwords should be stored in a location that is secure, but accessible to specific people within the organization. These lists can be stored in a sealed envelope with a responsible person's signature on it, and kept in a safe or some other place that can be locked inside a restricted area. When needed, the network administrator, manager, or other key personnel can open the envelope and use the password list. It is important that more than one person has the combination to the safe or key to the locked area, so that the list can be obtained if one or more of these people are unavailable. When it is no longer needed, the list is put in a new envelope, signed, sealed, and returned to the secure location. Following this procedure helps to ensure that anyone who isn't authorized to use the list will be unable to reuse the same envelope or duplicate the signature on a new one.

Remember that this information, or a copy of it, should be stored off-site (secured in the same way) in case the entire building is destroyed in the disaster.

NOTE

Rather than share the password to a critical account such as the built-in Administrator account, you can create secondary accounts for key persons and give those accounts administrative privileges, listing those account names and passwords on your sealed emergency document, to be revealed and used only in case of disaster.

Lists of important contact people should also be created and made accessible to members of the organization. One such list should provide contact information for members of the IT staff, so that certain employees (such as those working reception or the switchboard) can notify IT personnel of a potential problem. The list should provide information on what areas specific people are responsible for or have expertise in. That way, a programmer won't be called first about a network issue, or the network administrator won't be called about something he or she has no knowledge of. Another contact list should be created for members of the IT staff, so that they can contact vendors and con-tractors as needed. This list should include information for contacting companies responsible for repairing equipment, software support, phone service, ISP, and other technologies used in the business.

Procedures on how to handle specific problems should also be available to members of the IT staff, so that they can refer to them as needed. These documents can be stored in electronic format on the server, so that they can be easily accessed, but should also be printed so they can still be used if the server is unavailable. If you provide multiple methods for retrieving the same information, there is a greater chance that people will be able to access the information when needed.

As we'll discuss later in this chapter, a backup plan should be created and this should be one of the documents that is available to those who need it. Information in the backup plan should include steps on how to back up and restore data, where backed-up data is stored, and how long old backups are retained. If a server fails, or data needs to be restored for some other reason, these procedures can be used to restore the data and enable the business to resume using it.

In addition to documentation, installation CDs for all critical software should be stored in a place that's accessible to those who need it. Programs installed on the server might need to be repaired or reinstalled during a disaster, so it's important that these CDs be available when needed. IT staff should know where these CDs are located, so the functionality of necessary programs can be restored to the business.

The Windows Server 2003 and XenApp Server installation files should also be kept in a handy location, where they can be found and used when needed. These files can be used to repair system files or (if necessary) reinstall Windows Server 2003 and XenApp Server. They can also be used to run Recovery Console and ASR.

It is a good idea to store the original Windows Server 2003 CD and XenApp Server CD off-site in a secure location. You can make backup CDs to keep onsite if you don't have multiple original copies. You can also place the installation files on one or more servers, by copying the i386 folder on the installation CD to the server's hard disk and sharing the folder. If the network is functional, these files can be accessed across the network so that you don't need to bother with finding and using a CD.

Understanding Business Continuity Plans

Business continuity plans are used to identify key functions of a business and pinpoint the threats that are most likely to endanger them. By identifying such threats, processes can be created to ensure that normal business operations can be restored in the event of disaster. For example, if a company sells widgets, the business continuity plan is used to restore the organization's ability to sell its product and get that product to the customer. Because business continuity plans focus on restoring the business as a whole, they consist of many different plans and procedures that address different areas of the business.

The Elements of a Business Continuity Plan

Business continuity plans begin by identifying the key functions of departments within the company. These are the elements that must exist so that people within the department can do their jobs. Because jobs within the organization vary, many of these key functions also vary. However, some elements are constant. Having facilities to perform work-related duties is a common element, so the company might plan for workers to be relocated to branch offices if the building is damaged or destroyed in a disaster. By looking at what is needed to conduct business, contingency plans can be set in place to enable those functions to resume quickly in the face of catastrophe.

One of the plans included in a business continuity plan is the disaster recovery plan. Disaster recovery plans concentrate on restoring data and technology and implementing systems that can prevent or minimize disasters. As you'll see in later sections of this chapter, there are many countermeasures that can be taken to protect systems, and numerous tools that can be used to successfully restore systems and data when problems arise. Like business continuity plans, disaster recovery plans consist of many different plans and procedures, but narrow the focus to address individual areas of Information Technology (IT).

A major portion of protecting and restoring data and other files on a server is backing them up. As you'll see later in this chapter, backups create a copy of files and folders on other media, such as tapes, magneto-optical (MO) discs, CDs, or DVDs. When a problem occurs, these files and folders can then be copied back to the server, or to another server if the original is irretrievably lost. A backup plan creates a regimen of backing up data on a regular schedule, and outlines what data is to be backed up and the procedures that need to be followed when restoring it.

Just as data can be at risk in a disaster, so can the systems themselves. Problems might arise that prevent Windows Server 2003 from starting properly, or even starting at all. In these instances, network administrators or other members of the IT staff need to intervene and follow procedures to restore the system. Such procedures are found in a system recovery plan, which we'll discus in greater detail later in this chapter.

With any of these plans, it is important that the staff members who will be involved with using them be knowledgeable and well trained in their implementation. It is important for members of an organization to know that the plans exist, and the necessary parties must have a clear understanding of how to carry out the procedures involved. If this information is not disseminated to the proper parties and employees are not properly trained, people might fumble through the steps needed to complete certain tasks, while other tasks might be missed because no one knew they were required. The time to learn how a procedure should be carried out is before it is actually needed.

Backing Up Your Data

A backup enables data and system files on a computer to be archived to another location on the hard disk or to other media. You can compare backups to making a photocopy of an original document, which creates a duplicate that can be stored safely in case the original is destroyed. As with a photocopy, a backup of data is a duplicate of the original data on a computer at the time the backup was taken. Unlike a photocopy, however, the quality of the backup data is equal to the quality of the original.

When problems occur, the backed-up files can be restored to the location from which the data was originally copied or to another location such as a different directory or a different machine. The capability to restore the data is just as important as performing regular backups; if the backup cannot be restored, then the backed-up data is as lost as any original data you're attempting to recover.

Backing up and restoring data is a fundamental part of any disaster recovery plan. A backup plan provides procedures that detail which data should be backed up, how this data is to be backed up, and when it is to be backed up. The plan also provides information regarding the storage of backed-up data, and how it can be restored. Such information can be used during a disaster to restore system files and other data that might have been damaged or destroyed.

As we'll discuss in the sections that follow, there are many different elements to a good backup plan. In addition to knowing how the Backup utility can be used, you need to make decisions about what data will be backed up, where it will be stored, and other issues. Such decisions need to be made far in advance of any disasters. A good backup plan should be part of every network administrator's daily routine.

Backup Concepts

Backing up data begins with deciding what information needs to be archived. Critical data, such as trade secrets that the business relies on to function, along with other important data crucial to business needs, must be backed up. Other data, such as temporary files and applications, might not need to be backed up, as they can easily be reinstalled or aren't needed in the first place. Such decisions, however, will vary from company to company and even from department to department.

In addition to data, it is important to back up the System State data, which consists of files the operating system uses. These include the boot files, system files, the Registry, COM+ Class Registration database, and other files that Windows Server 2003 (depending on the server configuration) will require you to back up as a single unit. If the server fails at any point, these files can be used to restore the system to a functioning state.

Rather than simply backing up bits and pieces of your server, it is wise to back up everything on a server at the same time. This includes all data on the server and the System State data. If the hard disk on the server fails, or the entire server is lost in a disaster, then a full backup of everything can be used to restore the server quickly.

When creating a backup, you should always have the backup program create log files. A backup log shows which files were backed up, and the log can be saved or printed as a reference for restoring data. If you needed to restore a particular file or folder, the log would show whether a particular backup included it in the job.

When a backup is performed, the copied data is usually kept on media other than the local hard disk. After all, if the hard disk failed, both the original data on the disk and the backup would be lost. As we'll discuss later in greater detail, other media such as tapes can be used to store backups safely.

Microsoft recommends that three copies of the media be stored, with one copy kept off-site. This ensures that if one or two of the copies are destroyed in a disaster, the third can be used to restore data and the system.

To prevent backups from being stolen and used to restore data to another machine, it is important that backup devices and media be kept physically secure. Backup media should be stored in a secure location, such as a safe or locked storage device. The area in which it is stored shouldn't be easily accessible. In the same light, the devices used to create backups should also be secured. Removable devices should be stored in secure environments, while servers with backup devices installed on them should be kept secure (in locked server rooms). The physical security of devices and media should be as high as the security of data on the server.

Because backups are so important, it is important for personnel to be trained in how to perform backups and restores. Designated members of the IT staff should be knowledgeable in the steps involved in creating backups and restoring data, should know where media is stored, and should be aware of what data is to be backed up and when. If a disaster occurs, they should be able to follow the backup plan without incident. Before a disaster occurs, however, you should test whether data can actually be restored. If a device seems to back up data properly but is actually failing to do so, you might not be aware of it until you need to restore the data. Rather than assuming everything is being backed up properly, you should test your equipment by restoring data from a previous backup job. If files and folders can be restored properly, then you will have peace of mind that such data can be restored during a disaster.

Backup Media

There are many different types of media to which backed-up data can be stored. The type you choose will determine how much data can be stored on a single media target, and the speed at which backups can be performed. In choosing the type of media you'll use, you should estimate how much data will be copied during a backup job. Some types of media include:

- Magnetic tape (DAT, DLT)
- Hard disk
- Optical disk (CD/DVD)
- Solid state storage (USB devices, jump drives)
- Electronic vaulting (backups via links off-site)

Managing Media

Backups must be effectively managed so that there is a clear understanding of what's been backed up, when, and where it is currently stored. This enables people to know which tape they should use first to restore data, and where the tape (or other media) can be found. If media isn't managed properly, then a tape could be lost, accidentally erased, or overwritten.

When a backup is made, you should write the date on the media. This enables you and others to see that the backup is a duplicate of data from a given date. As you'll see later in this section, there could be numerous backups made in an organization, so you'll want to use the most current version.

This prevents users from having to reproduce more work than is needed. For example, let's say you made a backup of everything on your server on Monday and Tuesday, and the server crashed on Wednesday. If you restore the backup from Monday, any work that was performed after that time won't be included on the backup. This means that all work done by users on Tuesday will need to be redone. If the backup from Tuesday is restored, users will only need to redo work performed after that time (which would take hours rather than days).

Documenting the date also provides information on how many times a particular media type was used. Backup tapes can be used multiple times, but they don't last forever. Keep in mind that reusing the same magnetic tape over and over will slowly degrade the tape. When the tape holds your backed-up data, this can result in data being lost. To avoid this, you should record how many times a medium has been used, and not use it more than the number of times recommended by the manufacturer.

It is also unwise to keep all backup media in the same location or in the same area as the computers whose data you've backed up. Because you're backing up data to protect the business from data loss, keeping backups near the backed up computer can expose the backups to the same disaster that damages or destroys the original data on that computer. In the same light, if all the backups are together in the same location, they can all be destroyed simultaneously. If a fire or flood occurs and destroys the server room, all backup tapes stored in that room could also be destroyed. To protect your data, you should store the backups in different locations, so that they'll be safe until they're needed.

Off-Site Storage

Off-site storage can be achieved in a number of ways. If your company has multiple buildings, in different cities or different parts of the city, the backups from each site can be stored in one of the other buildings. Doing this makes it more likely that, if one location experiences a disaster, the original data or backups will remain safe. If this isn't possible, you can consider using a firm that provides off-site storage facilities. Some organizations store their off-site backups in a safe deposit box at a bank. The key is keeping the backups away from the physical location of the original data.

When deciding on an off-site storage facility, you should ensure that it is secure and has the environmental conditions necessary to keep the backups safe. You should ensure that the site has air conditioning and heating, as temperature changes could affect the integrity of data. It should also be protected from moisture and flooding, and have fire protection in case a disaster befalls the storage facility. The backups need to be locked up, and your organization should have policies that dictate who can pick up the data when needed. Otherwise, someone posing as a member of your organization could steal the data. Conversely, you want the data to be quickly accessible, so that you can acquire the data from the facility if you need it, without having to wait until the next time the building is open for business.

Configuring Security for Backup Operations

Being able to perform a backup requires that you have the proper permissions and rights. After all, if anyone could perform a backup, an unauthorized person could obtain a copy of the data stored on the computer. Note, however, that being able to back up data doesn't necessarily mean you are able to access and read it. Also note that a user who is authorized to back up data can back up and restore encrypted files without decrypting them.

The permissions and user rights needed to perform backup and restore operations in Windows Server 2003 are dependent on what is being backed up or restored, the permissions set on the files and folders, and the account being used to perform the backup and its group memberships.

To back up or restore any file or folder on the computer to which you are currently logged on as a user, you need to be a member of a group on that computer. Backup and restoration of files and folders on the local computer require you to be a member of the Administrators or Backup Operators local group. A local group is a group that's created on the computer (in contrast to a group that is created on the domain controller and used throughout the domain). A local group is assigned rights and permissions that apply only to that computer. Because the rights and permissions are limited to that machine, accounts that are a part of these groups cannot perform backup or restoration of data on other machines.

To back up or restore files and folders on any computer in a domain, you need to be a member of the Administrators or Backup Operators group on a domain controller. This also enables group members to back up or restore computers that are in a domain with which your domain has a two-way trust relationship. If you are not an Administrator or Backup Operator, there is still a chance that you might have the necessary permissions to perform a backup. The owner of a file or folder can generally back up his or her files. If the owner has one or more of the following permissions to a file or folder, then he or she can perform a backup:

- Read
- Read and execute
- Modify
- Full control

In addition to these rights and permissions, it is important that a user to whom you want to give the capability to back up and restore files doesn't have any disk-quota restrictions. Such restrictions make it impossible to perform backups of data. An administrator can also delegate the authority to perform backups to a user without placing that user in one of the authorized groups. Delegation of control can be done through the Delegation of Control Wizard or via Group Policy settings.

Understanding Backup Types

The types of backups you can choose in most commercial backup programs as well as the backup utility provided with Windows 2003 are as follows:

- Normal
- Incremental
- Differential
- Copy
- Daily

As you will see in the paragraphs that follow, different types of backups archive data in different ways. Because of this, the methods used to back up data will vary between businesses. One company might make normal backups every day, while another might use a combination of backup types. Regardless of the types used, however, it is important that data be backed up on a daily basis so that large amounts of data won't be lost in the event of a disaster.

NOTE

Some types of data require that you follow special procedures to back them up. The System State data, discussed in the text, is one such special situation.

Another special situation occurs when you want to back up files that are associated with Windows Media Services (WMS). To back up these files, you must follow the procedures that are outlined in the WMS Help files. You cannot use the normal backup procedures to back up and restore these files.

Microsoft recommends that if you want to back up database files on an SQL server, you should use the backup and restore utilities that are included with SQL Server instead of the Windows Server 2003 Backup utility.

If your Windows Server 2003 computer is running cluster services (Enterprise or Datacenter editions), you need to perform an ASR backup for each cluster node, back up the cluster disks in each node, and then back up individual applications that run on the nodes.

Before describing each of the backup types, it is important to understand that the type chosen will affect how the archive attribute is handled. The archive attribute is a property of a file or folder that's used to indicate whether a file has changed since the last time it was backed up. As you will see in the paragraphs that follow, depending on the backup type used, the archive attribute of a file is or is not cleared after it is backed up. When the file is modified, the archive attribute is set again to indicate it has changed and needs to be backed up again. Without the archive attribute, your backup program is unable to tell whether files need to be backed up or not. Here is a description of each backup type in more detail:

- **Full Backup** The full backup, as its name implies, backs up everything specified by the user performing the backup operation. A full backup can include the operating system, system state data, applications, and any other data. With a full backup, everything that is backed up has the file system archive bit reset (cleared). This allows the incremental and differential backup types to determine if the file needs to be backed up. If the bit is still clear, the other backup types know that the data has not changed. If the bit is set, the data has changed, and the file needs to be backed up. The full backup is usually the first backup performed on a server. It takes the longest of all the backup types to complete, because it backs up all specified files, regardless of the state of the archive attribute. A full backup consumes the largest amount of backup media of any backup type. Depending on the amount of information chosen to back up and the underlying backup technology involved, it may require multiple backup media to complete. The main advantage of the full backup type is the ability to rapidly restore the data. All of the information is contained in a single backup set when this type of backup is used. The disadvantages of full backups are high media consumption and long backup times.

- **Incremental Backups** During an incremental backup operation, all specified files have their archive bit examined. If the bit is set, the file is backed up, and then the bit is cleared. This backup type is used to back up data that has changed or been created since the last full (normal) or incremental backup. It can also be used after a copy or differential backup, but because these do not reset the archive attribute, there is no way for the incremental backup to tell which files have changed since one of those backups last ran. As a result, every file with the archive attribute set is backed up. The incremental backup type is used between full backups. It is quick to perform, collects the least amount of data, and consumes the smallest amount of media. A complete restore, however, requires the last full backup and every incremental backup (in sequence) since the full backup was performed. The primary benefits of using the full/incremental backup combination are time and media savings. The main drawback of this combination is longer and more complex restore operations if there are long periods between full backups.

■ **Differential Backups** The differential backup type is sometimes used as a substitute for the incremental type. A differential backup collects data that has changed or been created since the last full (normal) or incremental backup, but it does not clear the archive bit on the file. It can also be used after a copy or differential backup, but as with an incremental backup, every file with the archive attribute set is backed up. The differential backup is advantageous when you want to minimize the restoration time. A complete system restore with a full/ differential backup combination requires only the most recent full backup and the most recent differential backup. Differential backups start with small volumes of data after a recent full or incremental backup, but often grow in size each time, because the volume of changed data grows. This means that the time to perform a differential backup starts small but increases over time as well. In theory, if full or incremental backups are infrequent, a differential backup could end up taking as long and reaching the same volume as a full backup.

■ **Volume Shadow Copy** More of a Windows 2003 feature than a backup type, Volume Shadow Copy allows you to back up all files on the system, including files that are open by applications or processes. In previous versions of Windows, the applications would need to be stopped or users logged out to allow these files to be closed and backed up using a backup program. With Volume Shadow Copy, these files can continue to remain in use without affecting the integrity of the backup. This feature is enabled by default, but it may need to be disabled if data managed by some critical applications would be affected by the use of Volume Shadow Copy

WARNING

Not all backups are the same. Remember that normal and incremental backups set the archive attribute after backing up a file, but differential, copy, and daily backups do not. You can use normal, copy, and daily backups to restore files from a single backup job, whereas you can use incremental and differential backup types in conjunction with normal backups. This is because differential backups back up all files that have changed since the last normal backup (regardless of whether they were backed up by a previous differential backup), while incremental backups only back up files that have changed since the last normal or incremental backup and were not backed up previously.

Creating a System Recovery Plan

Because many types of disasters can affect an operating system's ability to start, Windows Server 2003 includes a variety of utilities that can be used to recover the system. These include the following:

- The capability to back up the System State data
- The creation of ASR sets
- The Recovery Console
- Startup options that appear when the computer is booted

Using these tools, you can remedy many of the problems that could prevent you from starting and using Windows Server 2003. In the next sections, we will discuss each of these tools in more detail.

Backing Up System State Data

The System State data is a set of files that the system uses to function; it must be backed up as a single unit. Windows Server 2003 requires these files to be backed up together, because the files included in the System State have dependencies, in which two or more files rely on one another to function. Because of this, you can't choose individual System State data files when performing a backup.

System State data files are specific to each computer running Windows Server 2003 and can't generally be swapped between servers. Since servers can have different hardware and software installed, swapping these files can result in devices, programs, and the operating system itself not functioning properly. Thus, when backing up System State data files, it is important to label the backup as belonging to a specific server so that you won't accidentally restore the wrong System State data files to a server.

NOTE

It is possible to restore the System State data to an alternate location, but if you do so, some components (the COM+ Class Registration database, the Active Directory database, and the Certificate Services database) are not restored.

Most backup programs can backup the System State data, including the Windows 2003 Backup utility. The files that are considered to be part of the System State can vary between computers. On Windows Server 2003, it always includes the following:

- The Registry
- The COM+ Class Registration database
- System files
- Boot files

In addition to these, your backup program might also include other files if the server is configured for a special purpose or has certain services installed, like XenApp. A domain controller has the Active

Directory and the SYSVOL directory included in the System State data, and a certificate server includes the Certificate Services database as part of the System State data. If the server is part of a cluster, cluster service information also is included in the System State data. If Windows Server 2003 is configured to be a Web server and has Internet Information Services (IIS) installed, the IIS Metadirectory is also included. As you can see, the role a server plays on a network and the services it has installed have a great impact on what is backed up as part of the System State data.

Primary, Nonauthoritative, and Authoritative Restores

There are different situations where you would restore Active Directory. In some cases, you might have only one domain controller on a network, while in other situations you might want the information on the backup to be replicated to other domain controllers on the network. Because situations will vary, Windows Server 2003 provides three different methods of restoring Active Directory:

- Primary
- Nonauthoritative (normal)
- Authoritative

Use a primary restore when you are restoring Active Directory to the only domain controller on your network or the first of multiple domain controllers being restored. This type of restore is commonly used when all of the domain controllers are no longer available (such as when a disaster has destroyed all servers or data), and you are rebuilding the network from scratch.

Use a nonauthoritative or normal restore when you are restoring Active Directory on a network with multiple domain controllers. When Active Directory is restored to the domain controller, it is generally older than the directory information stored on other DCs in the domain. To ensure all domain controllers have identical copies of Active Directory, these other domain controllers replicate updated data to the restored server.

The reason a nonauthoritative restore has its information updated from other domain controllers is because of the way updates to the directory are recorded. When the System State data changes on a domain controller that participates in replication, an update sequence number is incremented to indicate a change has occurred. Because the System State data on other domain controllers has a lower update sequence, they know that they don't have the most up-to-date data. The System State data with the higher update sequence number is then replicated to other domain controllers so they have duplicate information.

When a nonauthoritative restore is performed, the domain controller generally has older data restored to it. For example, a backup might have been performed several days ago, in which time a considerable number of changes could have been made on other domain controllers on the network. To ensure the domain controller being restored has the most recent information, information is replicated to it to bring it up-to-date.

This can be a problem in situations where you want the restored data to be used. For example, you might have made errors in modifying Active Directory objects, such as deleting a user account that is still needed. By performing the nonauthoritative restore, the deleted account is restored from the backup, but it is then deleted again when replication occurs. To enable restored data to not be affected by replication, you can use authoritative restores. An authoritative restore is similar to a nonauthoritative restore, in that Active Directory is restored to domain controllers participating in replication. The difference is that when it is restored, it is given a higher update sequence number, so it has the highest number in the Active Directory replication system. Because of this, other domain controllers are updated through replication with the restored data.

Creating an Automated System Recovery Set

An ASR set consists of files that are needed to restore Windows Server 2003 if the system cannot be started. When you create an ASR set, the following are backed up:

- System State data
- System services
- Disks that hold operating system components

In addition, a floppy disk is created that contains system settings. Because an ASR set focuses on the files needed to restore the system, data files are not included in the backup.

You should create an ASR set each time a major hardware change or a change to the operating system is made on the computer running Windows Server 2003. For example, if you install a new hard disk or network card, or apply a security patch or Service Pack, an ASR set should be created. Then if a problem occurs after upgrading the system in such ways, the ASR set can be used to restore the system to its previous state after other methods of system recovery have been attempted.

An ASR should not be used as the first step in recovering an operating system. In fact, Microsoft recommends that it be the last possible option for system recovery, to be used only after you've attempted other methods. In many cases, you'll be able to get back into the system using Safe Mode, Last Known Good Configuration (LKGC), or other options we'll discuss in later sections of this chapter.

ASR sets are easily created by using the Windows Server 2003 Backup utility. On the **Welcome** tab of the Backup utility, click the **Automated System Recovery Wizard** button. This starts the **Automated System Recovery Preparation Wizard**, which takes you through the steps of backing up the system files needed to recover Windows Server 2003 and create a floppy disk containing the information needed to restore the system.

You can restore an ASR set through the Windows Server 2003 setup by pressing **F2** in the text mode portion of setup. After doing this, the ASR restore starts recovery by reading configuration information that was stored on a floppy disk when the ASR set was created.

This information is used to restore disk signatures, volumes, partitions, and other disk configurations. A simple installation of Windows then starts and automatically begins restoring your system from the ASR set that was created with the Automated System Recover Wizard.

Installing and Using the Recovery Console

The Recovery Console is a text-mode command interpreter that can be used without starting Windows Server 2003. It enables you to access the hard disk and use commands to troubleshoot and manage problems that prevent the operating system from starting properly. With this tool, you can do the following:

- Enable and disable services
- Format hard disks

- Repair the master boot record and boot sector

- Read and write data on FAT16, FAT32, and NTFS drives

- Perform other tasks necessary to repairing the system

The Recovery Console can be started from the installation CD for Windows Server 2003, or you can install it on an x86-based computer. When installed on the computer, you can run it from a multiple-boot menu that appears when the computer is first started. Either method starts the same program and enables you to enter different commands to repair the system.

NOTE

You cannot install the Recovery Console on an Itanium running the 64-bit version of Windows Server 2003. You can still access the Recovery Console from the CD.

Configuring & Implementing...

Installing and Using the Recovery Console

Here is a brief step-by-step exercise for installing the Windows 2003 Recovery Console. To start the Recovery Console from the installation CD, run Windows Server 2003 Setup. Press **Enter** on your keyboard when the **Setup Notification** screen appears, and then press **R** on your keyboard to select the option of repairing the installation. This opens the Recovery Console and enables you to enter commands at the prompt.

To install the Recovery Console as a startup option, follow these steps:

1. Ensure that the Windows Server 2003 CD is in the CD-ROM drive.

2. Click **Start | Run**.

3. Enter the drive letter of your CD-ROM drive, then type **/I386/Winnt32.exe /cmdcons**.

4. A message box appears, asking if you'd like to install Recovery Console as a startup option and telling you that it takes approximately 7MB of disk space. Click **Yes**.

5. Windows Setup starts and the Recovery Console is installed.

Upon restarting your computer, you see a multiboot menu that enables you to start different operating systems installed on the computer. On this menu, you also

Continued

see an option labeled **Microsoft Windows Recovery Console**. Select it to highlight it and press **Enter** on your keyboard to start the Recovery Console.

When the Recovery Console starts, you must select the Windows installation you'd like to log onto, and enter the password for the Administrator account for that installation. The built-in Administrator account is the only account you can use to run the Recovery Console on Windows Server 2003.

The Recovery Console provides a prompt where you can enter text-based commands. The commands available to you are shown in Table 7.2.

Table 7.2 Commands for Recovery Console

Command	Description
ATTRIB	Enables you to view and change attributes on a file or directory
BATCH	Executes commands in a text file
BOOTCFG	Used for boot configuration and recovery. Enables you to scan disks for Windows installations, add an installation of Windows to the boot list, set the default boot entry, list entries in the boot list, and configure other parameters related to boot configuration.
CD	Displays the name of the current directory and enables you to change to a new directory
CHDIR	Displays the name of the current directory and enables you to change to a new directory
CHKDSK	Checks the disk for errors and displays results
CLS	Clears the screen
COPY	Copies a file to another location
DEL	Deletes a file
DELETE	Deletes a file
DIR	Displays the contents of a directory
DISABLE	Disables a service
DISKPART	Used to manage partitions on a hard disk. Enables you to add and delete partitions.
ENABLE	Enables a service
EXIT	Exits the Recovery Console and restarts the computer
EXPAND	Expands a compressed file
FIXBOOT	Creates a new boot sector on the system partition
FIXMBR	Used to repair the master boot record on the boot partition
FORMAT	Formats a disk

Continued

Table 7.2 Continued. Commands for Recovery Console

Command	Description
HELP	Displays commands available to use in the Recovery Console
LISTSVC	Lists available services and drivers
LOGON	Enables you to log on to an installation of Windows
MAP	Displays a list of drive letter mappings
MD	Creates a new directory
MKDIR	Creates a new directory
MORE	Displays a text file on the screen
RD	Deletes a directory
REN	Renames a file
RENAME	Renames a file
RMDIR	Deletes a directory
SYSTEMROOT	Sets the current directory to the systemroot
TYPE	Displays a text file on the screen

Using Windows Startup Options

Often, problems preventing Windows Server 2003 from running properly can be resolved by using the startup options. These are different options for starting Windows that can be accessed when you boot the computer. If you install new software, devices, or other components and find Windows Server 2003 doesn't load properly afterwards, the startup options can be used to load Windows with minimal drivers, VGA display, and other minimal settings. After the operating system starts, you can then use the utilities in Windows Server 2003 to resolve issues that prevent it from starting normally.

The Windows startup options can be displayed by pressing **F8** when the computer starts. This produces a menu of different options for starting the operating system. There are eight possible methods of starting Windows from this menu:

- Safe Mode

- Safe Mode with Networking

- Safe Mode with Command Prompt

- Enable Boot Logging

- Enable VGA Mode

- Last Known Good Configuration

- Directory Service Restore Mode

- Debugging Mode

In the following sections, we will look at each of these in a little more detail.

Safe Mode

Safe Mode starts Windows Server 2003 with the minimum files and drivers needed for it to load. This includes such elements as a mouse driver (except serial mice), keyboard, monitor, and base video, mass storage device drivers, and default system services. Starting Windows 2003 in this mode does not load the drivers and files required for network connectivity, thus making the server a stand-alone machine. After Windows Server 2003 loads in Safe Mode, you can then use the tools in Windows Server 2003 to adjust settings, or uninstall software that is preventing it from loading normally.

Safe Mode with Networking

Safe Mode with Networking starts Windows Server 2003 with the same minimum files and drivers as Safe Mode, but also loads the drivers needed to make connections to the network. With network connections, you can access resources that might be needed to restore your server to a working state. For example, if you need to uninstall a device driver that was causing problems, you might need to access documentation on the device or old drivers residing on another server. Without network connectivity, such resources might be inaccessible and the problem couldn't be fixed.

Safe Mode with Command Prompt

Safe Mode with Command Prompt enables you to start Windows Server 2003 with minimum files and drivers, but does not load the Windows Server 2003 Graphical User Interface (GUI). Instead, a command prompt is displayed, enabling you to enter text-based commands. This option is particularly important when the GUI interface fails to load properly, and the only way to access the system is through a command-line interface. It is also useful when you're comfortable using text-based commands, and using such an interface restores the system faster than waiting for a GUI interface to load.

Enable Boot Logging

When *Enable Boot Logging* is selected from the startup options, the drivers and services that are used by the system are loaded, and the results of loading them are logged to a file called ntblog.txt. The ntblog.txt file can be located in the directory containing Windows Server 2003 (the systemroot directory, named WINDOWS by default). By viewing this file after unsuccessfully attempting to start Windows Server 2003, you can determine where a problem occurred and at what point the operating system stopped loading properly.

Enable VGA Mode

Enable VGA Mode enables Windows Server 2003 to start with a basic VGA driver that provides minimal graphics support. This mode is useful when a graphics card has been installed or display settings have been changed, and consequently you can't view the Windows GUI interface or other elements of the system properly. By using Windows Server 2003 in VGA Mode, you are able to load and view Windows Server 2003's interface and then make changes to the system so the new settings or graphics driver won't be used. When you do so, you should then be able to restart Windows normally.

Last Known Good Configuration

As you've probably noticed when shutting down Windows Server 2003, the operating system takes some time to save system settings before actually shutting down the server. This information is used in case problems occur and you need to use the *Last Known Good Configuration* that's available on the startup menu. When Last Known Good Configuration is used, Windows starts using the Registry information and driver settings that were saved at the last successful logon. This option is particularly important if you incorrectly configured Windows Server 2003, because using the settings that were saved during the last successful logon will load the operating system as it was previous to these changes.

Directory Service Restore Mode

If you are having problems with a Windows Server 2003 computer acting as a domain controller, the startup options provide the *Directory Service Restore Mode*. This mode of starting Windows Server 2003 is used to restore the Active Directory database and the SYSVOL directory. Because this only applies to domain controllers, this option isn't available on servers that have not been promoted to domain controller status.

Debugging Mode

Debugging Mode is the final method of loading Windows from the startup options. Software developers use this mode, because they are the only ones who can reprogram Windows Server 2003 after finding bugs in the operating system code. When this mode is used, debugging information is sent through a serial cable to another computer as the system starts. The serial cable must be connected to COM1 port, and the baud rate must be set at 115,200 for this to work.

Updating and Patching the Network Operating System

Patching a large enterprise full of server and client systems has become something of an administrative nightmare in most IT shops because of the importance of staying on top of security patches that Microsoft releases frequently. Although Microsoft makes every effort to release patches in a timely manner, sometimes attackers themselves use security bulletins that inform them of a vulnerability to gain the ability to exploit it. With this awareness, an attacker can scan for companies whose machines have not been patched against the vulnerability, often severely damaging their systems. As the security specialist in your organization, you should have as part of your overall strategy a plan to analyze and quickly deploy the security patches that Microsoft releases.

To include new features and more functionality in newer versions of an OS, programmers have to write more lines of code. More lines of code mean more room for security holes, which leads to more patch releases. Not only do you need antivirus software to protect your system against malicious programs, you also need to worry about security patches so that hackers don't take advantage of a security hole. This was the case with the Blaster worm, which exploited the RPC/DCOM service and caused servers that didn't have the proper security patches to constantly reboot themselves, thus disrupting productivity by creating an unstable environment.

Designing a Windows Server Update Services Infrastructure

When deploying Windows Server Update Services (WSUS), it's important to be aware of not only its capabilities but also its limitations. WSUS certainly isn't a one-size-fits-all solution, and you should be certain that WSUS will meet your needs before you deploy it.

WSUS allows you to control which patches are visible to your users and automates the download and installation process so that no user intervention is required. Another important feature that is often overlooked is its ability to optimize bandwidth, especially for a large organization. Rather than having 5,000 clients each download a 3MB update (that's 15 gigabytes of information being pushed down your expensive Internet connection), you will be able to host the update locally and have clients download their information over an internal LAN connection.

In short, WSUS allows you to maintain what is effectively an internal Windows Update Web site, where your WSUS server contacts the actual Microsoft Update Web site and downloads updates that an administrator can review and approve for deployment. WSUS has many advantages over Windows Update, the most obvious of which is that with WSUS, you can control and approve the patches that are installed, as shown in Figure 7.6. As hard as Microsoft tries to build a software update package that will not break anything, sometimes patches that are not tested can damage a specific environment, rendering your computers unusable rather than tightening security on them.

Figure 7.6 Approving Critical Updates in WSUS

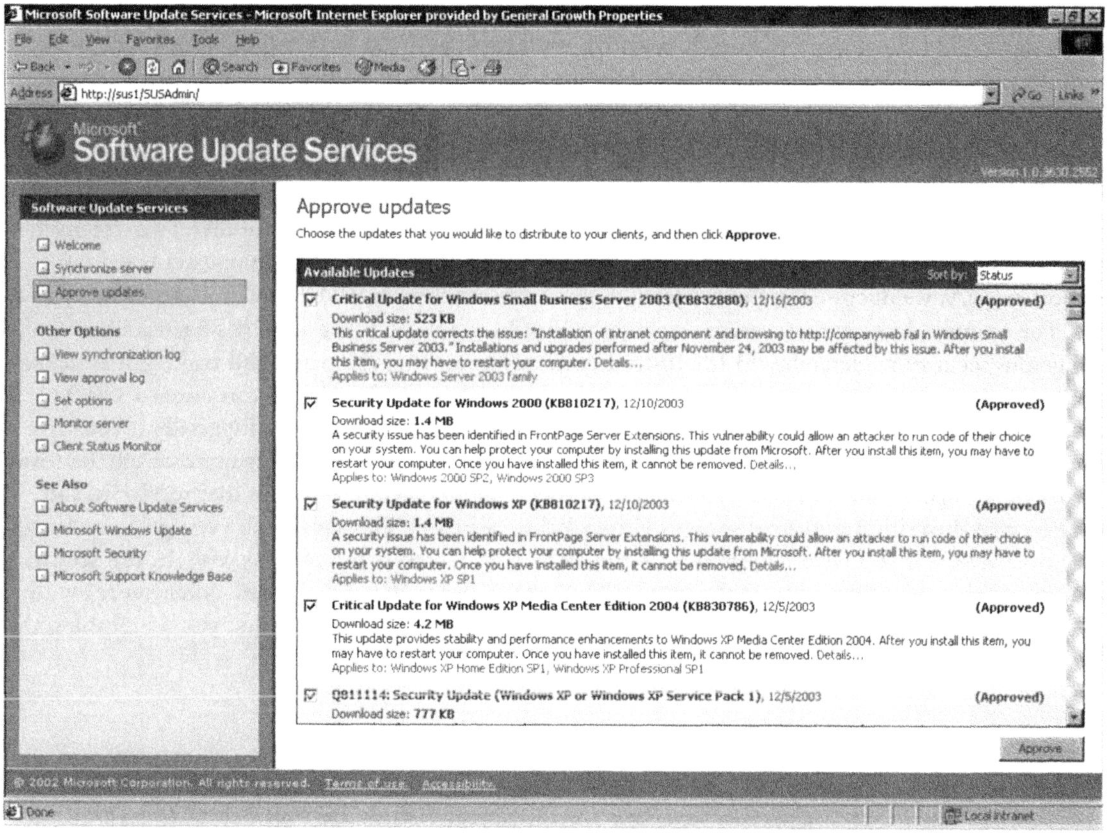

However, WSUS is far from a panacea, and it's important to remember its limitations. WSUS only allows you to deploy critical updates and service packs that you download from Microsoft. You cannot deploy other Windows Update files, including software updates and updated device drivers, using WSUS. Nor can you create your own .EXE or .MSI files and have WSUS deploy them for you; anything that WSUS deploys needs to be a critical update downloaded directly from Microsoft.

If you are working in an environment that supports many down-level or legacy clients, it's absolutely key to remember that WSUS will only deploy patches for "modern" Microsoft operating systems, a definition that extends to the following:

■ Windows 2000 with Service Pack 4

■ Windows XP with Service Pack 2

■ Windows Vista

■ Windows Server 2003

■ Windows Server 2008

If you are still supporting Windows NT or 9x clients, you will not be able to deploy patches for these operating systems using WSUS. On the server side, you can't automate the installation of updates for back-end applications such as SQL or Exchange Server. Finally, there's no good way to "push" installations to your clients, since WSUS is designed to operate in the background with no user intervention. So, if there is a newly released patch that you need to install on your client workstations right away, WSUS doesn't offer an intuitive way to force an update for your clients.

Using Group Policy to Deploy Software Updates

Group Policy is another great way you can deploy software in general and patches and updates in particular. Using GPOs, you can even customize who gets which updates and can thereby exert more granular control over the software distribution process, allowing you to prioritize updates based on importance. (As we discussed in the last section, this is something that WSUS will not allow you to do.)

For example, let's say that a security patch has just been released that addresses a particularly dangerous security vulnerability in IIS. Instead of simply approving the patch and making it available for everyone via WSUS and then crossing your fingers until it's deployed, you can create a GPO to forcibly update the OU, site, or domain that contains all your IIS Web servers. Especially if you have grouped your Web servers into a single discrete container such as an OU, this is quite an efficient way to deliver an update, since only the machines that need the update are the ones that receive it, and they receive the critical update as soon as Group Policy refreshes. This creates an even greater advantage over WSUS if you have remote offices and child WSUS servers to contend with. In this scenario, you would first need to wait until the child WSUS server in the Web servers' site synchronizes with the master server before that patch is even available to them. Using Group Policy, you are pushing the package to all the necessary servers regardless of geographic location.

TIP

Software installations in Group Policy can be applied to either computer or user configurations. Software packages applied to Computer Configurations are installed on computer startup. Packages applied to user configurations are installed at user logon.

Let's explore another situation; let's say that a critical security patch has been released for an application in use across your network. Before approving the update in WSUS, you find during testing that the update interferes with a development application that is used by your Web programmers. If your Web programmers are separated into their own OU, you can use the Block Inheritance setting within Group Policy to push this patch out to everyone *except* the Development OU. Even if the development users aren't separated into a single OU, you can still use access control lists (ACLs) to prevent the harmful patch from being deployed to their computers. But again, you have the option of pushing a software package in this manner only when you use Group Policy, as shown in Figure 7.7. WSUS does not offer this level of fine control.

Figure 7.7 Configuring Software Installation Policies

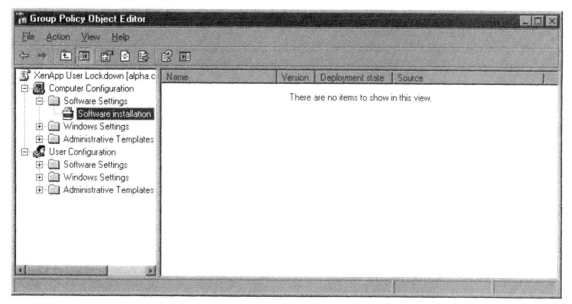

TIP

Remember that an object needs Read and Apply Group Policy permissions to a GPO to be able to have that GPO applied to that object. You can alter the ACL on a GPO to control which objects or groups will and will not have a GPO applied to them.

Design a Strategy for Identifying Computers That Are Not at the Current Patch Level

Now that you have configured your preferred method of pushing security patches to workstations and servers, how do you audit to make sure that your strategy is actually working? You'll need to perform some kind of audit to ensure that your machines are receiving the patches that they should receive and to identify machines on your network that do not possess the most up-to-date patch information.

This audit is necessary because you never know when a machine may be experiencing some issues whereby it is not getting the updates and is therefore susceptible to attack. Many tools are available to help you scan your network and generate reports of the current security patch level on machines. Microsoft offers several tools to assist with this task, including:

- **Microsoft Baseline Security Analyzer (MBSA)** This is a free utility that provides you with the ability to scan your domain or subnet periodically to check whether computers have failed to install patches or updates. MBSA can also report on a computer's compliance with some security best practices, such as strong password requirements. It can also check a computer to make sure that it is not open to any known security vulnerabilities (see Figure 4.8). What MBSA does not offer, however, is the ability to deploy the missing or failed patches. Once MBSA finds the vulnerability, you'll need to go back to SUS or GPO to redeploy the patches or else deploy them manually.

- **System Center Essentials 2007** This is a new management solution in the System Center family of IT systems management products specifically designed for midsize businesses (up to 500 PCs and 30 Servers). Essentials 2007 provides a unified management solution that enables IT professionals in midsize organizations to proactively manage their IT environment with increased efficiency.

- **System Center Configuration Manager 2007** This is an enterprisewide management utility for which the scope exceeds hardware and software inventories. However, if SMS is deployed in your organization, it can be used for the purposes of generating reports on the software that is installed on the server. SMS has recently added a SUS plug-in that further extends its functionality in this area.

To help organizations and security specialists with this huge burden of securing networks against security vulnerabilities, Microsoft has several options available to use as shown in Table 7.3. There are also many third party remediation tools that are covered elsewhere in this book.

Table 7.3 Comparing Different Microsoft Update Solutions

Product	Supported Software and Content	Content Types Supported
MBSA	Same as MU for security update detection. Windows, IE, Exchange and SQL config checks	Service Packs and Security Updates
Microsoft Update	Windows 2000+, Exchange 2000+, SQL Server 2000+, Office XP+ with expanding support	All software updates, driver updates, service packs (SPs), and feature packs (FPs)
WSUS	Same as Microsoft Update	Same as Microsoft Update with only critical driver updates

Continued

Table 7.3 Continued. Comparing Different Microsoft Update Solutions

Product	Supported Software and Content	Content Types Supported
Essentials 2007	Same as WSUS 3.0 + third-party and custom updates	All updates, SPs & FPs, + third-party and custom updates & .MSI & .EXE based app installs
SMS 2003	Same as WSUS + NT 4.0 & Win98* + can update any other Windows based software	All updates, SPs, & FPs + supports update & app installs for any Windows-based software.

A number of third-party tools and applications can also address this issue. Here are some of the more popular ones:

- **HP OpenView** (www.openview.hp.com) OpenView is infamous for its enterprisewide management capabilities. It operates at the same level as SMS and should be implemented as part of a larger management strategy, not just for patch management.

- **NetIQ Security Manager** (www.netiq.com) Security Manager by NetIQ offers a product designed for patch management. Everything from analysis and reporting to deployment of patches is included.

- **Gravity Storm Software Service Pack Manager 2000** (www.securitybastion.com) This product, like NetIQ, also offers a well-rounded method of gathering information about current computer patch levels and can even poll the corresponding Microsoft article if you are unsure what the missing or failed patch does. This product also offers the ability to deploy the missing patches and offers scheduling so that deployments do not adversely affect network traffic.

Recovering from Server Hardware Failure

Recovering from disasters isn't limited to being able to restart the server or restore deleted files. Anyone who's ever had hard disks fail and lost important data can testify to the importance of a computer's capability to recover from hardware failure. Similarly, if a server becomes unavailable due to a major problem, network users are unable to access resources. To deal with the possibility of hardware failure, Windows Server 2003 natively supports different methods of recovery, including the use of fault-tolerant disks and server clustering.

The Role of Fault-Tolerant Disks

Fault-tolerant disks enable a computer to recover from a disaster, so that data won't be lost or corrupted. RAID (Redundant Array of Independent—or Inexpensive—Disks) provides several methods of writing data across multiple disks. If one disk in an array fails, RAID enables you to replace the damaged disk and recover the data quickly. There are many different levels of RAID available, both as hardware and as software implementations. Windows Server 2003 supports only two built-in software implementations of RAID: RAID 1 and RAID 5.

RAID 1

RAID 1 is based on disk mirroring or duplexing. Data that's written to one disk is also written to another, so that each disk has an exact copy of the data and one disk's data is a mirror image of the other's. If one of the physical disks fails, the server can continue operating by using the other disk. Because data from one disk is mirrored to another, two disks must be used to implement RAID 1.

When mirroring is used on Windows Server 2003, the first disk in the set must contain files to be mirrored. The second disk must be at least the same size as the first, because information from the first disk needs to be written to it. If it were smaller, then all the data on the first disk couldn't be copied to the second. If the second disk is larger, the extra space is wasted.

The two disks in a mirror are seen as a single volume by the operating system and share a single drive letter. If one of the mirrors in a mirrored volume fails, the mirrored volume must be broken, using the Disk Management tool. This makes the other mirror a separate volume. This gives the still-functioning volume its own drive letter and enables you to create a new, mirrored volume using the free disk space on another disk, in order to restore fault tolerance.

Additional fault tolerance can be achieved with RAID 1 by using separate disk controllers for each disk; this is called duplexing. If only mirroring is used, both disks can become unavailable if the controller on which they are installed fails. With duplexing, each disk is installed on a different controller, so that if one of the disks fails or a controller fails, the data is still available through the other disk in the pair.

Mirroring disks not only provides fault tolerance, but can also impact performance. Multiple reads and writes to the disks are performed each time new data needs to be accessed or saved. Because data is read from both mirrored volumes, this can increase performance, because two different disks are reading the data at the same time. However, when data is written to the mirrored disks, there is a decrease in performance, because both disks must have the same data written to them.

RAID 5

RAID 5 is disk striping with parity. With this level of RAID, data is striped across three or more disks, with parity information stored across multiple disks. Parity is a calculated value that's used to restore data from the other drives if one of the drives in the set fails. It determines the number of odd and even bits in a number, and this information is used to reconstruct data if a sequence of numbers is lost, which is the case if one of the disks fail.

Because RAID 5 requires parity information to be calculated, the performance of your server can decrease when data is written using this level of RAID. However, performance can increase when data is read, because the data is read from multiple disks at once. Since there can be up to 32 disks making up RAID 5 array, this can be a significant advantage. However, when a disk fails, the performance decreases because the server must reconstruct the data from parity information on the other disks.

RAID 5 also offers better disk utilization than RAID 1. When you mirror a disk, you must purchase twice the amount of disk space that you'll actually use for data. Fifty percent of the total disk space is used for redundancy. With RAID 5, the amount of space used for parity is equal to one disk in the array, so the more disks you use, the higher your percentage of disk utilization. For example, if you have 10 disks in the array, only one-tenth of the total disk space is used for redundancy and nine-tenths of the space is available for data.

Planning Physical Security

One of the most important, and at the same time most overlooked aspects of a comprehensive network security plan is physical access control. This matter is often left up to facilities managers or plant security departments, or it is outsourced to security guard companies. Network administrators frequently concern themselves with sophisticated software and hardware solutions that prevent intruders from accessing internal computers remotely, while doing nothing to protect the servers, routers, cable, and other physical components of the network from direct access.

Notes from the Underground...

Being Blind to the Obvious

In far too many supposedly security-conscious organizations, computers are locked away from employees and visitors all day, only to be left open at night to the janitorial staff, which has keys to all offices. It is not at all uncommon for computer espionage experts to pose as members of the cleaning crew to gain physical access to machines that hold sensitive data. This is a favorite ploy for several reasons:

- Cleaning services are often contracted out, and workers in the industry are often transient, so that company employees may not be easily aware of who is or isn't a legitimate employee of the cleaning company.

- Cleaning is usually done late at night, when all or most company employees are gone, making it easier to surreptitiously steal data.

- Cleaning crew members are often paid little or no attention by company employees, who take their presence for granted and think nothing of their being in areas where the presence of others might be questioned.

Physically breaking into the server room and stealing the hard disk on which sensitive data resides may be a crude method; nonetheless, it happens. In some organizations, it may be the easiest way to gain unauthorized access, especially for an intruder who has help "on the inside."

Creating a Plan for Physical Security

Your physical security plan should include the building, data network, environmental controls, security controls and telecommunications equipment serving your environment. In most cases, the physical elements of data networking and security technology protecting that data should be dedicated and in a stand alone infrastructure.

This rule applies to data cabling, servers, switches, routers and any other physical element of the networked technology systems serving your environment. What this means is that you should protect those assets and data that are critical to the operations of your organization and take appropriate measures that would compromise their productivity and/or integrity.

Some of the more obvious areas that you should consider in a physical security plan include:

- Types of fire protection/suppression
- Electrical and power plant considerations
- Controlling physical access to HVAC and Humidity Controls
- Controlling physical access to the servers
- Controlling physical access to networked workstations
- Controlling physical access to network devices
- Controlling physical access to the cable
- Being aware of security considerations with wireless media
- Being aware of security considerations related to portable computers
- Recognizing the security risk of allowing data to be printed out
- Recognizing the security risks involving floppy disks, CDs, tapes, and other removable media

Network Resources That Require Physical Security

Let's look at why each of these is important and how you can implement a physical security plan that addresses all these factors.

Protecting the Servers

File servers on which sensitive data is stored and infrastructure servers that provide mission critical services such as logon authentication and access control should be placed in a highly secure location. At the minimum, servers should be in a locked room where only those who need to work directly with the servers have access. Keys should be distributed sparingly, and records should be kept of issuance and return.

If security needs are high due to the nature of the business or the nature of the data, access to the server room may be controlled by magnetic card, electronic locks requiring entry of a numerical code, or even biometric access control devices such as fingerprint or retinal scanners. Both ingress and egress should be controlled – ideally with logs, video cameras, and/or other means of recording both who enters and who exits.

Other security measures include monitor detectors or other alarm systems, activated during nonbusiness hours, and security cameras. A security guard or company should monitor these devices.

Keeping Workstations Secure

Many network security plans focus on the servers but ignore the risk posed by workstations with network access to those servers. It is not uncommon for employees to leave their computers unsecured when they leave for lunch or even when they leave for the evening. Often there will be a workstation in the receptionist area that is open to visitors who walk in off the street. If the receptionist must leave briefly, the computer – and the network to which it is connected – is vulnerable unless steps have been taken to ensure that it is secure.

A good security plan includes protection of all unmanned workstations. A secure client operating system such as Windows XP or Windows Vista requires an interactive logon with a valid account name and password in order to access the operating system (unlike older Windows 9x). This allows users to "lock" the workstation when they are going to be away from it so someone else can't just step up and start using the computer.

However, don't depend on access permissions and other software security methods alone to protect your network. If a potential intruder can gain physical access to a networked computer, he/she is that much closer to accessing your valuable data or introducing a virus onto your network. Ensure all workstation users adhere to a good password policy, as discussed elsewhere in this section and book.

Many modern PC cases come with some type of locking mechanism that will help prevent an unauthorized person from opening the case and stealing the hard disk.

Protecting Network Devices

Hubs, routers, switches and other network devices should be physically secured from unauthorized access. It is easy to forget that just because a device doesn't have a monitor on which you can see data, this does not mean the data can't be captured or destroyed at that access point.

For example, a traditional Ethernet hub sends all data out every port on the hub. An intruder who has access to the hub can plug a packet-sniffing device (or a laptop computer with sniffer software) that operates in "promiscuous mode" into a spare port and capture data sent to any computer on the segment, as shown in Figure 7.8.

Figure 7.8 An Intruder with Access to a Hub Can Easily Intercept Data

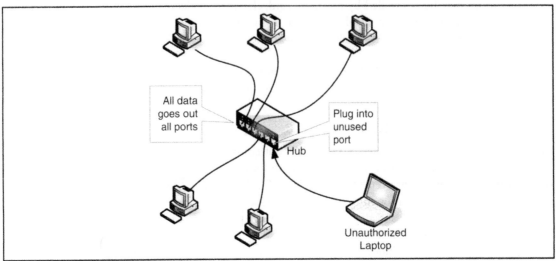

Although switches and routers are somewhat more secure, any device through which the data passes is a point of vulnerability. Replacing hubs with switches and routers makes it more difficult for an intruder to "sniff" on your network, but it is still possible to use techniques such as Address Resolution Protocol (ARP) spoofing. This is sometimes called router redirection, in which nearby machines are redirected to forward traffic through an intruder's machine by sending ARP packets that contain the router's Internet Protocol (IP) address mapped to the intruder's machine's MAC address. This results in other machines believing the intruder's machine is the router, and so they send their traffic to it.

A similar method uses Internet Control Message Protocol (ICMP) router advertisement messages. It is also possible, with certain switches, to overflow the address tables with multiple false Media Access Control (MAC) addresses or send a continuous flow of random garbage through the switch to trigger it to change from bridging mode to repeating mode. This means all frames will be broadcast on all ports, giving the intruder the same opportunity to access the data that he would have with a regular hub. This is called switch jamming.

It is often possible to detect an unauthorized packet sniffer on the wire using a device called a Time Domain Reflectometer (TDR), which sends a pulse down the cable and creates a graph of the reflections that are returned. Those who know how to read the graph can tell whether unauthorized devices are attached to the cable and where.

Other ways of detecting unauthorized connections include monitoring hub or switch lights using Simple Network Monitoring Protocol (SNMP) managers that log connections and disconnections or using one of the many tools designed for the specific purpose of detecting sniffers on the network. There are also several techniques using Packet Internetwork Groper (ping), ARP, and DNS that may help you to catch unauthorized sniffers.

Finally, if the switch has a special monitor port designed to be used with a sniffer for legitimate (network troubleshooting) purposes, an intruder who has physical access to the switch can simply plug into this port and capture network data. Your network devices should be placed in a locked room or closet and protected in the same manner as your servers.

Securing the Cable

The next step in protecting your network data is to secure the cable across which it travels. Twisted pair and coaxial cable are both vulnerable to data capture; an intruder who has access to the cable can tap into it and eavesdrop on messages being sent across it. A number of companies make "tapping" devices.

Fiber optic cable is more difficult to tap into because it does not produce electrical pulses, but instead, uses pulses of light to represent the 0s and 1s of binary data. It is, however, possible for a sophisticated intruder to use an optical splitter and tap into the signal on fiber optic media. Compro-mise of security at the physical level is a special threat when network cables are not contained in one facility but span a distance between buildings. There is even a name for this risk, "manhole manipulation," referring to the easy access intruders often have to cabling that runs through underground conduits.

Cable taps can sometimes be detected by using a TDR or optical TDR to measure the strength of the signal and determine where the tap is located.

Methods for Securing Facilities

Facility security is of paramount concern to any network environment. Campus level access, environment level access, and object level access protocols must all be implemented. Video surveillance and live surveillance by internal security are strongly recommended. With regard to general security, the entire facility should have at a minimum a two challenge system in place such that every entrant will be providing at least one validator at an automated checkpoint (i.e. biometric entry, external security card swipe, etc.) and one other independent manual or automatic validator (sign in at security desk, internal security card swipes, etc.)

Higher levels of access control should be applied to any infrastructure or workspace related to the really sensitive information. Each access attempt to the your network environment should be challenged by dual authentication and the access points should be under constant independent monitoring (i.e. cameras and access logging).

Dual authentication refers to two factor identification methodology. Two factor identification presumes any two personal identification factors will be challenged and both challenges must be successfully responded.

Challenge factors fall into the following identification categories.

- Something You Are – Biometric keys such as fingerprint or retinal scanner
- Something You Know – Password, PIN, etc.
- Something You Have – Security card, digital token, bingo card, etc.

Dual authentication across two categories of factors is recommended. A physical sign-in/out log is a useful supplemental tool for physical plant security even if a dual authentication protocol is in place; providing an ink-signature audit trail is useful for independent audit of security system performance and original handwriting can be used to investigate identity during security audit and review phases.

Security Measures and Objectives

There are many ways to break down the elements of your XenApp environment, but for the purposes of simplicity, we'll use three simple categories: *people*, *process*, and *technology*. As an IT professional, you understand the importance of the interplay among these three elements. Technology is implemented by people using specific processes. The better defined the processes are, the more reliable the results (typically). Technology is only as good as the people who designed and implemented it and the processes developed to utilize it. As we have discussed security measures in this book, you can see that we come back to these three elements repeatedly.

When planning your security measures and objectives, you should consider the interactions and limitations of people, processes, and technology. Figure 7.9 depicts the relative relationship of people, process, and technology in most companies. Infrastructure is part of the technology component, but is listed separately for clarity.

Figure 7.9 How People, Process, and Technology Interact

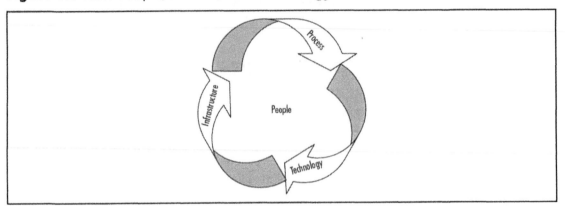

The term computer security encompasses many related but separate topics. These topics can be stated as security objectives:

- Control of physical accessibility to the computer(s) and/or network

- Prevention of accidental erasure, modification, or compromise of data

- Detection and prevention of intentional internal security breaches

- Detection and prevention of unauthorized external intrusions (hacking)

Network security measures can be loosely divided into three categories: *People*, *Processes*, and *Technology*. Earlier in this book we covered the basic security concepts and in this section we will provide more detail in how those security concepts apply to your XenApp environment. If your security goal is to have complete control over the data that comes into and goes out of your networks, you must define objective and measures that will help you reach that goal. We listed some general security objectives related to computer networks—especially those connected to an outside internetwork such as the Internet—as controlling physical access, preventing accidental compromise of data, detecting and preventing intentional internal security breaches, and detecting and preventing unauthorized external intrusions. In the following sections, we examine each of these objectives in detail.

People

The topic of network security might bring to mind a picture of evil corporate rivals determined to steal your company's most precious trade secrets or malevolent hackers bent on crashing your network and erasing all your data just for the sheer joy of it. Although these risks do exist, often the reality of network data loss is far less glamorous. A large proportion of erased, modified, or disclosed data is the result of the actions of employees or other authorized network personnel. Furthermore, a large percentage of that damage is the result of accidental compromise of the data.

Unintended errors in entering data or accessing network resources or carelessness in use of the computers and network can cause loss of data or crashing of individual computers, the server, and even the network. Your network security plan should address these unintended compromises, which can be just as disastrous as intentional breaches of security.

Know Your Users

To prevent accidental compromise of data, you should first know your users and their skill levels. Those with few technical skills should be given as little access as possible; allow them the access required to do their jobs, and no more. Too many network users have, in all innocence, destroyed or changed important files while attempting to clear space on their hard disks or troubleshoot a computer problem on their own.

Educate Your Users

Educating your users is one of the most important factors in eliminating or reducing such incidents. This does not necessarily mean upgrading the users' technical skills (although it can). Turning all your users into power users might not be cost-effective or otherwise desirable. What is essential is to train all your network users in the proper procedures and rules of use for the network. Every person who accesses your company network should be aware of your user policies and should agree to adhere to them. This includes notifying technical support personnel immediately of any hardware or software problems, refraining from installing any unauthorized software on their machines or downloading files from the Internet without authorization, and never dialing their personal ISPs or other networks or services from company machines without permission.

Control Your Users

In some cases, establishing clear-cut policies and making staffers and other users aware of them will be enough. In other cases, you will find that users are unable or unwilling to follow the rules, and you will have to take steps to enforce them—including locking down desktops with system or group policies and, with software such as ISA Server, implementing access rules and filtering to prevent unauthorized packets from being sent or received over the network. Luckily, most users will at least attempt to comply with the rules. A more serious problem is the "insider" who is looking to intentionally breach network security. This person could be simply a maverick employee who doesn't like being told what to do, or he or she could be someone with a darker motive.

Hiring and Human Resource Policies

In many cases, prevention starts with good human resources practices. That means that management should institute hiring policies aimed at recruiting people of good character. Background investigations should be conducted, especially for key positions that will have more than normal user network access.

The work environment should encourage high employee morale; in many cases, internal security breaches are committed as "revenge" by employees who feel underpaid, underappreciated, or even mistreated. Employees who are enthusiastic about their jobs and feel valued by the organization will be much more likely to comply with company rules in general and network security policies in particular.

Another motivation for internal breaches is money. If your company engages in a highly competitive business, competitors could approach employees with lucrative offers for trade secrets or other confidential data. If you are in a field that is vulnerable to corporate espionage, your security policies should lean toward the deny all access model, in which access for a particular network user starts at nothing and access is added on the basis of the user's need to know.

Physical Security

Ensuring a physically secure network environment is an important step in controlling access to your network's important data and system files, but it is only part of a good security plan. This is truer today than in the past, because networks have more "ways in" than they once did. A medium or large network may have multiple dial-in servers, VPN servers, and a dedicated full-time Internet connection. Even a small network is likely to be connected to the Internet part of the time.

A large part of physical security involves protecting systems from unauthorized physical access. Even if you've implemented strong security that prevents or limits access across a network, it will do little good if a person can sit at the server and make changes or (even worse) pick up the server and walk away with it. If people do not have physical access to systems, the chances of unauthorized data access are reduced.

Physical security also involves protecting servers and other assets from environmental disasters. Uninterruptible Power Supplies (UPSs) should be installed to provide electricity during power outages, and fire suppression systems to extinguish fires need to be in place (keep in mind that some fire suppression systems are not suitable for server rooms because they can destroy the servers in the process of extinguishing a fire). By considering natural risk sources within an area, you can determine which measures need to be taken to reduce or remove risks.

Physical security not only includes natural disasters, but also those caused by the workplace environment. Servers need to be stored in stable areas that adhere to the environmental requirements of the equipment, which can include temperature and humidity specifications.

Another part of physical security addresses requirements concerning granting access, revoking access, monitoring, and types of access. These could include when and where badge readers are required, when keys should and should not be used, office locks, access by service personnel, and so on.

The Paper Chase

Network security specialists and administrators tend to concentrate on protecting data in electronic form, but you should recognize that intruders can also steal confidential digital information by printing it or locating a hard copy that was printed by someone else. It does little good to implement strong password policies and network access controls if employees can print sensitive material and then leave it lying on desks, stored in unlocked file cabinets, or thrown into an easily accessed trash basket. "Dumpster diving" (searching the trash for company secrets) is a common form of corporate espionage—one that, surprisingly, often yields results.

If confidential data must be printed, the paper copy should be kept as physically secure as the digital version. Disposal should require shredding, and in cases of particularly high-security information, the shredded paper can be mixed with water to create a pulp that is impossible to put back together again.

Removable Storage Risks

Yet another potential point of failure in your network security plan involves saving data to removable media. Floppy diskettes, Zip and Jaz disks, USB memory sticks, jump drives, tapes, PC Cards, CDs, and DVDs containing sensitive data must be kept physically secured at all times.

Don't make the mistake of thinking that deleting the files on a disk, or even formatting the disk, completely erases the data; until it is overwritten, it is still there and can be retrieved using special software.

Although removable media can present a security threat to the network, they can also play a part in your overall security plan. Removable disks (including fully bootable large-capacity hard disks installed in mobile "nesting" racks) can be removed from the computer and locked in a safe or removed from the premises to protect the data that is stored there.

WARNING

The residual physical representation of data that has been "erased," from which that data can be reconstructed, is called data remanence. Methods used to prevent data remanence in high-security environments include degaussing, overwriting, and, in extreme cases, physical destruction of the media. Degaussing involves use of a device that generates a magnetic field to reduce the magnetic state of the media to zero, which restores it to an unrecorded state. Software (sometimes referred to as file shredder software) is available to overwrite all sectors of a disk with random bits in order to prevent recovery of the data. See http://packetstormsecurity.org/docs/rainbow-books/NCSC-TG-025.2.html for a detailed report on data remanence and the comparative merits of each solution.

Password Security

In the networking world, passwords (in combination with user account names) are normally the "keys to the kingdom" that provide access to network resources and data. It might seem simplistic to say that your comprehensive security plan should include an effective password policy, but it is a basic component that is more difficult to implement than it might appear at first glance.

In order to be effective, your password policy must require users to select passwords that are difficult to "crack" yet easy for them to remember so that they don't commit the common security breach of writing the password on a sticky note that will end up stuck to the monitor or sitting prominently in the top desk drawer.

A good password policy is the first line of defense in protecting your network from intruders. Careless password practices (choosing common passwords such as "god" or "love" or the user's spouse's name; choosing short, all-alpha, one-case passwords, writing passwords down or sending them across the network in plain text) are like leaving your car doors unlocked with the keys in the ignition.

Although some intruders might target a specific system, many others simply "browse" for a network that's easy to break into. Lack of a good password policy is an open invitation to them.

Strong passwords are more difficult to crack than simple ones. These types of passwords use a combination of keyboard characters from each of the following categories:

- Lowercase letters (a–z)

- Uppercase letters (A–Z)

- Numbers (0–9)

- Special characters (` ~ ! @ # $ % ^ & * ( ) _ + — = { } | [ ] \ :" ;' < > ? , . /)

The length of a password also affects how easy it is to crack. You can use security templates and group policies to control how long a password is valid, the length of a password, and other aspects of password management. Another requirement that is important to having secure passwords is making sure that each time users change their passwords, they use passwords that are different from previous passwords.

NOTE

Expensive, sophisticated firewalls and other strict security measures (short of biometric scanning devices that recognize fingerprints or retinal images) will not protect you if an intruder has knowledge of a valid username and password. It is particularly important to use strong passwords for administrative and service accounts.

To ensure domain controllers are secure, there are a number of password requirements that are enforced by default on Windows 2003 domain controllers:

- The password cannot contain any part of the user's account name.

- It must be a minimum of six characters in length.

- It must contain characters from three of the four categories: lowercase letters, uppercase letters, numbers, and special characters.

The best security policies in the world will be ineffective if the network users are unaware of them or if the policies are so restrictive and place so many inconveniences on users that they go out of their way to attempt to circumvent them. The security plan itself should contain a program for educating network users—not only regarding what the policies are but also why they are important and how users benefit from them. Users should also be instructed in the best ways to comply with the policies and what to do if they are unable to comply or if they observe a deliberate violation of the policies on the part of other users.

User Roles and Responsibilities

There is no single thing that you can do to prevent an insider threat. The concept of defense in depth applies here as it does to all areas of security. No single solution is going to make you secure. Only by putting many defense measures together will you be secure and those measures must encompass both preventive and detective measures.

Some of the key things that can be done to prevent or minimize the damage of the insider threat are the following:

- **Security awareness** Employees, contractors, and any other insiders need to be educated on how to protect corporate assets. They need to understand the dangers and methods of social engineering and be careful what information they give out. They also have to be cognizant that insiders could exist at their company and not only do their part to protect corporate assets (for example, locking their workstations), but they also have to look for indications of insider threat and report them to the correct parties.

- **Separation of duties** Any critical job function or access to critical information should involve two or more people. This prevents a single person from committing an inside attack.

- **Rotation of duties** All critical jobs should have multiple people who perform the roles and those people should be rotated through periodically. If a person knows that someone else is going to be performing a given role in two months, it will be much harder for them to commit fraud or other insider attacks, because there is a good chance someone might catch it later.

- **Least privilege** Any additional access that someone has can be used against the company. Although access is needed for people to perform their jobs, this access should be carefully controlled. People should be given only the access they need to do their jobs and nothing else.

Technology

Technology is clearly the piece of the puzzle that you, as an IT professional, will be most familiar. As you participate in your company's network security strategy, you will be in the best position to understand what happens with various technology components. Part of the reason for security planning is to look at your use of technology and understand which elements are vulnerable to which types of threats. A power outage, for example, impacts all the technology in a building. Suppose you have battery backup or generators for lights and certain computers but no power for air conditioning in Miami in July? Timing and circumstance come into play and working closely with your facilities person, for example, will help you look at the security plan in a more holistic (and realistic) manner than you might on your own.

Firewall Security

When it comes to securing networks, the first items that come to mind are firewalls, which are the primary gatekeepers between an organization's internal network and the outside world. While a properly implemented firewall can be one of the most effective security tools in your arsenal, it shouldn't be the only tool. The adage "defense-in-depth" means that you should have multiple layers of security. Using a defense-in-depth configuration, if one component of your defense failed or was defeated, there would still be a variety of other fallbacks to protect your network.

Remember that although the most common way to implement a firewall is between an internal network and the outside world (often the Internet), you should not limit yourself to placing firewalls only on the network edge. A firewall should be in any place you want to restrict the flow of traffic. With the current trend of security breeches originating from the inside of the network (often employees or ex-employees), companies are increasingly relying on firewalls to isolate and filter traffic between portions of the internal network.

Firewall Types

No discussion of firewalls would be complete without a discussion of the different types of firewalls. This is particularly true in this context, because it allows you to better understand exactly where in the spectrum the free firewall offerings lay. In the networking sense, a firewall is basically any component (software or hardware) that restricts the flow of network traffic. This is a sufficiently broad definition to allow for all of the various ways people have chosen to implement firewalls. Some firewalls are notoriously limited in capability and others are extremely easy to use.

Within the realm of firewalls there are many different ways to restrict network traffic. Most of these methods vary in the level of intelligence that is applied to the decision-making process. For example, to permit or deny traffic based on which network device is the sender or recipient, you would use a *packet-filtering firewall*. In reality, even the simplest packet filtering firewalls can typically make decisions based on the source Internet Protocol (IP) address, the destination IP address, and the source and/or destination port number. While this type of firewall may sound overly simplistic, consider if you have a server running a Web site for use on the Internet. In all likelihood, the only traffic that you need to allow to the server uses a destination port of Transmission Control Protocol (TCP) 80 or 443; thus, you could configure your firewall to permit only that traffic. These ports are used for HTTP and HTTPS, respectively. Because the server is available for the Internet, you can't filter traffic based on the source address or source port, which will be different for each connection.

The primary drawback with a simple packet filter is that the packet filtering firewall has to rely on very primitive means to determine when traffic should be allowed (e.g., synchronous [SYN] or acknowledgement [ACK] bits being set). While this was adequate in the early days of the Internet when security was not as big of a concern, it won't work any more. It is trivial to set the bits on the packet using freely available software to make the traffic look like it is a reply to another connection. Thus the *stateful inspection firewall* was born of necessity. This type of firewall monitors all connections (inbound or outbound), and as the connection is permitted (based on the firewall's configured rules) it enters this connection into a table. When the reply to this connection comes back, even if the reply uses a port that the firewall was not previously configured to permit, it can intelligently realize the traffic is a response to a permitted session and permit the traffic.

Unfortunately, as the firewalls get better so do the methods hackers use to circumvent them. Suppose you have configured your firewall perfectly and there are no holes: every permitted port is one you expressly want to allow. Using the previous example, no traffic is allowed to the Web server except Web traffic. Sounds good, but the problem is, if the firewall is completely secure, the server might not be. Flaws in the Web server software could allow the attacker to send the server an HTTP request that is 10,000 characters long, overflowing the buffers and allowing the attacker to execute the code of his choice. The packets used to transport the 10,000-character HTTP request are all legal TCP packets as far as the firewall is concerned: therefore, it would permit them to pass through to the Web server. The next step in firewall evolution serves to combat this type of attack. These types of firewalls are *application gateways*, or layer 7 firewalls.

This type of firewall not only filters network traffic based on the standard network parameters, but they also understand the higher layer protocol information contained within the packet, in this example HTTP. The firewall itself knows what a legitimate HTTP request looks like and can filter out a malformed or malicious request even though, from a network perspective, it might otherwise be a permitted packet. There is a down side to this type of approach, which is that the firewall must be programmed with all the same intelligence needed to filter normal traffic, plus the firewall must fully understand the protocols it is inspecting. This means additional programming for any protocol you want the firewall to understand. Most of the major commercial application gateways offer support for the major protocols such as HTTP, File Transfer Protocol (FTP), and Simple Mail Transfer Protocol (SMTP).

With all of this information circulating in your head, you're probably wondering which type is available for free? Generally speaking, you can find many free varieties of firewalls that perform some type of stateful inspection. Application layer gateways are not readily available for free. In reality, few organizations have the funds to use application gateways extensively. One ramification of *not* using an application gateway is that you need to ensure that the service that is exposed to untrusted traffic is configured as securely as possible and that the server itself is hardened against attack. Keeping the service patches up-to-date will help reduce the odds that an application-level attack will be successful.

Antivirus Software Security

It's not enough to provide virus protection at the server level; each client on your network needs to have antivirus software installed and updated with the latest virus definitions in order to provide the best defense for your systems and data. Viruses can often enter a corporate network through a single end user either opening an infected e-mail attachment or browsing to a Web site that contains malicious code. Because of this, you need to design virus protection for all systems on your network that interact with the Internet and the rest of the world at large. Are you running an e-mail server? Be sure that you are scanning incoming and outgoing e-mail messages for virus infections. Do your end users have Internet access from their desktops? Be sure that each network-connected workstation has antivirus software that provides real-time antivirus scanning. You can also install antivirus software at other points on your network, including at the firewall or proxy server that will scan all incoming network traffic for virus infections. While there are any number of commercial and freeware options available for virus protection, it's critical that a secure network design make allowances for its installation, use, and management.

Tip

Real-time protection refers to antivirus software's ability to scan files as they are created or accessed, thus providing instant notification if a downloaded file contains a virus or other form of malicious code. Most commercial antivirus software packages provide this feature.

Securing the File System

The NTFS file system used since Windows NT provides the base framework for file and folder security in Windows Server 2003. These permissions are set on the files and folders stored on the server's disk system and apply to authenticated users no matter how they access the file system (that is, whether they access it across the network or sitting at the local machine). By default, all users can read and execute files on the disk system, with the exception of certain system areas that are protected by default at installation. Applying NTFS permissions will control who has access to which areas of the disk system.

NTFS Permissions Defined

As an administrator, you can set NTFS permissions on files as well as folders. Table 7.4 describes the permissions available for NTFS folders, and Table 7.5 describes the permissions that can be applied to files. Even though the permissions are similar, there are some key differences when these permissions are applied to files and not to folders.

WARNING

Note that with shared-folder permissions, previously called share permissions (which we'll discuss later in this section), permissions can be set only at the folder level, not at the file level. Also note that shared-folder permissions apply only when accessing the resources across the network. These are the two most important ways in which NTFS permissions differ from shared-folder permissions.

Table 7.4 NTFS Folder Permissions

Permission	Function
Read	Enables objects to read the contents of a folder, including file attributes and permissions.
Write	Enables objects to create new files and folders within a folder, write attributes and extended attributes on files and folders, and can read permissions and attributes on files and folders.
List Folder Contents	Gives objects the same rights as the Read permission, but also enables the object to traverse the folder path beneath the folder where this permission is applied.
Read & Execute	Gives objects the same rights as the List Folder Contents permission, but also enables the object to execute program files stored in the folder.
Modify	Gives the object the same permissions as the Read, Write, List Folder Contents, and Read & Execute permissions, but also enables the object to delete files and folders within the designated folder.
Full Control	Gives objects full access to the entire contents, including the capability to take ownership of files and change permissions on files and folders.

Table 7.5 NTFS File/Folder Permissions

Permission	Function
Read	Enables objects to read the contents of a file, including file attributes and permissions.
Write	Enables objects to change the contents of or append to an existing file, as well as read the attributes and permissions on the file.
Read & Execute	Gives objects the same rights as the Read permission, but also enables the object to execute a program file.
Modify	Gives the object the same permissions as the Read, Write, and Read & Execute permissions, but also enables the object to delete the designated file.
Full Control	Gives objects full access to the file, including the capability to take ownership of the file and change permissions on the file.

When permissions are applied to a folder, those permissions apply to the files within the folder as well. For instance, if you set the Read permission on a folder, the object (user account or group) to which that permission applies is able to see the files stored in the folder and read the contents of the files within the folder. If you wanted to give a group access to write to a particular file in that folder, but not all files in the folder, you would assign the Write permission to the specific file.

To keep file system management reasonable, your best bet is to keep permission assignments as simple as possible. Because permissions assigned to a folder apply to all the files within a folder, you should make permission assignments at the folder level most of the time. A well-planned directory structure enables you to assign folder rights at a high level in the directory structure, keeping subsequent permissions changes further down in the directory structure to a minimum. In general, you should apply permissions to a specific file only when access to that file is significantly different from the other files in that folder. If you find that you are making file permission assignments to several files within a directory structure, it might be better to relocate those files to a different folder where the appropriate permissions can be assigned to the parent folder and not to the individual files.

Windows Group Policy

One of the most powerful tools for installing software updates is actually freely available for download from the Microsoft Web site, and integrates right into the Windows Server 2003 operating system. By using the Software Installation settings within Group Policy, you can automatically distribute security updates to an entire domain, site, or organizational unit (OU), or even to a single user or computer, from one centralized location. Unfortunately, there are a few drawbacks to relying solely on Group Policy. Remember that Software Installation settings do not apply when a client is logging on to Active Directory over a slow link (anything slower than 56Kbps.) This means that if you have a remote office that connects to a corporate LAN via a dial-up modem, no software installation settings will be propagated to the remote systems; if Group Policy is your only means of distributing patches, then these systems will remain unprotected. Group Policy also requires you to manually create and distribute software installation patches.

Citrix Policies

As in earlier Citrix versions, administrators are able to configure policies for users and user groups. XenApp Server allows creation and configuration of user and user group policies, and allows administrators to create and configure policies based on server groups, IP addresses, and client names. XenApp policy rules allow control across the board to affect features such as printing, bandwidth limits for connections, zone connection, and reliability preferences, to name a few.

At the heart of it, XenApp policies define connection settings. The capabilities provided by XenApp Server allow an administrator to define the policies for and servers, client machines, and IP addresses he wishes. A single policy can contain multiple rules that apply different settings to all of these entities in one shot.

Administrators can create policies and configure them to meet the needs of the users they support. Policies and the rules they contain can be made to support end users based on their geographic location, job function, and the method by which they connect to the network. XenApp policies can even be used cooperatively with Windows Group Policy to secure end-user connections via encryption and deny drive mapping.

Public Key Infrastructure

Public key security is not new in the technology world, but it has not been widely used until recently. Increased concerns about access control and data security have brought more and more public key solutions into the mainstream.

Understanding the Function of a PKI

Digital certificates are becoming more and more common in today's computing environment. These certificates offer a way for individuals to verify the authenticity of e-mail messages, encrypt files, and so on. Several third-party organizations have been providing digital certificates or other key services for a number of years. There can be a number of drawbacks to relying solely on third-party certificate providers to generate and verify user keys. One of the most significant roadblocks is cost. While the per-user cost of issuing a valid certificate has decreased recently, it can still be cost-prohibitive for a large organization to rely solely on external resources for certificate security. Ease of management is another drawback. Again, managing certificates through an external organization can be cumbersome, confusing, and time-consuming, especially for large organizations.

With a Windows-based network infrastructure, you have the option of developing and hosting your own PKI within your organization. Microsoft provides a number of tools for creating and managing digital certificates within Active Directory. There are a number of advantages to using an internal PKI structure. First, there is no per-user cost to generate digital certificates. So these certificates can be created for every individual within the organization, no matter how large. Second, certificates can be managed internally. You can monitor use of certificates within the organization and automatically revoke certificates when a user leaves the organization or no longer has the need to use a certificate. One of the drawbacks to using a completely internal PKI is that of trust. If all your certificates are generated and managed internally, you may have difficulty getting external organizations to recognize the validity of the certificates created within your organization.

The most complete implementation of a PKI includes certificates generated internally and externally. Acquiring a certificate from a trusted third-party organization lends credence to the validity of certificates used in your organization. Generating and managing internal certificates cuts down on the costs associated with public key security. Ultimately, how you implement your PKI depends largely on the needs you have for public key security within your organization.

Digital Certificates

One way to validate the key holder's identity is through the use of digital certificates. Either third-party organization trusted by the recipient of a set of keys or an internal Certificate Authority validates the authenticity of the keys and the key holder and generates a unique certificate to the user. The organization that issues the certificate takes the responsibility for validating the identity of the user and authenticates the certificate of the key holder. As long as you continue to trust the integrity of the issuing entity, you can trust that any digital certificates generated by them are valid, and therefore the identity of the key holder is valid as well.

The digital certificate is a document that contains information about the individual associated with the certificate, his or her public key information, an expiration date, and a digital signature for the issuer. Many applications now internally support digital certificates as a way of identifying users or systems, and a number of different hardware devices are in development or already on the market that make use of digital certificates for identification. Figure 7.10 shows a certificate as displayed in Microsoft Windows. In this figure, you can see the numeric thumbprint of the certificate file for the user.

Figure 7.10 Viewing a Digital Certificate

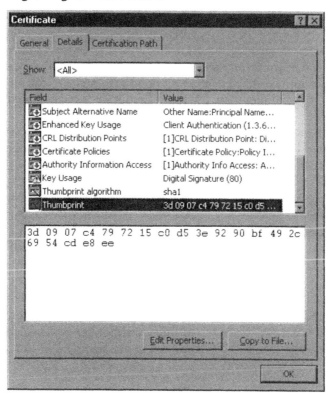

Users have two ways of requesting new certificates. One is using the Certificates MMC snap-in; the other is through Web enrollment. From within the Certificates console, users can expand the **Personal** object, right-click the **Certificates** folder, and select **Request New Certificate**. This sends a request to the CA to generate a new certificate for the user, and the newly generated certificate is stored in the user's certificate list.

Windows Server 2003 servers running Certificate Services also provide a Web interface for requesting and enrolling certificates. Users can point their browsers to http://*servername*/certsrv, where *servername* is the name of the server running Certificate Services. From the Web page, they can perform a basic certificate request, or select an advanced request where they can specify a certificate template to use, a specific cryptographic service provider, the size of the key, whether to generate a new key or use an existing one, and so on.

Certification Authorities

A provider that generates and validates digital certificates is known as a certification authority (CA). VeriSign, GlobalSign, Entrust, and other companies are third-party CAs that provide digital certificates, usually for a fee. For an enterprise organization, purchasing a digital certificate for every employee can be cost prohibitive, especially if the company is large or experiences high employee turnover. Microsoft provides tools to implement and maintain your own CAs within your organization, which enables you to generate and verify digital certificates "in house" at a significantly reduced cost. Depending on the nature of certificate use in your organization, using a completely internal CA structure may meet your needs. Or, you may choose to implement a hybrid structure that uses both internal and external CAs. Some agencies, for security reasons, may be required to rely completely on external CAs.

A root CA is the cornerstone of a PKI, no matter how large or small the organization. For small organizations, a single CA might be sufficient to handle the certificate verification process. A fully developed PKI generally has more than one CA set up in a hierarchical structure, and can include internal and external CAs in combination. Microsoft Certificate Services can function in any of the CA roles within the PKI.

Another important role within a PKI is managing revoked certificates. When an employee leaves a company or if a private key is compromised, the digital certificate for that employee should no longer be considered valid. CAs keep track of a certificate revocation list (CRL) and use the CRL when validating certificates upon request. When a validation request comes in for a certificate that is publis-hed on the CRL, the CA reports the certificate as revoked. Because an organization with a great degree of turnover can generate large CRLs, they can be time-consuming to distribute updates. A delta CRL can be used to minimize the update time. A delta CRL contains a list of changes to the last fully published CRL, and when a CA receives a delta CRL, it will combine the CRL it has on file with the delta CRL to generate an effective CRL, which will be used until a full CRL update is received.

In addition, if you implement an internal PKI, you can also specify specific CRL distribution points (CDPs) in the PKI structure. The CDP is the location that a client uses to check to see if a certificate is on the CRL. A CDP can be placed into a certificate as well, so that any client attempting to validate that certificate uses the CDP identified in the certificate instead of its default CDP.

Applying PKI Best Practices

Consider the following items when implementing a PKI in your organization:

- Determine early on if you are going to include third-party CAs as part of your PKI. If you are going to use third-party CAs, decide if you will use them for validation of certificates or generation of certificates as well. Be aware that using third-party CAs can be expensive and time-consuming.

- Keep the root CA on the network as secure as possible. The root CA is ultimately responsible for all certificate validation and trust in the PKI, and if the root CA is compromised, the entire PKI can be compromised as well.

- Use Microsoft's guidelines related to the performance of a Certificate Services server to determine how many CA servers you will need to install in your organization. This information, along with geographic and political restrictions, will help you plan for the count and locations of the CA servers.

Processes

Proper planning of a network infrastructure is essential to ensuring high performance, availability, and overall satisfaction with your network operations. In order to create a viable network design, you'll need an understanding of both the business requirements of your organization and current and emerging networking technologies. Accurate network planning will allow your organization to maximize the efficiency of its computer operations, lower costs, and enhance your overall business processes.

When planning for a new infrastructure or upgrading an existing network, you should take some or all of the following steps:

- Document the business requirements of your client or organization. Create a baseline of the performance of any existing hardware and network utilization.

- Determine the necessary capacity for the physical network installation, including client and server hardware, as well as allocating network and Internet bandwidth for network services and applications.

- Select an appropriate network protocol and create an addressing scheme that will provide for the existing size of the network and will allocate room for any foreseeable expansions, mergers, or acquisitions.

- Specify and implement the technologies that will meet the existing needs of your network while allowing room for future growth.

- Plan to upgrade and/or migrate any existing technologies, including server operating systems and routing protocols.

Security Patch Management

While Microsoft's focus on security is evident in Windows Server 2003, the fact remains that the discovery of new security vulnerabilities (and attacks that exploit them) is often simply a fact of life. As an administrator, you need to be able to determine which patches and updates are required by your enterprise computing systems, and the best way to deploy those updates as quickly and efficiently as possible. Creating an effective patch management scheme will reduce downtime and costs on your network associated with system outages or data corruption, and increase the overall security and integrity of your company's assets and intellectual property.

As a part of the Trusted Computing Initiative, Microsoft has attempted to streamline the patch management and installation process using both built-in functionality within Windows Server 2003 and freely available services and add-ons. The first step in effective patch management is obviously the ability to know that a patch is necessary and available. The Security Bulletin Notification Service provides e-mail bulletins whenever a security vulnerability for a Microsoft product has been reported and confirmed, usually along with information on how to obtain necessary patches or otherwise reconfigure vulnerable systems. The notification service classifies security vulnerabilities into one of four categories, as shown in Table 7.6. By remaining alert to the presence of security updates and patches, you can then define processes to distribute the necessary software updates to all of your network clients.

Table 7.6 The Microsoft Security Bulletin Classification System

Rating	Definition
Critical	A vulnerability of this severity could allow an Internet worm or virus to spread without user action, or even awareness.
Important	A vulnerability of this level can compromise the confidentiality, integrity, or availability of a user or company's data, or the availability of other network resources.
Moderate	The risk of this type of vulnerability is often greatly mitigated by factors such as the default configuration of the operating system, auditing, or difficulty of exploitation.
Low	A vulnerability whose exploitation is extremely difficult or whose impact is minimal.

Backup Policies

Data is a vital component of any business, but it does the business little good if the data can't be accessed from the server. Servers provide a variety of resources, and if they are unavailable, people within the company might be unable to do any work and the business won't be able to function. System recovery plans are used to prepare for circumstances that can affect a server's capability to run properly and address how the operating system and services can be restored in the event of a disaster.

System recovery plans document procedures on how to fix many of the problems that commonly result in the operating system failing to start. The plan should include information on the types of disasters that might affect a server, and how such problems can be fixed. Procedures provide step-by-step instructions on how to restore the system, and refer to other documents and plans (such as backup plans) that are used as part of system recovery.

Backup Rotation Schemes

Your goal in creating a backup schedule is to balance the number of tapes needed (cost effectiveness) with the amount of time that is required to restore the server's data completely (time effectiveness). This is most commonly done by *rotating* the type of backup made each day, week, and/or month.

A popular rotation scheme is the *Grandfather-Father-Son* (GFS) rotation, which organizes rotation into a daily, weekly, and monthly set of tapes. With a GFS backup schedule, at least one full backup is performed per week, with differential or incremental backups performed on other days of the week. At the end of the week, the daily and weekly backups are stored off-site and another set is used through the next week. To understand this better, assume the company is open from Monday to Friday. As shown in Table 7.7, a full backup of the server's volumes is performed every Monday, with differential backups performed Tuesday to Friday. On Friday, the tapes are then moved to another location, and another set of tapes is used for the following week.

Table 7.7 Sample Weekly Backup Schedule

Sun.	Mon.	Tue.	Wed.	Thu.	Fri.	Sat.
None	Full Backup	Differential	Differential	Differential	Differential, with week's tapes moved off-site	None

Because it would be too expensive to continually use new tapes, old tapes are reused for backups. A tape set for each week in the month is rotated back into service and reused. For example, at the beginning of each month, the tape set for the first week of the previous month would be rotated back into service and used for that week's backup jobs. Because one set of tapes is used for each week of the month, this means that you have most sets of tapes kept off-site. Even if one set were corrupted, the set of tapes for the week previous could still be used to restore data.

In the Grandfather-Father-Son rotation scheme, the full backup is considered the "Father," and the daily backup is considered the "Son." The "Grandfather" segment of the GFS rotation is an additional full backup that's performed monthly and stored off-site. The Grandfather tape isn't reused, but is permanently stored off-site. Each of the Grandfather tapes can be kept for a specific amount of time (such as a year), so that data can be restored from previous backups, even after the Father and Son tapes have been rotated back into service. If someone needs data restored from several months ago, the Grandfather tape enables the network administrator to retrieve the required files.

Auditing Policies and Audit Logging

Performance is not the only important thing to monitor in Windows Server 2003. In today's business environment, perhaps even more vital than ensuring top performance is the ability to ensure that sensitive data is kept secure. Security auditing enables you to track access to and modifications of objects, files, or folders, and to determine who has logged on (or attempted to do so) and when.

NOTE

You will want to make sure that you periodically back up audit information. The administrative account or administrative privileges are a prime target for hackers so there is always the possibility of intruders gaining administrator access to your system. With these privileges, an intruder can do malicious damage to your system and delete the audit events from the event log. If this happens, there will not be an audit trail to determine the cause and the damage to the system. To minimize the damage that would be caused by such an attack, duplicate the audit information periodically. You can use Microsoft Operations Manager (MOM) to copy audit events periodically and store them in a secure network drive; this provides a backup of the audit trail information.

Security events are logged in the security log, accessible by administrators via the Event Viewer. An audit entry can be either a Success or a Failure event in the security log. A list of audit entries that describes the life span of an object, file, or folder is referred to as an audit trail. The primary types of events that you can choose to audit include the following:

■ Computer logons and logoffs

■ System events (when a computer shuts down or reboots, or something happens that affects system security, such as the audit log being cleared, system time is changed, or an invalid procedure call port is used to try to impersonate a client)

■ User and computer account-management tasks (such as the creation of accounts or changes to account status or permissions)

■ Access to files, folders, and objects

Configuring security auditing helps you to track potential security issues and provide evidence in relation to security breaches. It is best practice to create an audit plan before you enable auditing on your system. The audit plan details the purpose and objectives of the audit. The audit plan should contain the following:

■ The type of information you want to audit

■ How much time you have to review audit logs

■ The resources you have for collecting and storing audit logs (disk space, memory and processor usage)

■ The intended scope of the audit

You'll need to ask yourself some questions as you prepare the audit plan. Is the purpose of the audit plan to prevent security breaches from unauthorized sources? If so, enable the audit failure events on logons and collect information on it. Is the objective of the auditing to get a snapshot of the organization's activities for forensic purposes? In that case, enable both success and failure events to collect data on all applications.

It is important to remember that the audit trail information can result in a very large amount of data if both the success and failure audits are enabled. Too wide a scope for the audit can also make it difficult for you to find the information you're looking for within a huge file that records thousands of events.

Change Management

You should have a change management policy in place and use that policy when you are implementing any changes to your system, whether it is a security patch, a password policy change, or a BIOS update – a good change management system will have ALL changes. Your policy should include several parts. For example, before you implement any change, you should document the impact the change will have on all users and customers. This should include any behaviors that users will have to change, or anything that will work differently after the change is made. It is important that you always remember to have management sign off before you make any of the required changes, to bring yourself into compliance. You should also always remember to test your change in a test environment before putting it into production. This is important to verify that it doesn't introduce other problems that must be resolved before you put it into production. You must also always have a back–out procedure in place just in case the change causes problems. After you have everything in place, make the update and then make sure you update any applicable documentation.

Summary

In this chapter, we took a look at protecting you servers and its collective parts. We showed you that by implementing a password on your server's system BIOS can add yet another preventative measure in your overall security plan. By using USB blockers you can prevent unauthorized users from gaining access to unnecessary resources. We then covered in depth Intrusion Detection Systems and how they work. We discussed how an intrusion detection system is much like a burglar alarm on your house and that an intrusion detection system can even be used to assist with compliancy of established corporate policies.

Next we discussed the issues surrounding the protection of your data. A major part of this discussion included the definitions of Business Continuity Planning (BCP) and Disaster Recovery (DR) Planning and how the two processes are closely tied together. We defined BCP as a methodology used to create and validate a plan for maintaining continuous business operations before, during, and after disasters and disruptive events. And we defined disaster recovery as a part of business continuity which deals with the immediate impact of an event. We also covered the importance of having a good backup plan for your environment. We also talked about creating a system recovery plan and the steps needed to accomplish this task. The topic of security and patch management was also covered and its importance in maintaining the overall security of your environment. We discussed the various methods that can be employed to assist with patch management. We also briefly discussed how RAID disks are yet another method to protect your data.

We told you that one of the most important, and at the same time most overlooked aspects of a comprehensive network security plan is physical access control. We discussed what measures could be put into place to assist in physical security control. We also covered which network resources should be included in the physical security plan.

We closed this chapter with a discussion of understanding security measures and objectives and how people, processes and technology affect our overall security posture. We discussed how knowing your users, educating your users and control your users will make your job easier. We reiterated the need for an effective password policy utilizing strong passwords. We also covered topics such as user roles and responsibilities, firewall security, antivirus software security and how all of these all have an important role in securing your XenApp environment.

Solutions Fast Track

Protecting Your Server (and Its Parts)

☑ To assist in the preventing the unauthorized access to your servers you can set the system BIOS to boot only from the hard disk and to also password protect the BIOS from changes.

☑ USB blockers can be installed to minimize the security risks imposed by using portable storage media and portable devices in your enterprise.

☑ You can utilize XenApp Resource Manager with or without the summary database to establish a means of producing alarms based on metrics you configure and want to monitor.

☑ When we speak of intrusion detection, we are referring to the act of detecting an unauthorized intrusion by a computer on a network. This unauthorized access, or intrusion, is an attempt to compromise, or otherwise do harm, to other network devices.

☑ Intrusion detection systems can also be used to monitor for compliance with your company's security policy.

Protecting Your Data

☑ Business continuity planning (BCP) is a methodology used to create and validate a plan for maintaining continuous business operations before, during, and after disasters and disruptive events. Disaster recovery is part of business continuity, and deals with the immediate impact of an event.

☑ A backup enables data and system files on a computer to be archived to another location on the hard disk or to other media. When problems occur, the backed-up files can be restored to the location from which the data was originally copied or to another location such as a different directory or a different machine. The capability to restore the data is just as important as performing regular backups; if the backup cannot be restored, then the backed-up data is as lost as any original data you're attempting to recover.

☑ Because many types of disasters can affect an operating system's ability to start, Windows Server 2003 includes a variety of utilities that can be used to recover the system.

☑ Patching a large enterprise full of server and client systems has become something of an administrative nightmare in most IT shops because of the importance of staying on top of security patches that Microsoft releases frequently.

☑ Fault-tolerant disks enable a computer to recover from a disaster, so that data won't be lost or corrupted. RAID (Redundant Array of Independent – or Inexpensive – Disks) provides several methods of writing data across multiple disks. If one disk in an array fails, RAID enables you to replace the damaged disk and recover the data quickly.

Planning Physical Security

☑ Your physical security plan should include the building, data network, environmental controls, security controls and telecommunications equipment serving your environment. In most cases, the physical elements of data networking and security technology protecting that data should be dedicated and in a stand alone infrastructure.

☑ File servers on which sensitive data is stored and infrastructure servers that provide mission critical services such as logon authentication and access control should be placed in a highly secure location. At the minimum, servers should be in a locked room where only those who need to work directly with the servers have access. Keys should be distributed sparingly, and records should be kept of issuance and return.

☑ Facility security is of paramount concern to any network environment. Campus level access, environment level access, and object level access protocols must all be implemented. Video surveillance and live surveillance by internal security are strongly recommended.

With regard to general security, the entire facility should have at a minimum a two challenge system in place such that every entrant will be providing at least one validator at an automated checkpoint (i.e. biometric entry, external security card swipe, etc.) and one other independent manual or automatic validator (sign in at security desk, internal security card swipes, etc.)

Security Measures and Objectives

☑ There are many ways to break down the elements of your XenApp environment, but for the purposes of simplicity, we'll use three simple categories: people, process, and technology. As an IT professional, you understand the importance of the interplay among these three elements. Technology is implemented by people using specific processes. The better defined the processes are, the more reliable the results (typically). Technology is only as good as the people who designed and implemented it and the processes developed to utilize it.

☑ The topic of network security might bring to mind a picture of evil corporate rivals determined to steal your company's most precious trade secrets or malevolent hackers bent on crashing your network and erasing all your data just for the sheer joy of it. Although these risks do exist, often the reality of network data loss is far less glamorous. A large proportion of erased, modified, or disclosed data is the result of the actions of employees or other authorized network personnel. Furthermore, a large percentage of that damage is the result of accidental compromise of the data.

☑ Technology is clearly the piece of the puzzle that you, as an IT professional, will be most familiar. As you participate in your company's network security strategy, you will be in the best position to understand what happens with various technology components. Part of the reason for security planning is to look at your use of technology and understand which elements are vulnerable to which types of threats.

☑ Proper planning of a network infrastructure is essential to ensuring high performance, availability, and overall satisfaction with your network operations. In order to create a viable network design, you'll need an understanding of both the business requirements of your organization and current and emerging networking technologies. Accurate network planning will allow your organization to maximize the efficiency of its computer operations, lower costs, and enhance your overall business processes.

Frequently Asked Questions

Q: Why is XenApp security broken down by the XenApp Security Model?

A: Implementing security based on the XenApp Security Model will assist you in protecting your network from different threats and different users.

Q: What is one security measure that is often overlooked that can help prevent the unauthorized access to server data?

A: Setting the BIOS password.

Q: What is the purpose of a USB blocker?

A: USB blockers can be installed to minimize the security risks imposed by using portable storage media and portable devices in your enterprise that utilize a USB connection.

Q: Which XenApp component can be configured to create alarms and alerts based on information you select?

A: You can utilize XenApp Resource Manager with or without the summary database to establish a means of producing alarms based on metrics you configure and want to monitor.

Q: What are the three points needed for an intrusion to exist?

A: Motive, Means and Opportunity

Q: What is the definition of an Intrusion Detection System (IDS)?

A: An Intrusion Detection System (IDS) is the high-tech equivalent of a burglar alarm—a burglar alarm configured to monitor access points, hostile activities, and known intruders.

Q: What is a Business Continuity Plan (BCP)?

A: Business continuity planning (BCP) is a methodology used to create and validate a plan for maintaining continuous business operations before, during, and after disasters and disruptive events.

Q: What is Disaster Recovery (DR)?

A: Disaster recovery is part of business continuity, and deals with the immediate impact of an event.

Q: What should be utilized to protect you when problems with data occur?

A: File and system backups. The backed-up files can be restored to the location from which the data was originally copied or to another location such as a different directory or a different machine.

Q: What are the parts of a System Recovery Plan?

A: The capability to back up the System State data, the creation of ASR sets, the Recovery Console, startup options that appear when the computer is booted

Q: What is WSUS?

A: WSUS stands for Windows Server Update Services and in short, WSUS allows you to maintain what is effectively an internal Windows Update Web site, where your WSUS server contacts the actual Microsoft Update Web site and downloads updates that an administrator can review and approve for deployment.

Q: What does RAID stand for?

A: Redundant Array of Independent (or Inexpensive) Disks

Q: What are some of the IT resources that require physical security?

A: Servers, workstations, network devices, cables

Q: When creating a physical security plan, what components should be reviewed and included?

A: Building, data network, environmental controls, security controls and telecommunications equipment serving your environment.

Q: What are the three categories of security measures and objectives?

A: People, processes and technology.

Q: Educating employees, contractors, and any other insiders on how to protect corporate assets and the dangers and methods of social engineering is called what?

A: Security Awareness

Q: What is rotation of duties?

A: All critical jobs should have multiple people who perform the roles and those people should be rotated through periodically. If a person knows that someone else is going to be performing a given role in two months, it will be much harder for them to commit fraud or other insider attacks, because there is a good chance someone might catch it later.

Q: What is least privilege?

A: Any additional access that someone has can be used against the company. Although access is needed for people to perform their jobs, this access should be carefully controlled. People should be given only the access they need to do their jobs and nothing else.

Q: What is PKI?

A: Public key infrastructure—the use of digital certificates to verify authenticity of e-mail messages, encrypt files, and so on.

Q: What is the Grandfather-Father-Son backup rotation?

A: Organizes rotation into a daily, weekly, and monthly set of tapes. With a GFS backup schedule, at least one full backup is performed per week, with differential or incremental backups performed on other days of the week. At the end of the week, the daily and weekly backups are stored off-site and another set is used through the next week.

Chapter 8

Security Guidance for ICA and Network Connections

Solutions in this chapter:

- **Understanding Network Protocols**

- **Defining Network Segregation**

- **Understanding Connections to a XenApp Server**

- **Understanding Internet Protocol Security**

- **Understanding Public Key Infrastructure**

- **Securing the Citrix License Server**

☑ Summary

☑ Solutions Fast Track

☑ Frequently Asked Questions

Introduction

Securing sensitive or mission-critical data is an important part of the network administrator's job. Data is especially vulnerable to interception as it travels across the network. Since its integration into Windows 2000, Terminal Services has proved to be an invaluable remote administration tool as well as a great application server platform—especially when used with Citrix XenApp. With Terminal Services and XenApp, you can log in to your Windows Server 2003 machines and perform administrative tasks from virtually any type of device, including Pocket PC devices and Windows CE devices. The power and convenience of Terminal Services and XenApp is obvious; however, this power comes with the potential to introduce security vulnerabilities into your network if the use of this technology isn't carefully managed. This risk is especially great because Terminal Services and XenApp are such a well-known application that it provides a tempting target for malicious users or hackers to attempt to gain access to your network. All that any attacker needs to know is the server's IP address, DNS, or NetBIOS name and he or she can try to access the Windows logon screen and attempt to log on to the server.

Understanding Network Protocols

A listener connection (also called the RDP-Tcp or the ICA-Tcp connection) must be configured and exist on the server for clients to successfully establish Terminal Services and Citrix sessions to that server. Administrators use the Terminal Services Configuration tool to create new listener connections and configure the ones that currently exist. This tool can also be used to configure connections for ICA (Citrix) clients using IPX, SPX, Asynchronous, or NetBIOS as well as TCP. Finally, the Configuration tool is also used to configure some server policy settings.

Microsoft recommends that you use Group Policy to configure Terminal Services connection settings, if possible. However, the Configuration tool enables you to specify settings separately for multiple connections on the same computer—something that you can't do with Group Policy. You can also use the Configuration tool for terminal servers that run pre-Windows Server 2003 operating systems.

In truth, it's pretty unusual for people to create their own listener connections, so the following section focuses on how to configure existing ones. All of the settings that relate to configuring listener connections also relate to settings you provide when you create one. You should also note that the term "listener connection" is an older term that is not used in Windows 2003. The Windows 2003 documentation refers to it as an RDP-TCP connection. We're using it here because there is no distinction made in the Windows Server 2003 Help files between a connection as configured in the Terminal Services Configuration tool, and a connection made from a client to Terminal Services running on a server. While we'll be using the term "listener connection" to help you keep them straight.

Configuration of the RDP Protocol

The Remote Desktop Protocol (RDP), handles the transfer of the screen information from the server to your client. It also ensures that your cursor movements and keystrokes make it from the client back to your session on the server. RDP was based on a set of International Telecommunications Union (ITU) T.120 protocol family. Windows 2000 Terminal Services included RDP v5.0, which increased performance. Windows XP and Server 2003 use RDP 5.1. In Windows Server 2003 Service Pack 1 (SP1), you can enhance the security of Terminal Server by configuring Terminal Services connections to use Transport Layer Security (TLS) 1.0 for server authentication, and to encrypt terminal server communications using RDP 5.2. RDP communicates on port 3389; it uses encryption to protect the information that is sent between the terminal server and the client computer.

For TLS authentication to function correctly, terminal servers must meet the following prerequisites:

- Terminal servers must run Windows Server 2003 SP1.

- You must have a RDP client that is TLS compliant.

- You must obtain a certificate for the terminal server (discussed later in this chapter).

Configuring & Implementing...

Configuring RDP for TLS Authentication

To configure RDP to use TLS authentication via the Terminal Services Configuration Tool as shown in Figure 8.1, follow these steps:

1. Select **Start | All Programs | Administrative Tools,** click on **Terminal Services Configuration** to execute the Terminal Services Configuration Tool.

2. Right click on the RDP-Tcp connection with which you want to modify and click **Properties**.

3. If not already displayed, click on the **General** tab.

4. In the security box, select **Negotiate** for the Security Layer.

5. For Encryption Level, select **High** or **FIPS Compliant**.

6. Click the **Edit** button for the certificate and select a certificate that has been installed on the server.

7. Click **OK** to close the RDP-Tcp properties, and exit the Terminal Services Configuration Tool.

Figure 8.1 Configuring RDP for TLS Authentication

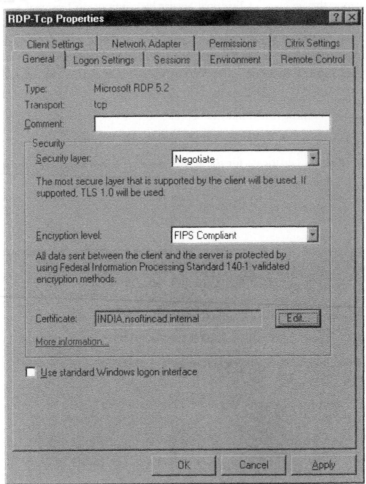

Listener connections can be configured for RDP only over TCP/IP, and only one listener can be configured for each network interface card (NIC) in the Terminal Services computer. By default, the RDP-Tcp listener is created that is bound to all of the NICs in the server. If the server has more than one NIC, an administrator can configure the default listener connection to only be associated with one NIC, and create new listener connections for each of the other NICs in the Terminal Services computer. You must be a member of the Administrators group, or be delegated the authority, in order to create new listener connections.

Creating new listener connections might be desirable if each NIC is attached to a separate segment, and only certain users should be enabled to access the Terminal Services computer from each segment. Permissions can be granted within the listener connection that specify who can and cannot connect. By default, only users of the Remote Desktop Users group are configured to connect using terminal servers. If you disable this in a user's properties, he or she will not be able to access any Terminal Services. If you want to enable a user to connect, but only from one segment that is attached to the terminal server, you can use the permissions associated with a listener connection to accomplish this.

The TCP/IP connection installed with Terminal Services comes with a set of default permissions. You can modify these default permissions by setting different permissions for different users or groups, adjusting them to fit the requirements of your organization. You must be logged on as a member of the Administrators group to manage connection permissions. The default permissions on Terminal Services objects are shown in Table 8.1.

Table 8.1 Standard RDP Permissions

Group	Permission
Administrators	Full control
LOCAL SERVICE	Service permissions
NETWORK SERVICE	Service permissions
Remote Desktop Users	User access
SYSTEM	Full control
Guest	Guest access

In most XenApp deployments you will want to limit a user's connectivity to only the ICA-tcp connection. To achieve this, it is recommended that you remove the Remote Desktop Users group and the Guest group from the RDP-Tcp permissions and only have Administrators able to connect, as shown in Figure 8.2.

Figure 8.2 Recommended RDP-Tcp Permissions

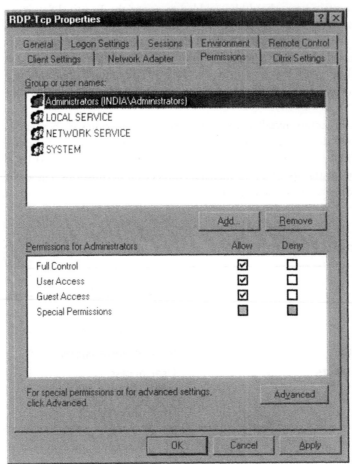

Controlling Connection Access

Use the permissions provided for Terminal Services to control how users and groups access the server. You can alter the default permissions to restrict individual users and groups from performing certain tasks, such as logging off a user from a session or ending sessions. You manage permissions from Terminal Services Configuration. You must be logged in as a member of the Administrators group to set permissions.

By default, there are three types of permissions:

- Full Control

- User Access

- Guest Access

You can configure these by setting permissions for which users or groups can use a specific task. You can set the following permissions as shown in Table 8.2.

Table 8.2 Default XenApp TCP Ports

Permission	Default Port
Query Information	Query sessions and servers for information
Set Information	Configure connection properties.
Remote Control	View or actively control another user's session.
Logon	Log on to a session on the server.
Logoff	Log off a user from a session. Be aware that logging off a user without warning can result in loss of data at the client.
Message	Send a message to another user's sessions.
Connect	Connect to another session.
Disconnect	Disconnect a session.
Virtual Channels	Use virtual channels. Be aware that turning off virtual channels disables some Terminal Services features such as clipboard and printer redirection.

TIP

Microsoft documentation states that you must use the Remote Desktop Users group to control remote access to Terminal Server and Remote Desktop for Administration. This is not entirely correct, because by modifying the default permissions on the RDP-Tcp protocol, you can choose which specific users and/or groups can have access to RDP and to what extent.

Configuration of the ICA Protocol

An ICA session is the communications link between clients and servers that users establish to run applications, which is very much like an RDP session. As you know, an ICA session transmits an application's screen display to the client and the client sends the user's keystrokes, mouse actions, and local data to the application running on the server. The default port on servers for inbound traffic from ICA sessions is 1494. The outbound port from the server used for the ICA session is allocated dynamically when the session is established.

NOTE

If session reliability is invoked, ICA traffic is tunneled through the Common Gateway Protocol, which uses TCP port 2598 by default. Like ICA traffic, the designated port is used for inbound sessions to Presentation Server, and a dynamically allocated port is used for outbound traffic. Ports 1494 and 2598 should be opened only to internal inbound traffic. Sessions originating from clients connecting over the Internet should be secured by means of the Citrix Secure Gateway or Citrix Access Gateway.

The configuration of the ICA protocol is very similar to the configuration of the RDP protocol and the methods described in the previous section can also be applied to the ICA-tcp session. The default permissions for the ICA-tcp protocol are shown in Figure 8.3.

Figure 8.3 Default ICA-tcp Permissions

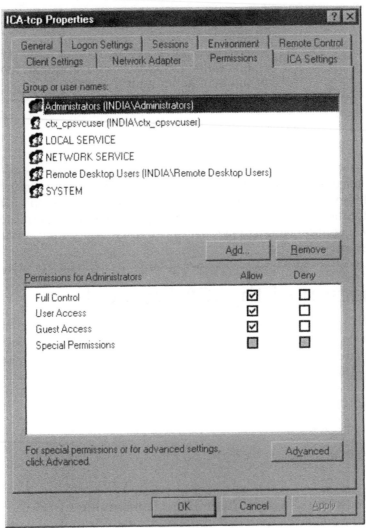

NOTE

You will notice that there is one additional user in the ICA-tcp permission list, which is the *Ctx_CpsvcUser*. The Ctx_CpsvcUser account provides the Citrix Print Manager Service with a server-local account to perform certain functions. By default, the account has only the necessary permissions, group memberships, and rights needed to perform those functions. Any deviation from this set of permissions and rights for the purpose of hardening or locking down the server might cause printers to not autocreate in an ICA session. The Ctx_CpsvcUser account belongs to the Power Users Group. Membership to this group gives account access to many resources not given to regular users. In addition, there are many security rights assigned specifically to this group. If your local security policies mandate that local accounts should not be used, you can configure the Citrix Print Manager Service to use a domain account. You should consult the Citrix web site, www.citrix.com, for specific information on how to do this.

Configuring TCP Ports

Table 8.3 lists the TCP/IP ports that XenApp servers, Citrix Clients, the IMA Service, and other Citrix services use in a server farm. This information can help you configure firewalls and troubleshoot port conflicts with other software.

Table 8.3 Default XenApp TCP Ports

Communication	Default Port
Citrix XML Service	80
Access Management Console	135
Citrix SSL Relay	443
ICA Sessions (clients to servers)	1494
Client-to-server (directed UDP)	1604
Server to server	2512
Presentation Server Console	2513
Session Reliability	2598
Server to MS SQL or Oracle server	139, 1433, or 443 for MS-SQL
License Management Console	8082
Server to license server	27000

Defining Network Segregation

Network interface cards (NICs) are the hardware used by your server to communicate with the rest of the network. NICs can communicate over several different wiring solutions, depending on design. Choosing a NIC is entirely dependent on the type of network infrastructure already in place. If you are running 10-Megabit switched Ethernet, then a 10/100-Megabit Ethernet card will do you little good beyond the initial 10-Megabit Ethernet capability. In a 100-Megabit Ethernet network, that same card will (theoretically) provide you with 10 times the communication speeds. The NIC will always be based on the type of infrastructure you already have or plan on having.

Some NICs even contain dual network ports on the same card and allow for failover if the first port should go dead. Some vendors offer server hardware that supports multiple network interface cards (NIC) that can either split up the traffic sent to the server from the same network segment (load balancing), or that can come online if the main NIC fails (failover redundancy). If you have a server that supports many concurrent users, you may discover that the network interface card is a bottleneck. To avoid this, you should select a server that can load balance the traffic between two or more NICs. If you wish to avoid the disastrous cost of a NIC failure, you should select a server that supports failover redundancy.

Multihomed servers

One consideration when choosing a NIC is whether to make a machine multihomed or not. A machine is *multihomed* when it contains two or more NICs that each connect to a network segment. These can be separate segments, or the same segment in the case of multihoming a machine for redundancy or speed issues. Multihomed machines can act as routers if an actual router is not available, but this will eat up the Central Processor Unit (CPU) to provide the routing service. Multihoming a XenApp server can be implemented for several reasons, which include:

- Servers that require redundant access
- Servers that require out of band management access (remote administration only)
- Servers that require a separate backup network
- Configuration of a private internal network
- Servers that require communication with resources outside the internal network.

Network bottlenecks can occur anytime an application that is executed by XenApp Server doesn't actually exist on the server itself. For instance, Microsoft Word will typically install locally on the XenApp Server, but the data normally exists somewhere else on the network. This is even more true for client-server applications such as PeopleSoft or SAP. While the bandwidth used by the sessions the server is hosting is relatively low, the network requirements for those sessions will be substantially higher. There are several ways to address this issue:

- Teamed cards to increase available bandwidth

- Collocation of the application and data on the Presentation Server

- Multihomed servers with network connects that separate session bandwidth from application bandwidth

Teaming network cards for redundancy is almost always a good idea. By aggregating multiple network cards together, their "physical" bandwidth can be logically totaled to provide for more "pipe." Most network cards today support teaming (in various forms), and in some cases the ability to team dissimilar network cards (such as a 10/100Mbps card with a 1Gbps card) if the need arises. We recommend that you always attempt to team identical cards to reduce the complexities and supportability issues that could arise otherwise.

Placing the application and data on the XenApp Server will certainly decrease the amount of traffic required to service the user request, thus eliminating the network as the potential bottleneck. However, this action means we have indirectly created a single point of failure for access to this application. If the data is located on a single XenApp Server, we will most likely not be able to "load balance" the application across the farm; therefore, this option isn't really a viable solution except in certain circumstances.

The last option of multihoming our XenApp Server presents many opportunities to increase performance and in a more limited way to increase fault tolerance. The concept of multihoming servers of all kinds has been around the networking world nearly as long as the network itself! Multihomed servers presented solutions to allow for fault tolerance, increase bandwidth, and in some cases, "private" networks for backup and authentication services. However, historically, XenApp's ancestors have had issues with multiple "paths" to a server. In the past, a Citrix server may inadvertently direct a user session to the "wrong" card in a multihomed server scenario, thus creating a denial of service .This problem has been long since fixed, so today we can discuss the benefit of multihoming our XenApp Servers to improve quality of service (QoS).

By multihoming your XenApp Servers you can segment our session traffic from our data traffic (and possibly the authentication and backup traffic as well). Placing two "legs" or "routes" to the network also can provide some measure of fault tolerance for access to the specific XenApp Server (although typically this is not as reliable or automatic as teaming).The situation arises due to the nature of application and network access. Let us consider the following scenario. Suppose you have a single XenApp Server that has a single NIC for all user sessions and network data access.The server is servicing 50 user sessions.The applications are all well behaved with the exception of your in-house database system for order tracking.When the application running on the XenApp Server (or client workstation) accesses the database for queries, large amounts of traffic are generated between the server and the database until the request is fulfilled.This translates into periods of slowness for the other user sessions on the server (even though the CPU, memory, and disk performance may be fine).Why? The answer is that all the user sessions and the application data access are contending for the same network link. Consider separating the user sessions and database access onto two separate network cards. Figure 8.4 demonstrates this concept of isolating the "data" network from the "session" network.

Figure 8.4 Multihomed XenApp Server

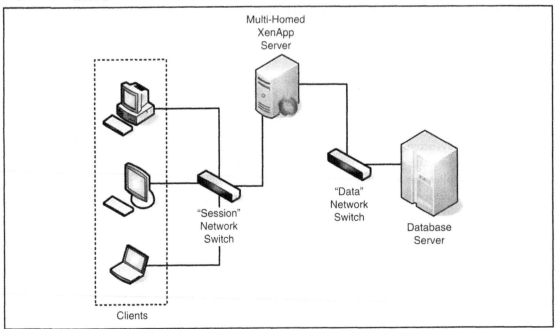

XenApp Zones

The servers within a farm can communicate at will with each other across IMA for the purposes of updating license usage counts, server load information, and so forth. As the farm grows, this traffic grows exponentially. To help control this flow of communications, Citrix uses the concept of a zone. A zone is a logical grouping of servers typically associated with subnets. Each zone has a data collector.

The data collector is responsible for complete knowledge of the dynamic information for the zone it is a member thereof. What is dynamic information, you may ask? Dynamic information is information that changes regularly within the farm, such as user session count on a given server, number of licenses consumed, number of disconnected sessions, status of a given connection, and so forth. The data collector typically is also responsible for all load information to allow for the decision as to where to load balance an incoming session. The data collector is very important and directly impacts the users' perception of performance.

Since the data collector is so important, let's review some best practices and general information about data collectors.

- By default, the first server built in a new farm is "selected" as the data collector.

- There is a single data collector per zone.

- A single zone may contain up to 256 servers. Larger or busier farms (five or more servers) should isolate a zone data collector (per zone) that will service application enumeration and load-balance requests to increase performance. This server should not service actual sessions, but instead redirect users' sessions to the appropriate servers.

- The role is dynamically reassigned in the event that the data collector should fail.

- Client software and Web interface servers typically should be pointed to the data collector for their zone for application enumeration (as it will be typically faster than crossing a WAN link).

Understanding Connections to a XenApp Server

As you might guess, the 32-bit Windows ICA client is intended for Microsoft Windows 32-bit operating systems, which include Windows 9x, Windows Me, Windows NT 4, Windows 2000, Windows 2003, Windows XP and Windows Vista. Citrix provides not one, but three 32-bit Windows clients, and you must decide which client or clients best suit your environment, the needs of your users, and the way you want to manage access to published resources. Your ICA client choices for 32-bit Windows operating systems are:

- Program Neighborhood Agent client

- Program Neighborhood client

- Web clients

Before you can decide the best client or clients for your environment, you need to thoroughly understand the differences between each client, what options each provides, and how configuration and deployment can be managed. There are several settings that can be configured on the ICA client in order to make it more secure. Some of the most notable that we will discuss are:

- Disabling the bitmap disk cache

- Using SSL/TLS for communications

- Not allowing user passwords to be saved

- Using two-factor authentication such as smart cards

- Disabling client device mapping (such has hard drives and the clipboard)

- Using Kerberos authentication for local client connections

Connections via Program Neighborhood Agent

The Program Neighborhood Agent (PNAgent) provides "transparent integration" of published applications to the user's Desktop. This means that users can have shortcuts on their Desktops, Start menu, and System Tray that will appear as though the applications were installed locally, but the shortcuts actually point to applications on the XenApp server. Thus, users will not be challenged with any new access methods.

As for client management and administration, the Program Neighborhood Agent is "centrally" managed from the Access Management Console on the Web Interface server. All user options such as logon method, shortcuts, shortcut placement, display, and audio settings are configured from the console and pushed out to the users. When modifications are made to the configuration, the changes are dynamically made when the client connects.

The Program Neighborhood Agent, as noted previously, requires the Web Interface to be installed. When a user clicks on a published application shortcut, the client uses HTTP or HTTPS to connect to the Web Interface where the configuration file is read and the user's Desktop is updated. Connections to the PNAgent should be made utilizing HTTPS as shown in Figure 8.5.

Figure 8.5 Configuring the Program Neighborhood Agent Client

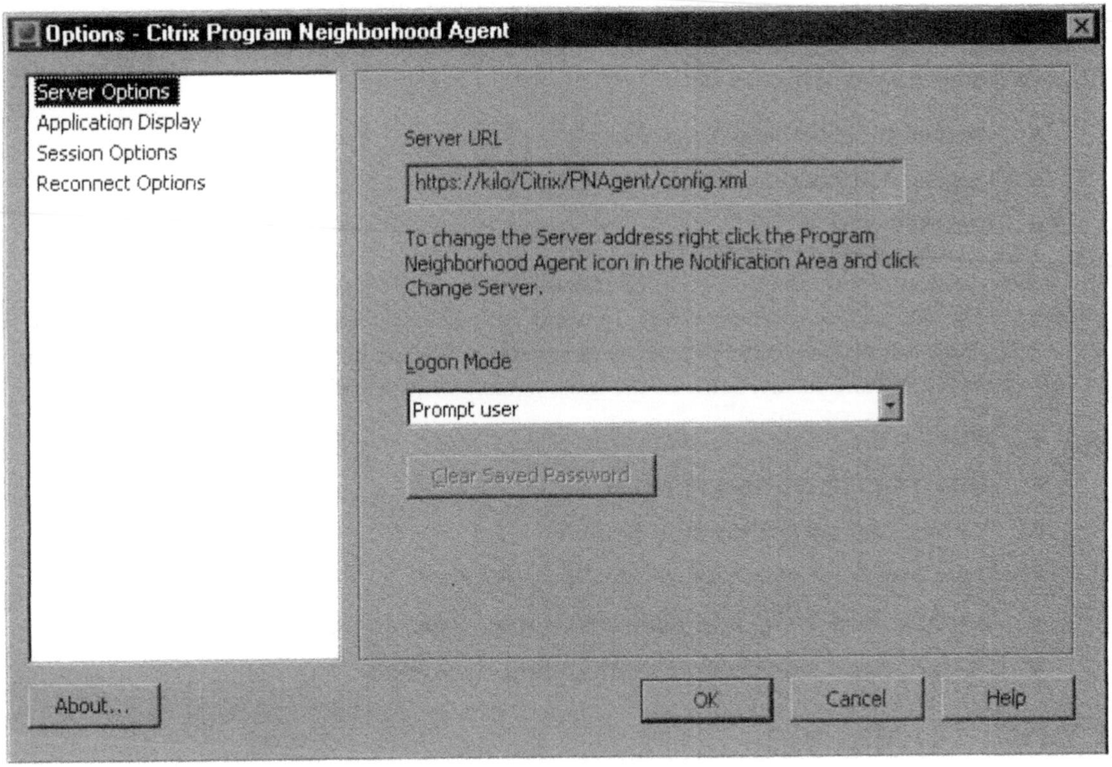

Connections via Program Neighborhood

The Win32 Program Neighborhood (PN) client provides users with access to published resources, application sets, and individual servers in the farm via its own unique user interface (see Figure 8.6). The PN client is the only Win32 ICA client that does not require the Web Interface, so if you are not running a Web server or the Web Interface, this is the client to choose. You can use this client with the

Web Interface, but once you look at the Program Neighborhood Agent and Web client features, you will not want to use the PN client. The downside to the PN client is that it is more complex and the only client that cannot be managed centrally or "pushed" out to the client preconfigured. It must be configured at the user's desktop and requires more administrative intervention. It could also be an issue if the users are unfamiliar with the client and the consequences of any changes they may make.

Figure 8.6 The Program Neighborhood Interface

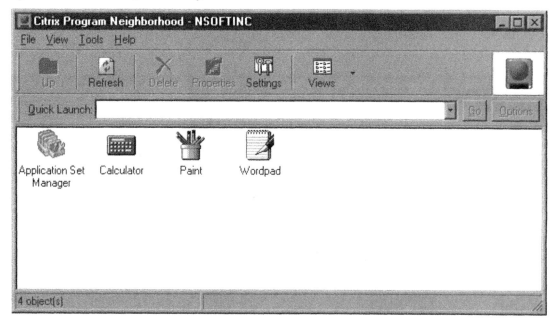

TIP

If you have not yet deployed ICA clients, Citrix strongly recommends installing the Web Interface and deploying the Program Neighborhood Agent or Web client rather than the Program Neighborhood client.

Kerberos Pass-Through Authentication

Kerberos, a network authentication protocol included in the Microsoft Windows operating systems, can be used in conjunction with Security Support Provider Interface (SSPI) to provide pass-through authentication with secret key cryptography and data integrity. When using Kerberos, the client does not need to handle the password and it is not sent over the network. This greatly reduces the risk of Trojan horse attacks on the client to access user's passwords. A more in-depth server side configuration of Kerberos is provided elsewhere in this book and must be followed in order for Kerberos authentication to work with an ICA client.

By default, the ICA client is not configured to use Kerberos authentication when logging on to a XenApp server. You must configure this functionality of the ICA client and you can configure Kerberos to use pass-through or explicit authentication.

Configuring & Implementing…

Configuring the ICA Client to Use Keberos Pass-Through Authentication

To restrict the client to use Kerberos authentication only you must perform the following steps:

1. Log on to the client as an administrator.

2. Launch Program Neighborhood. Click **Tools | ICA Settings**.

3. In the **General** tab, ensure that the **Pass-Through Authentication** setting is checked (as shown in Figure 8.7).

4. Exit Program Neighborhood.

5. Using a text editor such as notepad, open the WFClient.ini file located in the C:\Program Files\Citrix\ICA Client directory.

6. Ensure that the following settings exist under the [WFClient] section:

   SSPIEnabled=On

   UseSSPIOnly=On

7. Log off the client and then ensure that **Use local credentials to log on setting** is checked and that the **Pass-Through Authentication** setting is checked for each user.

Figure 8.7 Configuring the ICA Client to Use Kerberos

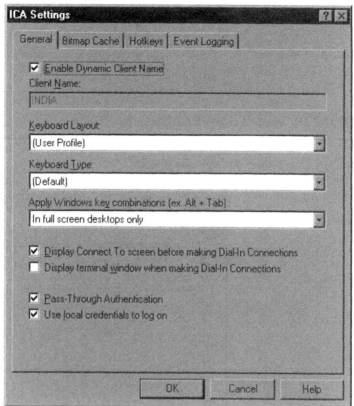

Selecting a Server Location Protocol

Our discussion thus far has assumed that the servers in question are Windows Server 2003 servers, so we will begin with the network protocols native to a Microsoft Windows network. The three options are:

- TCP/IP+HTTP
- SSL/TLS+HTTPS
- TCP/IP

Which option should you use? Citrix recommends using TCP/IP+HTTP as the Server Location network protocol because it provides several advantages over TCP/IP alone. One of the primary advantages is that TCP/IP uses User Datagram Protocol (UDP) broadcasts to locate XenApp servers.

UDP broadcasts can cause unnecessary network traffic, especially on slower networks. TCP/IP+HTTP does not. When an ICA client uses TCP/IP+HTTP to browse for a XenApp server to connect to, it uses HTTP encapsulated data that is sent to port 80 (by default) on the XenApp server. The XML service running on the server then provides the client with the address of a server in the farm that has the desired application. Once the client has the appropriate address, the ICA session is established and the user can begin using the application as shown in Figure 8.8.

Figure 8.8 TCP/IP+HTTP Server Location Protocol

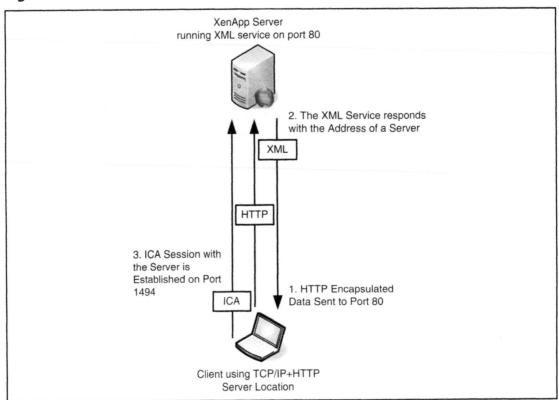

Citrix also recommends specifying servers to contact for ICA browsing. If no servers are specified in the Address List, the default name "ica" is used, and DNS or WINS will be relied on to resolve the name "ica" to a XenApp server address. If the name "ica" cannot be resolved, no server will be contacted.

Configuring & Implementing...

DNS Round Robin

DNS round robin can be used to map the hostname "ica" to multiple XenApp servers in your farm. Round robin refers to a technique that in simpler terms means "taking turns." The IP addresses of the servers are placed in a list, all resolving to the hostname "ica," and each time a request comes in to resolve the hostname, the DNS server hands out the first IP address in the list. That address then moves to the end, and the next time the request comes in for "ica," the DNS server provides the second IP address, and so on, until it loops back around to the first address. When used for Server Location addresses, it provides a work-around to configuring the client with individual addresses. The only caveat here is when the default XML port is changed. Even though you add the DNS entries mapping the "ica" hostname to valid server IP addresses, there is no way to set a specific port number from within DNS. ICA clients attempting to connect to the farm using "ica" in the server list will receive the error message "The ICA Browser did not return any names."

Since TCP/IP+HTTP is the preferred method for ICA browsing, you may wonder why plain old TCP/IP was provided as an option. After all, TCP/IP uses UDP and produces broadcast traffic on the network and is clearly less efficient than using TCP/IP+HTTP. Citrix retained TCP/IP as an option for those environments that still have older Citrix servers in use.

Citrix recommends using TCP/IP + HTTP protocol for Enumeration because it provides several advantages for most server farms:

- TCP/IP + HTTP uses XML data encapsulated in HTTP packets that the client sends to port 80 by default. Most firewalls are configured so port 80 is open for HTTP communication.

- TCP/IP + HTTP does not use (User Datagram Protocol) UDP or broadcasts to locate servers in the server farm.

- Routers pass TCP/IP packets between subnets, which allows clients to locate servers that are not on the same subnet.

SSL/TLS+HTTPS provides strong encryption appropriate for use over the Internet or through a proxy or firewall as well as server authentication. SSL, or Secure Socket Layer, operates between TCP and HTTP using port 443. The combination of SSL and HTTP is known as HTTPS. SSL establishes secure communications, delivers the server certificate, delivers the client certificate if there is one, verifies the integrity, and encrypts and decrypts the data. TLS, or Transport Layer Security, ensures the privacy between communicating applications and the Internet and uses port 443. If you opt to use SSL/TLS+HTTPS, the XenApp servers you want to communicate with must be configured to accept SSL or TLS communication.

Configuring & Implementing...

Configuring the ICA Client to Use SSL/TLS

To configure Program Neighborhood to utilize SSL/TLS you must perform the following steps:

1. Open Program Neighborhood.

2. To configure an application set to use SSL/TLS you must right click the application set to be configured and select **Application Set Settings**.

3. In the Settings dialog box, select **SSL/TLS+HTTPS** from the **Network Protocol** menu (as shown in Figure 8.9).

4. Click on **Add**, and then enter the fully qualified domain name of the SSL/TLS enabled XenApp servers to the **Address List** along with the appropriate TCP port. Click **OK**.

5. Click **OK** to exit the application set properties and save your settings.

Figure 8.9 Configuring the ICA Client to Use SSL/TLS

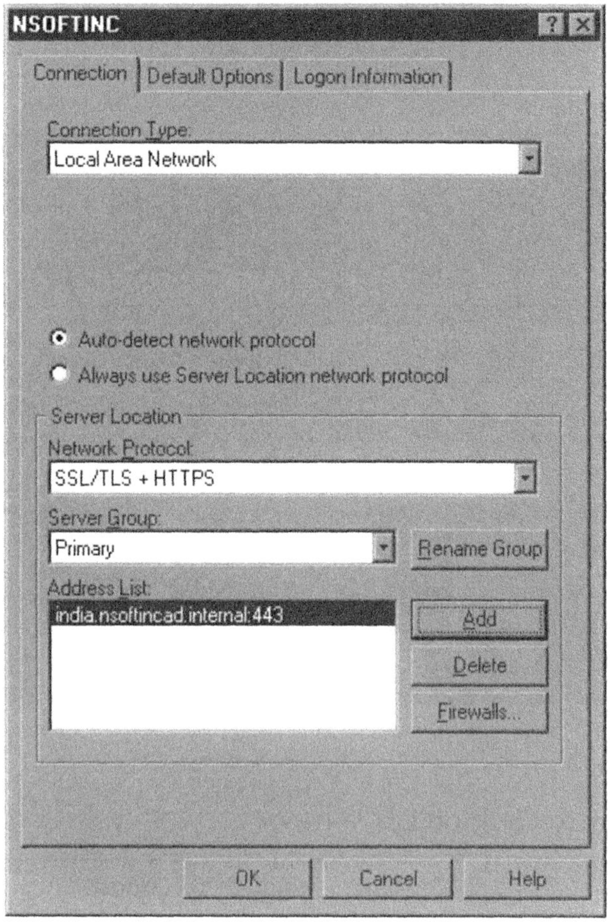

WARNING

In order to utilize SSL/TLS an appropriate root certificate must be installed on the client and the server. Additional information regarding certificates is covered later in this chapter.

Configuring Certificate Revocation List Checking

In order to fully utilize the features provided by SSL/TLS, you will need to configure Certificate Revocation List checking (CRL) for your ICA client.

When certificate revocation list checking is enabled, the clients check whether or not the server's certificate is revoked. By forcing clients to check this, you can improve the cryptographic authentication of the computer running XenApp and the overall security of the SSL/TLS connections.

For performance considerations in a large enterprise, the use of third-party CRL checking software should be used such as Tumbleweed.

Configuring & Implementing...

Configuring Certificate Revocation Checking

To configure Certificate Revocation List Checking you must perform the following steps:

1. On the server running the Web Interface, locate and open the Default.ica file with a text editor such as Notepad.

2. Locate the setting **SSLCertificateRevocationCheckPolicy** under the [WFClient] section. If the setting does not exist, you will need to add it.

3. Using the settings in Table 8.4, configure CRL checking to meet your organizational policies.

4. Save the Default.ica file.

Table 8.4 Certificate Revocation List Settings

Value	Snap-In to Choose
NoCheck	No certificate revocation list checking is performed
CheckWithNoNetworkAccess	The local list is checked
FullAccessCheck	The local list and any network lists are checked
FullAccessCheckAndCRLRequired	The local list and any network lists are checked; users can log on if all lists are verified. This setting forces mandatory CRL checking.

NOTE

If you do not set **SSLCertificationRevocationCheckPolicy**, it defaults to **NoCheck** for Windows NT 4.0. For Windows XP and Windows Server 2003, the default setting is **CheckWithNoNetworkAccess**.

Connections via the Web Interface

Citrix provides options of connecting to published resources by using the Web client. Connections using the Web client should be secured using SSL or TLS.

Configuring & Implementing…

Configuring Microsoft Internet Explorer for TLS 1.0 Only

On each client device ensure Microsoft Internet Explorer is configured for TLS 1.0 communication.

To configure Microsoft Internet Explorer for TLS 1.0

1. Launch Microsoft Internet Explorer. Click **Tools > Internet Options**. The Internet Options dialog box appears.

2. Select the **Advanced** tab to view the Settings. Within the Security section, ensure **Use TLS 1.0** is selected and ensure **Use SSL 2.0** and **Use SSL 3.0** are not selected, as shown in Figure 8.10.

3. Click **OK** to accept the changes and close the Internet Options dialog box.

4. Close Internet Explorer.

Figure 8.10 Setting TLS 1.0 in Microsoft Internet Explorer

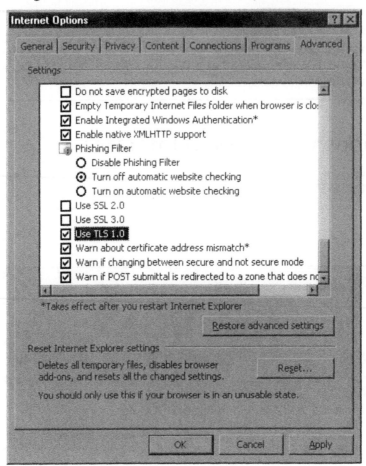

Connecting through a Proxy Server

Citrix provides several ways to improve security between the client devices and the XenApp server farm. For instance, if you are running SSL on your network, the ICA client can be configured to use a compatible protocol. The ICA client can also be configured to work with firewalls or the Citrix Secure Gateway. These settings can be configured for the entire enterprise, per Application Set, or per application or custom ICA connection. Some of the ways the ICA clients can support and integrate with your infrastructure security standards include:

■ Connecting through a SOCKS or secure proxy server such as an HTTPS proxy server or SSL tunneling proxy server

■ Integrating the ICA clients with Citrix Secure Gateway, Citrix Access Gateway or SSL Relay solutions with SSL and TLS protocols

■ Connecting through a firewall

What exactly is a proxy server and why do we need one? A proxy server is a server that acts as an intermediary between a client application such as a Web browser and another server such as a Web server. The proxy server is configured with certain rules that limit the access in to and out of a network. All requests in to and out of the network are intercepted by the proxy, and if the requests are legitimate, are forwarded on. Proxy servers also handle connections between ICA clients and XenApp servers. Citrix ICA clients support both the SOCKS and secure (HTTPS, SSL, or TLS) proxy protocols and can automatically detect and configure the client to work with the correct protocol.

Both the Program Neighborhood Agent and the Web Interface can be configured remotely to use proxy server settings, and the auto-client proxy detection is enabled by default. The Program Neighborhood client, however, must be configured at the user's workstation. In environments with multiple proxy servers, use the auto-client proxy detection feature. This feature will communicate with the Web browser to discover the information about the proxy server. It can also be helpful when configuring the client if you do not know which proxy server will be used. The auto-client proxy detection feature requires Internet Explorer 5.0 or later, or Netscape for Windows 4.78, 6.2, or later.

Configuring & Implementing...

To Set or Change Proxy Settings within the Program Neighborhood Client

1. Start Program Neighborhood.
2. Right-click either the **Application Set** or **Custom ICA Connection** you want to configure.
3. Select **Properties**.
4. From the **Connection** tab, click the **Firewalls** button. Your options on the Firewall Setting screen (shown in Figure 8.11) include:

- **Use alternate address for firewall connection.**
- **Automatically detect proxy.**
- **Use Web browser proxy settings** When enabled, this setting enables auto-client proxy detection.
- **Custom proxy settings** Here you can choose **None** for a direction connection, **SOCKS** or **Secure (HTTPS)** and enter the proxy address and port to be used.

Figure 8.11 Configuring the ICA Client to Use a Proxy Server

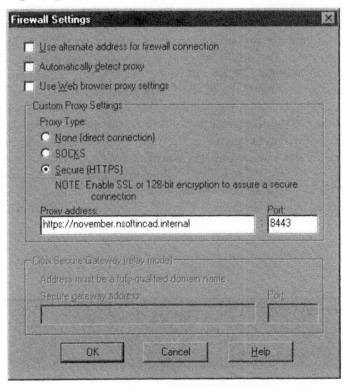

Additional Client Configuration Settings

Other settings that can improve the overall security posture of the ICA client that can be set both on the Web Interface and Program Neighborhood are:

- Disable Client Drive Mapping

- Disable any Unnecessary Device Mappings

- Disable Client Printer and Parallel Port Mappings

- Disable Serial Port Mapping

- Disable Personal Digital Assistant Mapping

- Disable Clipboard Mapping

Additionally, you can also disable Bitmap Disk Caching. This feature is provided as a performance measure for clients connecting over slow links. The directory where the bitmap cache is stored is protected by Windows permissions, allowing only the currently logged in user to access the data. Clients connecting over a high-speed connection do not need this capability and it should be disable to improve both performance and security.

Configuring & Implementing...

Disabling Bitmap Disk Caching

To disable bitmap disk caching, you must perform the following steps:

1. Using a text editor such as Notepad, open the Appsrv.ini file located in the user's Documents and Settings\Application Data\ICA Client directory.

2. Under the [WFClient] section, set the following value:

   ```
   PersistentCacheEnabled=Off
   ```

3. Save the changes to Appsrv.ini and exit Notepad.

TIP

Disabling serial port mapping typically disables personal digital assistant synchronization.

Understanding Internet Protocol Security

The two main goals of Internet Protocol Security (IPsec) are to protect IP packets and to give network administrators the ability to use packet filtering as a defense against network attacks.

Although we refer to IPsec as a protocol, it is actually a framework, or a collection of protocols and standards designed to protect IP data in transit. In this section, you'll learn about the protocols used by IPsec. These include the two primary protocols: the Authentication Header (AH) protocol and the Encapsulating Security Payload (ESP) protocol. We'll also discuss the roles of additional protocols used by IPsec, including the Internet Security and Key Management Protocol (ISAKMP), Internet Key Exchange (IKE), and the Oakley key-determination protocol, and the Diffie-Hellman key-agreement protocol.

Microsoft's Windows Server 2003 IPsec deployment includes the following features:

- Enhanced IPsec security monitoring with the MMC

- IPsec integration with Active Directory that allows for security policies to be centrally administered

- Use of Kerberos version 5 authentication as the default method by IPsec policies to verify the authenticity of connecting computers

- Backward compatibility with the Windows 2000 Security Framework

- Client and application transparency, because IPsec works at the Network layer of the OSI model

- Automatic security negotiation

IPsec is not required to be supported by any intermediary computer that routes data from the source to destination IP address, unless network address translation (NAT) or packet filtering has been implemented on the firewall. IPsec can be deployed with IPsec policy in Windows Server 2003 under any of these circumstances:

- Client-to-client and peer-to-peer support

- Gateway-to-gateway and router-to-router support

- Remote-access client dial-up and Internet access from private networks

The IP Security Policy Management MMC allows network administrators to set security policy settings and options that will allow the systems to negotiate with other systems regarding the traffic that is sent and received from that system.

How IPsec Works

Before secure data can be exchanged, a security agreement between the two communicating computers must be established. This security agreement is called a security association (SA). Both IPsec enabled computers agree on how to send and receive data, as well as how to protect the information contained in the data packets. Because IPsec SAs are unidirectional, at least two separate SAs are established to protect the data for every communication: one for inbound traffic and one for outbound traffic. There is a unique SA for each direction and for each protocol. Thus, if you are using both AH and ESP, there will be two SAs for AH and two for ESP.

Using the IP Security Policy Management console, you can configure the security policy to block, permit, or negotiate security within your networked environment. Because this security is transparent to users, it is easy to implement and administer.

Securing Data in Transit

An SA is a combination of three things:

- Security protocols

- A negotiated key

- A security parameters index (SPI)

These items together define the security settings that are used to protect the communication from the source IP to the destination IP. The SPI is a unique entry in the IPsec header of each packet and is used to identify which SA is being used to secure data. As mentioned earlier, there will always be separate SAs for inbound and outbound traffic. If a computer is communicating with multiple machines (for example, a database server with multiple clients sending queries), many SAs will exist. The receiving computer uses the SPI to determine which SA should be used to process incoming IP packets.

IPsec Cryptography

IPsec uses cryptography to provide three basic services:

- Authentication
- Data integrity
- Data confidentiality

There are times when only one or two of these services is needed, and other times when all of these services are needed. IPsec can use different methods to authenticate identities, including preshared keys, digital certificates, and Kerberos authentication. IPsec can also provide *anti-replay*. This refers to ensuring that an unauthorized person cannot capture the authentication credentials as they're sent across the network and "replay" them to establish a communications session with the server. IPsec uses the *hash* functions to ensure that the contents of the data packet have not changed between the time it was sent and the time it was received. IPsec provides data confidentiality only through the ESP protocol. AH does *not* provide for encryption of the data. ESP uses the 3DES and DES algorithms to ensure data confidentiality.

IPsec Modes

IPsec in Windows Server 2003 has two different modes: *tunnel* mode and *transport* mode. Your choice of which IPsec mode to use depends on your organizational needs. We will take a look at how each of these works and when each is appropriately used.

Tunnel Mode

In tunnel mode, IPsec encrypts the IP header and the payload, thereby securing the entire IP packet. It is used primarily when end systems or gateways do not support the L2TP/IPsec or the Point-to-Point Tunneling protocol (PPTP). In other words, tunnel mode allows you to use IPsec to create a tunnel, in addition to encrypting the data within the tunnel, with servers that cannot use the traditional VPN tunneling protocols (L2TP and PPTP). However, Windows Server 2003 does not support using IPsec as the tunneling protocol for remote access VPNs; it is only supported between gateways, routers, and servers. Remote-access clients must use PPTP or L2TP for VPN connections. The entire packet is encrypted by either AH or ESP.

Transport Mode

Transport mode, the default mode for IPsec, provides for end-to-end security. It can secure communications between a client and a server. When using the transport mode, only the IP payload is encrypted. AH or ESP provides protection for the IP payload. Typical IP payloads are TCP segments (containing a TCP header and TCP segment data), User Datagram Protocol (UDP) messages (containing a UDP header and UDP message data), and ICMP messages (containing an ICMP header and ICMP message data).

IPsec Protocols

As we mentioned earlier, IPsec itself is merely a framework within which a number of components work together. The primary IPsec protocols are ESP and AH. You can configure IPsec to use both of these protocols together to secure the data if you need both data encryption and integrity/authentication for the entire packet. Other IPsec protocols include ISAKMP, IKE, and Oakley, which uses the Diffie-Hellman algorithm.

Determine IPsec Protocol

Use the following steps to determine which IPsec protocol is in use by using the Network Monitor. This procedure assumes the Network Monitor has been installed via **Control Panel | Add/ Remove Programs**.

1. Select **Start | Programs | Administrative Tools | Network Monitor**.

2. When the Network Monitor opens, begin the capture by either clicking the **Capture** button and selecting **Start** or by pressing the **F10** key.

3. Allow the capture to run for a few minutes. To stop it, either click the **Capture** button, and then the **Stop and View** button, or press the **F11** key.

4. To view the IPsec protocol traffic on the captured packets, choose the **Display**, and then select the **Captured Data** option.

5. Choose **Display | Filter Data**. Then choose **Edit Expression** option and select the **Protocol** tab.

6. All protocols are enabled by default. You can chose to **Disable All** and then reenable the AH and ESP traffic. Enabled traffic will appear in the left pane, and disabled traffic will appear in the right pane.

7. Click **OK** after the IPsec protocols have been enabled.

8. Select the **OK** option again, and the frames should be displayed in the Network Monitor window. Notice that when you open a packet that is IPsec-secured, you are unable to read the data inside.

ESP

ESP provides confidentiality (in addition to authentication, integrity, and anti-replay protection) for the IP payload. ESP in transport mode does not sign the entire packet. Only the IP payload (not the IP header) is protected. ESP can be used alone or in combination with AH (in order to provide for signing of the entire packet).

Figure 8.12 illustrates how ESP affects the data. You can see that the IPsec AH header has been placed after the IP header and before the TCP header.

Figure 8.12 The Effects of the ESP Header in Tunnel Mode

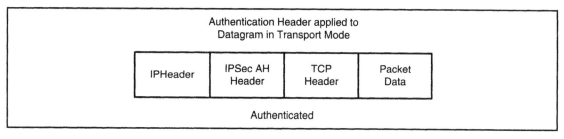

AH

AH does not provide confidentiality, which means that the data is not encrypted. Without data encryption, unauthorized people could use a sniffer-type program on your network to capture and read the packets, but they could not modify the data. AH works by using keyed hash algorithms, which are used to sign the packet for integrity verification. The AH packet signature is shown in Figure 8.13.

Figure 8.13 AH Using Transport Mode

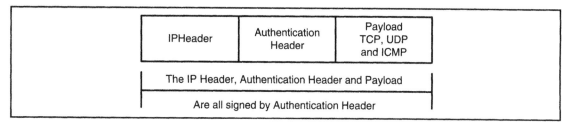

If you need both data integrity and authentication for the IP header, use ESP and AH in combination, as illustrated in Figure 8.14.

Figure 8.14 ESP Used with AH Transport Mode

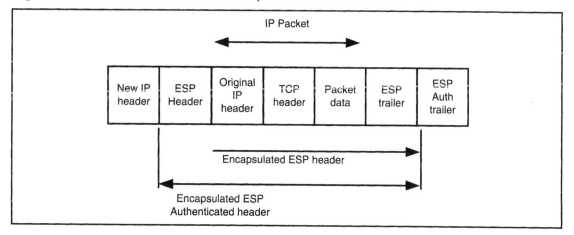

Additional Protocols

In addition to AH and ESP, the ISAKMP, IKE, and Oakley protocols and the Diffie-Hellman algorithm are used with IPsec. In the following subsections, we will briefly discuss each of these.

ISAKMP and IKE

ISAKMP is used by IPsec as a key management system by combining the ISAKMP protocol and another protocol named IKE. IKE is used to centralize SA management and to generate and manage the secret shared keys that are used to secure data in transport.

Often, firewalls, proxy servers, and security gateways must be configured to allow IPsec and IKE traffic to be forwarded. If the packets are not encrypted, the firewall, proxy server, or security gateway can inspect the packet contents or the TCP and UDP ports. If any type of modification has been made to the contents of these packets, the receiving IPsec computer will detect the modification and discard the packets.

In Windows 2000, a major drawback of IPsec was that it could not be used when one of the communicating computers was behind a NAT system. That is because NAT changes the IP headers when it translates multiple internal private IP addresses to a single public external address (which it does so that many computers can access the Internet via one public address). NAT has been an important mechanism for addressing the growing shortage of available public IP addresses, which is a limitation of the IPv4 protocol currently used for most Internet communications. Thus, many networks use NAT to reduce their need for additional public IP addresses.

However, Windows Server 2003's implementation of IPsec provides support for a new Internet specification that allows IPsec packets to be modified by a network address translator (NAT). This is called *NAT traversal*. IPsec's ESP packets can pass through NATs that allow UDP traffic. The IKE protocol automatically detects the presence of a NAT and uses UDP-ESP encapsulation to allow IPsec traffic to pass through the NAT.

Oakley

Oakley is a key-determination protocol. It is used to define how to acquire keying material after it has been authenticated. The Diffie-Hellman algorithm is the basic mechanism for the Oakley protocol.

Diffie-Hellman

The Diffie-Hellman key-exchange algorithm is a secure algorithm that offers high performance, allowing two computers to publicly exchange a shared value without using data encryption. The exchanged keying material that is shared by the two computers can be based on 768, 1024, or 2048 bits of keying material, known as Diffie-Hellman groups 1, 2, and 2048, respectively. Note that Diffie-Hellman does not provide authentication. For protection against man-in-the-middle attacks, identities are authenticated after the Diffie-Hellman exchange occurs. Diffie-Hellman algorithms can be embedded within a protocol that does provide for authentication.

IPsec Components

In addition to the protocols that operate within the IPsec framework, there are a number of operating system components involved in Microsoft's implementation of IPsec. The major IPsec components that are installed with Windows XP and Windows Server 2003 family are the IPsec Policy Agent service and the IPsec driver.

IPsec Policy Agent

The IPsec Policy Agent is a service that resides on each computer running the Windows Server 2003 operating system. It is shown in the Service console as IPsec services. The IPsec Policy Agent begins when the system is started.

For all domain member computers, the IPsec policy will be retrieved by the IPsec Policy Agent when the machine boots up or at the default Winlogon polling interval, unless an IPsec policy is in place that has the interval already set. Active Directory can be manually polled by typing the command **gpupdate** /*target:computer* at the command prompt.

If the IPsec Policy Agent is unable to find or connect to the Active Directory domain, it will wait for the policy to be activated or assigned. This is also true if there are no IPsec policies in Active Directory or the Registry.

IPsec Driver

The IPsec driver is used to match all packets against filters in the filter list. Once it finds a packet that matches the filter, it applies the appropriate filter action. If a packet does not match any filter, the packet is not changed and is sent back to the TCP/IP driver. The packet will then be either received or transmitted. After the transmission has been allowed by the filter action, the packet will be sent or received and not modified. If the packet is blocked by the filter action, it will be discarded. If the action requires security negotiation, main mode and quick mode SAs will be negotiated. The IPsec driver uses a database to store all current quick mode SAs. Any outbound packet that matches an IP filter list that is in need of security negotiation will be queued. After the packet has been queued, IKE is notified and will begin the security negotiation. After the negotiation has been successfully completed, the sending computer's IPsec driver will receive the session key from IKE. It will look in its database and locate the outbound SA, and then insert the SPI into the AH or ESP header. The packet will be signed, and if confidentiality is required, it will be encrypted and sent to the IP layer so it can be forwarded to the destination machine.

Deploying IPsec

With Windows Server 2003, Microsoft has made it relatively easy to deploy security for transmitted data throughout your organization by using the IP Security Policy Management MMC. However, before you begin to deploy IPsec on your network, you need to do your homework and determine the needs of your particular organization.

Determining Organizational Needs

It is very important to find a balance between protecting unauthorized access to data and choosing to make the information available to the largest group of users. The network administrator's dilemma is that security and accessibility are always at opposite ends of the continuum, and increasing one inevitably decreases the other.

After you've identified your organizational needs, you can begin to configure your policy. Only one policy configuration can be assigned at each of the following levels: domain, site, Organizational Unit (OU), and local level. Each IPsec policy consists of one or more IPsec rules. Each IPsec rule consists of the following:

- Selected filter list

- Selected filter action

- Selected authentication method or methods

- Selected connection type

- Selected tunnel setting

To configure IPsec policy, you can create a new policy, and then define the set of rules for the policy by adding filter lists and filter actions. Alternatively, you can create the set of filter lists and filter actions first, and then create the IPsec policies. Finally, you add rules that combine the appropriate filter list with the appropriate filter action. Additionally, you specify authentication methods, connection types, and tunnel settings.

Security Levels

When you begin to consider security levels within your organization, you must take into account the type of data each computer typically will be processing. For example, the configuration you would need for a Web server is different from the one you would need for a domain controller. When planning to deploy IPsec on your network, take into account the following general guidelines for each type of computing environment:

- **Minimal security** No sensitive data is exchanged and IPsec is not active by default.

- **Standard security** This guideline is most appropriate for file servers and similar computers. You can implement the Client (Respond Only) option or Server (Request Security) option for your IPsec policies. These policies enforce security when the client supports it, but they are also efficient because they do not require security if the client is not IPsec-enabled.

- **High security** The computers that need high security are the ones that contain sensitive or valuable data and/or are located in a public network setting. You can implement the Secure Server (Require Security) default policy on these machines. This requires IPsec protection for all traffic being sent to or received from the server (except initial inbound communication) with stronger security methods.

Managing IPsec

Windows Server 2003 comes with two handy tools for managing IPsec. These include the IP Security Policy Management MMC snap-in and the netsh utility (for those who love to use the command-line to execute commands).

Using the IP Security Policy Management MMC Snap-in

You can use the IPsec console to manage IPsec policies and to add and remove filters applied to the IPsec policies. IPsec filtering is used to permit or block certain types of IP traffic. With IPsec filtering, you can secure workstations from outside security hazards.

Configuring & Implementing...

Installing the IP Security Policy Management Console

Use the following steps to install and access the IP Security Policy Management console.

1. Select **Start | Run**, type mmc, and click **OK**.
2. In the empty console, select **File | Add/Remove Snap-In**.
3. Click the **Add** button and scroll down to the **IP Security Policy Management** snapin.
4. Click the **Add** button. The next window asks you to select the appropriate computer or domain that this snap-in will be used to configure. For this example, choose **Local computer**. Then click the **Finish** button.
5. Select **Close**, and then click **OK**. The IP Security Policy Management console will open.
6. Double-click **IP Security Policies on Local Computer**. The three basic policy templates are now displayed in the right pane, as shown in Figure 8.15.

Figure 8.15 The Three Standard IPsec Policies in the IP Security Policy Management Console

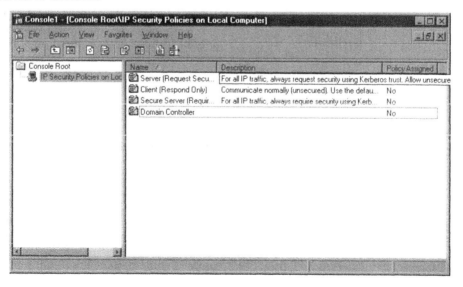

Default IPsec Policies

IPsec has a predefined set of default policies that can be implemented via the IP Security Policy Management console. The set includes Client (Respond Only), Server (Request Security), and Server (Require Security). The following sections explain the usage and settings for each default policy.

Client (Respond Only)

Client (Respond Only) is the least secure default policy. You might wish to implement this policy for intranet computers that need to respond to IPsec requests but do not require secure communications. If you implement this policy, the computer will use secured data communications when requested to do so by another computer.

This policy uses the default response rule, which creates dynamic IPsec filters for inbound/outbound traffic based on the port/protocol requested. The policy settings are as follows:

- IP Filter List: All

- Filter Action: None

- Authentication: Kerberos

- Tunnel Setting: None

- Connection Type: All

Server (Request Security)

The Server (Request Security) policy consists of three rules and can be used when a computer needs to be configured to accept unsecured traffic from other computers that are not IPsec enabled. However, it will always check for secure communication and use it if the other computer is able to use IPsec. The policy settings for the three rules are shown in Table 8.5.

Table 8.5 Policy Settings for Server (Request Security) Rules

Setting	First Rule	Second Rule	Third Rule (Default Response Rule)
IP Filter List	All IP Traffic	All ICMP Traffic	Dynamic
Filter Action	Request Security (Optional)	Permit	Default Response
Authentication	Kerberos	N/A	Kerberos
Tunnel Setting	None	None	None
Connection Type	All	All	All

Secure Server (Require Security)

The Secure Server (Require Security) policy consists of three rules and can be used for computers that require high security. Filters used in this policy require all outbound communication to be secured. This allows only initial inbound communication requests to be unsecured. The policy settings for the three rules are as shown in Table 8.6.

Table 8.6 Policy Settings for Secure Server (Require Security) Rules

Setting	First Rule	Second Rule	Third Rule (Default Response Rule)
IP Filter List	All IP Traffic	All ICMP Traffic	Dynamic
Filter Action	Require Security	Permit	Default Response
Authentication	N/A	Kerberos	Kerberos
Tunnel Setting	None	None	None
Connection Type	All	All	All

Custom Policies

In addition to the default policies that can be implemented with the IPsec Security Policy MMC, you can also create your own custom policies for implementation by using the **New IPsec Policy** in the IP Security Policy Management MMC.

To create your own custom policies with the IP Security Policy Management MMC, open the console and select the policy you wish to customize. Use the following steps to customize an IP Security Policy.

Configuring & Implementing…

Customizing IP Security Policy

1. Open the **IP Security Policy Management** console and click **IP Security Policies**.

2. Locate the policy you wish to customize in the right pane and double-click it, or right-click it and select **Properties**.

3. Click on the **Rules** tab, locate the rule you wish to modify and click **Edit**. Switch to the **Filter Action** tab, double-click the filter action that you want to modify.

4. Next, switch to the **Security Methods** tab, and do one of the following:

Continued

- To add a new security method, select the **Add** option.

- To modify an existing security method, select the security method that you want to modify and click the **Edit** option.

- To remove a security method, click the security method that you wish to delete and select the **Remove** option.

5. To add or modify a security method, select the **Security Method** tab, choose the **Custom** option button, and then click **Settings**.

6. Set the security method as follows, depending on your policy's need for encryption:

- Select the **Data and address integrity without encryption (AH)** check box if you need to provide data integrity for the packet's IP header and the data. Then for **Integrity algorithm**, select either **MD5** (which uses a 128-bit key) or **SHA1** (which uses a 160-bit key).

- If you need to provide both integrity and encryption for data confidentiality, select the **Data integrity and encryption (ESP)** check box. Then under **Integrity algorithm**, click **None** (for no data integrity; if you have AH enabled and for increased performance, you can choose this), **MD5**, or **SHA1**. Under **Encryption algorithm**, choose **None**, **DES**, or **3DES**.

7. You can also change the default session key lifetime settings, as follows:

- You can set the number of kilobytes of data that is transferred before a new key is generated by choosing the **Generate a new key every** check box and typing in a value in kilobytes.

- You can choose the **Generate a new key every** option to enter the number of seconds to elapse before a new session key is to be generated.

Using the IP Security Policy Wizard

You can open the IP Security Policy Management console by clicking **Start | Run** and typing **mmc**, and then clicking **OK**. Select **File | Add/Remove Snap-in**, and then click **Add**, Click **IP Security Policy Management**, and then click **Add**. For each computer scenario, you need to select a specific option. Table 8.7 shows the scenario and specific snap-in you would need to use.

Table 8.7 IPsec Policy Management Scenarios

Scenario	Snap-In to Choose
Manage IPsec policy for local computer	Select the **Local computer** snap-in
Manage IPsec policies for any domain members	Select the **Active Directory domain of which the computer is a member** snap-in
Manage IPsec policies for a domain that this computer is not a member	Select the **Another Active Directory domain** snap-in
Manage a remote computer	Select the **Another computer** snap-in

After you've chosen the snap-in, you can close the management console by selecting **Finish**, choosing **Close**, and clicking the **OK** button. To save your console settings select **File | Save**.

You can also access the IP Security Policy Management console from the Group Policy console. To do this, select **Start | Administrative Tools | Active Directory Users and Computers** and right-click the domain or OU for which you need to set Group Policy. (To open Active Directory Users and Computers utility, select **Start | Control Panel | Administrative Tools | Active Directory Users and Computers**.)

Configuring & Implementing...

Creating an IPsec Policy with the IP Security Policy Wizard

To create your own IPsec policy using the IP Security Wizard, follow these steps:

1. Open the IPsec Security Management Snap-in, right-click **IP Security Policies** in the left console pane, and then choose **Create IP Security Policy** from the context menu.

2. The IP Security Policy Wizard Welcome window appears. Click the **Next** button.

3. The IP Security Policy Name window appears, prompting you to give your IPsec policy a name and description. You can choose to accept the default name (not recommended, as it's not very descriptive), or you can enter a new name and description. Then click the **Next** button.

4. The next window allows you to specify how the policy will respond to requests. Accept the default (**Activate the default response rule**) or clear the check box, and then click the **Next** button.

Continued

5. The Default Rule Authentication Method window appears, as shown in Figure 8.16. Select a different authentication method or accept the default, **Active Directory default (Kerberos V5 protocol)**, and then click **Next**.

Figure 8.16 Select the Default Rule Authentication Method

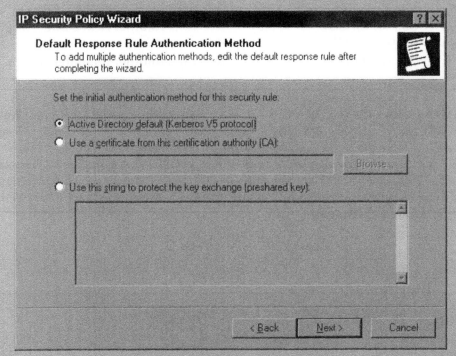

6. The **Completing the IP Security Policy Wizard** window appears. You can choose to edit the properties of the policy (the default) or clear the check box if you do not wish to edit the properties at this time. Click **Finish** to complete the Wizard. For this example, we will leave the **Edit properties** box selected.

7. When you select the option to edit properties, the **New IP Security Policy Properties** dialog box opens, as shown in Figure 8.17. This dialog box allows you to edit the IP security rules and change the general properties of the rule, such as the name and description. Click the **Edit** button in this dialog box.

Continued

Figure 8.17 IP Security Policy Properties

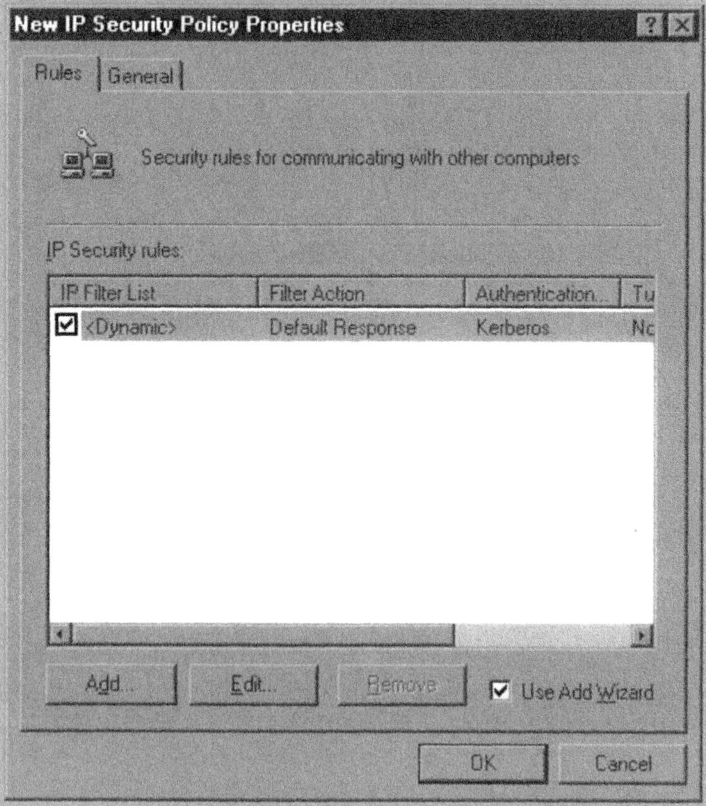

8. The Edit Rule Properties dialog box opens, as shown in Figure 8.18. Here, you can add, edit, or remove security methods; set the security methods that can be used when working with another machine; and select to use session key perfect forward secrecy (PFS). Next, click the **Authentication Methods** tab.

9. The **Authentication Methods** tab allows you to choose a trust method for communicating client computers. Click **Add** to add a method (again, your selections include using a certificate or a pre-shared key). Click **OK** to close the dialog box.

10. After the policy has been edited, you need to assign the policy. Before you assign the policy, make sure that you have the IPsec service started. To assign the policy, right-click the policy name in the right pane and select Assign, as shown in Figure 8.19.

Figure 8.18 Edit the IP Security Policy Security Methods

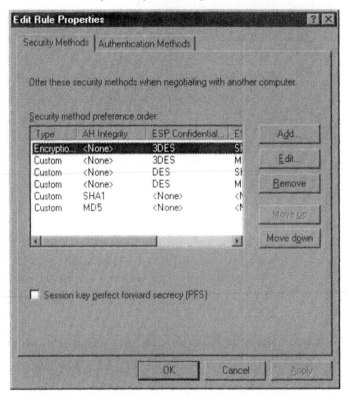

Figure 8.19 Assign the Newly Created IP Security Policy

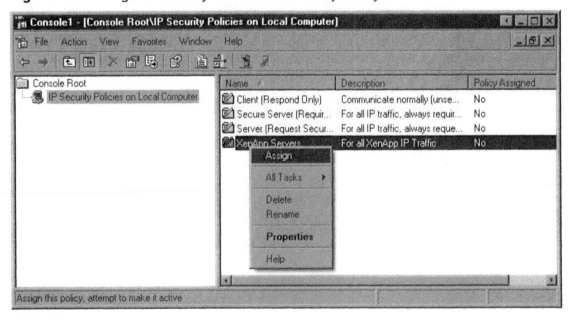

Managing Filter Lists and Filter Actions

To manage IP filter lists and filter actions, open the IP Security Policy Management MMC and select the policy you wish to modify by double-clicking that policy. In the **Rules** tab, select the rule you wish to modify that contains the IP filter and double-click it. Select the **IP Filter List** tab and double-click the IP filter that contains the filter list you want to configure. To edit or modify a filter in the IP Filter properties window, double-click the filter, choose the **Addresses** tab, and then select the **Source Address** drop-down box.

Assigning and Applying Policies in Group Policy

Now we will take a look at how to assign or unassign IPsec policy in Group Policy for Active Directory. These settings will take effect the next time Group Policy is refreshed, and if a new policy is assigned over an existing policy, the current policy is automatically unassigned. Use the **IP Security Policies on Active Directory** within the Group Policy console to assign policies to apply to Active Directory objects. To assign or unassign a local computer policy, select **Start | Run,** type **mmc**, and click **OK**. Then choose **File | Add/Remove Snap-in** and click **Add**. Click the **Group Policy Object Editor** and click **Add**. Choose **Finish,** click **Close,** and then click **OK**.

Active Directory Based IPsec Policies

Any IPsec policy that is applied for the domain will take precedence over local IPsec policy that is located on the member computer. After the IPsec policy has been applied to one of the Active Directory Group Policy Objects, it will be broadcast to all of the computer accounts that are affected by that GPO.

Group Policy has backup and restore tools that you can use to save policy information on assigned GPOs. These tools *do not* back up the IPsec policies. To back up and restore IPsec policies, use the **Export Policies and Import Policies** command in the **IP Security Policy Management** console. The Group Policy console will back up and restore only information pertaining to the IPsec policy assignments in relation to GPOs.

The IPsec Policy Agent on client computers running Windows XP Professional or a Windows Server 2003 operating system will poll Active Directory for updates to the assigned IPsec policy. This does not detect domain or OU changes or whether new IPsec policies have been assigned. The Winlogon service polls for these changes every 90 minutes. If a change has been made, the Winlogon service will notify the IPsec Policy Agent, and the IPsec policy changes will be applied.

Cached IPsec Policy

A copy of the currently assigned IPsec policy for a site, a domain, or an OU is cached in the local Registry of each computer to which it applies. If the computer that has the IPsec policy assigned cannot log on to the domain for any reason, the cache copy will be applied. The cache copy of the IPsec policy cannot be changed or managed.

Local Computer IPsec Policy

All Windows Server 2003 servers and Windows XP Professional computers have one local GPO called the local computer policy. With this local policy, Group Policy settings can be stored on individual computers, even when they are not Active Directory domain members. You can manage the local IPsec policy by using the IP Security Policy Management console. Alternatively, you can use the following netsh command at the prompt:

```
netsh ipsec static set store location=local
```

If a computer on which you've applied local IPsec policies later joins an Active Directory domain that has IPsec policies applied, the domain policies will override the local IPsec policy.

Addressing IPsec Security Considerations

As you begin to deploy IPsec throughout your organization, you will need to decide on the encryptions methods you wish to implement and whether to use firewall packet filtering. The following sections provide some guidelines to use when considering IPsec security.

Strong Encryption Algorithm (3DES)

DES and 3DES are *block ciphers*. This refers to an algorithm that takes a block of plaintext of a fixed length and changes it into a block of *ciphertext* (encrypted data) of the same length. The key length for DES is 64 bits total, but because 8 of the bits are used for parity information, the effective length is only 56 bits. With 3DES, the DES process is performed three times with different 56-bit keys, making the effective key length 168 bits. When using 3DES in encrypt-encrypt-encrypt (EEE) mode, 3DES works by processing each block as follows:

1.   A block of plaintext is encrypted with key one.

2.   The resulting block of ciphertext is encrypted with key two.

3.   The result of step 2 is encrypted with key three.

When using 3DES in encrypt-decrypt-encrypt (EDE) mode, step 2 is run in decryption mode. When 3DES is decrypting a packet, the process is done in reverse order. 3DES offers you the best mode for data confidentiality.

Firewall Packet Filtering

To allow for secured packets to be passed through a firewall, you need to configure the firewall or other device, such as a security gateway or router, to allow these packets to pass through the external interface.

The following ports and protocols can be used for firewall filtering:

■   IP protocol and port 50, ESP traffic

■   IP protocol and port 51, AH traffic

■   UDP port 500, IKE negotiation traffic

Diffie-Hellman Groups

As we discussed earlier in the chapter, Diffie-Hellman groups are used to define the length of the base prime numbers that are used during the key-exchange process. There are three types of Diffie-Hellman groups, as follows:

- **Diffie-Hellman group 1** This is the least secure group and it provides only 768 bits of keying strength.

- **Diffie-Hellman group 2** This group is set to a medium level, at 1024 bits of keying strength.

- **Diffie-Hellman group 3** This group is set to the highest level, at 2048 bits of keying strength.

Diffie-Hellman group 3 is available only on Windows Server 2003 family machines. If you wish to use this algorithm on Windows 2000 machines, you must have either Service Pack 2 or the High Encryption Pack installed. If you configure one client machine for a Diffie-Hellman group 1 key exchange and another client machine for the Diffie-Hellman group 3 exchange, negotiation will fail. For the best security, use the highest Diffie-Hellman group 3 key exchange. When using the quick mode, new keys are created from the Diffie-Hellman main mode master key material. If you have the master key or session key PFS enabled, a new master key will be created by performing a Diffie-Hellman exchange. The master key PFS will require a reauthentication of the main mode SA in addition to the Diffie-Hellman exchange. The session key PFS will not require this reauthentication.

Preshared Keys

To authenticate L2TP protocol and IPsec connections, you can select to use a pre-shared key. This is the simplest of three choices of authentication methods that you have with IPsec. The other two authentication methods are Kerberos and digital certificates. Before selecting to use a pre-shared key, you should be aware of all the implications of doing so.

A pre-shared key is a string of Unicode characters. You can use the Routing and Remote Access management console to configure connections to support authenticated VPN connections using the pre-shared key. A server that has the Windows Server 2003 operating system installed may also be configured to use a pre-shared key.

IPsec Configurations for XenApp

To utilize IPsec policies in your environment, you will need a full and comprehensive understanding of all network traffic flows in and out of your XenApp configuration. But in order to provide you a starting point with implementing IPsec policies you can use the policies in Table 8.8 as a guideline. The environment depicted by the settings in Table 8.8 are: a domain controller, two XenApp servers (one functioning as a Secure Ticket Authority), one Web Interface server and a Citrix Secure Gateway server.

Table 8.8. IPsec Policy Settings for a Highly Secure XenApp Environment

Rule	Source Address	Destination Address	Protocol	Source Port	Destination port	Action
DOMAIN CONTROLLER POLICY						
All IP Traffic	Any IP address	Any IP address	Any	Any	Any	Require security: 3DES/SHA-1 and certificate authentication
WEB INTERFACE POLICY						
All TCP/IP Traffic on port 443	Any IP address	My IP address	TCP	Any	443	Permit
All IP Traffic	Any IP address	Any IP address	Any	Any	Any	Require security: 3DES/SHA-1 and certificate authentication
SECURE GATEWAY POLICY						
STA Traffic	My IP address	IP address of primary XenApp server	TCP	Any	80	Require security: 3DES/SHA-1 and certificate authentication
ICA Traffic on port 1494 to primary XenApp server	My IP address	IP address of primary XenApp server	Any	Any	1494	Require security: 3DES/SHA-1 and certificate authentication
ICA Traffic on port 1494 to secondary XenApp server	My IP address	IP address of secondary XenApp server	Any	Any	1494	Require security: 3DES/SHA-1 and certificate authentication

Continued

Table 8.8. Continued. IPsec Policy Settings for a Highly Secure XenApp Environment

Rule	Source Address	Destination Address	Protocol	Source Port	Destination port	Action
CGP Traffic on port 2598 to primary XenApp server	My IP address	IP address of primary XenApp server	Any	Any	2598	Require security: 3DES/SHA-1 and certificate authentication
CGP Traffic on port 2598 to secondary XenApp server	My IP address	IP address of secondary XenApp server	Any	Any	2598	Require security: 3DES/SHA-1 and certificate authentication
All TCP/IP Traffic on port 443	Any IP address	My IP address	TCP	Any	443	Permit
All IP Traffic	Any IP address	Any IP address	Any	Any	Any	Block
PRIMARY XENAPP SERVER POLICY						
ICA Traffic on port 1494	Secure Gateway IP address	My IP address	TCP	Any	1494	Require security: 3DES/SHA-1 and certificate authentication
CGP Traffic on port 2598	Secure Gateway IP address	My IP address	TCP	Any	2598	Require security: 3DES/SHA-1 and certificate authentication
STA Traffic on port 80	Secure Gateway IP address	My IP address	TCP	Any	80	Require security: 3DES/SHA-1 and CA root certificate authentication

Continued

www.syngress.com

Table 8.8 Continued. IPsec Policy Settings for a Highly Secure XenApp Environment

Rule	Source Address	Destination Address	Protocol	Source Port	Destination port	Action
All IP Traffic (including TCP 2512)	Any IP address	Any IP address	Any	Any	Any	Require security: 3DES/SHA-1 and certificate authentication
SECONDARY XENAPP SERVER POLICY						
ICA Traffic on port 1494	Secure Gateway IP address	My IP address	TCP	Any	1494	Require security: 3DES/SHA-1 and certificate authentication
CGP Traffic on port 2598	Secure Gateway IP address	My IP address	TCP	Any	2598	Require security: 3DES/SHA-1 and certificate authentication
All IP Traffic (including TCP 2512)	Any IP address	Any IP address	Any	Any	Any	Require security: 3DES/SHA-1 and certificate authentication

NOTE

Note Reverse lookup zones must be enabled in Active Directory integrated DNS for all subnets within the IPsec environment.

Understanding Public Key Infrastructure

The Public Key Infrastructure (PKI) is the method of choice for handling authentication issues in large enterprise-level organizations today. Windows Server 2003 includes the tools you need to create a PKI for your company and issue digital certificates to users, computers, and applications. This section addresses the complex issues involved in planning a certificate-based PKI. We'll provide an overview of the basic terminology and concepts relating to the public key infrastructure, and you'll learn about public key cryptography and how it is used to authenticate the identity of users, computers, and applications/services. We'll discuss the role of digital certificates and the different types of certificates (user, machine, and application certificates).

You'll learn about certification authorities (CAs), the servers that issue certificates, including both public CAs and private CAs such as the ones you can implement on your own network using Windows Server 2003's certificate services. Next, we'll discuss the CA hierarchy and how root CAs and subordinate CAs act together to provide for your organization's certificate needs. You'll find out how the Microsoft certificate services work, and we'll walk you through the steps involved in implementing one or more certification authorities based on the needs of the organization. You'll learn to determine the appropriate CA type—enterprise or stand–alone CA—for a given situation and how to plan the CA hierarchy and provide for security of your CAs. We'll show you how to plan for enrollment and distribution of certificates, including the use of certificate requests, role-based administration, and auto-enrollment deployment.

To understand how a PKI works, you first need to understand what it is supposed to do. The goals of your infrastructure should include the following:

- Proper authentication

- Trust

- Confidentiality

- Integrity

- Nonrepudiation

By using the core PKI elements of public key cryptography, digital signatures, and certificates, all of these equally important goals can be met successfully. The good news is that the majority of the work involved in implementing these elements under Windows Server 2003 is taken care of automatically by the operating system and is done behind the scenes.

The Function of the PKI

Most of the functionality of a Windows Server 2003-based PKI comes from a few crucial components, which are described below. Although there are several third-party vendors, such as VeriSign (www.verisign.com), that offer similar technologies and components, using Windows Server 2003 can be a less costly and easier-to-implement option—especially for small- and medium-sized companies.

The Windows Server 2003 PKI does many things behind the scenes. Thanks in part to auto enrollment (discussed later in this chapter) and certificate stores (places where certificates are kept after their creation), some PKI-enabled features such as EFS work with no user intervention at all. Others, such as IPsec, require significantly less work than would be required without an advanced operating system.

Even though a majority of the PKI is handled by Windows Server 2003, it is still instructive to have an overview of how certificate services work.

1. First, a system or user generates a public/private key pair and then a certificate request.

2. The certificate request, which contains the public key and other identifying information such as user name, is forwarded to a CA.

3. The CA verifies the validity of the public key. If it is verified, the CA issues the certificate.

4. After it is issued, the certificate is ready for use and is kept in the certificate store, which can reside in Active Directory. Applications that require a certificate use this central repository when necessary.

In practice, it isn't terribly difficult to implement certificate services. Configuring the CA requires a bit more effort, as does planning the structure and hierarchy of the PKI—especially if you are designing an enterprisewide solution.

Components of the PKI

Properly planning for and deploying a PKI requires familiarity with a number of components, including but not limited to the following:

- Digital Certificates
- Certification Authorities
- Certificate Enrollment
- Certificate Revocation
- Encryption/Cryptography Services

In the following sections, we will discuss each of these in more detail.

Understanding Digital Certificates

Think of a certificate as a small and portable combination safe. The primary purpose of the safe is to hold a public key (although quite a bit of other information is also held there). Someone you trust must hold the combination to the safe—that trust is the basis for the entire PKI system. The main purpose of certificates is to facilitate the secure transfer of keys across an insecure network. Figure 8.20 shows the properties of a Windows certificate. Notice that the highlighted public key is only part of the certificate.

Figure 8.20 A Windows 2003 Certificate

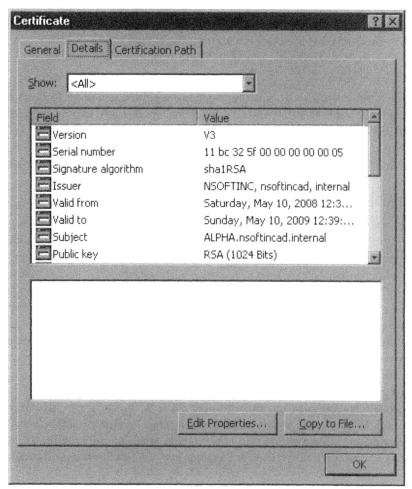

User Certificates

Of the three general types of certificates found in a Windows PKI, the *user certificate* is perhaps the most common. User certificates are certificates that enable the user to do something that would not otherwise be allowed. The Enrollment Agent certificate is one example. Without it, even an administrator is not able to enroll smart cards and configure them properly at an enrollment station. Under Windows Server 2003, required user certificates can be requested automatically by the client and subsequently issued by a certification authority (discussed below) with no user intervention necessary.

Machine Certificates

Also known as computer certificates, *machine certificates* (as the name implies) give the system—instead of the user—the capability to do something out of the ordinary. The main purpose for machine certificates is authentication, both client-side and server-side. As stated earlier, certificates are the main vehicle by which public keys are exchanged in a PKI. Machine certificates are mainly involved with these behind-the-scenes exchanges and are normally overseen by the operating system. Machine certificates have been able to take advantage of Windows' auto-enrollment feature since Windows 2000 Server was introduced. We will discuss auto-enrollment later in this chapter.

Application Certificates

The term *application certificate* refers to any certificate that is used with a specific PKI-enabled application. Examples include IPsec and S/MIME encryption for e-mail. Applications that need certificates are generally configured to automatically request them and are then placed in a waiting status until the required certificate arrives. Depending upon the application, the network administrator or even the user might have the capability to change or even delete certificate requests issued by the application.

Understanding Certification Authorities

Certificates are a way to transfer keys securely across an insecure network. If any arbitrary user were allowed to issue certificates, it would be no different from that user simply signing the data. For a certificate to be of any use, it must be issued by a trusted entity—an entity that both the sender and receiver trust. Such a trusted entity is known as a *certification authority* (CA). In a third-party, or external, PKI, it is up to the third-party CA to positively verify the identity of anyone requesting a certificate from it. Beginning with Windows 2000, Microsoft has allowed the creation of a trusted *internal* CA—possibly eliminating the need for an external third party. With a Windows Server 2003 CA, the CA verifies the identity of the user requesting a certificate by checking that user's authentication credentials (using Kerberos or NTLM). If the credentials of the requesting user check out, a certificate is issued to the user. When the user needs to transmit his or her public key to another user or application, the certificate is used to prove to the receiver that the public key inside can be used safely.

For a very small organization, it might be possible under Windows Server 2003 for you to use only one CA for all PKI functions. However, for larger groups, Microsoft outlines a three-tier hierarchical structure starting at the top with a root CA, moving downward to a midlevel CA, and finally an issuing-level CA. Both the midlevel CA and issuing-level CA are known as subordinate CAs.

Root CAs

When you first set up an internal PKI, no CA exists. The first CA created is known as the root CA, and it can be used to issue certificates to users or to other CAs. As mentioned above, in a large organization there usually is a hierarchy where the root CA is not the only certification authority. In this case, the sole purpose of the root CA is to issue certificates to other CAs to establish their authority.

The question then becomes: who issues the root CA a certificate? The answer is that a root CA issues its own certificate (this is called a *self-signed* certificate). Security is not compromised for two reasons. First, you will only implement one root CA in your organization and second, configuring a root CA requires administrative rights on the server. The root CA should be kept highly secured because it has so much authority.

Subordinate CAs

Any certification authority that is established after the root CA is a subordinate CA. Subordinate CAs gain their authority by requesting a certificate from either the root CA or a higher-level subordinate CA. After the subordinate CA receives the certificate, it can control CA policies and/or issue certificates itself, depending on your PKI structure and policies.

Certificate Requests

A client has three ways to request a certificate from a CA. The most common is auto-enrollment, and we'll discuss its deployment shortly. A client can also request a certificate by use of the **Certificates** snap-in. Clicking **Start | Run** and typing in **certmgr.msc** and pressing **Enter** can launch the snap-in. Note that the **Certificates** snap-in does *not* appear in the **Administrative Tools** folder as the **Certification Authority** snap-in does after installing certificate services.

Next, by expanding the **Personal** container and right-clicking the **Certificates** container beneath it, you can start the **Certificate Request Wizard** by choosing **All Tasks | Request New Certificate**. After the welcome screen, the first screen of the wizard enables you to choose the certificate type. You can only choose a type for which the receiving CA has a template. If you select the **Advanced** check box, the next screen (Figure 8.21) enables you to choose the Cryptographic Service Provider (CSP) and key length. You can also mark the key as exportable and/or enable strong private key encryption.

Figure 8.21 Cryptographic Service Provider Screen of the Certificate Request Wizard

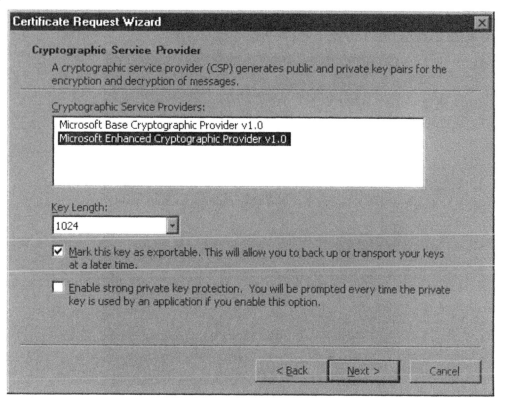

Continuing with the advanced options, you can choose **Browse the domain** to choose a CA to which you want to send the request. Finally, the wizard finishes by prompting you for a friendly name and description for the certificate. The last method for requesting a certificate is to use a Web browser on the client machine. Note that if you use this option, IIS must be installed on the CA.

Certificate Revocation

A CA's primary duty is to issue certificates, either to subordinate CAs or to PKI clients. However, each CA also has the capability to revoke those certificates when necessary. The tool that the CA uses for revocation is the *certificate revocation list*, or CRL. The act of revoking a certificate is simple: from the **Certification Authority** console, simply highlight the **Issued Certificates** container, right-click the certificate and choose **All | Revoke Certificate**. The certificate will then be located in the **Revoked Certificates** container.

When a PKI entity verifies a certificate's validity, that entity checks the CRL before giving approval. The question is: how does a client know where to check for the list? The answer is the CDPs, or CRL Distribution Points. CDPs are locations on the network to which a CA publishes the CRL; in the case of an enterprise CA under Windows Server 2003, Active Directory holds the CRL and for a standalone, the CRL is located in the *certsrv\certenroll* directory. Each certificate has a location listed for the CDP, and when the client views the certificate, it then understands where to go for the latest CRL. Figure 8.22 shows the Extensions tab of the CA property sheet, where you can modify the location of the CDP.

Figure 8.22 Extensions Tab of the CA Property Sheet

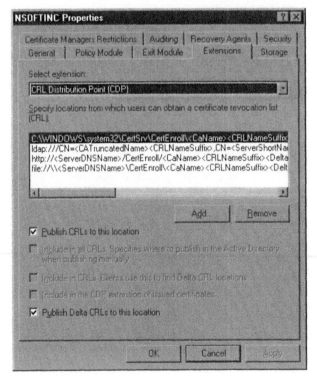

For a CA to publish a CRL, use the **Certification Authority** console to right-click the **Revoked Certificates** container and choose **All Tasks | Publish**. From there, you can choose to publish either a complete CRL or a Delta CRL Whether you select a New CRL or a Delta CRL, you are next prompted to enter a publication interval (the most frequent intervals chosen are one week for full CRLs and one day for Delta CRLs). Clients cache the CRL for this period of time and then check the CDP again when the period expires. If an updated CDP does not exist or cannot be located, the client automatically assumes that all certificates are invalid.

Securing the Citrix License Server

As mentioned in a previous chapter, every XenApp Server farm must include at least one license server. The license server stores the license files for the Citrix products that specify the parameters for the product usage. The license files replace the Activation Code that earlier Citrix products required for license activation.

The licensing architecture consists of three new licensing components:

- **The Citrix Licensing Server** The licensing server is required to use any of the XenApp products. It can be installed on a dedicated server or share space with other products on the same server. Where you install the licensing server will depend on the size of your environment and the resources available on the server hardware.

- **The License Management Console** License administration requires either Microsoft IIS or an Apache web server.

- **The License Allocation Process** The final piece is the license allocation process that involves obtaining the license files containing product usage information from MyCitrix. com, and storing them on the licensing server.

Each farm must have at least one licensing server, and that server must provide licenses for each XenApp product running in that farm. For instance, if you plan to run Password Manager in farm "A," licenses for Password Manager must be stored on the licensing server to which farm "A" points. You can have multiple server farms pointing to the same licensing server or to multiple licensing servers. How you choose to deploy your farm and licensing servers will depend on the size of your environment, usage, and physical location.

Multiple Licensing Servers

Multiple licensing servers should be used in large environments of 500 or more servers. In this case, Citrix recommends installing one dedicated licensing server for each Citrix product you use in your environment. There are other scenarios in which multiple licensing servers are recommended, such as when your servers are placed at different sites and need a local licensing server, or if you choose to segment departments within your company for security purposes.

Fault Tolerance

In environments in which it is critical for systems to remain available, you should consider implementing fault tolerance in the event of a license server failure. Fault tolerance can be implemented in various ways depending on the size or your environment and the resources it controls. One of the simplest ways to implement fault tolerance is to provide a backup license server. If your primary license server fails, you can manually point your servers to the backup server. Citrix provides a four-day grace period in the event of a failure, which should give you enough time to manually switch the license server or repair the primary.

When to Use a Shared or Dedicated Server

Aside from the system requirements, you must also consider the number of servers that will be connecting to your licensing server. If your environment is small and there are sufficient resources on a shared server, you need not install a dedicated licensing server. However, if the other applications on the server demand more resources, you will see a decrease in performance in both the other applications and the licensing server. Citrix has provided a rule of thumb to follow in determining when to use a dedicated versus a shared licensing server. Table 8.9 lists their recommendations.

Table 8.9 Deciding on Your License Servers

Total Servers	License Server Recommendations
Less than 50	A shared license server is fine for this installation.
50 to 500	A dedicated license server is recommended.
500 or more	Multiple dedicated license servers.

Securing Your License Server

As with any other component of your network, it is important to secure access to your License Management Console. Like the Access Management Console, you are allowed to add and remove authorized users who may perform administrative duties on a granular level. By default, the Licensing Console uses the credentials used when installing the license server. To add authorized users who can log in to and perform administrative tasks, or to delete or modify user accounts:

1. Open the License Server console. From the Welcome Page, select **User Administration**.
2. Click **Add New User** and then type the user's domain and username in the User box.
3. Select the administrative tasks you want to grant permissions for, and then click **Submit**.

Notes from the Underground…

The License Server and Grace Periods

Citrix recommends that you install the license server prior to adding your first XenApp server. This is an excellent recommendation because, as mentioned previously, you will be prompted for the license server name during the XenApp Server installation process, and because the XenApp Server will not accept user connections until it can contact a license server. Citrix provides a 96-hour initial grace period that will allow up to two users to connect while unable to connect to a license server. We recommend you use this period for testing your server before downloading license files.

Summary

In this chapter we started with network protocols and covered the basic concepts of the RDP-Tcp listener connection and the ICA-tcp listener connection and how you will need to secure the default installations of these protocols to prevent authorized user access. We showed you how modifying the permissions on these protocols could improve your system security.

Next we covered network segregation and multihoming. We explained that you can improve performance and provide additional security by separating ICA session traffic from other types of network traffic, especially when used for connections to databases or system backup software.

We then covered the various connections to a XenApp Server farm. We showed you how connecting via SSL/TLS is a more secure method of connecting to your XenApp resources and also provided instructions on how to configure your clients to utilize this configuration. We covered configurations for Program Neighborhood, Program Neighborhood Agent and the Web Interface and explained that the preferred client connection method was through the Web Interface because of the more granular control it provides for client configuration options. We also explained of the importance of implementing Certificate Revocation List (CRL) checking.

Next we covered the topic of IP Security and gave a general overview of what IP security is and the value it can provide for a highly secure network. We gave you an in-depth discussion of the components of IPsec so that you could have a better understanding of this feature if you choose to implement it in your environment. We finished the section by providing you a sample XenApp configuration deployment utilizing IPsec. Implementing IP Security along with other measures outlined in this book adds further security to your XenApp farm.

We also gave you an general over of how a Public Key Infrastructure (PKI) works. We explained that PKI is the method of choice for handling authentication issues in large enterprise-level organizations. If you were to view PKI, or a certificate, as a small and portable combination safe, you would see that the primary purpose of the safe is to securely hold something—in our case a public key (although quite a bit of other information is also held there). Someone you trust must hold the combination to the safe—that trust is the basis for the entire PKI system. The main purpose of certificates is to facilitate the secure transfer of keys across an insecure network.

We finished the chapter by giving you some options to consider when deploying your Citrix License Server. Perhaps the best tools to secure your license server are the use of NTFS permissions of critical files (like your license files with the file extension of .lic) and IPsec to control which servers are allowed access to the Citrix License Server.

Solutions Fast Track

Understanding Network Protocols

- ☑ A listener connection (also called the RDP-Tcp or the ICA-Tcp connection) must be configured and exist on the server for clients to successfully establish Terminal Services and Citrix sessions to that server.

- ☑ Configurations for the RDP-Tcp and ICA-tcp connections are very similar and most settings can be configured from the Terminal Services Configuration Tool or via Group Policy.

- ☑ A listener connection can only apply to a single network interface card or all interfaces.

Defining Network Segregation

☑ Multihoming a XenApp server can be implemented for several reasons, including servers that require redundant access; servers that require out-of-band management access (remote administration only); servers that require a separate backup network; configuration of a private internal network; and servers that require communication with resources outside the internal network.

☑ A zone is a logical grouping of servers typically associated with subnets. Each zone has a data collector.

☑ The data collector is responsible for complete knowledge of the dynamic information for the zone for which it is a member.

Understanding Connections to a XenApp Server

☑ There are several settings that can be configured on the ICA client in order to make it more secure. Some of the most notable that are:

☑ Disabling the bitmap disk cache

☑ Using SSL/TLS for communications

☑ Not allowing user passwords to be saved

☑ Using two-factor authentication such as smart cards

☑ Disabling client device mapping (such has hard drives and the clipboard)

☑ Using Kerberos authentication for local client connections

☑ You can connect to XenApp resources through three ICA client choices:

☑ Program Neighborhood Agent client

☑ Program Neighborhood client

☑ Web clients

Understanding Internet Protocol Security

☑ Microsoft's Windows Server 2003 IPsec deployment includes the following features:

☑ Enhanced IPsec security monitoring with the MMC

☑ IPsec integration with Active Directory that allows for security policies to be centrally administered

☑ Use of Kerberos version 5 authentication as the default method by IPsec policies to verify the authenticity of connecting computers

☑ Backward compatibility with the Windows 2000 Security Framework

☑ Client and application transparency, because IPsec works at the Network layer of the OSI model

- ☑ Automatic security negotiation

- ☑ In addition to the default policies that can be implemented with the IPsec Security Policy MMC, you can also create your own custom policies for implementation.

Understanding Public Key Infrastructure

- ☑ To understand how a PKI works, you first need to understand what it is supposed to do. The goals of your infrastructure should include the following:

- ☑ Proper authentication

- ☑ Trust

- ☑ Confidentiality

- ☑ Integrity

- ☑ Nonrepudiation

- ☑ Properly planning for and deploying a PKI requires familiarity with a number of components, including but not limited to the following:

- ☑ Digital Certificates

- ☑ Certification Authorities

- ☑ Certificate Enrollment

- ☑ Certificate Revocation

- ☑ Encryption/Cryptography Services

- ☑ Certificates are a way to transfer keys securely across an insecure network. If any arbitrary user were allowed to issue certificates, it would be no different from that user simply signing the data. For a certificate to be of any use, it must be issued by a trusted entity—an entity that both the sender and receiver trust. Such a trusted entity is known as a certification authority (CA).

Securing the Citrix License Server

- ☑ Every XenApp Server farm must include at least one license server. The license server stores the license files for the Citrix products that specify the parameters for the product usage.

- ☑ By default, the Licensing Console uses the credentials used when installing the license server.

Frequently Asked Questions

Q: How does Microsoft recommend that you configure Terminal Services connection settings, if possible?

A: Through the use of Group Policies.

Q: For TLS authentication to function correctly, terminal servers must meet what prerequisites?

A: Terminal servers must run Windows Server 2003 SP1, must have a RDP client that is TLS compliant, must obtain a certificate for the terminal server

Q: Can listener connections be configured for IPX/SPX for RDP?

A: No, listener connections can be configured for RDP only over TCP/IP.

Q: What is the concept of separating the user sessions and database access onto two separate network cards called?

A: This is called multihoming.

Q: What is a zone?

A: A zone is a logical grouping of servers typically associated with subnets.

Q: What are your choices for 32-bit Windows operating systems ICA clients?

A: Program Neighborhood Agent client, Program Neighborhood client, Web clients

Q: What setting is required in the WFClient.ini to enable Kerberos with Pass-Through Authentication?

A: SSPIEnabled=On and UseSSPIOnly=On

Q: What setting must be configured in the Default.ica on the Web Interface server to enforce mandatory CRL checking?

A: SSLCertificateRevocationCheckPolicy =FullAccessCheckAndCRLRequired

Q: What setting must be configured in the Appsrv.ini to disable bitmap disk caching?

A: PersistentCacheEnabled=Off

Q: What is the method of choice for handling authentication issues in large enterprise-level organizations today?

A: The Public Key Infrastructure (PKI)

Q: Of the three general types of certificates found in a Windows PKI, which one is considered the most common?

A: The user certificate is perhaps the most common.

Q: What is the minimum number of license servers required for a XenApp farm?

A: One. Every XenApp Server farm must include at least one license server.

Q: I have licenses for multiple Citrix products. How should I divide my license servers?

A: When possible, Citrix recommends having all of your licenses for the same product on the same license server.

Q: What are the two main goals of Internet Protocol Security (IPsec)?

A: To protect IP packets and to give network administrators the ability to use packet filtering as a defense against network attacks.

Q: What tool allows network administrators to set security policy settings and options that will allow the systems to negotiate with other systems regarding the traffic that is sent and received from that system?

A: The IP Security Policy Management MMC

Q: What are the three basic services that IPsec uses cryptography to provide?

A: Authentication, Data integrity, Data confidentiality

Q: What are the two IPsec modes?

A: Tunnel mode and Transport Mode

Chapter 9

Securing Access to XenApp Using Citrix Secure Gateway

Solutions in this chapter:

- Methods of Remote Access
- Configuring Citrix Secure Gateway

☑ Summary

☑ Solutions Fast Track

☑ Frequently Asked Questions

Introduction

One of the biggest challenges faced by many XenApp administrators is how to provide remote access to the farm resources without compromising the security of the network. Additionally, such access needs to be easy to use, very secure, and provide as close to local area network (LAN) performance as possible. Fortunately, Citrix has always been a company that produces products with a single goal in mind—access. Over the years, Presentation Server (and most recently, XenApp) has become a highly secure solution for allowing remote and mobile access to your company's internal network.

There are several methods of providing secure access to your remote and mobile users. As you investigate the complexities of leading user sessions through a firewall you will see how the methods of access you choose to implement will impact the firewall, the XenApp servers, and ultimately the users themselves as they attempt to make use of the solutions you provide them. Some of the methods that are available for allowing XenApp traffic to traverse firewalls include:

- Network Address Translation (NAT)
- Port Address Translation (PAT)
- Proxy servers
- HyperText Transfer Protocol (HTTP)
- SSL Relay
- Citrix Secure Gateway
- Citrix NetScaler
- Citrix Access Gateway

We spend most of our time and efforts in this chapter discussing the more modern ways of securing the communications between Citrix clients and XenApp servers via Citrix Secure Gateway server and the Citrix Access Gateway.

Methods of Remote Access

Remote and mobile access is one of the key benefits of Citrix XenApp. Remote access comes in many different levels of security, and we as network architects must consider all of the pieces that must go together to form a single cohesive secure solution for our users. Today's user populations require and often demand remote access to their office computing environment. XenApp Server provides the solution for users, whether a traveling salesperson operating out of a hotel or a work-from-home user who is looking for the easiest and best performing access to the corporate network. There is a wide variety of remote access solutions available with Citrix. We begin with a breakdown of the most typical solutions and examine the benefits and disadvantages of each.

Table 9.1 provides a quick overview of the various options for providing remote access to your XenApp servers (some secured and some unsecured).

Table 9.1 Recommended Remote Access Options

Remote Access Solution (1–5, 5 being most secure)	Secure	Ease of Implementation	Ease of Support	Costs
Network Address Translation (NAT)				
Port Address Translation (PAT)	1	Typically requires modifications to the firewall and clients to implement, and may require use of *ALTADDR* command on XenApp servers.	Firewall rules and *ALTADDR* commands are fairly static; client support can be a challenge.	$0, all features included in product.
Proxy servers	2	Similar to PAT, typically requires firewall modification and client software.	Same as NAT/PAT plus additional support concerns with proxies.	$0, all features are included in product to facilitate use of Proxy servers. The Proxy Servers have a wide range of costs and all can work so long as they support SOCKETS (SOCKS) version 5.
HTTP/HTTPS	3*	This solution requires the servers to have an SSL server certificate in order to be secure; otherwise, it is not secure.	Modern Citrix clients default to the use of HTTP/HTTPS, so supportability is easier. The only exception would be regular exchange of server certificates to secure the servers.	$300–$800 per XenApp server per year for public SSL server certificates. Internal or private certificate authorities can be used to eliminate this cost, but will require substantially greater support for both the public key infrastructure to support this and the deployment to the clients the root SSL certificate for the internal public key infrastructure (more on this later in this chapter).

Continued

Table 9.1 Continued. Recommended Remote Access Options

Remote Access Solution (1–5, 5 being most secure)	Secure	Ease of Implementation	Ease of Support	Costs
SSL Relay	3	Every XenApp server would require an SSL server certificate.	Same as HTTP/HTTPS.	This is similar to the HTTP/HTTPS. SSL Relay is a legacy service developed several versions ago prior to the release of the eXtensible Markup Language (XML) service that now exists on all servers and provides the HTTP/HTTPS functionality for query farm information.
Citrix Access Gateway	5	Short implementation time and centrally deployed client and updates to clients.	Centrally managed updates and changes to the client software.	$3000+. This is the Citrix hardware-based offering in the product line. Like all Citrix products, it is licensed per simultaneous connected user. The $3,000+ price tag is for the hardware itself.
Citrix Secure Gateway	5	More complicated than Access Gateway implementation, but more seamless.	Once configured and functioning, support requirements are minimal.	$0, there are no costs associated with the deployment of Secure Gateway, as all the required Citrix software components are included in the product. However, a properly designed deployment may include many new servers being added to the environment, so the cost of this hardware and the hosting operating systems and their support should be considered.

Securing Communications between XenApp Server and Client

The primary methods of securing remote access to our XenApp Servers:

- Secure ICA (ICA Encryption)
- Secure Socket Layer Relay (SSL Relay)
- Virtual private networking (VPN)
- Citrix Secure Gateway (CSG)
- Citrix Access Gateway or Citrix NetScaler

Each of these solutions has its benefits and disadvantages to deploying the solution. From Chapter 3 we know that Secure ICA is the oldest method of securing communications between Citrix client and server. Also from Chapter 3, we know that Secure Sockets Layer (SSL) was created to encrypt data transmitted between a client computer and a Web server, and that Citrix leverages the use of SSL through the implementation of the Citrix Secure Gateway, the Citrix Access Gateway and the Citrix NetScaler device. Each of these solutions has its benefits and disadvantages to deploying the solution. Let us examine these in more detail.

Secure ICA

Secure ICA can be implemented internally to your network or externally. It uses the same Transmission Control Protocol (TCP) port, 1494, as a nonencrypted ICA session. In many early solutions (prior to Secure Gateway or Access Gateway), many administrators would opt to use Secure ICA to encrypt their otherwise open solutions of NAT/PAT and proxy servers. Prior to Web Interface and XenApp Server policy, some administrators chose to implement multihomed servers to allow for control of when and how to encrypt data.

Figure 9.1 demonstrates a multihomed XenApp Server in which the internal network interface would not have Secure ICA enabled, but the external or demilitarized zone (DMZ) network interface would have Secure ICA 128-bit enabled.

Figure 9.1 MultiHomed XenApp Server with Secure ICA

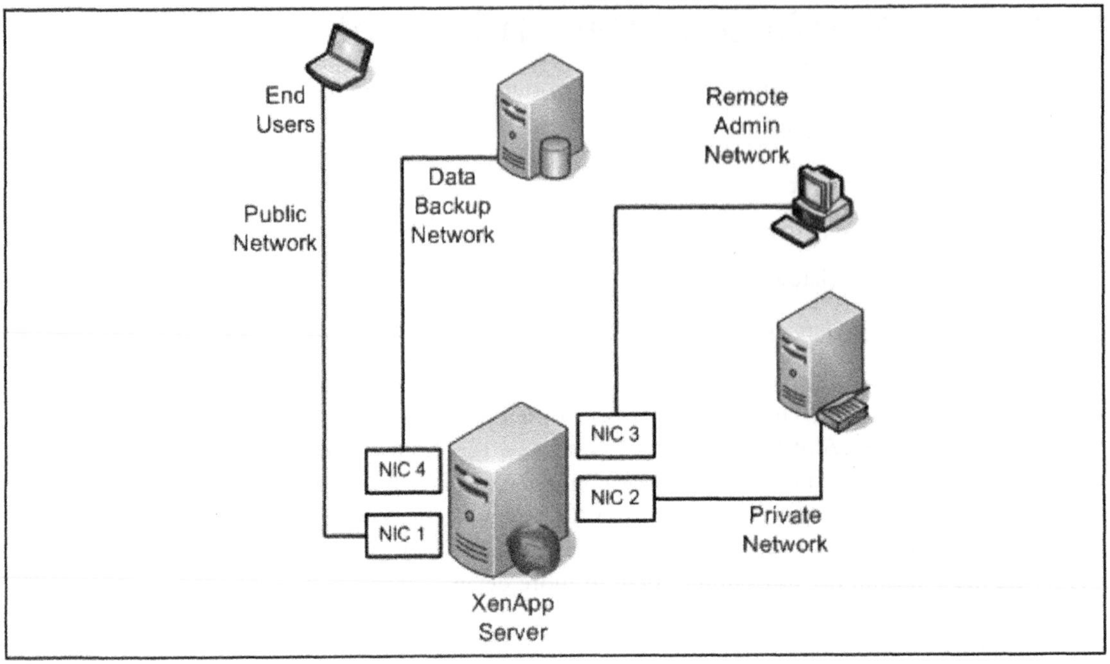

In this scenario, sessions originating from the production network would not be required to use encryption. External (nontrusted) network users would be denied connections if they didn't connect using encryption.

As previously mentioned, Secure ICA can be required on the network interface (via the Terminal Services Connection Configuration utility), on a published application by published application basis, or via XenApp policy. Published applications and XenApp Policy are "automatic" in allowing clients to connect with no changes required on the client end. If we configure the XenApp connection to require encryption, then any connection created (except those already published applications with encryption or policies requiring encryption) will require a setting adjustment on the client.

Let us begin by looking at the client side. Remember, a client can request encryption at any point (even if it isn't required from the server side). For clients to request encryption, they will have to change the configuration of their application sets or their custom connections.

Remember, a client can request encryption at any point (even if it isn't required from the server side). For clients to request encryption, they will have to change the configuration of their application sets or their custom connections. Figure 9.2 demonstrates the client changing the properties of a single custom connection to require encryption.

Figure 9.2 Client Enabling Encryption for a Custom Connection

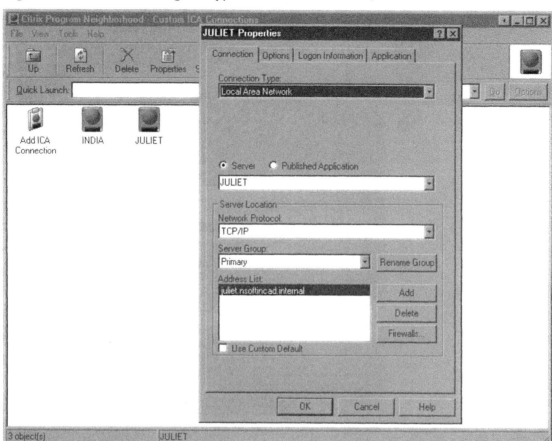

Figure 9.3 demonstrates the same concept for an application set (remember, security settings on an application set effect all applications in the set, while custom connections are set for each individual connection).

Figure 9.3 Client Enabling Encryption for an Application Set

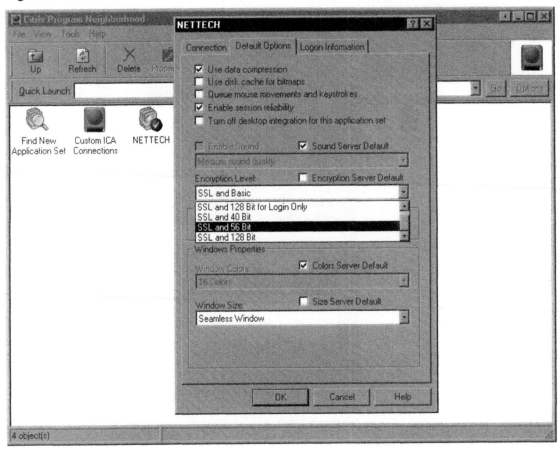

To confirm that a user is actually connected using encryption, the user simple needs to access the Program Neighborhood Connection Center in his or her systems tray (Win32 clients only), click on the correct connection, and select **Properties**. The Client Connection Status window should open and contain the encryption level as shown in Figure 9.4. Similar information may be gained by reviewing the connections in the Presentation Server Management Console.

Figure 9.4 Client Reviewing Connection Status to Ensure Encryption Is Being Used

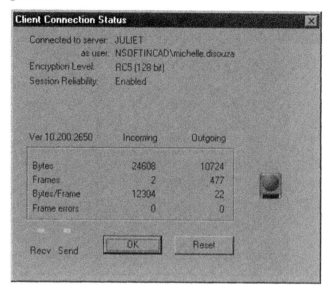

Secure ICA can be "enforced" from the server side via a number of methods. The most obvious way would be on the connection settings for ICA as we previously reviewed in Figure 9.1. Secure ICA or encryption can be enabled on a per-connection basis. By default, the ICA-TCP connection settings are shared between all adapters in the server. If you wanted to provide the scenario in Figure 9.1, you would simply create an additional connector and configure the connectors with the "internal" and "external" interfaces, respectively.

Setting the required encryption on the connection is the "oldest" of methods for encrypting a session with Secure ICA. In the past this was accomplished by using the Citrix Connection Configuration tool. Now, the same configuration can be accomplished using XenApp policies. Citrix also developed the option to allow us to publish applications requiring different levels of encryption. This flexibility allowed us to reserve the use of encryption for specific more security-conscious applications. This also allows us to publish the same application multiple times to different groups of users, and allow for some users to be forced into an encrypted session, perhaps for our chief financial officer (CFO). Enabling encryption on a given published application is a snap. Simply open the **Properties** of a given published application, navigate to the **Client Options** tab, and select the appropriate level of encryption as depicted in Figure 9.5.

Figure 9.5 Encryption Settings for Published Applications

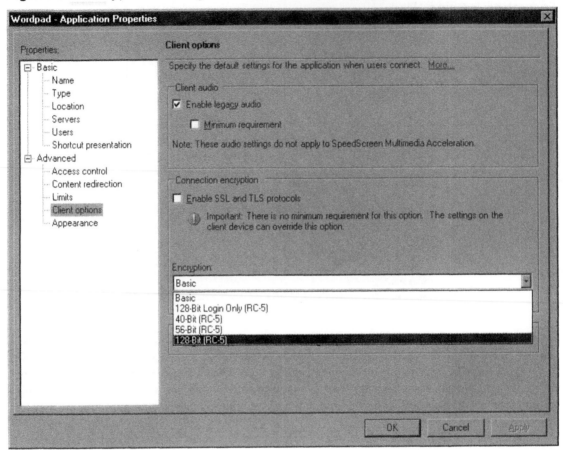

The final and arguably best method to require encryption of session data using Secure ICA is to enforce the encryption requirement through XenApp Policy. While we won't cover XenApp Policy in detail here, we mention it here as a way to enable encryption of a XenApp connection as demonstrated in Figure 9.6.

Figure 9.6 Enabling Encryption through Citrix Policy

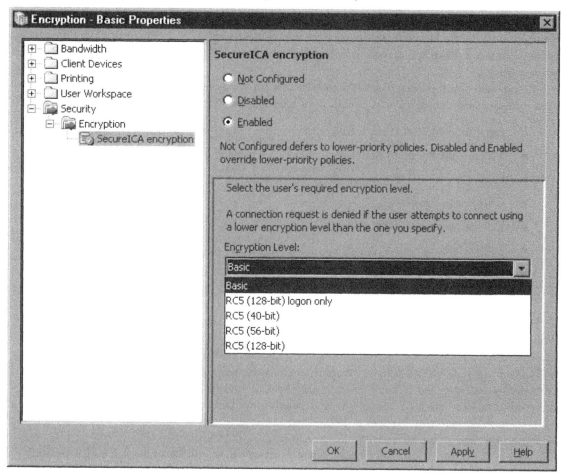

Secure Socket Layer Relay (SSL Relay)

Another security issue to consider is the way in which traffic is passed between the Web Interface server and the XML service on Citrix XenApp servers. In a process that is similar to standard Web traffic, data is transmitted in cleartext. This becomes a security concern when traffic between the Web Interface server and the Citrix XenApp farm is insecure. For example, many organizations will place a Web Interface server in the DMZ, or demilitarized zone, while maintaining a XenApp server farm in a more secure network. In the event Citrix XenApp servers are not located in a secure network environment, the use of the SSL Relay service will help to mitigate the security concern for unencrypted traffic. Although the password is slightly encrypted, it does not provide a secure alternative to the encryption methods discussed in this chapter. To assist you with this problem, Citrix has developed the SSL Relay service. This service allows you to configure all traffic passing between Web Interface servers and a Citrix XenApp Server to use SSL encryption.

Private Networking to Secure ICA Sessions

VPN initially appears to present the "simplest" solution for providing users' remote access to our XenApp server farms. However, this perception can be deceiving. VPN access to production networks brings with it a series of issues, some of which are specific to XenApp servers, and others that are more generic.

Before we delve too deep into VPN connectivity for servers and clients, let us first examine the primary issues surrounding VPN as a method of accessing our XenApp server farms.

- Installation of VPN client software

- Support of VPN client software

- Cost

- Complexity for users

- Latency and tunnel failure issues

- Split-tunneling

- Client is "part of the network"

- Worm/virus propagation

Installation of VPN client software can be a challenge for administrators and users alike. The installation programs, while typically automated, normally require administrative privileges over the computer on which the software is being installed. Additionally, the installation of the VPN client normally adds a "virtual" adapter to the workstation for the purposes of routing traffic correctly to the other end of the VPN concentrator. The existence of this VPN adapter modifies the routing tables of the local client, which, depending on the client's network, can lead to a series of issues with connectivity. Support of VPN client software is tied directly to the installation and ongoing help desk issues generated by the existence of the VPN software.

One of the largest factors to consider when deciding whether VPN access is the best method for your farm is cost. VPN client licenses are typically more costly than nearly any other alternative, and this typically doesn't include the cost associated with the hardware to install in your production network to provide the terminating end to client VPNs. Due to the higher cost associated with VPN access and the security concerns, most organizations elect to only provide access (if at all) to their internal users. Trusted business partners may be a case for this type of access, but even then, most administrators don't want to take on the support burden of a VPN client on noncompany-owned and managed hardware. That said, roving access from public or untrusted computers is pretty much out as far as this solution is concerned.

For those clients who are the "right fit" for this solution, using the VPN client software can be a challenge. Probably the single biggest complaint of VPN clients is the complexity of configuring and using the actual client, and the "strange effect" the software seems to have on the computer's connectivity. This complexity is typically so high and the repetitive use of the VPN solution required in truly learning the software is so low that many users simply give up and return to the office if system access is required. This by definition is not "simple" access.

Moving past the issues that VPNs present to the clients, several issues can cause us very serious internal concerns when a user does successfully establish a VPN. Latency in the underlying network connectivity between the client and the VPN concentrator can frequently be great enough to cause the tunnel to "hiccup." This pause or drop in the tunnel is an unacceptable solution for XenApp Server sessions. ICA is a presentation layer protocol of the OSI model. The relative position of the protocol makes it extremely susceptible to breaks or drops in connectivity. Latency can for the most part be overcome with a series of technologies from Citrix called Speed Screen, discussed elsewhere in this book. Breaks or drops such as those found in VPN connectivity can cause the user's sessions (once established) to simply disappear. This can be a serious issue to troubleshoot and resolve; it is not fun for you and definitely a bad experience for your customers, also known as your users.

Another issue more related to security is the dreaded split-tunnel. Split-tunneling is a concept in virtual private networking whereby the end device establishes the tunnel to your corporate network and is able to gain access to resources outside your corporate network. In simpler terms, the external computer has simultaneous access to corporate resources and public resources. This presents serious security issues, especially in situations where a client's computing device could have been turned into a "zombie" and some external "bad guy" has leveraged your user's computer as a free ticket into the corporate network. Fortunately, split-tunneling can be disabled in most cases. However, disabling it means that the user's access outside the tunnel disappears, and all requests are sent through the tunnel to include print request, Web sites, e-mail, and so forth, much of which may be unserviceable by the corporate network. Figure 9.7 demonstrates the concept of split-tunneling.

Figure 9.7 Effects of Split-Tunneling in VPN Access

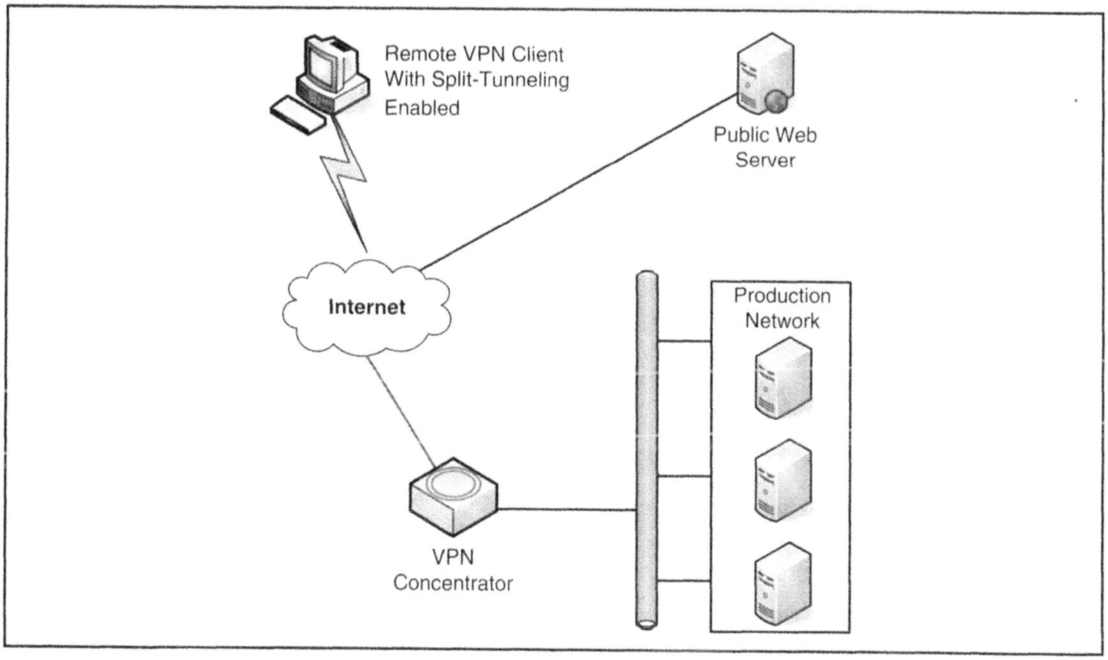

The last couple of security concerns for using VPN access as a remote access solution to XenApp servers are based on the following simple statement, "Clients are part of the corporate network." Once a VPN tunnel is established, virtually it is as if the remote computer were actually on your corporate network, bringing with it all of the issues and concerns that exist from supporting workstations. In our corporate networks, we spend a great deal of time securing, protecting, updating, and disinfecting our workstations through of a host of services and software. While these devices are not "easy" to support and manage, they are typically within our "sphere of power" and are controllable to some extent. Computing devices in users' homes or remote trusted networks are typically outside of our management scope. The unpatched vulnerabilities, viruses, and worms that they bring to our production network the instant they establish the tunnel should be of paramount concern to all network administrators. This last concern alone had nearly halted the adoption of VPN solutions in many environments. The recent advent of SSL-based VPNs and newer "hybrid" VPNs are taking some of the sting out of VPN solutions.

That being said, VPN access does provide one major advantage to XenApp Server users: there is no need to "reconfigure" their XenApp Server client software based on the fact that they are internal or external to the network. A single set of instructions for users could be issues whether the users access the farm from inside the network or outside (as when they are outside, they will simply establish the VPN tunnel). There is a variety of solutions surrounding VPN technology, but the basic issues of support, security, and simplicity are still challenges that more or less prohibit VPN access as serious contender for the best remote access method for XenApp servers.

Citrix Secure Gateway

Another methodology developed by Citrix allows the tunneling of all ICA client traffic using industry-standard security protocols such as Secure Sockets Layer (SSL) or Transport Layer Security (TLS). Citrix has developed a solution known as Citrix Secure Gateway that encrypts all Citrix client traffic such as ICA packets via industry-standard Internet encryption protocols to simplify the management of a secure infrastructure throughout your network. For example, by deploying a Citrix Secure Gateway in the corporate DMZ, the firewalls protecting your network from the Internet must only be configured to allow SSL packets to the Citrix Secure Gateway server from any ICA client. The Citrix Secure Gateway server will manage the connectivity and encryption across the public Internet and mask the XenApp server farm.

Not only does this provide a simplified security solution, it hides the server farm from potential intruders on the Internet. Although this offers security to the ICA clients, once the traffic passes through the Citrix Secure Gateway it is no longer encrypted. It is recommended to use one of the many other encryption techniques for the TCP\IP packets from the Citrix Secure Gateway to the XenApp Server farm.

The Citrix Secure Gateway is made up of the following components:

- **Secure Gateway Server** Central server that acts as "gateway" to the Citrix XenApp server farm. The Secure Gateway Server acts as the middleman and validates the ticket provided by the STA.

- **Secure Ticket Authority (STA)** Creates a ticket for each session offering a more secure access methodology.

- **Citrix XML Service** Provides the interface between a Citrix XenApp server and the Web Interface server.

- **Citrix XenApp Server Farm** Citrix XenApp server farm that provides published applications via the ICA Client.

Citrix Access Gateway

The Citrix Access Gateway is a hardened appliance deployed in an organization's DMZ that secures all traffic with standards-based SSL and TLS encryption. It serves as a complete replacement for Secure Gateway servers or traditional IPSec VPN devices.

> **NOTE**
>
> When deployed with XenApp Server Platinum Edition includes an Access Gateway Universal user license, allowing any Access Gateway edition to be deployed (appliances purchased separately).

Using Access Gateway with XenApp Server delivers the benefits of a hardened appliance, increasing security and extending user access to additional applications and resources. The *SmartAccess* component provides advanced policy-based control of XenApp Server applications and individual capabilities such as print and save. The *Citrix SmoothRoaming* functionality allows users to move seamlessly between access locations and devices, automatically adapting access to each unique access scenario.

The Citrix Access Gateway comes available in three editions to meet various business requirements:

- **Standard Edition** Designed for organizations with fewer than 500 concurrent users who are looking for an excellent secure remote access solution without the need for highly sophisticated policy deployment.

- **Advanced Edition** Designed for organizations with fewer than 500 concurrent users who are looking for an excellent secure remote access solution that includes highly sophisticated SmartAccess policy deployment, browser-only access and/or mobile device support.

- **Enterprise Edition** The best secure access solution for enterprise environments, offering market-leading scalability and performance, SmartAccess capabilities, high-availability options and integrated application acceleration and optimization.

One immediate advantage of the Citrix Access Gateway is the reduction of needed servers by supporting more users per appliance—up to 10,000 concurrent users on the Access Gateway 10000 series appliance (scalability varies according to appliance series), compared to 700 to 1,000 concurrent users per Secure Gateway server. Another advantage of the Citrix Access Gateway is the elimination of separate VPNs. Most organizations using Secure Gateway also deploy a separate VPN to secure other types of traffic, adding more expense and overhead. With Access Gateway, one SSL VPN can handle all of your organization's remote access needs. For detailed benefits are provided in Table 9.2.

Table 9.2 Access Gateway Features

Feature	Benefit	Standard Edition	Advanced Edition	Enterprise Edition
Support all applications and protocols	Provides access to all applications and data from anywhere	X	X	X
Web-deployed client	No need to pre-install or manage complex client software	X	X	X
XenApp integration	Replaces the Citrix Secure Gateway	X	X	X
Always-on access	Automatically reconnects users as soon as the network connection is restored	X	X	X
Integrated end-point scanning	Ensures the client device meets appropriate standards before connecting	X	X	X
Standards-based security	Information is protected using SSL/TLS encryption	X	X	X
SmartAccess	Policy-based technology determines what resources can be accessed		X	X
Access Interface	Provides "landing page" for users to access their applications, files and resources		X	X
Detailed Audit Trail	Gives admins visibility into all resources and services accessed by clients		X	X
Smart Card support	Protects resources by authenticating users with smart cards			X
Integrated high availability	Supports deployment of a high-availability pair of appliances, providing redundancy			X
Role-based and delegated administration	Simplifies management in large organizations and support multiple admins			X
Faster application response	Uses Citrix AppCompress technology and integrated SSL hardware acceleration			X
Quarantine Groups	Provides limited access for noncompliant devices			X
FIPS 140-2	Meets federal government FIPS 140-2 criteria		X	

Citrix Secure Gateway Components

Citrix Secure Gateway (CSG) is the most commonly implemented solution for securing remote access to XenApp and Presentation server farms. There are several reasons for this solution's popularity, but the most common are ease of use for the end users, no additional software costs (this product is included as part of Presentation Server and XenApp installation CDs), and the broad support of client operating systems. CSG has become the standard for remote access since its creation nearly three years ago. Secure gateway is itself a single server, but the solution requires several other components to work in concert toward a secure session for the user. A properly implemented CSG solution will include the Secure Gateway, a Web Interface server, a XenApp server farm with published applications, and a XenApp server serving as a Secure Ticket Authority. From a high-level, a typical implementation would look something like Figure 9.8.

Figure 9.8 Overview of Secure Gateway Components Placement

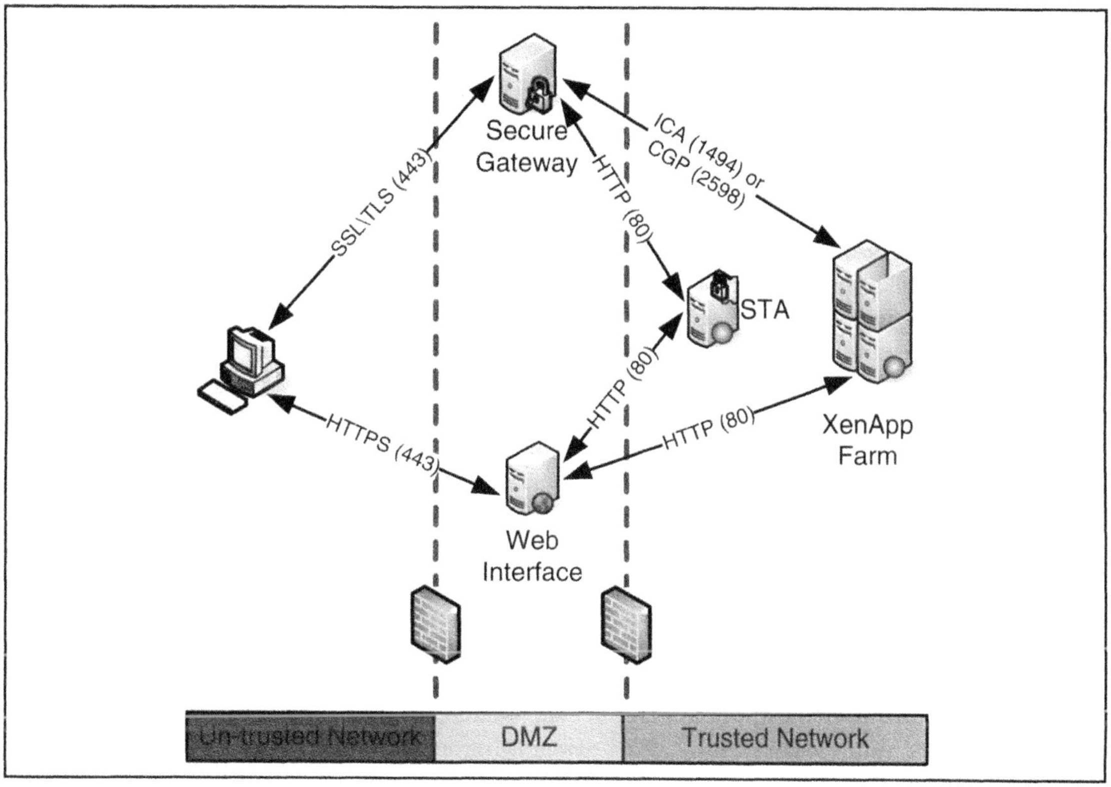

To correctly implement a Secure Gateway solution, careful planning and consideration must be given to each component. In this section, we discuss the planning and requirements for each component as it pertains to such as solution. After describing the requirements for each component, we will walk through the typical installation and configuration of that component (where applicable).

Secure Ticket Authority Configuration

The role of the Secure Ticket Authority (STA) is to issue session tickets in response to connection requests from Citrix Access Gateway or Web Interface servers. The STA also uses the tickets as the foundation for authentication and authorization for access to published applications in the farm(s). This authentication and authorization occurs when the Secure Gateway asks the STA to validate a ticket that a session has given the Secure Gateway.

The next question is whether to secure the communication between the "clients" and the STA service. The "clients" in this scenario would be the Secure Gateway and the Citrix Access Manager and/or Web Interface servers. The "client" requests are HTTP based and can be secured with a standard SSL certificate, thus allowing the "clients" to communicate with the STA using HTTPS.

Before we dig too much deeper into the configuration of the STA or Secure Gateway in general, we should briefly review certificate authorities (CAs) and the role that SSL certificates play in communications. Certificates are used to ensure that the parties communicating with each other are genuine. In today's computing world, there are three widely used types of certificates; the first is the root certificate.

The root certificate is created and issued by the CA. The purpose of the root certificate is simply to allow other devices to guarantee the authenticity of the two other types of certificates that the CA may issue, the client and server certificates. Anyone or any device may freely download and "add" the root certificate from a CA to their computer's "trusted roots." The action of adding a root certificate to a device implies that you "trust" the other certificates that the originating CA issues.

The client certificate is not as widely used today as the server certificate is. The client certificate is to allow the receiver of the communication to guarantee the caller is legitimate. Think of it this way: If a person walks up to your desk and asks you to let him into the server room, explaining that he works in IT for your company, you have no viable way of proving or disproving that statement, unless you ask to see his badge. The badge that he possesses functions as the client certificate in this case. Since you have seen other badges, you know the person who issues the badges, and you yourself have a badge, this knowledge functions as the root certificate (the one that allows you to trust). Client certificates are supported with Secure Gateway, although typically not implemented due to the cost and complexity of maintaining the infrastructure to issue and revoke these certificates.

Server certificates are our primary concern for this module. Server certificates allow you to confirm the legitimacy of the server on the other end. A perfect example of this is online shopping. Prior to purchasing the much-needed widget from eBay, you want to guarantee that the server on the other end—the one receiving your credit card information—is really an eBay server. Your Web browser does this by comparing the server certificate that the eBay Web server shows your computer with the root certificate issued by the same issuer of the server certificate. If, for instance, VeriSign issued the server certificate for the Web server we are building, we will need to ensure that the root certificate is added to the "clients" of that Web server. Most popular public CAs' root certificates are already added when you install the operating system on your computer or are updated when you apply services packs. Private CAs' root certificates could be added to your computer when you build them or through a management tool such as Active Directory if the computer exists within your management scope. Public CAs make their living by charging consumers for their services. Private CAs can typically be installed for free on many operating systems and have no cost associated with their operation other than the hardware and support needed. All of this brings us to this important point: public versus private CAs, and which to choose.

The decision to choose a public or private CA is easy, and can be based on a very simple set of rules:

- If the clients that will be "trusting" the root certificate (from the CA) are internal and under your management control, a private CA is a fine choice.

- If the clients that will be "trusting" the root certificate are outside of your management control—Internet users, remote users, home users, or trusted business partners—a public CA is the better choice.

Since the Secure Gateway, Citrix Access Gateway and Web Interface server will be acting as clients to the STA, we could choose to use either a public or private CA. Either way, we would ensure that the root certificates that matched the server certificate on the STA were added to the Secure Gateway, Citrix Access Gateway, and Web Interface. Figure 9.9 demonstrates the legs of communication that we are specifically securing by leveraging an SSL server certificate and the relationship between root certificates and server certificates.

Figure 9.9 Using SSL Certificates to Secure the Communication to the Secure Ticket Authority

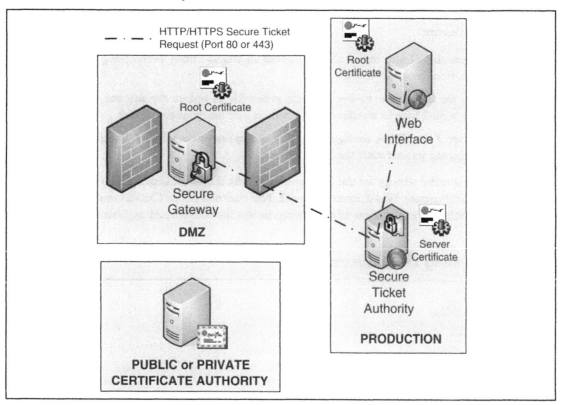

Once the decision is made as to whether to secure the network traffic between the "clients" and the STA, we now will look at redundancy considerations. A single STA is typically capable of handling the load of all but the largest environments. However, a single point of failure in our solution would be unacceptable. STAs can be load balanced or made more fault tolerant in a handful of ways. The basic rule of thumb is that the STA that issues the ticket must be the STA that validates the ticket. Web Interface provides a mechanism to load balance STAs inside the configuration, which is satisfactory for most implementations. If you elect to use Windows Network Load–Balancing Service or a hardware load balancer, pay special attention to the persistency, affinity, or "stickiness" of the connections. Again, it is imperative that the issuing and validating STA be the same.

For now, let us turn our attention to the configuration of the STA itself. In XenApp deployments that will utilize Citrix Secure Gateway (CSG), you must also configure at least one XenApp server to be an STA server. The CSG server does not perform authentication of incoming requests, it only defers authentication to an application enumeration server and uses the STA to guarantee that each user is authenticated. Application enumeration servers request tickets only for users who are already authenticated to the Web Interface. If users have a valid STA ticket, the gateway assumes that they passed the authentication checks at the Web Interface and should be allowed access.

This design allows the Citrix Secure Gateway server to inherit whatever authentication methods are in place on your Web server. For example, if your Web Interface server is protected with RSA SecurID, by design only SecurID–authenticated users can traverse the secure gateway server.

Since the STA shares its port with the XML service on a XenApp server, no additional configuration must be performed on a XenApp server, but there are changes to the STA configuration that will make it more secure:

■ Configure the STA to utilize SSL to prevent an attacker from intercepting the ticket as it travels from server to client

■ Reduce the ticket time–to–live as much as possible to reduce the amount of time an attacker would have to transfer the ticket from one machine to another

■ Use IPSec if the STA is configured on a XenApp server on which IIS is also installed and is sharing its port with the XML service

To configure specific settings for the STA, you must edit the CtxSta.config file typically found in the directory C:\Program Files\Citrix\System32. The contents of the CtxSta.config file are shown in Figure 9.10. An explanation of the settings in this file is described in Table 9.3.

Figure 9.10 Editing the CtxSta.config File

```
[GlobalConfig]
UID=STAA28FD497153B
TicketVersion=10
TicketTimeout=100000
MaxTickets=100000
LogLevel=0
MaxLogCount=10
```

```
MaxLogSize=20
LogDir=C:\Program Files\Citrix\system32\
; Allowed Client IP addresses
; To change, substitute * with client IP addresses. Use ";" to seperate
IP addresses/address ranges.
; To specify a range of IPs always use StartIP-EndIP.
; For example, AllowedClientIPList=192.168.1.1;10.8.1.12-10.8.1.18;123.1.2.3
AllowedClientIPList=192.168.1.50-75,
; SSL only mode
; If set to on, only requests sent through HTTPS are accepted
SSLOnly=off
```

Table 9.3 CtxSta.config File Settings

Setting	Description	Recommended Setting
UID	Unique identifier for the STA	Set by XenApp
TicketVersion	Version of the STA	Set by XenApp
TicketTimeout	Ticket timeout setting in milliseconds	No more than 10000 (100 seconds)
MaxTickets	Maximum number of tickets that can assigned	10000
LogLevel	Level of logging, 0 – minimal, 1 – XXX, 2 – XXX, 3	3 – Enables full logging of all STA traffic and errors
MaxLogCount	The number of STA logs that are maintained	At least 30 (this would be 30 days of logs)
MaxLogSize	The maximum size of the STA log	At least 20
LogDir	The directory where the STA log is maintained	Should be placed on a separate partition from system files and should configured to only be modified by system auditors
AllowedClientIPList	The list of IP addresses that are "trusted" by the STA	All IP addresses that will communicate with the STA
SSLOnly	Enable SSL encryption for the STA	On

TIP

If you are securing communications between the Secure Gateway and the STA, ensure that you install a server certificate on the server running the STA and implement SSL Relay. In most cases, internally generated certificates are used for this purpose.

NOTE

Configuration or reconfiguration of the STA requires the Internet Information Services to be restarted. This will disrupt the ticket issuing and validation process. Those connections already completed will be unaffected; however, new connections attempted during the restart or tickets issued but not yet validated will fail. Once restarted, the connection may be reattempted.

The STA's ID is simply a name given to this STA. This name is not network addressable and need not match the computer or hostname of the server on which the STA resides. The default name is STA01, which can be changed at any point. If you are using multiple STAs for load balancing and/or fault tolerance, selecting different STA IDs is required.

The ticket timeout defaults to 100 seconds, and is the value used to determine the "freshness" of the ticket. A ticket once issued must be used within this ticket timeout period, or the ticket will be invalidated. Most tickets are issued and validated in less than 30 seconds, so decreasing this number may assist in thwarting brute-force attacks on the STA.

The maximum tickets value defaults to 100,000 and determines the maximum number of tickets that will be allowed in this server's memory at any point. Decreasing this number will lower the amount of RAM consumed by the STA service.

Once the STA is configured (reconfigured), a restart of the XML service will be required to enforce the new settings.

Secure Gateway Installation and Configuration

The Secure Gateway service provides simplified secure remote access to your XenApp Server farms. The security is provided by the use of an SSL or TLS certificate to encrypt session data between the end-client device and the Secure Gateway. The Secure Gateway decrypts this traffic and then "proxies" the communication to the XenApp servers. The use of the Secure Gateway allows for a layer of defense and protection for your Presentation servers.

Planning the installation of the Secure Gateway server is a little more involved than the STA configuration. For starters, the most common problem faced by implementers is the type of certificate to use for the Secure Gateway. A server certificate that is 128-bit SSL or TLS is a minimum requirement for the construction of the service. The certificate can be either public or private, although nearly all organizations use public to allow for less interaction with the end-clients' workstations. For more information on certificates and CAs, review the previous section of this chapter on Secure Ticket Authority configuration.

Let's begin with the hardware and software requirements for Secure Gateway:

- Windows 2000 Server Family with the most recent service pack
- 512MB RAM
- 150MB hard drive space
- Network interface card (NIC)
- 128-bit SSL or TLS server certificate

Typically, for security reasons, the Secure Gateway is deployed on a server in the DMZ. This server would not have any other roles or services and is not necessarily joined to a domain. Secure Gateway servers can be load balanced and/or made highly available by using the Windows Network Load-Balancing or third-party hardware load balancers. As with STAs, care should be taken to ensure that session affinity is maintained.

NOTE

Secure Gateway also supports two other modes of operation. The first is Proxy mode, which allows for Secure Gateway servers to be installed in "chains" to allow for easier navigation through multistaged DMZs. Figure 9.11 demonstrates this concept. The second mode is where Secure Gateway and Web Interface are installed together on the same Windows server. This mode is known as Logon Agent mode. Due to security concerns surrounding IIS, we recommend separate servers for the installation and scalability of this solution. As most implementations are separate servers, the Logon Agent option will not be discussed in this chapter.

Figure 9.11 Secure Gateway Proxy Mode with Double-Hop DMZ

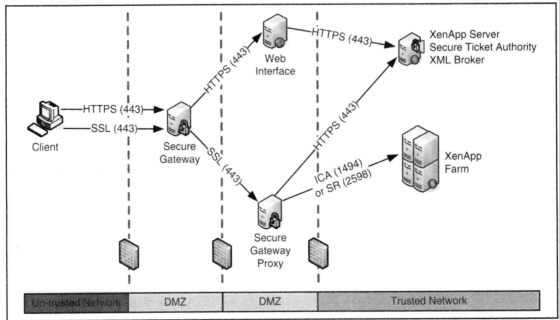

Installation and configuration of the Secure Gateway should begin with the task of obtaining a 128-bit SSL or TLS server certificate. While Secure Gateway can be installed prior to the server certificate being available, the service cannot be configured or function until the certificate has been added. While there are many ways to configure and request a server certificate, we will examine the most common methods, assume we are using a public CA (although we will be using a private CA, as the steps are nearly the same), and obtain an SSL certificate.

To obtain an SSL certificate:

1. The first step in obtaining an SSL server certificate is to generate a request from the Secure Gateway. The easiest way to generate the request is to use the Microsoft Management Console (MMC) and add the Certificates snap-in for the computer account for the local computer. To use this tool, click **Start | Run** and type **MMC**. From the **File** menu of the MMC, select **Add/remove snap-in and** complete the wizard as depicted in Figure 9.12.

Figure 9.12 Adding the Computer Account for the Local Computer's Certificates Snap-in to the MMC

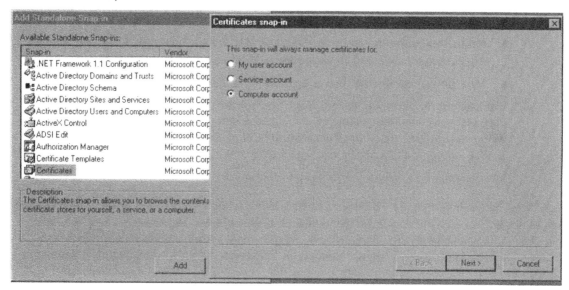

2. Once the Certificates snap-in is added, navigate the structure expanding **Personal** and **Certificates**. Right-click on **Certificates** and select **Request new certificate** as depicted in Figure 9.13.

Figure 9.13 Requesting a New Certificate

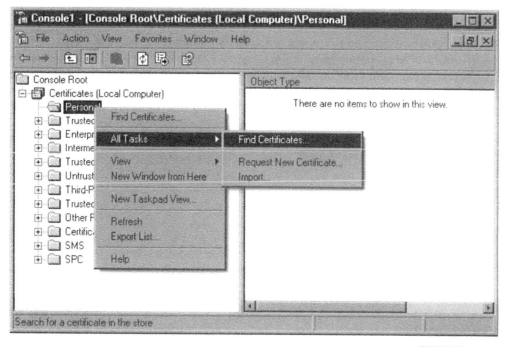

3. From there, complete the wizard with the following specifications:

   ■ **Friendly name** should be descriptive of purpose (but is not tied to DNS resolution).

   ■ **Bit length** minimum of 1024 (this is not the 128-bit key length).

   ■ **Common name** should be the fully qualified domain name (FQDN) (for example, csg.citrix.com) and must be resolvable by DNS.

   ■ Save the request to a file such as C:\CSG_SSL_Request.txt.

4. The next step to obtaining the certificate is to submit the request file's text to a CA. This can be accomplished online or with assistance from the many public CAs that exist. We recommend staying with a "name brand" CA to simplify the end-users' experience (as they will most likely already have the public CA's root certificate).

5. The final step is to add the certificate into the server.

Now that we have a correct SSL or TLS server certificate added to our soon-to-be Secure Gateway, we can begin the actual installation and configuration of the software. The Secure Gateway configuration will follow immediately after the install and may be completed, or cancelled and finished later. Please note that Secure Gateway requires a reboot of the server after installation. Future configuration changes to Secure Gateway do not require a reboot, but do restart the service (breaking all active sessions).

For now, let us turn our attention to the installation and configuration of the Secure Gateway. Once your server platform has met the requirements for installation, we can begin the install by inserting the Setup CD that shipped with our XenApp Server software, or you can download the components from the MyCitrix Web site. Begin the installation by running the **CSG_GWY.msi** from the CD.

The following section (and Figures 9.14–9.35) explains the install process and will aid in installing and configuring the Secure Gateway at any point.

1. First, we are asked some pretty tough installation questions. Installation mode can be either Normal or Proxy. Remember that Proxy is reserved for Double-Hop or complicated DMZ traversal, so most implementations will choose Normal. The Products to Secure section allows us to use Secure Gateway for Presentation servers, Secure Access Manager servers, or both. For the purposes of this book, we will choose **Presentation Servers only.** Make the appropriate choice and click **Next**.

Figure 9.14 Secure Gateway Installation

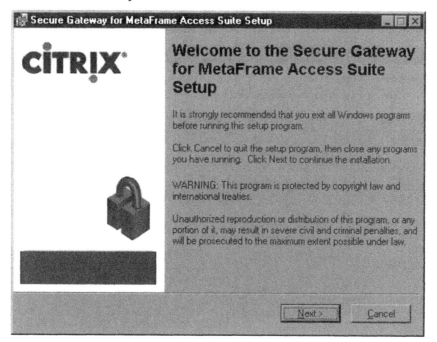

2. Click **Next**.

Figure 9.15 Secure Gateway Installation License Agreement

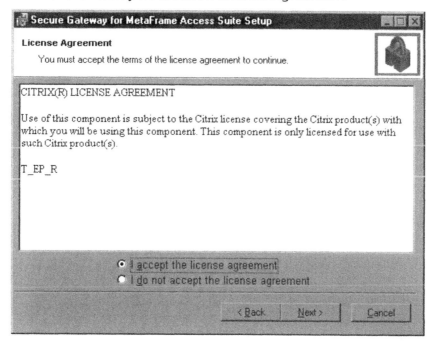

3. Accept the license agreement and click **Next**.

Figure 9.16 Secure Gateway Installation Mode

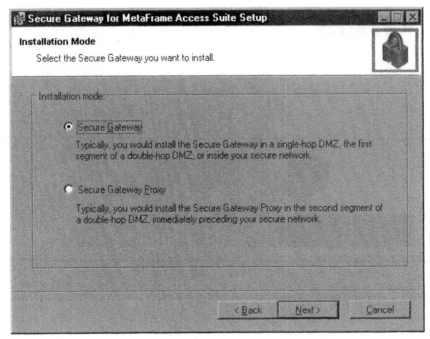

4. Select the installation mode, either **Secure Gateway** or **Secure Gateway Proxy**, and then Click **Next**.

Figure 9.17 Secure Gateway Installation Path

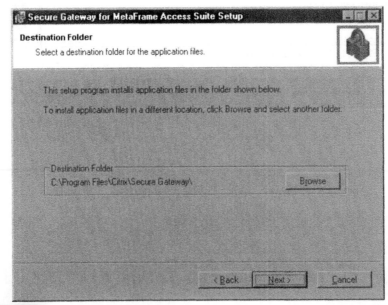

5. The Secure Gateway service is a small hard-disk footprint, consuming slightly more than 2MB. Choose the appropriate path and click **Next**.

Figure 9.18 Secure Gateway Service Account Configuration

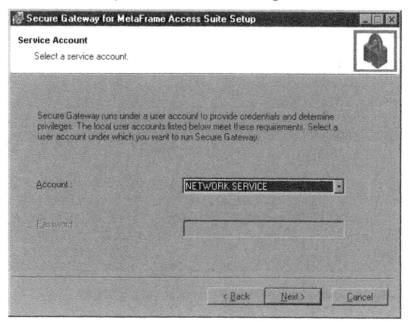

6. The Secure Gateway service runs under a user account to provide credentials and determine privileges. In most cases the **NETWORK SERVICE** account is sufficient. Choose a service account and click **Next**.

Figure 9.19 Secure Gateway Installation

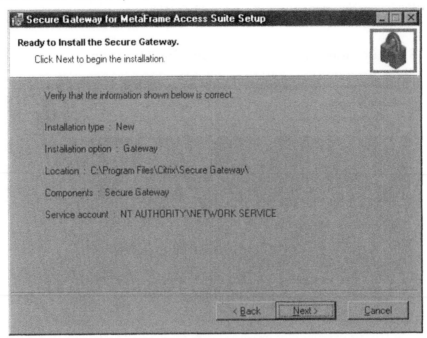

7. Verify that the installation information is correct and click **Next**.

Figure 9.20 Secure Gateway Installation Completion

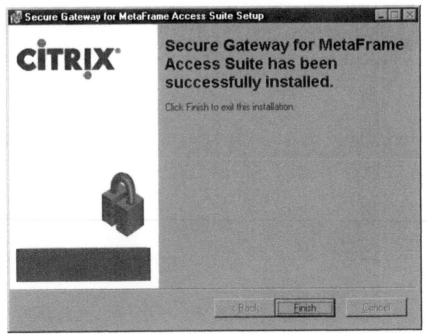

8. Click **Finish** to complete the installation.

Figure 9.21 Secure Gateway Configuration

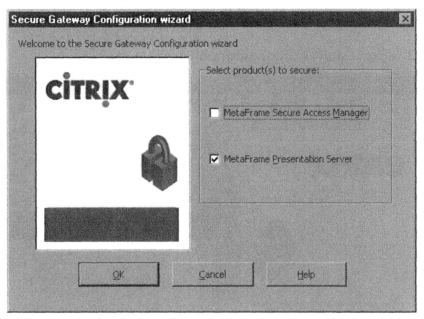

9. Immediately after the installation completes, the configuration wizard is launched. You will select the **MetaFrame Presentation Server** option and click **Next**.

Figure 9.22 Secure Gateway Configuration

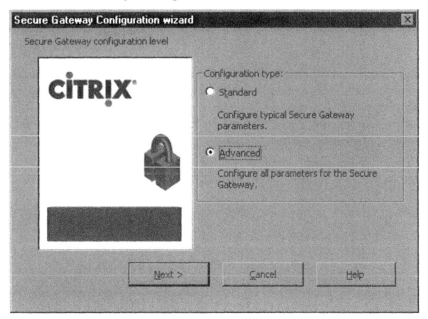

10.   As previously mentioned, this wizard can be cancelled and resumed at a later time (especially handy if building components while waiting on an SSL certificate). We can choose Standard or Advanced; for our purposes, we will choose **Advanced**, as we can see all the configuration options available to us with Secure Gateway. Select **Advanced** and click **Next**.

Figure 9.23 Secure Gateway Configuration Certificate Selection

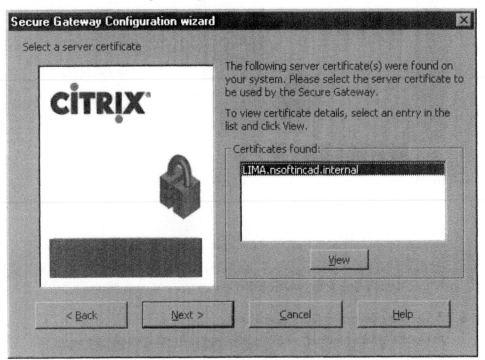

11.   At this point, we must select the server certificate that we added to the Secure Gateway server. If multiple certificates are available, take care to select the appropriate one and click **Next**. If there are no certificates listed, then none are added to the server on which you are attempting to install Secure Gateway. At least one certificate must be listed to continue with the configuration wizard.

Figure 9.24 Secure Gateway Configuration Protocol and Cipher Suite Selection

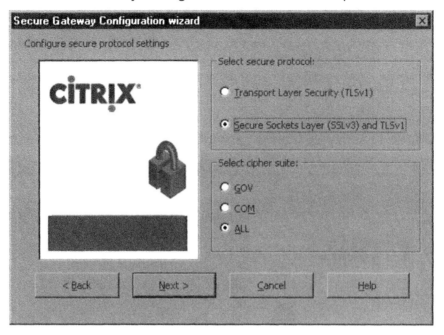

12. Select the protocol standard that you want to support based on your certificate and security needs. Most implementations will choose SSL and TLS. In addition, select the cipher suite to be used and click **Next**.

Figure 9.25 Secure Gateway Configuration Inbound Client Connections

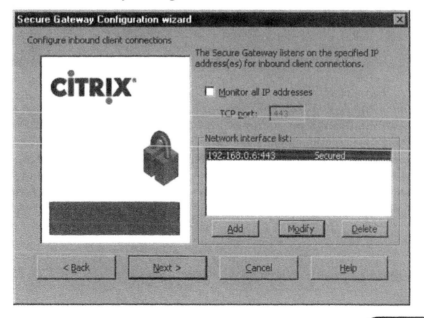

13.   The default behavior of the Secure Gateway is to monitor all IP addresses (thereby all network cards with an IP stack bound to them) for incoming connections. The default SSL-based port is 443. If your server performs roles other than Secure Gateway or has multiple network cards and you want to limit those that Secure Gateway monitors, remove the check for **Monitor all IP addresses** and configure the correct information in the **IP Interface and port list**. In most deployments, the defaults are correct so we will simply click **Next**.

Figure 9.26 Secure Gateway Configuration Outbound Connections Security

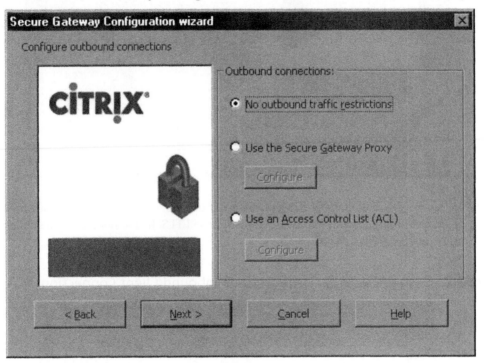

14.   In a simple single-hop DMZ and most typical implementations, we will choose **No outbound traffic restrictions**. However, if you have a double-hop DMZ, then you would specify the upstream Secure Gateway that is running in Proxy mode. Additionally, Secure Gateway has the capability to restrict which IP address, subnets, or networks from which to accept traffic; this would be configured with the **Use an access control list** option. Again, for most typical deployments, select **Default** and click **Next**.

NOTE

In a double-hop DMZ, ACLs can still be implemented, but they would be created on the upstream Secure Gateway server that is operating in Proxy mode.

Figure 9.27 Secure Gateway Configuration STA Information

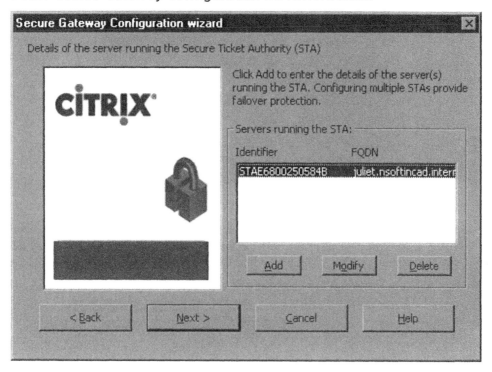

15.   In this window, we must list the STAs in the order in which the Secure Gateway is to contact them. To configure, click **Add**.

Figure 9.28 Secure Gateway Configuration Add STA Details

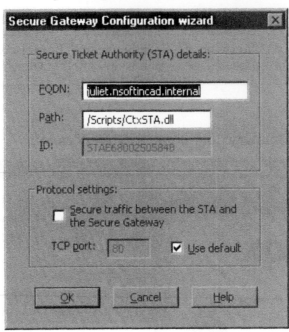

16. Specify the FQDN (such as Juliet.nsoftincad.internal), the path to the scripts directory and dll (the defaults are typically fine), and choose whether to communicate with the STA using HTTP or HTTPS (and the port number if different from the defaults). Click **OK**.

17. Once the STA is entered, the Identifier will be "queried" from the STA. You can add multiple STAs as previously mentioned, but they are contacted in the order in which they appear in the list. If the first in the list fails, it then goes to the second in the list, and so on. Confirm the configuration and click **Next**.

Figure 9.29 Secure Gateway Configuration Connection Parameters

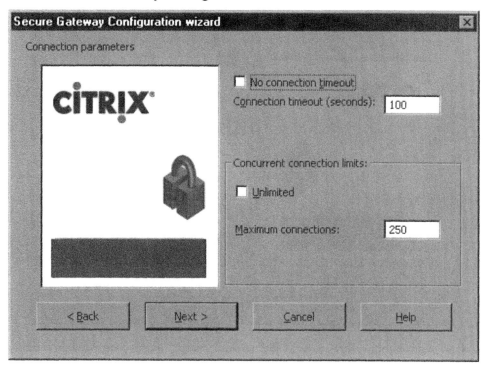

18.   The default connection parameters are typically fine. However, some environments want to change the **Connection limits** from Unlimited to some other number more suitable for the hardware in use. If Unlimited is unchecked, you can specify a **Maximum connections** and a **Connection resume**. The **Maximum connections** is just that, the value at which the server denies connections. The **Connection resume** should be about 10 percent below the maximum. The **Connection resume** is the value that the connection count must decrease to (once the maximum count has been reached) prior to new connections being accepted). Make your selections and click **Next**.

Figure 9.30 Secure Gateway Configuration Logging Exclusions

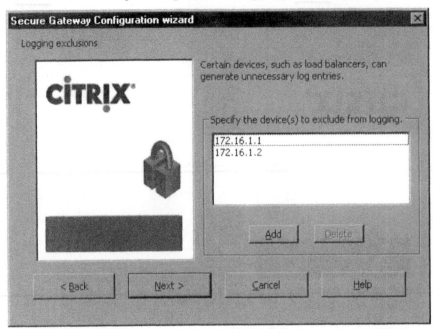

19. Logging exclusions allow us to ignore certain "chatty" devices that would otherwise generate a volume of useless entries in an otherwise usable log. Add those IP addresses to exclude and click **Next.**

Figure 9.31 Secure Gateway Configuration for Web Interface Server

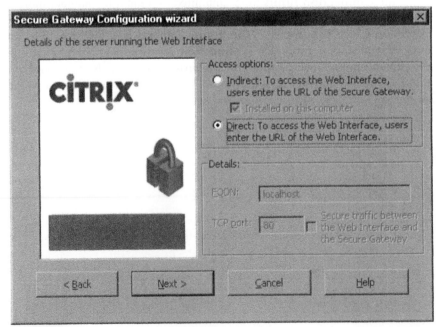

20.   All logging for Secure Gateway is written into the server's Application log in the Event Viewer tool and all events except informational ones are written. Set the value as you see fit and click **Next**.

Figure 9.32 Secure Gateway Configuration Logging Parameters

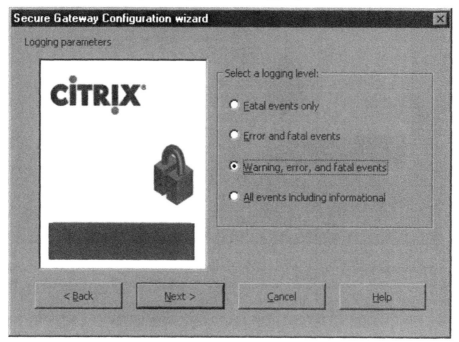

21.   If you install Web Interface on the same server as the Secure Gateway, choose **Installed on this computer**. Otherwise, choose **Installed on a different computer** and specify the server's name. If the Web Interface server also has a SSL server certificate, you may opt to secure the communications between the Secure Gateway server and the Web server using HTTPS. Specify your server's name and TCP port and click **Next**.

Figure 9.33 Secure Gateway Configuration Completion

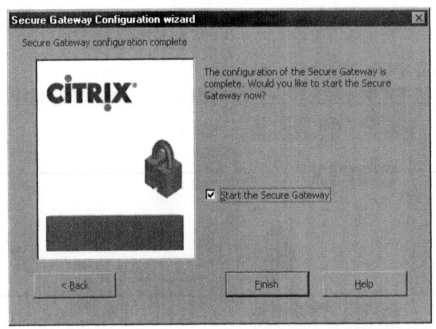

22. As previously stated, the initial install of Secure Gateway will require a reboot at the end of the configuration/installation. Subsequent reconfigurations will not require the reboot of the server, but will require the Secure Gateway service to restart, terminating all current connections. Upon completion of the service configuration wizard, click **Finish**.

Figure 9.34 Secure Gateway Hotfix Installation

23. After installation of the Secure Gateway Server software, you will want to apply the latest Secure Gateway hotfix that is available for download from the Citrix web site. The latest Secure Gateway hotfix is SGE300W008. Double-click on the SGE300W008.msi file to begin the installation.

24. Click **Next**, click **Finish**.

Figure 9.35 Secure Gateway Registry Modifications

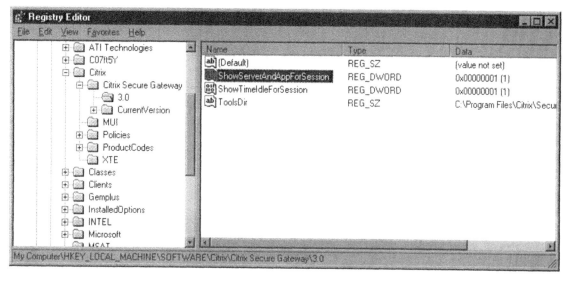

25. This hotfix allows you to show the server, resource, and time idle columns in the session information table. To configure these columns, edit the registry with the following values and then restart the Secure Gateway Management Console. When the specified registry values are set, the server, resource, and/or time idle columns are shown under session information. After installing the hotfix you will need to reboot the server.

Configuring & Implementing...

Updating the Registry for Hotfix SGE300W008

Here is the step-by-step procedure for updating the registry for this hotfix.

1. To show the server and resource columns in the session information, open the registry editor and navigate to HKEY_LOCAL_MACHINE\Software\ Citrix\Citrix Secure Gateway\3.0\

Continued

2. Right click in the right pane and select **New > DWORD** Value and enter **ShowServerAndAppForSession**. Double click the newly created entry and enter **1** for the value data.

3. Right click in the right pane and select **New > DWORD** Value and enter **ShowTimeIdleForSession**. Double click the newly created entry and enter **1** for the value data.

4. Restart the Secure Gateway Management Console.

After installation and configuration, Secure Gateway provides two tools for monitoring and maintaining the service. The first tool is the Secure Gateway Diagnostics. This tool, while very simple in function, can provide a wealth of information on configuration troubleshooting and issue resolution. By simply opening this tool, it will provide a detailed report of all components of the Secure Gateway service, including its capability to successfully communicate with other services, such as Web Interface. Additionally, the tool can generate reports that can be mailed to your support vendor or Citrix for further analysis and troubleshooting. Figure 9.36 demonstrates the tool.

Figure 9.36 Secure Gateway Diagnostics

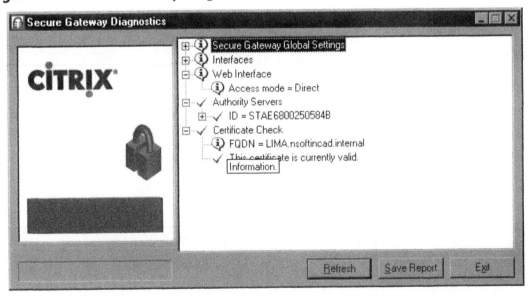

The second tool provided to manage and monitor the performance of the Secure Gateway is actually a preconfigured series of MMC snap-ins called the Secure Gateway Management Console (SGMC). The SGMC provides a single point of management and configuration for the entire function set of Secure Gateway. The SGMC contains reporting, logging, and performance analysis from a single seat. While configuration of this service occurs through the previously detailed Secure Gateway Service Configuration tool as demonstrated at the end of installation, the SGMC is primarily an information and troubleshooting tool. Figure 9.37 provides a glimpse of the features contained in this tool.

Figure 9.37 Secure Gateway Management Console

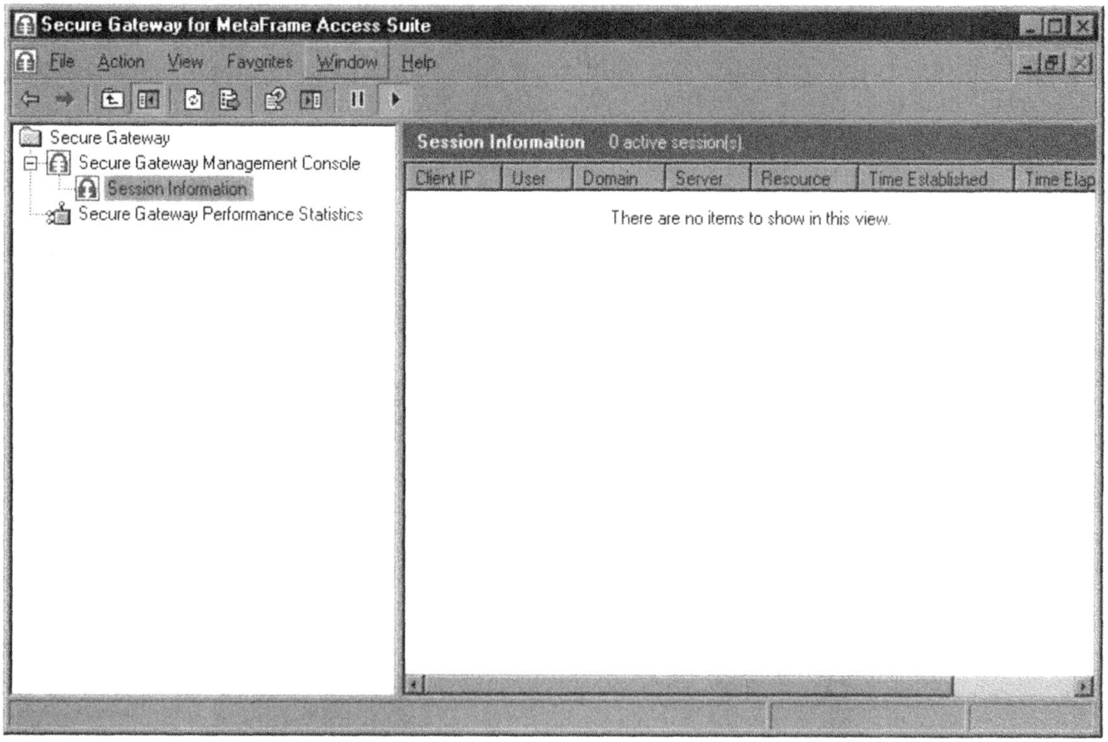

Web Interface Configuration to Allow for Secure Gateway Connections

The last step in configuring Secure Gateway and the various supporting components is to configure Web Interface to leverage our newly deployed Secure Gateway and STA. The Web Interface is a feature-rich product whose installation and configuration were covered elsewhere in this book. The information presented on Web Interface in this chapter is solely for the benefit of those who want to take advantage of the Secure Gateway services and need to gain the knowledge required to configure Web Interface for such integration.

We start by opening the **Access Management Console** on our Web Interface server and navigating to **Configuration Tools** folder and selecting **Web Interface**. Your already installed web interface site will be displayed. Click on the option **Manage Secure Client Access** and you will have four options:

- Edit DMZ Settings

- Edit Gateway Settings

- Edit Address Translations

- Display settings

From the Access Management console, we will be able to configure all the options necessary to integrate Web Interface into a newly deployed Secure Gateway solution. The first step is to edit the

DMZ settings and then select the access method as shown in Figure 9.38. You can configure client addresses, masks, and access methods using the Edit DMZ settings task. The order in which entries appear in the client address table is the order in which the rules are applied. If none of the rules are applicable, the default rule is applied. Click **Add** to add a new client route or **Edit** to edit an existing client route. Enter the network address and subnet mask that identify the client network.

Figure 9.38 Sample Secure Gateway Support Configuration for Web Interface

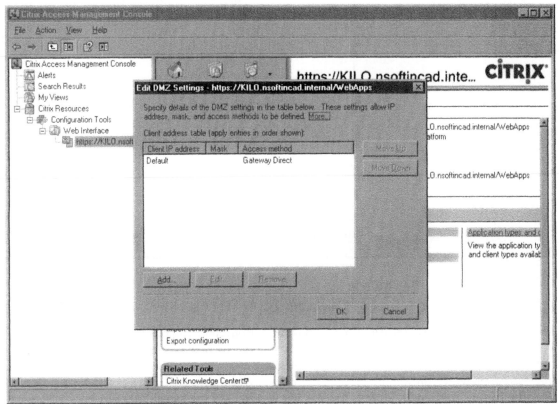

Select an access method from the following options:

- Select **Direct** if you want the actual address of the server to be given to the client. This is the default setting.

- Select **Alternate** if you want the alternate address of the server to be given to the client. The server must be configured with an alternate address and the firewall must be configured for network address translation.

- Select **Translated** if you want the address given to the client to be determined by the address translation mappings set in the Web Interface.

- Select **Gateway Direct** if you want the actual address of the server to be given to the gateway server.

- Select **Gateway Alternate** if you want the alternate address of the server to be given to the gateway server. The server running Presentation Server must be configured with an alternate address and the firewall must be configured for network address translation.

- Select **Gateway Translated** if you want the address given to the gateway server to be determined by the address translation mappings set in the Web Interface.

Click **OK** to save your settings.

Next, we must select Edit Gateway Settings as shown in Figure 9.39. We must enter the FQDN of our Secure Gateway server. The name entered should match the name on the server certificate used to install the Secure Gateway. The default port is 443 and should be correct unless you modified the port used by the Secure Gateway service. The next section requires us to enter the Secure Ticket Authority server information. Simply replace the **<SERVER>** section of the URL and click **Add**. Note that if you want to use SSL and have added an SSL server certificate to your STA, also change the protocol from **HTTP** to **HTTPS** before clicking **Add**. Your information should be similar to that shown in Figure 9.40.

Figure 9.39 Specific Address Translation Settings

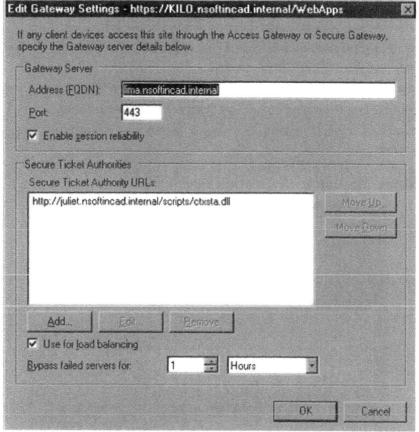

At this point, click **OK** at the bottom to save your changes.

Using the **Edit address translations** task, you can map the address of the server running XenApp Server to the address and port translated by the internal firewall, shown in Figure 9.40. Users can then launch applications through the Access Gateway or Secure Gateway if the address and port of the server are translated at the internal firewall.

You can use the Web Interface to define mappings from internal IP addresses to external IP addresses and ports. For example, if your server is not configured with an alternate address, you can configure the Web Interface to provide an alternate address to the client.

1. Click **Add** to add an address translation or **Edit** to edit an existing address translation.

2. In the **Access type** area, choose one of the following options:

   ■ If you want the client to use the translated address to connect to the server, select **Client route translation**.

   ■ If you want the gateway server to use the translated address to connect to the server, select **Gateway route translation**.

   ■ If you want both the client and the gateway server to use the translated address to connect to the server, select **Client and Gateway route translation.**

3. In the Internal IP address box, enter the normal (internal) IP address of the server.

4. In the **Internal port** box, enter the port number of the server.

5. In the **External address** box, enter the translated (external) IP address or host name that clients must use to connect to the server.

6. In the **External port** box, enter the port number of the server.

7. Click **OK**. The mapping appears in the **Address Translation Table**.

8. To remove a mapping, select the mapping in the **Address Translation Table** and click **Remove**.

Figure 9.40 Specific Address Translation Settings Map

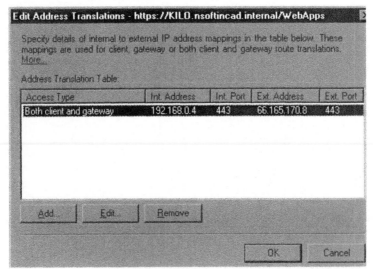

Summary

In this chapter, we examined the aspects of providing simple secure remote access to our Presentation server farm(s) leveraging various technologies. We explored the pros and cons to the various solutions and discussed the methods to implement most of these solutions.

We began with a thorough review of the bundled feature of encryption also known as Secure ICA. We explored the various ways of using Secure ICA from client-side settings to server-side. On the server side, we reviewed the options of connection settings, published applications, and Citrix policy to enforce the use of Secure ICA.

In the next section of the chapter, we briefly spoke of the Citrix Access Gateway and the features that it provides. Although the Access Gateway can replace the Citrix Secure Gateway many organizations still utilize the Citrix Secure Gateway to secure access for their remote users.

In the final section of this chapter, we reviewed the complete (and arguably complex) solution of Secure Gateway. We started with the planning, requirements, installation, and configuration of the Secure Ticket Authority (STA). We then planned for, installed, and configured the Secure Gateway itself, paying special attention to the areas that are typically stumbling blocks along the way. Finally, we configured the Web Interface to leverage our newly created Secure Gateway solution.

In conclusion, user communities and corporations demand a seamless, simple, and secure remote access solution for their remote offices, work-from-home users, and mobile workforce. The Citrix Access Suite—in particular, XenApp Server, Web Interface, and the Secure Gateway—can meet that requirement.

Solutions Fast Track

Methods of Remote Access

- ☑ The primary methods of securing remote access to XenApp include Secure ICA (ICA Encryption), Secure Socket Layer Relay (SSL Relay), virtual private networking (VPN), Citrix Secure Gateway (CSG), and Citrix Access Gateway or Citrix NetScaler.

- ☑ In the event Citrix XenApp servers are not located in a secure network environment, the use of the SSL Relay service will help to mitigate the security concern for unencrypted traffic.

- ☑ The Citrix Access Gateway is a hardened appliance deployed in an organization's DMZ that secures all traffic with standards-based SSL and TLS encryption. It serves as a complete replacement for Secure Gateway servers or traditional IPSec VPN devices.

Citrix Secure Gateway Components

- ☑ A properly implemented CSG solution will include the Secure Gateway, a Web Interface server, a XenApp server farm with published applications, and a XenApp server serving as a Secure Ticket Authority.

- ☑ After installation of the Secure Gateway Server software, you will want to apply the latest Secure Gateway hotfix that is available for download from the Citrix web site.

- ☑ Employing the use of IP Security policies and can provide greater security to your deployments by restricting access to defined ports.

Frequently Asked Questions

Q: I understand that Secure Gateway requires an SSL or TLS certificate. In an effort to save money, could I use my internal private certificate authority to generate the Secure Gateway's server certificate?

A: Yes. However, you must consider who the "customers" of this Secure Gateway will be. If you will be constructing the Secure Gateway as a remote access solution for your workforce and daily work use for the sales laptops you deploy to the field, then it can work well (as you can preinstall or add later the root certificate from your private CA). If, however, you are going to allow *any* device to connect, then distributing your internal private CA's root certificate may become a challenge.

Q: What tool is used for providing diagnostic and troubleshooting information regarding the Secure Gateway?

A: Secure Gateway Diagnostics Tool

Q: What tool is used for managing and monitoring the Secure Gateway?

A: Secure Gateway Management Console

Q: What hardware device provided by Citrix can replace the Secure Gateway?

A: Citrix Access Gateway

Chapter 10

Auditing and Security Incidents

Solutions in this chapter:

- **Introduction to Auditing**
- **Designing an Audit Policy**
- **Understanding Penetration Testing**
- **Understanding Vulnerability Assessments**
- **Creating an Incident Response Procedure**

- ☑ **Summary**
- ☑ **Solutions Fast Track**
- ☑ **Frequently Asked Questions**

Introduction

What is auditing? Auditing is an official examination and verification of information. Generally speaking, the best approach to auditing has been to find a middle ground in terms of effort and cost to meet the spirit of your organization's requirements, and then work with the auditor ahead of audit time to see how you've done. Generally, that approach reaps rewards that pay off in reduced "patching" of the effort. Obviously, meeting with the auditor before you start makes a lot of sense, but making certain the results meet with the auditor's approval is where your Return on Investment (ROI) will show up. If the auditor is happy, then the customer will be happy.

Introduction to Auditing

Whether it's your first on-site audit or your first vulnerability scan, it's pretty easy to fail an audit. And while this may not be the case for you, you should have a plan in place to deal with this if it happens. This may happen because you understood a requirement differently than what the auditor required, or it may be that you simply missed something. It's important to be prepared for this. As in all walks of life, whenever anything goes wrong we want to pass the buck. In this case, many times it's easy to pass the blame to the auditor. Having the right attitude came make all the difference. Generally, auditors are not going to be easy on you, because if they are too easy and don't correctly require companies to meet compliance to established standards, they can lose their auditing license.

In many organizations, the IT staff would like to put certain needed security measures in place but upper management says no because of cost. Remember, upper management's job is to help the company make money, not spend money. Even after you have done a careful cost-benefit analysis and have determined that the benefits outweigh the costs, upper management may still say no. A passed or failed audit (whether ongoing, external or internal) may be the perfect time to finally get them to say yes. If the auditor is requiring that you add something to come into compliance with a policy, you can use it as leverage with upper management to get that put in place. Again, submit a cost-benefit analysis, adding the cost of noncompliance to the total cost. Let them know that the auditor says you will not be compliant without that measure.

The Auditing Process

Security assessment and auditing can be thought of as incident prevention. Incidents are prevented by way of identification and remediation of vulnerabilities before they are exploited. By preventing even a single incident, you have effectively reduced the risk of a disruption or loss in confidentiality, integrity, and availability to your corporate assets. Depending on your business, these assets may not only *affect* the bottom line, they may *be* the bottom line.

The objective of an internal security audit is to evaluate the security of corporate hosts and networks. This evaluation will not only identify symptomatic security issues (vulnerabilities), but will also determine the systemic causes that led to those vulnerabilities (such as ineffective patch management). Organizations that effectively address both issues can effectively reduce current and future risk in their network environments.

Internal network security (also known as INS) is about identifying and addressing the vulnerabilities that have the greatest impact on your critical corporate assets. Remediation should be focused on a high return on investment. In most environments, the INS assessment-remediation lifecycle must be fast and cheap, but effective. We have already discussed steps such as asset inventory and prioritizing critical corporate assets, so what is the next step?

You need to take a hard look at the funds you have available to secure your internal network and make some documented decisions about the types of assessment that are right for you. My guess is that you will decide to break your network up into parts and assess each part differently. This will allow you to be comprehensive in your assessment of some, while only gathering the high-severity vulnerabilities from other networks.

Auditing Will Help You

When dealing with on-site auditors or approved scanning vendors, most people fit into one of three groups. Some people are intimated by auditors. They see them as someone with a lot of power, and they hope they will say and do the right things to get by. A second group seems to look at auditors as their enemy. They believe they must wrestle with the auditor and hopefully win in the end. The last set of people treat the auditor like a consultant they've brought in to help bring their company into compliance or as a second set of eyes on their network security posture. They respect the auditor's opinions and keep the auditor in the loop as they work out solutions. This last group will get the most out of their auditor and will have the best overall experience and be able to improve the overall security posture of their company with the least amount of hassle.

As hard as it might be to believe, auditors are there to help you. It's important to know how to work well with auditors so that your audit will go smoothly and efficiently, and ensure that you get your money's worth. A good auditor will go over your company's systems, practices, and policies with a fine-toothed comb, and tell you what you can do to improve your security. Hopefully, your primary goal is to have your company become more secure. When you realize that auditors provide you with a valuable service and that you're both on the same team working towards a common goal, you will have the right attitude.

Remember that auditors have moral and professional obligations to follow the guidelines and procedures they've been given for the audit. It is not appropriate to ask them to compromise those obligations. Auditors are trained and likely have performed many audits, and they can give you great advice on what you can do to bring yourself into compliance.

When you have the right attitude you will find ways to use your auditor to improve the security of your company. Seasoned auditors have a wealth of knowledge and can be a huge benefit to you to leverage it when bridging gaps in compliance.

They have seen many technologies, policies, and practices others have put into place to mitigate risks, and should be able to give you choices to help you meet requirements that work best for your situation. For example, if cost is your main concern, an auditor may know of a low cost or open source tool that you can use to help you comply with certain requirements. On the other hand if time is more important, the auditor may know of a solution that is quick to set up that will improve your security posture. As you work on your remediation, it's important to keep your auditor in the loop. This way he can give opinions on what you've chosen to do and can give further advice. It will also likely make your next audit much easier for both parties involved.

Why Is Auditing Important?

Auditing and Security policies are usually seen as a necessary compliance with some higher power, not as a necessity of function in a network operation. They are often overlooked and undervalued until they are really needed. We can create secure networks, write secure code, and build reliable, survivable systems with current technology today. If configured properly, using the principles outlined in this book, we can accomplish our goals. However, we still come down to the fundamental flaw with securing our networks: people.

People, unlike computers, don't follow instructions exactly as told. They have choices, and their choices can put cracks in the security walls. These cracks can be a personal dual-homed box connected to the outside, bypassing the firewall; they can be an insecure password that's easy to remember; or they can be a lazy system administrator that leaves ex-employee credentials in the authentication database. A properly implemented auditing and scanning policy can help prevent issues like this.

Identifying Threats to Internal Network Security

Most organizations have hardened network perimeters to lock out the bad guys. These strong walls provide a sense of security for the kingdom and allow trade and commerce to flourish—but it may be a false sense of security, for what measures have been deployed to protect the crown jewels from those *already inside* those walls?

Findings released by the FBI and the Computer Security Institute show that internal attacks account for a large percentage of security breaches that organizations experience, suggesting that internal security still needs to become more of a priority for security managers.

For example, worms have taken the probability of an unlikely and quasi-theoretical event like internal exploitation to the next level. If you take that threat, mix it with the value of your corporate assets, and add a dash of vulnerability, you have a recipe for disaster. There is no predictability to this madness; you must take fundamental security actions that will increase your overall security immediately. If your network is an Internet participant, you can't honestly say that the widespread, high-severity vulnerabilities living in your internal network are mitigated by limited exposure and threat.

To put things in perspective: The variance between the security of an Internet-facing network and an internal network is unnerving. In some cases, you could describe the security level of one by describing the inverse of the other. Although great effort is exerted maintaining the patch levels of Internet-facing devices, internal systems hosting far more sensitive data than a corporate Web server are frequently left several patch levels behind.

Have you considered the damage that could be done by disgruntled employees, contractors, building security guards, cleaning staff, or uninvited visitors connecting via an unsecured wireless access point? These potential attackers have immediate access to your networks and facilities, in fact they *require* this access in order to perform their jobs. These attackers are likely to have knowledge that would be unknown to an external attacker, such as the location of intellectual property or which systems would cripple the organization if damaged.

In today's computing environment, internal network security is now a requirement. Organizations must continuously examine both Internet-facing *and* private internal networks.

Internal Network Security Assessment Methodology

Assessing your internal network does not mean attempting to identify and remediate *all* vulnerabilities in your network. The sheer number of systems on your internal network, multiplied by an astronomical rate of network changes sets up this strategy for failure. And because securing every host on the internal network may not be plausible for most organizations, a number of departments within every company can be determined to deserve special attention. For varying reasons, these departments host data that could pose significant risk to the welfare of the organization as a whole. Assessing your internal network will require you to make difficult decisions about what to secure based on your available resources. You will need to secure the right assets, from the right risks, with the right measures.

Standardization and SAS70

The Statement on Auditing Standards (SAS) No. 70, Service Organizations, is a tool available to auditing firms and CPAs to conduct an audit of a company that already has implemented an information security program. The SAS70 does not contain a checklist of security controls, but rather allows an auditing firm to issue a statement of how well a company is adhering to their stated information security policy. The report issued can be of type I or type II: A type I includes the auditor's report and controls, and type II includes testing and verification of the security controls over a time of six months or more.

There has been some controversy over the applicability of the SAS70 to conduct a security review. Namely, it does not contain a checklist of recommended security controls, and verifies only that stated security controls are followed. If a corporation's information security program has omitted particular controls, as I have seen done with several clients, and I have mentioned previously, this is not noted in the SAS70 report. Because the audit is conducted by auditors who do not necessarily have an information security background, they may miss important gaps in the policy.

If you have already implemented a security policy based on a standard, such as the ISO17799, the SAS70 may give your information security program additional credibility. Having more accreditation groups stating that your program gets a "pass" grade doesn't necessarily mean you have a more secure program. However, it can help to make customers happy or meet federal or insurance requirements. Remember that the SAS70 is not appropriate for use as a checklist to create an information security policy.

Designing an Auditing Policy

When an architect or engineer goes about designing a computer environment, he or she will be aware of basic components in the form of capabilities that enable functionality at the various layers of the network. These are the things that make Internetworking of computer platforms possible across hubs and switches and routers. These are also the things that make monitoring of these networked components reliable. It is reliability that makes for a well-constructed monitoring solution that will stand the test of an audit, and survive scrutiny in a courtroom (should that necessity arise).

Any successful operating environment is designed from the ground up, or, in the case of a networking infrastructure and applications space, from the wires on up. It's important, therefore, to plan your auditing of your operating environment the same way you designed it.

Process for Planning an Audit Policy

One of the first components of an audit strategy is setting a logging level. A good audit and logging strategy is important to the proper maintenance of your network and the systems that are used on it. Before we get more deeply into defining your audit strategy, we need to deal with the logging question.

Just what you want to log will be one of the most important questions you'll ask yourself. Defining an extensive logging and auditing strategy will lower the performance of your server and of your network. Doing too little logging and auditing will leave you without the information you need to determine the source and cause of problems that arise. Your best option regarding logging is to log only those options you really need. Then, when you don't need a particular type of log data anymore, stop recording it.

Auditing of Active Directory Access

In some cases it is important to see who accesses Active Directory data. It is possible to log authorized and unauthorized access to Active Directory data. The audit records can be browsed in the Event viewer on the domain controller machines.

Auditing of Active Directory access is turned on by modifying Default Domain Controller Policy. You need to open the Active Directory Users And Computers tool, then choose **View | Advanced Features | Domain Controllers node | Properties**. Select the **Group Policy** tab. You should see the window shown in Figure 10.1.

Figure 10.1 Locating a Default Domain Controller's Policy

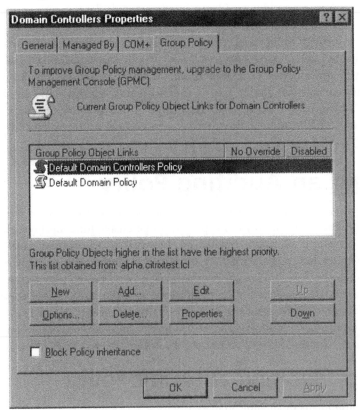

Click on the **Default Domain Controllers Policy** and select **Edit**. You will see a MMC console window with this policy open for editing. Expand the following nodes there: **Computer Configuration| Windows Settings | Security Settings| Local Policies | Audit Policy** (see Figure 10.2).

Figure 10.2 Audit Settings

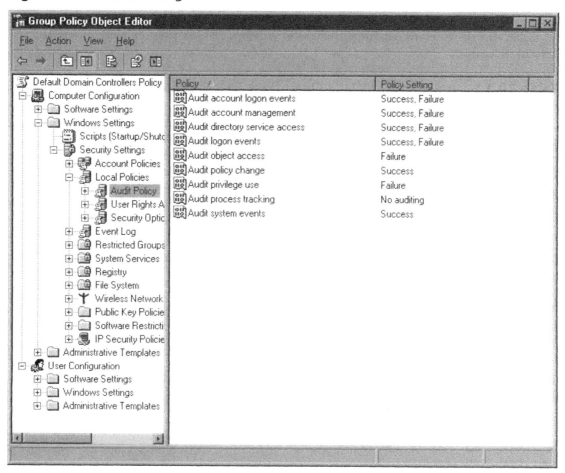

There are several entries under this branch of policy settings. We are interested in the *Audit directory services access* entry. If you double-click on this setting, you will be presented with a panel with check boxes that allow you to select **Audit Successful Attempts** or **Audit Failed Attempts** or both. Auditing of successful directory access events tends to produce a lot of information, so use this setting with care.

When you change the settings in a policy, these changes do not take place immediately. Domain controllers check for changes in their policies each five minutes, so this policy will become active on the domain controller at about this time. Other domain controllers will receive policy changes via replication later, depending on replication period settings.

Filtering of Active Directory-Related Traffic

One very important method of network services protection is using firewalls. MS Windows often uses many services and TCP/UDP ports for performing each operation—the logon process, for example, requires usage of four to seven ports. It is important to know which ports are used in each particular case, in order to configure firewalling correctly. Too often it happens that when domain controllers are separated by a traffic filtering device, administrators simply permit all traffic between them. This, of course, opens an extra hole for attacks.

Table 10.1 shows several standard operations in Windows 2003 that require usage of specific network services.

Table 10.1 Several Standard W2K3 Operations That Require Specific Network Services

Windows Operation	Network Service Required
Login and authentication (user or computer) Kerberos authentication (88/tcp, 88/udp)	Direct Host (445/tcp, 445/udp)
LDAP ping (389/udp)	
DNS (53/tcp, 53/udp)	
Establishing explicit trust between domains Kerberos authentication (88/tcp, 88/udp)	Direct Host (445/tcp, 445/udp)
LDAP ping (389/udp)	
LDAP (389/tcp or 686/tcp if using Secure Sockets Layer [SSL])	
DNS (53/tcp, 53/udp)	
Trust validation and authentication Kerberos authentication (88/tcp, 88/udp)	Direct Host (445/tcp, 445/udp)
LDAP ping (389/udp)	
LDAP (389/tcp or 686/tcp if using SSL)	
DNS (53/tcp, 53/udp)	
Netlogon (135/tcp plus other various ports, see below)	
Access file resource	Direct Host (445/tcp, 445/udp)
DNS traffic (e.g. locating a domain controller)	DNS (53/tcp, 53/udp)
Active Directory replication	Directory services RPC (various ports, see below)
Kerberos authentication (88/tcp, 88/udp)	

Continued

Table 10.1 Continued. Several Standard W2K3 Operations That Require Specific Network Services

Windows Operation	Network Service Required
LDAP ping (389/udp)	
LDAP (389/tcp or 686/tcp if using SSL)	
DNS (53/tcp, 53/udp)	
Direct Host (445/tcp, 445/udp)	

Netlogon service is provided via RPC portmapper on port 135/tcp. The range of dynamic RPC ports assigned by a particular machine can be limited manually by editing the system registry. Microsoft recommends that ports range starts above 5000 and consists of at least 20 ports. The key in the registry that needs to be changed is the following:

```
HKEY_LOCAL_MACHINE\SOFTWARE\Microsoft\Rpc\Internet
```

You need to add a new value:

```
"Ports"=REG_MULTI_SZ:5000-5030
```

This setting makes RPC services use only ports in the range 5000–5030. The machine needs to be rebooted after these changes have been made.

Directory services RPC ports used in the replication process can be set separately from the described range. The setting in the registry is located under the following:

```
HKEY_LOCAL_MACHINE\SYSTEM\CurrentControlSet\Services\NTDS\Parameters
```

You need to set a value:

```
"TCP/IP Port"=dword:0000c000
```

This hexadecimal number sets a fixed port (decimal 49152, this equals the number c000 in hex), which will be used by DS replication traffic.

What Time Is It?

During early development of computer networks, scientists discovered quickly that all systems had to have a common point of reference to develop context for the data they were handling. The context was obviously a reliable source of time, since computer systems have no human capacity for cognitive reconstruction or memory. The same holds true today for monitoring systems. We would all look a bit foolish troubleshooting three-week-old hardware failures, so hardware monitoring had it right from day one. It seems fairly straightforward that time and security event monitoring would go hand in hand.

Your source for time in your environment should be configured for acquiring time from specific, known and trusted time sources. Good monitoring systems (event management, network intrusion prevention) and forensic investigation tools rely on time. System time is frequently found to be arbitrary in a home or small office network. It's whatever time your server was set at, or if you designed your network for some level of reliance, you're systems are configured to obtain time synchronization from a reliable source, like the Naval Observatory Network Time Protocol (NTP) servers (see http://tycho.usno.navy.mil/ntp.html).

Subsequent network services on which your environment would rely include Domain Name System (DNS), directory services (such as Sun's or Microsoft's), and Simple Mail Transfer Protocol (SMTP) (e-mail). Each of these in turn rely on what are referred to as "time sources." Stratum 1 time sources are those devices acquiring time data from direct sources like the atomic clocks run by various government entities or Global Positioning System (GPS) satellites. Local hardware, in fact, is considered Stratum 1; it gets time from its own CMOS. Stratum 2 gets their time from Stratum 1, and so on. For most purposes, Stratum 2 is typically sufficient to "prove" time, as long as all systems in the environment synchronize their clocks with the Stratum 2 source.

The next area of concern is time synchronization. So what's the big deal, right? Event Management. That's the big deal. Here's the rub: What is your source for accurate time? How do you ensure that all your platforms have that same reference point so the event that occurred at 12:13 P.M. GMT is read by your event management systems as having occurred at 12:13 P.M. GMT instead of 12:13 A.M.?

There are two facets to the approach. One is to make sure you have a certified source of time into your environment (see: http://tf.nist.gov/ for a list of stratum 1 sources of time). Second is to make sure you have the means to reliably replicate time data across your network. Stratum 2, as mentioned, is an acceptable source for your monitoring environment, and that data can be acquired via the Internet from the National Institute of Standards & Technology (NIST) sources as described in the text. By using a durable directory service, the time data can be advertised to all systems, assuring no worse than a 20-second skew. In an Active Directory forest, for example, the Primary Domain Controller (PDC) emulator serves as a Stratum 2 source. Servers in the forest operating the parameters of W32Time service (based on Simple Network Time Protocol [SNTP]) adhering to RFC 2030, can therefore provide adequate time synchronization to within 20 seconds of all other servers in the AD forest.

Identity Management

One might suppose that the basics of any infrastructure mandate a good identity management solution—in the case of XenApp it is typically Microsoft Active Directory. Identity management solutions can be configured to have multiple roles per identity and multiple identities per user. It's important, therefore, to sort out how you need your solution to behave in the context of environment.

Roles-based identity has never been more difficult; therefore, many different industry and government regulations and standards call for them. Separation of duties is a concept that pervades throughout every business. Choosing the directory solution has everything to do with which platforms will operate in your environment. Either train or hire strong engineering and architectural staff to make sure this solution is deployed without a hitch. This text is not a discourse on identity solutions, but this is a worthwhile point.

With an Active Directory domain, you need to apply appropriate security settings to your directory. Security settings should be configured to basically track all access to systems in your directory domain. That is a good reason for having a dedicated domain in the first place; here, there are no safe systems and no assumptions of innocence. All access is tracked for audit. The system logs are sent to the event management solution immediately for correlation and archival. No opportunity for alteration must exist!

Establish the roles within the monitoring environment. There are really only two: system administrators and security log administrators. That's it. No one else should set foot (or network interface card [NIC]) in that environment. Make sure the system administrators are not the same individuals that manage your logging and auditing if you can help it. Each userid that is associated with logging and auditing must themselves be audited in much the same manner as within your user environment. Log each access. Each identity associated with your log monitoring environment must have a person attached to it. No guest IDs, no test IDs.

Event Management Storage

The amount of data a business deals with in this space can easily reach into the terabytes. Good thing disk space is so cheap! (Relatively speaking, of course, tools that handle and correlate this data might not be so cheap.) Logs add up quickly when you consider your sources:

- Firewalls

- Switches

- Servers

- Applications

- Databases

- IDS

- Other security software such as antivirus

Using storage area network (SAN) technology is the best way to go in terms of storage. You might consider a direct access storage device (DASD) connected to the various servers that handle log transfer, but what if you're dealing with appliance-based solutions? What if you're dealing with a combination?

SAN is really the best way to go for a hybrid-based solution (i.e., appliance and server based). You need this data in a reliable, separate architecture where it can exist for a long time (up to a year) and can be recalled on short notice (such as after a security incident).

Where all of this data will live is a bit different from where it will be stored. Storage can be connected to the appliances and servers via fiber channel either directly to a fiber channel (FC) card, or over the Internet Protocol (IP) network (see Figure 10.3). Accessing that data, therefore, can be different. The storage of the old data is not relevant to dashboards and alerting systems, but is more relevant to audits. The live or current data, therefore, may be stored closer to the correlation systems than the archive data.

Figure 10.3 Connecting Storage Devices

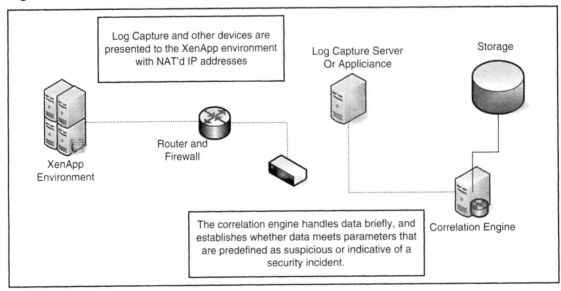

The enormous amount of data you will deal with in the course of logging and monitoring your environment means you must keep abreast of your available storage space and fabric capacity. As mentioned earlier, storage disk may be cheap, but acquiring EMC or other brands of SAN devices can be costly. Forecast your needs and have good capacity planning processes in hand!

As far as handling and then alerting on this data, you will need to select from a small population of security event/incident vendor technologies that automate this daunting task. The number of requirements you use during the selection process is significant.

Does the vendor support all your operating systems? Applications? Security tools? Develop your list of requirements, then start shopping. Deploying a security event management solution is critical to your success.

TIP

Don't be fooled by every magazine you pick up from the shelf at the book store. Selecting a good storage solution is a huge undertaking, because the costs can be high if you choose poorly. Refer to reports by groups such as Gartner (www.gartner.com) or Forrester (www.forrester.com) to understand where the market for such technologies are headed, which company has the best management tools, and which company is most viable. Nothing hurts an IT investment more than hanging your hat on a company that goes bankrupt six months after you signed the purchase order.

Determining What You Need to Monitor

Knowing what you are monitoring is half the battle in planning your storage needs as well as successfully deploying an auditable XenApp solution. Any well-intentioned system administrator can tell you the basic equations to develop the amount of storage needed for a firewall or a Network Intrusion Detection System (NIDS) device. It cannot be stressed enough, however, that trapping all that is logable is not the point. To do so would be counterproductive. The protection of your data and network is paramount, and therefore should be the focus of all logging activity.

Focus your monitoring on the files that perform transactions or serve as libraries to your SOAP, XML, or ActiveX transaction applications. Alterations in these files serve as ingress points for additional misbehavior. The obvious point here is that if the file is altered, someone with ill intent is already accessing your network.

In addition, look into your OS' critical files. Monitor and alert on odd behaviors. All the industry leading solutions in this space offer preconfigured solutions specific to varieties of software and operating systems. You should use these preconfigured packages to best protect your systems. However, applications that have been developed by small coding houses, or those you've written yourself, will need customization in order to be monitored. In this circumstance, your vendor must be willing to work with you to extend their technology to cover your gaps.

Again, if the vendor will not or cannot support your needs, take your business elsewhere!

Applications Services

It's best to break up the task of monitoring and logging into two less daunting components.

Best because the activity you are performing had best not interfere with the primary job of the components you're monitoring, which is providing services to customers.

Monitoring tools are meant to be unobtrusive, exhibiting a small resource footprint on their hosts and networks; if you overwhelm either, card transactions can be impacted. This would obviously be an undesirable situation that can create significant financial burdens and sudden career changes.

In this respect, we have grouped the "Application Services" of data storage and access. These systems are the honey of the hive, and are the point of aspiring to security compliance. This is our primary goal as well as that of any hacker looking for some data of return value.

Data Storage Points

Storage of user data may be a necessary evil in your environment. During the course of business, data transactions need to be quick and productive.

The storage points must be protected by a number of solutions, and typically are hosted on servers of some sort. Intrusion detection (such as TripWire), intrusion prevention, antivirus, and system logs are all sources of auditable data that must be captured and transmitted to your security event management solution.

Data Access Points

So, you have user data inbound and outbound via a XenApp solution, some is being stored, some is being sent on to an external source, some is being sent back to an internal system in the form of acknowledgements, approvals, and so on. How do you know that only your systems are able to see that data? How do you know that no other entity is intercepting or otherwise recording these data streams?

To make certain no hackers have gained access to these "supply chain" systems, the access of the systems is logged, best done via system logging (e.g., Windows-family servers event logging). Microsoft has published a paper regarding logging of privileged access, which can be found at http:// support.microsoft.com/kb/814595. Active Directory is an infrastructure component, and is frequently leveraged to grant access to applications resident on Windows Server hosts. As such, the access to the host is logged as well as access to the application.

Application logs can also be acquired using technology tailored to the task. Tools such as CA's Unicenter WSDM (for Windows platforms) and Oracle's WS-Security can be configured to acquire logs, then transfer them to your security event management solution.

Here, the point will be repeated; the logs will be moved to the event management solution for archival; no opportunity for alteration exists!

Infrastructure Components

The Infrastructure is the carrier and handler of user data. Operating systems and the management tools that support them do not care nor do they understand the content of the data streams that are occurring around them. Therefore, the code that runs on these components is necessarily low-level. We don't anticipate a Microsoft MOM agent to understand a Simple Object Access Protocol (SOAP) transaction, only its impact on central processing unit (CPU) and memory input/output (I/O).

Because of this, it is a safe assumption to make that this area is at least as important, if not more so, to watch with strong monitoring and alerting systems. It's also easier to overdo the solution, and impact the mission-critical services above. No matter how mission critical and infrastructure components are viewed, the care and feeding of one must not overwhelm the functionality of the other.

Infrastructure, by not having a good sense of what's happening at the applications layer, is an ideal place for a hacker to set up camp and search for good data of the sellable sort. A hijacked operating system or worse, a sniffer planted on the network by an insider, is a sure means of gathering such data.

Host Operating Systems (aka Servers)

The host operating system is probably the trickiest bit of the puzzle. Too many people have access to it, no matter how far you lock it down. There are system administrators, security administrators, and of course backup/restore folks. Each of these roles need to have a level of access, however, at no point should these folks be able to alter the system logs.

This is where Security Information Management (SIM) becomes quite handy in the area of system lockdown. When configuring the host, install a SNARE agent on it. Configure the agent to send the host system logs to your log collector. Also, configure the host to not retain logs for longer than 48 hours locally.

By configuring the host in this fashion, you have some local log data that is valuable to your administrators for technical reasons, but you've also moved the log data to a remote location. You've made it impossible for a hacker to cover his tracks.

A very important point: don't just move the logs then deleted them locally. Your system administrators and other support staff need these logs as well.

Network Objects

Wired and wireless. Routers, switches, hubs. Firewalls. Each of these components provide for intercommunication between and within networks. Each also generates logs of various levels of detail and size. Configure these platforms to send logs to your SIM solution.

Usually, you're not going to be able to load software on a supervisor card to route traffic logs; that's not how it works. You need skilled networking people to configure your infrastructure to send SNMP 2.0-compliant data to your SIM solution. The SIM will handle what it can in terms of load. This is where significant planning of your SIM solution comes into play.

The SIM itself must be very scalable if you're dealing with a large network with many subnets or bridged environments. The traffic is valuable to the correlation activities, so you want to capture as much of it as you can. That means you need a log collector proximate to your heaviest log-generating locations. Typically, a nexus of your network activities.

Integrity Monitoring

Tools like TripWire (www.tripwire.com) serve to monitor the Message Digest 5 (MD5) hash or checksum of the system files on your application or host. If alterations are made to these files, a good file integrity solution will detect and alert you to the issue.

To really make the best use of a configuration assurance tool, however, you will need to implement (assuming you have not already) a decent change management or configuration management database. You will also need solid processes around its use. An organization that is ISO-17799 compliant will typically have this sort of solution in hand already. Compliance can be a good thing! Solutions from NetIQ (www.netiq.com) can help in this area.

Common Auditing Tools and Sources

The simple statement "monitor everything" might be a wish in the dark for security professionals. After all, monitoring it all costs much more than the business might be bringing in the door. The cash margins still take precedent, but the balance of security cost versus loss of prestige and associated business must be weighed. Within that balance, establish what budget can be assigned to monitoring, then figure out "What will hurt my business if it is compromised?"

Security Information Management

A SIM solution at its heart is nothing more or less than a log collector and its correlation engine. The log collector's role is to acquire the log, normalize it (that is, translate the log data into the schema used by the vendor), then pass it on to the correlation engine.

The correlation engine uses rules, signatures (though not always), and sophisticated logic to deduce patterns and intent from the traffic it sees originating at the host operating system (OS) and network layers. Well-designed SIM technologies try to distribute much of the "heavy lifting" in terms of moving data, but the actual analysis of that data must be centralized in some form.

A SIM solution must be scalable! In other words, wherever your business has data, you should have some central point where a log collector is going to have a reasonable chance of receiving your logs, then passing them on. If you have an important subsidiary that handles significant volumes of data, you don't want your log collector at a remote office. You need to have it near where the data flows and where it is stored.

Security Event Alerting

When a correlation engine has determined that something is amiss (see "Are you 0wned?"), it will attempt to alert your security team in whatever fashion you configured. Typically, this alert is via e-mail or pager, though some folks use Windows popup messenger, a Web-based broadcast message, a ticket sent to a response center, or even a direct phone call from the alerting system.

Whichever means you decide on, make sure you do not use just one part of your infrastructure to deliver that message. If your business uses Voice-over-IP (VoIP) for phone services, a well-crafted network attack could disable your phone services. If an e-mail solution is disrupted by a spam attack or a highly virulent e-mail worm, you might not be able to receive the data from your SIM solution.

Make certain you use two separate forms of communication to send alerts from your SIM to your security team.

Are You Owned?

Getting Tipped Off That You Have a BOT on the Loose

When intrusion detection systems (IDSes) are configured correctly, your security team has spent time understanding which systems are expected to send data and initiate communications, and in what fashion. For instance, a Web server is not expected to initiate port 80 communications if it is configured to only support Secure Sockets Layer (SSL) communications for the purpose of completing online purchase transactions.

Similarly, the Web server is not expected to initiate communications to a foreign IP address using a port that supports I Seek You (ICQ) traffic. When IDS is configured correctly, your solution will detect such anomalies and alert you to their existence.

Understanding System and Network Logs

System and network logs are often called the "untapped riches." The now-famous humorous security calendar proclaims "Logs: Let'em Rot." Others just quietly choose to follow this maxim and ignore logs—at their own peril—altogether. On the other hand, as computer and Internet technology continues to spread and computers start playing an even more important role in our lives, the records that they produce, a.k.a. logs, start to play a bigger role. From firewalls and x to databases and enterprise applications, to wireless access points and Voice over Internet Protocol (VoIP) gateways, logs are being spewed forth at an ever-increasing pace.

Both security and other Information Technology (IT) components not only increase in numbers, but also often come with more logging enabled out of the box. An example of this trend includes Linux systems and Web servers that now ship with increased levels of logging. All those systems, both legacy and modern, are known to generate copious amounts of logs, audit trails, records, and alerts, that beg for constant attention. But this is easier said than done.

Immense volumes of log data are being generated on many corporate networks, necessitating more efficient ways of managing, storing, and searching through log data, both reactively—after a suspected incident—and proactively—in search of potential risks. For example, a typical retailer generates hundreds of thousands of log messages per day amounting to many terabytes per year. An online merchant can generate upwards of 500,000 log messages every day. One of America's largest retailers has more than 60 terabytes of log data on their systems at any given time. Unlike other companies, retailers often do not have the option of not using logging. With such vast amounts of log data available, a compromise between what is needed and what is unnecessary must be made in order to productively use logging information. Table 10.2 contains a sample list of technologies that produce logs. Though this list is not comprehensive, it is likely that you will find at least one system that you have in your environment and for which logs are not being collected, much less looked at.

Table 10.2 Log-Producing Technologies

Type	Example
Operating Systems	Linux, Solaris, Windows
Databases	Oracle, SQL Server, IBM DB2
Network Infrastructure	Cisco routers and switches, NetScaler, Access Gateway
Remote Access	IPSec, VPNs, SSL
Network Security	Checkpoint Firewall, Cisco PIX Firewall
Intrusion Detection	SNORT NIDS, ISS RealSecure
Enterprise Applications	SAP, PeopleSoft
Web Servers	Apache, IIS
Proxy Servers	BlueCoat, Squid, ISA
Email Servers	SendMail, Exchange
DNS Servers	MS DNS, Bind
Antivirus	Symantec, McAfee, TrendMicro
Physical Access Control	IDenticard, CoreStreet
Wireless Networking	Cisco Aironet AP, NetGear AP

NOTE

Table 10.2 is not a full list; everybody will have some esoteric and not so esoteric applications and devices that produce logs that are not covered in this table. In any case, if these devices are included in your XenApp environment, it is likely that these device logs will need to be collected, stored, and analyzed to satisfy your internal requirements as well as any externally mandated regulations.

Many companies and government agencies are trying to set up repeatable log collection, centralization, and analysis processes and tools. Despite the multitude of log sources and types, people typically start from network and firewall logs and then progress upward on the protocol stack as well as sideways towards other non-network applications.

For example, just about any firewall or network administrator will look at a simple summary of connections that his Private Internet Exchange (PIX) or Checkpoint is logging. Many firewalls log in standard syslog format and such logs are easy to collect and review. Reviewing network Intrusion etection System (IDS) logs (for those companies that chose to deploy this technology), while "interesting" in case of an incident, is often a very frustrating task since Network Intrusion Detection Systems (NIDSes) would sometimes produce "false alarms" and dutifully log them. Still, NIDS log analysis, at least the post-mortem kind for investigative purposes, often happens right after firewalls when organizations deploy their log management infrastructure for compliance, security, or operational uses since the value of such info for security is undeniable and logs can, in most cases, be easily centralized for analysis. Even though system administrators always knew to look at logs in case of problems, massive server operating system (both Windows and UNIX/Linux variants) log analysis didn't materialize until more recently. Collecting logs from Windows servers, for example, was hindered by the lack of agentless log collection tools, such as LASSO, that only emerged in the last year or two. On the other hand, UNIX server log analysis was severely undercut by a total lack of unified format for log content in syslog records.

Web server logs were long analyzed by marketing departments to check on their online campaign successes. Most Web server administrators would also not ignore those logs. However, since Web servers don't have native log forwarding capabilities (most log to files stored on the server itself), consistent centralized Web log analysis for both security and other IT purposes is still ramping up.

Similarly, e-mail tracking through e-mail server logs languishes in a somewhat similar manner: people only turn to e-mail logs when something goes wrong (e-mail failures) or horribly wrong (external party subpoenas your logs). Lack of native centralization and, to some extent, complicated log formats slowed down the e-mail log analysis initiatives.

Even more than e-mail, database logging wasn't on the radar of most Information Technology (IT) folks until recently. In fact, IT folks were perfectly happy with the fact that even though Relational Database Management Systems (RDBMSes) had extensive logging and data access auditing capabilities, most of them were never turned on. Oracle, Microsoft Structured Query Language (SQL) Server, IBM DB2, and MySQL all provide excellent logging, if you know how to enable it, configure it for your specific needs, and analyze and leverage the resulting onslaught of data. What's next? Web applications and large enterprise application frameworks largely lived in a world of their own, but now people are starting to realize that their log data provides unique insight into insider attacks, insider data theft, and other trusted access abuse. Additionally, desktop operating system log analysis from large numbers of deployed desktops will also follow.

Which Logs are Relevant?

Which logs are relevant to your environment? In some circumstances, the answer may be "all of them!" The following are a few common uses for log information:

- **Threat Detection** Historical Host Intrusion Detection Systems (HIDSes) from the 1990s looked at audit trails and logs in search of patterns and strings in logs, and raised alerts upon seeing them. Today, hunting for signs of hacking attempts (as well as successes in the form of "compromise detection") in logs is just as useful.

- **Incident Response and Troubleshooting** When a system is hacked, logs are the most informative, accessible and relatively easy to analyze (compared to full disk images) form of incident evidence.

- **E-discovery** While some say that a possibility of a subpoena or an e-discovery requests provides a compelling reason to not have logs, in reality, hiding one's head in the sand is unlikely to work in this case.

- **IT Performance Management and Troubleshooting** Network is slow? Looking at logs will help find out why.

- **Network Management** While log pundits might argue on whether a Simple Network Management Protocol (SNMP) trap is a kind of log record, logs are useful for many bandwidth management and network performance measurement tasks that are common in IT.

- **Compliance** Just about every recent regulatory compliance or "best practices" framework touches on audit logs.

Deciding Which Tools Will Help You Best

In this section we'll discuss various security tools.

Log Correlation

SIM tools provide incredible capabilities, and the best (and sometimes most questionable) include strong correlation capabilities. This means the system is able to acquire logs and events from disparate sources, normalize and compare the data presented, and make a logical deduction as to their meaning.

For instance, a series of calls outbound from a file server to an IP address over ICQ channels would tip off the SIM tools that a famous worm is running amok within the network. This in turn would generate an alert received by the Security Administrator, who then would have words with a certain System Administrator or two.

Log Searching

Generally, a database should be searchable in the same manner by a variety of tools, but the fact is that many vendors spend less effort on their retrieval tools than on their correlation and storage components—that's a situation generated by market forces.

If possible, using the same vendor for data retrieval is the best possible approach. However, if the retrieval capabilities show significant delay in reacquiring data (more than 24 hours), then consider another vendor.

Finding the best tool to mine log data after it has been archived (meaning, after it has been correlated and subjected to logic that detects attacks and such), is a very important bit of work. The point here is that after you've committed your terabytes of data to disk, you need a way to look for cookie crumbs if you've discovered an incident after-the-fact.

Data mining is a term normally associated with marketing activities. In this case, however, it's a valuable security discipline that allows the security professional to find clues and behaviors around intrusions of various sorts.

Some options for data mining include the use of the correlation tool you selected for security information management. In fact, most SIM tools now carry strong data mining tools that can be used to reconstruct events specific between IP and Media Access Control (MAC) identifiers.

The point is that the solution must be able to integrate at the schema layer. You don't want to invest in additional code just to make a data miner that typically looks for apples, to suddenly be able to look for oranges. If your current SIM vendor doesn't provide mining tools, insist on them, or take your business elsewhere.

Alerting Tools

Each vendor of SIM tools provides integration points to hook into sophisticated alerting systems. These take the form of management consoles that in turn provide SMTP, SNMP, and other means to transmit or broadcast information to whatever mode of communication is in play (e.g., pager, Smartphone, and so on).

Intrusion Detection and Prevention

Detection and prevention technologies have collided in recent months and are certain to converge to greater degrees over time. In the context of network and host activities, you should search for solutions and technologies where the best of breed is represented. Intrusion detection and prevention are more frequently housed on the same platform. This is an area where the business can see a better return in investment than on standalone solutions.

Intrusion Detection

Intrusion detection is a funny thing. Some focus on the network layer, some on the application layer. In a XenApp environment, you are typically dealing with application-layer traffic. Web services behaviors and transactions using eXtensible Markup Language (XML), SOAP, and so on. There are two sorts of IDS in this context: *network* and *applications*. In addition, there are two layers of IDS: *network* and *host*.

Network IDS is going to work in a similar vein to Intrusion Protection System (IPS), except that the purpose is to detect situations like distributed Denial of Service (DoS) attacks, while IPS is simply permitting or denying certain traffic.

Intrusion Prevention

When configuring IPS, the most important step is to catalog those data activities your network normally operates. Port 80 outbound from such-and-such server, 443 inbound and outbound, Network Basic Input/Output System (NetBios) and other Active Directory required protocols, File Transfer Protocol (FTP), and so on, each have legitimate purposes in most networks. The important point is to catalog the port, the expected origination, and the expected destination. Once that is documented, you can use that information to configure your IPS appropriately.

If you're configuring the network IPS, you'll need all the data relevant to that area of the network. If you're working on host IPS, you'll need expected transaction information for that host.

Dealing With Auditor's Mistakes

Auditors are human and will sometimes make mistakes. This rarely happens, but if it does there is a right way to deal with it. The first thing to do is to talk to the auditor and have him explain how he came to his or her conclusion. Many times the customer misunderstood a requirement or believed a compensating control mitigated a problem, but the auditor doesn't agree. Having good open dialogue about what you believe is a mistake, will often solve the problem quickly.

Sometimes an auditor will report a false positive. This is when an audit shows you have a vulnerability such as a missing patch or vulnerable system that really is not there. This seems to happen more with remote scans, since they have less access to systems, but even then they are very rare. Any good auditor knows how to keep false positives to a minimum. When you do get a false positive, your auditor should be able to work it out with you. They may want to get more details from you so they can verify that it is a false positive, and so they can fix the system so that they don't repeat them in the future.

Some approved scanning vendors basically run automated tools and do very little human checking. This generally works very well most of the time, but sometimes the scans can be very complicated, and because of some abnormality in your systems or something that happened during the test, a false positive occurs. Whenever you get a report that says you have a serious vulnerability, you should act as if it's true and see if there's something you can do to remediate the problem quickly. Depending on the situation, it may be a good idea to do some tests on your own. For example, the free tool Nessus has many of the same tests that an external scan will do. Depending on the type of vulnerability that was reported, you may be able also do some manual testing. For example if it's reported that a patch is missing, you may want to manually check on the system to verify if it is or is not. If after your testing you are unable to find the vulnerability, it may be time to challenge your scanning vendor's findings and report it as a false positive. They should do additional tests to determine why the false positive happened, and fix the problem for the future.

In some cases, you may need to push back. Pushing-back is when you challenge the auditor's results. This may happen because the auditor made a mistake, or because you don't feel like he adequately considered a mitigating control you had in place. When you push back you should be polite. Simply explain to the auditor your point of view and why you believe there was a mistake. If the auditor disagrees, ask him to explain his reasoning. If the auditor has explained why you didn't pass and you don't agree with his reasoning, you may need to talk to his manager about the situation. Normally, an auditor's manager will be a seasoned auditor who knows the process forward and backward. Explain your situation to the manager and why you think a mistake was made. Most of the time, the manager will talk to the auditor to get his side of the story before coming to any conclusions. If the auditor's manager agrees with the auditor, you will need to fix the problem to be compliant. Your only other option at this point is to find another auditor or scanning vendor. Usually the only reason to do this is if you feel the auditor is blatantly wrong. However, an auditor from a different company will likely come to the same conclusions.

Note

You may feel like you have mitigating controls in place to solve a problem but the auditor doesn't agree. In this case, it's the auditor who decides if a mitigating control mitigates the risk in question. The mitigating control should be at least as good, if not better, than what the requirement requires. Most of the time it's easier to follow the requirement exactly than to try to get a mitigating control to fix the problem.

Planning for Remediation

A good rule of thumb when doing remediation is that it should be as transparent as possible, so that it has a minimal impact on users. There may be times that remediation may have some impact on users. For example, implementing a much stricter password policy or disabling group accounts may have an effect on how users do their jobs. For the most part, patches and system updates should be transparent to users. The more transparent your remediation, the less problems you're likely to have implementing it. As you plan your remediation process, always keep transparency in mind.

The first thing you should do in planning for remediation is review your compliance gap with your auditor. Your compliance gap describes the difference from where you are now and where you should be to be compliant. You should get a report and be briefed on the details of the problems. It is important to ask your auditor which risks he considers high priority. For example, if the auditor feels that you have urgent risks that could easily be exploited at any time, you would want to work on mitigating these first. In a few cases, an auditor will find a risk that is being actively exploited. In this case, the auditor should let you know as soon as he finds the problem and not wait until the rest of his assessment is done. This would then become your top priority, and you should follow your company's procedure for dealing with attacks and call in your incident response team (see Figure 10.4).

Figure 10.4 Remediation Process

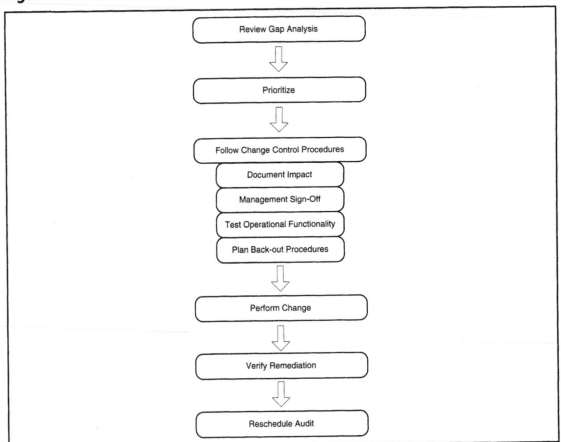

Now that you have your results and understand what needs to be done to come into compliance, it's time to prioritize our risks. With the help of your auditor and by doing your own research, you should work to determine which problem can be exploited easiest and can cause the most damage. These are the ones that should be fixed first. There are many tools that can be used to help you classify risks, including the many vulnerability Web sites. Here are some that you might find useful:

- **Common Vulnerability and Exposures (CVE)** This is a well-respected and much referred to listing of vulnerabilities in products. Many products use CVE number to reference vulnerabilities (http://cve.mitre.org/).

- **National Vulnerability Database** Supported by the Department of Homeland Security and has a great database of many types of vulnerabilities (http://nvd.nist.gov/).

- **Open Source Vulnerability Database (OSVDB)** A community run database of vulnerabilities. It will give you a lot of great information on a vulnerability, including references, ways to test your system, and how to mitigate the problem (www.osvdb.org).

- **Security Focus Bugtraq** A well-organized site that will give you a lot of information including what versions are effected, an overview of the problem, and examples of exploits. It uses Bugtraq IDs (bids) which are supported in many products (www.securityfocus.com/bid/

- **IBM Internet Security Systems (ISS-XForce)** A site backed by IBM that gives great overviews of many vulnerabilities (http://www.iss.net/).

- **Secunia** A Danish computer security company that lists and prioritizes vulnerabilities (http://secunia.com/).

Tools & Traps...

Common Vulnerability Scoring Systems (CVSS)

CVSS is a standard for scoring vulnerabilities that is becoming widely used. Most of the vulnerability databases will list CVSS scores, which are great in helping you determine the impact of a vulnerability. There are some vulnerabilities that may not have a CVSS score, but the *Forum for Incident Response and Security Teams* web site provides a listing of links and tools that can assist you in calculating calculate them, which can be found at www.first.org/cvss/scores.html.

For example, let's say that your report shows that you don't have your credit card area physically secured. Since this is not a specific vulnerability with a specific system, there won't be a CVSS score for it, but you can use CVSS to help you determine the priority.

Continued

In this example, we'll use a physical security issue to show you how this works. While this system is mainly for computer security issues, it works pretty well for physical vulnerabilities as well. Say your organization has a fax machine in a public area (such as a store lobby) where faxes containing orders that include cardholder data are received. Let's say that the location is not always closely monitored. For example, there may be times when the employees in the lobby are busy with customers and aren't watching the fax machine and therefore anybody could grab a fax.

On the calculator page, you would start with the Base Scoring Metrics. This gives CVSS a base score to work of off for the vulnerability.

Related exploit range is where an attacker would have to be to be able to exploit this vulnerability. If an attacker can compromise the system over the Internet or some other remote means, then it would be remote. In our case, with the credit card area not being physically secured properly, it would be Local.

Attack complexity is how hard it is to pull off the attack once an attacker has found the vulnerable target. If the attack requires other factors to be in place for it to work, it may make it complex. In our case, we'll say that this is Low complexity. Once an attacker knows where the credit card data is, it's easy for them to get to it, because our physical security is so bad.

The level of authentication needed is if an attacker must be authenticated to pull off an attack. This means that there is a test to verify who the user is that they have to bypass to attack the system. An example would be if to pull off our attack against the area with credit card data, we needed a fake badge. We're going to say that we don't (we can just walk in nobody will stop us) so the level will be **Not Required**.

Confidentiality impact is how the exploit will affect confidentiality of data that should be protected. In our case, if they can access cardholder data by simply walking into a protected area and walking off with a file cabinet with all cardholder data in it, it would be complete. We'll say that the filing cabinet is pretty safe, but we have faxes that come in with cardholder data on it and we don't protect it. In this case the confidentiality impact would be **Partial**.

Integrity impact is how the attack will impact the integrity of data. In our case, it's not likely that integrity will be compromised, so we'll use **None**.

Availability impact is the measure of how it will affect the availability of systems and data. Since the attacker can walk off with a fax, the data is no longer available, so we'll mark that as **Partial**.

Impact value weighting allows you to give more weight to confidentiality integrity, or availability. In our case, the biggest problem will be confidentiality, because the attacker just walked off with cardholder data, so we will chose **Weight confidentiality**.

At this point if we click Update Scores, we will get a base score of 3.7. Now we will do the temporal score metrics.

Availability of an exploit lets you determine if an exploit is actually available or not. In our case, we'll say that a **Functional exploit** exists since the attack would work much of the time, but there may be times when an employee would catch somebody.

The type of fix available allows us to specify if there is currently any way to remediate the problem. We'll say that we've asked employees to keep an eye on the

Continued

fax machine, which is a **Temporary fix** until we find a better place to move the fax machine to.

Level of verification that the vulnerability exists allows us to specify how sure we are the vulnerability is actually there. In our case, we know that the vulnerability exists so we'll choose **Confirmed**.

Now on to the environmental score metrics section. Here we will look at what kind of damage will happen.

Organization-specific potential for loss allows you to specify the physical impact the attack could have on your systems. Let's say one credit card number stolen on a fax likely won't bankrupt the company, so we'll say it has **Low (light loss)**.

The percentage of vulnerable systems allows us to choose how many of our systems are vulnerable to this attack. In our case, this is our only fax machine so we'll say all of them and chose **High (76 to 100 percent)**.

Now that we're done, we click the **Update Scores** button and get an overall score of 3.9.

There are many ways to prioritize risks, depending on how many and what types they are. You may want to use a simple or complex system for this. You should not spend a huge amount of time and effort prioritizing risks, since in the end they all need to be fixed. But it's good to have a general idea. We will discuss a quick way here and in the side bar titled CVSS, and we will discuss a slightly more complex way. We will score all vulnerabilities on a scale of 1 through 5 (5 being the worst) for risk level and probability of attack. We will then use these numbers to prioritize which ones to fix first.

NOTE

If you have a few gaps that will be remedied quickly, this quick classification system works best. If you have several vulnerabilities, some of which will take a long time to work out, then it's probably best to use the CVSS.

First we will classify vulnerabilities on a scale of 1 through 5 based on how bad these vulnerabilities are.

- **5** Urgent vulnerabilities that should be fixed as soon as possible. Basically this is when your system has been compromised and you should work to quickly get this fixed.

- **4** Critical vulnerabilities that have not been used to exploit your system yet, but may be in the near future. An example of this could include a patch to your systems are missing and there is a known worm crawling the Internet exploiting this problem. While this is not as bad as a system that is currently compromised, it's a close second and should be fixed soon.

- **3** High risk vulnerabilities that could be serious if exploited, but there is no worm or prolific exploit. An example of this might be a vulnerability that could be exploited by a script kiddie level malicious user.

■ **2** Medium level vulnerabilities are ones that would require a very sophisticated attacker to pull it off, but it's still possible. This could include a situation where a vulnerability is partially mitigated or there is a temporary fix in place.

■ **1** Low severity vulnerabilities, which include information disclosure or other type of vulnerability that doesn't pose much of a risk by itself, but if used with other information, may be exploited.

Next, we will give vulnerabilities a score of 1 through 5 based on the loss your organization will suffer if the vulnerability is exploited. When using this system, you should consider all forms of financial losses including loss of customers, cost to fix the problem after it happens, and so forth.

■ **5** The business will go bankrupt and no longer exists. You will not be able to survive a compromise of this kind.

■ **4** This likely won't shut the company down, but will have significant impact on the company financially.

■ **3** Your company will suffer a medium amount of loss. This will still be bad for the company, but they should be able to weather it without much problem.

■ **2** Your company will suffer a small but noticeable loss financially.

■ **1** The financial loss if this were exploited, would not really be noticed.

Now that we have classified all of our vulnerabilities based on the two systems, all you need to do is add up the two numbers for each vulnerability and you have its priority. Let's do an example to show you how this is done. Let's say that we have a vulnerable Web server. There is no worm that is actively crawling the Internet exploiting this problem, but there is exploit code available that is easy to use. In this case, we would give the vulnerability a severity risk of 3. Looking at the possible loss, we decide that it could be a pretty big deal. If an attacker was able to compromise our Web servers they could steal all incoming credit card information and could possibly use the Web server to get to other computers in the DMZ. There is also a possibility that an attacker can perform a pretty significant Denial of Service (DoS) attack against the Web servers. This would cost a decent amount of money, but wouldn't put us out of business. It's also important to consider penalties that could be levied because of noncompliance to whatever standards your organization must adhere. All of this considered, we decide to give the vulnerability a loss rating of 4. Now we simply add 3 and 4 and this vulnerability's priority is 7. The highest possible vulnerability is 10 (even though this would mean that a vulnerability is being actively exploited that will almost certainly result in your company going bankrupt).

TIP

After you've followed some system for prioritizing vulnerabilities for awhile, your instinct will tell you to fix one or more out of order. It's usually not a bad idea to follow your instinct.

Now that you have prioritized vulnerabilities, you should start fixing them from highest to lowest. You should have a change management policy in place and use that policy when you are implementing the changes. Your policy should include several parts. For example, before you implement any change, you should document the impact the change will have on all users and customers. This should include any behaviors that users will have to change, or anything that will work differently after the change is made. It is important that you always remember to have management sign off before you make any of the required changes, to bring yourself into compliance. You should also always remember to test your change in a test environment before putting it into production. This is important to verify that it doesn't introduce other problems that must be resolved before you put it into production. You must also always have a back-out procedure in place just in case the change causes problems. After you have everything in place, make the update and then make sure you update any applicable documentation.

Before you conduct another audit, it's a good idea to test your changes as best you can to verify that they are working as planned. For changes to systems, there are many tools that can help you do this. Nessus is a really good free vulnerability scanner that you can use to test for missed patches and other misconfigurations on many different systems.

Warning

Before running any type of scan on your network, you should always get management's approval.

Understanding Penetration Testing

In this section, we'll address the basic attributes that are common in all successful penetration testers. We're not going to cover the specific tools or include a ton of screenshots. Dozens of books already have that covered. Our goal is to identify those useful attributes so you can better address your own methodologies, as well as determine your weaknesses and areas for improvement.

Know the Security Analysis Life Cycle

Back in the days when we first started doing this type of work, it was all technical. That's all we did. We were the geeks, the freaks behind the keyboard; the ones that could work around the system controls. What we did seemed normal enough to us, but to the uninitiated, it was something akin to black magic or voodoo.

What was not realized at the time was that there are things that have to occur along all levels of the security life cycle in order for a penetration test to have the greatest value to the customer. The most basic of which is the fact that pen testing is just a piece of the overall security life cycle that must be addressed. As with most life cycles, things need to occur in their proper order (at least the large majority of the time); otherwise, the results could be meaningless or have significantly less value.

The standard security life cycle looks something like this: An organizational/programmatic assessment occurs; a full comprehensive technical evaluation is rendered; findings are presented to the customer; the customer takes appropriate the steps to close technical problems and implement defenses; and then a test of those defenses takes place. This is where the penetration comes into play. If we put this process into a flow chart or image, it would look like Figure 10.5.

Figure 10.5 The Basic Security Analysis Life Cycle

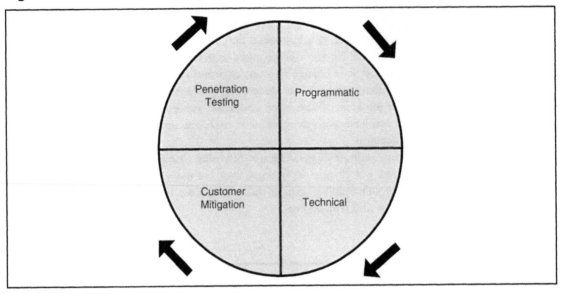

The truth of the matter is that this flow of activities and information is most advantageous to the customer. In other words, they can expect the absolute best possible results from a process similar to this one. Let's examine why that is.

Programmatic Testing

As a security professional, you understand that technical vulnerabilities can be found and fixed. But you also know that an organization that has not fixed the root cause of the issue will continue to have technical problems later on down the road. The findings may be different (in some cases they're the same, just on different systems), but technical vulnerabilities will continue to rear their ugly heads.

The root cause of those vulnerabilities is undefined, immature, or undocumented processes for areas of control within the organization. For example, a good deal of the vulnerabilities we find in technical evaluations or pen tests can be directly attributed to a lack of proper patching of applications and operating systems. Sure, we can find all the current technical issues and help the customer remedy those, but if the organization fails to address the actual patch process within the organization, they're going to continue having these findings in the future. The organizational, or programmatic, assessment locates these areas of procedural weakness in the organization and allows them to fix those issues. Once proper controls are in place, the number of findings in that area will lessen over time.

TIP

It's important to understand the entire security life cycle, even if you only work in a single area. By understanding how your area of expertise relates to the other areas in the life cycle, you'll be better prepared to answer customer questions, create useful output from your processes, and mature in your own professional experiences.

Technical Testing

But we all know that organizational findings aren't all there is when examining a customer. The technical piece is extremely important. A comprehensive technical evaluation will provide the customer with a clear picture of where those vulnerabilities lie and what the potential impact could be on their organization if those systems are compromised. The goal here is to allow the organization to understand what technical vulnerabilities currently exist, so they can close those while they're still working on creating a mature organizational security program.

Customer Responsibilities

Now that we've done the work, we want to provide the customer with a final report that details our findings, clearly and precisely. A poorly written report, or one that doesn't communicate with the intended managerial or executive audience, will seldom be of much use. But once the customer has received your well written report, they have to step up to the plate and roll up their sleeves.

This is where the rubber really meets the road, from a customer perspective. For each finding we've detailed, they need to implement a fix: a defense or mitigation. Think along the lines of fortifying a castle with a variety of defenses that will help stop an invading army. They'll implement moats, drawbridges, and towers. They'll employ guards, archers, and watchmen. Iron bars will be integrated into the stonework around all the sewer and water avenues in and out of the area. This analogy explains, basically, what the customer should be working on, based on your final report.

Penetration Testing

Finally, we're at the fun part (and the focus of this section), the penetration test. Once the customer has a full understanding of their security posture, both organizationally and technically, and they've had the opportunity to defend against their weaknesses, they'll need someone to test their defenses. This is similar to the television show where families hire a former burglar to try and break into their homes and prove whether it's possible or not. The thief doesn't need to find every way into the home, only one. Proving he/she can get into the home is the goal of the show, and that's also the goal of a penetration test.

Optimally, this life cycle will repeat itself every year or two. The shorter the time lapse from one life cycle to the next, the more secure and mature an organization has the opportunity to be. If the time between one full life cycle to the next is too long, the organization is likely to slip back into old habits and insecurity.

The Penetration Tester Mentality

The most important tool in any penetration tester's toolkit (more important than any application, script, or exploit) is his/her mind. Good pen testers have an uncanny ability to locate issues on-the-fly. And since every customer and situation is different, this is a "must have" attribute. Let's look at some of those attributes that make up a good penetration tester.

Know the Core Processes

There are certain things that every penetration tester does, with every client. We'll cover them in more detail in the next section, but as a quick prelude; we look at what information we can get publicly, we find out what components and services exist on the network, we locate all the known vulnerabilities, we break in to a target system, we escalate our privileges, we expand our reach, and we ensure our ability to get back into those systems later by installing backdoor applications.

It seems silly to think that hackers are that organized, but we are. We might not document all of these processes, but they are the basics used nearly every time. Understanding the methodology used provides a reliable structure for the successful penetration of customer systems. If you roll in to a customer site and just "wing it," things aren't likely to turn out so well. I've had dozens of customers call up concerned about a "prior engagement" with a security firm that lacked processes and had poor results.

> **Tip**
>
> Never underestimate the importance of following a standardized and mature process. Mature and repeatable processes allow for someone else to step into your shoes if you get hurt or are unable to complete your work.

Think for Yourself

Whereas core processes provide a foundation that can be taught to nearly everyone, creativity is the hallmark of all great penetration testers and is a much less tangible trait. Teaching people to think like a hacker is much more difficult; thus, this trait is normally what separates the wheat from the chaff. Every customer and situation you encounter as a penetration tester will be different. That's not to say there won't be similarities, but as a whole, each job is different.

When we discuss the difference, consider them in terms of different management, network architecture, applications, patch levels, policies, and employees. Each of these will impact your ability to have a successful penetration test. Penetration testers view each new organization as a puzzle. Imagine, if you will, that you're doing one of those maze puzzles found on the kids menu of the local hamburger joint. In the center of the maze you normally have the objective you must reach. Your starting point lies somewhere just outside the perimeter of the maze. Penetration testing is similar in that you come into the organization from an outside perspective and must find your way to the critical information that lies at the heart of that organization (the maze).

The real trick here is that each pathway to the data is littered with obstacles. To be successful, you'll need the ability to break through obstacles, or simply bypass them altogether. This is where creativity will really help. Remember, try to be flexible in your thought processes so every possible option will be available to you as you attempt to reach your goal.

Ethical Conduct

Over the years, we've seen any number of people try to differentiate between malicious hackers (often referred to as crackers) and penetration testers. The truth is that knowledgewise and mentally, they're nearly identical. The big differentiator is the ethical constraints that professional penetration testers apply to their conduct. Because they are employed by professional organizations, both commercially or for the federal government, there are ethical standards that need to be constantly monitored.

This should not be taken the wrong way. The desire to solve the puzzle, and the burn to be successful, still exists in the penetration tester, as it does in most hackers. We still enjoy the thrill of victory, as it were, but we also understand that the work we do could potentially put the customer at risk and should be performed with caution. When performed correctly, a penetration test can be used to improve the customer's defenses and improve their overall security posture.

Know When to Fold

Knowing when to fold your cards is a classic poker strategy that has paid off for smart card players for years. The same holds true when considering a penetration test. There will be times when you want to spend more time on a particular area that looks vulnerable. Sometimes this will pay off by providing you with a pathway into the network. Other times, it may be a complete waste of effort. Knowing when to back off from one area of examination and move on is a critical skill to have. The sooner you can come to terms with the idea that you can't compromise every vulnerability that exists, the sooner you can move on to more promising opportunities.

This is important to understand. We've seen folks get completely sucked into the process of compromising a single, potential vulnerability, all the while ignoring more promising issues elsewhere. Remember, the objective is to gain control of the customer network and get at its critical information; it's not to find every vulnerability. We're just trying to work our way through the vulnerabilities with the most likelihood of compromise; sometimes referred to as the low-hanging fruit. If you get too absorbed in one area, you may miss something that could be the difference between success and failure.

Use the Right Tools

Regardless of your skill level or how long you've been a penetration tester, you will always need the right tools. It's hard to argue with a jury of your peers, so the best place to look for the most popular and useful tools publicly available right now is at www.sectools.org. Fyodor, author of the legendary Nmap port scanning tool, compiles this list based on votes from professionals and hackers around the world. This top 100 list of applications is a must see for anyone in this line of business.

Build Your Own

Scripting and programming are your friends. That large majority of penetration testers, who are actually quite successful at what they do, have a knack for creating scripts and programs that do a lot of the manual labor for them. For instance, resolving a complete IP address block through a domain name server using reverse lookups could provide a lot of useful information, but doing that type of work manually would be time consuming. The creation of script might take an hour, but the time it would save in the long run would more than compensate for that. By building your own tools, you can be assured you understand what the tool is doing, create more efficient methods for performing your tests, and put the information into a format that works for your own penetration processes.

The Penetration Methodology

We mentioned it briefly earlier, but let's look at a standard methodology often used by hackers and professionals alike. The methodology is intended to start with a high level overview of the organization and slowly work itself into the details. As we move our way down the methodology, we gain a better understanding of how the organization processes, stores, transmits, and protects its critical information. We have eight steps in this penetration methodology that we'll discuss in more detail. You can see these steps in Figure 10.6.

NOTE

As you step through this process, it's important to take lots of notes. Make sure you detail which computers and accounts you've compromised, where you've installed backdoor software, and the avenues you took for each compromise. This information will be useful to the customer later when they need to implement defenses and clean up after your work.

Figure 10.6 An Example of Penetration Methodology

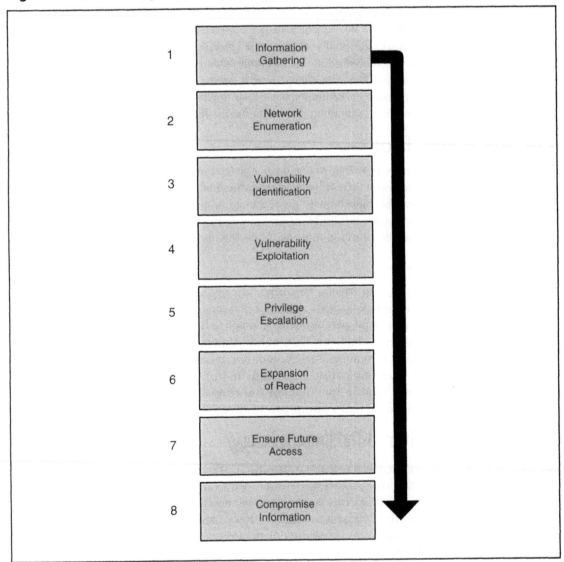

Information Gathering

The first task on any penetration test is identifying what information you can glean from public resources. The most notable, and most used, medium for this work is the Internet. It's amazing the information you can get simply by using search engines like Google, scouring newsgroup archives, perusing mailing list archives, and looking at public records that the company has willingly released into the wild.

Search Engines

We won't go into too much detail on search engines, but suffice to say that this will be one of your first tasks. Looking through search engines using the correct syntax can reveal a plethora of very useful information to a penetration tester. Most search engines will do queries based on postings to newsgroups, mailing lists, forums, and other forms of communication. They'll also search through information found on publicly available Web pages for your target, or their partner organizations. The most popular search engine used by penetration testers is undoubtedly Google. Regardless of what you use, though, make sure you understand the full list of options available to you in your search. For instance, Google comes with dozens and dozens of different search options that aren't commonly known and may help you in your searches.

Newsgroup Searches

Newsgroups have been a huge part of the Internet for decades now. The most well known is the USENET newsgroups. They were around before the Web was graphically based. These groups are basically huge message lists that users can subscribe to in order to watch for conversations or information on particular topics.

For those of us that have been in the online world for the past 20 years or more, we've most certainly used these groups in the past to communicate with other professionals or hobbyists. For instance, if you're having issues with your router configuration, you might decide to post your question to a newsgroup. his allows hundreds, if not thousands, of other readers to view your question and respond to it. The cool part is that these messages are all archived on the Internet in a variety of places and can be located later by doing search queries.

The following are some hints for performing these searches:

- Search for the company name
- Search for the company domain (for example, customer.org)
- Search for the name of individuals you know work there (say, Joe Schmo)
- Search for the company phone number
- Search for the public IP address space of the customer

Forums and Blogs

Forums and blogs have started to slowly replace newsgroups in the public eye. All sorts of useful information can be found on public blogs or technical support forums. Administrators will often post messages to these types of communities in order to get feedback on particular technical issues that might be causing them headaches. They're also known to post in response to posts from other people around the world. Posts such as these might contain valuable information about the architecture in use at the customer site. For instance, an administrator might post a response to a query on the forums stating something like, "In our organization, we use product X and I've found that if you configure it like this, the problem will go away." This information could help you focus your initial attacks on the organization.

Normal users and employees are oftentimes another way to find out what's in use at the organization. And because they're less likely to be educated in information security, they tend to provide more sensitive information in their posts. For example, let's say a user is having issues with a Web application in the organization. Instead of turning to their own administrators, which on multiple occasions have explained in clear, precise terms to the user how it's not really a problem, users will often post messages on forums instead. We've seen examples of information given out publicly to include application type, version number, patch level, configuration information, and, on occasion, actual code from the application. All of this information can be used to expand your attack.

Network Enumeration

Network enumeration is one of the most recognized hacker activities on the Internet. Because of its high-profile nature, dozens of tools and applications exist for performing these activities. The basic goal of network enumeration is to find out what components exist on the network, such as firewalls, computers, routers, switches, and printers. The port scan is the most familiar activity in this area. Port scans can be performed using any number of protocols, such as TCP, UDP, and ICMP. The most popular port scan tool is by far Nmap, but you can find many other similar tools at www.sectools.org.

Aside from finding out what components make up the target network, we also want to know what services, applications, and shared file systems are out there. Available services or applications may provide an avenue of attack, whereas shared file systems or printers could potentially allow an avenue of attack and access to sensitive information. Having this information will help you focus your attacks, saving time and effort on the penetration test.

Vulnerability Identification

Vulnerability scanning automates the process of determining what well-known vulnerabilities exist on the network. Imagine having to look at every computer manually, across the network, and trying to figure out what vulnerabilities existed. Some of these tools are freeware, such as Nessus (www.nessus. org), while others are commercial in nature, such as Saint (www.saintcorporation.com). The goal of this process is to collect as much useful information as we can in the shortest amount of time.

The two tools listed in the previous paragraph are general vulnerability scanners and will attempt to find issues in a large number of services and host types across an organization's network. Other tools, such as SPI Dynamic's WebInspect (www.spidynamics.com) or NGS's NGSSQuirrel (www. nextgenss.com), specialize in vulnerabilities on specific applications. For example, the NGS application is written by some of the world's foremost experts in database security and will help locate issues in databases that could provide an avenue into the network.

Vulnerability Exploitation

Exploiting the vulnerabilities is what separates the professionals from the script kiddies. The truth hurts, but a good many professionals in the security world depend wholly on the use of scripts and exploits written by other people. While this may be useful in some circumstances, the sole use of these exploits indicates the lack of maturity in the tester's knowledge and processes. A high quality tester will often have their own methods and scripts to help them break into a customer network.

The painful truth, however, is that we can't all know everything. So, based on that, there will be times when everyone will need to use someone else's work. The thing to understand is that you need to be absolutely certain that the code is safe to use on the customer's network. Although we're trying to break into the network to get a foothold in as many boxes as possible, we're still there to help the customer, not bring them down. In this case, it's really helpful if you already know how to program and read code.

The exploitation of vulnerabilities, whether taking advantage of a configuration issue or a software bug, provides us with the door into a single computer. This is the important first step that provides us with a normal user account. Everything else from here on out is based on this simple step.

Privilege Escalation

Once you find yourself in a target computer with a normal user account, you'll want to find a way to escalate your privilege to that of a root or Administrator user. In most cases, we'll concentrate on local Administrator or root access first, and then move on to the domain level access. The normal progression of access escalation is depicted in Figure 10.7.

Figure 10.7 The Access Escalation Process

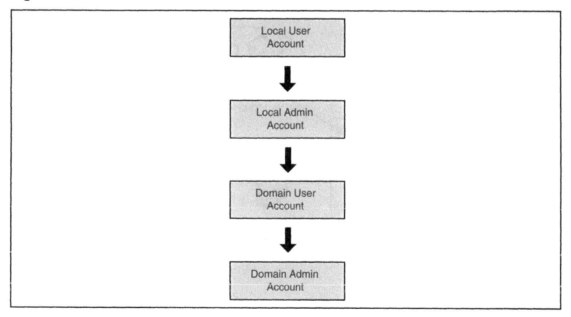

Expansion of Reach

Let's expand on the concept of access escalation a bit. In Figure 10.7, we kept things pretty simple by talking strictly about the access level of the accounts we were trying to compromise. If we take that one step further, we'll take the full network into account as well, versus a single host. Look at Figure 10.8 for an example.

TIP

Owning a single computer is great, but owning the entire network is optimal. Remember, when you're hired on for these engagements, you're most likely going to have a limited amount of time to compromise the customer resources. An attacker won't have those limitations, thus they can spend as much time breaking in as they need. What does this mean for you? It means you have to be better than an attacker in order to find those avenues into the customer network in a shorter period of time. You're going to have to go just as far in the network, if not further, with less time.

Figure 10.8 The Access Escalation Process for a Full Network

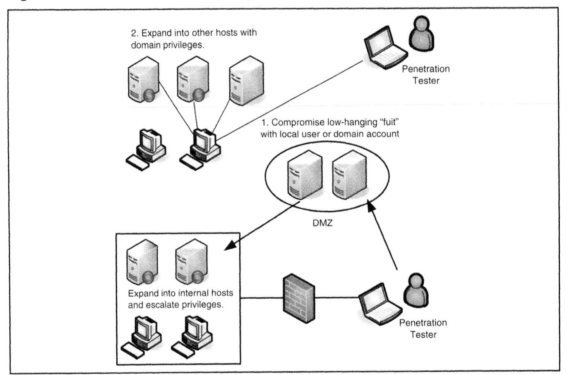

Ensure Future Access

Once you've gained the access to key systems in the customer network, you don't want that access removed right when you need it. Some customers may notice odd things occurring on their network. For instance, Bill Morrison from the accounting office doesn't normally log in to the server at 11 P.M., or maybe there has been an unusually high level of Web traffic occurring during off hours.

When this type of activity is noticed, the customer may cut off your access, either intentionally or unintentionally. To avoid this, you'll need to secure your future access to these systems through a number of possible means. These could include backdoor applications and/or additional privileged accounts.

Backdoor applications often run in the background on a compromised system, allowing access back into the system at a later date. They often run on nonpopular ports and require a username and/ or password to access the application. In instances of remote compromises, the backdoor will likely use a port that is allowed in and out through the firewall. Regardless of the port being utilized or the actual application in use, the goal is always the same: maintain and control access to compromised targets. In some cases, you may be able to simply create alternative administrative or root accounts. On systems that have hundreds of users, the new account isn't likely to ever be detected.

Warning

The use of some backdoor applications could cause more issues for your customer than good. For instance, there are a lot of these applications in the public space, but if you don't have access to the source code, you can never be sure of how they really operate. What if the application leaves the customer vulnerable beyond what you believe? How will you ever be able to ensure the customer is secured from that point forward? The same holds true with root kits. Always make sure you're using only approved backdoor applications that you know for sure can't be hijacked by a real attacker.

Compromise Information

At the core of any organization is certain information that is used on a daily basis to keep it profitable and in business. This could include customer data, such as credit card information, or it could include something much more sensitive, such as proprietary research and development data. This information is the actual goal of any penetration test. After all, it doesn't matter if you can get into the network if you can't compromise the information, does it?

You've gained account access, escalated that to administrative access, and expanded your access throughout the entire network. At this point, start looking for the treasure. Can you find those financial documents, research information, or patient health records?

Warning

Always remember that you're here to help the customer, not actually cause damage. If you download information, it needs to be stored securely on encrypted drive partitions. Never disseminate this information to third parties or outside entities. Protect all access and information at the highest level of sensitivity possible.

The Cleanup

Once the job is done, present your findings to the customer and get ready for the cleanup. What? Surely you didn't think you were done. You've taken over user accounts, created your own administrative accounts, installed backdoors, changed passwords, and taken sensitive information from the customer network. You need to set everything right now.

The first step is to go back through your notes and undo everything you've done. Let the customer know about all user accounts you had access to. They'll need to change passwords on all those accounts. Help the customer remove any backdoor applications you may have installed. Return all information you have obtained during your work and delete all soft copy information from your encrypted storage medium.

And finally, answer any and all questions the customer may have concerning how you achieved such resounding success on their network. Part of your ethical duty to the customer is to perform a knowledge transfer, ensuring that the customer has a better understanding of the thought processes and techniques that an attacker would use to compromise their network. Understanding this will help the customer better protect themselves and their customers.

Understanding Vulnerability Assessments

In the war zone that is the modern Internet, manually reviewing each networked system for security flaws is no longer feasible. Operating systems, applications, and network protocols have grown so complex over the last decade that it takes a dedicated security administrator to keep even a relatively small network shielded from attack.

Each technical advance brings wave after wave of security holes. A new protocol might result in dozens of actual implementations, each of which could contain exploitable programming errors. Logic errors, vendor-installed backdoors, and default configurations plague everything from modern operating systems to the simplest print server. Yesterday's viruses seem positively tame compared to the highly optimized Internet worms that continuously assault every system attached to the global Internet.

To combat these attacks, a network administrator needs the appropriate tools and knowledge to identify vulnerable systems and resolve their security problems before they can be exploited. One of the most powerful tools available today is the vulnerability assessment, and this chapter describes what it is, what it can provide you, and why you should be performing them as often as possible. Following this is an analysis of the different types of solutions available, the advantages of each, and the actual steps used by most tools during the assessment process. The next section describes two distinct approaches used by the current generation of assessment tools and how choosing the right tool can make a significant impact on the security of your network. Finally, the chapter closes with the issues and limitations that you can expect when using any of the available assessment tools.

What Is a Vulnerability Assessment?

To explain vulnerability assessments, we first need to define what a *vulnerability* is. For the purposes of this book, vulnerability refers to any programming error or misconfiguration that could allow an intruder to gain unauthorized access. This includes anything from a weak password on a router to an unpatched programming flaw in an exposed network service. Vulnerabilities are no longer just the realm of system crackers and security consultants; they have become the enabling factor behind most network worms, spyware applications, and e-mail viruses.

Spammers are increasingly relying on software vulnerabilities to hide their tracks; the open mail relays of the 1990s have been replaced by compromised "zombie" proxies of today, created through the mass exploitation of common vulnerabilities. A question often asked is, "Why would someone target my system?" The answer is that most exploited systems were not targeted; they were simply one more address in a network range being scanned by an attacker. They were targets of opportunity, not choice. Spammers do not care whether a system belongs to an international bank or your grandmother Edna; as long as they can install their relay software, it makes no difference to them.

Vulnerability assessments are simply the process of locating and reporting vulnerabilities. They provide you with a way to detect and resolve security problems before someone or something can exploit them. One of the most common uses for vulnerability assessments is their capability to validate security measures. If you recently installed a new intrusion detection system (IDS), a vulnerability assessment allows you to determine how well that solution works. If the assessment completes and your IDS didn't fire off a single alert, it might be time to have a chat with the vendor.

The actual process for vulnerability identification varies widely between solutions; however, they all focus on a single output—the report. This report provides a snapshot of all the identified vulnerabilities on the network at a given time. Components of this report usually include a list detailing each identified vulnerability, where it was found, what the potential risk is, and how it can be resolved. Figure 10.9 shows a sample Nessus Security Scanner report for a network of only five systems; the number of vulnerabilities is already over 100!

Figure 10.9 Sample Nessus Report

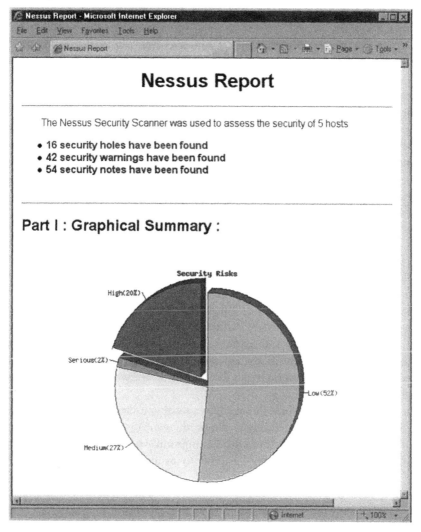

Why a Vulnerability Assessment?

Vulnerability assessments have become a critical component of many organizations' security infrastructures; the ability to perform a network-wide security snapshot supports a number of security vulnerability and administrative processes. When a new vulnerability is discovered, the network administrator can perform an assessment, discover which systems are vulnerable, and start the patch installation process. After the fixes are in place, another assessment can be run to verify that the vulnerabilities were actually resolved. This cycle of assess, patch, and reassess has become the standard method for many organizations to manage their security issues.

Many organizations have integrated vulnerability assessments into their system rollout process. Before a new server is installed, it first must go through a vulnerability assessment and pass with flying colors. This process is especially important for organizations that use a standard build image for each system; all too often, a new server can be imaged, configured, and installed without the administrator remembering to install the latest system patches. Additionally, many vulnerabilities can only be resolved through manual configuration changes; even an automated patch installation might not be enough to secure a newly imaged system. It's much easier to find these problems at build time when configuration changes are simple and risk-free than when that system is deployed in the field. We strongly recommend performing a vulnerability assessment against any new system before deploying it.

While many security solutions complicate system administration, vulnerability assessments can actually assist an administrator. Although the primary purpose of an assessment is to detect vulnerabilities, the assessment report can also be used as an inventory of the systems on the network and the services they expose. Since enumerating hosts and services is the first part of any vulnerability assessment, regular assessments can give you a current and very useful understanding of the services offered on your network. Assessments assist in crises: when a new worm is released, assessment reports are often used to generate task lists for the system administration staff, allowing them to prevent a worm outbreak before it reaches critical mass.

Asset classification is one of the most common nonsecurity uses for vulnerability assessment tools. Knowing how many and what types of printers are in use will help resource planning. Determining how many Windows 2000 systems still need to be upgraded can be as easy as looking at your latest report. The ability to glance quickly at a document and determine what network resources might be overtaxed or underutilized can be invaluable to topology planning.

Assessment tools are also capable of detecting corporate policy violations; many tools will report peer-to-peer services, shared directories full of illegally shared copyrighted materials, and unauthorized remote access tools. If a longtime system administrator leaves the company, an assessment tool can be used to detect that a backdoor was left in the firewall. If bandwidth use suddenly spikes, a vulnerability assessment can be used to locate workstations that have installed file-sharing software.

One of the most important uses for vulnerability assessment data is event correlation; if an intrusion does occur, a recent assessment report allows the security administrator to determine how it occurred, and what other assets might have been compromised. If the intruder gained access to a network consisting of unpatched Web servers, it is safe to assume that he gained access to those systems as well.

Notes from the Underground...

Intrusion Detection Systems

The difference between vulnerability assessments and an IDS is not always immediately clear. To understand the differences between these complimentary security systems, you will also need to understand how an IDS works. When people speak of IDSs, they are often referring to what is more specifically called a network intrusion detection system (NIDS). A NIDS' role is to monitor all network traffic, pick out malicious attacks from the normal data, and send out alerts when an attack is detected. This type of defense is known as a *reactive security measure* as it can only provide you with information after an attack has occurred. In contrast, a vulnerability assessment can provide you with the data about a vulnerability before it is used to compromise a system, allowing you to fix the problem and prevent the intrusion. For this reason, vulnerability assessments are considered a *proactive security measure.*

Assessment Types

The term *vulnerability assessment* is used to refer to many different types and levels of service. A host assessment normally refers to a security analysis against a single system, from that system, often using specialized tools and an administrative user account. In contrast, a network assessment is used to test an entire network of systems at once.

Host Assessments

Host assessment tools were one of the first proactive security measures available to system administrators and are still in use today. These tools require that the assessment software be installed on each system you want to assess. This software can either be run stand-alone or be linked to a central system on the network. A host assessment looks for system-level vulnerabilities such as insecure file permissions, missing software patches, noncompliant security policies, and outright backdoors and Trojan horse installations.

The depth of the testing performed by host assessment tools makes it the preferred method of monitoring the security of critical systems. The downside of host assessments is that they require a set of specialized tools for the operating system and software packages being used, in addition to administrative access to each system that should be tested. Combined with the substantial time investment required to perform the testing and the limited scalability, host assessments are often reserved for a few critical systems.

The number of available and up-to-date host assessment solutions has been decreasing over the last few years. Tools like COPS and Tiger that were used religiously by system administrators just a few years ago have now fallen so far behind as to be nearly useless. Many of the stand-alone tools have been replaced by agent-based systems that use a centralized reporting and management system. This transition has been fueled by a demand for scalable systems that can be deployed across larger server farms with a minimum of administrative effort. At the time of this publication the only stand-alone host assessment tools used with any frequency are those targeting nontechnical home users and part-time administrators for small business systems.

Although stand-alone tools have started to decline, the number of "enterprise security management" systems that include a host assessment component is still increasing dramatically. The dual requirements of scalability and ease of deployment have resulted in host assessments becoming a component of larger management systems. A number of established software companies offer commercial products in this space, including, but not limited to, Internet Security System's System Scanner, Computer Associates eTrust Access Control product line, and BindView's bvControl software.

Network Assessments

Network assessments have been around almost as long as host assessments, starting with the Security Administrator Tool for Analyzing Networks (SATAN), released by Dan Farmer and Wietse Venema in 1995. SATAN provided a new perspective to administrators who were used to host assessment and hardening tools. Instead of analyzing the local system for problems, it allowed you to look for common problems on any system connected to the network. This opened the gates for a still-expanding market of both open-source and commercial network-based assessment systems.

A network vulnerability assessment locates all live systems on a network, determines what network services are in use, and then analyzes those services for potential vulnerabilities. Unlike the host assessment solutions, this process does not require any configuration changes on the systems being assessed. Network assessments can be both scalable and efficient in terms of administrative requirements and are the only feasible method of gauging the security of large, complex networks of heterogeneous systems.

Although network assessments are very effective for identifying vulnerabilities, they do suffer from certain limitations. These include: not being able to detect certain types of backdoors, complications with firewalls, and the inability to test for certain vulnerabilities due to the testing process itself being dangerous. Network assessments can disrupt normal operations, interfere with many devices (especially printers), use large amounts of bandwidth, and create fill-up disks with log files on the systems being assessed. Additionally, many vulnerabilities are exploitable by an authorized but unprivileged user account and cannot be identified through a network assessment.

Automated Assessments

The first experience that many people have with vulnerability assessments is using a security consulting firm to provide a network audit. This type of audit is normally comprised of both manual and automated components; the auditors will use automated tools for much of the initial legwork and follow it up with manual system inspection. While this process can provide thorough results, it is often much more expensive than simply using an automated assessment tool to perform the process in-house.

The need for automated assessment tools has resulted in a number of advanced solutions being developed. These solutions range from simple graphical user inter face (GUI) software products to stand-alone appliances that are capable of being linked into massive distributed assessment architectures. Due to the overwhelming number of vulnerability tests needed to build even a simple tool, the commercial market is easily divided between a few well-funded independent products and literally hundreds of solutions built on the open-source Nessus Security Scanner. These automated assessment tools can be further broken into two types of products: those that are actually obtained, through either purchase or download, and those that are provided through a subscription service.

Stand-Alone vs. Subscription

The stand-alone category of products includes most open-source projects and about half of the serious commercial contenders. Some examples include the Nessus Security Scanner, eEye's Retina, Tenable Security's Lightning Proxy, and Microsoft's Security Baseline Scanner. These products are either provided as a software package that is installed on a workstation, or a hardware appliance that you simply plug in and access over the network.

The subscription service solutions take a slightly different approach; instead of requiring the user to perform the actual installation and deployment, the vendor handles the basic configuration and simply provides a Web interface to the client. This is primarily used to offer assessments for Internet-facing assets (external assessments), but can also be combined with an appliance to provided assessments for an organization's internal network. Examples of products that are provided as a subscription service include Qualys' QualysGuard, BeyondSecurity's Automated Scan, and Digital Defense's Frontline product.

The advantages of using a stand-alone product are obvious: all of your data stays in-house, and you decide exactly when, where, and how the product is used. One disadvantage, however, is that these products require the user to perform an update before every use to avoid an out-of-date vulnerability check set, potentially missing recent vulnerabilities. The advantages of a subscription service model are twofold: the updates are handled for you, and since the external assessment originates from the vendor's network, you are provided with a real-world view of how your network looks from the Internet.

The disadvantages to a subscription solution are the lack of control you have over the configuration of the device, and the potential storage of vulnerability data on the vendor's systems. Some hybrid subscription service solutions have emerged that resolve both of these issues through leased appliances in conjunction with user-provided storage media for the assessment data. One product that implements this approach is nCircles' IP360 system, which uses multiple dedicated appliances that store all sensitive data on a removable flash storage device.

The Assessment Process

Regardless of what automated assessment solution is used, it will more than likely follow the same general process. Each assessment begins with the user specifying what address or address ranges should be tested. This is often implemented as either a drop-down list of predefined ranges or a simple text widget where the network address and mask can be entered. Once the addresses are specified, the interface will often present the user with a set of configuration options for the assessment; this could include the port ranges to scan, the bandwidth settings to use, or any product-specific features. After all of this information is entered, the actual assessment phase starts.

Detecting Live Systems

The first stage of a network vulnerability assessment determines which Internet Protocol (IP) addresses specified in the target range actually map to online and accessible systems. For each address specified by the user, one or more probes are sent to elicit a response. If a response is received, the system will place that address in a list of valid hosts. In the case of heavily firewalled networks, most products have an option to force scan all addresses, regardless of whether a response is received during this stage.

These types of probes sent during this stage differ wildly between assessment tools; although almost all of them use Internet Control Message Protocol (ICMP) "ping" requests, the techniques beyond this are rarely similar between two products. Most commercial security scanners have the capability to use a series of TCP connection requests to a set of common ports to identify systems that might be blocking ICMP messages. This allows the scanner to identify systems behind firewalls or those specifically configured to ignore ICMP traffic. After a connection request is sent, any response received from that system will cause it to be added to the list of tested hosts. Many commercial tools include the capability to probe specific User Datagram Protocol (UDP) services in addition to the standard ICMP and TCP tests. This technique is useful for detecting systems that only allow specific UDP application requests through, as is commonly the case with external DNS and RADIUS servers.

Identifying Live Systems

After the initial host detection phase is complete, many products will use a variety of fingerprinting techniques to determine what type of system was found at each address in the live system list. These fingerprinting techniques range from Simple Network Management Protocol (SNMP) queries to complex TCP/IP stack-based operating system identification.

This stage can be crucial in preventing the assessment from interfering with the normal operation of the network; quite a few print servers, older UNIX systems, and network-enabled applications will crash when a vulnerability assessment is performed on them. Indeed, the biggest problem that most administrators encounter with automated assessment tools is that they can disrupt network operations. Often, the administrator will have to spend time rebooting devices, retrieving garbage printouts from network-attached print servers, and debugging user problems with network applications. This identification stage can often be used to detect and avoid problematic systems before the following stages can cause problems.

Enumerating Services

Once the host detection and identification steps are complete, the next stage is normally a port scan. A port scan is the process of determining what TCP and UDP services are open on a given system. TCP port scans are conducted by sending connection requests to a configured list of port numbers on each system. If the system responds with a message indicating that the port is open, the port number is logged and stored for later use. UDP port scanning can often provide inconsistent results, since the nature of the protocol makes obtaining consistent results difficult on most networks.

There are 65,536 available TCP ports; however, most assessment tools will only perform a port scan against a limited set of these. Limiting the scan to a subset of the available ports reduces the amount of time it takes to perform the assessment and substantially decreases the bandwidth required by the assessment (in terms of packets per second, not the total number of bytes). The downside of not scanning all available ports is that services that are bound to nonstandard, high port numbers are often completely ignored by the assessment. Most security scanners provide an option that allows the user to define how these ports are treated. The default is to consider all non-scanned TCP ports open, which can take quite a bit of time during the assessment, especially in cases where heavy packet filters or firewalls are in place.

Identifying Services

After the port scan phase, many assessment tools will try to perform service identification on each open port. This process starts with sending some common application requests and analyzing the responses against a set of signatures. When a signature matches a known application, this information is stored for the later use and the next service is tested. Although not all assessment tools perform this stage, the ones that do can provide much more accurate results, simply by knowing which vulnerabilities to check for on what ports.

Most security scanners include a robust service identification engine, capable of detecting more than 90 different application protocols. This engine uses a set of application probes to elicit responses from each service. After each probe is sent, the result is matched against a list of known application signatures. When a matching signature is found, the port number and protocol are stored for future use and the engine continues with the next service. If the Secure Sockets Layer (SSL) transport protocol is detected, the engine will automatically negotiate SSL on the service before sending the application probes. This combination of transport-level and service-level identification allows the system to accurately detect vulnerabilities even when the affected service is on a nonstandard port.

The HyperText Transfer Protocol (HTTP) is a great example of a service that is often found on a port other than the default. Although almost all standard Web servers will use TCP port 80, literally thousands of applications install an HTTP service on a port other than 80. Web configuration interfaces for many Web application servers, hardware devices, and security tools will use nonstandard ports. Email protocols such as Simple Mail Transfer Protocol (SMTP), Post Office Protocol 3 (POP3), and Internet Message Access Protocol (IMAP) are often configured with the SSL transport protocol and installed on nonstandard ports as well. A common misconfiguration is to block spam relaying on the primary SMTP service, but trust all messages accepted through the SSL-wrapped SMTP service on a different port.

Additionally, this phase prevents an application running on a port normally reserved for another protocol from being ignored completely by the scan or resulting in false positives.

Identifying Applications

Once the service detection phase is complete, the next step is to determine the actual application in use for each detected service. The goal of this stage is to identify the vendor, type, and version of every service detected in the previous stage. This information is critical, as the vulnerability tests for one application can actually cause another application to crash. An example of this is if a Web server is vulnerable to a long pathname overflow. If any other vulnerability tests send a request longer than what is expected by this system, the application will crash. To accurately detect this vulnerability on the Web server instead of crashing it, the system must first identify that specific application and then prevent any of the problematic vulnerability tests from running against it.

One of the most common problems with most assessment tools is that of the false positive where the tool reports a vulnerability that does not actually exist on the tested systems. False positives can produce a huge amount of verification work for the assessment engineer. When application identification information is either missing or incomplete, test results will often include false positives. When the developers of these assessment tools write the vulnerability tests, they often assume that the system they are interacting with is always going to be the product in which the vulnerability was discovered. Different applications that offer the same service will often respond to a probe in such a way that the vulnerability test logic registers a vulnerability. For this reason, application identification has become one of the most critical components of modern assessment tools.

Identifying Vulnerabilities

After every online host has been identified, each open port has been mapped to a known service, and the known services have been mapped to specific applications, the system is finally ready to begin testing for vulnerabilities. This process often starts with basic information-gathering techniques, followed by active configuration probes, and finally a set of custom attacks that can identify whether a particular vulnerability exists on the tested system.

The vulnerability identification process can vary from simple banner matching and version tests, to complete exploitation of the tested flaw. When version detection and banner matching are used to identify a vulnerability, false positives often result due to application vendors providing updated software that still displays the banner of the vulnerable version. For this reason, version numbers are often consulted only when there is no other way to safely verify whether the vulnerability exists.

Many common vulnerabilities can only be identified by attempting to exploit the flaw. This often means using the vulnerability to execute a command, display a system file, or otherwise verify that the system is indeed vulnerable to an attack by a remote intruder. Many buffer overflow and input manipulation vulnerabilities can be detected by triggering just enough of the flaw to indicate that the system has not been patched, but not enough to actually take down the service. The assessment tool has to walk a fine line between reliable vulnerability identification and destructive side effects.

Vulnerability tests that use banner checks will encounter problems when the tested service has been patched, either by the vendor or system administrator, but the version number displayed to the network has not been updated, or at least when it has not been updated in the way the vulnerability test expects. This is a relatively common practice with open-source UNIX-based platforms and certain Linux distributions.

Reporting Vulnerabilities

After the analysis is finished, the final stage of the assessment process is reporting. Each product has a unique perspective on how reports should be generated, what they should include, and in what formats to provide them. Regardless of the product, the assessment report will list the systems discovered during the assessment and any vulnerabilities that were identified on them. Many products offer different levels of reporting depending on the audience; it is useful to provide a high-level summary to management giving a system administrator a report that tells him or her what systems need to be fixed and how to do so. One of the popular features in many assessment tools is the capability to show trend reports of how a given network fared over time.

Two Approaches

When performing an automated vulnerability assessment, the actual perspective of the test can have a huge impact on the depth and quality of the results. Essentially, there are two different approaches to vulnerability testing: administrative and outsider. Each has distinct advantages and disadvantages, such that many of the better assessment tools have migrated to a hybrid model that combines the best features of both approaches. Understanding these different approaches can provide insight into why two different assessment tools can provide such completely different results when used to test the same network.

Administrative Approach

The administrative approach performs the assessment from the perspective of a normal, authenticated system administrator. The assessment tool might require that it be launched by an authenticated administrative user or provided with a user account and password. These credentials can be used to detect missing patches, insecure configuration settings, and potentially vulnerable client-side software (such as e-mail clients and Web browsers).

This is a powerful approach for networks that consist of mostly Windows-based systems that all authenticate against the same domain. It combines much of the deep analysis of a host assessment with the network assessment's scalability advantages. Since almost all of the vulnerability tests are performed using either remote registry or remote file system access, there is little chance that an assessment tool using this method can adversely affect the tested systems. This allows assessments to be conducted during the day, while the systems are actively being used, without fear of disrupting a business activity.

The administrative approach is especially useful when trying to detect and resolve client-side vulnerabilities on a network of workstations. Many worms, Trojans, and viruses propagate by exploiting vulnerabilities in e-mail clients and Web browser software. An assessment tool using this approach can access the registry of each system and determine whether the latest patches have been installed, whether the proper security settings have been applied, and often whether the system has already been successfully attacked. Client-side security is one of the most overlooked entry points on most corporate networks; there have been numerous cases of a network with a well-secured perimeter being overtaken by a network simply because a user visited the wrong Web site with an outdated Web browser.

Unfortunately, these products often have some severe limitations as well. Since the testing process uses the standard Windows administrative channels—namely, the NetBIOS services and an administrative user account—anything preventing this channel from being accessed will result in inaccurate scan results. Any system on the network that is configured with a different authentication source (running in stand-alone mode, on a different domain, or authenticating to a Novell server) will not be correctly assessed. Additionally, these products may have issues similar to the issues of host-based assessment tools, network devices, UNIX-based servers, and IP-enabled phone systems may also be completely missed or return incomplete results.

Network and host-based firewalls can also interfere with the assessment. This interference is a common occurrence when performing assessments against a system hosted on a different network segment, such as a demilitarized zone (DMZ) or external segment behind a dedicated firewall. Additionally, network devices, UNIX-based servers, and IP-enabled phone systems might also be either completely missed or have only minimal results returned. An example of this is a certain Windows-based commercial assessment tool that will report missing Internet Information Server (IIS) patches even when the Web server has not been enabled or configured.

This type of testing is very helpful to verify a network-wide patch deployment, but should not be relied upon as the only method of security testing. Microsoft's Security Baseline Scanner is the best example of an assessment tool that uses this approach alone. Many of the commercial assessment tool offerings were originally based on this approach and have only recently started to integrate different techniques into their vulnerability tests. The differences between administrative and hybrid solutions is discussed at length in the section The Hybrid Approach.

The Outsider Approach

The outsider approach takes the perspective of the unauthenticated malicious intruder who is trying to break into the network. The assessment process is able to make decisions about the security of a system only through a combination of application fingerprinting, version identification, and actual exploitation attempts. Assessment tools built on this approach are often capable of detecting vulnerabilities across a much wider range of operating systems and devices than their administrative approach counterparts can.

When conducting a large-scale assessment against a network consisting of many different operating systems and network devices, the outsider approach is the only technique that has a chance of returning accurate, consistent results about each discovered system. If a system is behind a firewall, only the exposed services will be tested, providing you with the same information that an intruder would see in a real-life attack. The reports provided by tools that use this hybrid approach are geared to prevent common attacks; this is in contrast to those tools using the administrative approach that often focus on missing patches and insecure configuration settings. In essence, the outsider approach presents a much more targeted list of problems for remediation, allowing the administrator to focus on the issues that would be the first choices for a potential intruder.

Although this approach is the only plausible method of conducting a vulnerability assessment on a heterogeneous network, it also suffers from a significant set of drawbacks. Many vulnerabilities simply cannot be tested without crashing the application, device, or operating system. The result is that any assessment tools that test for these types of vulnerabilities either provide an option for "intrusive" testing, or always trigger a warning when a potentially vulnerable service is discovered. Since the outsider approach can only detect what is visible from the point in the network where the assessment was launched, it might not report a vulnerable service bound to a different interface on the same system. This is an issue with reporting more than anything else, as someone reviewing the assessment report might not consider the network perspective when creating a list of remediation tasks for that system.

The Hybrid Approach

Over the last few years, more and more tools have switched to a hybrid approach for network assessments. They use administrative credentials when possible, but fall back to remote fingerprinting techniques if an account is either not available or not accepted on the tested system. The quality of these hybrid solutions varies greatly; the products were originally designed with only the administrative approach in mind have a difficult time when administrative credentials are not available, whereas the products based on the outsider approach often contain glitches when using an administrative account for tests. It seems that the latter has better chances at overcoming its hurdles without requiring a rewrite. Overall, though, these products provide results that are often superior to those using a single approach. The Nessus Security Scanner and eEye's Retina product are examples of tools that use this approach.

One of the greatest advantages of tools using the outsider approach is that they are often able to determine whether a given vulnerability exists, regardless of whether a patch was applied. As many Windows network administrators know, installing an operating system patch does not actually guarantee that the vulnerability has been removed. A recent vulnerability in the Microsoft Windows Network Messenger service allowed a remote attacker to execute arbitrary code on a vulnerable system. Public exploits for the vulnerability started circulating, and companies were frantically trying to install the patch on all their internal workstations. Something that was overlooked was that for the patch to take effect, the system had to be rebooted after it was applied. Many sites used automated patch installation tools to update all their vulnerable systems, but completely forgot about the reboot requirement.

The result was that when an assessment was run using a tool that took the administrative approach, it reported the systems as patched. However, when an assessment was run using a tool such as the Nessus Security Scanner, it reported these systems as vulnerable. The tool using the administrative approach simply checked the registry of each system to determine whether the patch had been applied, whereas the Nessus scan actually probed the vulnerability to determine if it was still vulnerable. Without this second assessment, the organization would have left hundreds of workstations exposed, even though the patches had been applied. The registry analysis used by many tools that take the administrative approach can miss vulnerabilities for a number of other reasons as well. The most common occurrence is when a hotfix has been applied to resolve a vulnerability, and then an older service pack is reapplied over the entire system. The changes installed by the hotfix were overwritten, but the registry entry stating that the patch was applied still exists. This problem primarily affects Windows operating systems; however, a number of commercial UNIX vendors have had similar issues with tracking installed patches and determining which ones still need to be applied.

Recently, many of the administrative and hybrid tools have developed new techniques for verifying that an installed patch actually exists. Shavlik Technology's HFNetChk Pro will actually check the last reboot time and compare it to the hotfix install date. Many scanners actually access the affected executables across the network and verify the embedded version numbers.

The drawbacks to the hybrid approach are normally not apparent until the results of a few large scans are observed; because the administrative approach is used opportunistically, vulnerabilities that are reported on a system that accepts the provided user account might not be reported on a similar system that uses a different authentication realm. If the administrator does not realize that the other system might be vulnerable as well, it could lead to a false sense of security. These missed vulnerabilities can be difficult to track down and can fall under the radar of the administrator. Because there is a higher chance of these systems not being patched, the hybrid approach can actually result in more damage during an intrusion or worm outbreak. Although the administrative approach suffers from the same issue, tools using the administrative approach take it for granted that systems outside of the authentication realm will not be tested.

Realistic Expectations

When the first commercial vulnerability assessment tools started becoming popular, they were advertised as being able to magically identify every security hole on your network. A few years ago, this might have been close to the truth. The number of publicly documented vulnerabilities was still quite small, and tracking vulnerability information was an obscure hobby. These days, the scenario is much different, whereas there were a few hundred well-documented vulnerabilities before, there are literally thousands of them now, and they don't even begin to scratch the surface when it comes to the number of flaws that can be used to penetrate a corporate network.

In addition to the avalanche of vulnerabilities, the number and type of devices found on an average corporate network has exploded. Some of these devices will crash, misbehave, or slow to a crawl during a network vulnerability assessment. A vulnerability test designed for one system might cause another application or device to stop functioning altogether, annoying the users of those systems and potentially interrupting the work flow. Assessment tools have a tough job; they have to identify as many vulnerabilities as possible on systems that must be analyzed and categorized on the fly, without reporting false positives, and at the same time avoid crashing devices and applications that simply weren't designed with security in mind. Some tools fare better than others; however, all current assessment tools exhibit this problem in one form or another.

When someone first starts to use a vulnerability assessment system, he or she often notices that the results between subsequent scans can differ significantly. This issue is encountered more frequently on larger networks that are connected through slower links. There are quite a few different reasons for this, but the core issue is that unlike most software processes, remote vulnerability testing is more of an art form than a science. Many assessment tools define a hard timeout for establishing connections to a service or receiving the result of a query. If an extra second or two of latency occurs on the network, the test could miss a valid response. These types of timing issues are common among assessment tools; however, many other factors can play into the consistency of scan results.

Many network devices provide a Telnet console that allows an administrator to reconfigure the system remotely. These devices will often set a hard limit on the number of concurrent network connections allowed to this service. When a vulnerability assessment is launched, it might perform multiple tests on a given port at the same time; this can cause one check to receive a valid response, while another gets an error message indicating that all available connections are being used. If that second check was responsible for testing for a default password on this particular device, it might completely miss the vulnerability. If the same scan was run later, but the default password test ran before one of the others, it would accurately detect the vulnerability at the expense of the other tests. This type of timing problem is much more common on network devices and older UNIX systems than on most modern workstations and servers, but can ultimately lead to inconsistent assessment results.

Dynamic systems are the bane of the vulnerability assessment tools. If an assessment is in full swing and a user decides to reboot his workstation, the assessment tool will start receiving connection timeouts for the vulnerability tests. Once the system comes back online, any subsequent tests will run normally; however, all tests launched during the period of downtime will result in missing vulnerability results for that system. This type of problem is incredibly difficult to detect when wading through a massive assessment report, and at this time only a handful of commercial systems offer the capability to detect and rescan systems that restart during the assessment process.

Despite the extraordinary amount of refinement and testing that most assessment tools have undergone, false positives continue to annoy network administrators and security consultants alike. As we discussed earlier in the chapter, a false positive is simply a vulnerability that is reported, but does not actually exist on the tested system. These annoyances can build to quite a bit of verification work— before you throw out any vulnerability assessment application for the false positive load, take the time to tune it as we show you later in this book. Nonstandard Web servers, backported software packages, and permissive match strings inside vulnerability test scripts are the top causes for false positives.

The Web server software that provides a configuration console for many network devices is notorious for causing false positives; instead of returning a standard "404" error response for nonexistent files, these systems will often return a success message for any file that is requested from the system. In response, almost all of the popular assessment tools have developed some form of Web server fingerprinting that allows their system to work around these strange Web servers.

The Limitations of Automation

Vulnerability assessment tools are still no replacement for a manual security audit by a team of trained security experts. Although many assessment tools will do their best to find common vulnerabilities in all exposed services, relatively simple vulnerabilities are often missed. Custom web applications, written under tight deadlines and for small user bases, often perform inadequate security checks on user input, but automated assessment systems may not find these flaws. Although the chances of an automated assessment tool being able to find a vulnerability in this software are slim, a security analyst experienced with Web application testing could easily pinpoint a number of security issues in a short period of time. Just because an automated assessment does not find any vulnerabilities does not mean that none exist.

Creating an Incident Response Procedure

The most basic rule about planning for incidents is this: Keep it simple. The more complicated your incident response plans are, the less likely they will be effective in a real incident. It's sometimes easy to overengineer a plan in the relative calm of everyday business activities. When an incident strikes, people are not likely to remember a lot of rules, procedures, and details.

What to Include in a Communication Plan

Incident communications covers a lot of territory and may involve numerous teams working in a coordinated fashion, but the messages being communicated should originate from or be approved by a single Incident Manager (IM). In an security incident, you should avoid having multiple sources of communications going out since it can cause confusion, error, frustration, and worse. Though you don't want to create a bottleneck in your communication stream, in the early stages after a business disruption, strive to have the IM clear any messages going out. This not only will ensure that the message is correct and consistent, it will keep the IM in the loop as well. This establishes a two-way communication channel between the IM and the teams working on security incident activities and helps in the coordination of activities and teams.

Security Checklist

- Make certain that users are aware of what they can do to help protect company resources. If a user in your organization suspected that they might have just released a virus, what would they do? Do they know who to call? More importantly, would they be afraid to call?

- Periodically review basic internal network security, and document your findings. Use the results to provide justification for continued internal protection initiatives. How chewy is your network? Use common enumeration techniques to try and build a blueprint of your company's network. Can you access departmental servers? How about databases? If a motivated hacker sat down at a desk in one of your facilities, how much critical data could be compromised?

- Determine whether you have adequate border policing. Try to download and run some common rogue applications, like file-sharing networks or instant messaging program. Are your acceptable use policy documents up to date with what you actually permit use to? Make sure these documents are kept up to date and frequently communicated to users.

- Work with the administrators and management staff necessary to make sure you can answer each of these questions. If one of your users uploaded company-owned intellectual property to a public Web site, could you prove it? Are logs managed effectively? Is authentication required to access external network resources? What if the user sent the intellectual property via e-mail?

Activation Checklists

You may find it helpful to develop a variety of checklists, which can be extremely useful in making quick decisions for moving forward. Since you and your team may not have time to rehearse these plans frequently, checklists can help remind you of critical steps to take, regardless of the situation. Activation checklists should delineate all the activities and triggers that should take place prior to and during incident plan activation. This begins with some sort of disruptive event occurring, someone notifying the Incident Management team team, and someone determining that the security incident plan should be activated as a result of the disruptive event. Remember, there may be some minor events that do not trigger the activation of the security incident plan, so deciding what criteria will be used to activate the plan in whole or in part should be part of the process.

Process for Planning an Incident Response Procedure

Most IT departments have some process in place for addressing and managing a computer incident. An incident is defined as any activity outside normal operations, whether intentional or not; whether man-made or not. For example, the theft in the middle of the night of a corporate server is an incident. A Web site hack or a network security breach is also an incident. A database corruption issue or a failed hard drive is also an incident, but for the purposes of this discussion, we're going to stick with the emergency kinds of incidents and leave the more routine incident handling to your existing IT operations procedures. For example, we'll assume you can handle a bad hard drive or a failed router through standard operating procedures and we won't cover that here. What we will cover are the incidents that require a swift and decisive action to stop the incident from continuing. This includes events such as a network security breach or a denial of service attack and events such as a fire in the server room or a flood in the building.

Incident Response Plan

The purpose of incident response (IRP) plans and procedures is to provide a systematic approach as well as a general guideline for your organization's staff on procedures to be followed whenever abnormal or unusual situations occur, which may affect daily operations and ultimately compromise corporate data. Another purpose for incident response procedures existence is ensuring business continuity in a timely but organized manner to include documenting the event in a manner so that management can analyze procedures undertaken and address short comings if the event occurs again in the future.

It is important that IRPs are supported throughout the organization, and tested regularly. A good incident response plan cannot only minimize the affects of a security incident, but can also reduce any negative publicity that often follows. There is something to be said about the positive aspect of knowing that a security incident will occur. It allows your Computer Incident Response Team (CIRT) to develop the appropriate course of action to minimize damages. Combining this course of action with subject matter expertise allows the CIRT to respond to incidents in a systematic and formal manner.

The IRP should be clear and concise and executed quickly. When an IRP is executed, there is little room for error. For this reason, the IRP should be practiced regularly and scenarios staged to provide as much exposure to the procedures to the staff on specific incidents. Testing makes it possible for methodologies to be developed that allow for timeliness and accuracy, minimizing the impact and damages in the event of an actual compromise. An IRP has a number of requirements, to include, but not limited to:

- The creation of an CIRT to execute the plan.

- Legal approval

- An appropriate budget

- Upper management buy-in/support

- An action plan

- Appropriate resources (i.e., standby systems (hot, cold), backup devices/services, redundant storage)

Computer Incident Response Team

The first step in this process is to form a *Computer Incident Response Team*. You may already have a team in place that addresses computer incidents such as security breaches. If that's the case you have the foundation of a computer incident response team (CIRT) that can be used in the event of a more widespread disruption such as a fire, earthquake or flood. The members of the team, like the ERT, should have defined roles and responsibilities. As with the ERT, team members should also be trained in their roles. For example, if you have staff responsible for monitoring network security and they notice a potential breach through a particular port, they should also know how to shut down that port and have the network permissions that enable them to do so. If all they know how to do is monitor the log file or traffic, for example, and have no idea how to shut down a port or stop the problem, it could be hours before the problem is addressed. Therefore, members of your CIRT should have training and appropriate network permissions to address these problems.

The steps needed to create an effective CIRT are:

- Procure equipment and provide the infrastructure to support the team's mission.

- Develop the policies and procedures to support CIRT services.

- Define the specifications for and build your incident-tracking system.

- Develop incident-reporting guidelines for your organization and clientele. Incident reporting procedures include as much detail as possible to alleviate confusion. They should include what medium can be used for submitting reports (e.g., e-mail, pager, phone, Web forms, and so on). It should also include details about what type of information should be included in the report.

- Develop a process for responding to incidents. This includes how the CIRT will prioritize and respond to received reports, response timeframes, and notifications. Also, an after-action report should be created to discuss lessons learned and to provide closure to the original party reporting the incident.

The primary function of the CIRT is to execute the Incident Response Plan when a security incident occurs. In order for the CIRT to be effective, its duties must be well defined. There are five major areas of responsibility for the CIRT team. These are:

- Monitor
- Alert and Mobilize
- Assess and Stabilize
- Resolve
- Review

Monitor

Every network must be monitored for a variety of events. Some of these are failure events that indicate a problem has occurred such as a hardware failure or the failure of a particular software service to start or stop appropriately. Other events are tracked in log files for later review or auditing. These might include failed login attempts or notification of a change to security settings, for example. Other incidents may include unusual increases in certain types of network traffic or excessive attempts to login to secure areas of the network. Whether the event stems from intentional or unintentional acts, the network needs to be monitored. The CIRT should be involved with helping to determine what should be monitored as well as assisting in monitoring the network. Not all events have significance and sometimes it's only through seeing recurring events that a pattern can be discerned. Therefore, having experienced team members monitor the network will help reduce the lag time between an unwanted event and a response.

While a serious security breach might not cause you to activate all or part of your Business Continuity plan, suppose you had some very strange activity on four of your corporate servers and the CIRT member couldn't determine the source of the anomalies. Is this a disaster or not? If it's caused by fire in the server room, yes. If it's caused by an errant software update that was just applied, maybe not. The point is that your CIRT team should monitor the network activity and take appropriate action regardless of the source of the problem. In some cases, this will involve activation of the Business Continuity or Disaster Recovery (BC/DR) plans, in other cases it won't.

Alert and Mobilize

Once an unusual, unwanted, or suspicious event has occurred, the CIRT member should alert appropriate team members and mobilize for action. This may involve shutting down servers, firewalls, e-mail, or other services. As part of a BC/DR plan, this can also include being alerted that the event or disaster disrupted network services, such as a data center fire or theft of a corporate server after a fire in another part of the building. Alerting and mobilizing should have the effect of stopping the immediate impact of the event.

Assess and Stabilize

After the immediate threat has been halted, the CIRT team assesses the situation and attempts to stabilize it. For example, if data has been stolen or databases have been corrupted, the nature and extent of the event must be assessed and steps must be taken to stabilize the situation. In many cases, this phase takes the longest because determining exactly what happened can be challenging. If you have members of your team that have been trained in computer forensics, they would head up this segment of work. If you do not have members of your team trained in this area, you should decide whether it would be advisable to provide this training to staff or hire an outside computer forensics expert. Outside consultants can be helpful in this case for the simple fact that they work in this arena day in and day out and are most likely more up-to-date and experienced in this area than staff that occasionally goes to training and rarely (if ever) puts that training to use. he decision is yours based on the skills, expertise, and budget of your company. Having in-house expertise can be a good first step and you can always hire an outside expert on an as-needed basis.

Keep in mind that you have defined maximum tolerable downtime and other recovery metrics. A review of these should be included as part of the assess and stabilize procedures so that plans and actions can accommodate these requirements.

Resolve

After determining the nature and extent of the incident, the CIRT can determine the best resolution and implement it. Resolution may involve restoring from backups, updating operating systems or applications, modifying permissions, or changing settings on servers, firewalls, or routers.

Review

Once the event has been resolved, the CIRT should convene a meeting to determine how the incident occurred, what lessons were learned, and what could be done to avoid such a problem in the future. Within the scope of a BC/DR plan, this might involve understanding how the recovery process worked and what could be done differently in the future to decrease downtime, decrease impact, and improve time to resolution.

NOTE

Computer Emergency Response Team (CERT)

There are numerous terms and acronyms floating around regarding computer emergencies, computer incidents, and computer security. The grandfather of them all, however, is the concept of computer emergency response developed by the Software Engineering Institute (SEI) at Carnegie Mellon University. We mentioned this resource earlier in the book and thought this would be a good time to mention it again. The Web site has a vast array of information and resources you can access. When developing your BC/DR plan for the IT portion of your business, read up on the latest trends and knowledge on the Web site at www.cert.org. Head to this URL for details on creating a CERT team: http://www.cert.org/csirts/action_list.html. It's a great resource for IT professionals even outside the scope of BC/DR planning as well.

Other Considerations Regarding Security Incidents
Forensics

Your organization may need to communicate with outside parties regarding an incident. This includes reporting incidents to organizations such as the Federal Computer Incident Response Center and law enforcement, and also fielding inquiries from the media. One reason that many security-related incidents do not result in convictions is that organizations do not properly contact law enforcement. Several levels of law enforcement are available to investigate incidents:

- The Federal Bureau of Investigation [FBI]
- The U.S. Secret Service
- District Attorney Office
- State Law Enforcement
- Local (e.g., county) law enforcement

Law enforcement should be contacted through designated individuals in a manner consistent with these procedures. The spokesperson will be familiar with the reporting procedures for all relevant law enforcement agencies and well prepared to recommend which agency, if any, should be contacted.

Customer notice should be provided whenever it becomes aware of an incident of unauthorized access to customer information and, at the conclusion of a reasonable investigation, determines that misuse of the information has occurred or it is reasonably possible that misuse will occur. Customer notice should be given in a clear and conspicuous manner. The notice should include the following items:

- Description of the incident
- Type of information subject to unauthorized access
- Measures taken by the institution to protect customers from further unauthorized access
- Telephone number customers can call for information and assistance
- Remind customers to remain vigilant over next 12 to 24 four months, and report suspected identity theft incidents to the institution

Additionally, customer notice should be delivered in a manner designed to ensure that a customer can reasonably be expected to receive it. For example, the institution may choose to contact all customers affected by telephone or by mail, or by electronic mail for those customers for whom it has a valid e-mail address and who have agreed to receive communications electronically.

IT Recovery Tasks

The tasks needed to recover IT systems are probably quite familiar to you, but they should be delineated within your BC/DR and IRP plans. Each subteam should have a clear set of guidelines and procedures for how and when they will perform their work. Be sure to note dependencies within the checklist so that teams don't work at cross-purposes. You can add items to the checklist as checkpoints for these purposes, much like milestones are used in project plans. IT recovery checklists are also included in the Appendix of this book. Part of IT recovery involves responding to, stopping, and repairing problems caused by system failures, security breaches, or intentional data corruption or destruction. Depending on the nature or severity of the attack or incident, you may need to activate a computer incident response team (CIRT).

Training Is Not Optional

When disaster strikes, most people resort to what they know best; they fall back on their training. The same is true of IT professionals. In the face of a major system outage or security breach, IT staff will do what they've been trained to do. Training is not an option for emergency preparedness, it is a requirement. Emergencies by their very nature are incredibly stressful and chaotic. People, by their very nature, feel most comfortable in any situation when they know what to expect and what to do. In an emergency, they won't necessarily know what to expect, but they will know what to do if they've been trained. Training is also important for CIRT teams because security incidents can be devastating to a company. CIRT members should know what to look for and exactly what actions to take in order to address a potential security breach or other serious incident. It doesn't help to shut down a server if the firewall has been breached; it doesn't help to shut down e-mail if the virus has infected a server. In addition to general IT skills, CIRT members should represent the various areas of expertise required in your IT department including servers, infrastructure, security, database administration, and applications, to name a few. CIRT members also should have checklists or step-by-step instructions to follow for standard incident types such as security breach, firewall breach, virus outbreak, and so on. This helps reduce stress and ensures everyone follows standard procedures to halt the immediate impact of any computer-related incident.

Summary

In this chapter, we provided an overview of the auditing process. We explained how security assessment and auditing can be thought of as incident prevention and by having a sound auditing strategy in place could potentially save you money and legal liabilities later. We explained that the objective of an internal security audit is to evaluate the security of corporate hosts and networks and that this evaluation will identify symptomatic security issues (vulnerabilities). We also covered how auditing will help you with maintaining a healthy and secure environment. We showed why auditing is important—people, unlike computers, don't follow instructions exactly as told; people have choices, and their choices can put cracks in the security walls.

We explained how a properly implemented auditing and scanning policy can help prevent issues like this. We further explained how to identifying threats to your internal network security and how to develop an internal network security assessment methodology. Standardization and SAS70 topics were also covered. We showed you how to design an auditing policy and outlined the process for planning an audit policy. We also covered the importance of time synchronization, identity management and event management storage. We provided information on what you need to monitor such as applications services (data storage points and data access points), infrastructure components (host operating systems [aka servers]), and network objects. Integrity monitoring and the use of common auditing tools were covered. Finally, we discussed how to deal with an auditor and the issues connected with remediation.

We learned about the importance of penetration testing and how it can aid in improving your overall security posture. We defined the security analysis life cycle and covered the differences between programmatic and technical testing. Customer responsibilities were also defined. We covered the penetration methodology that includes information gathering, network enumeration, vulnerability identification, vulnerability exploitation and privilege escalation.

In this chapter we discussed using vulnerability assessment scanning and why it is important in maintaining a secure network. We explained the different assessment types and the assessment process. We also explained the realistic expectations that we can expect from the usage of a vulnerability assessment scanning tool.

We finished the chapter with defining what an incident response procedure is. That a good incident response procedure includes effective communications and planning. We defined the requirements for establishing an incident response plan and the roles and responsibilities of a computer incident response team. The topics of forensics, IT recovery tasks and the importance or training were also discussed.

Solutions Fast Track

Introduction to Auditing

☑ Auditing is an official examination and verification of information. Generally speaking, the best approach to auditing has been to find a middle ground in terms of effort and cost to meet the spirit of your organization's requirements, and then work with the auditor ahead of audit time to see how you've done.

☑ The Statement on Auditing Standards (SAS) No. 70, Service Organizations, is a tool available to auditing firms and CPAs to conduct an audit of a company that already has implemented an information security program.

☑ Knowing what you are monitoring is half the battle in planning your storage needs as well as successfully deploying an auditable XenApp solution.

Designing an Audit Policy

☑ Any successful operating environment is designed from the ground up, or, in the case of a networking infrastructure and applications space, from the wires on up. It's important, therefore, to plan your auditing of your operating environment the same way you designed it.

☑ Just what you want to log will be one of the most important questions you'll ask yourself. Defining an extensive logging and auditing strategy will lower the performance of your server and of your network. Doing too little logging and auditing will leave you without the information you need to determine the source and cause of problems that arise. Your best option regarding logging is to log only those options you really need.

☑ A good rule of thumb when doing remediation is that it should be as transparent as possible, so that it has a minimal impact on users.

Understanding Penetration Testing

☑ As a security professional, you understand that technical vulnerabilities can be found and fixed. But you also know that an organization that has not fixed the root cause of the issue will continue to have technical problems later on down the road. The findings may be different (in some cases they're the same, just on different systems), but technical vulnerabilities will continue to rear their ugly heads.

☑ The most important tool in any penetration tester's toolkit (more important than any application, script, or exploit) is his/her mind. Good pen testers have an uncanny ability to locate issues on-the-fly. And since every customer and situation is different, this is a "must have" attribute. Let's look at some of those attributes that make up a good penetration tester.

☑ Exploiting the vulnerabilities is what separates the professionals from the script kiddies. The truth hurts, but a good many professionals in the security world depend wholly on the use of scripts and exploits written by other people. While this may be useful in some circumstances, the sole use of these exploits indicates the lack of maturity in the tester's knowledge and processes. A high quality tester will often have their own methods and scripts to help them break into a customer network.

Understanding Vulnerability Assessments

☑ Vulnerability assessments are simply the process of locating and reporting vulnerabilities. They provide you with a way to detect and resolve security problems before someone or something can exploit them. One of the most common uses for vulnerability assessments is their capability to validate security measures.

☑ There are two types of vulnerability assessments: host and network.

☑ Vulnerability assessment tools are still no replacement for a manual security audit by a team of trained security experts. Although many assessment tools will do their best to find common vulnerabilities in all exposed services, relatively simple vulnerabilities are often missed.

Creating an Incident Response Procedure

☑ The most basic rule about planning for incidents is this: Keep it simple. The more complicated your incident response plans are, the less likely they will be effective in a real incident.

☑ An Incident Response Plan (IRP) has a number of requirements, including legal approval, an appropriate budget, upper management buy-in/support, an action plan, and appropriate resources (i.e., standby systems [hot, cold], backup devices/services, and redundant storage)

☑ When disaster strikes, most people resort to what they know best; they fall back on their training. The same is true of IT professionals. In the face of a major system outage or security breach, IT staff will do what they've been trained to do. Training is not an option for emergency preparedness, it is a requirement.

Frequently Asked Questions

Q: What is auditing?

A: Auditing is an official examination and verification of information.

Q: What is SAS70?

A: SAS70 stands for *Statement on Auditing Standards (SAS) No. 70*. This is a tool available to auditing firms and CPAs to conduct an audit of a company that already has implemented an information security program. The SAS70 does not contain a checklist of security controls, but rather allows an auditing firm to issue a statement of how well a company is adhering to their stated information security policy.

Q: What is the purpose of a correlation engine?

A: The correlation engine uses rules, signatures (though not always), and sophisticated logic to deduce patterns and intent from the traffic it sees originating at the host operating system (OS) and network layers.

Q: How are logs relevant?

A: Threat Detection, Incident Response and Troubleshooting, E-discovery, IT Performance Management and Troubleshooting, Network Management, Compliance

Q: What is a good rule of thumb when doing remediation?

A: It should be as transparent as possible.

Q: How can vulnerabilities be classified?

A: On a scale of 5 to 1. 5: Urgent, 4: Critical, 3: High Risk, 2: Medium Level, 1: Low Severity

Q: Before running any type of scan on your network, you should always do what?

A: You should get management's approval.

Q: What are the four parts of the standard security life cycle?

A: An organizational/programmatic assessment occurs; a full comprehensive technical evaluation is rendered; findings are presented to the customer and the customer takes appropriate the steps to close technical problems and implement defenses; and then a test of those defenses takes place.

Q: What is considered to be the most important tool in the penetration tester's toolkit?

A: The most important tool in any penetration tester's toolkit (more important than any application, script, or exploit) is his/her mind. Good pen testers have an uncanny ability to locate issues on-the-fly.

Q: What are the eight steps of the penetration methodology?

A: Information gathering, network enumeration, vulnerability identification, vulnerability exploitation, privilege escalation, expansion of reach, ensure future access, compromise information.

Q: Name two resources penetration testers can use to find useful information regarding penetration testing?

A: Search engines, newsgroups, forums, blogs, books, peers

Q: What is a vulnerability?

A: A vulnerability refers to any programming error or misconfiguration that could allow an intruder to gain unauthorized access.

Q: What are vulnerability assessments?

A: Vulnerability assessments are simply the process of locating and reporting vulnerabilities.

Q: What is the main difference between a host and network assessment?

A: A host assessment normally refers to a security analysis against a single system, from that system, often using specialized tools and an administrative user account. In contrast, a network assessment is used to test an entire network of systems at once.

Q: What is an "incident"?

A: An incident is defined as any activity outside normal operations, whether intentional or not; whether man-made or not.

Q: What is the most basic rule about planning for incidents?

A: Keep it simple.

Q: What tools can be used to assist you in carrying out an effective communications plan?

A: Security Checklist and Activation Checklists

Q: What are the five major areas of responsibility for the CIRT team?

A: Monitor, Alert and Mobilize, Assess and Stabilize, Resolve, Review

Index

Printed and bound by CPI Group (UK) Ltd, Croydon, CR0 4YY

03/10/2024

01040343-0018